Developing Library and
Information Center Collections

Developing Library and Information Center Collections

Fifth Edition

G. EDWARD EVANS
and
MARGARET ZARNOSKY SAPONARO

Library and Information Science Text Series

LIBRARIES
UNLIMITED
A Member of the Greenwood Publishing Group
Westport, Connecticut • London

Library of Congress Cataloging-in-Publication Data

Evans, G. Edward, 1937–
    Developing library and information center collections / by G. Edward
Evans and Margaret Zarnosky Saponaro.—5th ed.
        p.   cm.—(Library and information science text series)
    Includes bibliographical references and index.
    ISBN 1–59158–218–0 (alk. paper)—ISBN 1–59158–219–9 (pbk. : alk.
paper)
    1. Collection development (Libraries)—United States.
    2. Information services—United States. I. Saponaro,
Margaret Zarnosky. II. Title. III. Series.
    Z687.E918 2005
    025.2'1—dc22   2005016098

British Library Cataloguing in Publication Data is available.

Library of Congress Catalog Card Number: 2005016098
ISBN: 1–59158–218–0
        1–59158–219–9 (pbk.)

First published in 2005

Libraries Unlimited, 88 Post Road West, Westport, CT 06881
A Member of the Greenwood Publishing Group, Inc.
www.lu.com

Printed in the United States of America

The paper used in this book complies with the
Permanent Paper Standard issued by the National
Information Standards Organization (Z39.48–1984).

10 9 8 7 6 5 4 3 2

No Library of One Million Volumes can be all BAD!
—from a cover, *Antiquarian Bookman*

We were told that if one put one million monkeys at one million typewriters,
they would, in time, produce the complete works of Shakespeare.
Now that we have the Internet, we know that is just not true.

I worry more about poor quality of information online,
and students' lack of skills for evaluating information,
than . . . about frequently discussed evils like pornography.
—John Leland
"Beyond Littleton: The Secret Life of Teens,"
Newsweek, May 10, 1999

We wish to dedicate this edition
to all the students,
who will begin developing the collections of the future,
and their instructors who will assist them in their learning.

As a personal dedication:
to the young readers
Travis and Trenton Evans

And to Frank Saponaro
for his support

Contents

List of Illustrations

Preface to the Fourth Edition

Less than six years have passed since the issuance of the third edition. When the call came suggesting that it was time to start work on a new edition, it seemed much too soon. However, after reviewing what might require updating and thinking about new sections, it became clear that it was indeed time to get to work.

Electronic issues now pervade collection development and management activities. The underlying basics remain, but the whats and hows are changing rather quickly. As a result, this is a somewhat longer edition, and almost every chapter contains something about electronic resources, reflecting the changing environment of collection management.

As with the prior editions, I asked for user feedback to help plan the contents of the new edition. To that end, 61 instructors who used the third edition received a questionnaire/survey form. That form listed sections where I thought additions would be appropriate, as well as suggestions for dropping sections to keep the book to a reasonable length. Forty-seven individuals took the time to reply; some even included their students in the process. To all those who took the time to respond, my very sincere thanks. This edition does in fact reflect your feedback.

One of the surprises in the responses was a rather consistent reluctance to have material dropped. This posed a problem in terms of the overall length of the projected new edition. The final solution was to drop sections that 40 percent of the respondents agreed could be eliminated. Nevertheless, the final manuscript was longer than first envisioned, so much longer that major cuts became necessary in order to keep the final book to a reasonable length.

One of the biggest departures from previous editions of this text occurred as a result of all the additions. For the first time, materials from the text are now available via the Internet. Specifically, the contents of what was Chapter 4 in earlier editions (Selection Process: Theory), and the two Appendices—"Book and Electronic Collection Policies" and the International Coalition of Library Consortia (ICOLC) "Statement of Current Perspective and Preferred Practices for the Selection and Purchase of Electronic Information"—are available from two websites <http://lib.lmu.edu/dlc4> and <http://www.lu.com/evanszarn.cfm>. In addition, there are some examples of needs assessment forms on the websites. We regret that space considerations prevented us from including this material in the main body of the text but encourage you to refer to this material in your studies.

Most of the individuals who devoted some hours to reading one or more chapters for the third edition once again contributed time, thought, and critical comment for material in this edition. To that list I must add Professor F. Jay Dougherty (Loyola Law School), who provided very valuable advice about copyright material, especially on the Digital Millennium Copyright Act; Mr. Evan A. Reader (Director, CSU-Software and Electronic Information Resources, Office of the Chancellor, California State University System); Mr. Lynn F. Sipe (Associate Director for Collections, University of Southern California and 1999 Chair of the American Library Association, Association for Library Collections and Technical Services' Collection Management Section), who read many of the chapters and also provided ideas for various other chapters; and Ms. Ann Williams (American Health Care Association), who provided a special library perspective.

I also wish to thank those who provided policies for Appendix One: David R. Bender (Executive Director, Special Libraries Association); Mary Lou Calvin (Director of Library Services, Warner, Norcross & Judd); Marcia Findley (Loyola Marymount University); Paul Metz (Virginia Polytechnic Institute and State University); John Stemmer (Xavier University); Phyllis Young (Collections Development Coordinator, Los Angeles County Library System); and Ann Williams (Director, Information Resource Center, American Health Care Association).

Lastly, as one can see from the title page, I decided that it was time to bring in another person to assist in the preparation of this and future editions. Margaret Zarnosky is serving as a "junior" author on this edition, after having provided excellent comments and ideas for the last edition.

G. Edward Evans
Los Angeles, California

This volume has provided me with a unique opportunity, and I have very much enjoyed assisting in its preparation. Beyond those individuals mentioned above, who deserve thanks for their assistance, I also wish to acknowledge several individuals for their efforts on behalf of this project. In particular, Annemarie Anderson and Sylvia Rortvedt (Northern Virginia Community College, Alexandria Campus) both deserve special thanks. Annemarie provided a critical "library student's perspective" of the work in progress, including the newly added tables in chapter 4. Sylvia, as Collection Development Officer, was always available to provide insight and suggestions for the text, as well as needed research support. Finally, a very special thank-you to my parents for their love and support.

Margaret R. Zarnosky
Alexandria, Virginia

Preface to the Fifth Edition

Just as libraries and information centers have changed dramatically in the span of five years since the last edition of this text, so has the role of the collection development officer. This edition attempts to reflect those changes.

As has been our practice, a survey was distributed to instructors who used the fourth edition. Keeping this edition to a reasonable length was an important goal for us. Therefore, the users' feedback on what to add and drop proved invaluable. We owe a very special thanks to the twenty-six instructors and collection development officers who took the time and offered suggestions and commented on chapter content.

Although survey respondents did suggest material to drop, it was still necessary to cut additional material in order to achieve the desired length of this text. Providing proper coverage while maintaining a reasonable book length was a challenge that required compromise. The option we chose was to develop a CD for supplementary material and for material from the fourth edition. We also have a website (<http://www.lu.com/dlc5/>) to update and expand upon websites referenced throughout the text.

Some of the major changes in this edition are as follows. Readers will note the chapter count is down by one as the result of combining serials (print and electronic) into a single chapter—6. Additionally, the chapters on other electronic materials (chapter 7), government information (chapter 8), audiovisual materials (chapter 9), and resource sharing (chapter 15) have been almost completely rewritten. Chapter 1 (Information Age—Information Society) has likewise been heavily edited to reflect suggestions from instructors. All of the remaining chapters contain extensive revisions, reflecting changing practices, policies, and technologies.

This edition would not have been possible without the contributions of a great number of individuals. We are especially grateful for the assistance of Christina Hennessey and Glenn Johnson-Grau, who provided valuable text for chapter 7, as well as those who read draft chapters—Rhonda Rosen from the Loyola Marymount University Staff, Sandra Beeson from Northern Virginia Community College, and Marianne Ryan and Yvonne Carignan from the University of Maryland Libraries. Mary Goldberg from Camarillo Public Library and Carla McCaffrey from Woodlin Elementary

School also provided input, which was greatly appreciated. We would also like to extend a very special thanks to Dr. Donald Davis from the University of Texas for reading the entire manuscript and for his many invaluable comments and suggestions. As always, the input of each of these individuals greatly improved the manuscript. However, they are not responsible for errors in content.

We hope this edition will prove as useful to students and others as did previous editions.

G. Edward Evans
Los Angeles, California
Margaret Z. Saponaro
College Park, Maryland

1
Information Age—Information Society

Reading is the opposite of dissipation;
it is a mental and moral practice of concentration
which leads us to unknown worlds.

—Octavio Paz[1]

More than eight years have passed since *Angels From Russia* (1998) was nominated for the prestigious Booker McConnell Prize, an event that created a controversy. (The Booker Prize goes to the best full-length novel in English by an author who is a citizen of the U.K., the Commonwealth, Ireland, Pakistan, or South Africa.) What created the stir was that a person could not buy a copy of the novel in a bookstore; it was solely a virtual book. The judges debated "when is a book a book" and literary merit versus format. As far as we know, there is no information available about how far *Angels* went in the consideration process; what we do know is it did not win the prize. At the time and very much today, the issue of "physical versus virtual" book existence plays a role in the minds of many people. The U.S. National Book Awards Committee did not clarify the issue in 2001, when it announced e-books would be eligible for a prize but only if the publisher submitted "a hard copy of the work, printed and bound on 8½ by 11-inch paper."[2]

It has been suggested that books and reading are something like horses.[3] That is, in the late 19th century, horses were the primary mode of transportation. Today, we still have horses, but primarily for pleasure use, and only a few people ride for pleasure. Perhaps some time in the future, books and reading will be the "horses" of information. However, even if it becomes possible to deliver all information to all individuals everywhere electronically, we believe that the current interest in the technology that

1

makes information available misses a key point, as reflected in the Paz quotation, which goes on to state:

> . . . to read is to discover unsuspected paths that lead to our own selves. It is recognition. In the era of advertising and instantaneous communication, how many people are able to read this way? Very few. But the continuity of our civilization lies with them.[4]

What Is a Book?

Definitively answering this question is probably not possible at this time. As David Greetham noted,[5] the *Oxford English Dictionary* has more than 120 separate meanings for "book." He concludes his fifteen-page essay on what a book is by stating that "there is enough critical meat here to keep me busy for many months ahead, and (as I threatened before), possibly to produce 'a book' (if by then I know what that is)."[6] Given there is such a semantic range in usage of the word *book*, it is perhaps understandable that the "information industry" uses the word with a wide range of meanings.

The late 1990s was a time when predictions abounded that print books were dead and the e-book's time had come. Traditional publishers were announcing new e-book programs, and new e-book companies formed. The conventional wisdom developing during this time was that print was out, and e-resources would rule. This did not come to pass completely as planned, and, to paraphrase Mark Twain, the news of the demise of print was/is premature. However, that also does not mean that e-books have gone the way of 8-track tapes and stereoscopes. In fact, as we prepared this edition, a program for the American Library Association (ALA) summer 2004 convention was announced with the title "E-Book Update." As noted in the ALA preliminary program description, "E-books are not dead! Steady progress is being made in publishing, marketing, and distributing e-books. Important standards are reaching a mature stage. E-book promoters see a strong foundation for future success of this digital product."[7]

One reason that a person might think e-books are dead is the steady stream of announcements seen as early as 2001 and continuing up to the time we wrote this chapter about failed e-book projects. Some examples include AOL Time Warner laying off most of its digital book employees due to poor sales in December 2001,[8] Gemstar eBooks[9] announcement in June 2003 that they were "winding down" their e-book operations, and *Library Hotline*'s September 2003 news article discussing the decision by Barnes & Noble to drop e-book venture due to issues with sales and viewing.[10] One company that made a name for itself, NetLibrary (<http://www.netlibrary .com/>), still existed in the summer of 2004, but not as the stand-alone for-profit organization it was intended to be when launched in 1998. Instead, it became part of OCLC, which acquired the company in 2002, when it went into bankruptcy.

It was not as though these happenings came as a complete surprise. Two articles published in 2001 provided a cautionary note about the speed with which e-books would become the dominant format. D. T. Max's[11] "The Last Book" asks the question, "If computers finally replace trusted hardcover and paperback, will our culture ever be the same?" His answer is that when (if) it happens, it is critical that one reads and does so widely. We would add, "Read with a critical eye and think about the content." Steven Sottong[12] was more skeptical about the speed of change from print to e-book in his work "E-Book Technology: Waiting for the 'False Pretender.'"

Despite the sometimes gloomy prospects for their futures, we do not believe print or e-books are dead. Rather, we think, at present and for some time to come, e-books have a niche market for supplying quick factual information. When the technology makes it easy to curl up comfortably in bed to read a "trashy" e-novel or to read an e-book at the beach or in the backyard on a sunny day, its time may indeed have arrived. At present, few people read more than a couple of pages of an e-document on their computer screen. Instead, many choose to print long documents to read as a "traditional" print format. As is true of most information formats, digital is very good for some things and not so good for others. It seems very likely that paper and digital materials will coexist for a very long time, with each format doing what it does best.

Libraries, Collections, and the Virtual World

For some time now, the popular press has put forward the idea that the "virtual" world has arrived and that institutions such as libraries and print formats are dying, if not already dead. Some, perhaps many, people seem to believe that everything important is to be found only in some type of digital format.

An early example of such blind faith in electronic resources appeared in a book one of this text's authors reviewed some years ago. Åsebrit Sundquist reworked her doctoral dissertation and published it as *Pocahontas & Co.: The Fictional American Indian Woman in Nineteenth-Century Literature*. In an otherwise fine study, her faith in electronic resources, especially at such an early date, was surprising. Given the time period she covered, it is very surprising her doctoral committee did not raise questions about her apparent overdependence on electronic databases. In several sections of her book, she made statements to the effect that there were few research studies of 19th-century Native American women to be found. At one point she went so far as to declare, "There are very few historical or anthropological studies about American Indian women in particular. *A database search (DIALOG) confirmed this*" (emphasis in the original).[13] A quick check of print bibliographies in the reviewer's office yielded twenty-eight 19th-century articles by and about Native American women in probably less time than it took to conduct the DIALOG search. Our purpose is *not* to disparage the study but to make the point that there has been, and is, a widespread misunderstanding of just what is and is not in electronic form.

In a more recent example (2003), during an initial fund-raising planning meeting for the construction of a new library, the person who would lead the funding activities said he did not see why it was necessary to build a new library, as books were dead and everything his daughter needed for her education was available on the Web. His comments were somewhat echoed in a short article in the *Economist*[14] with the title "Dumbing–Down, Mind Games." The article explored the societal problems arising from sound bites, predigested news, instant analysis, and so on and noted that, at least in the U.K., book and literary festivals were growing in popularity, which the editors saw as a counterbalance to a general "dumbing" down of society.

Given the shift toward more complex technologies to distribute information, a question that appears before us is—are libraries and books two of the 21st-century "dinosaurs"? We do not believe that is the case. Without question, we are at the start of a transition/transformation of both libraries and books caused by technology. Libraries have a substantial institutional history—more than 5,000 years—while books are relative newcomers. People forget, if they ever thought about it, that society developed and maintained the concept of a library for thousands of years. One of the first libraries, at least identified in the archaeological record, was in the city of Ur (Akkadian civilization) dating to about 2850 B.C.

Throughout the ensuing millennium complex societies around the world have had four constant values/beliefs about libraries:

- it is physical place;
- it is a collection of what is deemed to be important information materials;
- it organizes those materials and provides assistance in their use; and
- it preserves the materials for future users.

This last point is important to note, as libraries need to be considered for both their potential impact upon society and their use of some form of physical space. Libraries are part of the "information highway" that connects people to the world of knowledge. They use the knowledge to build and improve their society, and in the process they create new knowledge that needs preservation. Thus, there is an ever-growing need for space to house print and digital materials.

In today's environment, we talk about information and electronic resources. While "information" is what libraries have always been about, for many people, libraries will be forever linked to, and equated with, books. (A discussion of the characteristics of information may be found on the CD accompanying this text.) This is not the true picture of today's libraries, nor, for that matter, has this been an accurate representation of the scope of library collections for many years.

The fact is, over time, libraries have added or adapted many formats or technologies in their role of organizing and preserving information. Ur's library was a collection of clay tablets. At some point in history, there was probably concern when a new technology—the scroll—came on the scene, in that it did not seem very permanent. Egyptian libraries' collections were papyrus scrolls, while Roman libraries' collections were vellum scrolls. When the codex/book appeared, another transition was necessary. During the Middle Ages, the vellum manuscript books were so costly to produce that collections were chained down. With the development of paper-based books and the printing press yet another change took place. Surely, just as the scroll was likely met with some skepticism by those who used clay tablets to store information, it is very likely that some angst about cheap paper books occurred at their inception. Some may have even gone so far as to say there would be no need for libraries anymore. After all, at this point, anyone could have their own books and personal libraries. Although personal libraries did arise, libraries became even more important as the volume of information increased. The 20th century brought with it an expansion in the formats libraries collected—microforms, sound recordings, CD-ROMs, videocassettes, etc. By the end of the century, electronic resources started to become important components in library collections, while other formats continued to be collected. Thus, libraries have changed and adapted over time, but their basic functions have remained constant.

In 2003, Ann Okerson published an article in which she outlined her personal view of the digital library. In the article she wrote about eight "eternal verities" or assumptions that library collection managers bring to an electronic world. These assumptions are as valid for e-resources as they are for "traditional" formats. Her primary message that libraries are adapting and will continue to adapt to the digital environment is summed up in one of her concluding sentences: "May we all go boldly together where no libraries have gone before."[15]

Libraries have been going "boldly together" toward the future for more than 5,000 years. As Patricia Sabosik[16] noted, the turmoil in today's publishing is almost the same as it was in the 15th century. Just as the printing press shifted access to information from a few to many people in the mid-17th century, we are seeing a similar shift today. Sabosik suggested that the shift today is from libraries to end users. In her view, libraries are becoming intermediaries, rather than storehouses, of information. Certainly some of the shifting she described has already taken place and is likely to grow in scope; however, the process will probably take a long time to complete—that is, assuming that the virtual library, or knowledge center, of the future does ultimately become little more than an electronic switching center service.

The net effect of the many advances in technology we see on a daily basis is a new phenomenon that raises unique issues for libraries and society. Many problems relate to handling the economic aspects of information and access to that information (often written about in terms of ownership versus access). Although a detailed discussion of these problems is beyond the scope of this book, we will mention them where they have an influence on collection development and resource management.

Our view is that the future of libraries will lie somewhere between the technologists' projections and what exists today. The idea of fiction, essays, literature, poetry, and biographies becoming the "horses" of the information future is most unappealing and in our opinion highly unlikely.

What does all this have to do with collection development? Everything, we believe. Even if the "brave new world" of electronic information comes to pass, there will still exist a need for locally maintained resources, if for no other reason than cost control. It is crucial to understand that the availability of information in an electronic format does not reduce costs but rather shifts them. Securing information from locally maintained databases, for high-use sources, will most likely remain less expensive than paying for the information plus the telecommunication charges for accessing a remote database on an as-needed basis. Knowing who is using what, for what purposes, and how often, as well as knowing what sources exist that can supply the information in the most cost-effective way, is the keystone of present and foreseeable collection development work. It matters little what the format is. What does matter in the long run is the ability of the end user to have access to the appropriate resources to read and ponder.

Admittedly, when librarians think of online resources, they are thinking of "scholarly" electronic (fee-based) subscription databases, while the general public thinks in terms of the Internet. Librarians make a distinction between the two while using both resources; most end users do not. "The Web" is a highly mixed bag of the "the good, the bad and the very ugly." Norman Oder, in a *Library Journal* article, outlined some of the problems that exist in finding information on the Internet.[17] The essence of the article was who could—and how to—"tame" the Web: commercial for-profit organizations or librarians? On the "free-available" commercial side, only *Yahoo!* (<http://www.yahoo.com>) even attempts to impose a semblance of order on Internet materials. However, with the number of pages being posted to the Web increasing by the minute, Yahoo!'s efforts cover only a small portion of the total available. As for efforts of individual libraries to "tame" the Web, reference librarians and collection development officers have been "selecting," establishing appropriate links (acquisition), arranging (cataloging), and periodically reviewing (evaluation) Internet sites for some time. One need only look to Librarian's Index to the Internet (<http://www.lii.org>) and the Internet Public Library (<http://www.ipl. org>) as examples. The process of "collection building" appropriate sites draws on the same skills and principles that librarians have employed for years with print materials (see pages 15–16), demonstrating that the skills of the collection development librarian apply no matter what medium is involved.

In fact, no matter what form the future "megalibrary" may take, it is certain that its basis will be a collection of information resources. Unless there is a *plan* for what the collection will contain, the megalibrary will have limited, if any, value. The purpose of this book is to assist individuals in gaining an understanding of the process of developing an intelligent and useful collection for the end users of that collection.

Concepts and Terms

Regardless of the type of clientele they serve, the primary purpose of all libraries and information centers is to assist in the transfer of information and the development of knowledge. Figure 1.1, page 17, illustrates the process involved, using nine circles to represent the transfer cycle. There is the *identification* stage, during which the organization segregates appropriate from inappropriate information. In most instances, there is more appropriate information available than the organization can handle. Thus, there is a need to *select* the most appropriate or important information to *acquire*. After acquisition, the organization *organizes* the information in some manner. Upon completion of the organizing action comes the *preparation* of the information for *storage*, which should ensure the information is easily retrievable. Users often need assistance to describe their needs in a manner that leads to locating and retrieving the desired information (*interpretation*). Finally, users draw upon the secured information to aid them in their activities/work (*utilization*) and disseminate the outcome of the work to the internal or external environment or both. If the transfer process is to function properly, there must be procedures, policies, and people in place to carry out the necessary *operational* steps. As always, there must be coordination and money for the operations to do what they were set up to do; this is the administrative and managerial aspect of information work.

The foregoing discussion helps set the stage for this book, which focuses on the process of building information collections for long- and short-term storage. Collection development, or information acquisition, is one

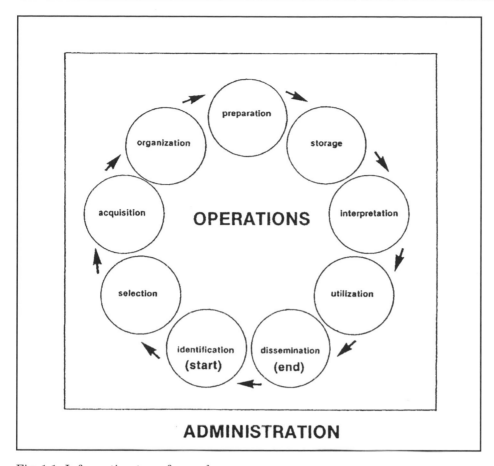

Fig. 1.1. Information transfer work.

area common to both librarianship and information resource management. As in prior editions, we define collection development as "the process of identifying the strengths and weaknesses of a library's materials collection in terms of patron needs and community resources, and attempting to correct existing weaknesses, if any." With only minor modifications, this definition can apply to both libraries and information centers in any organization collecting materials in any format. Thus, collection development is the process of meeting the information needs of the people (a service population) in a timely and economical manner using information resources locally held, as well as from other organizations. This new definition is broader in scope and places emphasis on thoughtful (timely and economical) collection building and on seeking out both internal and external information resources. It is worth noting that Ross Atkinson suggested that the phrases *collection development* and *collection management* are being used interchangeably and that there is no consensus on which term is more comprehensive in scope.[18]

Collection development is a universal process for libraries and information centers. Figure 1.2, page 8, illustrates the six major components of the process. One can see a relationship between figures 1.1 and 1.2 in that collection development involves three of the nine information transfer ele-

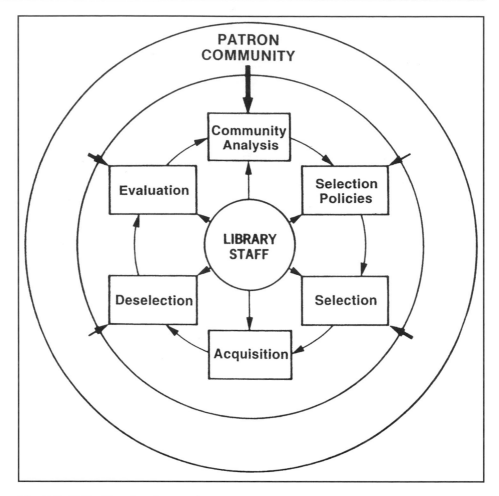

Fig. 1.2. Collection development process.

ments (identification, selection, acquisition). As implied by the circle, collection development is a constant cycle that continues as long as the library or information center exists. All of the elements in the cycle are discussed in subsequent chapters.

Because of our philosophy of collection development, which has a focus on meeting the information needs of the community the collection serves, we begin the discussion of collection development with the needs assessment (community analysis) element. The terms *needs assessment, community analysis*, or *user community*, as used throughout this book, mean the group of persons that the library exists to serve. They do *not* refer only to the active users but include everyone within the library's or information center's defined service limits. Thus, a community might be an entire political unit (i.e., a nation, region, state, province, county, city, or town). Alternatively, a community may be a more specialized grouping or association (i.e., a university, college, school, government agency, or private organization). Also, the number of people that the library is to serve may range from a very few to millions. As discussed in chapter 2, data for the analysis comes from a variety of sources, not just staff-generated material. For collection development personnel, the assessment process provides data on what information the clientele needs. It also establishes a valuable mechanism for user input into the process of collection development. (Note the size of the arrow in figure 1.2 from the community to collection development; the size indicates the level of "community" input appropriate for each element.)

One use for the data collected in a needs assessment is as part of the preparation for collection development policy. Clearly delineated policies on both collection development and selection (covered in chapter 3) provide collection development staff with guidelines for choosing items for inclusion in the collection. (Note that collection policies cover a wider range of topics than just selection policies. For example, *selection* policies normally provide only information useful in deciding which items to purchase, whereas *collection* policies cover that topic in addition to such related issues as gifts, weeding, and cooperation.) Most libraries have some of the required information available for their collection development personnel, although they do not always label it "policy." Some libraries call it an *acquisitions* policy, some a *selection* policy, some a *collection development* policy, and others simply a *statement*. Whatever the local label, the intent is the same: to define the library's goals for its collection(s) and to help staff members select and acquire the most appropriate materials.

At this point, the staff begins the procedures for selecting materials (covered in chapters 4 through 9), using whatever written policies or statements the library has prepared. For many people, this is the most interesting element in the collection development process. One constant factor in collection development is that there is never enough money available to buy everything that might be of value to the service community. Naturally, this means that someone, usually one or more professional staff members, must decide which items to buy. *Selection* is this process of deciding which materials to acquire for a library collection. It may involve deciding among items that provide information about the same subject; deciding whether the information contained in an item is worth the price; or determining whether an item could stand up to the use it would receive. In essence, it is a matter of systematically determining quality and value. Selection is a form of decision making. Most of the time it is not just a matter of identifying appropriate materials but of deciding among items that are essential, important, needed, marginal, nice, or luxurious. Where to place any item in the sequence from essential to luxurious depends, of course, on the individual selector's point of view. It is just a matter of perception. So it is with library materials.

Individuals buying an item for themselves normally do not have to justify the expenditure to anyone. However, when it is a question of spending the library community's money, whether derived from taxes or an organization's budget, the problem becomes more complex. The question of whose perception of value to use is one of the challenges in collection development. Needs assessments and policies help determine the answer, but there is a long-standing question in the field: How much emphasis should selectors place on clientele demand and how much on content quality? Often the question of perception comes up when someone objects to the presence of an item in the collection (see chapter 18).

Once the selectors make their decisions, the acquisition work begins (see chapters 10, 11, and 12). *Acquisition work* is the process of securing materials for the library's collection, whether by purchase, as gifts, or through exchange programs. This is the only point in the collection development process that involves little or no community input; it is a fairly straightforward business operation. Once the staff decides to purchase an item, the acquisition department proceeds with the preparation of an order form and the selection of a vendor, eventually recording the receipt of the item and finally paying the bill (invoice). Though details vary, the basic routines remain the same around the world, just as they do in either a manual or automated work environment. (Note that the *acquisition* process does not always mean buying an item. Gift and exchange programs can also be useful means of acquiring needed material.)

After receipt, an item goes through a series of internal library operations (beyond the scope of this book), such as cataloging, and is eventually made available to the patron community. Over time, nearly every item outlives its original usefulness in the collection. Often the decision is to remove these items from the main collection. The activity of examining items in the library and determining their current value to that library's collection (and to the service community) has several labels, the oldest being *weeding* (see chapter 13). Another term for this process is *deselection* (the opposite of selection). In the United Kingdom, the term used is *stock relegation*. Regardless of the label used for this activity, the end result is the same. When a library decides that a given item is no longer of value, it will dispose of the item (by selling it, giving it away, or even throwing it away). If the item still has some value for the library, the decision may be to transfer the item to a less accessible and usually less expensive storage location.

Evaluation (see chapter 14) is the last element in the collection development process. To some extent, weeding is an evaluation activity, but weeding is also more of an internal library operation. Evaluation of a collection may serve many different purposes, both inside and outside the library. For example, it may help to increase funding for the library. It may aid in the library's gaining some form of recognition, such as high standing in a comparative survey. Additionally, it may help to determine the quality of the work done by the collection development staff. For effective evaluation to occur, the service community's needs must be considered, which leads back to community analysis.

There is little reason to define library materials other than to emphasize that this volume covers various formats, not just books. Different authors writing about library collections use a number of related terms: *print, nonprint, visual materials, audiovisuals, AV, other media*, and so on. There is no single term encompassing all forms that has gained universal acceptance among librarians. *Library materials* (or simply, *materials*) is a nonspecific term with respect to format that is otherwise inclusive. Thus, we use it throughout this text. Library materials may include books, periodicals, pamphlets, reports, manuscripts, microformats, motion pictures, videotapes or audiotapes, DVDs, CDs, sound recordings, realia, and so forth. In effect, almost any physical object that conveys information, thoughts, or feelings potentially can be part of an information collection.

Before we go further, several other commonly used terms must also be defined: *collection management, information resource management, knowledge management, content management,* and *records management*. The terms cover similar activities and differ primarily in organizational context. *Collection management* is a broad-based activity encompassing all the aspects of collection development discussed above, as well as other issues related to the collection such as preservation, legal concerns, access, and resource sharing. The process usually places emphasis on collecting materials produced by other organizations. *Information resource management*, as used today, relates to any organizational context, often without any centralized collection of materials, in which the information resource manager is responsible for identifying and making available both internal and external sources of information. Practitioners in computer science and information systems generally define *knowledge management* as the "management of objects that can be identified and handled in information systems."[19] Martin White defined *content management* as software that "provides a platform for managing the creation, review, filing, updating, distribution, and storage of structured and unstructured content."[20] *Records management* is the process of handling the working records of an organization with an emphasis on retention, retrieval, and access issues. No matter which term is most familiar to you, the resulting goal of each of the activities defined by these terms is to provide accurate information in a timely and cost-effective manner to all members of the service community.

Collection Development and the Community

As seen in our earlier review of the "evolution" of library technology from clay tablets to the gigabyte, factors inside and outside the library influence collection development. Among these factors are the library's structure and organization, the production and distribution of the information materials, and the presence of other libraries in the area. Figure 1.3, page 12, illustrates some of the interrelationships among the library organization, the producers and distributors of materials, and other libraries.

Traditionally, libraries have organized their internal activities into public and technical services. Those activities in which the staff has daily contact with clientele are considered public services; almost all other activities are frequently considered a part of technical services. Collection development work bridges this traditional division. With the automation of library functions, the boundaries between public and technical services are disappearing. In fact, they are becoming so undefined that some libraries are doing away with these labels. In the "traditional" model of collection development, library staff responsible for collection development provides information to the acquisition department, which in turn orders the desired items from the materials producer or a distributor. After receiving the materials and clearing the records, the acquisition department sends the items on to the cataloging department for processing. Eventually, the processed items go onto shelves, into cabinets, or onto websites as links to databases or as full-text files. No matter the format, the end result is that the materials are placed where the public can use them. Both the public service staff and the individuals using the collections provide input to the collection development staff concerning the "value" of individual items. The selection staff then considers the input when performing deselection and evaluation activities. The information generated from these sources may eventually influence the library's written policies for collection development.

Materials producers exert many significant influences. Obviously, they control what is available for library purchase by their choice of whether or not to produce any given item. (Chapters 4 and 5 describe some of the factors in such decisions.) Furthermore, their business requirements occa-

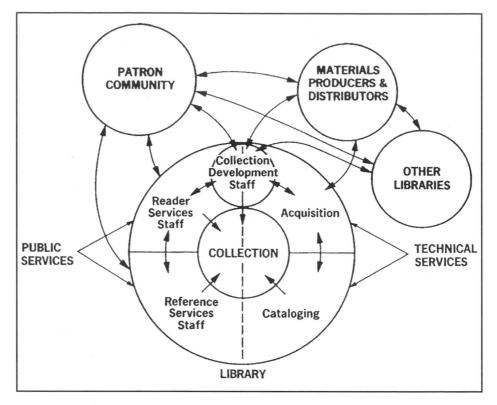

Fig. 1.3. Collection development, the library, and the community.

sionally cause libraries to modify their acquisition procedures; however, most producers and vendors are very good about accommodating unusual library requirements. Finally, producers market their products directly to the community, thus generating a demand. Despite fears that libraries are not used as heavily as they once were, people often communicate this demand to the library rather than buying the item, thus causing an indirect response to the marketing activities of the material producers.

Collections and services in other libraries and information centers used by the service population also influence collection development. Cooperative collection development programs enable libraries to provide better service, a wider range of materials, or both. Resource sharing projects can also reduce the duplication of materials that results from overlapping service communities and user influence on collection development. For example, a person might engage in business research while in the company's library. The person may take evening classes at an academic institution, using that library for class-related and business-related materials alike. That same individual may also rely on a local public library—because of its convenience—to supply information on job-related, class assignments, and recreational concerns. Thus, one person's requests for job-related materials could influence three different types of libraries in the same area to collect the same material. Despite their numerous advantages, effective cooperative programs can still be difficult to manage (see chapter 15 for a further discussion of this issue).

Collection Development and Institutional Environments

The variety of institutional settings in which one finds information services is large. However, it is possible to group our discussion around four general categories: education, business, government, and research. These categories share some basic characteristics. All have a specific service population, all collect and preserve materials in a form suitable for use by the service population, and each organizes materials in a manner designed to aid in the rapid identification and retrieval of desired material(s). The definitions given earlier also apply to all of these categories. Differences emerge because of both the specific service population and the limits set by the library's or information center's governing body.

Collection development is a universal process for all types of libraries. As one moves from one environmental setting to another, however, differences in emphasis on the various elements of the collection development process become apparent. For example, some education (school) and government (public) libraries tend to place more emphasis on library staff selection activities than do business and research libraries. Also, differences in emphasis occur within a type of library, so that occasionally a community college library (education) might more closely resemble a large public library (government) in its collection development activities than it does a university library (education). The approach taken in this book is to present a general overview of these activities, noting when necessary the differences among and within the types.

To some extent, the chapters in this book reflect these differences in emphasis. For several reasons, needs analysis is very important in public and school libraries, as well as in information centers (in a business), but it receives less emphasis in college and university libraries. In public libraries, selection is usually the responsibility of librarians, whereas in other types of information centers patrons have a stronger direct voice in the selection process. Public libraries need the information derived from such an analysis to build an effective collection; therefore, chapter 2 on information needs assessment has a public library's slant. School libraries often employ teacher/librarian selection methods that place an emphasis on published reviews.

The size of a library's service community has a definite bearing on collection development. Three facts of collection development are universal:

1. As the size of the service community increases, the degree of divergence in individual information needs increases.

2. As the degree of divergence in individual information needs increases, the need for resource sharing increases.

3. It will never be possible to satisfy *all* of the information needs of any individual or class of clientele in the service community.

Even special libraries and information centers, serving a limited number of persons, encounter problems in relation to these laws. Because no two persons are identical, it is impossible for their materials needs and interests to entirely coincide. In the special library environment, the interests of users can be, and often are, very similar, but even within a team of research workers exploring a single problem, individual needs will vary. The needs of a small group are not as homogeneous as they may appear at first.

The element of collection development that varies the least is collection development policy. Simply put, as the collection grows in size, the need for more complex and detailed policy statements increases. Thus, large academic and research libraries generally have the most comprehensive collection policy statements. We review collection development policies in chapter 3.

Selection is the element that varies the most among and within the types. Because of those many variations, it is difficult to make many generalizations. However, with that in mind, the following are some general statements about the variations:

1. Public libraries emphasize title-by-title selection, and librarians do the selecting.

2. School libraries also emphasize title-by-title selection. Although the media specialist may make the final decision, a committee composed of librarians, teachers, administrators, and parents may have a strong voice in the process.

3. Special and corporate libraries select materials in rather narrow subject fields for specific research and business purposes. Often the client is the primary selector.

4. Academic libraries select materials in subject areas for educational and research purposes, with selection done by several different methods: faculty only, joint faculty/library committees, librarians only, or subject specialists.

Selection also varies by the role the library has in the "parent" organization of which it is part. The academic libraries' role is in the dissemination and creation of knowledge. School media centers focus on dissemination and the development of knowledge, while public and special libraries' roles are the dissemination and utilization of knowledge.

The size of the collection is also a factor in determining the who and the how of selection. In small public libraries, most of the librarians do some selection work. (Very often there is only one librarian to do all the professional work.) As the library system grows, adds branches, and expands services, the library director delegates work. More often than not, it is the department heads and branch library supervisors who have selection responsibilities. Large metropolitan systems frequently assign selection activities to a committee composed of representatives from all of the service programs, though not always from every branch. This committee generates a list of titles from which individual services and branches select. In essence, the selection committee does the initial screening and identification work for the system.

A similar relationship of size and selection exists in academic libraries and some special libraries. However, the selectors in these cases, more often than not, are the users: academic faculty or company staff. Even when librarians are responsible for selection in libraries serving institutions with hundreds of subject specialists, the faculty members or researchers have a significant voice in the selection process. Obviously, the in-depth knowledge of a subject specialist can become the deciding factor in making a selection. A common practice in both types of libraries is to hire librarians with graduate degrees in both librarianship and one other subject area. Even then, because of the advanced and sometimes esoteric nature of the research reported in the materials, the library must draw on all of the subject expertise at the institution.

In small academic, school, and special libraries, selection is in the hands of the subject specialist (faculty or researcher), unless the librarian is also an expert in the field. Indeed, small teaching institutions often expect the faculty to build the library collection. As budgets for materials increase and the collection grows proportionally, the librarians become more involved in selection activities.

Eventually, a collection will fill all available shelf space. Some time before that happens, the library must decide either to reduce the collection size (deselection) or to create additional storage space. In school and public libraries, this does not present a great problem; patrons often wear out popular items, freeing up shelf space. Often, such libraries buy multiple copies of items. Then, by retaining just one copy after demand drops, they regain some shelf space. Also, only exceptionally large public libraries have major archival responsibilities; thus, weeding is somewhat easier. Academic and research libraries seldom buy multiple copies and have significant archival responsibilities, making deselection an involved process. Special (business) libraries perform deselection on a regular basis because of space limitations. Often this results in rules for weeding (for instance, discard all monographs that are five years old). Rules of this kind help to solve one problem: lack of staff time for deselection. However, this less thoughtful approach to the problem may increase the demand for interlibrary loan of items discarded. More research has been performed on weeding/deselection in academic libraries than for all of the other types of libraries combined, and chapter 13, with its emphasis on academic libraries, includes a further discussion of this issue.

Although the final phase of the process, collection evaluation, takes place in all types of libraries, it is especially significant in libraries serving educational organizations. One form of evaluation is performed by an outside agency that determines the quality of education provided (accreditation) by schools and academic institutions. If nothing more, the agency (government or private) that funds the institution will require periodic assessments, which will invariably include the library and its collection. For such libraries, the evaluation process may have far-reaching effects. Naturally, librarians in educational institutions have a strong interest in improving the evaluation process, and they have written a great deal about the topic. Chapter 14 draws heavily upon this literature, as well as the literature on accreditation.

Collection development is a dynamic process that should involve both the information professional and the service community. Few information professionals question the need or value of client input; the question is how much there should be. The best answer is, as much as the organization can handle and still carry out its basic functions and as much as the community is willing to provide.

In the end, the following statements are the philosophical foundations of this work:

1. Collection development should be geared primarily to identified needs rather than to abstract standards of quality; however, an identified need can be a long-term need (more than five years into the future), not just an immediate need.

2. Collection development, to be effective, must be responsive to the *total* community's needs, not just to those of the current or the most active users.

3. Collection development should be carried out with knowledge of, and participation in, cooperative programs at the local, regional, state, national, and international levels.

4. Collection development should consider all information formats for inclusion in the collection.

5. Collection development was, is, and always will be subjective, biased work. A periodic review of the selector's personal biases and their effects on the selection process is the best check against developing a collection that reflects personal interests rather than user interests.

6. Collection development is not learned entirely in the classroom or from reading. Only through practice, taking risks, and learning from mistakes will a person become proficient in the process of developing a collection.

Summary

Without doubt, technology is changing the way libraries and information centers do business. Some writers, as noted earlier, suggest that the "virtual library" means the demise of collection development. However, those who understand the concept know that the issue of selection and collection building will remain an important function in whatever environment technology brings.

One can engage in collection development in libraries and information centers that are either formally or informally organized. Although organization labels will vary, the process is the same. Most large organizations now view information and its management and control to be as essential as any other resource they employ. In fact, obtaining the right information at the right time and being able to analyze and apply it successfully are crucial to an organization's success and survival. As a result, organizations are training and hiring people who know how to acquire and manage information resources. Though many organizations will not call these individuals librarians, and they may not work in libraries, they need and use many of the same skills librarians traditionally employ in collection building. Whatever environment one works in, collection development is an exciting challenge that requires lifelong learning. Throughout this text, we will highlight various means of keeping current in this ever-changing field.

Notes

1.   Octavio Paz, *The Other Voice: Essays on Modern Poetry* (San Diego: Harcourt Brace Jovanovich, 1991), 88.

2.   Roger Durbin, James Nalen, Diana Chlebek, and Nancy Pitre, "eBook Collection Development and Management: The Quandary of Establishing Policies and Guidelines for Academic Library Collections," in *Advances in Library Administration and Organization*, vol. 19, ed. Edward Garten and Delmus Williams, 61 (Greenwich, CT: JAI Press, 2002).

3.   James Lictenberg, "Reading: Does the Future Even Require It?" *Liberal Education* 79 (Winter 1993): 11.

4.   Paz, *The Other Voice*, 88.

5.   David Greetham, "What Is a Book?" *Journal of Scholarly Publishing* 34 (July 2003): 182–97.

6.   Ibid., 196.

7.   American Library Association, *Preliminary Tracks Program: As of 11/9/03* (Chicago: American Library Association, 2003), 16.

8.   David D. Kirkpatrick, "AOL Retreats From Big Push for E-Books," e-mail to alta-l@ala1.ala.org discussion list, December 5, 2001.

9.   "A Very Important Ebook Announcement," June 18, 2003, <http://www.gemstarebook.com/cgi-bin/WebObjects/eBookstore.woa/wo/0.0.5.0.23.1.0.5>.

10.   "Barnes & Noble Drops eBooks Citing Sales, Unwieldy Devices," *Library Hotline* 32, no. 38 (September 22, 2003): 1.

11.   D. T. Max, "The Last Book," *UTNE Reader* 104 (March–April 2001): 74–80.

12.   Stephen Sottong, "E-Book Technology: Waiting for the 'False Pretender,'" *Information Technology and Libraries* 20, no. 2 (2001): 72–80.

13.   Åsebrit Sundquist, *Pocahontas & Co.: The Fictional American Indian Woman in Nineteenth-Century Literature* (Atlantic Highlands, NJ: Humanities Press International, 1981), 209.

14.   "Dumbing–Down, Mind Games," *Economist* 368 (August 2, 2003): 53.

15.   Ann Okerson, "Asteroids, Moore's Law and the Star Alliance," *Journal of Academic Librarianship* 29, no. 5 (2003): 285.

16.   Patricia Sabosik, "Document Delivery Services: Today's Electronic Scriptoria," *Computers in Libraries* 12 (December 1992): 16–17.

17.   Norman Oder, "Cataloging the Net: Can We Do It?" *Library Journal* 123 (October 1, 1998): 47–51.

18.   Ross Atkinson, "Managing Traditional Materials in an Online Environment," *Library Resources & Technical Services* 42 (January 1998): 10.

19.   Mark Brogan, Philip Hingston, and Vicky Wilson, "A Rich Storehouse for the Relief of Man's Estate," in *Advances in Library Administration and Organization*, vol. 19, ed. Edward Garten and Delmus Williams, 2 (Greenwich, CT: JAI Press, 2002).

20.   Martin White, "Content Management," *Online* 26, no. 6 (2002): 20.

Further Reading

Alsmeyer, D. "Reinventing the Corporate Library." *Multimedia Information and Technology* 27 (February 2001): 64–68.

Brooks, S. "Integration of Information Resources and Collection Development Strategy." *Journal of Academic Librarianship* 27 (July 2001): 316–19.

Buchanan, W. E. "Developing Library Collections When Everyone Thinks the Internet Is Everything." *Rural Libraries* 22, no. 1 (2002): 31–40.

Chandler, Y. J., et al. "Libraries and Librarians: The Key to Growth and Survival? The Relationship Between Corporate Productivity and Information Services." *INSPEL* 36, no. 4 (2002): 223–53.

Clay, E. S. "Collection Development: Getting the Point." *Public Libraries* 40 (September–October 2001): 265.

"Collection Development." (Special issue.) *School Libraries in Canada* 21, no. 4 (2002): 1–40.

Crowley, B., and D. Ginsberg. "Professional Values: Priceless." *American Libraries* 36, no. 1 (January 2005): 52–55.

De Rosa, C., L. Dempsey, and A. Wilson. *The 2003 OCLC Environmental Scan: Pattern Recognition.* Dublin, OH: OCLC Online Computer Library Center (2004) <http://www.oclc.org/membership/escan/>.

Dilevko, J., et al. "The Challenge of Building Multilingual Collections in Canadian Public Libraries." *Library Resources & Technical Services* 46 (October 2002): 116–37.

Dobson, C. "Beyond the Information Audit: Checking the Health of an Organization's Information System." *Searcher* 10 (July–August 2002): 32–37.

Edwards, P. M. "Collection Development and Maintenance across Libraries, Archives, and Museums." *Library Resources & Technical Services* 48 (January 2004): 26–33.

Foster, J. B. "Collection Development, from Text to Technology." *Computers in Libraries* 20 (June 2000): 34–39.

Gordon, I. "Asserting Our Collection Development Roles: Academic Librarians Must Take Responsibility for the Collection." *College & Research Libraries News* 61 (September 2000): 687–89.

Greenstein, D., and S. E. Thorin. *The Digital Library: A Biography.* 2nd ed. Washington, DC: Council on Library and Information Resources (2002) <http://www.clir.org/pubs/abstract/pub109abst.html>.

Hutley, S. "E-books in Public Libraries." *Multimedia Information and Technology* 28 (February 2002): 23–24.

Intner, S. S. "Ten Steps to Great Collections." *Technicalities* 22 (July–August 2002): 1, 5–7, 24.

"It's a Marriage—Not a Choice." (Print v. electronic resources in school libraries.) *The School Librarian's Workshop* 23 (January 2003): 7.

Johnson, D. "Print & Electronic Library Resources: A Match Made in Heaven." *School Libraries in Canada* 21, no. 4 (2002): 5–6.

Johnson, M. A. "Dollars and Sense in Collection Development: Skills and Competencies for Collection Development and Management." *Technicalities* 19 (May 1999): 7–9.

Kerby, R. "What Practicing School Media Specialists Say about Collection Development." *School Library Media Activities Monthly* 18 (May 2002): 26–27.

Lee, H. "Collection Development as a Social Process." *Journal of Academic Librarianship* 29 (January 2003): 23–31.

"Managing Books and Technology: Survey Results—Part II." *The School Librarian's Workshop* 23 (October 2002): 6–7.

Miller, R. H. "Electronic Resources and Academic Libraries, 1980–2000: A Historical Perspective." *Library Trends* 48 (Spring 2000): 645–70.

Nielsen, T. "Four Steps I Took That Transformed My Solo Corporate Library." *Computers in Libraries* 23 (October 2003): 22–24.

Stratigos, A., et al. "Going Virtual with the Corporate Library." *Online* 25 (March–April 2001): 66–68.

Tucker, J. C., and M. Torrence. "Collection Development for New Librarians: Advice from the Trenches." *Library Collections, Acquisitions, and Technical Services* 28, no. 4 (Winter 2004): 397–409.

Wiegand, W. W. "Critiquing the Curriculum." *American Libraries* 36, no. 1 (January 2005): 58–61.

Wolf, M. T. "Building Library Collections: The Horse Is Riding Us." *Journal of Educational Media and Library Sciences* 40 (June 2003): 429–37.

2
Information Needs Assessment

Library services and collections should be developed based on an understanding of the service community's information wants and needs. It is virtually impossible, and also unnecessary, to collect information about all aspects of the service community. However, the more the collection development officers know about users' work roles, general interests, education, information or communication behavior, values, and related characteristics, the more likely it is that the collection will provide the desired information at the time desired. Another reason for collecting data about the service population is that with limited resources to serve a wide range of interests, even in a small research and development unit, one must have a solid database of client information in order to prepare an effective collection development plan. In today's collection development environment with its increasing emphasis on e-resources, one should have information about end user technology capabilities, or lack of access in some cases, in order to make sound acquisitions decisions. The cost of e-titles/packages tends to be several times higher than most print and audiovisual (AV) materials, which makes purchasing decisions more critical.

Data collected about users are valuable in policy formulation, selection activities, and evaluation projects. Selection officers should base policy formulation and modification on the data collected. Although the data will seldom provide complete help in the selection of a specific item, it will establish selection parameters. Any assessment of the collection should include a consideration of how well it meets the expectations and needs of the users.

There are many similarities between "need assessment projects" and marketing studies, and they frequently employ the same data-collecting methods. Both focus on gaining insights about the people ("target populations") being studied. Often their goals are similar in that they want to improve the usefulness/value of a service or "product." Additionally, both can produce data valuable for other projects. In some cases it is possible to combine two activities into a single project, as long as one limits the goal(s). Libraries of all types need to market themselves, especially in today's environment, and one builds useful/effective collections, in part, through a solid understanding of the service population. Both types of projects can provide data for accomplishing these purposes. We explore the methods later in this chapter.

Researchers use several terms for the concepts and processes of learning more about a target population: community analysis, information needs analysis, needs analysis, needs assessment, role analysis, user studies, information audit, and market analysis. On a general level, the terms are identical, but they differ greatly in the specifics of application and purpose. *Community analysis* usually refers to a broad study of the service community (public libraries most often engage in this type of study). Sometimes the term *planning process* more accurately identifies the purpose of the activity. The terms *information audit, needs analysis*, and *needs assessment* generally apply to small groups or individual "target groups" (special library, information center, or information brokers employ this approach). (Both needs analysis and needs assessment are discussed in more detail later in this chapter.) *User studies* generally denote research projects designed to gain insight into how, why, when, and where people seek information and use information resources (academic libraries engage in this type of study). *Market analyses* are studies of communities or people to assess interest in, or reactions to, a service or product. All the approaches have value in building the cost-effective collection.

There are several terms—information need, information want, expressed demand, satisfied demand, information behavior—that one will encounter in the literature. (A good article on this subject is T. D. Wilson's "On User Studies and Information Needs."[1]) It is far beyond the scope of this chapter to address all these terms. However, we believe defining three terms, *needs*, *wants*, and *demands*, is important for the purpose of this book. *Needs* are situations (community, institutional, or personal) that require solution; it does not always follow that a need is something the group or person wants. *Wants* are things that the group or person is willing to expend time, effort, or money to acquire; it does not always follow that the thing wanted is good for the group or person. *Demands* are things the group or person wants and is willing to act in concert (writing letters, making telephone calls, testifying, or demonstrating) to acquire. From a library or information center perspective, the ideal outcome of a study is identification of a need that is wanted and demanded.

Conceptual Background

People seek information from both formal and informal systems. Typical informal systems are friends, colleagues, and organizations not designed as formal information sources (community centers, parent–teachers associations, professional associations, clubs, etc.). Clearly, the informal systems provide the bulk of an individual's everyday, or common, information. Daily living activities generate dozens—perhaps hundreds—of information wants, ranging from what is good in the cafeteria today to the interest rate on loans for buying a home, what the weather is like, etc. Depending upon the urgency of the situation, a person locates the information with greater or lesser effort, speed, and accuracy. Most of the daily living and activities information requirements are local in nature. Mass-market sources, such as newspapers, radio, and television, answer most of the broader local information wants. However, even these sources often serve an area so large or diverse that information is not as precise as some people may require. (E.g., in large urban areas major newspapers often publish regional editions.)

As the importance of the information increases (needs), so do the amounts of money, time, and other resources devoted to securing precise, accurate information. A weather forecast (covering 18 to 24 hours) prepared and printed in a newspaper several hours before it is read is adequate for most people. For many people, the weather forecast is of marginal importance, so they expend little time, effort, or money to secure up-to-the-minute, accurate weather information. In contrast, for airline pilots and those who fly with them, weather information is much more important. As a result, airlines commit significant resources to having the latest, most accurate data. When there is a space shuttle launch, a worldwide meteorological network supplies information. From the individual to the largest organization, all information seekers place a value on each type of information used, often without being fully aware that they are doing so. Several factors influence the information's value, such as the role it plays in decision making; the type of information needed (text, numeric, graphic, or audio); and the format of the information package (book, journal, database, cassette, etc.). One important factor is accessibility and the effort required to gain access to information. This factor is governed by what may be called the "law of least effort."

According to the law of least effort, people and organizations expend as little as possible of their resources (time, money, or effort) to secure information. Frequently, when a person is preparing a document, there is a need for more accurate or current information. A typical reaction is to turn first to materials at hand, although the person knows there is only a slight chance that those materials will contain the needed information. Most people try this even when they know where they can secure the appropriate information, just because the known source is less convenient. In a work environment, individuals ask fellow workers before consulting formal information resources. In a variation on this method, scholars and researchers make frequent and successful use of the so-called invisible college, which is a communication network linking people interested in particular topics. One reason for the success of informal information systems is that the formal information system is frequently slow to distribute data.

Collection development staff should know what informal sources exist within the service community. In some cases, it is possible to incorporate some of these informal sources into a formal system, thereby providing better service. Occasionally, such incorporation improves the quality or retrievability of information. Many libraries and information centers offer referral services that supply names of people or organizations expert in an area and willing to supply information. Equally important is knowing how people use the informal system. This may influence both the structure of a formal information system (e.g., a library collection) and the contents of that collection.

Research on both formal and informal information systems has been ongoing for some time. Such studies use and examine terms such as information user (who), information need (what and why), information-seeking behavior (how), and information retrieval success and failure (why). We know that a number of variables (demographics) affect the individual when seeking information.

Level of education is a factor in using the formal information system. Individuals with high school or less education tend not to use the formal information systems. High school graduates up to those with postgraduate degrees tend to be frequent users of the formal systems. At the postgraduate level, usage of the "invisible college" plays an ever-increasing role.

Another factor is level of income, which is often reflective of the attained educational level. Thus, it is not surprising that low-income individuals tend to use libraries less than do middle-income people. High-income people are more likely to either purchase the information they need or have someone get it for them.

Cultural background is yet another consideration, as it creates the individual's basic values and attitudes toward information. Knowing about the service population's cultural backgrounds and attitudes about formal information systems is essential in planning effective services and collections. Few formal information systems have a monocultural service population. It is important that collection development officers take the time to study and understand, to some extent, the cultural contexts represented in the service community.

Group membership, reference groups, and the invisible college all influence how an individual responds to formal information systems. In the work situation, the organization and work responsibilities also enter the picture. Organizations establish special, if not unique, values regarding information. They determine what constitutes information for them, how valuable or important information is, and how much of the organization's resources should go into providing information services. Within that context, departments and work units establish their value systems.

Economic considerations are more and more a factor in decision making in the information center environment. Twenty years ago in the United States, few people questioned the idea of a totally subsidized public library or the desirability of having such a library in every community. In the mid-1970s, there was a discussion of costs and benefits in terms of library services and materials. Now there is more and more frequent discussion of partial, if not full, cost recovery.

The following articles represent the variety of studies that are appropriate in library settings. They also give a sense of the range of issues the studies can address.

Polly P. Frank, "Student Artists in the Library: An Investigation of How They Use General Academic Libraries for Their Creative Needs," *Journal of Academic Librarianship* 25, no. 6 (1999): 445–55.
Frank studied 181 visual art students from a dozen academic institutions to ascertain what resources they used as well as how they used the material.

Roger Strouse, "Corporate Information Centers in the Year of Accountability," *Online* 25, no. 4 (2001): 86–88.
This brief article discusses the experiences of a corporate library being asked to demonstrate its value to the parent corporation. Clearly, how well the collections meet users' needs is an important aspect in the process of determining value.

Daniel O. O'Connor and Robert Fortenbaugh, "Socioeconomic Indicators and Library Use," *Public Libraries* 38, no. 3 (1999): 156–64.
The authors examined the linkages between socioeconomic indicators and library usage from eighteen New Jersey public library data sets

to determine if there were factors that could promote greater library development.

Lynn Westbrook, "Understanding Faculty Information Needs in a Special Education Setting," *Knowledge Quest* 30, no. 2 (2001): 39–42.
"The librarian and school administrator who participated in this study gathered data on previously unknown faculty information needs in the areas of information literacy instruction and specific areas of collection development" (pg. 39).

Studies of users and the service community can provide information needed for effective planning. As pointed out by T. D. Wilson, there are several reasons why studying information behavior is important:

- our concern is with uncovering the facts of the everyday life of the service population;

- by uncovering those facts, we may come to understand the needs that push the individual into information-seeking behavior;

- by better understanding those needs, we are better able to understand what meaning information has in people's everyday lives; and

- by all of the foregoing, we should gain a better understanding of the user and be able to design more cost-effective information systems.[2]

Some years ago, Colin Mick pointed out some issues relating to the difficulties of basing plans on studies of the service population:

There is now a backlog of nearly 1,000 information needs and use studies, but they provide little information which can be applied to problems involving either the management of information work or the design of information products and services. In short, the reason information innovations are technology and content driven is because information behavior studies have failed to provide information which can be used in the design of systems and services.[3]

In the years that have passed since Mick wrote that, there has been a steady increase in the pool of useful information available. However, Douglas Zweizig, who published several pieces on community analysis, was pessimistic about the real value of such studies:

Community analysis will not result in direct identification of community information needs. False expectation is associated with community analysis. It is raised by rhetoric that urges community analysis so we may be "responsive to the information needs of the community." . . . [B]y studying the community, we can diagnose information needs and prescribe appropriate materials and services. . . . But the metaphor only serves to conceal our ignorance from even ourselves. . . . "[I]nformation need" is only our idea, not necessarily something that exists in the minds of our patrons. . . . [F]indings have advanced our understanding of individual information seeking but, as libraries are presently organized, the findings do not provide guidance on what programs to plan or what materials to buy.[4]

Despite his cautious view of the value of user or community studies, Dr. Zweizig realized the importance of conducting and using the results of such studies. Recognizing the limitations and dangers involved is important, and knowing what to do with the results is critical for a successful study. Using a conceptual framework is important. (Mick, Lindsey, and Callahan outline one good model for framing such a study.[5])

Practical Aspects

There are several uses for the data collected in a survey, and though one may design a project to meet only one objective, the data may be of value in a later project as well. Surveys are a starting point, and when properly conducted, they provide a database that the information center can use for a variety of purposes. Through other techniques of information gathering and by using quantitative analysis, collection development staff can more accurately assess information needs. However, first the staff must gain an accurate picture of the service community. During the years Dr. Evans taught at the University of California, Los Angeles (UCLA) library school, many students elected to do their master's thesis on some aspect of collection development, and several did some form of user/community analysis project. As a result of these projects, we identified seven areas where survey data can assist in planning and managing library or information center activities:

- developing collections;
- planning new services;
- locating service points;
- assessing physical facility requirements;
- adjusting staffing patterns;
- assessing collections and services; and
- planning budgets.

Obviously, collection development is a major research area. Studies for this purpose range from broad surveys to identify basic characteristics of the service population, to in-depth analysis of who makes the heaviest use of the collection and why, as well as how people use the materials. One student study was done in response to a statement from the Los Angeles city attorney's office that the Los Angeles Public Library (LAPL) system might be violating several civil rights laws relating to equal access and service. The city attorney's investigation noted a marked difference between branches serving white and nonwhite communities. Differences existed in all areas: staffing, service hours, collection size, amount spent on materials, and space. The branches in nonwhite communities had substantially less in all areas. The investigation showed that there was no intent on the part of LAPL to discriminate; the differences resulted from a complex series of events occurring over a long time and were primarily the result of relying on a budgeting system based on circulation data. Collections did not change as quickly as the service population. One finding was that some branches had decreased circulation, which translated into lower funding. Failure to consistently monitor changes in the service community also contributed to the problem. The student studied the relationship between branch collections, service area demographic data, and commercial information materials available in the service area. There was a stronger correlation between branch collections than there was between the collections of low-funded branches and their service communities (as measured by materials sold in the local retail outlets), especially in the area of non-English publications.

Librarians often think they should add "innovative" or, at least, new services. Which services and what optimum service levels to offer are complex questions to answer. Data from a properly constructed survey can provide decision makers with the basis for predicting user reactions to new or modified services. Should we offer computer software? What databases should we add? Would "filtering" online searches become a problem for adult users? Can we charge for printing, and how much? In the absence of sound data from a survey, the decision makers can only guess at the answers. One interesting study of a public library compared four groups' ranking of desired services: the library users, part-time workers in the library, clerical and paraprofessional staff, and the professional staff. Professional staff estimates of what would be desirable differed significantly from the users' views, but the part-time employee rankings were very similar to those of the community. Although this study was too small in scope to generalize beyond one community, it does suggest that a cautious approach to instituting new services would be wise, especially in the absence of user input.

Two related uses of assessment studies are determining *service points* and changing *physical facilities requirements*. With the ability to deliver information electronically, the questions of whether there should be service points and, if so, where to locate them become very important. Commitments from funding authorities for capital expenditures for new facilities or long-term leases of space will be harder to secure. Many individuals question mobile delivery services (bookmobiles or media mobiles) because of high energy and maintenance costs. These factors, along with other economic concerns, often suggest that electronic delivery should be the solution. However, electronic delivery has long-term cost implications and raises questions regarding how the library will provide access to electronic systems and to whom. Data from an assessment project will be helpful in making informed decisions. Sharon Baker and Karen Wallace devoted an entire chapter to the question of service points in their book *The Responsive Public Library Collection.*[6]

Many older buildings were not designed with the needs of the disabled and elderly in mind, much less the inescapable proliferation of technology needed in today's libraries. With steadily improving health care and increased longevity, an increasing number of individuals in the service population are in one or both of these categories. The passage of the Americans with Disabilities Act of 1990 (ADA) has implications for services in all types of libraries and information centers. Knowing the size of the affected population can help in planning budgets, services, and equipment needs. Complying with ADA regulations often requires changes in public access areas.

A decision to add a substantial amount of technology often requires additional power at a facility, as well as new or expanded data and telecommunications closets. Modification of existing structures is generally more expensive per square foot than new construction due to demolition expenses on top of the new construction. Having a clear understanding of the service population's access needs—both physical and virtual—will make the planning process more effective.

All libraries and information centers depend on the good will of their users. Complaints to funding authorities, be they profit or nonprofit, cause those authorities to question the effectiveness of the library or information center. A regular *assessment program* can be helpful in gauging the service population's attitudes about services and collections. Having current information readily available may make the difference between receiving quick approval of a project or budget and undergoing a long, possibly painful review and justification process.

As community demographics change, there may be a need to *adjust the staffing pattern* of the library or information center. Changes in subject expertise (in an academic or business setting); a need for bilingual skills; attention to special population groups (e.g., children, the institutionalized, or the elderly); a need for more technical skills in various electronic fields or in indexing, abstracting, or information consolidation—all of these may require the library or information center to have more or different staff with new skills and knowledge.

Hiring staff always takes more time than one expects; if you add to the hiring process redefining or restructuring an existing position, the process takes even longer. Survey data about the shifts in the service community can assist in projecting when one should start planning for staff changes. Such projections allow the library or information center to respond in a timely manner.

All of the areas discussed have cost and *budget implications*. Funding authorities look with greater favor on budget requests that the library supports with objective data and that come from individuals whose past requests were generally accurate. Survey data can prove useful in the budgeting process.

The preceding list of possible uses of survey data is not exhaustive but illustrates the many processes that can benefit from assessment studies. Again, such surveys can serve multiple purposes, not just collection development.

Assessment and Marketing

As we noted earlier, needs assessment projects and market research share several characteristics. Both types of studies often seek the following types of information:

- Why a person does or does not use a particular product or service.

- How the person uses the product or service.

- Where the person acquires and uses the product.

- What is good and bad about the product or service.

- What new products or services would be of interest.

- Occasionally, how much the person would be willing to expend, in terms of time, money, or effort, for a product or service.

Assessment and marketing projects are most easily accomplished and useful when they have a relatively narrow focus. "Target populations" or "market segments" are essentially the same thing—identifying a distinctive set of characteristics in the overall population to study, to communicate with, to provide service to, etc. Both the Frank and Westbrook articles mentioned earlier are examples of targeted/segmented groups. Two other examples, from the public library sector, are Solina Marquis' "Collections and Services for the Spanish-Speaking"[7] and Annie Armstrong et al.'s[8] "Information Needs of Low-Income Residents in South King County." Clearly, the first step in a project is to identify the target population.

When considering an assessment project, some basic concerns about the outcome arise. Careful planning, using sound research methods, will take care of technical issues, such as sample size, pretesting requirements, question bias, and interviewer influence. Questions that one must answer include:

1.   Is the target population knowledgeable or interested enough to respond to complex questions? Would several simple questions covering a complex question be better?

2.   Is there staff available, with the requisite skills, to carry out the project?

3.   To what extent will the data accurately reflect the attitudes, opinions, needs, and issues important to respondents instead of information that the respondent thinks the data collectors want?

4.   How will you analyze the data?

5.   Will the survey process result in unrealistic expectations in both respondents and staff?

It is sometimes possible to locate a recent study conducted for another purpose—unrelated to the library—that contains data useful for the library's current project. In such cases, the risk of having data biased by respondents giving answers they think the current project planners want does not exist (although it may have existed for the original study). For example, marketers often collect "lifestyle" data and occasionally have a question or two about library usage such as "How frequently did you use the library in the last year?" Because the survey was performed by an advertising agency, more people will answer such a usage question honestly than they would if a library had sent the survey. Still, some bias undoubtedly exists in the data, because people tend to think that using the library is a good thing to do, and they respond in a way that will make them look good. Locating such studies can save time and effort and perhaps provide more reliable data.

In developing the assessment tool, you or a consultant will have to develop a set of questions to ask. First-time surveyors will benefit from having the services of a consultant, at least during the planning phase of the project. Several resources exist that can assist in formulating a project. Many basic textbooks on research methods outline the fundamental techniques of survey research, as do many marketing books. Beyond the fundamental research methodology level, there are some practical guides available. Keeping in mind that currency is less an issue than having guides with sound track records, some useful titles include:

Everhart, Nancy. *Evaluating the School Library Media Center: Analysis Techniques and Research Practices.* Westport, CT: Libraries Unlimited, 1998.
    Although the focus of this work is evaluation, many of the techniques and practices included have value when thinking about, and conducting, needs assessment projects.

Henczel, Susan. *The Information Audit: A Practical Guide.* Munchen: K. G. Saur, 2001.

While the "information audit" is most often associated with the special library, this book has useful ideas for any type of library; it also contains three case studies.

Horton, Forest W. *How to Harness Information Resources*. Cleveland, OH: Association for Systems Management, 1974. *Information Management Workbook*. Washington, DC: Information Management Press, 1983.
These titles are of great interest to special libraries, information brokers, and others in less traditional information center environments.

Kaufman, Roger, and Fenwick English. *Needs Assessment*. Englewood Cliffs, NJ: Educational Technology Publications, 1979.
A useful book that provides an excellent overview of the process.

Lauffer, Armand. *Assessment Tools for Practitioners, Managers and Trainers*. Newbury Park, CA: Sage Publications, 1982.
A practical guide to assessment methods.

Nichols, David. *Assessing Information Needs: Tools and Techniques*. London: Aslib, 1996.
This concise guide to assessing information needs covers how to frame a project, methods of data collecting, and how to set realistic goals/outcomes.

Nickerns, J. M., A. J. Purga, and P. P. Noriega. *Research Methods for Needs Assessment*. Washington, DC: University Press of America, 1980.
A sound work for developing a needs assessment project.

Rossman, Marlene L. *Multicultural Marketing*. New York: American Management Association, 1994.
Written for businesses wishing to become more effective in marketing products to a wider base, this book provides excellent insights that apply to library needs assessments. Particularly good for public libraries.

Warren, Roland L. *Studying Your Community*. New York: Russell Sage Foundation, 1955.
This is a classic for anyone planning a public library assessment project.

Large-scale studies are expensive and time-consuming, but they must be done occasionally for accreditation purposes, because of major shifts in the library's parent organization, or for other related reasons. Between such projects, libraries and information centers can conduct smaller-scale efforts. Small studies can produce reliable and useful data. The following section contains suggestions for the content of both large- and small-scale projects, focusing on how collection development activities may be improved as a result.

Elements of the Study

As soon as you decide to conduct an assessment project, you must answer several questions, including (1) Who is to collect the information? (2) What information do the planners want? (3) What methods will produce the desired data? (4) How will the planners use the data?

Who Will Do the Study?

Who or how many people will be responsible for supervising and running the study depends on several factors: financial support (library budget or supplemental funds), the number and qualifications of personnel available (staff members or outside consultants), and the depth and breadth of the study.

Any survey of major proportions should have financial backing sufficient to hire a consultant to assist in planning the study. This is true even if one or more staff members have expertise in designing assessment projects. An outsider's view can be helpful in catching problems insiders are too close to see. Whether or not the library hires a consultant, the involvement of collection development personnel and other staff is essential to the project's success.

When planning a large-scale project, budgeting for paid data collectors is essential. Small-scale projects may have the potential for using existing staff. Few libraries have staffing patterns that would allow staff to be doing special project work for any significant amount of time. The exception would be where assessment activities were factored into the job description.

One way to overcome lack of staff time and experience in assessment work is to build such projects into the regular collection development activities. Many larger academic libraries moved in this direction through the use of subject specialists. However, only relatively recently have assessment activities become part of the typical job description.

Using the library staff as the assessment team does offer some advantages. The staff members collecting the data fully understand how the results will be used. A staff team comes to the task with useful information about needs gained through day-to-day work. For example, the staff members have taken requests for or attempted to locate information for users that is not available in-house.

Another benefit is that the staff on the team gains or increases their commitment to the assessment process and its value as they learn more about the service community. Generally, staff involved in a project show a greater willingness to accept and implement the results and to use them daily. In addition, when one uses an internal research team, they need less time to inform the rest of the staff about the results, because staff social interaction cuts across departmental boundaries. Using an outside person or firm to conduct the study normally results in one or two presentations to the staff or circulation of draft documents for comment. Because of time constraints, the process often leads to staff misunderstandings and, occasionally, resistance to the entire project.

A helpful step, especially to secure community support, is to establish an advisory board for the project. The board should represent all the major groups covered by the assessment project (e.g., students, faculty, researchers, administrators, young people, adults, various ethnic groups, etc.). Though the committee must be advisory in nature, it can provide invaluable insight into problems the project team may encounter in collecting data. For example, what are some of the pressing information needs of the target populations? When and where should data gatherers make contact with the sample group? What are some ideas about how to approach people to enlist their full cooperation? In addition to helping answer these questions, the advisory board can help set project priorities and assist in interpreting the collected data.

Developing a clear statement of the study's objectives and a detailed list of the steps to take and the questions to ask is essential. Unclear goals lead to disastrous results and open the way for self-serving interpretations of the data.

What Will Be Studied?

Each type of library or information center has a slightly different definition of their service *community*. In the context of the public library, community means the political jurisdiction that the library serves. For academic and school libraries, the community is the parent institution. In the case of special libraries, it is the company, business, institution, or foundation that provides the operating library's funds. In the corporate setting, the community may be a division or unit of the parent company. With these distinctions in mind, it is possible to identify eleven broad categories of data that apply to all types of libraries.

Historical data is useful in several ways. Understanding a community's historical development may lead to a better, and sometimes quicker, understanding of where that community stands today. Although corporate libraries may not have any long-term collection preservation functions, an understanding of the history of the library or information center and its service community can help clarify or restructure current collection development objectives. Historical background information also provides clues about areas of the collection to weed or areas in which it is no longer necessary to acquire material.

Geographical information may be used to answer questions such as: In which physical directions is the community growing? (This is an issue for large academic campuses as well as for public libraries.) What is the distribution of the population (or departments or offices) over the geographic area? This can also be an issue for schools where there is a busing program. This type of information helps the library staff determine service points, which, in turn, may influence the number of duplicate titles acquired, which reduces the number of titles the library can buy.

Transportation availability data, combined with geographic factors, are important in the library's decision-making process regarding how many service points to establish and where to locate them. The aforementioned "law of least effort" is a factor to keep in mind when thinking about "transportation" in a library environment. Merely noting the existence of a bus or shuttle service does not provide enough information for a meaningful analysis. How often is the service provided? What does it cost? What are the hours of service? What is the level of use? Answers to these questions are vital in determining service points and service hours. As noted in the previous paragraph, the number of service points affects plans for developing the collection. Often, large academic and industrial organizations provide their own transportation systems, especially in urban areas. The existence of a good internal transportation system may help a library to build a more varied collection. A courier or document delivery system may help alleviate the need for as many (or as large) branch operations. Reduction in the number of branches, while still maintaining the same level of service, can reduce the need for duplicate materials.

Legal issues will not be too difficult to determine, nor will the amount of data accumulated be large. Nevertheless, there may be legal implications for collection development. In some academic institutions, the teaching faculty has the legal right to expend all book funds. Preparing for a possible problem is less difficult than dealing with an existing one or with an unexpected surprise. Clear policies about the delegation of selection authority and responsibility may help to avoid a problem and will certainly help to solve those that do arise.

Some other areas where legal issues and collection development intersect are accountability, copyright, and depository status. To which bodies is the library accountable, especially for collection development? Are there any legal restrictions on what the library may buy with monies allocated for collection development? Some jurisdictions have regulations regarding the acquisition of certain types of materials or formats. In addition to purchasing, there may be legal restrictions on how long a library must keep material and regulations regarding disposition of the material removed from the collection. Today, copyright compliance is a significant issue, especially for educational and special libraries, and it does have an impact on collection development. Libraries that are depositories for government publications are subject to a substantial body of regulations regarding the retention, usage, and disposal of the material. In a corporate information center or archives, government regulations as well as professional guidelines may affect records retention. Some regulations specify not only how the organization must retain the records but also their format (paper, microfilm, or electronic). How does one go about changing the regulations? Knowledge of the library's legal position will help answer this question.

Political information, both formal and informal, has a relationship with legal data, much like the link between geographic and transportation information. There are "politics" in any organization, so informal issues will exist, like it or not. On the formal level, questions include: To what extent is the library a political issue? If political parties exist, how do their attitudes toward library and information services differ? What is the distribution of party affiliations in the community? Are some areas of the community more politically conservative or liberal than others? Should library service-point collections reflect these philosophical differences? On the informal level, some questions to consider are: How do the politics of the community work? Who influences fiscal decisions? In academic, school, and special libraries, what are the politics of the allocation process for collection development funds? Answers to most of these questions will not have a direct bearing on which titles go into the collection, but they may influence the way in which the library secures and allocates funds and how much money is available for collection development.

Demographic data is essential in formulating an effective collection development program in all libraries. Basic changes in the composition of the population are inevitable, but only by monitoring the community can collection development staff anticipate changes in the composition of the population. Waiting until change takes place creates an image of an institution that is slow to adapt. Census data should be the starting point for any public or school library assessment project. Using such data today is much easier than it was just a few years ago, and in some cases useful maps already exist on American Community Survey (ACS), produced by the Census Bureau <http://www.census.gov/acs/www/>. ACS is an annual survey that produces SF3-like data for the noninstitutionalized population. The sample methodology employed is the same as SF3's. As of 2004, data is available for "places" with populations of 250,000 or greater. By 2006, data for 2005 should be available for areas with 65,000 + populations. The plan is that by 2010, ACS data will be available at the tract level nationwide and will fully replace the ten-year census cycle.

Data from the U.S. Census long form (SF3, STF3, and STF3A) are the most commonly used data sets for library projects. These files are especially

useful for gaining census tract, block group, and block information. Among
the data you can find total population, age, gender, race/ethnicity, housing
units, household relationships, income, education, workforce, ancestry, citi-
zenship, and language. As an example of a small-scale project using such
data, a public library thinking about an after-school program could determine how many children ages five to seventeen live in single-family homes
and where the parent works live in the census tracts or zip codes in the
service area.

For most projects, the "geography" to use is one of the following—
county (Los Angeles), place (Santa Monica), tract (population between 3,000
and 9,000 people), block group (a series of blocks within a tract), or block
(bounded by streets). It is also possible to use zip codes for large-scale projects in "Metropolitan Statistical Areas." There are five maps on this book's
CD that illustrate how a region of Los Angeles-Santa Monica changed over
five census periods. Textual material related to the maps that appeared in
the fourth edition is also available on the CD. (An important note: it is not
possible to make direct racial comparisons between the 1990 and 2000 census due to the addition of multiracial response categories in the 2000 data
collection process. For that reason, we did not create a 2000 map.)

If one has access to Geographical Information System (GIS) software,
one can make even greater use of census data. C. Koontz has written extensively about GIS techniques that can be useful to library managers, as
well as collection development officers; another good article is by Denice
Adkins and Denyse Sturges (see the Further Readings section for full references).

Economic data are useful for both general planning and collection development purposes. Knowledge of the existing economic base of the community and of possible changes may help the library better plan its
collection development activities. That is, anticipating increases or decreases in funding can lead to a more even collection, especially for serial
publications. An economy based on semiskilled or unskilled workers calls
for one type of collection, a skill-based economy calls for another, and an
economy based on knowledge workers calls for still another. Communities
with a seasonal economy or a predominantly migrant population face several problems. What type of service and which formats would best serve the
seasonal population? When you know the answers to these and similar
questions, you can begin to build a useful collection.

Communication systems available within the community are important to the library's service mission. Closed circuit and cable television, as
well as telecommunication systems, have become valuable resources for delivering information directly to users. Long important in primary and secondary schools, television is becoming a factor in higher education and in
the education of the whole community. Public access to cable television—
one channel reserved for community use and sometimes a second channel
for the school district—has had an impact on some libraries and their services. Community reference services combining cable television and telephone are possible, and some libraries offer story hours on cable. Another
developing phenomenon is electronic villages, for example, Blacksburg, Virginia, where the entire community is connected to the Internet.

Social and educational organizations reflect community values. Although social patterns are slower to change than individual attitudes, the
library must consider such pattern shifts in planning an integrated
collection-building program. Social clubs, unions, and service organizations
affect and reflect community interests. The most important group of or-

ganizations is educational. An academic institution no longer offers only two-year, four-year, and postgraduate degree programs. Evening adult education classes, day and night degree programs, off-campus, compressed video, online classes, and even some remedial high school-level courses create complex instructional programs, each facet having different information needs. A public library's concern must be broader than public and private primary and secondary schools; it should also consider adult vocational programs and higher education. Special libraries in business exist to serve research and development and planning needs; however, other areas, such as in-house training and development, may require library support.

Cultural and recreational organizations also reflect community interests. As with social organizations, these formal groups provide useful clues to highly specialized interest areas with enough community interest to sustain a formal group. Many of these groups, when given library service, join the library's most solid and influential supporters. This category does not apply to special libraries, as there is seldom a question about who their users are. (For a discussion of cultural diversity and needs assessment, see an article by Dr. Evans in the journal *Collection Building*.[9])

Other *community information services* are, in some respects, the most important elements in the collection development program. If the library identifies several community information sources, and if the various sources can develop a working cooperative agreement, everyone will benefit. All too often public, school, and academic libraries in the same political jurisdiction operate as if they existed in isolation. When a group of publicly supported libraries in a local area fails to develop cooperative programs, considerable resources and services go to waste. The first step in achieving a cooperative arrangement is to know what resources each library holds. In addition to knowing what library resources exist in the community, the librarian should know about other information resources, such as bookstores, video and music stores, newspapers, radio and television stations, and motion picture theaters. Some writers have suggested that fewer recreational materials are necessary in the library if other recreational outlets are available to the community.

How and Where Is Data Collected?

Knowing what you need to know is only one-third of the battle. Knowing how to get the information and how to analyze it represent the remaining two-thirds. The fields of social welfare and sociology have developed a number of methods for systematically studying a community. One may divide community studies into four primary types: (1) key informant, (2) community forum, (3) social indicators, and (4) field survey. Libraries can use all of these methods, singly or in combination, depending on the specific project. Combining approaches is a good technique because it helps to ensure that valid, unbiased data is obtained. (A good book to review for planning a combined approach is Jack McKillip's *Needs Analysis*.[10])

As suggested above, there are several factors to consider when deciding what data collecting methods to use. One obvious factor is the target population's willingness/ability to respond to a particular method. The goal/purpose of the project is another consideration, as are qualitative needs and the degree of comprehensiveness desired. Each factor translates into more or less time, money, and effort for the project. (Issues surrounding community participation in needs assessment are described in the supplemental material for this chapter, located on the CD accompanying this text.)

Key informants and community forums primarily use some form of interview/focus group techniques. Social indicator and field survey projects, while using the interview method, often rely on questionnaire data and results of behavior observations. Occasionally, in educational situations they can employ the diary method. Large-scale projects almost always use a combination of methods, as each has certain strengths and weaknesses.

Key Informant

Key informants are individuals who are in a position to be aware of the needs of the people in the community. Included in this group are public officials, officers of community organizations, business leaders, educators, the clergy, and unofficial leaders (those who do not hold office) in the community who are influential and whom other people view as knowledgeable about community affairs. The project team interviews these individuals to ascertain their opinions and ideas concerning the community's information needs. Another term that is sometimes used for key informant is *gatekeeper*. (A particularly good article on gatekeepers and libraries is by Cheryl Metoyer-Duran.[11]) Often, data collected from key informants forms the base of a field survey project.

To be effective, one must carefully pretest an interview schedule by generating a set of proposed questions and then trying them out with individuals who have backgrounds or positions similar to those of the people who will be part of the study. The purpose of pretesting is to learn what responses the researcher may expect to receive and whether the answers will, in fact, address the project issues. Frequently, the pretest answers are not what were expected, and the team must refine the questions in order to address the project goals or achieve consistent results. Consistency in this case means having questions that respondents will interpret/understand in the same way. Pretesting questions allows a team to reduce the range of interpretation by rewording ambiguous or confusing questions. Keeping the number of interviewers to as few as possible, unless they have already had extensive experience in interviewing, will also help reduce inconsistency. The more interviewers there are, the greater the chance of "interviewer bias" causing problems of reliability and consistency.

Potential shortcomings of the key informant approach include the fact that key informants do not fully represent the community. Because their selection is not random, the researchers cannot treat the data as if it represents the community population. The opinions of key informants reflect personal biases; their perceptions of a community's information needs may differ from the perceptions of people who do not hold positions of influence. In essence, this type of data supplies subjective, but useful, information about how people of influence perceive the community information needs.

The key informant approach is relatively easy to prepare and implement. It requires the least amount of time to collect data, and it is very helpful in making key people aware of the information problems of a diverse community. However, when using this approach, one must supplement data from key informant interviews with published (objective) data and, when possible, with a representative cross-section of community opinion. In a corporate setting, the interview method is the most useful technique.

Community Forum

The *community forum* is a type of town meeting. Recently, the focus group methodology has gained popularity as a substitute for the open community forum. Again, the advisory committee can be useful in setting up such meetings and encouraging community members to attend. This approach avoids selection bias by the researcher, as anyone in the community can express his or her opinion at a number of public meetings or volunteer for a focus group. The key to success for this approach lies in extensive publicity. In a large community, a number of meetings may be necessary in order to keep the groups small enough so people will feel comfortable expressing their opinions. Smaller, more numerous meetings also allow for adequate time to fully hear all points of view. To make these meetings useful, the research team must provide some structure for the meetings, which is very similar to what a focus group leader does in preparation for a session. A typical approach is to design sets of questions/issues to raise at the meetings. The team must also leave time to handle questions from the audience. It is usually desirable to have the entire survey team present at "town hall" meetings or at least to tape the proceeding for later review.

Two advantages of the community forum are that it is easy to arrange and relatively inexpensive. Forums also help identify individuals who have an interest in improving the quality of library service in their community. When it comes time to implement new programs, the library may be able to draw on these people to assist in the work. One clear disadvantage of the community forum is that people who do not use the library probably will not attend the meetings. If they feel they have no need for the library, why should they spend time talking about its services? Another major disadvantage is that the data obtained are impressionistic and subjective. These data are extremely difficult to categorize and are not readily amenable to systematic analysis. Although these disadvantages are serious, the community forum is useful as a major grassroots democratic process for soliciting opinions, ideas, and criticism from the general population. When exploring options for starting a service to an unserved cultural or ethnic group, the community itself is an essential part of the process.

Social Indicators

Social scientists have developed a method that makes use of *social indicators* to determine the needs of various segments of a community. It has been noted that "the notion of the city as a constellation of 'natural areas' has . . . proven useful as a method of describing social subdivisions within communities."[12] A natural area is a unit within the community that can be set apart from other units or areas by certain characteristics. Those characteristics, or social indicators, may be geographical features, such as rivers or transportation patterns; sociodemographic characteristics, such as age, sex, income, education, and ethnicity; population factors, including distribution, density, mobility, and migration; the spatial arrangements of institutions; and health and social well-being characteristics, such as condition of housing or suicide rates.[13]

By using descriptive statistics found in public records and reports, the library involved in a community analysis can deduce certain information needs of the community's population. By selecting factors that researchers think are highly correlated with those groups in need of information, surveyors may be able to extrapolate the information needs of the whole community. What these social indicators (also called factors, variables, or characteristics) may be is a point of much disagreement among researchers in library and information science. Some social indicators include age, health, sex, employment, education, marital status, income, and location of domicile or work site.

What are the implications of those indicators for library users? The following are some broad generalizations based on library research:

- Use of libraries and information centers tends to decrease with age, especially among adults over the age of fifty-five. (One reason for decreased use is deteriorating vision and other health problems.)

- Senior faculty, researchers, and organization officials tend to use libraries and information centers less as they increase in status and age. (They still use information; however, the actual gathering is done by junior or support staff, who tend to be younger.)

- Women make greater use of libraries and information centers than men, regardless of the library's institutional environment (public, academic, or corporate).

- As the number of years of education increases, so does use of libraries, up to about sixteen years of formal education. After earning a bachelor's degree, a person's library use curves downward. (Apparently, graduate and postgraduate education moves the person into the invisible college network, so there is less need to use formal information systems.)

- Income level and use of formal information systems also show a J-shaped curve. That is, low income usually translates into low use; use rises through middle and upper-middle income levels; and use sharply decreases at high income. (Apparently, persons with high incomes can purchase a large percentage of the information they require.)

- Generally, as health declines, there is a decrease in the use of formal information systems. (However, with proper equipment and special services, libraries can reverse this tendency.)

- Persons employed in manual labor tend not to use formal information systems. Information use tends to increase in direct relationship to increased levels of skills required to perform the work.

- The law of least effort is clearly evident in the finding that as the distance of the residence or workstation from the information center increases, there is a corresponding drop in use.

- Single persons and married couples with no children tend to use formal information systems less than couples with children, and as the number of children rises, so does use.

After researchers select the indicators, they can start to collect data from a variety of existing sources. In addition to census data, there are other sources for up-to-date local information. Regional, county, or city planning agencies gather statistics and make projections that can be useful, as do school boards, chambers of commerce, social service agencies (public and private), and police departments.

Field Surveys

The *field survey* approach to community analysis depends on the collection of data from either a sample or the entire service population of people. An important goal of many field surveys is to contact nonusers as well as users. The most common means of collecting data is through interview schedules or questionnaires. The methods most frequently used are telephone interviews, person-to-person interviews, and mailed questionnaires. Questions often elicit data from an individual or household regarding frequency of use of the library, research, study, reading habits, economic and/or educational background, or any other information that the library believes will provide information into need, use, and especially nonuse of the library. Comparing these data to those one derives from census sources may provide insights into differences in the user/nonuser populations.

One choice the team must make is between a structured or unstructured format for the survey. Open-ended questions (unstructured format) take more time to answer than fixed-alternative, or closed, questions (structured format). The type of question asked can affect both the response rate and data analysis. Open-ended questions are much more difficult to code and analyze, and there are fewer methods of statistical analysis that one can apply to them. With the structured format, data are homogeneous and are more easily coded and analyzed. The structured format is much easier to use, especially when volunteers are conducting interviews or coding and analyzing the data. However, even when using the structured format, the researcher must carefully prepare instructions to volunteers to assure accurate results.

If some of the target population does not speak English, it is necessary to translate the questions into the language(s) of the target population, if one wants to understand all the information needs. Respondents should be offered both versions of the questionnaire; offering only the translated version may be interpreted as an insult. A native speaker should do the translation; slang or local usage may not follow formal speech patterns that nonnative speakers tend to use.

The next step in the field survey is to select a sample. According to Warheit, "The selection of the sample depends largely upon the information needed: the unit for analysis, i.e., individuals, households, etc.; the type of data gathering techniques used; and the size it must be to adequately represent the population from which it is drawn."[14]

Cost is an important issue when selecting a sample size. A large sample may call for complex selection methods, and more time will be required to complete the survey. This is an area where the services of a paid consultant are valuable to determine the most appropriate type of sample and sample size as well as the most useful statistical tests to use on the data.

A popular method of obtaining information from respondents is through the personal interview. This permits face-to-face contact, stimulates a free exchange of ideas, and usually has a high response rate. The telephone interview, though popular, has the disadvantage of a limit to the amount of time that the interviewer can hold the interest of the respondent. Twenty minutes is about the maximum length for telephone interviews that have a good response rate. They also may limit the number of lower-income respondents. (It should be noted that, contrary to popular belief, telephone surveys are not covered under the domain of the "National Do Not Call Registry," implemented in October 2003.)

Mail surveys require less staffing and training than surveys that depend on in-person or telephone interviews. These two advantages can significantly reduce the cost, in both time and money, of conducting a survey. However, there are two significant disadvantages to the mailed survey. First, most mailed surveys have a low response rate. Organizations conducting mail surveys have reported a response rate as low as 35 percent, and such rates can seriously affect the validity and reliability of the collected data. Even with repeated mailings the response is frequently low, and the cost of keeping track of who has or has not responded is high. Second, some persons in the community are unable to respond to anything but the simplest of questions. This may be especially true in bilingual or multilingual communities. Of course, the problem of language can be overcome by printing the questionnaire in all the appropriate languages, but there will still be the problem of literacy level, regardless of the language used. With an interview, a trained interviewer can detect, from the respondent's verbal and nonverbal signals, when there is something not quite right about a question. Because of these disadvantages, libraries using a mail survey must carefully design the questionnaire and use the simplest and most succinct language possible while still meeting the established objectives. The libraries should also attempt to determine what an acceptable response rate will be before expending the time and money for a survey that could be of questionable value.

The survey approach, like the other needs assessment approaches, has certain advantages and disadvantages. The primary disadvantage is its cost. Designing a survey of a large sample, conducting extensive interviews, and performing advanced statistical analysis, for example, tend to cost more than other methods. Another disadvantage is that many individuals refuse to supply information about themselves or other family members. In many communities, the refusal or nonreturn rate may be so high as to make the data of questionable value.

However, one important advantage of the survey approach is that, if carefully designed and administered, it will produce the most accurate and reliable data for use in determining the information needs of the service community. The other community needs assessment approaches are useful, but they have drawbacks. The key informant approach is not fully representative of the community. The community forum does not attract nonusers. Variables indicating library use and the benefits derived from that use are not fully established for the social indicators approach. When one combines the field survey with one or more of the other methods, the shortfalls of each individual method are mitigated. The combined approach allows the team to compare results from the different methods; especially valuable is the comparison of data from a user study with the data gathered by a field survey.

Some other data-collecting techniques are observation, diaries, transaction logs, and citation analysis. Observation of user behavior can serve as a cross-check on what users report as their behavior in an interview, questionnaire, or diary. A concern about observation data is how much the observer's presence affects the observed behavior. Diaries can be excellent sources of detailed information about what, when, where, and how information was sought and used. Getting participant cooperation is an issue, as recording activities can be viewed as unnecessary extra work. In educational situations where the diary is linked to a classroom activity, it works well. One can also get satisfactory results in a corporate setting where only a few individuals participate. There is a concern that since the data is self-reported, it would be biased toward making the reporter "look good" rather than reflect actual behavior. This is where the observation method can come into play as a cross-check.

Electronic databases do, or should, provide "management reports" or "transaction logs" that can supply very important information about when and what was accessed. With cost of the resources being so high, checking such reports/logs should be a regularly scheduled activity. In most cases, one will not be able to determine who (type of user) accessed the database, but there should be data on when, how, and how often it was used.

Citation analysis is a helpful tool for collection development. It can assist in identifying "core" collections, weaknesses as well as strengths of an existing collection. We explore this method in chapter 4.

How Is Data to Be Interpreted?

Analyzing the data takes time and skill and begins with tabulating the data. The tabulation method selected depends on how the team collected the data and the capabilities of the agency or group performing the analysis. Tally sheets are one way to start the process. These sheets list each aspect or question of the study, its value or range of responses, and overall totals. After tabulating the data, one can perform elementary statistical analysis, such as averages and standard deviations.

One simple and inexpensive method of analysis is to prepare maps indicating the study units (e.g., census tracts) and the variables or responses analyzed. If one has access to GIS software, such as *ArchExplorer*™, making the maps will be easier and in many cases more informative. Adding map overlays improves this method, as they can illustrate distributions of, and relationships among, the selected variables. This produces the most useful results when there are a small number of variables. Analysis involving a large number of variables requires more sophisticated techniques. Today's powerful desktop computers allow the research team to employ more sophisticated types of analysis that were costly to perform in the past. However, the team must have sound reasons for using each type of analysis. The ability to do something is not reason enough to do it. It can be just as difficult to draw conclusions from a mass of statistical test results as it is from raw data.

Most assessment projects yield large quantities of data that one can manipulate statistically. However, statistics give only one level of probability and statistical significance. The main question—how to interpret the data—remains. One way to interpret data is in terms of social needs. Some years ago, J. Bradshaw discussed four types of social needs: normative, felt, expressed, and comparative.[15]

Normative needs often are based on expert opinion. One commonly cited normative need is the need to increase the literacy level. Teachers, librarians, and others, in their professional roles, express this normative need. To some degree, the general public accepts this need, but little funding is available to meet it.

Felt needs come from the population or community based on its insight into its problems. How appropriate or realistic felt needs may be is not the issue; they are a reflection of a problem. However, just as normative needs are not always what the community wants, felt needs do not always reflect what is good for the community. Where normative and felt needs conflict, interpretation and compromise come into play.

Expressed needs reflect behavior. Individuals often say they want or need something, but their behavior shows they really want or need something else. Libraries and information centers respond well to expressed needs; that is, they are more likely to meet a greater percentage of the information needs of active users than the needs of infrequent users. Libraries react to expressed needs by adding more material about the subject to the collection. Though that is not wrong, it does risk unbalanced spending or failure to respond to real, though unexpressed, information needs. The needs assessment project can reveal whether the library is overre-sponding to active users' needs.

Comparative needs are the result of comparing the target population to other populations. One such comparison might be the number of items checked out, per capita, by the target group versus overall usage by regis-tered borrowers. When making such comparisons, the services for the two groups must be the same. One advantage of focusing on comparative needs is that they usually result in some quantitative measures that can be use-ful in setting goals for new services or programs according to the results of the assessment project.

The project team and its advisory board can begin analysis and inter-pretation by considering a series of questions. The following is a sample of the types of questions these groups might review before preparing a draft report. Each project generates its own set of questions.

- What are the most important felt needs within the community?

- What are the most important normative needs as identified by the experts?

- Which needs are the most relevant to the mission and experience of the library or information center?

- How can you reconcile the multiple and conflicting needs?

- What is a realistic expectation for resources to respond to the needs?

- What are the clients' costs for each alternative?

- What are the direct and indirect costs to the institution or parent organization for each option?

- What impact or outcome is likely for each alternative? Are they measurable?

- Are timelines feasible to set up an effective program?

- Are the materials available to provide the service?

- How will the option(s) fit into the existing service structure?[16]

To present the findings of the study, the team must choose the most suitable format for the community. The selection factors relate to the char-acter of the community, the type of survey, and the intended audience. Ad-vanced statistical analysis may be a suitable format for audiences that can understand the assumptions and implications of such tests (e.g., academic and corporate environments). For public libraries, the target audience is more varied, from highly literate to illiterate. Thus, the team must present the results in such a way that individuals in the community, in public of-fice, and in the library can easily understand the implications. One way to achieve such broad coverage is by employing descriptive summaries, charts, diagrams, and other visual aids.

The examination of the data by several individuals and groups helps the team identify action areas. One method is to use group discussions (focus groups) to consider possibilities. If the preliminary conclusions are weak or unsubstantiated, group discussions are likely to reveal the prob-lem. Such public discussion can help create a strong commitment among all interested parties to seeing that action is taken to improve services. Another advantage of involving several groups in the analysis is the identification of certain unmet needs and interests of the community that are not the responsibility of the library. Public disclosure of such community problems will bring them to the forefront and possibly motivate an agency or group to assume responsibility for taking corrective action.

After the project staff gathers all the comments, suggestions, and other feedback, it should analyze the conclusions once more in preparation for the final report. The final report should include the objectives of the study, the methodology used to collect the data, a list of the identified problem areas, and a prioritized list of recommendations.

The most important question to ask following a needs assessment is: Do the present objectives of the library coincide with its new knowledge of the community? Are the objectives in line with the current needs of the community, do they reflect a past need, or are they merely self-serving? The findings of the study should answer these questions, and if the objectives of the library do not reflect the needs and interests of its community, staff recommendations should ensure that the proper changes will occur.

The study may reveal segments of the community that should receive better service. The findings should indicate what areas of library service contributed to the failure to achieve the desired level of service. Hours of service, location or lack of service points, attitude of staff, and citizens' lack of knowledge about library programs may all be causes of failure. Ways to solve the problems should be recommended. For example, an extensive publicity campaign, using newspapers, radio, posters, and bulletins, may be effective in informing the community of existing programs.

Recommendations should include those that can be easily and economically implemented as well as those that call for extensive programming changes, but all recommendations should be realistic and economical. "Blue sky" reports, in which recommendations are uneconomical or unfeasible, seldom receive favorable consideration by those who are responsible for resource allocation. Present and future resources should be a factor in formulating the recommendations. Starting in the 1990s, most libraries had, and still have, little prospect of receiving large infusions of additional funds. Thus, establishing new services necessitates reducing existing services, making it all the more essential that recommendations are realistic.

Adjusting the collection development policy is easy to do after the research team identifies the information needs and interests of the community. For example, more older people may have moved into the community, requiring large-print books and materials dealing with living on a limited income. Justifying a change in the collection development policy to reflect the change in service population is easy, given accurate survey data.

As soon as the library completes a major needs assessment project, it should establish an ongoing analysis program. Statistical information is easy to keep current, and staff can gather additional information using smaller samples than employed in the original survey. The amount of time and staff effort needed for continuing analysis will be a fraction of that devoted to the original study. This means that the staff can continuously adjust the library's objectives, programs, and collection to meet the changing information needs and interests of the service community.

Type of Library

Much of the focus in the preceding section was placed on the public library, in part because public libraries have a long history of assessing community needs. Today, any library hoping to maintain—not to mention in-crease—its funding must know its service community.

Public Libraries

King County Library System (KCLS) in Washington has an extensive and ongoing community assessment program that must be the envy of all public library systems.[17] With a service area of more than 2,000 square miles, the system has been studying its service areas for some time. Be-tween 1991 and 1997, twenty-four of forty service areas had in-depth stud-ies done. The plan was to conduct four such studies each year, and hopefully they will continue to fund the work to make it an ongoing cycle.

KCLS uses a variation of a method Dr. Evans employed when con-sulting on needs assessment—a visualization of the service area. In their case, they drive the team through the area, making stops at various points. (Dr. Evans would also drive the area, then return to photograph "typical" areas. In working with the branch staff, he would mix the photographs with some from other service areas and determine just how well the staff knew their service area.) KCLS uses its data for more than collection develop-ment purposes, just as suggested earlier in this chapter. They plan services, collections, hours, programs, etc. around, at least in part, the data gathered during the survey/assessment activities.

Academic Libraries

Some years ago, Norman Roberts and Thomas Wilson wrote, in refer-ence to academic libraries and assessment, that "such studies should be a normal method of obtaining management data at regularly repeated inter-vals."[18] One university library that has studied its service population is the University of Michigan.[19] They employed a methodology often used in mar-keting studies—focus groups. These are seldom used to generalize to a larger population group because often they are self-selected. (Dr. Evans has used focus groups of undergraduate and graduate students to assist in eval-uating services at the Loyola Marymount libraries.)

At the University of Michigan, the focus group information led to the formulation of a telephone survey. With the assistance of a marketing firm, the library designed a study to assure that there would be statistically re-liable and valid data. (In an academic or special library environment, the telephone survey can be an effective and time-saving method.) The primary focus was five open-ended themes/questions:

- When you need information for your work or studies, what do you do?

- What role does the library play in your work or studies? How does the library compare to other sources of information you may use?

- Are you comfortable with your level of awareness of the library and its services?

- When you come to the library, does the facility assist you or impede you in your work?

- In your wildest dreams, what does the library of the future look like to you and how do you see it serving you?[20]

In today's atmosphere of technology and "virtual" environments, academic libraries might specifically focus on aspects such as:

- What electronic databases do you use more than once a month?
- When preparing the results of your research, do you prefer print or electronic "notes" and resources?
- What are the major or critical problems you encounter when using digital resources?
- What type(s) of assistance would you like to have available when using electronic resources?

School Library Media Centers

For the school library media center, key issues are:

- How well does the collection meet the needs of the curriculum?
- To what degree does it assist teacher's class preparation activities?
- What is the right balance between print and media, and has it been achieved?
- How much of the budget can/should go toward e-resources?
- What is the relationship with the local public library?
- To what extent must students depend upon the public library collections and e-resources to complete class assignments?

Formal surveys/assessment projects are necessary to answer these and other questions that parents, teachers, and administrators can, and do, raise from time to time.

Special Libraries/ Information Centers

In the special library or information center environment, the focus tends to be on small groups and individuals. Thus, the techniques used by larger academic or public libraries are seldom necessary. Corporations, research institutes, professional organizations, and the like seldom have a sound knowledge of the basic issues related to acquisition and use of information within themselves, unless there are regular information assessments/audits. Some of the key issues are:

- What information resources are currently in use?
- How are these resources used?
- What are the outcomes, if any, of their use?
- What equipment is required to use the information, and who uses that information?
- What is the cost of the information and its associated equipment?
- What is the "value" of the results? That is, what is the cost/benefit of information acquisition and use within the organization?

Information audits are one assessment technique for special/corporate libraries. Such audits can help ensure that maximum value is realized from the organizations' expenditures on information resources. They are usually company- or division-wide in scope and take into consideration all information resources, not just the resources housed or made available through the library. DiMattia and Blumenstein[21] reported on a survey they conducted about the value of information audits. They noted, "The audits detect gaps and duplication in services and resources" (pg. 48). They identified four goals for information audits based on their study. An audit should identify:

1. information needs to meet organizational targets;

2. overall information resources;

3. knowledge and expertise resources of the organization; and

4. where information resides, who uses it, the barriers to its use, and the gaps that need to be filled.[22]

The authors suggest that one of the driving forces leading to an audit is the need to make the organization's intranet better/more effective. They also noted that using outside consultants to at least assist in, if not fully carry out, the audit process is a common practice.

In addition to the methods mentioned earlier in this chapter, several methods are particularly good when addressing a small group environment. Five such methods are activities, data analysis, decision making, problem solving, and empirical analysis. (F. W. Horton's books, listed on page 29, provide detailed information about these assessment techniques.)

The *activities* approach uses an in-depth interview with an individual or group and has as its objective the outlining of all the activities of a typical day or project. The focus is on decisions made, actions taken, topics discussed, letters or memos written and received, and forms processed. The approach is based on the assumptions that daily activities fall into a regular pattern and that once a pattern is identified, the information officer can translate the activities into specific information requirements. One problem with the method is that people often forget important, but infrequently performed, tasks. Another drawback is the tendency to overemphasize the most recent problems or activities.

Data analysis is a method in which the investigator examines information sources used and materials produced by the person or study group. This approach circumvents the problems of forgetfulness and overemphasis on recent work. Reports, files, letters, and forms are the focal point of the study. The documents are studied to determine what information was used in creating them. After finishing the examination, the researcher discusses each item in some depth with the person(s) concerned to determine which resources they consulted in preparing the documents. Through this process, it is possible to identify unnecessary information sources and to determine unmet needs.

The *decision-making* approach is similar to data analysis, but it focuses on the decision-making process. Again, the researcher is interested in the information used to formulate decisions and the origin of that information. The researcher also looks at the information received but not used. During the interview the researcher explores how the cost of not having the right information or not having it as soon as required affected the decision-making process. In the profit sector, either or both factors can have serious financial implications for the organization.

The *problem-solving* approach is similar to the decision-making approach, except that the focus shifts to problem solving. Frequently, a problem-solving activity cuts across several departments or units and takes more time to complete than a decision-making process. The problem-solving approach provides a better organizational picture more quickly than the decision-making approach does.

All of the preceding approaches depend on the user providing accurate information about what she or he did or did not do. *Empirical studies*, in contrast, are based on observations of what is done (expressed needs), how users act, and information sources used. If a formal information center exists, it might conduct experiments, such as varying the location of information sources or removing them, to determine whether the users' perceptions of the value of an item translate into use.

Summary

Effective collection development is possible only when it is based on sound knowledge of the service community. All types of libraries should engage in needs assessment. The methods covered in this chapter, though emphasizing the public library environment because of its complex service population, can be modified for use in any type of library or information center environment.

Notes

1.   T. D. Wilson, "On User Studies and Information Needs," *Journal of Documentation* 37 (March 1981): 3–15.

2.   Ibid.

3.   Colin Mick et al., "Toward Usable User Studies," *Journal of the American Society for Information Science* 31 (September 1980): 347–56.

4.   Douglas Zweizig, "Community Analysis," in *Local Public Library Administration*, 2nd ed., ed. E. Altman, 38–46 (Chicago: American Library Association, 1980).

5.   Mick et al., "Toward Usable User Studies."

6.   Sharon L. Baker and Karen Wallace, *The Responsive Public Library Collection*, 2nd ed. (Englewood, CO: Libraries Unlimited, 2002).

7.   Solina Kasten Marquis, "Collections and Services for the Spanish-Speaking: Issues and Resources," *Public Libraries* 42, no. 2 (2003): 106–12.

8.   Annie Armstrong, Catherine Lord, and Judith Zeletr, "Information Needs of Low-Income Residents in South King County," *Public Libraries* 39, no. 6 (2000): 330–35.

9.   G. Edward Evans, "Needs Analysis and Collection Development Policies for Culturally Diverse Populations," *Collection Building* 11, no. 4 (1992): 16–27.

10.   Jack McKillip, *Needs Analysis: Tools for the Human Services and Education* (Beverly Hills, CA: Sage Publications, 1987).

11.   Cheryl Metoyer-Duran, "Information-Seeking Behavior of Gatekeepers in Ethnolinguistic Communities," *Library and Information Science Research* 13 (October–December 1991): 319–46.

12.   G. J. Warheit et al., *Planning for Change: Needs Assessment Approaches* (Rockville, MD: Alcohol, Drug Abuse and Mental Health Administration, n.d.), 48.

13. Ibid.

14. Ibid.

15. J. Bradshaw, "The Concept of Social Need," *New Society* 30 (1972): 640–43.

16. Evans, "Needs Analysis and Collection Development Policies," 18.

17. Jeanne Thorsen, "Community Studies: Raising the Roof and Other Recommendations," *Acquisitions Librarian* 20 (1998): 5–13.

18. Norman Roberts and Thomas Wilson, "The Development of User Studies at Sheffield University, 1963–88," *Journal of Librarianship* 20 (October 1988): 271.

19. Margo Crist, Peggy Daub, and Barbara MacAdam, "User Studies: Reality Check and Future Perfect," *Wilson Library Bulletin* 68 (February 1994): 38–41.

20. Ibid., 38.

21. Susan DiMattia and Lynn Blumenstein, "In Search of the Information Audit: Essential Tool or Cumbersome Process?" *Library Journal* 125, no. 4 (2000): 48–50.

22. Ibid., 48.

Selected Websites*

(See also resources on the DLC5 website: <http://www.lu.com/dlc5>)

Community Analysis—IS560
<http://web.utk.edu/~wrobinso/560_lec_commun-analysis.html>
William C. Robinson's list of community analysis provides an overview of such topics as SWOT (Strengths, weaknesses, opportunities, and threats) analysis and environmental scanning.

Community Analysis for Libraries and Librarians
<http://skyways.lib.ks.us/pathway/ca_homepage.html>
This site provides background information, methodologies, and sample models for community analysis.

Indiana Community Analysis Resources on the WWW
<http://www.ibrc.indiana.edu/presentations/community_scan.html>
Prepared by the Indiana State Library and Indiana University (IU), this site provides a series of questions to ask when completing a community analysis and accompanying sources of statistical information.

Library Research Service: Community Analysis
<http://www.lrs.org/asp_public/community.asp>
Sponsored by the Colorado Department of Education, this site provides links to several resources for community analysis at both the state and national levels.

Public Library Geographic Database
<http://www.geolib.org/PLGDB.cfm>
A part of GeoLib, sponsored by the Florida Resources and Environmental Analysis Center, PLGB provides a listing of the locations of over 16,000 public libraries in the United States with accompanying statistics from the Census Bureau and National Center for Educational Statistics.

Public Library Planning Process: Community Analysis Methods and Evaluative Options (CAMEO Handbook)
<http://skyways.lib.ks.us/pathway/cameo/>
The CAMEO Handbook covers the "looking around" method of analysis and provides detailed lists of resources and sample worksheets.

South Carolina State Library—Public Library Community Analysis Online
    <http://www.state.sc.us/scsl/lib/commscan.html>
    Includes twenty-one questions for analysis, with accompanying links.

*These sites were accessed May 5, 2005.

Further Reading

Adkins, D., and D. Sturges. "Library Service Planning with GIS and Census Data."
    Public Libraries 43 (May/June 2004): 165–70.

Blake, J. C., and S. P. Schleper. "From Data to Decisions: Using Surveys and Statis-
    tics to Make Collection Management Decisions." *Library Collections, Acquisi-
    tions, and Technical Services* 28, no. 4 (Winter 2004): 460–64.

Doll, C. A., and P. P. Brown. *Managing and Analyzing Your Collection: A Practical
    Guide for Small Libraries and School Media Centers*. Chicago: American Li-
    brary Association, 2002.

Duff, W. M., and C. A. Johnson. "A Virtual Expression of Need: An Analysis of E-mail
    Reference Questions." *American Archivist* 64 (Spring/Summer 2001): 43–60.

Koonttz, C., and D. Jue. "Unlock Your Demographics." *Library Journal* 129 (March
    1, 2004): 32–33.

Marquis, S. K. "Collections and Services for the Spanish-Speaking: Accessibility."
    Public Libraries 42 (May/June 2003): 172–77.

Osa, J. O. "Collection Development: Curriculum Materials Center." *Acquisitions Li-
    brarian* 30 (2003): 131–53.

Paul, K. "Collection Mapping." *School Libraries in Canada* 21, no. 4 (2002): 2.

Rogers, M. "Serving Up World Languages." *Library Journal* 128 (June 15, 2003): 42–
    44.

Steffen, N. O., and K. C. Lance. "Who's Doing What: Outcome-Based Evaluation and
    Demographics in the Counting on Results Project." *Public Libraries* 41 (Sep-
    tember/October 2002): 271–79.

Westbrook, L., and S. T. Tucker. "Understanding Faculty Information Needs."
    Reference & User Services Quarterly 42 (Winter 2002): 144–48.

3
Collection Development Policies

Lois Cherepon and Andrew Sankowski, in writing about the need for revising a collection development policy, made the following point:

> Collection development in the 21st century has become a balancing act for academic libraries. Deciding what to purchase in electronic format, what to continue to purchase in print, and what to purchase in both formats becomes increasingly difficult. . . . The answer involves compromise, keeping current with both technology and resources, creating or recreating a collection development policy. . . . [1]

Although their reference point is the academic library, the issues they raise are of concern to all types of libraries. We would also suggest that effective collection development has always been a balancing act of formats. What e-resources have done is add yet another layer of complexity to the process, albeit probably the most costly and complex layer. The complexity requires an up-to-date written policy statement for reasons we outline below.

A collection development policy, when properly prepared, is, in fact, the library's master plan for building and maintaining its collections. Like all good plans, the collection development policy must reflect and relate to the library's other plans, especially those that are long-range and strategic in character. It also must be up-to-date in terms of the library's overall mission and goals.

Collection development policies, selection policies, acquisition policies—are they just different names for the same thing? They are different—the latter two would address only one of the collection development functions, while the first one covers all aspects. However, many librarians use the terms interchangeably, perhaps because there is some overlap in what such policies cover. This assumes, of course, that the library has a written policy. One library school professor who taught collection development told her classes, "On the first day you go to work in collection development, ask to see the written policy so you can study it. When they tell you they don't have one, faint. By the way, you need to practice fainting and falling so you don't hurt yourselves—not many libraries have written collection development policies." This is less true today than it was in the 1970s and 1980s. However, it also is true that many of the existing policies have not been reviewed, much less revised, in many years. It also is true that there is still a substantial number of libraries that do not have such a written policy.

Joseph Straw[2] conducted a survey of ARL (Association of Research Libraries) library websites to determine how many had Web-based collection development statements. Fifty-four (44 percent) had no such Web statements, and in all likelihood many of those institutions did/do not have a current written policy either. In the same issue of the *Acquisition Librarian* as the Straw article, James Spohrer[3] wrote about the fact that the University of California, Berkeley library's collection development policy had not been revised since 1980—well over twenty years.

When there is a revised policy in place, it tends to focus on electronic resources due to the complexity arising from this format and the cost impact on collection development. Unfortunately, little attention is paid to other formats during the revision process. A discussion of the issues related to e-materials and policies appears on pages 64–65.

What Are Collection Development Policies?

Although selection and acquisition policy statements may contain much of the same information found in a good collection development policy, they do not cover some important topics. Selection policies often omit references to evaluation, deselection, and intellectual freedom. Acquisition policies tend to focus on the mechanics of acquiring materials instead of the selection process or collection building.

As we discussed in chapter 1, *collection development* is the process of making certain the library meets the information needs of its service population in a timely and economical manner, using information resources produced both inside and outside the organization. Effective collection development requires creating a plan to correct collection weaknesses while maintaining its strengths. A collection development policy provides guidance for those doing the selection work. Specifically, the staff consults the collection development policy when considering which subject areas to augment and determining how much emphasis to give each area. At the same time, the policy should be a mechanism for communication with the library's service population, as well as with those who provide its funding.

Why Have a Collection Development Policy?

As noted earlier, hundreds of libraries and information centers do not have a written policy and yet have sound collections. Luck plays a role in having a sound (much less an excellent) collection without also having a written policy—that is, the luck of having had individuals charged with the responsibility of building the collection who were highly intelligent and motivated by a deep commitment to the library and its collections. As a result, these individuals stayed at that library for most, if not all, of their careers and had extensive knowledge of the collection's content as well as the needs of the library's service community. In talking to such individuals, one often finds that they do have a plan/policy; it's just not on paper. The question is, what happens when that person leaves/retires? Will the replacement person have any sense of what the plan was/is? Maybe, maybe not; this is where some of the luck comes into play.

Electronic resources create new challenges that cannot be left to chance. If nothing else, e-materials have finally broken down the idea that library collections can, and should, be solely print-based. As Dan Hazen suggested, there is a need to be flexible in our collection policies, whether a single comprehensive document or, as he proposed, a series of shorter descriptions.[4] It is also clear that we must embrace all the appropriate formats for the collection and the service population.

Another argument for a written collection development policy is the problem of lack of continuity in both staff and funding. A written policy helps assure continuity and consistency in the collecting program despite changes in staff and funding. Collection development policies are even more important for school libraries because of the many attacks on materials from individuals and groups who seek to limit children's access to certain materials.

Finally, collection development policies can be used as the foundation for the development of a practical manual or handbook to assist librarians in the selection of materials for the library. One such handbook, developed by the Library of Congress, is available online at <http://lcweb.loc.gov/acq/colldev/handbook.html>.

An interesting article that places some of these reasons in a public library context is Merle Jacob's "Get It in Writing."[5] One technique that she employed in proposing the policy was to issue a questionnaire to the selectors to complete. To complete the survey, selectors had to look at the materials in the collection within their areas of responsibility, as well as review past selection decisions. It should be noted, however, that comprehensive plans are never short.

Arguments Against Writing a Collection Development Policy

Why have many libraries not formulated or updated a collection development policy? One of the major reasons is that a good policy statement requires large quantities of data. It is necessary to know (1) the strengths and weaknesses of your collection; (2) the community you are serving and how it is changing; and (3) other resources available to your patrons locally or accessible through interlibrary loan. Only when you have all of this knowledge in hand are you ready to start developing a collection development policy.

Another reason policies are lacking is that they require a great deal of thought. A policy must change to reflect the changing community; therefore, collection development staff never finishes collecting data and thinking about the changes. Some librarians say it is not worth the trouble: as soon as the plan is on paper, the situation changes so much that the plan is almost immediately out of date. Of course, after the library completes the basic work and writes the policy, updating the policy should not be a monumental problem. Updating does take time, but if it is done annually, it is almost painless.

Without question, there is a growing concern about the value of policies that are hundreds of pages long and that are seldom consulted as a result. However, everyone agrees there must be some plan in writing—whether on paper, the Web, or both—that addresses the direction in which the collection should go.

Uses of a Collection Development Policy

A policy statement provides a framework within which individuals can exercise judgment. Unless the library is highly atypical, its collection development work will involve several persons at any one time and a great many persons throughout the library's history. Whenever a number of persons make decisions without some written guidelines, slightly different views of the library's purpose will probably emerge. In the absence of some guidance, this leads to divergences of opinion, which in turn usually lead to inconsistencies in the collection. With a collection development policy statement, everyone has a reference point. In such situations, working agreements are possible even when total agreement is impossible. In a school media center setting, differences of opinion about what should or should not be in the collection can, and sometimes do, lead to the courtroom rather than the classroom.

In an academic situation, with faculty in charge of selection, many points of view come into play. For example, four different anthropology professors might be selectors in four successive years. Lacking a policy statement, each professor would be free to, and sometimes would, buy heavily in a particular area of personal interest. The result might be one year of almost exclusive purchasing of North American ethnology, one of Bantu studies, one of physical anthropology, and one of Oceanic material. Given enough changes in professors and their personal interests, it might be possible to cover the entire field. Still, many fields would receive little or no attention during most years. A professor might not stay long enough to fully develop a collection in an area, with the result being that the library cannot claim strength in any one area. If the professors have full authorization for the selection process, the library can do little to keep a bad situation under control.

Special libraries may or may not have a written collection development policy. One reason many do not have a policy is that the mission statement of the library is so specific—as to service community, formats, and subject areas collected—that a collection policy would be redundant. Where the service population and areas of interest diversify, there is a need to develop a written policy covering all or some of the topics discussed in this chapter.

Admittedly, a written policy statement will not solve all problems, because selectors normally have authority to make the final decisions. However, if the library has a document outlining the fields requiring coverage, the policy can serve as a reminder that areas other than the selector's favorites need consideration. Even the small public library will find a written collection development policy useful, especially if there is community involvement in its approval or preparation. Among its many uses, the collection development policy

- informs everyone about the nature and scope of the collection;
- informs everyone of collecting priorities;
- forces thinking about organizational priorities for the collection;
- generates some degree of commitment to meeting organizational goals;
- sets standards for inclusion and exclusion;
- reduces the influence of a single selector and personal biases;
- provides a training and orientation tool for new staff;
- helps ensure a degree of consistency over time and regardless of staff turnover;
- guides staff in handling complaints;
- aids in weeding and evaluating the collection;
- aids in rationalizing budget allocations;
- provides a public relations document;
- provides a means of assessing overall performance of the collection development program; and
- provides outsiders with information about the purpose of collection development (an accountability tool).

Some people suggest that a collection development policy would be more practical if it consisted of minipolicies for subject areas or specialized service programs.

Providing information about the characteristics of the user population, in addition to simply identifying who the library serves, is essential for newly hired bibliographers in understanding the user base. It probably is best done with a separate document. Data about what and how the primary user groups use information materials aids in selecting the right material at the right time. Outlining the character of the various subject fields the library collects, as well as information about the major producers of the materials collected, will assist individuals taking over a new subject responsibility. Including data about review sources will further enhance the usefulness of the manual. Statements about subject and format priorities also are beneficial, especially when combined with an indication of the percentage of the materials budget normally expended on a subject.

Elements of a Collection Development Policy

In addition to the advantages outlined earlier, a collection development policy statement can provide a useful means of communicating with end users. Though a complete policy statement runs to many pages, longer than most people care to read, a summary of its major points can be valuable. This is especially true if the individuals have had some say in the policy formulation. Posting the policy on the Web provides 24/7 access.

What elements belong in a good collection development statement? The following discussion of the three major elements—overview, details of subject areas and formats collected, and miscellaneous issues—illustrates why policy formulation is so time-consuming and why it is critical to success. Certainly, all U.S. libraries should consult two American Library Association (ALA) publications: *Guide for Written Collection Policy Statements* (2nd ed., 1996) and the earlier *Guide for Writing a Bibliographer's Manual* (1987, O.P.). School library media centers can benefit from consulting *Information Power: Building Partnerships for Learning*.[6]

Element One: Overview

The first element consists of a clear statement of overall institutional objectives for the library. Statements such as "geared to serve the information needs of the community" have little value or concrete meaning. To ensure that the statement will help selectors and has specific meaning, all of the following factors should be present in the first section:

1. Organizational mission and goals. Having a short statement about parent organizational goals and how the library's mission links to the broader mission helps place the document into a larger context.

2. A brief general description of the service community (town, country, school, or business). What is the composition of the community, and what changes are occurring? If you have done a thorough job of community analysis (see chapter 2), this part of the policy and many of the following sections will be easy to prepare.

3. Specific identification of the service clientele. Does this include anyone who walks in the door? Who are the primary clients? Does this group include all local citizens, all staff and students of the educational institution, all employees of the business? Will you serve others? If so, to what degree? Will the service to others be free, or will there be a fee? Are there other differences in service to various groups (e.g., adults, children, faculty, or students)? Must patrons come to the library? Will there be service for the disabled, the institutionalized, and users with below-average reading ability or other communication problems? These are but a sample of the questions one might ask about the service population. There are no universal answers; there is a right answer for a particular library at a particular time, and this answer will change over time.

4. A general statement regarding the parameters of the collection. In what subject fields will the library collect? Are there any limitations on the types of format that the library will acquire (e.g., only printed materials, such as books, periodicals, and newspapers)? What are the limits in audiovisual areas? This section should provide an overview of the items covered in detail in the second major element of the policy.

5. A detailed description of the types of programs or patron needs that the collection must meet. In a public library, to what degree is the collection oriented toward educational purposes, that is, toward the support of formal educational programs and self-education? Will the library meet recreational needs? If so, to what degree? Will the collection circulate, or is it for on-site reference only? (For public libraries with specialized service programs, this

is the place to outline service goals. When developing an ethnic collection, the goals can be different for different groups.)

Dr. Evans developed the following list, based on the book *Understanding You and Them*, to illustrate different service goals one could have for various purposes (the target population will decide which goal will be most desirable):

- The root culture, to help maintain its heritage and social values.
- The experiences of the ethnic group in the United States.
- Survival skills and general information about life in the United States.
- The changing nature of society, with an emphasis on social changes in the root culture.
- Relations with other ethnic groups.
- Materials that reflect the current situation of the group in the United States.
- The future of the group in American society.
- Educational materials that will help adults and children in various formal and informal educational programs.[7]

Academic libraries need to consider how much emphasis to place on research material in comparison to instructional material. Again, statements about collection goals are appropriate. Gale Hannigan and Janis Brown suggested five collection development goals in the area of microcomputing. These guidelines can be used in either academic or special libraries. The suggested goals are

- to provide computer-based instructional programs to support the clinical years of the medical school curriculum;
- to provide a central facility for expensive resources needed by individuals on an occasional basis, such as interactive videodisc;
- to provide productivity tools (e.g., word processing) to increase student computer literacy;
- to provide a facility for evaluation of clinically oriented software; and
- to provide end users with access to computerized databases, either online or CD-ROM.[8]

These goals may appear unrelated to the collection; however, by changing the wording to relate the goals to the service population, they could apply to most libraries or information centers. In special libraries, the question tends to focus on which classes of users to serve.

The overview section should also address general limitations and priorities, including an outline of how the library will develop the collection. To what degree will the library collect retrospective materials? One important issue to cover in this section of the policy is whether the library will buy duplicate copies of an item. If so, what factors will the library use to determine the number of copies to acquire and how long to retain them? One excellent book on the topic of duplicate copies is Michael Buckland's *Book Availability and the Library Users*.[9] This book provides information essential to members and potential members of a collection development staff.

Another element should be a discussion of the library's role in cooperative collection development programs. To be effective, this section must leave no doubt in a reader's mind as to whether the basic philosophy is one of self-sufficiency or cooperation. If the reader is in doubt, it means the policy writers either did not want to make a decision on this critical issue or wanted to avoid taking a public stand. Furthermore, when the library is part of one or more cooperative programs, this section should identify those programs and identify the subject areas for which the library has a major collecting responsibility. For subject areas that the library does not collect, the policy should list the libraries that do collect them.

Element Two: Details of Subject Areas and Formats Collected

Policy writers should break down the collections into constituent subject areas, identify types of material collected, and specify the primary user group for each subject. This may sound like a lot of work—it is. Collection development officers must spend hours talking to users about what subject areas they use and spend many more hours thinking about what they have learned. After collecting the data, someone must assign priorities to each area, perhaps by format within each area. All of this work is done with the goals of achieving a proper balance of subjects and supplying the information needs of the service community. A complete listing of patron groups and formats could run to several pages if each of the major categories is subdivided. The following list provides the major categories.

Patrons

Adults
Young adults
School-age children
Preschool children
Physically disabled (e.g., the blind, visually impaired, and persons who use wheelchairs)
Shut-ins and persons in institutions (e.g., hospitals, residential care facilities, and prisons)
Teaching faculty
Researchers
Staff and administrators
Undergraduate students
Graduate students
Postgraduate students
Alumni

Formats

Books (hardbound or paperback)
Newspapers
Periodicals (paper, microform, and electronic)

Microforms
Slides
Films and videos
Pictures
Audio recordings
Online resources (Internet and other services)
Musical scores
Pamphlets
Manuscripts and archival materials
Maps
Government documents
CD-ROMs and DVDs
Realia
Games and toys
Specimens
Software, databases, and other electronic formats

The lists provide a clear picture of the magnitude of the project, especially when one adds in subject-area considerations and changing formats.

Although this process may seem too time-consuming, remember that few libraries collect all categories, formats, or subjects. Libraries set priorities, or levels of collecting intensity, in several ways. The ALA guidelines suggest a five-level system: comprehensive, research, study, basic, and minimal. The Research Library Group (RLG), an organization of large research libraries in the United States, developed a multipurpose conspectus that identifies collecting levels. The Association of Research Libraries (ARL) also adopted the conspectus model. European and Canadian academic libraries have also employed the conspectus concept. A 2003 article by McGuigan and White[10] discusses the rationale and framework for the subject-specific section of the policy.

Nonacademic groups have modified the conspectus concept to meet the needs of all types of libraries. Some of these groups include Alaska Statewide Inventory Project, Colorado State Library Project, Illinois Statewide Collection Development Project, Metropolitan Reference and Research Agency of New York, and, most notably, the Pacific Northwest Collection Assessment Project. The conspectus model has become the de facto standard for assigning a numerical value to the existing collections and the level of collecting the library wishes to maintain or achieve. It serves as a tool for both collection policy development and assessment.

The conspectus model helps in formulating a collection policy because it forces collection development staff to engage in detailed subject analysis. Normally, it uses the Library of Congress Classification System, with conversion tables for the Dewey Decimal Classification numbers, as the basis for subject analysis.

More than 200 libraries of all types have successfully employed the Pacific Northwest model. It employs the basic conspectus structure but provides a coding system that all types of libraries can use. There are four possible subject level approaches a library may select from:

- 20 major LC divisions (the least detailed and most appropriate for small and medium-sized nonspecialized libraries);

- 200 subject level (this is the level many colleges use);

- 500 field level (the most common level for medium-sized academic and most large public libraries); and

- 5,000 topic level (this is the level one needs to employ with a research collection).

In most of the models, a collection development officer assigns a numerical value to each subject area in terms of both current collecting levels and existing collection strength. With some models the library may also indicate the desired level of collecting, if it differs from existing values. The RLG system of coding employs five values: 0—out of scope; 1—minimal; 2—basic information; 3—instructional level; and 4—research level. The *Pacific Northwest Collection Assessment Manual* offers a more detailed division of the coding: 1a, 1b, 2a, 2b, 3a (basic), 3b (intermediate), and 3c (advanced).[11]

One of the major concerns or criticisms about the conspectus method relates to how different selectors, in the same or different libraries, apply the codes. It is important that all selectors apply the codes in the same way to ensure some degree of consistency among libraries. Until the *Pacific Northwest Manual* appeared, the process of assigning values was highly subjective. However, the *Manual* offers quantitative guidelines to help selectors assign consistent values. The following are the major points:

1. Monographic Coverage in a Division (will vary according to publishing output)

   1a = out-of-scope
   1b = (or less) fewer than 2,500 titles
   2a = 2,500–5,000 titles
   2b = 5,000–8,000 titles
   3a = 8,000–12,000 titles representing a range of monographs
   3b = (or more) more than 12,000 titles representing a wider range than 3a

2. Percentage of Holdings in Major, Standard Subject Bibliographies

   1b (or less) = 5% or below
   2a = less than 10%
   2b = less than 15% holdings of major subject bibliographies
   3a = 15–20%
   3b = 30–40%
   3c = 50–70%
   4 (or more) = 75–80%

3. Periodical and Periodical Index Coverage

   1b = some general periodicals + *Readers' Guide to Periodical Literature* and/or other major general indexes
   2a = some general periodicals + *Readers' Guide to Periodical Literature* and other major general indexes
   2b = 2a + wider selection of general periodicals + 30% or more of the titles indexed in the appropriate Wilson subject index + access to the index
   3a = 50% of the titles indexed in the appropriate Wilson subject index and access to the index(es)

3b = 75% of the titles indexed in the appropriate Wilson subject index and/or other appropriate major subject indexes + access to the indexes + a wide range of basic serials + access to nonbibliographic databases

3c = 3b + 90% of the titles indexed in the appropriate Wilson subject indexes + access to the major indexing and abstracting services in the field.[12]

Because the categories are not mutually exclusive, there is a wide margin for interpreting what value one might assign. However, the system is much tighter than the RLG system, which provides no such guidelines.

Elizabeth Futas' interesting article about genre literature suggests that one might use categories called recreational, informational, instructional, and reference for genre materials when preparing a policy statement:

The level that makes the most sense for genre literature is the recreational level, which indicates the best current titles on the market. Some of the better known and still read genre authors might fall into one of two other levels available for public library selection, general information level, indicating a large number of current titles, or instructional level, a good selection of current titles and a good selection of retrospective titles. As an example of authors in each, take the Mystery genre:

Level	Author
Recreational	Lillian Jackson Braun, Joe Gores
Informational	Mary Higgins Clark, Ed McBain
Instructional	P. D. James, Elmore Leonard
Reference	Dorothy Sayers, Dashiell Hammett[13]

After the detailed subject information (a complete conspectus) is available, a selector can focus attention on the items appropriate for the collection. Policy statements are only guidelines, with ample room for individual interpretation, but they do narrow the scope of a person's work. Combine the subject intensity section with the patron list and format listing, and the result is a solid framework on which to build a sound collection.

Most subject areas fall into one of the middle intensity ranges. Few libraries have more than one or two topics at the upper levels; libraries usually restrict such categories to a person (e.g., Goethe or Sir Thomas More) or a narrow topic (e.g., pre-Columbian writing systems or 19th-century Paris theater).

The next part of the policy is short but important. It identifies where responsibility for collection development lies. Ultimately, responsibility lies with the head of the library, as it does for all library activities. However, unless the library is very small, no one expects the head librarian to personally perform all the tasks for which she or he is responsible. Because the collections are important to the success of the library's programs, the question of who will actually develop them is vital. The answer requires a careful examination of the needs of the library and the nature of the service community. This section of the collection development policy should contain a clear statement of who will be responsible for selection, what guidelines the selectors are to use in making their decisions, and the basis for evaluating the selectors' performance. Media center selection responsibility can be particularly troublesome because of possible conflicts about who controls collection content—parents, teachers, media specialists, or the school board. The U.S. Supreme Court ruling in *Board of Education, Island Trees Union Free School District v. Pico*[14] limited the power of school boards to add, remove, or limit access to materials. (Chapter 18 contains additional information about the *Island Trees* case.)

Who Shall Select?

Potential selectors include

- end users;
- librarians from public service areas, with no special background or training beyond basic library education;
- librarians from technical service areas, with no special background or training beyond basic library education;
- subject or service specialists with advanced training in a subject or service area;
- department heads; and
- the head librarian.

A library may utilize one or more of the groups listed here.

How Shall They Select?

Delegation of selection responsibility in any given library depends on the type of library and local conditions. Whatever the decision regarding who will select, it must be in the policy so there will be no question where the responsibility and accountability lie. Selection decisions may be made by

1. independent selectors;
2. committees; and
3. individuals or groups using a centrally prepared list from which selections are made.

One can make a few generalizations about differences in where selection responsibility lies in different types of libraries. Many exceptions to these generalizations exist, but broad patterns are apparent in most areas. Educational institution libraries usually have more user (teachers and students) involvement and greater use of subject specialists than is seen in public libraries. Special or technical library staff often have advanced training in the field in which their library specializes. That staff, with substantial input from the primary users, is responsible for selection. Public libraries normally use librarians, often department heads from public service areas, as selectors, working through selection committees or from lists prepared by a central agency.

When nonlibrarians have an active voice in the selection process, most of their input relates to the working collection. Usually, members of the library staff have primary responsibility for the reference collection. Thus, users recommend current books and monographs, and librarians do most of the retrospective buying and selecting of serials and other media for the collection.

In addition to specifying how selectors will select, this section of the policy should provide general guidelines concerning what, and what not, to select. Normally, such written guidelines are more important in public libraries and school library media centers than in academic or special libraries. This is because there are more groups with an interest in the content of the collection and concern about its impact upon the children and young adults using it. The following are some sample selection guideline statements:

- Select items useful to clients.
- Select and replace items found in standard lists and catalogs.
- Select only those items favorably reviewed in two or more selection aids.
- Do not select items that received a negative review.
- Try to provide both, or all, points of view on controversial subjects.
- Do not select textbooks.
- Do not select items of a sensational, violent, or inflammatory nature.
- Select only items of lasting literary or social value.
- Avoid items that, though useful to a client, are more appropriately held by another local library.

The list could go on and on. See chapters 6 and 7 for additional discussion about selection criteria. Whatever criteria the library chooses, the collection development policy must clearly state the criteria to answer questions that may arise about why something is or is not in the collection.

Element Three: Miscellaneous Issues

This section of the collection development policy statement deals with gifts, deselection and discards, evaluation, as well as complaints and censorship. Each topic is important. However, each can stand alone, and some libraries develop longer, separate policy statements for each. Because they do have some relationship to collection development, the collection policy writers incorporate an abstract or summary of those policies instead of preparing something new.

Gifts

The golden rule for gifts is: Do not add a gift unless it is something the library would buy. Selectors must resist the temptation to add an item because it is free. No donated item is ever "free." Processing costs are the same for gifts and purchased materials. Expending library resources to add something to the collection just because it was a gift, when it does not match the library's collection profile, is a very poor practice. Applying the same standards to gifts as you do to purchased items will also reduce later weeding problems.

A written gift policy must make it clear whether the library accepts only items matching the collection profile or accepts anything with the proviso that the library may dispose of unwanted items in any manner deemed appropriate. Equally important is a statement regarding conditional gifts. Will the library accept a private collection and house it separately, if the donor provides the funds? Will it accept funds earmarked for certain classes of materials and use them to acquire new materials? If the library is trying to expand the collection through gifts and endowment monies, who will be responsible for this activity? How will the library coordinate the activities? These are some of the major questions that the policy writers should address in a section on gifts.

Gifts and endowment monies are excellent means of developing a collection, provided the library has maximum freedom in their use. Naturally, the library must answer an important public relations question regarding gifts: Is it better to accept all gifts, regardless of the conditions attached to them, or should the library avoid conditional gifts? If there is a clearly reasoned statement as to why the library does not accept conditional gifts, there should be fewer public relations problems.

Deselection and Discards

Deselection programs vary from library to library, but all libraries eventually must face the issue. Even the largest libraries must decide what materials to store in less accessible facilities; all large libraries have some type of limited-access storage facility. (Chapter 14 provides a detailed discussion of this issue.) The policy statement records staff decisions regarding the criteria, scope, frequency, and purpose of a deselection program.

At present, deselection questions seldom arise for anything but books and periodicals. In media centers and public libraries where other media are in high demand, especially audio and video recordings, there is a greater need for replacing worn-out items than for weeding unused materials.

Multiple copies of bestsellers and other books in high demand are issues in most public and educational libraries. The questions are, how many copies should the library purchase, and for how long should the library retain multiple copies? To some extent, the McNaughton Plan, which provides for short-term rental, can help reduce the cost of popular titles and reduce long-term storage of books in high demand for short periods of time. However, rental plans do not resolve the question of how many extra copies to retain or what the retention period should be.

Questions about multiple copies are not limited to popular or mass-market titles in public libraries. Similar issues arise concerning textbooks in educational libraries. There are no easy solutions to the problem of extra textbooks in educational settings, unless the library operates a rental system. Some policy guidelines for academic libraries are:

- Buy one copy for every ten potential readers during a six-month period.

- Buy one copy for the general collection and acquire one copy for every five readers during X months for the high-use or rental collection.

- Buy one copy for every ten students for required reserve reading use.

The length of time, number of readers, nature of use, and local conditions influence how many textbooks are purchased and how long they are retained.

Evaluation

Evaluation is essential to collection development. Chapter 14 outlines the major issues and needs the policy should cover. The policy should indicate whether the evaluation process is for internal purposes (e.g., identifying collection strengths and weaknesses), for comparative purposes, or perhaps for reviewing selectors' job performance. Each purpose requires different evaluation techniques or emphases. Making decisions about the how and why of evaluation ahead of time, putting them in writing, and getting them approved will save time and trouble for staff, patrons, funding agencies, and governing bodies.

Complaints and Censorship

The final section of the collection development policy statement outlines the steps to be taken in handling complaints about the collection. Eventually, every library will receive complaints about what is or is not in the collection. It is easier to handle questions about what is not there. (The library can always try to buy a missing item.) The major problem will be complaints about what is in the collection or questions as to why the policy limits collecting areas in a certain way.

When faced with a borrower or parent who is livid because of an item's inclusion in the collection, how does one defuse the situation? Passing the buck to the supervisor will only increase the patron's frustration. However, without guidelines for handling this type of situation, it is dangerous to try to solve the problem alone.

Usually, the person wants the offending item taken out of the collection. The librarian should not promise to remove the item but instead should agree to review it, if the library has an established review procedure. It is necessary to identify who, how, and when the library will handle the review process. Usually, the process begins by asking the patron to fill out a form. Though this response may appear bureaucratic to the individual, it does help identify the exact nature of the complaint. Complaint forms should consist of two parts, one explaining the library's review procedure, the other asking the person to identify the offending sections or qualities of the item. Because the staff is offering to take action, the individual usually becomes less angry. (Chapter 18 explores the issues of censorship and intellectual freedom.)

It is important that the library establish procedures for handling complaints *before* the first complaint arises. Ad hoc decisions in this area can cause community relations problems for the library. In this instance, the merits of consistency far outweigh the drawbacks. Whatever system for handling complaints the library chooses, it must become part of the written collection development policy.

There are books of policies one can use as models, for example, E. Futas' *Collection Development Policies and Procedures*, 3rd ed. (Phoenix, AZ: Oryx Press, 1995) and Richard Wood and Frank Hoffman's *Library Collection Development Policies: A Reference and Writers' Handbook,* 2nd ed. (Lanham, MD: Scarecrow, 2003). On the Internet, there are two very useful sources of collection development policies for all types of libraries that are worth visiting—AcqWeb's Directory of Policies on the Web available at <http://www.acqweb.org/cd_policy.html> and Electronic Collections Policies at <http://www.library.yale.edu/~okerson/ecd.html>.

Electronic Resources

Turning now to e-materials and policies, there are both similarities and differences in the structure of the policy or policies. In many ways, the similarities are such that a single comprehensive policy would be possible. However, given the length of most print policies, incorporating more material into them probably will make them too long to use effectively. Two other factors in favor of separate policies are the current concern about e-resources and the relative ease of creating a separate document. Some libraries make a distinction on the basis of "ownership"—print equals ownership and one type of policy; leased equals e-resources and another policy. That leaves a variety of electronic resources without a policy home.

Like the print policy, there ought to be an overview section in the electronic policy that defines terms and outlines the context of the policy. What does the policy cover? Does it include onetime purchases of CD-ROM products, only ongoing subscription services, or both? What about data sets? Does it cover the library's linking to various websites?

When there is agreement on the scope of the policy, just as with the print policy, there should be a statement about users. There are some thorny issues related to Internet access and certain classes of users, particularly children (see chapter 18). There are also some user issues associated with some companies' license agreements. Some libraries, especially U.S. government depositories, provide different levels of service to different types of databases. Both the differences in service levels and, if appropriate, the type(s) of user eligible to receive the service should be in the policy.

Content is, of course, a factor. Therefore, some type of statement about comparing print and electronic versions, when both exist, should be part of the policy. Peter Clayton and G. E. Gorman[15] published an interesting article proposing a method of using the conspectus approach for e-resources. The policy is probably the best place to have a statement regarding the role of electronic materials: whether they are replacements for print, supplements to print, duplicates of print, or some variation on the theme. Roger Durbin et al. wrote an insightful essay[16] about the need for an e-book policy. Although policies are guidelines rather than ironclad rules, outlining expectations for electronic materials is often easier at the abstract policy level than in a heated debate about a given product. Related to the question of role is an assessment of how an electronic version of a title compares to a print version—is it a total or partial duplication, or is it complete with added features? If the e-version duplicates a paper one, is there a time delay between the availability of one of the formats? Sometimes (more often than one would expect based on the popular press about technology) the print version appears months ahead of the electronic one.

Because the cost associated with electronic materials is high, and the items involved are often packages of titles rather than the print single-title approach, the policy ought to have a section devoted to cost assessment. Technology upgrades, both hardware and software, may be "hidden" costs of a product. Statements about how many, if any, upgrades are acceptable could go into this section. A related cost factor is whether the library is to buy or lease the product. If an annual lease is used, does the library get to retain anything when it ceases to pay the annual fee? Some guidelines about the preferred approach will help the selectors.

Training and support issues and how to assess them should be part of the policy as well. A list of factors to investigate will help avoid surprises later. For instance, does the product use a search interface already in use by other products in the library? What level of online/telephone vendor support (days and hours available) exists? If the product is Web-based, how stable and reliable is the host site? Erratic or uneven connection rates can cause the staff extra work and stress because they must handle users who are upset by being locked out or disconnected or by other problems that do not allow the search to be successfully completed.

A section that is particular to electronic resources is one on technical issues and license agreements. Many libraries do not have enough staff and expertise to support all types of e-resources. The policy is the place to outline what is and is not supported. A few libraries, especially those with limited staff or expertise, appear to be limiting themselves to Web products and few, if any, networked CD-ROMs. (As more and more products become Web-based, the decision not to support local tape mounting and/or networking of CD-ROMs is less problematic.) Decisions about licensing—who signs, what changes to seek, who is responsible, etc.—should be part of the policy.

Getting the Policy Approved

Having invested considerable staff time to preparing a comprehensive collection development policy, it is important that the library's governing board approve that policy. With board approval, everyone agrees on ground rules for building a collection that will serve the community.

An ideal policy approval process might consist of the following:

1. The director appoints a staff committee to draft a basic policy statement for submission to the director.

2. The director reviews and comments on the draft and distributes it to the library staff for comments and suggestions.

3. The original committee incorporates the comments and suggestions into an interim draft. Perhaps the committee will call a general meeting to discuss the interim draft before preparing the final version.

4. The director presents the final draft statement to the governing board for review, possible revision, and approval.

5. Between board review and final approval, the library holds an open meeting for community feedback about the proposed policy. At the meeting, members of the drafting committee, the director, and representatives of the governing board explain, describe, and, if necessary, defend and modify the statement.

6. The final step is to prepare multiple copies of the final statement for the library staff and patrons who request a copy. A good public relations device is to prepare a condensed version for distribution to each new user of the library.

Following these steps ensures community, staff, and administrative consensus about issues before a problem arises. It is much easier to agree on evaluation procedures, review procedures, levels and areas of collecting, and so on in advance than to try to handle them in the heat of a specific disagreement. An approved policy makes it easier to resolve disagreements, because it provides a body of established and agreed-upon rules.

Summary

Collection development is a complex process that is highly subjective, rife with problems and traps for the unwary. A comprehensive written policy, developed with the advice and involvement of all parties concerned, helps regulate the process and makes it less problematic.

Notes

1.   Lois Cherepon and Andrew Sankowski, "Collection Development at SJU Libraries: Compromise, Missions, and Transitions," in *Collection Development Policies: New Directions for Changing Collections,* ed. Daniel Mack, 64 (New York: Haworth Press, 2003).

2.   Joseph Straw, "Collection Management Statements on the World Wide Web," *Acquisitions Librarian* 30 (2003): 77–86.

3.   James Spoher, "The End of an American (Library) Dream: The Rise and Decline of the Collection Development Policy Statement at Berkeley," *Acquisitions Librarian* 30 (2003): 33–47.

4.   Dan C. Hazen, "Collection Development Policies in the Information Age," *College & Research Libraries* 56 (January 1995): 29–31.

5.   Merle Jacob, "Get It in Writing: A Collection Development Plan for the Skokie Public Library," *Library Journal* 115 (September 1, 1990): 166–69.

6.   *Information Power: Building Partnerships for Learning* (Chicago: American Association of School Librarians and Association for Educational Communication and Technology, 1998).

7.   For a more complete discussion of items in the list, see G. Edward Evans, "Needs Analysis and Collection Development Polices for Culturally Diverse Populations," *Collection Building* 11, no. 4 (1992): 167. The list was based on C. E. Cortes, F. Metcalf, and S. Hawke, *Understanding You and Them* (Boulder, CO: Social Science Education Consortium, 1976).

8.   Gale Hannigan and Janis F. Brown, *Managing Public Access Microcomputers in Health Sciences Libraries* (Chicago: Medical Library Association, 1992), 90.

9.   Michael Buckland, *Book Availability and the Library Users* (New York: Pergamon Press, 1975).

10.   Glen S. McGuigan and Gary White, "Subject-Specific Policy Statements: A Rationale and Framework for Collection Development," *Acquisitions Librarian* 30 (2003): 15–32.

11.   *Pacific Northwest Collection Assessment Manual,* 4th ed. (Lacey, WA: Western Library Network, 1992).

12.   Ibid., 48.

13.   Elizabeth Futas, "Collection Development of Genre Literature," *Collection Building* 12, nos. 3/4 (1993): 39–45.

14.   457 U.S. 853, 102 S. Ct. 2799 (1981).

15.   Peter Clayton and G. E. Gorman, "Updating Conspectus for a Digital Age," *Library Collections, Acquisitions & Technical Services* 26 (2002): 253–58.

16.   Roger Durbin, James Nalen, Diana Chlebek, and Nancy Pitre, "eBook Collection Development and Management: The Quandary of Establishing Policies and Guidelines for Academic Library Collections," in *Advances in Library Administration and Organization,* vol. 19, ed. D. E. Williams and E. D. Gartan, 59–84 (Greenwich, CT: JAI Press, 2002).

Further Reading

American Library Association. "Guidelines for Developing Beginning Genealogical Collections and Services." *RQ* 32 (Fall 1992): 31–32.

Atkinson, R. "Old Forms, New Forms: The Challenge of Collection Development." *College & Research Libraries* 50 (Summer 1991): 507–20.

Boge, K. D. "Integrating Electronic Resources into Collection Development Policies." *Collection Management* 21, no. 2 (1996): 65–76.

Boyarski, J. S., and K. Hickey, eds. *Collection Management in the Electronic Age: A Manual for Creating Community College Collection Development Policy Statements.* Chicago: ACRL, 1994.

Callison, D. "Evolution of School Library Collection Development Policies." *School Library Media Quarterly* 19 (Fall 1990): 27–34.

Carter, N. F. "Bibliographer's Manual: A New Life, A New Process." *Collection Management* 29, no. 1 (2004): 31–42.

Caywood, C. "Nonprint Media Selection Guidelines." *Journal of Youth Services in Libraries* 2 (Fall 1988): 90–94.

Feehan, P. "Youth Services Collection Development Issues." *Collection Building* 10, nos. 1/2 (1990): 55–60.

Forte, E., C. Chiu, S. Barnes, S. DeDecker, G. Colmenar, C. Pickett, S. Lewis, and C. Johns. "Developing a Training Program for Collection Managers." *Library Collections, Acquisitions, and Technical Services* 26, no. 3 (Autumn 2002): 299–306.

Gerhardt, L. N. "Matters of Policy." *School Library Journal* 39 (January 1993): 4.

Gorman, G. E. "An Embarrassment of Riches, or Just an Embarrassment?" *Australian Library Review* 8 (November 1991): 381–88.

Harloe, B., and J. M. Budd. "Collection Development and Scholarly Communication in the Era of Electronic Access." *Journal of Academic Librarianship* 20 (January 1995): 29–31.

Hodge, S. P., D. Calvin, and G. E. Rike. "Formulating an Integrated Library Government Documents Policy." *Government Information Quarterly* 6, no. 2 (1989): 199–213.

Hoolihand, C. "Collection Development Policies in Medical Rare Book Collections." *Collection Management* 11, nos. 3/4 (1989): 167–69.

Hopkins, D. M. "Put It in Writing." *School Library Journal* 39 (January 1993): 26–30.

Hughes-Hassell, S., and J. C. Mancall. *Collection Development for Youth: Responding to the Needs of Learners.* Chicago: American Library Association, 2005.

Hutchinson, C. A. "Collection Development: Bordering on Dysfunction." *Teacher Librarian* 29 no. 5 (2002): 54–55.

Intner, S. S. "Using a Collection Development Curriculum as a Model for Developing Policy Documents in Practice." *Acquisitions Librarian* 15, no. 30 (2003): 49–62.

Jacob, M. "Get It in Writing: A Collection Development Plan for the Skokie Public Library." *Library Journal* 115 (September 1, 1990): 166–69.

Johnson, M. A. "Writing Collection Development Policy Statements: Getting Started." *Technicalities* 14 (October 1994): 2–5.

Johnson, S. "Gifts: Are They Worth It?" In *Charleston Conference Proceedings 2002,* edited by R. Bazirjian and V. Speck, 119–24. Westport, CT: Libraries Unlimited, 2003.

LaGuardia, C., and S. Bentley. "Electronic Databases: Will Old Collection Development Policies Still Work?" *Online* 16 (July 1992): 60–63.

Latham, J. M. "To Link, or Not to Link." *Library Journal* 127 (Spring 2002): 20–22.

Lein, E. "Suggestions for Formulating Collection Development Policy Statements for Music Score Collections." *Collection Management* 9 (Winter 1987): 69–101.

Mancall, J. "(Un)changing Factors in the Searching Environment: Collections, Collectors and Users." *School Library Media Quarterly* 19 (Winter 1991): 84–89.

Maple, A., and J. Morrow. *Guide to Writing Collection Development Policies for Music*. Lanham, MD: Scarecrow Press, 2001.

Okpokwasili, N. P., and M. L. Bundy. "A Study of Selection and Acquisition Policies of Agricultural Libraries in the United States." *Libri* 39 (December 1989): 319–30.

Pappas, M. L. "Selection Policies." *School Library Media Activities Monthly* 21, no. 2 (October 2004): 41–43.

Perez, A. J., ed. *Reference Collection Development: A Manual*. 2nd ed. Chicago: American Library Association, 2004.

Robinson, A. "Acquisitions Policy for Contemporary Topics in an Academic Library." *The Acquisitions Librarian* 15, no. 30 (2003): 87–100.

Shreeves, E. "Between Visionaries and the Luddites." *Library Trends* 40 (Spring 1992): 579–95.

Smith, L. "Interactive Multimedia and Electronic Media in Academic Libraries—Policy Implication." *Reference Librarian* 38 (1993): 229–44.

Stacy-Bates, K. K., et al. "Competencies for Bibliographers: A Process for Writing a Collection Development Competencies Document." *Reference & User Services Quarterly* 41 (Spring 2003): 235–41.

Thomas, V. C. "Formulating a Federal Depository Collection Development Statement." *Legal Reference Services Quarterly* 11, nos. 1/2 (1991): 11–16.

U.S. National Library of Medicine. *Collection Development Manual*. Bethesda, MD: National Institutes of Health, 2004 <http://www.nlm.nih.gov/tsd/acquisitions/cdm/>.

White, G. W., and G. A. Crawford. "Developing an Electronic Information Resources Collection Development Policy." *Collection Building* 16, no. 2 (1997): 53–57.

Wykle, H. H. "Collection Development Policies for Academic Visual Resources Collections." *Art Documentation* 7 (Spring 1988): 22–26.

4
Selection Process in Practice

In the first chapters of this book, we focused on the nature of information and the theory behind the collection development process. We discussed the importance of both understanding the needs of your users and developing a comprehensive collection development policy, both of which provide a necessary foundation for the actual selection process. With this foundation, we may now move into the practical side of this process by exploring what takes place in the real world of libraries and information centers. To do this, we examine how different environmental settings influence selection work and describe the major categories of selection and acquisition aids. The tools used from institution to institution will differ, just as the selection process itself varies between and even within institutions. However, the tools listed here provide a valuable framework for the selection of materials. While reviewing this chapter, it is a good idea to keep in mind the advice offered by Patrick Jones:

> Collection development isn't about buying new books; it is about mixing new releases with standard titles. It is about weeding and maintaining, not just ordering everything on [a "best of"] list. It requires a balancing act between quality and popularity, single copies and multiples, old and new.[1]

What Happens in Selection

Before we examine the differences in how the various types of libraries approach collection development, it is useful to review some of the basic points of the selection process. No matter what type of library one works in, there are several common steps in the selection process. First, selectors must identify collection needs in terms of subjects and specific types of material. (This is especially important in the absence of a written collection development policy.) The next steps involve determining how much money is available for collection development and allocating a specific amount for each category or subject; developing a plan for identifying potentially useful materials to acquire; and finally, conducting the search for the desired materials. In most situations, the identification of potential acquisitions draws heavily from published lists, catalogs, flyers, e-mail and print announcements, and bibliographies. After securing the list of potential titles, a person or group assesses the worth of various titles on the same topic. In some cases, only one title is available. When that occurs, only two questions remain. First, is the price reasonable for the level of use that the item will receive? Second, is the item physically suitable for the proposed use? If the answer to both questions is the same (yes or no), the issue is resolved. When the answers are different, one must secure more information about the level of need before ordering the item.

More often than not, one makes the assessment using published information rather than a physical examination of the book. Although an item-by-item physical examination and reading, listening, or viewing are the ideal, most libraries lack the staff resources or the time to secure examination copies and review each title. Typically, school and public libraries devote more time to looking over approval copies than do academic libraries, although university and research libraries do use approval plans.

Most wholesalers and jobbers provide examination copies if they can reasonably expect that the libraries will purchase most of the titles sent or will order multiple copies of some of the titles. For example, if a librarian requested 100 titles on approval and kept 90, the jobber would probably send other titles on approval. However, if the library kept only 65 titles, it would become necessary to convince the jobber that there was good reason for this high rejection rate, or the firm might cancel the program. (If the library orders multiple copies of most of the retained titles, most vendors would continue to ship approval materials.) The reason is simple: it costs as much to select, pack, and ship an approval order as it does a firm order. (This is true for both the library and the vendor.) Thus, the more a library can depend on published selection aids to reduce the need for examination copies, the better off everyone will be. Many academic libraries use a jobber approval program, but the principle remains the same for all types of libraries: the return rate must be low. Some vendors will reassess a plan if the return rate rises much above 5 percent.

Selection Concepts and Terms

Before we go any further, it is useful to examine some common terms used in selection and acquisition work. Four related terms are *standing order*, *blanket order*, *approval plan*, and *Till Forbidden*. Although some people use these terms imprecisely, each has a specific meaning. *Standing orders* and *blanket orders* are similar; in both cases, the library commits to purchasing everything sent by a publisher or vendor, provided the materials match the terms of a formal agreement. (From a collection management point of view, such orders create a high degree of uncertainty in terms of the total annual cost, although some libraries do set an upper limit on total cost of materials a jobber may send without permission. The best one can do to make an estimate is to use the prior year's cost and an inflation factor, but variations in publishing schedules can cause marked variations in actual costs.) A *standing order* is normally placed for a series (e.g., Routledge's Literary Criticism and Cultural Theory series). A *blanket order* is placed for a subject field, grade level, or country's publications (e.g., all books about politics in Latin America, all books for undergraduates, or all the books published in Finnish in Finland). *Approval plans*, as noted earlier, allow the library to examine items before deciding to buy. They are not firm orders, which are legal contracts. Finally, serials librarians frequently use *Till Forbidden* to indicate that the publisher or supplier of a journal should automatically renew a subscription without any further approval from the library. This system saves time and money for both the library and publisher or supplier by reducing the amount of paperwork required to maintain subscriptions. For more details on acquisitions, see pages 229–47.

Each of these mechanisms plays a role in effective and efficient collection development, and each clearly affects selection activities. When selectors know the library needs everything on a subject or all of one type of information material or when selectors can satisfactorily define the scope and depth of need, a standing or blanket order is best. Such orders free selectors' time for more difficult decision-making activities. If selectors have less precise information about needs but know the library will need large numbers of titles, an approval plan may be best. However, the approval plan requires selectors to examine each shipment to decide which titles to keep and which to return.

Variations in Selection

Due to the different institutional environments in which the selection activities occur, there are naturally variations in the process. Given the universal nature of information and the diversity of institutional settings in which an information specialist may work during a career, no single method of categorizing institutional environments is completely satisfactory. However, for convenience of presentation, this section employs the traditional categories of libraries: academic, public, school, and special. There are great differences even within each category, and what follows provides only a broad overview of the thousands of variations that may exist.

Academic Libraries

Community or Junior Colleges

In the United States and many other countries, there are at least two broad types of postsecondary schools: vocational and academic. Publicly supported vocational programs in the United States are commonly referred to as community or junior colleges; however, most of these institutions have both vocational and academic programs. The academic program is roughly equivalent to the first two years in a college or university and serves as a transfer program to a four-year college or university. Frequently, the quality of education is just as good as that of a four-year college. If the transfer program is to succeed in providing the equivalent of the first two years of a four-year undergraduate degree, then the scope of the program must be just as comprehensive as that of the university program.

Collection development officers in a community college library have a challenging job. Not only must they focus on the academic programs, but they must also give equal attention to a wide range of vocational programs and user needs—and do so with a modest budget. Unfortunately, from a cost perspective, it is seldom possible to find materials that are useful in both programs. Also, many vocational programs need more visual than print materials, which accounts in part for the fact that American community college libraries tend to be leaders in the use of audiovisual (AV) materials. Strength in the AV collection means that the selection staff must know more about AV selection than their colleagues in other types of academic libraries. Community college librarians normally have other duties assigned to them aside from their collection development responsibilities, such as administration, reference, and instruction, which prevent them from devoting their entire focus to collection development.

Many community colleges must serve a broad student population composed of traditional, nontraditional, international and first-time college students enrolled in a mixture of in-person, televised, and online courses. In addition, most community or junior colleges offer extensive adult education or continuing education programs, which all too often have little or no relationship to the degree programs. While most academic institutions offer some form of adult, or nondegree, courses and programs, their libraries may not support this curriculum as extensively as their core courses. However, in most community colleges the library, or learning resource center (LRC), must handle all programmatic information needs. As LRCs serve a heterogeneous community, their collections must often reflect a diverse population with varying levels of language skills. Given the diversity of subjects and levels of user ability, the community college library resembles the public library more than it does its larger relation, the university library.

As a result of space and budgetary restrictions, selection in LRCs is usually item by item, with less use of blanket orders and approval plans than in other types of academic libraries. Collections generally contain at least a few items in all the standard educational formats, and as a result, selection personnel generally use a greater variety of selection aids than their colleagues in other types of libraries. Very little out-of-print searching and buying occurs, with the exception of replacing lost or worn-out materials. (Chapter 11 discusses sources for acquiring out-of-print materials.) Faculty involvement in LRC selection work is desirable, just as it is in other educational settings, and such support can be just as difficult to secure in LRCs as it is elsewhere.

College Libraries

Although college libraries serving primarily bachelor's degree programs are diverse, each serves a highly homogeneous user group. (Only the small special library that caters to a company or research group is likely to have a more homogeneous service community.) One characteristic of bachelor's degree programs is that, within a particular college, all the students who graduate, regardless of their major, complete some type of general education program. A program of core courses means that students select from a limited number of courses during their first two years. Less variety in course offerings makes selection work for that aspect of the institution's activities less complex (provided that sufficient networking occurs with the faculty and that the library is well aware of changes in the overall curriculum and in individual courses). Support of the curriculum is the primary objective of the college library collection. Collections in college libraries may offer some support for faculty research, but, unlike universities, colleges seldom emphasize research. With the curriculum as the focus for collection development activities, selectors have definite limits within which to work. Faculty members frequently play an active role in selection, more so than in the LRC or university context.

Most of the items selected for the American college library are current works in English. College libraries in general have fewer AV materials than do LRCs, but there is a growing trend to include all formats in the collection. Most institutions have a music audio collection and art slides or CDs to support the core curriculum survey courses in music and art. Retrospective collection building (identifying and acquiring out-of-print items) is not a major activity in the college library. Many college libraries have rare book rooms and spend a small percentage of their materials budget on rare items. A few college libraries have a strong special collection in a narrow subject field. Even without a rare book or special collection, some retrospective buying takes place. Most of the out-of-print searching and buying activities are to replace worn-out and lost books.

Because of their numbers (more than 900 in the United States) and their long history, college libraries have developed a series of standards, some quantitative and some qualitative. In June 2004, ACRL issued new "Standards for Libraries in Higher Education," which includes basic guidelines for resources.[2] (Two noteworthy articles reviewing such standards and the issues surrounding them are by Fernekes and Nelson[3] and Kaser.[4]) Although standards may provide a basic framework for discussion, they do not have any influence in selection work, at least on a day-to-day basis.

Without question, the most widely used selection aid in American college libraries is *Choice* (published by the American Library Association). ALA created *Choice* to meet the specific needs of college library collection development officers by reviewing publications aimed at the undergraduate market. Subject experts, including librarians, write the reviews with an emphasis on the subject content and the title's overall suitability for undergraduate, rather than research, use. With small staffs (typically ten to fifteen people), few college libraries have sufficient subject expertise to evaluate all the potentially useful titles published each year, even with help from the teaching faculty. Because *Choice* annually reviews more than 7,000 titles of "potential use by undergraduates"[5] and because of its widespread use as a selection aid, several librarians have studied *Choice* to determine whether it is an effective selection aid. For example, do items receiving positive reviews receive more use than titles receiving neutral reviews? One such study concluded that *Choice*

> reviews appear helpful in identifying the most worthy titles, as those most likely to be used repeatedly. . . . [T]itles appealing primarily to a more elite audience of specialists ought to be scrutinized if the selector is concerned about maximum use. The question of the level on which the book is written is an important one. . . . [S]electing strictly on the basis of probable popularity runs the risk of developing a collection which could be categorized as "lightweight" academically.[6]

The authors also noted that a collection based on *Choice*'s so-called worthy titles may or may not address the needs of the particular institution. Despite such analyses, *Choice* remains a popular resource for selection in a variety of settings.

University Libraries

The interests and needs of university and research libraries dominate the professional literature, as evidenced by the number of books and articles published about academic collection development in recent years. This domination arises from several types of numerical superiority. Though these libraries are not as numerous as libraries of other types, the size of their collections and the number of their staff, as well as monies expended per year on operations, far surpass the combined totals for all the other types of libraries. University and research libraries have collections ranging from a few hundred thousand to more than 10 million volumes. As an example, Tozzer Library (Harvard University) is a relatively small library in the world of research libraries, given its collection size. However, since it collects only in the fields of anthropology and archaeology, it is one of the two largest anthropology libraries in the world. Like all research libraries, Tozzer spends a good deal of money on materials each year, does much work that is retrospective, and collects in most languages.

Collection development and selection work require more time and attention in university research libraries than in other academic libraries. Typically, there are full-time collection development officers who to some degree or another establish liaison relationships with their subject faculty. In other academic libraries, collection development is one of many duties a librarian performs. Looking at the history and development of U.S. academic libraries, one can see a changing pattern in regard to who does the book selection. In small libraries with limited funds, there is strong faculty involvement; sometimes the faculty has sole responsibility for building the collection. As the collection, institution, and budget grow, there tends to be a shift to more and more librarian involvement and responsibility. At the university and research library level, subject specialists come back into the selection picture, but they are members of the library staff rather than the teaching faculty. Many, if not most, of the persons responsible for collection development in research libraries have one or more subject graduate degrees in addition to a degree in library science. Such individuals are usually responsible for developing the collection in a specific subject or language. As such, knowledge of one or more foreign languages is a must if one wishes to be a collection development officer at the university level.

There is no single method by which academic libraries divide the universe of knowledge among subject specialists. Local needs and historical precedents determine how the library distributes these responsibilities. Some universities use broad areas (social sciences or humanities), others use geographic divisions (Oceania or Latin America), and still others use small subject fields (anthropology or economic botany) and languages (Slavic or Arabic). It is not uncommon to find a mix of all methods.

A significant problem in large university and research library systems with departmental or subject libraries is coordinating collection development activities. No matter the size of the collection budget, there is always more material than money. Unintentional duplication is always a concern, but the biggest problem is determining whose responsibility it is to collect in a given subject. As the number of persons involved grows and the scope of each person's responsibility diminishes, the danger of missing important items increases. Working together, sending one another announcements, and checking with colleagues about their decisions become major activities for university collection development officers. (Joint collection development activities with the "conspectus" approach were covered in chapter 3.)

University libraries have traditionally depended heavily on standing and blanket orders, as well as approval plans, as means of reducing workloads while assuring adequate collection building. At times, even leased collections—more commonly seen in public libraries—find their way into academic settings. (For a discussion of this practice, see the articles by Odess-Harnish[7] and Van Fleet.[8]) Using such programs allows selectors more time for retrospective buying and for tracking down items from countries where the book trade is not well developed. However, with many university libraries grappling with journal inflation rates and the cost of online materials, it remains to be seen to what extent a dependence on blanket orders can continue.

Public Libraries

As is seen in junior or community college library clientele, diversity is the primary characteristic of public libraries' selection practices (arising from the heterogeneous nature of the communities they serve). A wide variety of practices exist, as it is obvious that communities of a few hundred people, with a small library open only a few hours per week with no professional or full-time staff, do not follow the same practices as their large urban counterparts. Collection sizes range from several hundred items (Mancos, Colorado) to large research collections of millions of volumes (New York City).

Despite this variety, some generalizations can be applied to most public libraries. The service population normally consists of many unrelated constituencies: persons from various ethnic groups, of all ages, with various educational backgrounds and levels of skill and knowledge and with a variety of information needs. All these groups fall within the public library's service population. Community need is the dominant factor in selection, all too often because funding and good sense permit no other choice. Although librarians do the selecting, occasionally they employ a committee format with patron involvement. Growth of the collection is modest because of limited budgets, stack space, and the removal of worn-out or outdated materials. Most selections are current imprints, with retrospective buying generally limited to replacement titles. Medium-sized and large public libraries commonly collect audio and video recordings as well as a variety of other AV formats. Perhaps the main differences in collection development between public libraries and libraries of other types are need to develop collections for a wide range of ages (from infants to adults) and their strong emphasis on recreational needs, in addition to educational and informational materials. Trade publishers count on a strong public library market for most of their new releases. Without the library market, book buyers would see even higher prices, because only a fraction of the new books published would become strong sellers, much less bestsellers.

For larger libraries, there are two important issues in selection: speed and coordination. Most of the larger libraries are systems with a main library and one or more branches. The reading public likes to read new books while they are new, not six to nine months after interest wanes. Often interest is fleeting, especially in fiction. So, having the new books on the shelf and ready to circulate when the demand arises is important. With several service points, a system must control costs. One way to help control cost is to place one order for multiple copies of desired items rather than ordering one now, another later, and still more even later.

Anticipating public interest is a challenge for the public library selector, and it probably would be impossible without several aids. Unquestionably, two of the most important aids are an understanding of the needs of the library users and the selectors' inquiring, active minds and their commitment to read, read, read. In addition, one of the most useful aids is Reed Business Information's *Publishers Weekly* (*PW*). Reading each issue cover-to-cover provides a wealth of information about what publishers plan to do to market new titles. Clues such as "30,000 first printing; major ad promo; author tour"; "BOMC, Cooking and Crafts Club alternative"; "major national advertising"; "soon to be a TV miniseries"; or "author to appear on the *Tonight Show*" can help the selector to identify potentially high-interest items before demand arises. *PW* bases its information on publishers' stated plans, and the information appears well in advance of implementation, so there is time to order and process the items before patron requests begin to materialize. Needless to say, not all the highly promoted titles generate the interest the publisher hopes for. Occasionally, *PW* has an article that covers publishers' successes and failures.[9] Additional resources include *Library Journal* (*LJ*; Reed Business Information) and *Booklist* (American Library Association), which provide "Prepub alerts" and "upfront preview" listings. All three publications include such information in both their print and online publications.[10] By knowing the community and the publishers, a selector can, in time, predict with reasonable accuracy the titles that will likely be of high interest to their users. The McNaughton Plan (rental plan) is one way to meet high, short-term demand for multiple copies. (See chapter 11 for more information on this service.) Another way in which collection budgets may be "stretched" is through the use of a "floating" collection, in which titles are owned by a system, rather than a specific library. (See Ann Cress' article in *LJ* for a discussion of this concept.[11])

The need to coordinate order placement is one reason many public libraries use selection committees or centralized selection. Selection committees, especially if they include a representative from each service location, reduce the problem of order coordination. In large systems with dozens of branches and mobile service points, such as the Los Angeles Public Library, total representation is impractical. In such cases, the selection committee develops a recommended buying list, and the service locations have a period of time to order from the list. Though not a perfect system, it does help achieve some degree of coordinated buying and cost control. Sullivan identified further advantages of centralized selection, noting:

> Most public libraries have chosen to centralize selection because they need front-line librarians to concentrate on duties more directly related to customer service. Some systems use centralized selection to streamline technical services processes and ensure all users derive the same quality of service by receiving new materials at the same time. Many systems find that one of the major benefits of centralized selection is meeting the patron expectation to have access to titles nearer to the publication date.[12]

Small public libraries may not experience all of the same problems of large libraries; however, they are likewise concerned about the availability of funds and having the time to buy materials. Reviews play a vital role in helping selectors at the small library locate the best possible buys with limited funds. More and more public libraries, including the smallest, participate in some type of cooperative network, which benefits collection development. Thus, small libraries sometimes can draw on the expertise of the network for identifying appropriate materials and can use selection aids they could never justify having if they were on their own. Some cooperatives engage in joint purchasing to gain discounts on high-volume purchases. In such cases, the smaller libraries use the purchasing list approach that large systems use. Even for small U.S. public libraries that are part of a cooperative, *Booklist* is the most important selection aid. Although *Booklist* contains only recommended titles, it also reviews a wide range of nonprint materials and reference items.

As mentioned previously, another distinctive feature of public library collection development is the need to collect children's materials. In many public libraries, children's books get the highest use. Most libraries depend on positive reviews when making selection decisions about children's books. Often, the staff members examine the title when it arrives to make certain it fits collection guidelines. One of the first specialist positions a growing public library tries to create is for children's materials and services.

It should be noted that while there is some overlap between children's materials in schools and those in public libraries, it is not large. Throughout the United States and in other countries as well, requirements for being a school librarian and for being a children's librarian in a public library vary. In addition, academic librarians may be called upon to select children's materials, particularly to support education programs. (For an overview of this issue, see Bay's article on the topic.[13])

Two other special features of public library collection development are noteworthy. First, the public library, historically, has been a place to which citizens turn for self-education materials. Self-education needs range from basic language and survival for the recent immigrant, to improving skills gained in schools, to maintaining current knowledge of a subject studied in college. In addition to the true educational function of the preceding, there is the self-help and education aspect exemplified by learning how to repair a car, how to fix a sticky door, how to prepare a special meal, or how to win friends and influence people. Selecting materials for the varied educational wants and desires of a diverse population can be a real challenge and a specialty in itself.

The last feature of note is the selection of genre fiction, a staple in most public library collections. Most people read only a few types of fiction regularly, whether it be mysteries, spy novels, or science fiction. Thus, learning about the various types of fiction and their authors can be a challenge, especially as few review sources include such works. (It might be a good idea for all public librarians to have a course in genre novels while in library school.) A good resource that can be of help in learning about such fiction is *Genreflecting: A Guide to Reading Interests in Genre Fiction.*[14] For example, although one may think that all westerns are the same, some readers will devour any western about range wars but will not touch a title about mountain men. In the area of westerns alone, *Genreflecting* lists thirty-two distinct themes and the names of authors who specialize in each one. This work is kept current by the companion *Genrefluent* website (<http://www.genrefluent.com>), maintained by the author. Genre literature is also included in resources such as *BooksinPrint.Com*.

Learning about the different categories and their authors is not only fun but useful for anyone developing a public library collection. (Of course, genre works are not limited to print titles, and some libraries take advantage of programs such as *Automatically Yours*, provided by Baker and Taylor, which provides standing orders for Anime videos.) Senkevitch and

Sweetland found that certain "core" fiction items remain in the collection from year to year, so the entire genre collection would not likely have to be replaced from year to year.[15]

School Library Media Centers

As curriculum support dominates school library media center (LMC) collection development, some similarities exist among community college, college, and school media center selection activities. Each emphasizes providing materials directly tied to teaching requirements, and each uses instructor input in the selection process. An emphasis on current material, with limited retrospective buying, is common. Community college and school media centers share the distinction of having the greatest number and variety of AV materials in their collections, but both school and community college media centers must serve an immense range of student abilities.

Although similarities do exist, the differences between school media centers and other educational libraries far outweigh the similarities. For example, in the area of curriculum support, school media centers have limited funds for collection development, thus resembling the small public library. With limited funds and limited staff (often there is only one professional on the staff), most of the money goes to purchasing items that directly support specific instructional units. Teachers and LMC staff must plan effectively to assure that scarce funds meet topical requirements and that cooperation with other school, public, and academic libraries will maximize student access to needed materials. As Dorion put it, librarians must consider the "bang for the buck" of a title, selecting those items that will be widely used throughout the school.[16] School libraries in particular realize that excellent access for children builds expectations for the future and a willingness to fund all types of libraries as intellectual needs expand.

Library media specialists often build a core collection that provides some breadth and then concentrate on building emphasis collections that target curricular goals. For example, the media specialist might combine textbook and LMC funds to build rotating classroom and LMC collections of fiction and literary nonfiction to support a literature-based reading program. A hands-on math collection of manipulatives and fun, math-oriented literature might be used to support a move to meet the National Council of Teachers of Mathematics curriculum standards. Science department and LMC funds could be combined to access resources such as *SIRS Discoverer on the Web*.

Published reviews play a significant role in media center selection. Often, school districts secure published reviews and also inspect items before making purchase decisions. The reasons for this are parental and school board interest in the collection's content and the need to spend limited funds on materials that will actually meet teachers' specific needs. The most widely used review sources are ALA's *Booklist;* Reed Business Information's *School Library Journal;* and Wilson's *Children's Catalog.* Brodart offers an online series of "Recommended titles" for students in the K–6 and 7–12 grade levels, which can also be useful in selection. To a lesser degree, school libraries also use *Library Journal.* Finding reviews that provide adequate coverage of nonprint formats is a challenge; although *Booklist, LJ,* and *School Library Journal* all contain some AV reviews, they cover only a small percentage of the total output. Information about grade level and effectiveness in the classroom are two crucial concerns for the media specialist. Grade level information is generally available, but it is very difficult to locate data about classroom effectiveness. Usually, the time involved in gathering effectiveness data is too great to make it useful in media center collection development.

Normally, teachers and media specialists serve on committees that review and select items for purchase. There may also be some parent representation on the committee as well. Whatever the committee composition, the media specialist must take the responsibility for identifying potentially useful items, preparing a list of suggestions, and securing examination or preview copies for group consideration. Most importantly, the committee must have a clear sense of collection emphasis, of how the items under consideration support current curriculum, and of how the collection will grow as the curriculum evolves.

Although selection responsibility lies with the library media specialist, parents and others have legitimate concerns about both formats and content of materials to which children have access. Some parents and religious groups have strong objections to certain ideas in books and journals. As such, the need for a collection development policy may be more acute in the school media center than in other settings.

School library media centers are probably the most closely monitored of all types of libraries. However, public libraries receive their share of monitoring, especially in the area of children's materials. Media centers handle an ongoing flow of questions about, and legal challenges to, the content of the collection. An illustration of this scrutiny was the tongue-in-cheek *Reader's Guide to Non-Controversial Books*, published by the National Committee for Good Reading. This publication listed items that would not be "offensive to any of the cultural or religious values in our society." Its proposed users were to be children, young adults, and "discriminating" adults in the United States. The publication contained ten blank pages.[17] Concern over controlling, influencing, developing, or expanding (or a number of other labels) children's minds generates challenges. At times, both liberal and conservative pressure groups question why a certain item is, or is not, in a collection. Written policies and advisory committees are two means of answering such questions.

The term *library media specialist* denotes a person who knows about all types of information formats and the equipment necessary for using the formats. Today, at least in the United States, most school library media centers also serve as computer centers. Selection of instructional computer software is a common responsibility, and, not infrequently, so is teaching students and staff how to use computers and software. Given that many schools are equipped with technology in each classroom, library media specialists must do more than build a centralized collection. In addition, they must continue to expand areas in the school for instant access (high-tech teaching stations) or on-call access (we will get the material if you give us advance warning), or they must help get students to a location where the materials or technology can be used (the school's LMC, the public library, or an academic library).

Building the school media center collection is probably the most rewarding and the most frustrating of all types of collection building. Normally, the center serves a relatively small population, and each user is known on a personal level seldom found in other types of libraries. The frustration comes from having too little money to buy all the needed material, understaffing, and the difficulty in finding both appropriate material and necessary reviews.

Special Libraries and Information Centers

Almost any general statement about special libraries and information centers is inaccurate for any individual special library, because of the diversity of environmental settings. In a sense, this is a catchall category. As a result, this category may be the largest and the least homogeneous. Dividing this category into three subclasses—scientific and technical, corporate and industrial, and subject and research—allows some useful generalizations. However, even these subclasses are not always mutually exclusive. A hospital library can have both a scientific and a corporate orientation if it has a responsibility to support both the medical and the administrative staff. In teaching hospitals, there is an educational aspect to collection building as well. There may even be a flavor of a public library, if the library offers a patient-service program. Some corporations establish two types of information centers, technical and management; others have a single facility to serve both activities. A geology library in a large research university may have more in common with an energy corporation library than it does with other libraries in its own institution. Independent research libraries, such as the Research Library at the Getty Research Institute, would also be included within the category of special libraries, as they have no ties to government or educational institutions. Similar in mission to subject (or branch) libraries at universities, as a whole "independent research libraries, especially those founded in the eighteenth and nineteenth centuries, often driven by fiscal constraint . . . have sharpened their collecting focus to establish expertise and identity in limited, specialized subject areas."[18]

Special libraries in the United States and Canada number over 9,000. Despite their substantial numbers, special libraries have not influenced professional practice as much as one would expect. This does not mean that special libraries have not made important contributions or developed innovative practices; it merely means that circumstances often make it difficult or impossible for special libraries to share information about their activities in the same manner as other libraries. Their diversity in character and operational environment is one reason for special libraries' modest influence. Another reason is that libraries and information centers in profit-oriented organizations frequently limit the reporting of activities and new systems for proprietary reasons; knowing what a competitor is working on may provide a company with an advantage. Such concerns often limit the amount of cooperative activities in which corporate libraries may engage. One way to learn about an organization's current interests is to study the materials in its library.

Two widely shared characteristics of special libraries are lack of space and their reliance on online resources. Limited space for all services, but particularly for collection storage, is a frequent complaint of the special librarian. Although all libraries eventually experience lack of space, a special library seldom expects to expand beyond its assigned area. Deselection becomes, more often than not, a regular part of the special library's cycle. Accurate information about the most useful core items for the collection and how long these items will remain useful assists the librarian in providing cost-effective service. Special librarians and information officers make good use of data generated by bibliometric techniques in selecting and maintaining collections of the most needed serials. Bradford's law, Lotka's law, Zipf's law, and citation analysis have contributed to the effective operation of special libraries. Two examples illustrate the use of bibliometric data. Researchers have identified the half-lives of journals for many scientific fields. For example, the half-life of a physics journal is 4.6 years. This means that half of the references in a current physics journal carry a publication date within the last 4.6 years. In addition to half-life, researchers also study journals' impact, importance, or influence. When one knows which journals receive the most bibliometric citations, one can decide which titles to acquire and keep. Like any statistical data, information from bibliometric studies is approximate. Therefore, though helpful in collection building and management, these studies assist only in decision making and cannot serve as a substitute for professional judgment. (Other libraries will likely make increasing use of these techniques as they come under the economic and space pressures faced by special libraries.)

Most special libraries have very current collections and, in terms of collection policy, would be considered level 4 (research), but without the retrospective element. Despite the heavy emphasis on current materials, the best-known selection aids provide little help to persons responsible for collection building in special libraries. Most of the material acquired for special libraries is very technical and of interest to only a few specialists; as a result, no meaningful market exists for review services. Recommendations of clients and knowledge of their information needs become the key elements in deciding what to buy.

The term *Information Center* is a reasonable label for most special libraries, because they collect many information formats seldom found in other libraries. For example, special libraries frequently acquire patent and trademark information. In some cases, the library conducts regular searches for new information that may be of interest to the organization; most typically, it makes occasional searches for specific items. Some special libraries may go so far as to collect seemingly unusual items such as well logs and remote sensing data. Well logs are records of drilling operations and are of interest to most energy companies involved in exploration. Remote sensing data take many forms but are normally from satellite sources; these data, depending on their specific content, can be of interest to farmers, archaeologists, mining engineers, geologists, military officials, and others. Both formats are secured from specialized sources. Most are generally expensive (normally, cost is less important than access and speed of delivery) and require special handling. A number of special libraries also handle restricted information. The restricted material may be labeled as classified by law or government agency, or it may take the form of internal documents that are important or sensitive. Staff members working with classified information are usually investigated and given clearances before they begin handling classified material.

Special library collections tend to be *now* collections. Their purpose is to meet immediate needs, not future needs. When needed, the library secures historical material through interlibrary loan. Order placement takes place by phone or e-mail, and librarians charge the costs to credit cards. Sometimes, acquiring a title means placing an order from overseas, next-day air express delivery, with the delivery costs equaling or exceeding the cost of the item ordered. When that happens—and certainly it is not an everyday occurrence—it does give one a sense of how valuable information is in some organizations.

Online database access is prevalent in most special libraries. Unlike other libraries, which tend to emphasize bibliographic databases, special libraries access numeric, bibliographic, and full-text services. A particular concern for today's special librarian is deciding when to utilize a database service for occasional access to information and when to acquire a hard copy of the same data. Indeed, this type of cost-benefit question confronts all types of libraries to some degree.

Understanding user needs is a major part of the special library program, to a greater degree than in other types of libraries. Selective dissemination of information (SDI) is a technique often used in special libraries. By developing and maintaining user interest profiles, the library can continually monitor the information needs and interests of its service population, allowing more effective collection building, and distribution of electronic content. The technique also serves as a public relations activity. Every SDI notification serves as a reminder of the library's existence and value. Usually, SDI services are ineffective for large service populations, because the services are too costly to operate; however, several commercial firms offer SDI-like services. The Institute for Scientific Information (ISI), a subsidiary of Thomson, is one commercial organization that offers SDI-like services; it also publishes several indexing and abstracting tools to which many special libraries subscribe (*Science Citation Index*, *Web of Science*, etc.). These firms also provide bibliometric data (including information about half-lives and impact) about the titles they cover.

Selection Aids

Although they may not be utilized to their fullest extent, everyone involved in collection development recognizes the importance of bibliographies and review sources in building a library collection. If no selection aids existed, the size of the library staff would have to increase dramatically or the number of items acquired would drop. The aids provide, to some degree, an overview of the output of publishers and media producers. Without bibliographies or review sources, each publisher and media producer would flood the library with catalogs and announcements of products, and the filing and retrieval system for that material would add significantly to the library's workload. Finding the answer to the question, "How many books exist on vegetable gardening?" would entail going through thousands of catalogs and announcements to cull all relevant items. This merely underscores the fact that, despite their shortcomings and librarians' complaints about specific selection aids, they are time-saving tools essential to the efficient function of the library.

This section describes six categories of selection aids (summarized in table 4.1, with serials, audiovisual, and government documents selection aids appearing in the chapters about those formats) and mentions a few representative titles. All of the aids save time and frustration if one takes the time to study the titles in each one. As with any reference tool, the first step is to read the introductory material that the publisher or producer provides.

The categories covered in this chapter are:

1. current sources for in-print books;

2. catalogs, flyers, and announcements;

Table 4.1. Selection aids.

Type of Selection Aid	Characteristics	Advantages	Disadvantages	Example
Current sources for in-print books	Contain citation information	Identify new materials as they become available; particularly useful in large libraries attempting to achieve broad coverage	Usually provide only for author searches; subject searches are time-consuming; may not contain review/content information	*American Book Publishing Record (ABPR) Books in Print*
Catalogs, flyers, and announcements	Marketing material designed and distributed by publishers	May contain more information than in-print lists	Brief information; advertising copy tends to present the item in its most favorable light	*ALA Editions for ALA publications*
Current review sources	Designed to promote or evaluate works Three types of reviews: 1. Reviews for persons making their living buying books 2. Reviews for subject specialists 3. Reviews for the general public	Save staff time in locating/reviewing newly published works	"Differential marketing" may affect promotion of titles; only a small percentage of total book output reviewed; delay in review's appearance in print; reviewer competence varies; reviews tend not to be critical in nature	*Library Journal (LJ) Choice Booklist New York Times Sunday Book Review Amazon.Com*
Bibliographic databases	Cooperative and individual library catalogs; serve as partial replacement for national bibliographies	Access to millions of records worldwide; usually do not need separate access to national bibliography; useful for verification work; information can be downloaded and serve as bibliographic record in online catalog	Not all countries well represented in online systems	OCLC RLIN

(*continued*)

Table 4.1—*Continued.*

Type of Selection Aid	Characteristics	Advantages	Disadvantages	Example
Recommended, best, and core collection lists	Lists of items recommended for purchase	Useful when used carefully	Impractical to strive to collect every item listed; list becomes dated immediately upon publication	*Public Library Catalog* J. Gillespie, *Best Books for Children: Preschool Through Age Six*, 7th ed. (Westport, CT: Bowker-Greenwood, 2002)
Subject bibliographies	Listings prepared by subject experts and including critical evaluations	Can exist for virtually any subject	Currency and selectivity issues exist	J. H. Sweetland, *Fundamental Reference Sources*, 3rd ed. (Chicago: ALA, 2001)

3. current reviews;

4. bibliographic databases;

5. best books, recommended lists, and core collections; and

6. subject bibliographies.

The examples within each category are selective at best. To give complete, worldwide coverage to all the titles in each group would require one or two books at least as long as table 4.1.

Current Sources for In-Print Books

National in-print lists are key tools in selection because they identify new materials as they become available. To be effective, individuals involved in selection and acquisition work must be familiar with these tools. New books (those acquired during the year they are published) represent the majority of the materials acquired by most libraries. In some large research or archival libraries, this may not be the case, but even in such libraries, new books represent a large percentage of the total annual acquisitions. Every country in the world with any significant amount of publishing has a publication that attempts to list that nation's books in print. Naturally, the degree of success varies, and access to such international lists may be easy or difficult. For countries with a high volume of publishing (such as the United States, Great Britain, and other industrialized countries), there may be weekly lists of new books. (An example is VNU Entertainment Media's—formerly Whitaker's—*Bookseller*.) Most listings of in-print books provide information about the author, title, publisher, place of publication, date of publication, and price. In addition, the listing may offer information about length; special features; series information; International Standard Book Number (ISBN); and cataloging information, including subject headings. Cataloging information can be helpful in selection because, too often, the title of a book does not provide enough information to allow anyone to make an informed judgment about its content. Additionally, "while there are certainly exceptions, a book's in-print status says something about its reputation and popularity."[19]

In-print lists are issued weekly and are cumulated into monthly publications such as *American Book Publishing Record* (Bowker). Such monthly lists offer the same information contained in weekly listings, while providing several means of access, usually subject, author, and title. In a few countries, prepublication announcements appear in a single source, such as *Forthcoming Books* (Bowker). Although such aids can be of some value in planning purchases of new books, two major factors limit their use: first, announced books do not always appear on schedule; and second, a few announced titles never appear. While printed weekly lists facilitate only an author search (and make subject searches time-consuming), publishers' websites can facilitate faster, more up-to-date searches.

In many countries, an annual list is the only list, or at least the only one that a library outside the country can acquire. Annual lists range from a few hundred pages to multivolume sets. All contain the basic bibliographic information required to order a specific book (author, title, publisher, date); most include many of the features included in weekly or monthly lists, including author, title, and subject access. Examples of annual lists are *Books in Print* (Bowker); *British Books in Print* (available online from Whitaker via DIALOG and included within Bowker's *GlobalBooksinPrint.Com*); *Les Livres Disponibles* (Editions du Cercle de la Librairie); and *Verzeichnis Lieferbarer Bucher* (Verlag der Buchhandler-Vereinigung GmbH). There is an in-print book list corresponding to almost every major language in which there is active publishing.

It should be noted that regardless of their format, most comprehensive in-print lists issued by commercial publishers are not complete. In most cases, the comprehensiveness of the resource depends on information submitted by book and media publishers. Even online in-print resources (such as *BooksinPrint.Com*) may not be completely up-to-date (although they will be more current than a print counterpart). The in-print list publisher has neither the staff nor the time to attempt to track down all possible titles for inclusion. Thus, if a publisher forgets or does not wish to submit data about a title or group of titles, nothing appears for those items. Because libraries and retail outlets use in-print lists as a buying tool, larger publishers tend to send in the information, while many smaller publishers do not. One should never assume that, because a specific title does not appear in the national in-print list, the item is out of print or does not exist. Even if other titles by the same publisher do appear, it is wise to contact the publisher to inquire about the availability of the missing item. Some persons have suggested that a few publishers do not appear in commercial in-print lists because of commercial competition. To date, no evidence shows that this did, or does, happen. However, an annual list that is based on copyright deposit data is more likely to be complete than is a commercial list.

Large and small libraries alike rely on in-print tools—in print or electronic format—especially where reviews are not as critical in selection decisions (although an added feature of many electronic in-print lists is access to reviews). These tools allow the selector to see a broader spectrum of the current output and help assure a better expenditure of limited funds, which is particularly helpful in smaller libraries. There is a slight danger that some items appearing in a less frequent list will be out of print, but for most small libraries, this is hardly a concern, because their "wish lists" far exceed the funds available.

Catalogs, Flyers, and Announcements

Publishers market their products through catalogs and other forms of promotional material. Some publishers use direct marketing via mail or e-mail almost exclusively. They believe that their publications become lost among too many others in national in-print resources and that these lists do not provide enough information to sell their books. Such publishers distribute catalogs listing all their available products and send out flyers and e-mail announcements of new titles. Even publishers who participate in combined in-print lists employ these sales methods.

Generally, such announcements contain more information about a book and its author(s) than do national in-print resources. When one cannot secure a review copy or find a published review, catalogs and flyers can provide useful selection data. It is necessary to use such information with caution. The purpose of the catalogs and flyers is to sell merchandise; though few publishers would lie about an item, advertising copy presents the item in its most favorable light. As the selector becomes familiar with publishers, she or he learns which publishers are objective and which puff up their products more than the content warrants.

Unfortunately, a few unscrupulous individuals attempt to deceive libraries and individual book buyers. For example, Dr. Evans has a large personal collection of Native American reference works, of which two titles illustrate our point. One is a three-volume set (5×8 inches) titled *Dictionary of Indians of North America*, with the imprint Scholarly Press, St. Clair Shores, Michigan (1978). The other is a two-volume set (7×10 inches) titled *Biographical Dictionary of Indians of the Americas*, with the imprint American Indian Publishers, Newport Beach, California (1983). The content of both works is identical. The owners of these and many other imprints were convicted of fraud. However, their convictions did nothing to help the many libraries that paid for materials that were never delivered or that duplicated existing material. All one can do when confronted with information about what appears to be a title of high interest from an unfamiliar publisher is to ask for an examination copy and to ask selectors in other libraries if they know the firm. In time, one may associate a company name or location with potential problems. Flyers from unknown publishers, offering large discounts for prepaid orders, deserve a second, third, and fourth look before committing funds. One may never see the publication or get the money back. Discussion lists, such as COLLDV-L, can be one resource for finding out information about such titles. (See the Further Reading list for subscription information.)

Libraries that make heavy use of announcements, flyers, and catalogs for selection must set up an efficient storage and retrieval system. In the past, commercial firms attempted to collect publishers' catalogs and sell the collections to libraries, such as Bowker's *Publisher's Trade List Annual (PTLA),* which was discontinued in 2001. Since the collections were almost immediately incomplete, fewer and fewer libraries bought it, depending instead on their own filing system. Of course, libraries generally keep catalogs only from publishers and dealers that they use on a regular basis.

Books in Print can serve as one substitute for catalogs and is available in a number of formats, including an annual print edition, as well as on CD (*Books in Print with Reviews*) and online (*BooksinPrint.com*—in "Professional" and "Patron" versions, as well as Spanish-language, children's, and international editions). Other sources of information include Brodart's TIPS program. TIPS is an acronym that stands for *Title Information Preview Ser-*

vice, which provides reviews, customized to the profile of the subscribing library, of new and forthcoming titles. Information about this service is available at (<http://www.books.brodart.com/services/tips.htm>).

Current Review Sources

Wherever a flourishing book trade exists, so does an equally strong book-reviewing system. One can divide book reviews into three types: (1) reviews for persons making their living buying books (trade and professional booksellers and librarians), (2) reviews for subject specialists, and (3) reviews for the general public. Book selectors use all three types, but those of greatest utility are the trade and professional reviews. Some differences in emphasis do exist among types of libraries. Special libraries make the least use of reviews, but when they do need a review, the first two categories receive the greatest credence, with a preference for the specialist reviews. Academic and school collection development personnel make extensive use of the first two types of reviews but seldom examine popular reviews. Public libraries frequently consult mass-market review sources along with the other types of sources.

Trade and professional reviews are of two types: those designed to promote and those designed to evaluate. Although the primary market of such trade journals as *Publishers Weekly* and *Bookseller* is booksellers (both wholesale and retail), librarians can, and do, make effective use of their reviews. The reviews alert booksellers to new titles that will receive heavy promotion. Publishers have a reasonably good grasp of which titles will sell well and which will not. Because of this, not all titles are promoted in the same manner or with equal funding. This is called *differential marketing*. In differential marketing, each title's marketing "allowance" varies based on its anticipated sales, as does the approach taken for the promotion of that title. A potentially good seller may receive extra promotional effort and funding to cultivate the book into a bestseller. Bookstore owners want to know about such titles ahead of time so they can order enough copies to meet the demand at its peak (usually no more than one or two months). Like book buyers, library patrons want to read bestsellers when they are bestsellers, not after demand subsides. Like bookstore owners, selection personnel read trade reviews to assure that bestsellers are in the collection by the time interest peaks. Trade reviews may miss an unexpected bestseller or predict greater popularity than some books achieve, but they do help selectors identify which items will be in top demand.

Evaluative reviews prepared by librarians or by specialists for librarians are also extremely important in selection, especially in public and school libraries. One will find these reviews in almost all library publications, such as *Library Journal, Library and Information Update* (Chartered Institute of Library and Information Professionals), and *C&RL News* (Association of College and Research Libraries). Normally, such reviews are descriptive and evaluative; occasionally, they are comparative. Reviews of this type are particularly useful because the reviewers prepare them with library needs in mind. A variety of online resources for book reviews exist. Two websites worth consulting include AcqWeb's *Directory of Book Reviews on the Web* (<http://www.acqweb.org/bookrev.html>) and *BookPage* (<http://www.bookpage.com>). A specialized resource focusing on reviews of materials in the humanities and social sciences is H-Net Reviews (<http://www.h-net.org/reviews>).

As useful as they are, current review sources are not without their problems. One of the biggest problems is lack of comprehensive coverage. Although many library publications contain book reviews, only a small percentage of the total annual publishing output is reviewed. Some titles appear to garner more reviews than their content warrants; others never receive a single review. Each *Bowker Annual: Library and Book Trade Almanac* (Information Today) contains information about the number of titles reviewed. The 2004 volume shows the following pattern for 2003 books:

Booklist	8,729 (down 365 from 2002)
Bulletin of the Center for Children's Books	847 (up 129 from 2002)
Choice	6,520 (down 291 from 2002)
Horn Book Guide	4,728 (up 432 from 2002)
Library Journal*	6,205 (up 88 from 2002)
New York Times Sunday Book Review	1,206 (down 716 from 2002)
Publishers Weekly	9,055 (up 551 from 2002)
School Library Journal	4,193 (down 128 from 2002)

*Not included in this total are reviews of online and audiovisual materials, or "Prepub Alert" items.

The Bowker Annual lists fifteen review sources, which published a total of 50,754 reviews, 6,011 of which appeared in newspapers.[20] The magnitude of the problem of coverage is clear when one realizes that at least 146,371 titles appeared in 2003.[21] If even only minimal overlap existed (and everyone knows that overlap is fairly extensive), the average number of reviews would be less than one for every three titles.

Choice covers the largest percentage of new books of primary interest to academic libraries. However, during 2003 publishers released 15,327 titles in the fields of sociology and economics. If one adds history (7,929 new titles), there is a total of more than 23,000 new titles in those three fields alone. With only 6,520 reviews in 2003, *Choice* could not have completely reviewed even those three fields, to say nothing of other fields of academic interest.

Another sign of the problem in review coverage of new titles is found in Wilson's *Book Review Digest (BRD)*. Each year *BRD* publishes citations to, and summaries of, approximately 8,000 new books. A nonfiction title must receive at least two reviews to be included in *BRD*. To find the reviews, *BRD* editors examine leading journals and newspapers that have large book review sections. Even with this large pool of potential sources, only 5,000 to 6,000 new books, out of an annual output of more than 100,000 titles, meet the inclusion criteria. What are the implications of incomplete review coverage? First, no one source of book reviews covers more than a fraction of the total output. Second, even if every book did get reviewed, there would be less than one review per title. Third, many new titles never receive even one review. (Even in Great Britain, where there exists very high interest in the book trade and a strong tradition of reviewing, most books seldom receive more than one review, and a fairly large number of new books get none.)

Another limit on the usefulness of reviews is the speed with which they appear. Most trade reviews appear on or before the publication date, whereas most professional (library) reviews appear several months after publication. One reason for the delay is that librarians and subject specialists write the reviews—one of the strong points of this approach. But first, the title must get to a review editor, who decides which titles ought to be reviewed and identifies an appropriate reviewer. The reviewer may or may not be able to review the item immediately. Eventually, the reviewer returns a review to the editor, who then edits the text and fits the review into the publishing schedule. This is a complex process, but it is necessary to disseminate professional opinions about new titles. For most journals, the only compensation a reviewer receives is the title she or he reviews. Using unpaid reviewers minimizes costs to the journals; hiring professionals to review books would greatly increase the journals' expenditures.

Some professional journals focus on a particular type of library, for example, *School Library Journal*, *Choice* (academic), and *Booklist* (public and school). Some materials are useful in more than one type of library, and journal editors try to make their publications useful to several types of libraries. Nevertheless, each journal has a primary emphasis, focusing on certain classes of books and using qualified reviewers who make value judgments about the materials covered. A few journals (e.g., *Booklist*) publish only positive reviews. This approach leaves one wondering why a certain title failed to appear. Was it because of a negative evaluation, or did the editors decide not to review it? Just as the general professional review sources cannot cover every new title, neither can the specialty sources. If a library depends on published reviews, this drawback can be important. One can wait a long time before being reasonably certain that no review will appear, and even then there are nagging questions as to why no review appeared.

When reading reviews, one must consider reviewer competence. Nonfiction titles require reviewers with subject expertise. For general trade books (titles intended for the general reader), it is not essential that the reviewer have in-depth subject knowledge for every book reviewed. When one gets beyond introductory texts and average readers' guides, the need for depth in background increases, until one reaches the level where one expert is reviewing another expert's publication for a few other experts in the field. Most academic disciplines have one or two journals that publish scholarly reviews for the field. Expert reviews of this type could be, but seldom are, of great assistance in developing a collection. A major reason for their lack of usefulness is that the reviews are slow to appear; often books are one or two years old by the time a review is published. Such delays are unacceptable in libraries with patrons who need up-to-date material. Adding to the problem are scholarly publishers' small press runs (small quantities printed); the item may be out of print by the time a librarian sees its review.

Online bookstore websites (such as *Amazon.Com*) are gaining popularity with patrons and librarians alike. However, the reviews contained in such widely accessible sources should be carefully considered, as any reader may be a "reviewer." (In some cases, reader reviews have appeared in these sources for titles that have yet to be published, leading one to question the credibility of the "reviewer.")

The best source for the broadest coverage of academic titles from the United States is *Choice. Choice* reviewers are subject experts, and the reviews normally appear within a year of publication, often within three or four months after the title's release. To provide wide coverage, the reviews are relatively short, one or two paragraphs; thus, one sacrifices depth to gain coverage and speed. However, the reviews do include a synopsis "Summing Up" section—listing the reviewer's overall recommendation and an assessment of the reading level of the material at hand. *Choice* provides libraries a variety of options to receive reviews, by making them available electronically (*ChoiceReviews.online*, <http://www.choicereviews.org>), as well as through preprinted cards containing individual reviews (*Choice* Reviews on Cards).

A final category of review sources focuses upon the interests of the general reader or user of a format (e.g., the *New York Times Book Review*, *Times Literary Supplement*, and *Video Librarian*). Editors of popular review sources must keep in touch with current interests and tastes to hold their readership. Because they can review only a small percentage of the new titles, their selections are made with great care and an eye on popular current interests. One knows that thousands of people will read the reviews, and demand for the reviewed titles will likely increase. Because of the need to be up-to-date and the fact that most popular press reviewers are paid, reviews of most titles appear within a month or two after the title's release.

It is important to note that many reviewers who write for the popular press are friends of the authors they are reviewing.[22] Thus, one needs to be careful when using popular press reviews for anything more than identifying titles that may experience high demand.

Data about the number of book reviews published each year makes it clear that one will probably face a search problem (Where has that book been reviewed?) if one must use reviews for selection purposes. To some extent, indexing services that cover book reviews help, but they provide little assistance in tracking down the most current titles (from publication date to about eight months old). Two factors account for the problem. First, it takes time to produce and publish a review; second, after the review appears, it takes the indexing service time to prepare and publish its index. However, for older titles, the indexes can be major time-savers. *Book Review Digest* (*BRD*) and *Book Review Index* (*BRI*) are two major American tools of this type. *BRI*, which does not include any annotations, lists the reviews that appear in about 500 journals and provides citations to more than 130,000 reviews each year. (Again, one might think that number means every title receives at least one review—not so, as some books receive multiple reviews. The 2003 edition of *BRI* included 136,700 reviews but covered only 78,000 titles.) Multiple years of *BRD* may be accessed online via *Book Review Digest Plus* (Wilson), while a cumulative version of *BRI* is available via DIALOG. The price of gaining access to review citations is time. Certainly, *BRI* is a useful tool, but only for older titles. Two additional resources are *Book Index with Reviews* and *BookSource: Nonfiction*, both available online from EBSCO. *Book Index with Reviews* includes large-print and books-on-tape editions of various titles, while *BookSource: Nonfiction* does as its name implies, providing reviews solely for popular nonfiction titles. (The difference in these resources lies in the fact that they are designed with end users, not librarians, in mind.)

A final limit of book reviews is that, as a whole, they are not very critical. A reviewer does not work from the assumption that a book is bad. Rather, the expectation is that the book will be good, if not great. As a result, the vast majority of reviews are positive or noncommittal.

Certainly, reviews are helpful when used with care. Book reviews can, and do, save libraries valuable staff time, as no library has staff with enough time to read and review all of the potentially useful new titles that appear each year. However, a library should not employ reviews as a substitute for local judgment. Just because review X claims that an item is great does not mean that the item fits local needs. Reviews aid in the selection process, but they should never be the sole basis for selection. When selectors gain familiarity with book review editors and reviewers' biases, these tools become more valuable.

Bibliographic Databases

Bibliographic databases, in the form of both cooperative and individual library catalogs, are, in a way, replacements for national bibliographies, such as the *National Union Catalog* (*NUC*). With organizations such as OCLC and RLG providing access to databases of millions of records from thousands of libraries around the world, most libraries no longer need access to national bibliographies for collection development. Certainly, for retrospective work, national bibliographies are important, and for countries not well represented in the online systems, they are essential. However, for most libraries in the United States, bibliographic databases are much more useful.

For verification work, bibliographic databases often prove to be the best single source. Not only can searchers verify the existence of a title, but, with proper equipment, they can also download the information to the library's acquisition system, thus eliminating the need to key in entries. Further, once the library receives and catalogs the item, the information from the online service can serve as the bibliographic record in the library's online public catalog. Another use of the online databases is in selection. Because systems like OCLC and RLIN provide information about which libraries hold certain titles, it is possible for a selector to determine which local libraries already hold an item under consideration. If resource-sharing agreements are in place, and the selector thinks the item will have low use, the decision may be not to purchase the title. (See the article by Coates and Kiegel in the Further Reading section for a more complete discussion of advantages of automated selection.)

Yet another use of the databases is for collection evaluation. A library can buy reports containing holdings information about a particular group of libraries, as well as its own holdings. The data comes from one of the large bibliographic utilities. Using this data, the library can make a variety of comparisons of its holdings against other libraries.

Best Books, Recommended Lists, and Core Collections

"Best of" lists or lists of items recommended for purchase are useful when selectors employ them carefully. As Jones noted, "While the various lists represent the best books published in one year . . . as chosen by a group of informed observers, they may or may not indicate which are the best books for the customers you serve, or want to serve."[23] A brief examination of the amount of material in such lists will dispel any doubts about the subjectivity of the selection process. Titles such as *Public Library Catalog* (*PLC*, Wilson), *Hot, Hotter, Hottest: The Best of the YA Hotline* (Scarecrow Press), or *Best Books for Middle School and Junior High Readers: Grades 6–9* (Libraries Unlimited) show some overlap but also some differences. The differences arise from the purposes of the lists and the individuals who make the selections. Personal opinions vary, and these lists reflect either one person's opinion or a composite of opinions about the value of a particular title. (For an in-depth examination of the selection practices of *PLC*, see the review by Dilevko and Gottlieb.[24])

Few specialists in collection development would claim that a library ought to hold any title just because of its presence on two or more recommended lists. Consider a list that contains basic books for undergraduate programs in mathematics, published by a national association of mathematics teachers. One would expect a library that serves an undergraduate mathematics program to hold a high percentage of the listed titles, but even in such a case, one should not expect to find every title. Why not? A major reason is the emphasis of the school's program; there may be no need for a particular title. Another reason is that, often, several equally good alternatives exist. A final reason is that the list is out-of-date on its publication date (unless the work is updated online), as new titles supersede the titles listed. Also, trying to get a copy of every title on a list can be extremely time-consuming. Unless there is agreement that it is important to secure every title, it is wise not to spend the time; retrospective buying requires much more time than buying in-print titles. Despite these disadvantages, core lists are useful to consult at times and can "provide a benchmark for beginning a collection, evaluating an existing collection, or maintaining a collection with current material."[25]

Subject Bibliographies

Subject bibliographies suffer from many of the same limitations as lists of best or recommended items: currency and selectivity. When subject experts prepare a bibliography and write critical evaluations for the items listed, such publications provide useful information for both selection and collection evaluation activities. Only the imagination of the compilers limits the range of subject bibliographies. A quick review of some publishers' catalogs proves that compilers have unlimited imagination. In most broad fields, at least one such bibliography exists, and for most fields several are available. When there have been multiple editions, it is advisable to check on the amount of change between editions. Do new editions merely add more titles, or is there a real revision, with older, superseded titles dropped and new assessments made of all the items? One should not depend on published reviews but do one's own checking before using such a bibliography as a selection aid.

Using Citation Information for Selection

Although useful for identifying new titles, many selection aids provide only the basic bibliographic information about an item. Selectors using only citation information select thousands of titles to add to library collections each year. How do they make their decisions from such limited data? Most bibliographic citations follow a convention for the presentation—the content and order—of the entry. (More and more selection aids follow ANSI Z39.29–1977, the American National Standard for Bibliographic References.) The standard means that the selector can expect to see the same pattern in entries in various selection aids. That order provides "information" regarding the item cited. With experience, one's judgment about an item may change as one examines each element of a citation.

For example, a selector reading a citation about conditions on the

Dakota reservations in South Dakota would make different judgments about the content of the cited item depending on whether the citation read "Washington, D.C., 2004" or "Pine Ridge, S.D., 1999." Similarly, the selector's judgment of a title about apartheid would depend on whether its imprint was "Johannesburg, 2003" or "Maseru, 2003." Another example of how an element could modify a judgment is a title implying comprehensive or comparative treatment of a broad or complex subject, with pagination indicating a much shorter book than would be reasonable for the topic. Who authored the title is a key factor in the selection process. When the citation string includes subject descriptors, profound modification in judgment can occur. An entry in a selection aid may seem appropriate for Tozzer Library (Harvard University) until one encounters the subject heading *juvenile*. Without the supplemental context, it is possible and even probable that the library would order some inappropriate items because of inadequate information. (This is a good reason to follow Ranganathan's rule to know the publishers; even then one may be fooled occasionally.)

As aptly noted by Metz and Stemmer, "even the best bibliographers can be expected to be familiar with only a minority of authors in their fields, and because titles provide limited information, knowledge of the publisher often furnishes the decisive element in selection decisions."[26] The authors surveyed collection development officers at ARL and Oberlin group institutions as to their perceptions of the reputations of academic and larger commercial publishing firms. Their research indicated that "although not the most important factor in selecting a book, the reputation of the publisher does play a significant role in collection development."[27]

As long as individuals and not machines assign subject headings and classification numbers in selection aids, selectors must realize there is a large element of subjectivity in the process. Normally, only one class number appears; the problem is that another person might reach a different opinion about the item and assign other headings and classification numbers. If a selector uses several sources with overlapping coverage, and they also supply subject assignments, the selector may gain some additional insight as to subject content. However, more often than not, the selector makes her or his decision on only one source of information. One seldom has time to track down entries in several sources, especially if the initial findings are positive.

Another type of supplemental information is the source in which the citation appears. In national bibliographies, compilers make no value judgments regarding the merits of an item, whereas in a publication like *Booklist*, one knows it contains only recommended items. Thus, each selection aid carries with it a form of supplemental context. Finally, a patron request may be the supplemental information that determines the selection decision, regardless of any other contextual information. This is especially true in special libraries.

Ross Atkinson proposed a model for analyzing citation data that every beginning selector should read.[28] (Two other good sources are Schwartz's "Book Selection, Collection Development, and Bounded Rationality"[29] and Rutledge and Swindler's "The Selection Decision.")[30]

Selection in Action

Now that we have reviewed the different contexts in which collection development occurs, as well as some of the selection tools, we will outline the steps we follow when using selection aids that supply subject information. For example, Dr. Evans usually selects in the area of anthropology and sociology. One quickly learns that, for anthropology, appropriate material can appear under a wide variety of class numbers or subject headings. If one confines one's search to the anthropology class numbers, one will miss important new titles. Thus, one must scan long lists of titles to identify the appropriate title for the library. To do this quickly and effectively, one needs a system for thinking about the titles scanned.

Here is one way to approach the process. When examining subject information, first, ask yourself: Does this fall within the areas of our collecting? If the answer is yes, then consider whether the material is of interest to the library's clientele. If it is, then consider: How much do we already have on this subject (what formats, how old)? If the title remains viable at this point, think about the cost of the item: Can the library afford to acquire it? Also consider the quality of the work, taking publisher and author track records into account. If the item is not a one-time purchase, think about the library's ability to maintain the acquisition. Occasionally, you may encounter a reprint of a title already in the collection. When this happens, try to determine whether there is new material in the reprint (frequently, there is a new introduction or other additions) and how much new material has been added. Also consider the condition and use pattern of the item currently in the collection. More and more frequently, there is a question about the need for special handling, as is the case with CD-ROMs that come with traditional books. Another somewhat daunting decision may be whether or not to purchase the item in print or electronic format (see Stewart's essay for a detailed discussion of this topic[31]). Two final questions to consider are: What is the source of the information under consideration— that is, are you looking at review media, a publisher's flyer, vendor announcement, trade or professional publication, national bibliography, or other source? Also ask yourself if acquisition of the item caused a problem, such as objections, mutilation, or theft.

This approach requires selectors to know the user population, collection content, collection priorities, materials budget status, primary authors and publishers or producers in the selector's areas of responsibility, and review sources and general production levels in the selector's areas of responsibility. However, knowledge of these items can only help the selector make appropriate decisions for their collection.

Summary

While this has been a lengthy discussion, it still covers only the high points and basic issues of book selection. The tools listed here are not perfect, but by using them regularly, one learns the advantages and disadvantages of each. (A good article to consult is by Agee, who provides a list of criteria for evaluating selection tools.[32]) To increase their chances of making appropriate choices for their users, selectors must know their service population, what exists in the collection, types of formats and materials that meet the needs of a given situation, and vendor sources that can supply appropriate materials. In addition, selectors must be able to choose among a variety of items and formats to get the most cost-effective items for a given situation; determine quality and its many variations; balance quantities, qualities, and costs; and recognize the real value or nonvalue of gifts. Learning to be a book selector is a lifelong process, and the items listed in the bibliography provide leads to material about various aspects of this challenging, exciting, and rewarding area of information work.

Notes

1. Patrick Jones, "To the Teen Core," *School Library Journal* 49, no. 3 (March 2003): 48.

2. Association of College and Research Libraries, "Standards for Libraries in Higher Education," Chicago: American Library Association (2004), <http://www.ala.org/ala/acrl/acrlstandards/standardslibraries.htm>.

3. Robert Fernekes and William Nelson, "How Practical Are the ACRL 'Standards for College Libraries'?" *College & Research Libraries News* 63, no. 10 (November 2002): 711–13.

4. David Kaser, "Standards for College Libraries," *Library Trends* 31 (Summer 1982): 7–18.

5. "Introduction," *Choice* 1 (March 1964): ii.

6. J. P. Schmitt and S. Saunders, "Assessment of *Choice* as a Tool for Selection," *College & Research Libraries* 44 (September 1983): 375–80.

7. Kerri Odess-Harnish, "Making Sense of Leased Popular Literature Collections," *Collection Management* 27, no. 2 (2002): 55–74.

8. Connie Van Fleet, "Popular Fiction Collections in Academic and Public Libraries," *The Acquisitions Librarian* 29 (2003): 63–85.

9. For an overview of the British publishing industry, see John Baker's "Trying to Adjust in an Unsettled Time," *Publishers Weekly* 251, no. 10 (March 8, 2004): S2–S14, S23–S24. Claire Kirch's article "Graywolf Press Celebrates Success," *Publishers Weekly* 251, no. 13 (March 29, 2004): 15–18 presents another example of industry news.

10. Readers are encouraged to visit the following websites to view how each of the three publishers provide reviews of current works: *Booklist* <http://www.ala.org/ala/booklist/booklist.htm>; *Library Journal* <http://www.ljdigital.com>; and *PW Interactive* <http://www.publishersweekly.com/index.asp>.

11. Ann Cress, "The Latest Wave," *Library Journal* 129, no. 16 (October 1, 2004): 48–50.

12. Kathleen Sullivan, "Beyond Cookie Cutter Selection," *Library Journal* 129, no. 11 (June 15, 2004): 45.

13. Mark T. Bay, "Selecting Children's Literature for Academic Librarians: Tips from the Trenches," *Behavioral and Social Sciences Librarian* 19, no. 2 (2001): 1–6.

14. Diane Tixier Herald, *Genreflecting: A Guide to Reading Interests in Genre Fiction*, 5th ed. (Englewood, CO: Libraries Unlimited, 2000).

15. Judith Senkevitch and James H. Sweetland, "Public Libraries and Adult Fiction: Another Look at a Core List of Classics," *Library Resources & Technical Services* 42, no. 2 (April 1998): 102–12.

16. Ray Dorion, "An Administrator's Guide to Collection Development," *School Libraries in Canada* 21, no. 4 (2002): 20.

17. National Committee for Good Reading, *Reader's Guide to Non-Controversial Books* (Castle Rock, CO: Hi Willow Research and Publishing, 1986).

18. Susan M. Allen, "Special Collections Outside the Ivory Tower," *Library Trends* 52, no. 1 (Summer 2003): 64.

19. Jones, 49.

20. *The Bowker Annual Library and Book Trade Almanac*, 49th ed. (Medford, NJ: Information Today, 2004), 533.

21. Ibid., 508.

22. Katherine Dalton, "Books and Book Reviewing, or Why All Press Is Good Press," *Chronicles* 18 (January 1989): 20–22.

23. Jones, 48.

24. Juris Dilevko and Lisa Gottlieb, "The Politics of Standard Selection Guides: The Case of the Public Library Catalog," *Library Quarterly* 73, no. 3 (2003): 289–337.

25. Jim Agee, "Selecting Materials: A Review of Print and Online Sources," *Collection Building* 22, no. 3 (2003): 138.

26. Paul Metz and John Stemmer, "A Reputational Study of Academic Publishers," *College & Research Libraries* 57 (May 1996): 235.

27. Ibid., 245.

28. Ross Atkinson, "The Citation as Intertext: Toward a Theory of the Selection Process," *Library Resources & Technical Services* 28 (April/June 1984): 109–19.

29. Charles A. Schwartz, "Book Selection, Collection Development, and Bounded Rationality," *College & Research Libraries* 50 (May 1989): 328–43.

30. John Rutledge and Luke Swindler, "The Selection Decision: Defining Criteria and Establishing Priorities," *College & Research Libraries* 48 (March 1987): 123–31.

31. Lou Ann Stewart, "Choosing Between Print and Electronic Sources: The Selection Dilemma," *The Reference Librarian* 71 (2000): 79–97.

32. Agee, 140.

Further Reading

Alabaster, C. *Developing and Outstanding Core Collection: A Guide for Libraries*. Chicago: American Library Association, 2002.

Baker, S. L., and K. L. Wallace. *The Responsive Public Library: How to Develop and Market a Winning Collection*. 2nd ed. Englewood, CO: Libraries Unlimited, 2002.

Calhoun, J. C. "Reviews, Holdings, and Presses and Publishers in Academic Library Book Acquisitions." *Library Resources and Technical Services* 45 (July 2001): 127–77.

Casey, A. M. "Collection Development for Distance Learning." *Journal of Library Administration* 36, no. 3 (2002): 59–72.

Coates, J., and J. Kiegel. "Automating the Nexus of Book Selection, Acquisitions, and Rapid Copy Cataloging." *Library Collections, Acquisitions, and Technical Services* 27 (2003): 33–44.

COLLDV-L. Library Collection Development Discussion List. To subscribe to the list, send the following message to Listproc@usc.edu: subscribe Colldv-l. Your-first-name Your-last-name.

Crawford, G. A., and M. Harris. "Best Sellers in Academic Libraries." *College & Research Libraries* 62, no. 3 (2001): 216–25.

Credaro, A. "Walking Through the Valley of the Shadow of Happy Talk: Book Reviews and Collection Development." *Library Media Connection* 23, no. 3 (November–December 2004): 51.

Dewe, M., ed. *Local Studies Collection Management*. Aldershot, UK: Ashgate, 2002.

Dilevko, J., and K. Dali. "The Challenge of Building Multilingual Collections in Canadian Public Libraries." *Library Resources and Technical Services* 46, no. 4 (October 2002): 116–37.

Fenner, A., ed. *Selecting Materials for Library Collections*. Binghamton, NY: Haworth Press, 2004.

Herald, D. T. *Teen Genreflecting: A Guide to Reading Interests*. 2nd ed. Englewood, CO: Libraries Unlimited, 2003.

Hill, G. R. "Music Publishers' Catalogs." *Notes* 59, no. 3 (March 2003): 730–38.

Hughes-Hassell, S., and J. C. Mancall. *Collection Management for Youth: Responding to the Needs of Learners*. Chicago: American Library Association, 2005.

Jenkins, P. O. "Book Reviews and Faculty Book Selection." *Collection Building* 18, no. 1 (1999): 4–5.

Johnson, P. *Fundamentals of Collection Development and Management*. Chicago: American Library Association, 2004.

Jones, P., P. Taylor, and K. Edwards. *A Core Collection for Young Adults*. New York: Neal-Schuman, 2003.

Katz, B. "Best Books and Readers." *Acquisitions Librarian* 13, no. 25 (2001): 189–94.

Kerby, R. N. "Selection Sources." *School Library Media Activities Monthly* 18, no. 8 (April 2002): 24–26.

Lare, G. A. *Acquiring and Organizing Curriculum Materials: A Guide and Directory of Resources*. 2nd ed. Lanham, MD: Scarecrow, 2004.

Luttmann, S. "Selection of Music Materials." *The Acquisitions Librarian* 16, nos. 31/32 (2004): 11–25.

Manitoba Library Association. *Canadian Review of Materials*. <http://www.umanitoba.ca/cm>.

Marquis, S. K. "Collections and Services for the Spanish-Speaking: Issues and Resources." *Public Libraries* 42, no. 2 (March/April 2003): 106–12.

McGrath, E. L., W. F. Metz, and J. B. Rutledge. "H-Net Book Reviews: Enhancing Scholarly Communication with Technology." *College & Research Libraries* 66, no. 1 (January 2005): 8–19.

Miller, S. *Developing and Promoting Graphic Novel Collections*. New York: Neal-Schuman, 2004.

Owens, J. "Nursing Tools for the Selection of Library Resources." *Acquisitions Librarian* 16, nos. 31/32 (2004): 89–99.

Pasterczyk, C. E. "Checklist for the New Selector." *College & Research Libraries News* 49 (July/August 1988): 434–35.

Resource Links: Connecting Classrooms, Libraries and Canadian Learning Resources. <http://resourcelinks.ca>.

Rockwood, I. E. "Choice: The FAQ." *Choice* 40, no. 4 (December 2002): 576.

Schiffrin, A. *The Business of Books: How International Conglomerates Took Over Publishing and Changed the Way We Read*. London: Verso, 2000.

Snider, A. "Thinking Sidewise: Tips for Building an Alternate History Collection." *School Library Journal* 50, no. 4 (April 2004): 41–43.

Terry, A. A. "How Today's Technology Affects Libraries' Collection Choices." *Computers in Libraries* 20, no. 6 (June 2000): 51–55.

Wren-Estes, B. "Online Selection Tools: The Future for Collection Development in Public Schools." *Colorado Libraries* 28, no. 1 (Spring 2002): 14–15.

5
Producers of
Information Materials

Chapter 1 discussed several technology issues that are impacting libraries. Those same issues affect the producers of information products—books, journals, recordings, graphics, etc. Producers of information materials are grappling with technology issues just as much as libraries are. The opening paragraph in the first chapter raised the question of what *is* a book; later in that same chapter, the issue of how to handle pricing of electronic materials was introduced. Product cost has become a very sore point between producers and libraries, especially electronic packages, but even print costs seem to have escalated well beyond the Consumer Price Index (CPI) rate.

While technology has caused producers to adjust/change the way they conduct their day-to-day activities, the underlying functions remain stable, as we discuss a little later in this chapter. As was true of promises of cost savings from using technology in libraries, producers have *not* found that technology has reduced their costs of doing business. It seems clear that "going digital" does not save anyone any money. So, for both the producers and consumers the question is, What is the correct balance between traditional formats and electronics?

In "Pages, Pixels, and the Profession," George Bornstein[1] explored some of the pros and cons of print and digital formats. His view is that digital success lies in increasing machine-searchable text projects such as "Project Gutenberg" and "Pandora" or commercial databases like Chadwyck-Healey's *American Poetry Database*. The other major plus for digital is having journals available online. Essentially, he sees speed and accessibility as the primary pluses of digital. Although he does not state it, one can infer from his piece that he sees digital, at present, as very good for quick information and traditional (print) as still the format of choice for study and reading. Costs are a long-term concern for digital formats, and the most pressing cost issues include encoding to increase searchability (SGML,

XML, etc.), long-term maintenance of the digital material, intellectual property rights, and data accuracy/integrity. Costs for any format become a concern, especially for scholarly material producers, as library budgets often remain static for years, if they do not shrink in size.

Richard Cox addressed some of these same issues in his article "Taking Sides on the Future of the Book,"[2] in which he commented on the Internet, books-on-demand, electronic books, and other nonprint/nonlinear electronic resources. At one point he wrote, "I still read books as well as navigate the Internet. I still write books as well as upload electronic texts on the World Wide Web. I still browse bookstores as well as scan electronic library catalogs."[3] Those words are probably reasonable descriptors of the behavior of a great many of us and, in our opinion, will remain so for some time to come. They are also probably good indicators for what a great many producers of information materials are, and will be, doing for some time: producing a mix of traditional and electronic products.

In the past, one could categorize information producers by product: (1) those who produced printed matter (books, periodicals, newspapers, and the like) and (2) those who produced audiovisual materials. Seldom did a producer work in both areas. Today, although some companies are solely devoted to the production of print or audiovisual materials, most print publishers also have one or more electronic and audiovisual lines. University presses and other scholarly publishers are also moving into electronic publishing for what previously might have been a print publication. An example is the University of North Carolina Press' CD-ROM *Excavating Occaneechi Town.*[4] A common approach is what we have done here: produce a print book with an accompanying CD-ROM, often to provide more information and contain costs. Another method is to place supplemental material on a website.

Some sense of the "staying power" of print is found in sources such as *Books in Print (BIP)*. A check of *BooksinPrint.Com* in mid-2004 indicated there were over 9 million English-language titles in the database. (These numbers are based upon unique ISBNs; thus, many titles would be double-counted if there were both hardcover and paper versions in print. Some popular titles might even be triple-counted, if there was also an audio version available.) Certainly, electronic products are being produced, but as of 2005 they had not noticeably slowed the production of print materials. The 2003–2004 edition of *BIP* listed 203,000 *new* titles.

A major reason for the staying power of books is that paper copies still provide the least expensive means of distributing large quantities of timely information to a large number of people in the format they read and use. Certainly, one can mount a long document (300 or more pages) on the Internet; many people do. Further, it is obvious that any number of individuals can simultaneously read that document. However, very few individuals using that material attempt to read it off the computer screen. Rather, they print some portion or the entire file and read the material in printed form. (Anyone with experience in a reference department is well aware of the volume of printing being done of electronic data, most of which is in relatively short files.)

Also, some people are uncomfortable with technology-based information sources. There is always some question, with electronic files, about the integrity of the material: is what one sees on the screen what the author originally input? With journal articles graphics may be missing. For marketing people, the fact that ads are seldom made available in the online version is a problem. Finally, many people still like to read in bed, on the subway, at the beach, and other places where technology-based systems are inconvenient, if not impossible, to use.

What Is Publishing?

What is publishing? That question has been with us, at least in the United States, for more than 300 years. Publishers and others have debated whether publishing's purpose was/is cultural or commercial in nature or both.

In the abstract and to some degree in the real world, "the book" is a cultural artifact as well as an essential means of recording and preserving the culture of a society. Certainly, libraries of all types have, to a greater or lesser degree, some role to play in preserving and passing on their society's cultural values and heritage. Thus, books have had a special aura of importance—some might even say sacredness—that is very different from that of, say, clothes, cars, or cameras. Discarding worn-out items like the latter may bring some scowls from a few people. However, there is widespread disapproval of doing the same with a book. From early childhood one hears, "don't bend the pages," "wash your hands before using your books," "treat your books with respect"—and having the label "book burner" is something no one wants.

Because of the cultural and literary aspects involved in the production of books, there is some sense that a literate society *must* have a publishing program of some type. Further, that publishing program *must* produce books for the good of society. Sometimes supporters of the cultural purpose seem to paint a picture of noble people—from writer, to editor, to owner—who are free of the concerns of economics and profit. (A less flattering view might be that they act as the gatekeepers to, or controllers of, knowledge.) Does that mean, then, that there should be no concern with costs? Clearly not.

The romantic view of publishing is nice but unrealistic; even most government publications have a price. (As we see in chapter 8 on government information, the cost of that information is also rising.) The fact is, the bottom line of publishing is the bottom line. Without an expectation of a reasonable return, why would anyone invest time and money in publishing? Certainly, one can debate what "reasonable" means, but no one should question the need for a return beyond that of survival. The return ought to be greater than that of putting the money in an insured savings account, as there are substantial risks in publishing—not everything sells as fast as one might hope, if it sells at all. Publishers are in the commercial world, and most of them have stockholders to take into account as well as the interests of readers and society.

Albert Greco summed up the present situation in U.S. publishing as follows:

> Many industry analysts believe that publishing is in disarray, dangerously weakened by steep returns, stark sales figures, fickle and price sensitive customer base, the "rise" of chains and superstores and price clubs and the concomitant "decline" of independent book store[s], a population more interested in watching television than in reading books, paper thin profit margins, staggering technological challenges, and author advances that dumbfound even seasoned industry veterans. . . . Its best

days are indeed ahead, a fact that excites tens of thousands of people every day about this wonderful, funny, and, at times, hard business.[5]

Publishing is both a cultural and a commercial activity, but without the commercial there would be no cultural purpose.

When one is going to work day in and day out with an industry, even if one is just buying its products, some knowledge of that industry will make everyone's life a little easier. An understanding of the publishing trade's characteristics—such as how producers determine prices, how they distribute products, and what services one can expect—can improve communication between producers and buyers. Under the best of circumstances, a great deal of communication must exist between the parties if one is to build effective collections.

Such knowledge provides the librarian with some understanding of, if not sympathy for, the problems of producers. Publishers who depend on library sales know (or should know) a great deal about library problems and operations. They often joke about how uninformed librarians are about the trade. Today's strained relationship between libraries and publishers developed, in part, because neither group fully understood or tried to understand the other's position on issues such as copyright and pricing. Yet, we also know that when two parties discuss problems with mutual understanding of the other's position, the working relationship will be more pleasant. Each is more willing to make an occasional concession to the other's needs; this flexibility can, in turn, foster mutually beneficial alliances.

Collection development courses in library schools usually touch only lightly on publishers and their problems due to time constraints. Further, courses in the history of the book trade seldom have time to deal with the contemporary situation, because it is not yet history. Most schools' curricula do not have a place for a course in contemporary production. Even if they did, most students would not have time for it in their tight course of study. For this reason, students lack information that could prove invaluable, because knowing what happens in publishing can affect the selection process. First, knowing something about publishing helps selectors identify the most likely sources of materials, that is, which among the thousands of producers are most likely to produce the needed material. Second, by keeping up-to-date with what is happening in publishing, one can anticipate changes in quality and format. Third, librarians may be able to influence publishing decisions, if the publisher is aware that the librarian is knowledgeable about the issues involved in developing profitable books.

How Publishing Works

Book publishers have evolved from single-person hand press operations to highly specialized, computerized multinational corporations. Over the past ten to fifteen years, publishing has changed in many ways. Most of the change is technology-related and results from making increasing use of electronic publishing. An early hope was that there would be a cost saving from moving into e-publishing, but like so many other hoped-for technology cost savings, they failed to materialize, at least for those who purchased the output. A good essay outlining the impact of technological changes, especially on processes, is seen in Peter Adams' "Technology in

Publishing: A Century of Progress."[6] Although processes may be changing, the basic functions of publishing remain the same.

Publishers supply the capital and editorial assistance required to transform an author's manuscript/ideas into books and other information products. Generally, publishers perform six functions regardless of what format they work with—print, nonprint, or electronic:

1. Tap sources of materials (concepts).

2. Raise and supply the capital to produce salable products.

3. Aid in the development of the material.

4. Contract for the manufacturing (duplication, packaging, etc.) of the product.

5. Distribute materials, including promoting and advertising.

6. Maintain records of sales, contracts, and correspondence relating to the production and sale of the materials.

For a thumbnail sketch of the basic development of publishing, refer to the supplemental material on CD for this text.

When it comes to the tapping sources of materials, there is a significant difference between paper-based and nonprint (video, soundings, etc.) producers. For book and professional journal producers, the majority of their materials originate with manuscripts from authors who had an idea or story they think is worth telling. Certainly, publishers of books and journals do put forward ideas/commission works on a topic that the publisher thinks will sell well. However, even in those cases the author has great freedom in terms of structure and approach taken to the subject. Nonprint producers, especially those in the documentary/educational market, exercise very tight control over the topic, content, and treatment. They usually hire all the personnel needed to translate the idea into a salable product.

Another difference is that most print materials are used by an individual, whereas educational nonprint formats are intended primarily for groups. The group usage is a major factor in the need for tighter control over the entire process—costs are higher to produce a marketable product, and sales potential is smaller, thus making risks greater.

All producers raise the capital required to transform an idea into a marketable title. As we noted, costs are considerably higher for good-quality nonprint products, so it is not surprising to learn that such producers tend to offer significantly fewer titles than do book publishers. Costs are also of a different type for the nonprint title—primarily technology and people— while for print titles the people costs are much smaller. A person can gain a sense of difference in thinking about the resources (people, time, and equipment) between rewriting a chapter of a book and reshooting a fifteen-minute scene for a documentary.

In terms of aiding in the development of an idea, the two types are opposite in character. While book editors provide encouragement and feedback to authors in the final analysis, the authors are ultimately responsible for the final content. Editors work with authors in developing an idea, perhaps send out an outline/prospectus for review, and even read some early chapters and provide commentary. They also make the decision if the final manuscript is acceptable for publication. Sometimes through keeping up-to-date with development in a field, editors have an idea for a title and seek out an author to write the book. Sometimes an author approaches the editor with an idea, and occasionally there are "over-the transom" full manuscripts that arrive in the mail (not many of these are published—at least in their mailed-in form). "Editorial development" is a key factor in a book publisher's success or failure; however, it is not the tight control exercised by nonprint producers. If one book publisher rejects the manuscript, it may be, and occasionally is, "picked up" by another publisher.

Given the nature of the documentary/educational nonprint market, it is not surprising producers keep the development of a product under tight supervision and control. Many people are involved—just check the printed material that accompanies one of your favorite CD sound recordings. There are a number of names beyond the artist(s) who played important roles in the final product, something seldom found in books much beyond a "thank-you" to the editor.

The last three functional areas—contracting, distribution, and record keeping—are basically the same for both print and nonprint producers. They contract for the duplication and packaging of their materials, as well as handling a variety of administrative issues. Record keeping, as for any business, is very important, especially tracking how many copies have been sold and what royalties are due. Distribution of books tends to be more complex than is the case for periodicals and nonprint titles. Nonprint producers primarily distribute directly to end buyers (see chapter 9 for more information about acquisition options of AV materials). Book publishers have warehouses filled with current and backlist titles, while nonprint producers tend to have relatively small inventories.

There is one aspect of nonprint that can be problematic for libraries. We mentioned above the high cost of producing nonprint materials; we should have qualified that by adding "reputable" to "nonprint producers." Low-end equipment is widely available, which makes it possible to start a "nonprint" operation and to market poor-quality products. Because the nonprint field lacks many of the infrastructure features of the book publishing—trade bibliographies, a host of review sources, etc.—it is more difficult to assess quality prior to purchase, unless the vendor allows for previewing the material.

Another difference is that nonprint producers, except in the areas of video and sound recording, are much more dependent on the institutional (schools and libraries) market than are print publishers. This, combined with the cost associated with quality products, means there is a limited range available in terms of topics and treatments. Risks and costs are high, especially if one thinks in terms of units of information conveyed. The educational area has a very large number of "single concept" nonprint materials that cost two or three times what a multiple-concept book costs.

Table 5.1 provides a summary of some of the major collection development factors that vary between print and nonprint producers. Other chapters covering serials, AV, and government information provide more detailed information. The balance of this chapter focuses on books.

Types of Publishers

The publication *Book Industry Trends* (Book Industry Study Group) employs a nine-category system for grouping books:

Table 5.1. Differences between media producers and book publishers.

	Media Producers	Book Publishers
Audience	Individual as part of a group	Individual
Idea Authorship	Company generated	Agent generated
Use	Group and sequential, equipment paced	Single and nonsequential, self-paced
Cost per concept	High	Low
Selection process in library	Usually group	Individual
Cost to enter field	Relatively low, except for interactive formats	Moderately high, desktop publishing low
Inventory	Low	High
Market	Clearly defined	Highly variable
Potential sales volume	Low (except audio and video recordings)	Medium
Cost per copy to buy	Moderate	Relatively low
Ease of copying	Easy to copy, high sales price	Easy to copy, low sales price
Distribution	Mostly single source	Multiple source
Changes in format and equipment	Very rapid with high rate of obsolescence	Relatively slow

- trade;
- mass market;
- book clubs;
- mail order (including e-mail);
- religious;
- professional;
- university presses;
- el-hi; and
- college textbook.

Because of what are primarily economic interests, publishers can, and do, have several "lines"; thus, the above grouping is not as clear-cut as data-collecting categories present. Below we provide an overview of twelve types of publishing firms, some of which mirror the categories used by *Book Industry Trends*, and some of which are more reflective of the overall book trade.

Trade publishers produce a wide range of titles, both fiction and non-fiction, that have wide sales potential—for the so-called general reader.

HarperCollins; Alfred A. Knopf; Doubleday; Macmillan Publishers; Little, Brown and Company; Thames & Hudson; and Random House are typical trade publishers. Many trade publishers have divisions that produce specialty titles, such as children's, college textbooks, paperback, reference, and so forth. Trade publishers have three primary markets: bookstores, wholesalers, and libraries. They have two important subsidiary markets—book clubs and mass market paperbacks. To sell their products, publishers send sales representatives to visit buyers in businesses or institutions in each of the markets.

Specialty publishers restrict output to a few areas or subjects. Thomson Gale is an example of a specialty publisher. Specialty publishers' audiences are smaller and more critical than trade publishers' audiences. The categories of specialty publishers include reference, paperback, children's, microform, music, cartographic, and one or two subject areas. Libraries are a significant market for this type of publisher.

Textbook publishers, especially those that target the primary and secondary schools (el-hi), occupy one of the highest-risk areas of publishing. Most publishers in this area develop a line of textbooks for several grades, for example, a social studies series. Preparation of such texts requires large amounts of time, energy, and money. Printing costs are high because most school texts feature expensive color illustrations and other specialized presswork. Such projects require large upfront investments that must be recouped before a profit can be realized. If enough school districts adopt a text, profits can be substantial, but failure to secure adoption can mean tremendous loss. Textbook firms, such as Arnold Publishing, Saxon Publishers, and Scott, Foresman/Addison, produce several series to help ensure a profit or to cushion against loss. Why would a company take the risk this type of publishing involves? Consider the amount of money spent on textbooks each year: more than $4.289 billion in 2001 for el-hi texts and $3.468 billion for college textbooks.[7] Because of the scheduling practices in school textbook adoption (usually occurring once a year), textbook publishers can reduce warehousing costs, thus adding to the margin of profit. From time to time, U.S. el-hi publishers face pressure to change the content of their publications from a variety of special-interest groups (see chapter 18—censorship). This pressure adds yet another element of risk to textbook publishing.

Subject specialty publishers share some of the characteristics of textbook houses. Many have narrow markets that are easy to identify. Focusing marketing efforts on a limited number of buyers allows specialty publishers to achieve a reasonable return with less risk than a trade publisher takes on a nonfiction title. Specialty houses exist for a variety of fields; examples include art (Harry N. Abrams), music (E. C. Schirmer), scientific (Academic Press), technical (American Technical Publishers), law (West Publishing), and medical (W. B. Saunders). Many specialty books require expensive graphic preparation or presswork. Such presswork increases production costs, which is one of the reasons art, music, and science and technology titles are so costly. Another factor in their cost is the smaller market as compared to the market for a trade title. A smaller market means that the publisher must recover production costs from fewer books. Although the risk level is greater for specialty publishing than for trade publishing, it is much lower than that of el-hi publishers.

Vanity presses, or subsidy publishers, differ from other publishing houses in that they receive most of their operating funds from the authors whose works they publish. An example is AuthorHouse. Vanity presses always show a profit and never lack material to produce. They offer editing assistance for a fee, and they arrange to print as many copies of the book as the author can afford. Distribution is the author's chore. Although such presses provide many of the same functions as other publishers, they do not share the same risks. Many authors who use vanity presses give copies of their books to local libraries, but such gifts often arrive with no indication that they are gifts.

Private presses are not business operations in the sense that the owners expect to make money. Most private presses are an avocation rather than a vocation for the owners. Examples are Henry Morris, Bird, and Poull Press. In many instances, the owners do not sell their products but give them away instead. Individuals who enjoy fine printing and experimenting with type fonts and design own most private presses. As one might expect, when the owner gives away the end product (often produced on a hand-press), only a few copies are printed. In the past, many developments in type and book design originated with private presses. Some of the most beautiful examples of typographic and book design originated at private presses. Thus, large research libraries often attempt to secure copies of items produced by private presses.

Scholarly publishers, as part of not-for-profit organizations, receive subsidies. Most are part of an academic institution (University of California Press), museum (Museum of Northern Arizona), research institution (Getty Institute), or learned society (American Philosophical Society). Such presses exist to produce scholarly books that would not be acceptable (profitable) to commercial publishers. Most scholarly books have limited sales appeal. A commercial, or for-profit, publisher considering a scholarly manuscript has three choices: (1) publish it and try to sell it at a price that ensures cost recovery; (2) publish it, sell it at a price comparable to commercial titles, and lose money; or (3) do not publish the item. Because of economic factors and a need to disseminate scholarly information regardless of cost (i.e., even if it will lose money) the subsidized (by tax exemption, if nothing else), not-for-profit press exists. As publishing costs have skyrocketed, it has been necessary to fully subsidize some scholarly books, almost in the manner of a vanity press.

The role of the scholarly press in the economical and open dissemination of knowledge is critical. Every country needs some form of this type of press. Without scholarly presses, important works with limited appeal do not get published. Certainly, there are times when a commercial house publishes a book that will not show a profit simply because the publisher thinks the book is important, but relying on that type of willingness, in the long run, means that many important works will never appear in print.

Like their for-profit counterparts, scholarly presses are making ever-greater use of electronic publishing techniques. Two good survey articles about how electronics are changing scholarly publishing are R. M. Borrong et al.'s "The Crisis in Scholarly Publishing"[8] and Ann Okerson's "Publishing Through the Network."[9] Though the networks hold promise, they also hold the possibility of higher information costs. As Freeman noted,

> If profit rather than commitment to scholarly communication becomes the primary goal of those controlling access to the Internet, university presses would find themselves unable to afford to publish the scholarly works that are the core of their activities. Thus the public nature of the Internet must be carefully guarded if we want to realize the true benefits of a democratic networked

environment: broad access to scholarly research and information not driven by financial concerns. A diverse range of independent, nonprofit publishers is critical to that goal.[10]

Another serious problem with Web-based publishing is the instability of websites. In a recent article, Micheal Bugeja and Daniela Dimitrova were quoted as saying that "scholarly citations in cyberspace are like atoms in various states of decay."[11] The author of the article in which that comment appeared was reporting on the "half-life" of Internet footnotes (which researchers now suggest is fifteen months). That is, the Web address cited for a scholarly article becomes outdated, broken, or changed in a relatively short period of time. This factor, combined with concerns about the integrity of the material after time has passed, means there is a serious problem if one relies on the Web too much for long-term access to scholarly material.

Government presses are the world's largest publishers. The combined annual output of government publications—international (UNESCO), national (U.S. Government Printing Office), and state, regional, and local (Los Angeles or state of California)—dwarfs commercial output. In the past, many people thought of government publications as characterized by poor physical quality or as uninteresting items that governments gave away. Today, some government publications rival the best offerings of commercial publishers and cost much less. (The government price does not fully recover production costs, so the price can be lower.) Most government publishing activity goes well beyond the printing of legislative hearings or actions and occasional executive materials. Often, national governments publish essential and inexpensive (frequently free) materials on nutrition, farming, building trades, travel, and many other topics. As is seen with scholarly presses, many government publications are currently being converted to e-only production. (See chapter 8 for more detailed information about government publications.)

Paperback publishers produce two types of work: quality trade paperbacks and mass-market paperbacks. A trade publisher may have a quality paperback division or may issue the paperbound version of a book through the same division that issued the hardcover edition. The publisher may publish original paperbacks, that is, a first edition in paperback. Distribution of quality paperbacks is the same as for hardcover books. Mass-market paperback publishers issue only reprints, or publications that first appeared in hardcover. Their distribution differs from other book distribution. Their low price is based, in part, on the concept of mass sales. Therefore, they sell anywhere the publisher can get someone to handle them. The paperback books on sale in train and bus stations, airline terminals, corner stores, and kiosks are mass-market paperbacks. These books have a short shelf life compared to that of hardcovers.

People talk about the paperback revolution, but it is hard to think of it as a revolution. Certainly, the paperback has affected publishers' and a few authors' incomes. Also, some readers are unwilling to accept a hardcover when the smaller, more compact paperback is available. The low price of a paperback also appeals to book buyers.

Books with paper covers are not new. In some countries all books come out with paper covers, and buyers must bind the books they wish to keep. The major difference is that most people think of only mass-market paperbacks as paperbacks. The emphasis on popular, previously published titles issued in new and colorful covers and sold at a low price is apparent. Those are the elements of the paperback revolution, not the paper cover or even the relatively compact form. Nor has the paperback created a whole new group of readers, as some overenthusiastic writers claim. It has merely tapped an existing market for low-cost, popular books.

Contrary to popular belief, using a paper cover rather than a hard cover only reduces the unit cost of a book by between twenty and thirty cents. Original paperbacks incur the same costs, except for the cover material, as a hardcover title, which is why their cost is so much higher than reprint paperbacks. The reason the price of "mass market" paperbacks is so much lower than the same title in hardcover is that they first appeared in hardcover. The title sold well in hardcover (otherwise, there would be no reason to bring out a paper version) and had shown some profit. This means that the publisher has already recovered some of the major production costs. Having recovered the editorial costs, with marketing costs recouped and title awareness good, makes it possible to substantially reduce the price. Economies of scale, or high sales volume and low per-unit profits, also reduce the price.

Newspaper and periodical publishers are a different class of publisher. Usually, book publishers depend on persons outside their organization to prepare the material that they publish. Newspaper and periodical publishers retain reporters or writers as members of their staffs. Of course, there are exceptions to the exception. For instance, some popular (and most scholarly) periodicals consist of articles written by persons not employed by the organization that publishes the journal. In general, in newspaper or periodical publishing, one finds the same range of activities found in book publishing. In other words, there are commercial publishers of popular materials, specialty publishers, children's publishers, scholarly or academic publishers, and government publishers. All subcategories share the characteristics of their book publishing counterparts; some are divisions of book publishing organizations.

Supplying current information is the primary objective of newspaper and journal publishers. With books, one can assume that most of the material published is at least six months old at the time of publication. The newspaper or periodical format provides the means for more rapid publishing, from two or three months to less than one day. (Major exceptions are some scholarly and academic periodicals, which frequently are one, two, or more years behind in publishing accepted articles.) To provide the most current information available, the library must acquire the newspapers or periodicals that suit the community's needs and interests. (Chapter 6 discusses problems concerning control and selection of these materials.)

Two other types of publishing activities deserving mention are *associations* and *reprint houses*. Professional and special interest groups and associations frequently establish their own publishing houses. The American Library Association is one such organization. These organizations may publish only a professional journal, but they also may issue books and audiovisual materials. The operating funds come from the association, but the association hopes to recover its costs. Professional associations are often tax-exempt, and thus their publishing activities are similar to those of scholarly presses: limited-appeal titles, small press runs, relatively high prices, and indirect government subsidies. Some associations do not have paid publication staff and use volunteer members instead; they contract with a commercial publisher to print the group's journal, conference proceedings, and other publications. Association publications, whether published by the organization itself or by contract, can provide the library with numerous bibliographic control headaches. For example, they announce ti-tles as forthcoming, but the items never get published. Many publications are papers from meetings and conventions (called "Transactions of . . ." or "Proceedings of . . ."); the titles of such publications frequently change two or three times before they appear in hardcover. Many of these publications do not find their way into trade bibliographies.

Reprint publishers, as the name implies, focus on reprinting items no longer in print. Most of the sales by reprint houses are to libraries and scholars, and many of the titles that these publishers reprint are in the public domain (i.e., no longer covered by copyright). The other major source of reprinted material is the purchase of rights to an out-of-print title from another publisher. Although many of the basic costs of creating a book do not exist for the reprint house (e.g., editing, design, and royalties), reprints are expensive because of their limited sales appeal. (In the past, some pub-lishers would announce a new release with a prepublication flyer that in-cluded an order form. Later, the company would announce the cancellation of the title. Some suspicious librarians suggested that such cancellations were the result of insufficient response to the prepublication announce-ment.) Sometimes reprints cause as many or more bibliographic headaches for libraries than do association titles. Despite the many problems, reprint houses are an essential source of titles for collection development programs concerned with retrospective materials.

Small presses are important for some libraries. Some people, including librarians, think of small presses as literary presses. Anyone reading the annual "Small Press Round-Up" in *Library Journal* could reasonably reach the same conclusion. The reality is that small presses are as diverse as the international publishing conglomerates. Size is the only real difference; in functions and interests small presses are no different from large trade pub-lishers.

Small Press Record of Books in Print (*SPRBIP*) lists over 50,000 titles from more than 5,000 small publishers for 2003.[12] Many of these presses are one-person operations, done as a sideline from the publisher's home. Such presses seldom publish more than four titles per year. The listings in *SPRBIP* show the broad range of subject interests of small presses and show that there are both book and periodical presses in this category. Some people assume that the content of small press publications is poor. This is incorrect, for small presses do not produce, proportionally, any more worth-less titles than do the large publishers. Often, it is only through the small press that one can find information on less popular topics. Two examples of very popular books that were originally published by small presses are *Ruby Fruit Jungle* by Rita Mae Brown and the Boston Women's Health Book Collective's *Our Bodies, Ourselves*.

Another factor that sets small presses apart from their larger coun-terparts is economics. Large publishers have high costs and need substan-tial sales to recover their costs, but small presses can produce a book for a limited market at a reasonable cost and still expect some profit. Small presses also can produce books more quickly than their larger counterparts.

From a collection development point of view, small presses represent a challenge. Tracking down new releases can present a variety of problems. Locating a correct current address is one common problem. Another is learning about the title before it goes out of print. With *SPRBIP*, Len Ful-ton of Dustbooks (<http://www.dustbooks.com/sprbip.htm>) tries to provide the best possible access, and he has succeeded to a surprising degree, given the nature of the field. However, waiting for his annual *SPRBIP* may take too long, because small presses frequently move about, and their press runs are small (i.e., only a limited quantity of books is printed). In essence, few small presses are part of the organized trade or national bibliographic network.

Very few of these presses advertise, and even fewer of their titles receive reviews in national journals. There are three publications/sources of information about current small press titles, Dustbook's *Small Press Review,* Midwest Book Review's *Small Press Bookwatch* (<http://www.mid westbookreview.com/sbw>), and Greenfield's *Small Press Book Review*. Lack of reviews in more traditional review sources is not the result of book review editors discriminating against small press publications. Rather, it is a function of too many small press operators not understanding how items get reviewed and failing to send out review copies.

Functional Areas of Publishing

Publishing consists of five basic functional/operational areas, which apply equally to print and nonprint materials: administration, editorial, production, marketing, and fulfillment. A publisher must be successful in all five areas if the organization is to survive for any length of time. Just because the organization is not for profit does not mean it has any less need for success in each of these areas. Administration deals with overseeing the activities, ensuring the coordination, and making certain there are adequate funds available to do the desired work. It is in the editorial area that publishing houses decide what to produce. As noted earlier, acquisition and managing editors discuss and review ideas for books or articles. Large book publishers develop *trade lists* (a combination of prior publications, manuscripts in production, and titles under contract) to achieve a profit while avoiding unnecessary competition with other publishers.

Book selectors ought to learn something about the senior editors in the major publishing houses with which they deal. As with reviewing, the view of what is good or bad material is personal, so knowing the editors will help in planning selection activities. The editors' opinions about what to accept for publication determine what will be available on the annual list.

The *annual list* is the group of books that a publisher has accepted for publication and plans to release during the next six to twelve months. The *backlist* comprises titles published in previous years that are still available. A strong backlist of steadily selling titles is the dream of most publishers. Editors spend a great deal of time planning their lists. They do not want to have two new books on the same topic appear at the same time unless those books complement one another. They want a list that will have good balance and strong sales appeal as well as fit with the titles still in print.

In 1998, the *New York Times* published an article about rising book production, loss of editors, and the increase in errors in books. This article noted there was a 16 percent drop in the publishing workforce in New York City between 1990 and 1998 and that the decrease was primarily in the editorial category. It also speculated about the role mergers played in the situation. One editor was quoted as saying, "It's all become a big, fat, screaming, mean, vicious, greedy, rude, and crude feast. . . . So little of your time is spent doing creative work that I'm seriously considering leaving."[13] Editors are critical to the publishing process, so one hopes that the New

York City situation is not representative of the field as a whole; however, the situation appears to be much the same at the time we prepared this edition.

Production and marketing join with the editorial team to make the final decisions regarding production details. Most publishers can package and price publications in a variety of ways. Some years ago, the Association of University Publishers released an interesting book entitled *One Book Five Ways* (for a full citation, refer to Further Readings at the end of this chapter). The book provides a fascinating picture of how five different university presses would handle the same project. In all five functional areas, the presses would have proceeded differently, from contract agreement (administration), to copyediting (editorial), to physical format (production), to pricing and advertising (marketing), and to distribution (fulfillment).

Production staff considers issues such as page size, typeface, number and type of illustrative materials, and cover design, as well as typesetting, printing, and binding. Their input and the decision made regarding the physical form of the item play a major role in how much the title will cost. Although technology has changed how and who performs some production activities, the basic issues of design, layout, use of illustrations, and use of color remain unchanged.

Marketing departments are responsible for promoting and selling the product. They provide input about the sales potential of the title. Further, this unit often decides how many review copies to distribute and to what review sources. Decisions about where, when, or whether to place an ad are the responsibility of the marketing department. All of these decisions influence the cost of the items produced. Many small publishers use direct mail (catalogs and brochures) to market their books. Publishers' sales representatives visit stores, wholesalers, schools, and libraries. When salespeople visit the library or information center, they keep the visits short and to the point. Each visit represents a cost to the publisher, and the company recovers the cost in some manner, most often in the price of the material. One activity for which most marketing units are responsible is exhibits. For library personnel, convention exhibits are one of the best places to meet publishers' representatives and have some input into the decision-making process. From the publishers' point of view, if the conferees go to the exhibits, conventions can be a cost-effective way of reaching a large number of potential customers in a brief time. Librarians should also remember that the fees exhibitors pay help underwrite the cost of the convention.

Fulfillment activities are those needed to process an order, including warehousing of the materials. In many ways, fulfillment is the least controllable cost factor for a publisher. Some publishers are using their electronically archive "typesetting" files for backlist titles to provide on-demand printing capability and keep inventory/warehousing costs as low as possible. Libraries and information centers sometimes add to the cost of their purchases by requiring special handling of their orders. Keeping special needs to a minimum can help keep prices in check. Speeding up payments to publishers and vendors will also help slow price increases, because the longer a publisher has to carry an outstanding account, the more interest has to be paid. Ultimately, most increases in the cost of doing business result in a higher price for the buyer, so whatever libraries can do to help publishers control their fulfillment costs will also help collection development budgets.

For various reasons, despite strong marketing efforts, some publications do not sell as well as expected. When this happens, sooner or later the publisher has to dispose of the material; many times, these become re-maindered items. A decision by the Internal Revenue Service influenced press runs and the speed with which publishers remainder slow-moving warehouse stock (*Thor Power Tool Co. v. Commissioner of Internal Revenue*, 439 U.S. 522 [1979]). Remaindered items sell for a small fraction of their actual production cost. Prior to the *Thor* decision, businesses would write down the value of their inventories, or warehouse stock, to a nominal level at the end of the tax year. The resulting loss in the value of the inventory (which was, by and large, on paper only) then became a tax deduction for the company, increasing its profit. Since *Thor*, publishers can take such a deduction only if the material is defective or offered for sale below actual production cost. Under the previous method, publishers could find it prof-itable to keep slow-selling titles in their warehouses for years. Thus far, ef-forts to get an exemption from the ruling for publishers have been unsuccessful. At first, the ruling increased the number of remaindered books, but now most publishers have cut back on the size of their print runs in an attempt to match inventories to sales volume. More often than not, this means higher unit costs and retail prices. Despite all the problems for the field, total net sales income for book publishing has increased steadily, from $14.1 billion in 1989 to an estimated $26.87 billion in 2002.[14]

Several times in this chapter we mention the publisher's goal of profit or reasonable return. What is "typical" for a 250-page trade book selling for $25.00? Let's take a look at a hypothetical first press run:

Suggested Retail Price	$25.00	
Printing/binding	– 2.00	(a cost no matter the number of
	23.00	items sold)
Warehouse/Distribution	– 2.00	(also a given "at best"
	21.00	warehousing)
Discount to retailer	– 12.50	
	8.50	
Overhead (including editorial)	– 2.00	
	6.50	
Marketing	– 1.50	
	4.00	
Author royalty (10%–15%)	– 1.25	(This is a high number as it
	2.75	represents 10% of list price. Most royalties are based on net sales income, which is always lower.)

Werner Rebsamen published some percentages of costs he was provided by a major New York publisher to use at his presentation at the Book Manu-facturing Institute[15]:

- 24.1% Royalties and Guarantees
- 5.7% Editorial Production

- 16.4% Marketing
- 24.2% Manufacturing
- 9.2% Returns
- 8.4% Fulfillment
- 9.3% General Administration

One can find data on annual sales in a variety of sources: *PW*, *The Bowker Annual of Library & Book Trade Almanac*, Standard and Poor's *Industry Surveys*, and so forth. Anyone concerned with collection development must make use of statistical data about publishing to develop intelligent budgets and work plans. Statistical data about the number of new titles available as paperbacks, reprints, and so forth can be useful in planning the workload for the next fiscal year. For example, perhaps the library will need to hire more staff or redirect efforts of existing staff if the volume of acquisitions increases. Knowing the pricing patterns over a period of years and the expected acquisitions budget allows one to project the workload. The two most accessible sources of publishing statistics for the United States are *PW* and *The Bowker Annual*. Data in both sources and almost all other printed statistical data about publishing come from the American Book Producers Association (ABPA). Remember that the statistics represent information drawn from ABPA members, and not all publishers belong to that group. In fact, a great many small and regional publishers do not.

Publishers use a variety of distribution outlets, selling directly to individuals, institutions, retailers, and wholesalers. Distribution is a major problem for both publishers and libraries because of the number of channels and the implications for acquiring a specific publication. Each channel has a different discount, and one accesses them through different sources. Figure 5.1 illustrates in a general way the complexity of the system. Production and distribution of information materials, whether print or nonprint, consist of several elements, all interacting with one another. Writers and creators of the material can, and do, distribute their output in several ways: directly to the community or public; to agents, who in turn pass it on to producers; or directly to the producers. Producers seeking writers often approach agents with publication ideas. The figure illustrates the variety of channels publishers use to distribute their publications to the consumer.

Most publishers use all these sales channels. Wholesalers, direct mail companies, and retail store operators act as middlemen; a retailer may buy from the jobber or directly from the publisher. Each seller will have different discounts for different categories of buyers, ranging from no discount to more than 50 percent. Not only are there a great many choices available to the buyer, but the sources also compete with one another. These factors combine to push up the cost of distributing a publication, which in turn increases its list price. With multiple outlets, different discounts, and different credit conditions, the publishing industry has created a cumbersome, uneconomical distribution system.

Selling practices vary by title and publisher; however, one can make a few generalizations. Advertising will help a good book, but it seldom, if ever, makes a success out of a poor book. Publishers use both publicity and advertising, which are two different marketing devices. An interview with the author or a review of the book on a national radio or television program is

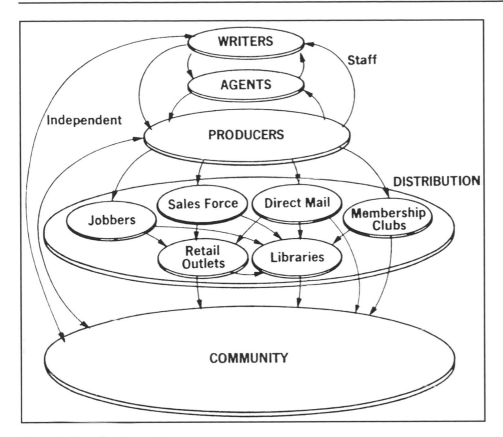

Fig. 5.1. Distribution system.

an example of publicity. Normally free, publicity will do a great deal for the sales of a book. However, the book's topic, or at least its author, must be of national interest or the title will not attract attention. Changes in current events can change a slow-moving book into a bestseller overnight, something that no amount of advertising can accomplish.

Publishers advertise in several ways. First, they use trade advertising directed toward retail outlets and institutional buyers. Second, they make an effort to get items reviewed in major professional and general review media. (Reviews are technically promotion rather than advertising, because one does not pay to have a title reviewed. However, a lead review can be worth more than a full-page advertisement.) Third, they place announcements and ads in professional journals, where the emphasis is on reaching individual buyers, both personal and institutional. Fourth, they employ cooperative advertisements (co-op ads) in the book review sections of many newspapers. A co-op ad is one in which the publisher and a retail store share the cost of the advertisement. The publisher determines which titles are eligible for cooperative advertising. Finally, for books with a defined audience for which there is a good mailing list, the publisher often uses a direct mail campaign, again with individuals and institutional buyers as the targets.

This brief overview outlined the most basic elements of publishing. Its purpose is to start a collection development novice thinking about the trade. The next section presents a discussion of some of the problems facing producers today, which is also important for the new collection development officer to recognize and understand.

Producers' Problems and Collection Development

Collection development personnel need to understand some of the important issues and problems facing producers, because those factors inevitably have an impact on their collections. Rising costs create problems for everyone, but publishers and media producers have some special problems. Information producers experience pressure from two sides. On the one hand, the rising costs of materials and labor put pressure on them to raise the prices of their products. On the other hand, if they do raise prices, they must realize that this may cut into sales, thus cutting into their profits more than the cost increases themselves. The consumer must meet basic needs first, and during periods of inflation, meeting basic needs cuts into funds available for luxury items. For most individual buyers, books and media are among the first items to be cut.

Producers are likely to continue increasing their prices as the personal buyer market continues to shrink. Institutional buyers will continue to buy materials, but a static materials budget over two or three years, in combination with increasing costs of materials, means that the library buys fewer items each year. Most libraries do not receive large budget increases even during inflationary periods. The increases they do receive do no more than keep pace with inflation; thus, for all practical purposes, the budget is static. These two factors effectively limit the number of items purchased, and producers must carefully weigh these concerns before raising prices. This, in turn, forces them to be more and more selective about the items they produce. They will carry few, if any, materials that do not show a profit.

If producers could simplify their distribution system, they could achieve significant savings. Why should the general consumer (individual or institution) be able to purchase an item directly from the producer or from a wholesaler or retailer? The distribution system as it now operates is cumbersome and costly. For book publishers, it is a matter of having a typical marketing system (producer to wholesaler to retailer), but at the same time the system allows any individual customer access to any level of the system to make a purchase. Media producers, in contrast, use direct sales. Both systems are costly for everyone. The book system requires complex handling procedures at each level because of different classes of customers. For the media system, shipping single-item orders to numerous locations increases the cost of placing and filling an order. The impact on collection development is that more money goes into paperwork and administrative procedures and less is available to collection development. Both producers and librarians must strive to solve this problem.

Perhaps the most difficult question concerns the right to use knowledge resources, or, rather, how one may use them. As noted earlier, copyright has become a central issue among librarians, educators, and other users of knowledge resources on the one hand and the producers on the other. Yet, without copyright, there is little incentive for anyone to produce a work. The problem is how far society can go to provide and protect such incentives and still ensure adequate access to material at a fair price. Libraries want open, free access and use, and producers want limited free access. This issue, of course, has an important role to play in determining how one develops a collection, with electronic information making the issue ever more complex.

Summary

In this chapter, we reviewed the history of publishing, the main types of publishers, and their main product lines in order to introduce this complex and sometimes misunderstood field. Producers of information materials grapple with many of the same issues as do libraries, such as coping with the effect of technology and rising costs. By understanding some of the challenges faced in the publishing industry, it is hoped librarians can more easily cultivate a productive relationship with information producers.

Notes

1. George Bornstein, "Pages, Pixels, and the Profession," *Journal of Scholarly Publishing* 34 (July 2003): 197–207.

2. Richard J. Cox, "Taking Sides on the Future of the Book," *American Libraries* 28 (February 1997): 52–55.

3. Ibid., 53.

4. R.P.S. Davis, P.C. Livingood, H.T. Ward, and V.P. Steponaitis, *Excavating Occaneechi Town* (CD-ROM) (University of North Carolina Press, 1998).

5. Albert N. Greco, *The Book Publishing Industry* (Boston: Allyn & Bacon, 1997), x–xi.

6. Peter Adams, "Technology in Publishing: A Century of Progress," in *Scholarly Publishing*, ed. R.E. Abel and L.W. Newlin, 29–39 (New York: Wiley & Sons, 2003).

7. *Bowker Annual: Library and Book Trade Almanac—2003* (Medford, NJ: Information Today, 2003), 519.

8. R.M. Berrong et al., "The Crisis in Scholarly Publishing," *PMLA* 118 (October 2003): 1338–43.

9. Ann Okerson, "Publishing Through the Network: The 1990s Debutante," *Scholarly Publishing* 23 (April 1992): 170–77.

10. Lisa Freeman, "Big Challenges Face University Presses in the Electronic Age," *Chronicle of Higher Education* 39, no. 34 (April 28, 1993): A44.

11. Scott Carlson, "Here Today, Gone Tomorrow: Studying How Online Footnotes Vanish," *Chronicle of Higher Education* 51 (April 30, 2004): A33.

12. *Small Press Record of Books in Print* (Paradise, CA: Dustbooks, 1975–   ).

13. Doreen Carvajal, "The More the Books, The Fewer the Editors," *New York Times*, Monday, June 29, 1998, at B1, B3.

14. *Bowker Annual*, 519.

15. Werner Rebsamen, "Trends in Publishing, New Technologies and Opportunities," *New Library Scene* 16 (December 1997): 10–12.

Further Reading

Adams, L. "Librarians Tell Publishers What They Really Need." *Journal of Youth Services in Libraries* 14 (Summer 2001): 32–34.

Dave, R. *The Private Press*. 2nd ed. New York: R. R. Bowker, 1983.

Davidson, C. N. "Understanding the Economic Burden of Scholarly Publishing." *Chronicle of Higher Education* 50 (October 3, 2003): B7–B10.

Eaglen, A. B. "Publishers' Sales Strategies: A Questionable Business." *School Library Journal* 34 (February 1988): 19–21.

———. "Publishers' Trade Discounts and Public Libraries." *Library Acquisitions: Practice and Theory* 8, no. 2 (1984): 95–97.

———. "Shell Game: Publishers, Vendors and the Myth of the Backlist." *School Library Journal* 38 (November 1992): 24–28.

Eaton, N., B. Macewan, and P. J. Potter. "Learning to Work Together—the Libraries and the University Press at Penn State." *ARL* 233 (April 2004): 1–3.

Greco, Albert N. *The Book Publishing Industry*. Boston: Allyn & Bacon, 1997.

Helfer, D. S. "Is the Big Deal Dead? Status of the Crisis in Scholarly Publishing." *Searcher* 12 (March 2004): 27–32.

Hutton, F. *Early Black Press in America, 1827–1860*. Westport, CT: Greenwood Press, 1993.

Kopka, M. "Backlist: How to Use It." *Publishers Weekly* 240 (October 4, 1993): 24–25.

Lawal, I. "Scholarly Communication at the Turn of Millennium: A Bibliographic Essay." *Journal of Scholarly Publishing* 32 (April 2001): 136–54.

Marmion, D. "Editorial: Looking at the Publishing Process." *Information Technology and Libraries* 21 (December 2002): 146.

Misek, M. "eScholars of the World Unite!" *EContent* 27 (March 2004): 36–40.

One Book Five Ways. Los Altos, CA: William Kaufmann, 1977.

Pfund, N. "Sidestepping Fate." *Library Journal* 129, no. 19 (November 15, 2004): 27–29.

Primich, T., et al. "A Corporate Library Making the Transition from Traditional to Web Publishing." *Computers in Libraries* 19 (November–December 1999): 58–61.

Quandt, R. E. "Scholarly Materials: Paper or Digital." *Library Trends* 51 (Winter 2003): 349–75.

Quint, B. "Digital Books: More Value Added, Please." *Information Today* 22, no. 1 (January 2005): 7.

Tafuri, N. A. Seaberg, and G. Handman. *Guide to Out-of-Print Materials*. ALCTS Acquisitions Guides Series No. 12. Chicago: American Library Association, 2004.

Tenopir, C. "Electronic Publishing." *Library Trends* 51 (Spring 2003): 614–35.

Reid, C. "Breaking Even Is Hard to Do." *Publishers Weekly* 249 (April 29, 2002): 29.

Rogers, M., et al. "E-Book Aftermath: Three More Publishers Fold Electronic Imprints." *School Library Journal*, Net Connect 127 (Summer 2002): 4, 8.

Velterop, J., and D. Goodman. "Challenging Current Publishing Models." *Serials Librarian* 44, nos. 1/2 (2003): 73–75.

Watson, P. D. *E-Publishing Impact on Acquisition and Interlibrary Loan.* Chicago: American Library Association, 2004.

Wilson, S. "Beacon's Modern Era: 1945–2003." *Journal of Scholarly Publishing* 35 (July 2004): 200–209.

6
Serials—
Print and Electronic

Serials are one of the two most important components of any library or information center collection, based on the percentage of the collection development funds expended on them. Unlike monographs, serials come in a variety of formats and represent an ongoing financial commitment for the library. Regardless of their format, serials are a primary source of current information for people, as information appearing in recent issues of serials is usually the most current available on the topic covered. As a rule, the information contained in serial publications is usually not as comprehensive as one finds in monographs on the topic; thus, books/monographs and serials are complementary information resources rather than competitors. However, in library settings, serials do compete for the funds available for building the collection.

Currently, there is a substantial body of literature about e- versus print serials. At present, the issue is not one of either/or, but rather how to balance the need for both. Additionally, for the most common types of serials—magazines and journals (more about this later)—the basics are the same for both print and electronic—selection, acquisition, handling, evaluation, preservation, and, of course, costs. We address all of these topics in this chapter.

The 21st century will, in all likelihood, be one in which we see a steady decrease in paper-based serials and a steady rise in the number of electronic titles available to end users. Such a trend is already well under way, and the role of electronic serials has grown quickly since the fourth edition of this book went to press. However, for the lifetime of this edition, it is likely both print and electronic serials will continue to coexist.

Regardless of the way they are accessed, print, microform, Internet/Web-based, CD-ROM, and online services all create user expectations that present challenges for collection development officers as well as all the library staff. A key challenge is providing the most cost-effective mix of serials that will come as close as fiscal limits permit to meeting user needs and desires. (Anyone with experience with serials knows that no matter how many titles one has, users always seem to want more!)

What Is a Serial?

Answering the above question is not as simple as one might expect. Individuals (users and librarians alike) frequently use the words *journals, magazines, periodicals,* and *serials* interchangeably, with no great misunderstanding resulting from the imprecise usage. Thomas Nisonger, in his fine book on serials management,[1] devoted more than six pages to how different groups have attempted to define the material covered in this chapter. For the purposes of this chapter, the following definitions from the ALA *Glossary of Library and Information Science* will suffice for two key terms:

> *Serial*—"a publication issued in successive parts, usually at regular intervals, and, as a rule, intended to be continued indefinitely. Serials include periodicals, annuals (reports, yearbooks, etc.) and memoirs, proceedings, and transactions of societies."

> *Periodical*—"a publication with a distinctive title intended to appear in successive (usually unbound) numbers of parts at stated or regular intervals and, as a rule, for an indefinite time. Each part generally contains articles by several contributors. Newspapers, whose chief function it is to disseminate news, and the memoirs, proceedings, journals, etc. of societies are not considered periodicals."[2]

Definitions in general dictionaries have more overlap:

> *Journal*—"a periodical publication especially dealing with matters of current interest—often used for official or semi-official publications of special groups."

> *Magazine*—"a periodical that usually contains a miscellaneous collection of articles, stories, poems, and pictures and is directed at the general reading public."

> *Periodical*—"a magazine or other publication of which the issues appear at stated or regular intervals—usually for a publication appearing more frequently than annually but infrequently used for a newspaper."

> *Serial*—"a publication (as a newspaper, journal, yearbook, or bulletin) issued as one of a consecutively numbered and indefinitely continued series."[3]

We have chosen to use the term *serials*, because it represents the broadest spectrum of materials.

Just as there are several terms for paper-based serials, so there are for the digital format: *electronic journals, online journals, digital journals,* and the more all-embracing *electronic resources* are used interchangeably. (To date on the electronic side there has been no attempt to differentiate between serial types.) As noted by Nisonger, there is no standard accepted definition of an electronic journal/serial.[4] In the interest of space, for this discussion we will use *e-serial*. Producers take three broad approaches with e-serials: an electronic-only version of a new title, an electronic-only version of a title converted from a paper version, and a version available both in print and electronically. However, some caution is necessary when it comes to interpreting just what "full text" means. At present (2005), full text often does not guarantee that one will find the graphic material and photographs from the print version accompanying the online text. There may be more graphic material—such as sound or video files—accompanying the online version of a title. Alternatively, some items such as letters to the editor, position announcements, or advertisements may be omitted from the electronic version of a print title.

Some years ago, Fritz Machlup and others developed an eighteen-part classification system for serials.[5] These categories apply to both print and electronic formats. The following discussion uses their classification system because it covers all types of serials, including serials "not elsewhere classified." We have yet to encounter a serial that does not fit into one of his other seventeen categories.

Institutional reports are annual, semiannual, quarterly, or occasional reports of corporations, financial institutions, and organizations serving business and finance. Most of the reports available to libraries and information centers are free for the asking. Some organizations will add a library to their distribution lists, but others will respond only to requests for the current edition.

Yearbooks and proceedings are annuals, biennials, occasional publications, bound or stapled, including yearbooks, almanacs, proceedings, transactions, memoirs, directories, and reports of societies and associations. Many libraries collect serials in this class, especially academic, special, and large public libraries. Although it is possible to secure some of these serials through a vendor, there are a significant number that one must secure directly from the society or association.

Superseding serials consist of two additional labor-intensive collecting categories. First are the superseding serial services (each new issue superseding previous ones, which are usually discarded), including telephone directories, catalogs, loose-leaf data sheets, etc. Second are nonsuperseding serial services bound, sewn, stapled, or loose-leaf, including bibliographic and statistical data. One must acquire most of the materials in these classes directly from the publisher. Superseding serials are important but problematic: important because people need the correct or current information and problematic as they can be difficult to track and sometimes to secure. Loose-leaf services are particularly important in U.S. law libraries and accounting firms (two examples are *Labor Relations Reporter*, from the Bureau of National Affairs, and *Standard Federal Tax Reporter*, from Commerce Clearing House). Nonsuperseding serials are less of a problem, and some are available from serial jobbers.

Newspapers are daily, weekly, and monthly unbound publications of local, regional, national, and international interest. All types of libraries, with the exception of elementary school media centers, collect newspapers. Serial jobbers handle subscriptions to major newspapers for libraries, while local papers and some regional papers must be ordered directly from the publisher. At the time one places the order, selectors and collection development officers must establish the value of the newspapers' content to the local users, in the sense of the demand or need to have the latest issue in the shortest time. For example, one can receive the *Times* (London) in hard copy in a variety of packages, each with a different cost: daily airmail edition by air freight, daily airmail edition by airmail (the most expensive option), daily regular edition by air freight, daily regular edition in weekly packets (the least expensive option), or microfilm edition. The *New York Times* similarly offers a wider variety of hard copy editions: city edition, late city edition, national edition, New York edition, large-type weekly, same day, next day, two-day, weekly packets, and microfilm.

Most of the major national and international newspapers, such as the aforementioned *Times* and *New York Times*, are now available online—some from a vendor (e.g., Lexis/Nexis), some only through the publisher. A number of papers, such as the *Washington Post*, have their own websites that offer content that differs from the print edition of the paper, such as in-depth local news or photographic essays. (The "catch" of these sites is often that current content may be freely accessible, but access to online backfiles may require registration and/or payment of a subscription fee. This is generally not the version to which libraries subscribe, but it is a version patrons may be more accustomed to using.) Electronic versions may solve some of the storage issues associated with newspaper backfiles. They also work well for many readers, as the articles are not very long, and people are more willing to read a short article without wanting to print a hard copy. Often, however, people demand good-quality printing capability for electronic journal articles because of their length. In any event, choosing the electronic version would lessen the "housekeeping" (storage, reshelving, claims) costs for the print versions held, not to mention that an electronic version is more easily searchable than a print counterpart.

Newsletters are irregular publications such as leaflets, news releases, regularly scheduled newsletters, and similar materials published by various organizations. This category can be of major importance for some libraries. Special libraries are the most likely to become involved in the ongoing collection of this class of serial. Many of the items in this class are very inexpensive or free. Others, especially specialized newsletters, can cost thousands of dollars. In either case, someone must put in the time and effort to identify the sources and get on the appropriate mailing lists.

What are the most common serials? Eleven of Machlup's categories cover the variations in the common serials—magazines and journals (scholarly publications). According to Machlup's definition, magazines are mass-market serials, the ones that almost any serial jobber will handle for a library. His *magazine* categories include:

- Mass-market serials, weekly or monthly newsmagazines (such as *Newsweek*).

- Popular magazines dealing with fiction, pictures, sports, travel, fashion, sex, humor, and comics (an example is *Sports Illustrated*).

- Magazines that popularize science, social, political, and cultural affairs (*Smithsonian*).

- Magazines focusing particularly on opinion and criticism—social, political, literary, artistic, aesthetic, or religious (an example is *Foreign Affairs*).

- "Other magazines not elsewhere classified" category. An example of an item in this last category is an organization publication (governmental or private) that is really a public relations vehicle, sometimes called a *house organ*.

Machlup similarly divided *journals* into four subcategories, with one category divided into two smaller units:

- Nonspecialized journals for the intelligentsia well informed on literature, art, social affairs, politics, etc. (*Science* is an example).

- Learned journals for specialists—primary research journals and secondary research journals (*American Indian Culture and Research Journal*).

- Practical professional journals in applied fields, including technology, medicine, law, agriculture, management, library science, business, and trades (*RQ*).

- Parochial journals of any type but addressed chiefly to a parochial audience, whether local or regional (*Plateau Journal*).

Again, most titles in these categories are available through vendors, although one must place direct orders for some of the more specialized learned journals. Most parochial journals must be purchased directly from the publisher; local history and regional archaeological publications are examples of this class of serial.

Machlup's final serials category is *government publications*, reports, bulletins, statistical series, releases, etc. by public agencies, executive, legislative and judiciary, local, state, national, foreign, and international. Because we cover this group in chapter 8, we offer no further discussion here.

With the preceding variations in serials in mind, you can understand why there is confusion about terms and challenges in collecting and preserving them. Each type fills a niche in the information dissemination system. Although they do create special handling challenges, they are a necessary part of any library's collection, and the public service staff must deal with them.

Selection of Serials

Selection of serials focuses on three basic issues: titles currently in the collection, existing titles not in the collection, and newly published titles. One uses slightly different criteria in assessing each group. When reexamining titles in the collection, subscription price and use patterns are the two primary issues (see page 126 for an explanation of why periodic reexamination is necessary). Electronic serials often have the added element of requiring the consideration of a group of titles rather than a title-by-title approach.

Looking at interlibrary loan (ILL) data and citation analysis information helps one decide whether an existing title that is not in the collection ought to be. For new titles, the subject area, cost, and—when available—reviews are the key elements in deciding whether to place a subscription. As with books, one can incorporate some macro selection decisions into the collection development policy for serials. Some possible macro decisions are:

- Subscribe to any titles requested by users that match collected subject areas (this rule is often used in special libraries).

- Subscribe to any title borrowed through ILL more than X number of times.

- Subscribe to all core titles, as identified through citation analysis, in subject areas collected.

- Do not subscribe to unindexed titles (print only consideration).

- Do not subscribe to journals that contain unrefereed articles.

The list could go on; the point is, the more macro decisions there are, the easier serials management becomes.

One can also make other broad generalizations about serials selection. The fields of science, technology, and medicine (commonly abbreviated as STM in the literature) are very dependent on serial publications. At the opposite end of the spectrum are the humanities, which depend more on books than on serials. Between these two are the social sciences, some of which are more similar to the science disciplines (e.g., psychology, linguistics, physical anthropology), and others of which are more similar to the humanities (e.g., political science, education, and social anthropology).

A decision to subscribe to, or place a standing order for, a serial is a much bigger decision than similar decisions for monographs. Several factors account for the difference. Because serials are ongoing, they can become a standing budgetary commitment from a number of points of view.

Because serials arrive in the library or information center in parts, there usually is an ongoing process for receiving the parts and maintaining records about what did or did not arrive (see page 139 for further coverage of these topics). Unfortunately, few serials arrive in a form that allows for easy long-term storage or heavy use; therefore, libraries must bind or otherwise develop a means to preserve them. In addition, print serials occupy large amounts of storage space, which over time becomes scarce. Gaining access to the contents of print serials usually requires use of indexing and abstracting services, which are in themselves serials. Adding a new indexing or abstracting service typically results in additional work for the ILL unit, unless the library subscribes to all of the titles covered by the service. A serials collection that does not provide for quick, easy, and inexpensive photocopy services will quickly become a collection of covers and advertisements; the articles will disappear. When adding a title that has been in existence for some time, one must consider the question of backfiles. Finally, serial titles and frequencies change over time, which may require changes in its OPAC record. As we discuss later in this chapter, electronic serials also require the resources to access them—meaning libraries must minimally invest in computing and printing resources for users, as well as very likely offering a means of off-site access to electronic titles through a proxy server. These are the most important differences between selecting a book and selecting a serial.

Serials subscriptions require renewals, but with most vendor plans the renewal process is automatic, requiring no action on the part of the collection development staff. When the subscription renewal requires a positive decision by the library staff, the serials holdings are more likely to reflect the current interests of the library's users. With automatic renewal, there is a substantial chance that the library will continue inappropriate serials long after the serial ceases to meet community needs.

A long-term commitment means with rapidly rising prices and small budget increases, each year serials take up a larger proportion of the total materials budget. Chapter 12 on fiscal management provides more information about this problem, but in general, serials prices have been increasing at a much faster rate than general inflation. Thus, each year the amount of money required to maintain the present serials subscriptions increases at a rate greater than many libraries are able to sustain.

An important consideration in serials selection is how users gain access to the information each issue contains. Going through each issue is not efficient, and few people are willing to do this. Many print serials produce an annual index, but this is of no help with current issues. Over time, an entire industry has developed around providing access to serials. A variety of indexing and abstracting companies now provide services that assist in locating information in serials. Naturally, most of these services are expensive and are an overlooked cost of building a serials collection. Although Harvard's Tozzer Library (an anthropology library) is atypical, it illustrates the nature of the problem. That library receives more than 1,200 anthropology serials each year. If it did not do its own indexing, the library would have to spend more than $30,000 per year for indexing and abstracting services to achieve only 83 percent coverage of its serials holdings. Tozzer's solution to the indexing problem is to index all the serials it receives. It publishes the index as *Anthropological Literature*, which helps offset the indexing costs.

One selection question is, Should one subscribe only to commercially indexed serials? If a library subscribes to an unindexed title (such as a small local newspaper), does the library do anything to help users locate information in the new serial? In-house indexing of a title, although useful to patrons, does become a workload issue. Even using specialized (subject) indexing services can increase workload factors, as frequently use of such services generates user requests for titles indexed in the service but not held by the library. The library must then decide whether to add yet another title to the serials list, increase the interlibrary loan (ILL) department's workload, or make patrons unhappy. Copyright law limits the library's ability to use ILL in place of subscribing to a particular title; copyright law imposes legal constraints on the frequency with which one may borrow articles from a single serial title (see chapter 17).

One alternative to placing a subscription is to use a commercial document delivery service. Even with a substantial royalty fee, the occasional article from a seldom requested title may well be the most cost-effective option for meeting a user's needs. Louis Houle and Chris Beckett explored this approach in their article "Just in Time vs. Just in Case."[6]

Serials tend to increase the volume of copying activities—photocopy and printing. Serials articles are short (seldom more than twenty-five pages); as a result, many people prefer a hard copy of an article to consult at their leisure. Also, many libraries do not allow print serials to circulate, which further encourages copying.

When a library does not start a subscription with volume 1, number 1, the librarian must decide whether and to what extent to acquire back issue volumes. Are backfiles needed? Some serials publishers have full runs available, but most do not. Titles widely held by libraries may be available from reprint houses or online vendors. Print backfiles are expensive, they may be difficult to find, they may require binding, they certainly take up valuable shelf space, and many receive little use. Additionally, libraries cannot assume that vendors handling online full-text serials will maintain backfiles or make them available for all titles.

Serials can, and do, change over time. New editors, governing boards, or owners make major and minor shifts in the content and orientation. A major shift in emphasis usually is well publicized. As selectors become aware of such shifts, they should reassess the serial. A title change is something librarians frequently complain about, primarily because of internal concerns (see articles by Foggin[7] and Nelson[8]). From a collection development point of view, a title change should be welcome because it very likely signals a significant change in the serial's content. For that reason, the selectors should review the changes in content to determine whether the item is still appropriate for the collection. More difficult to identify is a slow shift over a number of years as editors change. The final result may be a greater difference in content than a well-publicized major change, but few people will notice the shift. Periodic examination of incoming serials by the selection officers is an excellent method for checking on changes in emphasis.

There are a number of issues to ponder in the interplay between digitized and paper-based serials. One issue is how to provide access. Digital serials, in theory, are accessible anywhere, anytime, as long as there is a connection between a computer and the database containing the desired material. Many users and technology supporters see this as the ideal future: anywhere, anytime. Library literature generally approaches this issue in terms of ownership versus access.

When a library subscribes to a paper journal, the library owns the copies of those titles, for which it paid the appropriate fee. Electronic formats are often a different matter. Producers of electronic material usually include a license agreement that limits the library's ability to use the material and normally states that the library has access rights only so long as the annual fee is current. In essence, the library only leases the data. If a library has any responsibility for long-term retention of information, leasing is a problematic policy, even if the producer says it will archive the files and gives the library the right to access the files for the years for which it paid a lease fee.

Other aspects of serials are the issues of "just-in-case" and "just-in-time." Long-term preservation is, in a sense, just-in-case, that is, working on the assumption that someone at some time will require the information. Just-in-time is locating the desired material at the time the user needs it, most often from somewhere other than the home library collection. Digitized data make just-in-time delivery a realistic option. One reality is that fewer and fewer libraries can continue to subscribe to thousands of serials titles just-in-case. If there is a paper subscription, it must be for high-demand items, not the seldom-used titles.

Leasing and just-in-time delivery work well, but one cannot help but wonder about how far profit-oriented producers will go to maintain back-files or, for that matter, who will still be in business twenty years in the future (see pages 142–43 for more about preservation). There are serious concerns about who, how, and for how long electronic data will be available (archived).

Given all of these factors, one can see why serials selection is a major decision. Yet, all too often, libraries treat it as being no different from the decision to acquire a monograph.

Special E-Serial Selection Issues

Is the process of selecting e-serials different from that followed for print serials? The answer is no, not really; however, there are some additional steps. We believe that all the factors that apply to selecting paper titles also apply to e-journals. One factor that differs is that often, at least in the case of journal aggregator services, the purchasing decision is made for a package of titles rather than title by title. (We return to this issue later in this chapter in the section on Acquisitions/Serial Vendors.) That, in turn, means that the cost being considered is substantially higher than for any single, typical library paper subscription. Additionally, some vendors may have exclusive rights for certain titles, thereby "forcing" the decision to select a specific vendor in order to have access to a title. Thus, one adds factors of new costs, vendor support, and a "package" of titles to the list of issues that must be considered.

Another factor complicating the decision is that electronic resource decisions involve more staff than is typical for paper-based selection decisions. If nothing else, there are questions about technology requirements and capabilities that systems staff must answer. In addition, more of the public service staff becomes involved in supporting users of electronic resources. Few users need assistance in opening a paper journal, but many may need it when locating and using an electronic title. Packages from either producers or other vendors often employ different search engines; this requires staff to remember which database operates in which manner. Thus, public service staff often want a voice in deciding what, if any, new electronic products to add to the service program.

Mary Jean Pavelsek outlined a set of eleven "guidelines" for evaluating e-journals and their providers[9] (we modified some of her phrasing slightly):

- economics;
- ease of use/user flexibility;
- archival implications;
- future accessibility;
- access;
- licensing, copyright, and distribution restrictions;
- single or multiple publisher;
- print versus electronic comparisons;
- user support;
- if a package, is it "all or nothing"?; and
- planned enhancements.

To her list we would add cost per user, technological issues, and aggregators.

Deciding on aggregator packages usually entails accepting a number—sometimes a substantial number—of titles one would never subscribe to in print. Few of the aggregators allow a library to take only the titles of interest. Naturally, that means the library pays for titles it does not want. Thus, one question to consider is if the overall cost is really appropriate for the number of titles the library *does* want.

One system for evaluating aggregator as well as publisher/producer titles is the weighted system developed by the California State University Libraries (CSUL) for deciding on systemwide purchases. CSUL has a committee of twelve members, representing the twenty-three campuses of the system, each of whom serves for two years. Evaluations are made independently by each committee member, using the weighted system, during a two-week trial period. (Results of their evaluations are available on the system's web page <http://seir.calstate.edu/reviews/index.shtml>).

Technical issues of network capability, stability, and compliance with general standards are all key factors. Also, how much support is available from the vendor and during what hours? If required, how is authentication handled? Domain access—recognizing Internet Protocol (IP) ranges—is a low-cost option for the library; however, remote users with private Internet service providers will not have access unless the library provides it via a proxy server. Stefanie Wittenbach covered the above issues and more in her article "Everything You Always Wanted to Know About Electronic Journals But Were Afraid to Ask."[10]

Content concerns relate to the usual subject issues and also to how complete the material is, assuming there is a print counterpart. Another concern should be whether there are "additions" to the product and whether they are necessary or beneficial. Some vendors/producers add some form of multimedia—sound or video clips—to their material. Often this is of the "gee whiz, look what technology allows us to do" variety rather than being a true added value. Such additions create hardware and software compatibility problems for some library-owned machines and certainly for some remote users' machines.

Another issue to consider is what the library can or cannot do with the electronic material. Some vendors place restrictions on who can use the material, even in a public access setting. Such restrictions create problems for the public service staff—how to identify user types and monitoring what is being used. For example, *Academic Universe*® from Lexis/Nexis is contractually limited to the students, staff, and faculty of the purchasing institution. Individuals not affiliated with the institution are not permitted to use the service. What happens if the purchase was through a consortium, and a person is visiting another campus that is part of the consortium? Can the visitor use the service without violating the license agreement, since the home institution also has the service? Logically, one would think that such use would be acceptable; however, unless the consortium's agreement so indicates, there is a chance that such use would be a violation. Another concern is that all contracts call for the purchaser to be responsible for copyright violations. The whole question of license agreements is complex, and we discuss these matters more fully in chapter 17 on legal issues.

Long-term access to, and preservation of, material is usually a concern. Who will archive the material? How will it be archived, and for how long? These are questions one needs to consider at the point of making a selection decision. Programs operated by libraries, such as JSTOR or LOCKSS, are more likely to provide the electronic long-term archiving that both librarians and scholars expect with print materials. Commercial ventures are profit-driven and are unlikely to maintain a service that loses money for very long. Although the current purpose of JSTOR—a not-for-profit organization—is the selective digital conversion of retrospective files of print journals of scholarly interest, it may be complemented by a similar service called LOCKSS ("Lots of Copies Keeps Stuff Safe"), sponsored by Stanford University. Although LOCKSS is newer to the scene than JSTOR, it champions the use of agreements between libraries and publishers for long-term access to electronic journals (<http://lockss.stanford.edu>). (Another program, sponsored by the National Library of Medicine [NLM] and the Wellcome Trust, is mentioned in the section on Administration later in this chapter.)

Print serials are expensive, and in many ways e-serials are even more of an investment, especially when one factors in the technology costs. Studies as well as causal observation show that end users like, if not prefer, electronic resources, especially those that are Internet-based. Unfortunately, Web searching using Google or other tools is very often the method employed by end users, essentially ignoring the library's investment in databases. Students, at all levels, are prone to look for *an* answer, which a Web search almost always produces, rather than looking for *the* answer, which the database is more likely to provide. Judy Luther suggested that metasearching may be the way to maximize the library's expenditure on e-resources in "Trumping Google: Metasearching's Promise."[11]

Selection Models

There are five basic approaches to selection: cost, citation analysis, worth or use, polling, and core lists. There are many variations, but the five listed form the basis for models for selecting serials. Much of the work done in this area is relatively recent and more the result of having to cancel, rather than to start, subscriptions.

Cost models of selection are the oldest and have the greatest number of variations. One of the most complex models deals with the real annual cost of a serial. The annual cost consists of six elements: acquisition cost, processing cost, maintenance cost, storage cost, utility or use cost, and subscription price. *Acquisition costs* include such things as selection, order placement, and time spent in working with the subscription agent or publisher. *Processing costs* cover check-in, claiming, routing, cataloging or other labeling, adding security strips, and shelving in public service for the first time. *Maintenance costs* involve binding, microfilming or acquiring microform, repair, selecting for remote storage, and possibly discarding. *Storage costs* entail calculating the linear feet of storage space (either or both shelf and cabinet space) used by the title and the cost of the space. *Utility* or *use costs* are the most complex to calculate. They incorporate costs of time for such things as retrieval from a storage location (library staff only), pickup and reshelving, answering questions about the title ("Do you have . . . ?", "I can't find . . .", and "What is the latest issue you have?"), and all other required assistance (e.g., assistance with microform readers). The last, and often the lowest, cost is the subscription price. The sum of these costs represents the real annual cost of the title for the library. Looking over the list of costs makes it clear that it will take some time to calculate the individual cost centers. However, once one determines the unit costs (e.g., the average time to shelve an issue), it is fairly easy to calculate the cost for a given number of issues of a title. With an annual cost for each title, selectors can determine which titles to continue or discontinue. Several articles describing variations on this approach are included in the Further Reading section at the end of this chapter.

Like cost models, citation analysis paradigms take several forms. The main objective, from a selection point of view, is to identify frequently cited titles. Citation analysis can help identify a core collection for a field and provide a listing of titles ranked by the frequency with which they are cited. Another collection development use of citation analysis is in evaluating a collection. (Could a set of papers/reports have been done using this collection?) Citation analysis information is most useful in large or specialized research collections, although core collection information is valuable to smaller and nonspecialized collections as well.

It is important to understand certain assumptions about citation analysis before deciding to use this approach. The underlying assumption is that the subject content of the cited document relates to that of the citing document. A second assumption is that the number of times a document receives a citation is proportional to the value or intrinsic worth of the document. Another assumption is that all the publications an author cites were, in fact, used. (A related assumption is that authors list all the sources they used.) One other major assumption is that the sources used to secure the citation data are representative of the field under investigation. These are the major assumptions; others do exist. However, many people do not accept all the assumptions. If one cannot accept the assumptions, one should not use citation data for collection building.

There are two major sources of citation data: research reports and articles in the professional press, and data from the publishing firm Thomson/ISI (Institute for Scientific Information). Thomson/ISI publishes *Science Citation Index* (*SCI*), *Social Sciences Citation Index* (*SSCI*), and *Arts & Humanities Citation Index* (*AHCI*). These publications provide citation information for many journals. For example, *SSCI* covers over 1,700 social science titles and provides selective coverage of about 3,300 nonsocial science journals that contain some social science material. On an annual basis, Thomson/ISI also produces *Journal Citation Reports* (*JCR*), which provides a useful analysis of the journals Thomson/ISI covers.

Some of the major features of *JCR* are

- a listing of the number of articles a title contained for the year;
- how many citations were made to articles that appeared in the title through time;
- a ratio of articles published to articles cited (impact factor);
- a ratio of articles published during the year to citations to those articles (immediacy index); and
- a cited half-life, that is, how far back in time one needs to go to retrieve 50 percent of all citations appearing during a year to all articles that ever appeared in the title.

Such information can be helpful in making continuation and storage or deselection decisions.

Using the Bradford Distribution, one can rank titles to develop information for collection policy use as well to make decisions regarding current subscriptions.[12] The goal of this ranking is to identify all journals containing articles relevant to a given subject and to rank them in order based on the number of relevant articles they publish in a year. The pattern, according to Bradford's Law of Scattering, will show that a few journals publish the majority of articles and that a large number of journals publish only one or two cited articles. If one equates a basic collection (level 2 in the conspectus concept; see pages 58–59) with holding journals that contain 20 percent of the relevant material, one might subscribe to only three or four titles. For libraries with a comprehensive collection (level 5), the subscription list may contain several hundred titles. For example, Tozzer Library has a current subscription list of more than 1,200 titles for its coverage of anthropology. Journal worth models usually involve some information about title usage along with other data. Dawn Bick and Reeta Sinha described one of the many worth models,[13] which can be reasonably easy to implement. The model involves cost, use, impact factor, and information about the nature of the publication (e.g., core subject) to calculate a cost-benefit ratio.

As one might assume, most of the models require a substantial amount of data collection. If their only utility lay in making selection decisions, few libraries would use them. Their major value comes into play when the library must cut subscriptions. Having collected data that are similar for all the titles makes the unpleasant task a little easier. What librarians hoped would be a rare occurrence has, for some libraries, become an almost annual task. Each time the task becomes more difficult, and the models demonstrate their value.

Polling experts and using lists of recommended journals are other methods for identifying what to buy or keep. Both suffer from being less directly linked to the local situation, unless the experts are local users. One can find lists of journals in relatively narrow subjects, often listed with recommendations, or at least comments, in journals like *Serials Librarian* (Haworth) and *Serials Review* (Elsevier).

Maria Janowska described a rather complex model to use when making the choice between paper and electronic materials.[14] She drew on a publishing method known as Multiple Criteria Evaluation (MCE). Her approach used content, publication cycle, number of subscribers, overall cost, and price as the criteria. She then used a matrix that allows one to compare the criteria against one another, which allows consistency in the decision-making process. The process is somewhat complex but is worth considering when making a series of decisions regarding paper or electronic journals.

Identifying Serials

Serials employ a different bibliographic network from that used for monographs. Few of the selection aids for books cover serials. However, there are several general and specialized guides to serial publications. Reviews of serials are few and far between. The "Magazines" column published in *Library Journal* six times a year is one source of serial reviews. In the past, when publishers would supply several free sample copies of a title for the library to examine, the lack of reviews was not a problem. Today, many publishers charge for sample issues, and though it depletes the funds for subscribing to serials and adds to the time it takes to acquire them, it is useful to get sample issues before committing the library to a new serial.

Four useful general guides are *Ulrich's Periodicals Directory* (R. R. Bowker), *Magazines for Libraries* (R. R. Bowker), *Serials Directory* (EBSCO), and *Standard Periodical Directory* (Oxbridge Communications). All employ a subject arrangement, and entries provide all necessary ordering information. EBSCO's *Serials Directory* is available online and on CD-ROM, and Bowker's annual print edition of *Ulrich's* is complemented electronically via *Ulrichsweb.Com* or the quarterly CD-ROM version, *Ulrichs on Disc. Standard Periodical Directory* covers American and Canadian titles and has a reputation for providing the best coverage of publications with small circulations, lesser-known organizations, and processed materials.

These sources are very useful for acquisition information; however, they should be used with a degree of caution for selection purposes. This is especially true when seeking scholarly, peer-reviewed journals, as Robert Bachand and Pamela Sawillis noted.[15]

Newspapers, newsletters, and serials published at least five times a year are identifiable in guides like *Gale Directory of Publications and Broadcast Media* (Thomson/Gale) and *Willings' Press Guide* (Thomas Skinner Directories). For literary publications, one should use *International Directory of Little Magazines and Small Presses* (Dustbooks), *MLA International Bibliography* (Modern Language Association), and *L'Année Philologique* (Société International de Bibliographie Classique).

Many of the titles above that are annual publications have limited value in identifying new titles, because the information they contain is at least several months old. Obviously, online versions of products such as *Ulrichsweb.Com, Serials Directory*, or *MLA* will provide more current information. (As noted earlier, serials change in a variety of ways—titles, frequency, editorial policy, and so on—and keeping up with existing titles is enough of a problem without adding the need to identify newly created serials.)

Using a review of serials presents certain difficulties. Most serials that receive reviews are popular magazines rather than scholarly journals. Given the propensity of serials for change, a completely accurate assessment of a title is possible only when the serial ceases publication and the reviewer can examine all the issues. All that one should expect from a review of a serial is an accurate description of the content of the issue(s) available to the reviewer, rarely more than six issues. What a selector wants from the review is as much information about the purpose, audience, and editorial policy as the reviewer can identify; information about publisher, price, frequency, and other technical matters; and, if appropriate, comparisons to other related serials. Unfortunately, some of those limited data may be lacking, because it is sometimes difficult to determine purpose and editorial policy, even with the volume 1, number 1 issue in hand. Information about the publisher is less important in serials selection than in monograph selection because many times the serial is the publisher's only publication, and only time will reveal the publisher's reliability.

Serials Review publishes some reviews prepared by serials librarians and, occasionally, subject experts. The journal started as both a reviewing journal and a professional journal for serials librarians. Today it is primarily a professional journal, with only an occasional appearance of a review for a new or established serial. When reviews of established journals appear, they are useful in helping librarians monitor changes in the editorial policy of titles to which the library subscribes.

Library Journal (*LJ*; Reed Business Information) offers a regular column focusing on new periodicals. These columns contain brief annotations describing selected serials titles. A "Periodicals Information Directory" is also available online from the *LJ* companion website (<http://www.libraryjournal.com>). Because of the breadth of coverage, most types of libraries will find some titles of interest covered in the course of a year. An additional resource, compiled every few years, is *Magazines for Libraries*, which includes approximately 7,000 recommended titles.[16]

One can also use "core" or recommended lists for a variety of subject fields. Two examples are the "Brandon/Hill Selected List of Print Books and Journals in Allied Health," *Journal of the Medical Library Association* 91, no. 10 (January 2003): 18–32 by Dorothy R. Hills and colleagues, and Susan

Patron's "Miles of Magazines," *School Library Journal* 50, no. 3 (March 2004): 52–57. However, as was mentioned in chapter 4, some caution is in order when using core lists; one must understand the methodology employed to generate the list and know that it fits the needs of the library.

Acquisitions/Serial Vendors

For most libraries, it is not economical to place all of its serials subscriptions directly with the publisher. The amount of work required to monitor expiration dates, place renewals, and approve payments repeatedly for each title is too great. In any sizable serials collection, a few titles will be direct orders to the publisher; however, if a library uses a serials vendor for most orders, there will be more time for other problem-solving activities related to serials.

Today print vendors (subscription agents) also must deal with electronic serials and a few, such as EBSCO, also serve as aggregators. In addition to subscription agents, there are a number of aggregators of e-serials, such as *ProQuest*, Lexis/Nexis, Thomson/Gale, and H. W. Wilson. Aggregators secure licenses from publishers to mount one or more of their titles in a database with a proprietary search engine (such as *EBSCOhost*). Such databases often contain hundreds, if not thousands, of titles. The title selection will likely include some of the titles to which the library subscribes and very many more that the library does not take in a print format. In almost all cases, one subscribes/leases the package as a whole, not to individual titles—so it becomes an "all or nothing" proposition. Publishers gain by not having to invest in the technology, and they maintain a database and a search engine, as well as gaining some additional revenue. Libraries gain by having access to databases with large number of titles searchable through a single search engine. (The fewer variations there are for users to learn, the better it is for the public service staff.) Aggregators presumably gain income through the difference between their license fees, technology costs, and so on and what they charge libraries.

There is a second type of aggregator—not-for-profit organizations. They operate in much the same manner as their commercial counterparts. Examples are OCLC's Electronic Collections Online (available via *FirstSearch*), Johns Hopkins' Project MUSE, and JSTOR. While the first two aggregators focus on recent materials, JSTOR focuses on journal backfiles rather than current issues.

A third way to secure electronic titles is directly from the publishers. Publishers may offer packages or access to individual titles. By doing so, they may increase their revenue by cutting out the agent. Those offering packages may place restrictions on how many, if any, of the print subscriptions the library may cancel as a result of having electronic access to the title. Examples of publishers offering searchable packages are Elsevier, MCB, Sage, and Wiley.

An excellent source for details about e-journal acquisitions is the March/April 2003 issue of *Library Technology Reports*. The entire issue is devoted to e-journal vendors and acquisitions. A good book on the acquisition aspects of serials work is N. Bernard Basch and Judy McQueen's *Buying Serials*.[17]

Serials jobbers tend not to handle monographs, just as book jobbers tend not to handle serials. *Tend* is the key word here, given the variety of serials; in the area of annuals and numbered monograph series, lines become blurred, and jobbers overlap. Given the nature of serials publications, one is better served by an experienced serials jobber than by a friendly and willing book jobber who offers to handle the serials list along with book orders. Many serials librarians find it best to use domestic dealers for domestic serials and international dealers for international titles. Choosing a foreign dealer out of the country can be a challenge. It is advisable to ask other librarians about their experience with the dealers one is considering. One means for doing so is through a discussion list such as SERIALST (subscription instructions are in the Selected Websites section). If the librarian cannot identify anyone using a dealer, he or she might start by placing one or two subscriptions with the dealer and increase the volume of business if service is satisfactory.

Service is what one is looking for in a serials vendor. To provide service, the company must make a profit. How does it do that? In the past, vendors offered discounts. Today, libraries pay a service charge based on a percentage of the total subscription price. Serial vendors have one minor and two major sources of income. One major source is the discount publishers offer vendors. (Publishers offer these discounts because it is more convenient for them to deal with one billing/ordering source rather than subscriptions to many individual subscribers.) Recently, librarians have blamed publishers for rising subscription costs, but a few publishers claim that vendors share the blame because vendors are not passing on a share of the discount they receive from the publishers. Whatever the case may be, vendors depend on publishers' discounts to make a profit.

The second major revenue source for vendors is the service charge they add to their invoices to libraries. The service charge varies from library to library, depending on several factors. It often requires a good deal of work to determine just what the service charge is. When a subscription list contains thousands of titles, it is unlikely that there will be only one invoice, if for no other reason than that prices change during the year; supplementary invoices will arrive. Sales representatives may not know all the factors involved in calculating the charge and can give only an overview explanation. There may be various rates for various types of publications; in part, the service charge depends on the size of the discount the vendor receives.

Another variable in the calculation of a library's service charge is what services the library uses. Often, there is an extra charge for handling unusual serials, such as government publications. The types and number of management reports the library receives from the vendor also affect the service charge. Title mix is another factor, just as it is with book jobbers. For serials vendors, it is more a matter of knowing which titles generate additional work for the vendor, rather than a bookseller's pricing concerns with popular titles (low price/high discount) versus scholarly titles (high price/low discount). If a library has a high percentage of problem titles, its service charge may be somewhat higher than for another library with a similar number of subscriptions, costing about the same but with fewer problem titles. As a result, setting the service charge becomes an art, and the service charge is open to negotiation.

If print serial pricing with discounts and service charges is confusing at times, how vendors/producers set prices for e-serials is positively mystifying. There are a variety of methods for pricing e-resources—pay per document, concurrent users, price per search, and service population size, to name but a few. A 1998 study[18] of e-pricing identified sixteen distinct approaches; today, if anything, there are even more variations. To make things even more confusing, vendors occasionally change their method, making predictions of next year's cost even less certain. Add to this the widespread practice of purchasing an e-package through a consortium, which makes it almost impossible to know what "the price" really is; about the only thing that is known is how much the library paid the last time.

Even if one could determine "the price," there will naturally be differences in prices for single titles and packages. E-only titles are the most straightforward and more or less mirror pricing of a print title in the same field. When it becomes an e-version of a print title, pricing becomes murky once again. Sometimes the publishers, at least initially, provide the e-edition free of charge with a paid print subscription; other times there is an additional fee. Typically, the fee is some percentage of the print subscription as long as that stays fully paid. Taking just the e-version of a title is usually the most costly route, often several times the print price. (The higher price may be warranted if the print title carries advertising and/or there is a mailing list market—both areas are sources of revenue for journal publishers that do not exist in the e-environment. Clearly, if the e-version is an Adobe PDF (Portable Document Format) file of the print edition, then the advertising factor is not present.)

Package pricing from aggregators can truly be bewildering. At the most fundamental level, one finds pricing varies by type of library, perhaps based on the notion that the greater the value to the library's users, the higher the price should be. Thus, a corporate library may face a higher charge than an academic or public library for the identical package. While one expects vendors to create specialized packages for different markets (school districts have different needs from those of research institutions) and thus have different costs associated with the package, having different prices for a package-based type of library seems unfair. What might be more surprising is that there is at least one package existing for corporate and law libraries that other libraries may not lease, even when they have users who need and have used the package in the past. This can, and does, create challenges for the library staff when trying to explain why they cannot provide access.

While today there are two choices for acquiring access to a package—going it alone or purchasing it as part of a consortial "deal"—the typical approach is to look for consortial opportunities. It seems to be the best method for getting the best price—"seems" because one can never be certain that another consortium did not get a better price or even that going it alone might have been quicker and no more costly.

We regret to say that acquiring access to some of these packages through consortia is rather like purchasing an automobile; for a car there are manufacturer's suggested list price, the dealer's price, fleet price, cash price, trade-in price, and the price you actually pay. Although there are fewer prices in a consortial package "big deal," the process of getting the final cost really does bring to mind the car-buying experience. There is the vendor's announced price based on what pricing model the firm uses, there probably is some discussion of a consortial price, and there is perhaps even a "estimated price" if all consortial members sign up. However, none of these are likely to be the final price.

The reason for the frequent variation in price and the amount of time it takes to reach the final cost is the way many consortia operate, not because of the vendor(s). The selection process usually begins with the question, "Who would be interested in purchasing product X?" The question quickly becomes, "It depends; how much would it cost?" The vendor provides an answer normally based on the notion that all members will take part in the "deal." At that point, some of the members decide they cannot afford the product and say they are dropping out. If the product is a new one, there will be a request to have a trial period—thirty or sixty days is most common. More often than not, all the members will have access to the product during the trial, even those that said they did not think they would be interested. At the end of the trial a count is taken of who is interested, and the vendor develops a new quote based on that number. Commonly, some of the libraries that thought they were interested find the price too high for them and drop out. That normally means yet another quote from the vendor; frequently, the result is a higher cost per library, leading to still further changes in the number willing to take part. Reaching a final "deal" can take several months, with libraries dropping out and occasionally back in as the price changes. (Cooperative collection development and consortia are more fully discussed in chapter 15.)

Some of the other pricing complexities faced by single-institution and consortial purchasers alike include the number of authorized IP addresses and the question of what a "site" is, as well as who will have access to the resource. Taking the last point first, many licenses state that only the "primary clientele" are covered. If you paid on an institutional full time equivalent (FTE) basis, should you allow others not included in that count to have access? (This is primarily an issue for educational libraries, where the FTE number usually reflects the student population, not faculty, staff, or others who may use the library.) From a legal point of view the answer would be no. A license agreement that takes a more inclusive definition of the primary clientele is better for the library or increasing the FTE number to better reflect the potential user population would satisfy the more limited definition. The problem with the latter approach is that probably a large, but unknown, number of staff never would use the service, and the cost of leasing the product goes up.

When it comes to IP addresses, the question becomes, What about remote access? This is an issue when part of the agreement calls for a listing of authorized IPs. To some degree, the IP and site issue are interrelated, as often the assumption is that the IP range relates to a single geographic location as well as proxy for the number of users. Today with proxy servers in operation in many libraries, the IP range is probably worthless as a true gauge of physical location.

For school districts, public libraries, and academic institutions with distance education programs, the license definition of "site" is very important. There are two common meanings. One, as expected, is in terms of a physical location (any location within X distance of the leasing location is authorized). The second definition is administrative in nature—any location administered by the leasing location, regardless of distance, is authorized. Clearly, the latter definition is better in many situations. It will also save money, as the geographic definition would lead to extra fees for locations beyond the defined distance.

Advantages of Vendors

What does the customer receive from a vendor beyond the basic advantage of one order, one invoice, and one check for multiple subscriptions? Automatic renewal by a vendor saves library staff time, and when the invoice arrives, there is the opportunity to cancel titles no longer needed. Jobbers may offer multiple-year subscription rates that will save the library money. Notifying libraries about discontinuations, mergers, changes in frequency, and other publication alterations is a standard service provided by a serials jobber. The jobber is more likely to learn of changes before a library does, especially if the jobber has placed hundreds of subscriptions with the publisher.

Vendors also provide some assistance in the claiming process (missing issues, breaks in service, and damaged copies). Several of the larger American subscription agents (such as EBSCO) have fully automated serials systems that libraries use to handle their serials management programs, including online claiming. For libraries with manual claiming systems, most vendors offer two forms of claims: one by which the library notifies the vendor, which in turn contacts the supplier; and one by which the vendor supplies forms for the library to use to contact the publisher. Assistance in claiming has become more important in the past ten to fifteen years as more and more popular-market publishers use fulfillment centers. These centers serve as a publisher's jobber; that is, a center handles a number of different publishers' titles by receiving, entering subscriptions, and sending copies to subscribers. (For such centers, the mailing label is the key to solving problems; until recently, few libraries worried about serials' mailing labels.) Often the subscription vendor is more effective in resolving a problem with a fulfillment center than is a single library.

Management information is another service serials vendors offer. Their information regarding price changes can be most useful in preparing budget requests. Other types of management information that may be available (at an extra cost) are reports that sort the subscription list by subject or classification category, accompanied by the total amount spent for each group or (if there are several groups) a record of how many titles and how much money were charged to each group.

A good place to learn about the variety of services available and about who offers which services is at the national meetings of various library associations. For example, representatives of most national serials vendors, as well as a number of foreign vendors, attend the ALA annual conventions and North American Serials Interest Group (NASIG) conferences. They will supply more than enough promotional material to fill a suitcase. Collect the information (including a formal request to quote), make comparisons, review the vendor's website, and talk with other librarians about their experiences with various vendors; this is the best way to go about selecting a vendor for one's library.

Before leaving this section, there are a few points we need to raise about vendors and acquisitions of e-serials. They are related to the phrase "long-term." As is true of the book-publishing industry, there are issues of shifting relationships/ownership among vendors (publishers, vendors, and aggregators alike). Often it makes no real difference who owns whom or who has a special relationship, but occasionally it does, as when an aggregator has a special relationship with a publisher. An example is *EBSCOhost*'s exclusive license with Harvard for access to the e-version of the *Harvard Business Review*, a title of interest to a wide variety of libraries and which was in several aggregator databases prior to the exclusive agreement.

Related to ownership is the question of financial viability of the vendor/aggregator/publisher. In 2002/2003, a number of libraries as well as publishers learned of the demise of Faxon/RoweCom, a firm that was a major serials vendor.[19] While this was an unusual event, it does happen from time to time and can be costly and disruptive when it does. In this case, libraries had paid for subscriptions, but the publishers had not received any payment. With the firm declaring bankruptcy, there were major concerns about how the costs would be handled—there were hundreds of thousands of dollars involved for some libraries.

Perhaps the most frustrating "long-term" issue with e-packages occurs when what you thought you paid for is not necessarily what you get—at least for the full term of the agreement. One problem is a title suddenly being withdrawn from a package, usually not by the aggregator's choice but rather the publisher's (the *Harvard Business Review* is an example). Two other examples are Chemical Abstract Services' (CAS) decision to remove its products from DIALOG and *EBSCOhost* and Sage's (a scholarly journal publisher) decision to pull its publications out of *EBSCOhost* and *ProQuest* and to start a joint project with CAS.[20]

Another problem, which is probably the most common, is the announcement that title X will now have a six-/nine-month "embargo" on the e-edition. The embargo means that a certain amount of time must pass between the release of the print edition and when an e-version will become available.

Administration/Handling of Serials

Serials represent a major percentage of the collection development funds for most types of libraries. Accountability is an important issue for those handling funds, and part of accountability is being certain one gets what one has paid for. Traditionally, assuring one has gotten what one paid for is higher for serials than for monographs on a title-by-title basis. The reason for this is the ongoing nature of the serials commitment and the fact that serials arrive in parts.

When ordering and receiving a monograph, the library incurs a one-time cost. Serials, in most libraries, have ongoing receiving and renewal costs, in addition to the cost of placing the initial order. Claiming missing issues of print titles is a normal part of maintaining a serials operation. A staff member records each issue when it arrives in the library. When the person notes that an issue is missing or that a number has been skipped, the library contacts the publisher or agent to attempt to secure the missing material. (This is called *placing a claim*.) Acting promptly on claims can be important, because serials publishers print only slightly more copies than the number of subscribers. Serials publishers know that a certain percentage of issues sent will go astray in the mail, and they print extra copies to cover the expected claims. However, at times the number of claims is greater than the number of available copies. When that happens, a number of unlucky libraries receive out-of-print notices. The closer the claim is made to the publication date, the greater the chances are of receiving the missing issue. (The consequences of small print runs appear again when it is time to bind the volume, and the library discovers that one of the issues is missing. Locating a copy can be time-consuming, if not impossible.) Daily serials check-in is assumed to be a must to avoid missing issues. Automated serials systems help speed routine serials work, including providing automatic claiming, but in a library with a large serials list, one or more full-time staff may work exclusively on processing serials. Clearly, each new serial adds to the workload on an ongoing basis.

In the case of e-serials, as we mentioned in the section on selection, someone must assure that the technical issues have been addressed before the service is implemented. If the access is Web-based and domain in nature, providing IP ranges is fairly straightforward. However, password verification is still a requirement of some systems, and libraries must decide who will have access to these passwords. Will users log on individually, or will certain users (such as faculty members) be given the password to use as needed? There must be testing to determine compatibility with other services (e.g., changes in hardware or software configurations). Libraries must also consider what, if anything, will appear in the library's OPAC about the product. If a package of, say, 1,000 full-text journals is purchased, will the library add a note to the holdings statements for titles the library also has in a print format? What about entries for the "new" titles, even those that may not be important to the library's user base? Will the OPAC reflect just title, electronic address only, or both? Will there be a "hot link" in the OPAC or on the library website? If images are included in the package, does the library need "helper" applications (such as Adobe's *Acrobat Reader*) installed on its public machines?

Additionally, every library using electronic materials needs one person or office that handles and maintains a file of license agreements. Someone must review the agreement and notify staff of any new requirements.

Public service staff will need time for familiarization and training in using the new product. Vendor support telephone numbers and/or Internet addresses should be available to the appropriate staff. End users may also need assistance, especially if they want to print, e-mail, or download an article from the product for the first or second time. If the journals are accessible from off-site, whether through a proxy server or other means, what support exists in the library and at the institution for off-site patrons who have trouble using the resource? A good article outlining all the steps and issues in implementing a new e-serial is Cindy Stewart Kaag's "Collection Development for Online Serials."[21]

In 1998, Janet Hughes and Catherine Lee published an interesting article[22] that can serve as a case study of the process of selecting, acquiring, and implementing a full-text journal package. Part of what makes this article interesting is that it addresses issues related to multiple service points. The authors described the process used at Pennsylvania State University and its statewide twenty-three-campus system. They concluded by stating, "Overall, although the experience of implementing the first networked full-text databases at Penn State was a positive one, its success depended upon careful planning and dedicated inter-departmental and campus cooperation. These qualities will be needed to make future forays into full-text equally successful."[23]

Managing e-serials has become a complex activity for both libraries and vendors alike. When one adds in consortial packages, which raise questions of who gets in touch with whom when there is a problem, the complexity becomes even greater. From the library perspective, e-serials generally call for staff with higher-level skills or training than called for with print titles.

One of the activities that require a different set of skills is working with the publisher/vendor to enable users to gain access to the material and that the access functions properly. This can be easy or very difficult depending upon local circumstances. Deciding how to handle "denial of access" takes time. Was the problem in the subscription, the local network, the Internet, the suppliers or maintaining the links?

Given the complexities and costs involved, libraries are outsourcing some of their e-serials administration. There are several companies at the time we prepared this text that provide outsourcing possibilities. Serials

Solutions provides a system to track and report full-text journals in aggregator databases as well as independent e-serials, if the library supplies subscription information. They offer other services such as an alphabetical list of serials that can be loaded on a local server or that can be hosted by the company and "overlap analysis," which will identify which resources appear in multiple databases. TDNET (which acquired the services of Journal WebCite) also offers hosted and local server options for the database. TDNET also provides usage statistics and offers an option for table of contents linkage to a document delivery service.

In this section, we used the terms "traditionally" and "normally" several times as modifiers for serials administrative activities. While it is true that most libraries undertake the activities described, there are a few that are making significant changes due to the costs associated with the operation. One growing trend is to stop binding all but the most heavily used titles. Another change is that some libraries, such as the University of Nevada–Reno, have basically done away with print serials check-in.[24] It seems likely that more and more libraries will take hard looks at the costs and benefits of some of the administrative activities for both print and e-serials. An excellent study of such costs is "Library Periodical Expenses: Comparison of Non-Subscription Costs of Print and Electronic Formats on a Life-Cycle Basis."[25]

Up until this point, our discussion of print and electronic serials has focused upon some of the more standard entries: scholarly journals, magazines, newspapers, and the like. There is a type of literature that does not receive much discussion, the so-called grey literature. In the past, some research and special libraries made an effort to collect this type of material. Today, with electronic "publishing" on the Internet a fact of life, grey literature takes on a new meaning. Grey literature was, and is, primarily of scholarly interest, particularly in the sciences, and tends to be the output of the "invisible college." A widely accepted definition of grey literature has yet to be formulated. *Harrod's Librarians' Glossary* defines these items as "semipublished material, for example reports, internal documents, theses, etc. not formally published or available commercially, and consequently difficult to trace bibliographically."[26] Julia Gelfand stated, "The definition of grey literature has changed rather drastically since the First International Conference, held in Amsterdam, four years ago [1993]."[27] One of the reasons for the changing nature of the concept of grey literature is electronic publishing.

To some degree, what we now call the Internet was developed so that scientists and scholars could more quickly share results (grey literature) and work together from different physical locations (the invisible college). Today, technology and the Internet are creating new types of grey literature, not just online preprint services and technical report access. Perhaps the most striking change is the ability to describe phenomena in other than textual terms, via online modeling, movement, sound, and true interactive collaborative work. Julia Gelfand suggested,

> Learning about this new grey literature is in itself a non-traditional role for librarians and scholars. . . . Training and bibliographic familiarity in this age is, indeed, quite different, because one does not follow a curriculum or set of readers or textbooks, but instead studies by doing, engaging in online time, discovering what the digital literati in different fields contribute as resources for good, appropriate, critical, sought after information. Usually, a strong needs assessment for the information, coupled

with this new facility in making it readily available without enhanced packaging, encourages its use.[28]

Is grey literature a serial? As it tends to be ongoing in nature, one can consider it at least a semiserial. To what degree the library tries to provide access to such material is very much a matter of local need and close collaboration between the library and its users.

Preserving the Investment

By their nature, print serials arrive in successive issues, normally as paperbacks. If the library maintains serials for long periods of time, or the titles receive relatively heavy use, the library usually repackages the serial for more convenient handling. One method is to store the loose issues in a cardboard or metal container (sometimes referred to as a Princeton File) that keeps a limited number of issues together in a vertical position. This makes it easier to shelve the loose issues alongside bound materials. The container must have room on its outfacing side to record the title and issue or volume number of the items in the box. The most common long-term storage treatment is binding. A third alternative, microformat storage, represents an additional cost. Whatever choice is made, there is an ongoing cost to package each serial year after year.

Eventually, finding storage space for collections becomes a problem for all libraries and information centers. Storing long runs of serials can consume large quantities of limited shelf space. Using microforms as the long-term storage format for long runs of low-use serials will help with the space problem for a time. However, microforms also present their own challenges. Users usually resist and complain about using microforms, so there is a public relations issue to address when shifting to microforms. Microforms also mean acquiring equipment: microform readers at a minimum, with reader-printers being a common solution and with new digital film scanners that even make it possible for patrons to burn images to CD being the latest technological enhancement. Libraries usually have at least two types of microform readers, film and fiche. Most machines have several lenses to accommodate various reduction ratios. The library must maintain the equipment and provide users with assistance as needed, especially when it is necessary to change lenses. As the size of the microform collection increases, more equipment will be needed to meet user demands. Finally, microform storage cabinets are heavy when empty and very heavy when full. Libraries may face problems in locating a growing collection of such cabinets if the floor cannot sustain their combined weight. Clearly, microform brings with it new costs and concerns.

Digitization of journal content appears to be an attractive alternative to microfilming backfiles of journals. One project devoted to journal digitization is PubMed Central, in which NLM, in collaboration with the Wellcome Trust and the U.K. Joint Information Systems Committee (JISC), aims to provide free access to a number of historic medical journals.[29]

Another solution for storage is to move low-use items to a less accessible and less costly facility. Yet another solution is to deselect some titles. As space becomes scarce, decisions about what to keep and for how long become more and more difficult, although the presence of archive e-titles may ease these problems. Given the current nature of most serials, older holdings are prime candidates for remote storage. After making the first, relatively easy decisions about which titles to store, weeding decisions become increasingly complex, take more time, and can lead to conflicts between staff and users. This is discussed in more detail in chapter 13.

Going with a document delivery option saves space, and the cost of requested materials may never equal the cost of the microforms. Gale Etschmaier and Marifran Bustion discussed the pros and cons of such services in an article about the experience of Gelman Library at George Washington University in implementing a document delivery service. The situation they described was a major journal cancelation project in which the library canceled 1,031 journal titles in 1993–1994. One of their interesting findings was that, as of early 1997, only 35 of those titles (roughly 3 percent) had been the subject of any requests for articles.[30] They concluded by stating, "The data gathered through monitoring direct requests through document delivery and interlibrary loan services can be monitored and analyzed as an aid to collection development."[31]

Print is just one of several serials preservation issues. Perhaps a greater long-term question has to do with access to e-serials over time. Digital archiving of e-resources is a major concern for libraries, at least those serving academic institutions. Since a library generally only leases access, and the vendor/publisher owns the material, who *is* responsible for preserving the information? At present there is no definitive answer to that question, but projects such as JSTOR and LOCKSS are steps in the right direction toward comprehensive preservation of e-serials.

Deselection

If there is a single theme to this chapter beyond serials, it is "cost." Serials, whether in print or electronic format, are expensive to acquire and maintain. Subscription prices seem to escalate far beyond almost any other commodity. With most library budgets remaining more or less static, it is the exceptional library that has not had to face the challenge of canceling magazine and journal subscriptions, standing orders, and other serials at least once or twice in the past five years. Although deselection is covered more extensively in chapter 13, some comments are appropriate here.

One question is, Should one cancel print subscriptions when an e-version is available in the library? The answer is, as is often the case, It all depends on the circumstances. With some aggregator packages print cancellations are very limited or nonexistent. Canceling too many may create a greater cost than the "savings" from the canceled titles. Canceling titles that have an e-embargo on them probably will create a great many public relations problems for the public service staff. Keep in mind just what "full text" means for the title under consideration—even the lack of color can be a problem when it comes to color tables, charts, or illustrations. Other questions to ponder are, What is the e-format (HTML, PDF, etc.), and how does the typical user use the material? Although HTML versions of articles do not require helper applications such as Adobe *Acrobat*, a title offered in a format other than PDF (representing the journal as laid out in print) may create citation problems for the users. These are but a few of the "circumstances" that need to be thought through prior to canceling a print title because an e-version is available.

Usage studies can be of some help in a cancellation project if the data are sound. The problem is getting the sound data for make good judgments. Lacking circulation data, in most cases, means that some type of in-house usage data must be collected, and frequent users are prone to returning issues to the shelf rather than leaving for the staff to reshelve. That type of activity can cause some decision to be made that ought not happen.

Canceling titles is a frustrating and unpleasant experience for staff, users, and suppliers. Chapter 13 provides some guidance for how to make the process somewhat less painful.

Issues and Concerns

Several major issues face libraries today in regard to their serials collections. Cost is perhaps the major concern (cost of subscriptions, processing, storing, changing value of currencies, and tight budgets). Another issue is the delivery of serials information to users without subscribing to the title by using document delivery or, as some librarians phrase it, "just-in-time rather than just-in-case." Related to document delivery are questions about copyright and traditional ILL services; on a percentage basis, ILL is more often used for serials than monographs.

Continued growth in the number of serials and their spiraling costs are two issues of grave concern, especially for scholarly journals. Areas of knowledge are constantly being divided into smaller and smaller segments; at the same time, these smaller audiences want more information about the narrower topic.

Costs of producing a special-interest journal will rise, no matter how many or how few people are interested in reading about the subject. When a journal reaches a certain price level, the number of individual subscribers drops quickly. More often than not, any price increase to individual subscribers only makes the problem worse. Increasingly, scholarly journal publishers employ a dual pricing system, one price for individuals and another, higher price (often double or triple the individual rate) for institutions (read: libraries). The publishers' premise is that an institutional subscription serves the needs of many readers, which justifies the higher price. An interesting ethical question for librarians in general and collection development personnel in particular is: Is it ethical for a library to regularly accept an individual's gift of a journal that has a high dual-rate subscription? (Our view is that no, the library should not do that. If not for ethical reasons, there are practical concerns about the regularity with which the person delivers the issues, as well as with securing missing issues.)

There are two types of journal price studies with which collection development staff should become familiar: macro pricing and micro pricing. Macro information deals with subscription prices, rates of increase, and projections of coming price increases. One can obtain this type of data about the library's subscription list from the library's serials vendor. Information about overall price changes appears in several sources for U.S. serials, including *Library Journal* and *American Libraries*. One problem for many libraries is that data about projected price changes appear at a time when they are of little help in preparing the budget request for the next fiscal year. The data may be useful, but they are about a year behind the budget. That is, one uses 2005 projections for preparing the 2006–2007 budget requests. (See chapter 12 for more information about budgeting.) What was clear at the time we prepared this edition was that no relief is in sight in terms of price increases. This pattern has been facing libraries for many years. Publishers do not understand why libraries cut their subscription lists, and libraries and users do not understand why the prices must rise by so much more than the consumer price index.

Microstudies examine cost of the information in the journal, number of articles per volume, number of pages, page size, and cost per 1,000 words or characters. Such studies are helpful in the retention and cancellation activities in which more and more libraries must engage on an annual basis. (Finding micro studies takes a little effort; one good article dealing with the subject and presenting some examples is by Barbara Meyers and Janice Fleming.[32]) Not all publishers are pleased to see micro studies published, but such studies do provide useful data for building a cost-effective serials collection. Naturally, one must use these data in conjunction with other information, such as local use patterns.

It should not come as a surprise that e-serials do not save either the producer or the library money. Perhaps at some point in the past there was a reasonable expectation of such savings. However, by the mid-1990s it was clear to both vendors and libraries that this would not be the case. For example, as Robert Marks noted, the American Chemical Society estimated that its CD-ROM journals cost 25 to 33 percent more to produce than their print versions. The higher cost was attributed to the need to provide and maintain a search engine.[33] In another article, Tom Abate reported the American Institute of Physics' estimate that providing both a print and an electronic copy of a title cost between 10 and 15 percent more than just offering a print version of the same title.[34] Conversations with publishers of electronic-only serials indicate that they see no difference in costs; they claim it costs just as much for an e-only version as it does for print-only. Janet Fischer of MIT Press indicated that the reason producers of e-only serials see costs as equal was not so much a function of production costs as it was an overall loss of revenue—no back-issue sales, no renting of subscriber mailing lists, and, perhaps most importantly, the loss of advertising income.[35]

Librarians and scholars are exploring the concept of "open access" to combat ever-escalating prices of scholarly journals. Open access at its most fundamental level is a system for online availability, free of charge, of peer-reviewed research publications. It is essentially a different model for handling the publication of *scholarly* material where profit and commercial copyright cease to be issues. What the concept would do is shift the cost burden to the research institutions in a more direct and hopefully less costly manner than now exists. Two examples of open access projects are the *Public Library of Science* (<http://www.publiclibraryofscience.org/>) and BioMed Central (<http://www.biomedcentral.com/>). It is something of an open question whether the concept can work outside the science and technology fields, but then STM serials titles are the most expensive, on average, of all the academic disciplines. Institutional repositories, discussed in the next chapter, are a variation on the open access theme.

Cooperation in Serials Work

No library can acquire and keep all the serials that its patrons need or will at some time request. Knowing who has what serials holdings is important to serials librarians and anyone involved in interlibrary loan activities. The CONSER project helps to identify holdings in American and Canadian libraries. It is interesting to note that, despite the longtime concern about serials holdings, it was not until early 1986 that a national standard for serials holding statements was adopted in the United States (ANSI Z39.44). The standard provides for the same data areas, data elements, and punctuation in summary holding statements in both manual and automated systems.

Although the Center for Research Libraries (CRL) is much more than a cooperative serials program, CRL serials holdings have been effective in holding down the amount of duplication of low-use serials titles in American and Canadian research libraries. Bibliographic utilities such as OCLC and RLIN, whose databases include serials holdings, provide a type of union list service that H. W. Wilson's *Union List of Serials* provided so well in the past. To some extent, even vendor-based systems offer a form of union listing. Though it is possible to use such union lists and shared holdings to cover some low-use serials requirements, the librarian must be certain to comply with copyright regulations before deciding not to buy.

Summary

Serials are a vital part of any information collection. They are complex and costly, regardless of their format, with cost likely to remain the primary concern for some time. For the past fifteen years, serials prices have had double-digit rate increases, higher than anything else a library adds to its collection. Thus, serials continually take a larger and larger share of the materials budget, or the library must begin to cancel titles and provide access to the information in some other manner. Technology is changing the way libraries handle serials and is making it possible to provide access to more titles. However, technology will not solve the economic concerns of either the publishers and producers or the consumers. How the two groups will solve the problem is impossible to predict. It is likely that the serials price problem will be present for some time.

Notes

1.   Thomas Nisonger, *Management of Serials in Libraries* (Englewood, CO: Libraries Unlimited, 1998).

2.   Heartsill Young, ed., *ALA Glossary of Library and Information Science* (Chicago: American Library Association, 1983).

3.   *Webster's Third New International Dictionary* (Springfield, MA: G & C Merriam, 1976).

4.   Thomas Nisonger, "Electronic Journal Collection Development Issues," *Collection Building* 16, no. 2 (1997): 58.

5.   Fritz Machlup et al., *Information Through the Printed Word* (New York: Praeger Publishers, 1978).

6.   Louis Houle and Chris Beckett, "Just in Time vs. Just in Case: Examining the Benefits of Subsidized Unmediated Ordering (SUMO) vs. Subscriptions," *Serials Librarian* 44, nos. 3/4 (2003): 265–69.

7.   Carol Foggin, "Title Changes: Another View," *Serials Librarian* 23, nos. 1/2 (1992): 71–83.

8.   Nancy Nelson, "Serials Title Changes: What's in a Name?" *Computers in Libraries* 13 (February 1993): 4.

9.   Mary Jean Pavelsek, "Guidelines for Evaluating E-Journal Providers," *Advances in Librarianship* 22 (1998): 39–58.

10.   Stefanie Wittenbach, "Everything You Always Wanted to Know About Electronic Journals But Were Afraid to Ask," *Serials Librarian* 44, nos. 1/2 (2003): 11–24.

11.   Judy Luther, "Trumping Google: Metsearching's Promise," *Library Journal* 128 (October 2003): 36–39.

12.   Robert Sivers, "Partitioned Bradford Ranking and the Serials Problem in Academic Libraries," *Collection Building* 8, no. 2 (1986): 12–19.

13.   Dawn Bick and Reeta Sinha, "Maintaining a High-Quality, Cost-Effective Journal Collection," *College & Research Libraries News* 51 (September 1991): 485–90.

14.   Maria A. Janowska, "Printed versus Electronic: Policy Issues in the Case of Environmental Journals," *Serials Review* 20 (Fall 1994): 17–22.

15.   Robert Bachand and Pamela Sawallis, "Accuracy in the Identification of Scholarly and Peer Reviewed Journals," *Serials Librarian* 45, no. 2 (2003): 29–59.

16.   Cheryl LaGuardia, Bill Katz, and Linda Sternberg Katz, *Magazines for Libraries*, 12th ed. (New York: R. R. Bowker, 2003).

17.   N. Bernard Basch and Judy McQueen, *Buying Serials* (New York: Neal-Schuman, 1990).

18.   Nancy Knight and Susan Hillson, "Electronic Pub Pricing in the Web Era," *Information Today* 15 (September 1998): 39–40.

19.   "RoweCom Sale Set for $7 Mil. Dependent on Deal Support," *Library Hotline* 32 (April 14, 2003): 2, 4.

20.   Carol Tenopir, Gayle Baker, and William Robinson, "The Art of Conjuring E-Content," *Library Journal* 128 (May 15, 2003): 38.

21.   Cindy Stewart Kaag, "Collection Development for Online Serials: Who Needs to Do What, and Why, and When," *Serials Librarian* 33, nos. 1/2 (1998): 107–22.

22.   Janet Hughes and Catherine Lee, "Giving Patrons What They Want: The Promise, the Process, and the Pitfalls of Providing Full-Text Access to Journals," *Collection Building* 17, no. 4 (1998): 148–53.

23.   Ibid., 153.

24.   Rick Anderson and Steven Zink, "Implementing the Unthinkable: The Demise of Periodical Check-in at the University of Nevada-Reno," *Library Collections, Acquisitions & Technical Services* 27, no. 1 (Spring 2003): 61–71.

25.   Roger Schonfeld, Donald King, Ann Okerson, and Eileen Fenton, "Library Periodical Expenses: Comparison of Non-Subscription Costs of Print and Electronic Formats on a Life-Cycle Basis," *D-Lib Magazine* 10 (January 2004): 1–16.

26.   R. Prytherch, comp., *Harrod's Librarians' Glossary* (Aldershot, UK: Gower, 1995), 285.

27.   Julia Gelfand, "Teaching and Exposing Grey Literature," *Collection Building* 17, no. 4 (1998): 159.

28.   Ibid., 160–61.

29.   National Library of Medicine. "International Agreement to Expand PubMed Central," <http://www.nlm.nih.gov/news/press_releases/intlpubmed04.html>.

30.   Gale Etschmaier and Marifran Bustion, "Document Delivery and Collection Development: An Evolving Relationship," *Serials Librarian* 31, no. 3 (1997): 24.

31.   Ibid., 26.

32.   Barbara Meyers and Janice Fleming, "Price Analysis and the Serial Situation: Trying to Solve an Age-Old Problem," *Journal of Academic Librarianship* 17 (May 1991): 86–92.

33.   Robert Marks, "The Economic Challenges of Publishing Electronic Journals," *Serials Review* 21 (Spring 1995): 85–88.

34.   Tom Abate, "Publishing Scientific Journals Online," *Bioscience* 47 (March 1997): 175–79.

35.   Janet Fischer, "True Costs of an Electronic Journal," *Serials Review* 21 (Spring 1995): 88–90.

Selected Websites
and Discussion Lists*

(See also resources on the DLC5 website: <http://www.lu.com/dlc5>)

Back Issues and Exchange Services
    <http://www.uvm.edu/~bmaclenn/backexch.html>
    A source of missing issues and exchange of serials and other materials. Maintained by Birdie MacLennan; her main site (<http://www.uvm.edu/~bmaclenn/>) is "Serials in Cyberspace," a collection of resources and services of use to serials librarians.

CONSER Program Home Page
    <http://lcweb.loc.gov/acq/conser/>
    The Library of Congress' website for information about the Cooperative Online Serials Program (CONSER).

The Daily Press
    <http://www.sispain.org/english/media/press.html>
    A website in English providing information about print and electronic newspapers in Spain.

Ejournal Site Guide
    <http://www.library.ubc.ca/ejour>
    Joseph Jones' website with annotated links to sites for e-journals.

Electronic Journal Miner
    <http://ejournal.coalliance.org>
    The Colorado Alliance of Research Libraries site that provides information on almost 3,000 e-journals.

E-zine list: John Labovitz's e-zine-list
    <http://www.e-zine-list.com>
    John Labovitz's site for electronic 'zines available via the Web, FTP, or otherwise electronically.

Gold Rush
    <http://grweb.coalliance.org>
    A set of resources to manage e-serials originally established for members of the Colorado Alliance of Research Libraries (CARL), made available to libraries outside the consortium.

ICOLC Statement on Electronic Information
    <http://www.library.yale.edu/consortia/statement.html>
    Site for information on the International Coalition of Library Consortia (ICOLC), which deals with consortial purchases of electronic resources.

JAKE: Jointly Administered Knowledge Environment
    <http://jake.openly.com>
    Sponsored by the Cushing/Whitley medical library at Yale University, a service for searching, managing, and linking to e-serials.

The Journal of Electronic Publishing
    <http://www.press.umich.edu/jep/>

A good source of information about e-publishing, from the University of Michigan Press.

JSTOR—The Scholarly Journal Archive
    <http://www.jstor.org>
    Journal Storage (JSTOR)'s home page.

Liblicense: Licensing Digital Information
    <http://www.library.yale.edu/~llicense/>
    Archive for LIBLICENSE-L discussion list.

Library Oriented Lists and Electronic Serials
    <http://www.aladin.wrlc.org/gsdl/cgi-bin/library?p=about&c=liblists>
    Sponsored by the Washington Regional Library Consortium (WRLC).

LOCKSS: Lots of Copies Keeps Stuff Safe
    <http://lockss.stanford.edu>
    LOCKSS project home page, including links to sample vendor agreements and a list of current participants and titles.

NewJour
    <http://gort.ucsd.edu/newjour/>
    List of archived networked e-journals.

North American Serials Interest Group
    <http://www.nasig.org>
    Website of NASIG, an important group in serial management programming and information.

Project MUSE
    <http://muse.jhu.edu>
    Created by Johns Hopkins University, Project MUSE provides the full text of approximately 250 journals in the arts and humanities from forty scholarly publishers.

PubList.Com
    <http://www.PubList.com>
    An Internet directory of publications.

PubMed Central
    <http://www.pubmedcentral.gov/>
    A free digital archive of biomedical and life sciences journal literature, sponsored by the National Library of Medicine (NLM). Of particular note is the page devoted to "Digitizing Back Issues of Journals," available at: <http://www.pubmedcentral.gov/about/scanning.html>.

Scholarly Electronic Publishing Bibliography
    <http://info.lib.uh.edu/sepb/sepb.html>
    References on electronic publishing.

Scholarly Journals Distributed Via the World-Wide Web
    <http://info.lib.uh.edu/wj/webjour.html>
    From the University of Houston Libraries; lists more than 120 free Web-based academic journals.

Serials in Libraries Discussion Forum (SERIALST)
    LISTSERV@list.uvm.edu.
    To subscribe, send the following message: SUBSCRIBE SERIALST Your-First-Name Your-Last-Name. For detailed information regarding SERIALST, visit <http://www.uvm.edu/~bmaclenn/serialst.html>.

UK Serials Group Homepage (UKSG)
    <http://www.uksg.org>
    An excellent source of information about UK and European serials vendors and services.

United States Book Exchange
<http://www.usbe.com/>
A mainstay for serials librarians as a source of missing journal issues and exchange of serials.

University of Georgia Electronic Journal Locator
<http://www.libs.uga.edu/ejournals/menu.html>

*These sites were accessed May 5, 2005.

Further Reading

Albitz, R. "Pricing Policies for Electronic Resources." *The Acquisitions Librarian* 15, no. 30 (2003): 3–13.

Allen, R., and L. Y. Hsiung. "Web-Based Tracking Systems for Electronic Resources Management." *Serials Librarian* 44, nos. 3/4 (2003): 293–97.

Antelman, K. "Do Open Access Articles Have a Greater Research Impact?" *College & Research Libraries* 65, no. 5 (September 2004): 372–82.

Bartel, J. *From A to Zine: Building a Winning Zine Collection in Your Library*. Chicago: American Library Association, 2004.

Bevis, M., and J. B. Graham. "The Evolution of an Integrated Electronic Journals Collection." *Journal of Academic Librarianship* 29, no. 2 (March 2003): 115–19.

Black, S. "Scholarly Journals Should Be Treated as a Public Good." *Serials Librarian* 44, nos. 1/2 (2003): 53–63.

———. "Using Citation Analysis to Pursue a Core Collection of Journals for Communication Disorders." *Library Resources and Technical Services* 45 (January 2001): 3–9.

Bluh, P., ed. *Managing Electronic Serials*. ALCTS Papers on Library Technical Services & Collections, no. 9. Chicago: ALA, 2001.

Brogan, M. *A Survey of Digital Library Aggregation Services*. Washington, DC: Digital Library Federation and Council on Library and Information Resources, 2003.

Brooks, S. "Academic Journal Embargoes and Full Text Databases." *Library Quarterly* 73, no. 3 (July 2003): 243–61.

Canepi, K. "Microfilm Serial Backfiles: Are They Still Cost Effective?" *Serials Review* 29, no. 4 (Winter 2003): 282–86.

Carnevale, D. "Libraries With Tight Budgets Renew Complaints About Elsevier's Online Pricing." *Chronicle of Higher Education* 50, no. 17 (December 19, 2003): A33.

Case, M. M. "Reassessment of Aggregate Subscriptions to Electronic Journals: Trends and Questions." *Vantage Point*. Birmingham, AL: EBSCO, 2003.

Clouten, K., and M. Gane. "New Directions in Serials Management." *Collection Management* 27, no. 1 (2002): 27–39.

Duranceau, E. F. "Pricing of Digital Resources: An Interview with Simon Tanner." *Serials Review* 29, no. 2 (2003): 121–26.

Enssle, H. R., and M. L. Wilde. "So You Have to Cancel Journals? Statistics That Help." *Library Collections, Acquisitions, and Technical Services* 26, no. 3 (Autumn 2002): 259–81.

Fowler, D., ed. *E-Serials Collection Management: Transitions, Trends and Technicalities*. New York: Haworth Information Press, 2004.

Goodman, D. "The Criteria for Open Access." *Serials Review* 30, no. 4 (2004): 258–70.

Greiner, T. "The Case of the Disappearing Article." *Library Journal* 129, no. 7 (April 15, 2004): 58–59.

Guterman, L. "The Promise and Peril of Open Access." *Chronicle of Higher Education* 50, no. 21 (January 30, 2004): A10–14.

Gyeszly, S. "Electronic or Paper Journals? Budgetary, Collection Development, and User Satisfaction Questions." *Collection Building* 20, no. 1 (2001): 5–10.

Hahn, K., and L. Faulkner. "Evaluative Usage-Based Metrics for the Selection of E-Journals." *College & Research Libraries* 63 (May 2002): 215–27.

Hoover, L. "Developing an E-Journal Collection." *Serials Librarian* 45, no. 2 (2003): 129–37.

Jaguszewski, J. M., and L. K. Probst. "The Impact of Electronic Resources on Serial Cancellations and Remote Storage Decisions in Academic Research Libraries." *Library Trends* 48, no. 4 (Spring 2000): 799–820.

Jewell, T. R. *Selection and Presentation of Commercially Available Electronic Resources: Issues and Practices*. Washington, DC: Council on Library and Information Resources, 2001 <http://www.clir.org/pubs/abstract/pub99abst.html>.

Johnson, K. G. "The Dog Ate My Issue and Other Reasons for Gaps in the Periodical Volume." *Serials Review* 30, no. 3 (2004): 214–19.

Johnson, K., and M. Manoff. "Report of the Death of the Catalog Is Greatly Exaggerated: The E-Journal Access Journey at the University of Tennessee." *Serials Librarian* 44, nos. 3/4 (2003): 285–92.

Kara, B., and C. Stamison. "Keeping the Connection: Maintaining E-Journal Subscriptions." *Serials Librarian* 46, nos. 3/4 (2004): 309–13.

King, D., P. B. Boyce, C. H. Montgomery, and C. Tenopir. "Library Economic Metrics: Examples of the Comparison of Electronic and Print Journal Collections and Collection Services." *Library Trends* 51 (Winter 2003): 376–400.

Kovacs, D. *Building Electronic Library Collections*. New York: Neal-Schuman, 2000.

Krumenaker, L. "Tribunes and Tribulation: The Top 100 Newspaper Archives (Or Lack Thereof)." *Searcher* 11, no. 7 (July/August 2003): 28–35.

Mabe, M. A. "Revolution or Evolution: Digital Myths and Journal Futures: Sifting Fact from Fiction." In *Charleston Conference Proceedings 2001*, edited by K. Strauch, 37–50. Westport, CT: Libraries Unlimited, 2003.

Magazines in Special Media. Washington, DC: Library of Congress, National Library Service for the Blind and Physically Handicapped, 2003.

McBride, R. C., and K. Behm. "A Journal Usage Study in an Academic Library: Evaluation of Selected Criteria." *Serials Librarian* 45, no. 3 (2003): 23–37.

McCracken, P. "Management of Electronic Serials, Outsourcing and Bringing New Products to the Marketplace." *Serials Librarian* 44, nos. 1/2 (2003): 115–23.

Mobley, E. R. "Serial Challenges and Solutions: The View from the Director's Chair." *Serials Librarian* 44, nos. 1/2 (2003): 37–44.

Nisonger, T., ed. "Collection Development in an Electronic Environment." *Library Trends* 48 (Spring 2000): 639–44.

Oberg, S. "Which Route Do I Take? A Viewpoint on Locally Developed versus Commercially Available Journal Management Solutions." *Serials Review* 30, no. 2 (2004): 122–26.

———. "Gold Rush: An Electronic Journal Management and Linking Project." *Serials Review* 29, no. 3 (2003): 230–32.

Peterson, J. W. "Stretch Your Budget! How to Select Web-Based Subscription Resources." *Computers in Libraries* 23, no. 2 (February 2003): 20–24.

Reich, V. "LOCKSS: Lots of Copies Keeps Stuff Safe: Creating a Permanent Web Publishing and Access System." In *Charleston Conference Proceedings 2001*, edited by K. Strauch, 83–87. Westport, CT: Libraries Unlimited, 2003.

Rhind-Tutt, S. "Pricing Models for Electronic Products—As Tangled As Ever?" In *Charleston Conference Proceedings 2002*, edited by R. Bazirjian and V. Speck, 79–85. Westport, CT: Libraries Unlimited, 2003.

Rupp-Serrano, K., S. Robbins, and D. Cain. "Canceling Print Serials in Favor of Electronic: Criteria for Decision Making." *Library Collections, Acquisitions, & Technical Services* 26 (2002): 369–78.

Schonfeld, R. C. *JSTOR: A History*. Princeton, NJ: Princeton University Press, 2003.

Schonfeld, R. C., D. W. King, A. Okerson, and E. G. Fenton. *The Nonsubscription Side of Periodicals: Changes in Library Operations and Costs between Print and Electronic Formats*. Washington, DC: Council on Library and Information Resources, 2004, <http://www.clir.org/pubs/abstract/pub127abst.html>.

Seeds, R. S. "Impact of a Digital Journal (JSTOR) on Print Collection Use." *Collection Building* 21, no. 3 (2002): 120–22.

Szczyrbak, G., and L. Pierce. "E-Journal Subscription Management Systems and Beyond." *Serials Librarian* 44, nos. 3/4 (2003): 157–62.

Tenopir, C. "Electronic Journal Use: A Glimpse into the Future with Information from the Past and Present." In *Charleston Conference Proceedings 2002*, edited by R. Bazirjian and V. Speck, 36–41. Westport, CT: Libraries Unlimited, 2003.

Tenopir, C., with B. Hitchcock and A. Pillow. *Use and Users of Electronic Library Resources: An Overview and Analysis of Recent Research Studies*. Washington, DC: Council on Library and Information Resources, 2004, <http://www.clir.org/pubs/abstract/pub120abst.html>.

Tucker, J., and M. S. Hoyle. "Understanding Embargoes and Utilizing Other Services." *Serials Librarian* 45, no. 3 (2003): 115–17.

Turner, R. "E-Journal Administration—Fragmentation or Integration?" *Serials Librarian* 45, no. 1 (2003): 75–84.

Van Orsdel, L., and K. Born. "Closing in on Open Access." *Library Journal* 129, no. 7 (April 15, 2004): 45–50.

Walker, J. "OpenURL and SFX Linking." *Serials Librarian* 45, no. 3 (2003): 87–100.

Weiss, A. K., and J. P. Abbott. "Print Journal: Off Site? Out of Site? Out of Mind?" *Serials Librarian* 44, nos. 3/4 (2003): 271–78.

Wilson, P. "Managing Full-Text Electronic Serials." *Public Libraries* 42 (July/August 2003): 228–29.

Zhang, X. "Combining Traditional Journal Check-In and Claiming Activities with Electronic Journal Initiation and Maintenance Activities." *Library Resources & Technical Services* 47, no. 4 (October 2003): 208–14.

7
Other Electronic Materials

Library collections, no matter the setting, are normally composed of a combination of formats, including those in print (book, serial, or journal) and audiovisual formats. We discussed print materials and e-serials in earlier chapters. In this chapter, we focus our attention on some of the other e-resources that could be appropriate for the collection, including numeric databases and music, and we touch upon the issue of institutional repositories. We also touch on some of the general issues associated with e-resources to the collection. It should be noted that chapter 8 examines government information and also contains substantial information about electronic access. All of the materials covered in these chapters do carry legal concerns for the library, and to avoid duplication as much as possible, we provide a detailed discussion of these concerns in chapter 17.

The opening sentence of the Library of Congress' publication *Collection Development and the Internet* concisely stated the reason for this chapter: "The Internet has the potential to change radically much of our work, whether it be as reference specialists or as recommending officers."[1] Today that statement is more accurately phrased as, "The Internet *has* radically changed. . . ." Libraries are making ever-increasing use of Internet resources in their service programs and as part of their "virtual collections." Certainly, the electronic environment goes well beyond just Internet/Web resources, but those resources are becoming more and more dominant.

A frequently asked question is: Are electronic materials merely another type of storage media, like microforms? They are, indeed, another storage format in one sense, because digitized data does allow compact storage of large quantities of information. However, digital formats also allow data manipulation in ways that are not cost-effective in other formats. Further, the electronic environment allows both free-text and Boolean searching. Downloading information from electronic resources to a user's computer and being able to cut, paste, move, add, and delete as much as desired are now possible. (This is possible either with or without complying with copyright; the new copyright law has special implication for libraries in this regard; see chapter 17.) Such capabilities make electronic information the preferred information format for many users, especially students at all levels.

Electronic formats cause libraries and information centers to concentrate their attention on overall operations and rethink systems and services in a way never before required. To some degree, it may be a question of the survival of our field. Electronic information producers can deliver the product directly to the end user at home or in the office, and increasingly they are doing so. Proper planning, realistic goals, and intelligent reorganization of operations will ensure that libraries play an ever-expanding role in the information transfer process in the electronic age.

Electronic delivery of information requires delivery methods, equipment, software, substantial user support, and time to assess the various services and products that producers offer. Few users have the time, energy, inclination, or funds to handle all these activities effectively. Libraries can, and should, undertake these tasks. If we do not, someone else will.

Background and Needs Assessment

The electronic environment creates several challenges for libraries and information centers: print versus electronic; ownership versus access; user need versus institutional need; free versus fee; and librarian as gatekeeper versus user selection. It is not a matter of either/or; rather, it is a matter of determining the proper local mix. Clearly, one cannot make the necessary judgments about these issues without knowing the local users, what information they want and need, how and where they use the information, what type of equipment they have, what network and telecommunication capabilities exist, and what monetary and equipment resources are available to the library or information center.

Print and electronic information sources are both complementary and competitive. Users with an interest in historical information and data certainly will require, in most cases, print collections. The amount of pre-1970s e-resources, while growing, is still not comprehensive. This is changing over time, but at the moment, recent information is in highest demand, and it is not surprising that commercial vendors focus on the highest-demand areas first. (One example of a change in backfile access is JSTOR [<http://www.jstor.org>]; however, as mentioned in chapter 6, this is a library-initiated, rather than commercially run, project.) One obvious advantage of print sources is that they do not malfunction, and one can use them in a variety of locations without having to consider power, network connections, and similar technical issues. However, electronic sources have a clear advantage in terms of locating and manipulating information. They also do not require physical storage space (beyond space requirements for any in-house servers required), which can be a major issue with print collections. In any case, it is imperative to have an understanding of the end users' preferences for print and electronic information.

Traditionally, libraries and information centers depended on an ownership-of-materials model as the primary means of meeting user information needs. Interlibrary loans (ILL) for books and photocopies of journal articles more or less filled any gaps between the local collections and local needs. Interlibrary loan adheres to the ownership-of-materials model in that it requires other libraries to own the loaned material. Some e-resource vendor licenses carry a restriction on the use of their material for ILL purposes, although pressure from libraries, particularly from consortia, are persuading publishers to adopt more realistic and flexible ILL policies.

Electronic materials and methods of information dissemination present the opportunity for libraries and information centers to provide access to more resources than they can realistically expect to acquire and house. Access can be directed to a user's home or workplace, allowing end users to make independent choices about what they want, from what source, and how quickly. Access may be a more cost-effective option for the library or information center. (Cost issues are covered later in this chapter.)

The balancing of individual and institutional needs raises the issue of free versus fee services. There is the long-standing tradition of free library service. Although maintaining this tradition is the goal of many information professionals, it has been some time since all services were free. Charging for services began with charging for photocopying, and the practice has expanded steadily over the years. In the electronic environment, it is easy to associate service costs with individual users, and there are a greater variety of costs (e.g., charges for per document viewing, number of simultaneous users, printing, or copyright/royalties). Because it is easier to associate costs with an individual in the electronic environment than it is in the print environment, it is possible to pass the charges on to the user. To some degree, the new costs are not new; they were merely hidden or too time-consuming to track in the print world. Again, how far one goes in charging fees depends on the local situation and service community.

Libraries supporting educational programs are more likely to absorb the costs for electronic information that directly supports instruction and pass on charges for noninstructional uses. Some institutions have a sliding scale, allowing for a base level of free access and some form of cost sharing as the individual's use increases. Public libraries must consider the economic differences in the community with the goal of assuring that those who cannot afford to pay the fees do not become information-poor. Special libraries, on the other hand, may pass costs to project teams or departments to answer an organization's desire to track actual operating costs of various units; in other situations, the costs are considered overhead and are not assigned to any unit other than the information center.

The roles of the library, computing services, and users in electronic information transfer are a topic of debate at conferences, on discussion lists, and in electronic discussion groups, as well as in the literature and in the institution. Who has primary responsibility? If shared, how is it shared? Who decides what will be available? Who supports and maintains the service(s)? Not one of these questions, like many related ones, has clear answers. We are in the process of developing models based on experience. Efforts to merge the various institutional players have not proven successful. However, it is clear that text, numeric, voice, and image data technologies are becoming integrated, and, at some point, institutions must come to grips with the need to coordinate the various activities.

One aspect of the debate is whether there should be preselection of electronic materials. In preselection, the library or information center plays the role of gatekeeper, rather than letting users choose among all information resources independently. Although the terms are different, the fundamental issue is as old as libraries and collection development. Years ago, a favorite examination question in collection development courses was, "Is collection development selection or censorship?" On one side are those who believe that no one should predetermine what resources best fit the organization's mission and profile. Their position is, let the user find what she or he needs without preselection by someone else. The opposite view is that preselection and guidance are in the best interests of both the users and the organization. As in the past, libraries, information centers, and organizations cannot provide access to everything. Thus, choices are inevitable; someone or some group must function as a gatekeeper or, at the very least, as a cost controller.

Refusing to perform the gatekeeper function is akin to putting a person in the middle of a multimillion-volume storehouse, with only a floor plan keyed to broad classification groupings, and saying to this person, "You are on your own." That will waste not only the individual's time but also the institution's resources. In a sense, this view is a return to the research library philosophy of the 1950s, 1960s, and early 1970s: "Get everything possible, just in case." A gatekeeper who points the way to potentially useful materials, perhaps by adding pointers on the library's website or through a federated search, aids the user in the long run and maximizes the benefit of the institution's funding for information services. When the library or information center provides such assistance, it does not deny the user access to other electronic resources available through other services. The case for some assistance and evaluation is summed up in the following 1994 quote, which still holds true today:

> Still in its infancy—with only a hint of its future richness—networked information is currently anarchic and pretty much "use at your own risk." One writer characterized the Internet as "awash with information, both useful and banal." Data files are incomplete and unverified, there is little or no documentation or support, it is difficult to pin down author responsibility, and there are few evaluative resources.[2]

One advantage of electronic collection building, compared with building print collections, is more effective tracking of categories of who is using the information and what resources she or he used. (Although most online circulation systems allow one to easily retrieve somewhat similar information about circulated items, for in-house use, the best one can do is track the items used, not who used them.) Many of the better commercial electronic products have management report software that allows one to learn how, when, and what classification of users accessed the material, as well as the type of search. One gets more accurate and complete data with less effort in the electronic environment. It is up to librarians to make effective use of the data to provide the right information at the right time at the right cost.

Issues in
Electronic Collection Building

E-resources and their associated technology share two unfortunate characteristics with audiovisual materials—speedy rates of change and lack of stability. The "half-life" of websites was mentioned in chapter 5. William Fisher also addressed this issue in his 2003 article "Now You See It; Now You Don't: The Elusive Nature of Electronic Information."[3] He makes a critical point that "the number of options available makes it more difficult to identify the individual titles in the most appropriate formats we need for our collections. It takes longer to evaluate the choices we make, and with fewer dollars it is more difficult to rectify mistakes or misjudgments."[4]

Although there have been some successful experiments,[5] for the most part, libraries that were quick to move into e-books and especially those that also started a loan program for e-book readers know about e-resource misjudgments. While one does not want to be too far "behind the curve," being an early adopter can be very costly.

One issue that makes processing some e-materials challenging, especially Web/Internet materials, is that they do not usually remain "fixed" in the way print materials do. Anyone with any amount of experience with Web/Internet materials has at least once encountered a message indicating that the URL one bookmarked is no longer operative. Sometimes a new address is provided on a "transition page," but often there is no referring link. Not only are addresses variable, but so is the content of the site. "This document last modified on . . ." is a message found on many websites; another message is "under construction." Both messages make it clear that what you see today may not be what or all you will see tomorrow.

We are not alone in our belief that electronic materials and the Internet have indeed radically changed collection development. Kathleen Kluegel wrote that "it is time to see if the traditional models of technical processes, collection development, and collection management still fit the needs of the library and its users."[6] Certainly, she is correct in that electronic resources require different cataloging processing (we address some of these views later in this chapter). The basic question, however, is whether e-resources are really so different as to require radical changes in processing activities. The fact that libraries are leasing or renting the data does not really change the acquisition process. Certainly, there are echoes of the old approval plan in the free trial that many e-materials vendors offer. (The major concern with trials is whether one has access to the full product or just a sample; only a full product should be reviewed.)

An aspect of e-materials that is seldom addressed is how to deal with bytes rather than books. This is an area where we *do* need to make radical changes in how we deal with collection statistics. Many agencies that collect data about libraries do not ask about electronic resources—in some cases they ask only about "volumes." Volumes are something funding bodies understand; they can see and hold them. The fact that one "rents" rather than owns the material, at least in many instances, also raises questions in funders' mind about what they and the library have to show for expending substantial amounts of money on e-materials.

With packages of e-materials, the vendors and producers decide what is or is not included, as well as for how long. It is not uncommon for packages' content to change even during a single lease period. That, of course, raises the question of what to count. For example, is a package such as OCLC's *FirstSearch* one package or *N* number of databases? If one counted just the packages, one could not compare libraries very accurately, because libraries can turn off access to individual databases or individual journals. Why do that? Because the OCLC pricing model is based on the number of searches used, libraries can and do turn off databases that are least useful to local users but may generate a significant number of searches to users not understanding the content of the database.

In the past, a library's "status" was, at least in part, a function of the size of the collection—the more volumes, the higher the status. Changeable packages make for variable counts, assuming that one counts databases, and create fluctuating statistics that are difficult to quickly explain to non-librarians.

When adding a printed item into one's OPAC, one has a reasonable expectation that the only time one needs to make a change to the record is if the item is withdrawn. (We know that subject heading and authority records do change and can cause additional changes to the item's "bibliographic record" in the system; however, such changes generally affect only a small percentage of items. Also, some libraries do not make the changes unless it is clear that users know and will use the new form.) With websites, if one adds a record to the OPAC, that means that either someone must check the site on a regular basis and make any needed adjustments in the OPAC record or that the library must accept the fact many such records no longer reflect reality. Although it is possible to "automate" the process of checking links, it still requires people power to check content, make decisions about any needed changes, and input the new information. Some commercial products available now also make this process easier by tracking changes to the larger electronic packages for you and providing updated MARC records with these changes, so librarians do not have to track the changes in a constantly changing database such as Lexis/Nexis or *ProQuest*.

Types of Electronic Materials

Full Text

Of today's major types of electronic resources, full text is the most challenging and replete with options. We covered the issues of e-serials in chapter 6. Here we will just remind readers there are two categories—electronic only and electronic/print—of interest in this chapter. Certainly, the technical, legal, and financial issues addressed later in this chapter must be considered, but collection development issues are easily dealt with.

Full-text material comes in four formats: online, CD- or DVD-ROM, print, and microform. In some cases, there are cost differences when both print and electronic formats are available. As we mentioned in chapter 6, the vendor or publisher frequently has one price for the print version, a different price for the electronic version, and then a third price to subscribe to both the print and electronic version. Although sometimes the formula for the print plus electronic version is 10 percent over the cost of just the print version, there is no standard rule, and the rules are always changing and vary across publishers. Sometimes the electronic subscription is offered for free for a short time, perhaps to get users hooked on the subscription before the vendor starts to charge for the service. An advantage to having both formats becomes obvious during, for example, a network outage when users still have access to the print version, and one owns it without further cost.

The definition of *full text* varies between print and electronic versions. Sometimes, in the online version, this means text without graphics or tables. The reason for the qualification is that images (charts, tables, and other illustrations such as advertisements) require substantial amounts of memory and delivery time, as well as delivery platforms capable of handling those images. Graphic display often requires powerful PCs, more powerful than many PC owners might own. In addition, even if an end user has a high-speed Internet connection, downloading online images can be a slow process. On the other hand, some online versions include *more* graphics and tables, as it is cheaper to post these online than to print them, and online versions also can contain multimedia elements such as sounds or videos that are not possible in a print version of a document.

Although we covered e-serials in chapter 6, we also need to give some attention to e-books. We opened this edition with a brief discussion of the controversy surrounding literary book awards and the question of "when a book is a book." Just as there are variations in e-serials, so there are with e-books. Some, like Patricia le Roy's *Angels of Russia*, are available only in an electronic version. (One website to consult for e-books is "Alex Catalogue of Electronic Texts," <http://www.infomotions.com/alex2>.)

One of the oldest efforts in digitizing existing books is Project Gutenberg. The original goal of that project was to have 10,000 titles available, a target long since past, as the collection now numbers over 13,000 titles (<http://www.gutenberg.org>). Titles in the project are all public domain items (no longer covered by copyright). Other projects include the University of Michigan's (UM) "Humanities Text Initiative" (<http://www.hti. umich.edu>), which focuses on Middle English materials and American poetry, as well as recent releases from the UM Press. From Brown University, there is "The Women Writers Project" (<http://www.wwp.brown.edu>). This subscription-based project's goal is to create a full-text database of the publications in English written by women between 1330 and 1830. Since 1992, the "Electronic Text Center at the University of Virginia (<http://etext.lib.virginia.edu>) has been working to create a unique collection of online materials. By early 2005, the collection included "70,000 on- and off-line humanities texts in thirteen languages with more than 350,000 related images (book illustrations, covers, manuscripts, newspaper pages, page images of Special Collections books, museum objects, etc.)."[7] Another project in the works was announced by Google in late 2004. This Web search service has partnered with five major libraries, including Harvard, the University of Oxford, and New York Public Library, to digitize collections and make them available online.[8] The ultimate success of the project remains to be seen, but this is certainly one of the most extensive initiatives attempted to date.

With any full-text material, whether book or serial, one issue to consider is the way the text was formatted: ASCII, Adobe PDF, HTML, XML, or SGML. ASCII is the oldest and, in many ways, the easiest approach. However, one loses most of the formatting of the original document, as well as any images. Adobe Acrobat PDF is an approach that retains formatting and images and is frequently encountered on the Internet but is a proprietary format of Adobe. HTML (Hypertext Markup Language) is probably the most common method used on the World Wide Web and the simplest. XML (eXtensible Markup Language) is gaining popularity on the Web and is more customizable than HTML, including the use of "stylesheets" (which move the coding of "style" away from the text of the document). Both HTML and XML are subsets of the more complex and thorough SGML (Standard Generalized Markup Language). Many organizations use SGML to digitize their internal documents. There are several advantages to using SGML; it is an international standard, it is device-independent, and it is system-independent. Having documents in SGML makes it easier to change systems without incurring significant document conversion costs.

Music

Although we address music more extensively in chapter 9, we need to include in our discussion of electronic resources music in recorded form, which is available on the Internet, some of it free and some for a fee. MP3 files and file sharing have become a significant issue at the start of this century. Most of what is available through file-sharing activities is illegally copied and distributed material. This is obviously an issue that concerns the music industry, which has become more aggressive at enforcing copyright infringement against both individuals and institutions (consider the cases mentioned in chapter 17). Libraries now have increased options to find legal recordings at recording company websites or other fee-based services. Two such services for the library market are Classical Music Library, owned by Alexander Street Press (<http://www.classical.com>), or Naxos Music Library (<http://www.NaxosMusicLibrary.com>), both of which provide a streaming-audio service of classical music. The audio files do not reside on the desktop computer or on a library's server; instead the music is streamed to the desktop computer but cannot be saved or downloaded to that system. Apple Computer's iTunes (<http://www.itunes.com>), Listen.Com's Rhapsody (<http://www.rhapsody.com>), and Napster (<http://www.napster.com>) are three popular consumer-based legal streaming-audio services. Such subscription-based services allow users unlimited listening time to full albums, singles, or access to programmed music stations through streaming-audio, as well as offering subscribers an opportunity to choose to purchase digital versions of particular albums or songs for a set price, usually for a cheaper price than buying the single or the album in a physical form.

Music scores are also available on the Web. One source is MuseData, a fee-based source of classical music scores sponsored by Stanford University's Center for Computer Assisted Research in the Humanities (<http://musedata.stanford.edu>). Commercial sources for musical scores include *MusicNotes.Com* (<http://www.musicnotes.com>), Sheet Music Direct (<http://www.sheetmusicdirect.com>), and Freehand Systems' Sunhawk (<http://www.sunhawk.com>). These sites have a variety of music types—pop, rock, gospel, country western, jazz, etc.

We address electronic access to other nonprint formats, such as photographs, maps, and videos, in chapter 9.

Numeric Databases

Numeric databases have been part of library or information center collecting activities for at least twenty-five years. Generally, libraries acquired these data sets, such as the U.S. Census, as tapes that were mounted on a mainframe. Today, researchers can gain access to such sets online.

A source for numeric data sets is the Inter-University Consortium for Political and Social Research (ICPSR) at the University of Michigan (<http://www.icpsr.umich.edu>). Over 500 colleges and universities from the United States, as well as numerous institutions from around the world, are members of ICPSR. This consortium serves as a central repository and dissemination service for social science electronic data sets. Since its establishment in 1962, ICPSR has collected data sets that cover a broad range of topics. Beginning with a few major surveys of the American electorate, the holdings of the archive have now broadened to include comparable information from diverse settings and for extended periods. Data ranging from nineteenth-century French census materials to recent sessions of the United Nations, from American elections in the 1790s to the socioeconomic structure of Polish *poviats*, from characteristics of Knights of Labor Assemblies to expectations of American consumers, are contained in the archive. It also hosts archives such as International Archive of Education Data (from the National Center for Education Statistics), Health and Medical Care Archive (the archive of the Robert Wood Johnson Foundation), and Child Care and Early Education Research Connections.

When considering numeric collection building, one must remember that these tend to be very large files, and format or compatibility may be issues to consider, as well as the quality of the documentation. In the case of ICPSR, data sets are available from the website for members or via CD-ROM for larger data sets or for those institutions without high-speed connections.

Support for use of ICPSR data depends both on people with the skills and knowledge to do the technical work and on sound documentation. Anyone who has seen the documentation that accompanies many commercial products can imagine the quality of documentation for data sets from researchers whose primary purpose was their own project. Library staff will probably not have experience with all the various statistical packages on the market (such as SPSS and SAS). Support means institutional costs. Again, there are costs associated with either mode of access (online or CD-ROM). Careful consideration of both options and how to handle the charges is essential before moving into the business of acquiring data sets.

"Traditional" Reference Materials

Bibliographies, indexes, abstracts, and tables of contents are the traditional types of reference materials. With the data in electronic form, the publishers or producers can generate more and more specialized products. Public service users frequently prefer online or CD-ROM products over print versions. User expectations or beliefs about electronic information also create challenges for the staff. Too often, users think the electronic data (particularly Web-based content) is both the most current and the most comprehensive, and this is not always true.

Software

Although some libraries in the past started collecting software, few still do except to the extent it comes as a supplement to a print publication. School media centers, if they have responsibility for computing services, are the most likely to maintain collections of educational application programs. Libraries are acquiring more and more books that come with software on CD-ROM or on an associated website that is integral to the use of the printed material.

Institutional Repositories

In the time since the last edition of this text was produced, there has been a growing interest among librarians, especially in academic settings, in the concept of the "institutional repository" (IR). While any library serving a parent organization that creates digital information could consider starting a program, it seems only large and medium-sized academic libraries are currently pursuing the idea.

At the time we prepared this book, there was no established definition of the concept; however, Clifford Lynch's view is reflective of most, if not all, of the issues involved:

> In my view, a university-based institutional repository is a set of services that a university offers to the members of the community for the management and dissemination of digital materials created by the institution and its community members. It is essentially an organization commitment to the stewardship of these digital materials, including long-term preservation where appropriate, as well as organization and access or distribution.[9]

To some degree, the concept is a logical extension of the paper-based institutional archive. Digital storage capacity and costs are now such that large-scale capacity and long-term storage are feasible.

Just what one should include in an IR is very much an open question. Some libraries are starting with traditional library materials such as electronic theses and dissertations or scanned or digitized manuscript material from their archives/special collections—essentially, starting with materials at hand that can demonstrate the usefulness of the concept. Getting faculty and others to contribute research reports, pre- and postprint articles, "white" papers, research data, etc. can be a challenge.

Perhaps the best-known project, based on press coverage, is Massachusetts Institute of Technology's (MIT) DSpace repository project (<http://www.dspace.org>). In 2000, MIT began collaborating with Hewlett-Packard to develop DSpace, an open source software package designed to facilitate digital storage and access as well as the sharing of archived material. DSpace was released in 2002, and number of universities, including Cambridge (<http://www.lib.cam.ac.uk/dspace/>) and the University of Maryland (<http://drum.umd.edu/dspace/index.jsp>), adopted the system. Today, any research institution can acquire a free copy of the program, and there is an active community of users of the product. Other notable digital repository examples in the United States include the University of Michigan's "Digital General Collection" (<http://www.hti.umich.edu/g/genpub/>), Virginia Tech's "Digital Library and Archives" (<http://scholar.lib.vt.edu/>), and the University of California's "eScholarship Repository" (<http://repositories.cdlib.org/escholarship/>). International examples include the Netherlands' "Digital Academic Repositories" (<http://www.darenet.nl/en/>), the U.K.'s Focus on Access to Institutional Resources (FAIR) Programme, sponsored by the Joint Information Systems Committee (<http://www.jisc.ac.uk/index.cfm?name=programme_fair>), and the University of British Columbia's Public Knowledge Project (<http://www.pkp.ubc.ca>).

As with any new project, there are policy and procedural concerns as well as long-term funding issues that require careful thought before launching an IR. Starting with limited goals and expectations is often the best approach. An article that appeared in the *Chronicle of Higher Education* in June 2004 reported on the fact that many faculty members, even at MIT, are reluctant to provide less traditional library materials for the repository.[10] Reasons for the reluctance are not surprising—wanting only the final work posted, concern that a posting would be viewed as "prior publication," making it difficult to get final work published, the value of IR-published papers at tenure evaluation time, and concerns about granting distribution rights to the institution.

When starting down the road to establish an IR, the library must be certain it has the resources to carry it through. It is one thing to gather already digitized materials and quite another to have to collect materials and then digitize them. Technical needs must be considered, such as a server to house the IR documents and perhaps a scanner for digitizing new materials. The library will also need someone to manage the IR, both philosophically (deciding what will be included in the IR, what will be the submission process) and technically (who will set up the IR software, who will troubleshoot technical problems with the IR). A good article providing background on the history and administration of institutional repositories is by Miriam Drake.[11]

Without a doubt, even without going the route of establishing an institutional repository, libraries and collection development officers will face increasing pressure to add electronic formats. Cost, legal, and selection issues each will become more complex as time goes by. Balancing the various needs will present challenges for all concerned.

Selection Issues

Loyola Marymount University (LMU) considers four broad categories of issues when evaluating a new electronic product: content, access, support, and cost. The approach is similar to what other libraries do in this area.

Content

As with any format, content issues should be the first consideration. There is some temptation to acquire an electronic format because it is new, because others have it, because it is attractive or entertaining, because it is multimedia-based, or because it will interface with existing equipment. None of these are valid reasons for adding a title. Instead, care should be taken to make certain the item matches up with both library and institutional goals. In an ideal situation, the item will match several goals.

Given the relatively high cost of electronic formats, it is important that the material be useful to a large number of potential users. It is not unreasonable to purchase a $50 or $75 book for a single known user and a few potential users. Similarly, a library might subscribe to a $1,000 journal to serve the needs of a department and, in an academic environment, the needs of departmental majors. However, in today's tight budget environment, with the exception of specialized research environments, most libraries would think long and hard about committing $2,000 or more to any product that did not meet multiple-user needs.

Although popularity, or high demand, is a basic reason for selecting an item, it also creates some public service concerns. One can lease or buy multiple copies of bestseller books, develop request lists, and have a few rental copies of high-demand items. Few libraries or information centers circulate their journals, so current journals are usually available when a user seeks them. A single-user license for a CD-ROM or online product, however, can create queues and substantial paper and ink/toner costs (if there is a printer attached to the computer) as well as a need for equipment maintenance of heavily used hardware. Thus, even though multiple users are an important factor in the selection decision, the consequences of that popularity also must be taken into account. A popular item may require purchasing a multiple-user license that adds significantly to the cost.

Content of the product is the key issue, as it is for any addition to the collection. If the product is bibliographic or statistical in nature, one must consider how far back in time the data go. What use characteristics of the subject field are represented in the product? The myth that older literature in the sciences is obsolete has little research documentation.[12] Though it is true of all fields that use declines with age, that does not mean that use, or importance to the field, ceases entirely. Understanding local use patterns is a key issue in making the selection decision.

Questions to consider about content include: How often is the product updated? Are there plans to add to the backfiles? If so, how soon will they be added, how far back will they go, and will there be an additional charge for the backfile materials? These are key questions for products that incorporate bibliographic and abstracting data. Occasionally, vendors advertise greater coverage than the product actually offers. One tool that can assist in determining the amount of overlap between selected electronic products is the "CUFTS Resource Comparison" search feature developed at the Simon Fraser University Library for the Canadian Council of Prairie and Pacific University Libraries (<http://cufts.lib.sfu.ca/tools.shtml>).

Problems like those mentioned above make it important to seek out reviews *and* require at least a thirty-day trial for new products. Clearly, the public service staff will need to be fully aware of the various product limitations, so that they can make the end users equally aware of the situation. This is one excellent reason that library and information center staffs need to continue to serve as interpreters and guides to information services, whether electronic or print.

In selecting any product for the collection, aspects like quality, accuracy, authoritativeness, and currency of data are factors that any collection development officer will consider. With electronic products, these factors can be even more significant than with other formats. Many people have great respect for anything in print and transfer that faith to electronic products, which they believe always contains the most current, complete, and accurate information available. This almost-blind end-user acceptance of electronic information means that selection personnel must be careful in their decisions about electronic formats.

As mentioned previously, long-term availability is another concern. Online material sometimes disappears overnight. The person operating a discussion list or website may simply stop maintaining the service or may make a significant change in a server; some users don't learn of the change, and they lose that connection. As a result of the Tasini decision, covered in chapter 17, some content has actually been removed from electronic databases. With a print version in the collection, there is a reasonable degree of certainty that the data will always be available, as long as the book remains a part of the collection.

A real concern is how long the CD-ROM/DVD formats will be with us. Full text on CD-ROM has already started to become the next "problem" format, rather like sound recordings. How many times must a library or information center acquire the same information? For example, the sound recordings of Handel's *Water Music* are available in many forms—first as a 78-rpm disk, then as a 33⅓-rpm disk, then as an 8-track tape, then as a cassette, and now CDs, MP3, and streaming audio. (See chapter 9 for more about this issue.) If one of the library's or information center's goals is to preserve information for future generations, then format viability and support must be a concern.

Migration to new formats is a real concern in preserving data. Someone will need to migrate the data from one platform to the next, which is a cost someone must underwrite on a regular basis. Will systems fifty or even ten years in the future have the capability to handle "ancient" material in an ASCII format? More to the point, who will own that data, and what will it cost to have access? These questions have no ready answers. We do know that print has served humankind very well for centuries and that it can continue to do so without regard to operating systems or hardware delivery platforms.

A final item on the list of content considerations is whether the product offers some value-added advantage over existing print versions. Especially important is any type of customization that the producer offers that more closely links the product's content to the local collections. For example, databases that are customized to show which indexed titles are locally available would have added value. Almost all electronic products offer easier searching, more search options, and generally faster results than their print counterparts. Because of this, it is important to try to find some other value-added feature before committing funds. As Matthew Ciolek[13] suggested, a danger exists that electronic material, especially on the Web, will move from WWW to MMM (Multi-Media Mediocrity). We must always focus first on content.

Access

Being able to customize a product to indicate local holdings brings us to the second major category of selection issues: *access*. One aspect of access is availability of materials. This issue applies primarily to the indexing, abstracting, and table of contents products. As noted in chapter 6, when the library adds a new indexing or abstracting service, users will see citations to some publications that are not in the local collection. A decision to give users access to the tables of contents of thousands of periodicals might generate numerous requests for articles from titles not available locally. One should not ignore the impact on ILL service when making this decision.

Returning to other access issues, one question that requires an answer is: How compatible is the product with the local network or library OPAC? Related to compatibility is the question of licensing; that is, what is the difference in cost between single-user and multiple-user licenses? Also of concern is the type of search engine or interface used by the product. One must consider how different it is from other electronic products already locally available. In the past, one could assume Boolean logic searching, but today some vendors are using statistical searching or weighted terms. (*Weighted term searching* is a system that retrieves on the basis of word-frequency matches of search terms to words in the document and presents the user with the most frequent matches first.) The popularity of the latter system in commercial text imaging and retrieval systems (e.g., a records management application) is causing products like Westlaw and Lexis/Nexis to use statistical searching engines. Strategies for a successful search are very different for the two search engines. This will translate into extra training for staff and users alike.

A final access issue is how a user from your institution will be recognized as a valid user by the electronic resource's authentication process. Individuals using computers within the walls of the library or entire institution can be recognized either through an IP address or a password. All the IP addresses for your site will be given to the vendor for authentication purposes, or the vendor will give you a user name and password intended for your users only. Users at home or "off-site" can also use the electronic resources by authenticating through a proxy server using special passwords or a library card number.

Not surprisingly, the overarching access issue is the user. Where (library, office, home), when (during library operating hours, 24 hours per day), and how (local network, Internet, commercial service) does the end user gain access to the information? As a general rule, as accessibility goes up, so does the cost. An as-yet-unavailable ideal solution is having everything available 24 hours a day, from any authorized location, with full cost control capability and no need for local support.

Support

Just as user access is a key decision point, support should also be a prime consideration during the selection process. How much training does a user need to successfully use the product? Having only similar interfaces or having only a few variations in how one can use products means that the public service staff will have less support activity. This leads to another question: How much initial and ongoing staff training is necessary to provide user support? The answers to these questions depend on the quality of the documentation that accompanies the product. Usually, a phone call to vendor support or an e-mail to the vendor works well only when the individual posing the question has good to fair technical knowledge of the product. Usually, this means that staff members rather than end users must contact the vendor.

Anyone with public service experience knows that most people follow the directions only when everything else fails. Reading introductory material about how to use print resources was never a strong point with general users. They are no more likely to take the time to read instructions for electronic products, some of which come with extensive user manuals or online help. A rule of thumb is that the bigger the manual or the more extensive the online help, the more help the public service staff will have to provide. Information about ease of use and size or usefulness of manuals may appear in product reviews (if a review can be found). Some review sources to consult are *The Charleston Advisor: Critical Reviews of Web Products for Information Professionals* (Charleston Co.) and *ARBA* (Libraries Unlimited). Often, information about ease of use and size of the manual text is available only after the library receives the product. Discussing the product with a library that already has the product is worthwhile, especially for products costing more than a few thousand dollars. However, your library may receive a later version of the product that incorporates significant changes, so the experiences of libraries with previous versions may not apply to the new version.

Questions about vendor/producer reliability are important support considerations. Reliability of the producer is a more significant issue with electronic products than it is with print products. Will the telephone number or e-mail address for customer help remain active, and is help available at times when it would likely be needed? What is the response time for e-mail questions to the vendor? What are the systems (computing resource) requirements? Will new versions result in retraining users or reconfiguring the local system? What is the relationship between vendor support service hours and the library's hours? Just because the producer of the electronic product is one the library staff knows from its nonelectronic products does not mean that the transition to the new format will be smooth. It also does not mean that the producer will stay with the format or support existing products if the company decides to drop the format. Just as technology changes rapidly, so do the producers of electronic materials.

Some software can be unreliable and troublesome. Invariably, some products have one or more bugs that take time and effort to eliminate. A few seem to have bugs in each new release, although, in a sense, this is better than the occasional bug. When there is a consistent pattern, one can plan how to do the debugging, instead of encountering unexpected problems. Specialized products, often from smaller publishers, are more likely to have homegrown, nonstandard solutions that can require more support (e.g., *Catholic and Periodical Literature Index* [Catholic Library Association] or *Bible Windows* [Silver Mountain]). Compatibility of hardware and software is also a key issue in selecting a format for mounting electronic information.

Support issues affect the impact new products have on existing services and activities. Some new products reduce pressure on the staff (e.g., the full text of materials frequently requested through ILL). In some instances, it may be possible to reduce staff work by giving particular end users thorough training in using a product and assigning those users their own accounts and passwords. Other times, there will be a substantial increase in the staff workload. In those cases, staff discussions about the impact and the value of the product are an essential part of the decision-making process.

This section could have appeared in pieces in various chapters, but we thought that bringing them all together would make the information stand out more clearly. A variety of websites exist that are useful to collection development officers. A very good article on this area is by Shelley Arlen and her colleagues.[14]

A starting point for anyone interested in collection management is the COLLDV-L discussion list described in chapter 4. Another source is the Internet, where most major publishers as well as vendors and suppliers have websites. Notable examples include YBP Library Services (<http://www.ybp.com>) and EBSCO (<http://www.ebsco.com>). Generally, these sites contain searchable versions of the print catalogs, as well as promotional materials. What one usually gains from looking at such websites is the most current pricing information, as well as information about recent releases or new services. Something akin to a "catalog of catalogs" is a site maintained by Northern Lights Internet Solutions, titled "Publisher's Catalogues" (<http://www.lights.com/publisher>). Obviously, the ability to go to one site to access multiple publisher catalogs can save selection staff time and effort.

Probably the most comprehensive site for acquisitions is *AcqWeb*, a source that was created by the staff at the Vanderbilt Law School Library and that migrated to Appalachian State University in the fall of 2004 (<http://www.acqweb.org/>). This site also has an excellent directory of publishers and vendors. We mentioned a number of sites to consult for serials in chapter 6. For government documents, a good starting point is the *GPO*

Access Online Resources page (<http://www.gpoaccess.gov/databases.html>), with a number of other resources covered in chapter 8.

Many types of libraries use reviews in their selection processes for print resources, and these tools can provide guidance for electronic resources as well. As noted in chapter 4, most useful sites for reviews are available to libraries by subscription and include Bowker's *Global Books in Print* (<http://www.globalbooksinprint.com/GlobalBooksInPrint/>), Libraries Unlimited's *ARBA Online* (<http://www.arbaonline.com/>), and ALA's *ChoiceReviewsOnline* (<http://www.choicereviews.org>). All three of these titles include reviews by professional librarians. Selectors can also locate book reviews published in many U.S. newspapers such as the *New York Times Book Review* (<http://www.nytimes.com/pages/books/>) or *Los Angeles Times Book Review* (<http://www.calendarlive.com/books/bookreview/more/>), both of which require free user registration to gain access to the reviews. For free, selectors can find reviews at *Amazon.com* (<http://www.amazon.com>), which includes reviews from all the sources listed above but also contains reviews from nonprofessionals, which can be useful for more obscure items or newer items not reviewed by the major review sources. Keep in mind, as we noted in chapter 4, that *anyone* can post reviews at Amazon, including those with a bias toward your library purchasing or not purchasing that particular book.

Cost

While addressing questions of content, access, and support, the selection process must also deal with cost. The most obvious costs are the initial cost of the product and ongoing charges for updates or annual subscription fees. Although the most obvious, these may not be the largest costs in the long run. Information is an economic good that does not follow traditional pricing models. As we noted in earlier chapters, producers employ a variety of pricing strategies. This makes it more complicated to calculate what electronic information will really cost the library or information center and makes it difficult to accurately compare prices of various products offering similar information. Likewise, it is a time-consuming task to attempt to compare the unit cost of a print periodical subscription or electronic access to the cost of securing the article from one of several document delivery services. As an example, how does one compare the *Grove Dictionary of Art Online* (Oxford University Press, <http://www.groveart.com>) with the thirty-four-volume set in paper (Grove's Dictionaries)? Can cost really be a factor in the comparison? To assign a logical monetary value to ease of use and speed of access is difficult. It depends on local circumstances. At best, one can look at the expected use or cost of each format and decide whether the value is reasonable for the library.

To further complicate the equation, some electronic resources can be purchased outright instead of leased. This would incur a onetime, up-front cost that would be much larger and may need to come from a different budget than a cost spread over several years. Additional cost considerations for one or more electronic formats may include display or print charges; downloading charges; customization charges; optional features, such as saved searches; and charges for management reports or software.

In addition to vendor costs, local library costs are a factor in the decision-making process. The computers and other hardware required to use electronic materials are generally more expensive to buy and maintain than other media playback equipment. As programmable units, they are susceptible to system failure, to loss of information because of power fluctuations and inadvertent user error, to tampering by computer hackers, to viruses, and to theft. All of these factors generate additional costs (equipment; security devices; service contracts and maintenance; and, all too often, replacement).

An estimate of the amount of printing or downloading activity the product will generate is another cost factor that cannot be ignored. Even without a royalty fee, there are printing costs, assuming that the decision is to allow users to print information. Paper, ink, or toner cartridge costs can and do mount quickly, if there is no effort to control them. Libraries and information centers employ several techniques to control such costs. One obvious method is to assess a printing charge. (There are coin and debit-card units that work with printers, and money can be added to library cards.) Another method is to allocate a number of free copies per user, with the staff providing the appropriate number of sheets of paper and charging for additional paper. This approach generates a cost in staff time to provide the paper and, occasionally, to put the paper into the printer or troubleshoot paper jams. Some libraries allow downloading to disk instead of printing. There are several drawbacks to this approach. Some products do not allow downloading. Another serious disadvantage is that not all customers can use downloaded data, which means that the library *must* allow some printing or risk having a single user tie up a product for extended periods. Plus, allowing patrons to download opens the risk of their inserting a virus-infected disk into the computer—if the computers have not been made to scan disks before use.

For popular products, libraries want to keep the user turnover rate as high as possible, which means offering both printing and downloading. Users can print to disk rather than to paper, which is useful for programs that are not set up for downloading. Another method for handling printing costs is to locate a system printer, perhaps connected to a local area network, in a staff area, making it possible to monitor and charge for printing activities. This option generates staff costs but establishes a distribution system that assures that each user gets the right printout. If the institution is networked, printing charges, as well as other costs of use, could become automatic debits against individual user accounts. An additional option, which is becoming more and more popular for Web-based resources, is to e-mail articles to the patron's own account. This assumes that users have the capability to send and receive e-mail—but free options such as Hotmail or Yahoo! do exist. This can transfer printing costs to the individual user and save valuable library resources.

In 1994, Peter Young stressed the need to create a paradigm for libraries and librarians, addressing the need to evaluate resources as quantifiable commodities and products.[15] In that same year, a team of British researchers outlined a scenario in which information as a commodity was examined not only in terms of the set price of the commodity (such as an online database) but also in terms of the total cost of all the elements of an electronic resource.[16] Karen Svenningsen wrote a very good survey article on this topic and provided several models one can employ for conducting cost analysis.[17] Meanwhile, White and Crawford[18] described a cost-benefit analysis for electronic resources at Penn State University that could be used in almost any setting.

The overall goal is to select the most cost-effective format that will meet the needs of a large number of users. This is no easy task, given the cost and pricing variables that exist. By seriously considering the factors outlined in the preceding sections, one has a better chance of successfully achieving this objective.

Other Issues

The legal, financial, and technical issues relating to electronic acquisitions and processing work, as well as to other activities and services, are important enough to merit extra emphasis.

One question that becomes increasingly important as one advances into the arena of electronic collection development is how users know the material is available. Providing lists of possible Internet sites or creating and maintaining a library web page with direct links to the available resources works reasonably well as long as the list is manageable and resources are available to create and maintain the website. As the listing grows in length, grouping by subject is a frequent next step. A way to match the right resource to the user inquiry is through a federated searching product, which searches a chosen number of the library's resources simultaneously (including the catalog), presenting relevant results from all the resources. An example of a systemwide application of this concept is *Research Port* (<http://researchport.umd.edu>), developed for the University System of Maryland and Affiliated Institutions (<http://usmai.umd.edu/>). By following such a scheme, libraries can avoid developing what amounts to a second online catalog.

OCLC began looking at Internet resources in 1991 and by 1993 was testing the suitability and usefulness of the MARC format and AACR2 for cataloging sites and materials found. By 1995, it was apparent that "traditional" cataloging systems would work for most Internet resources and that linking the catalog record to the resource site was highly desirable. After some discussion, the USMARC record added the 856 field (Electronic Location and Access). That field is now the location of URL (Uniform Resource Locator) information.

In 1997, Erik Jul noted in an article, "Cataloging Internet resources raises many critical questions, among which three stand out as fundamental: (1) Are Internet resources worth cataloging? (2) Is traditional MARC/AACR2 cataloging appropriate for Internet resources? (3) What about resources that change location?"[19] One might add to his last question the phrase "or that simply disappear." Certainly, it seems reasonable, since we employ cataloging methods for other information formats in our collections, that we do the same with Internet materials deemed appropriate for our service population.

Jul suggests that the answer to his first question is clearly yes. However, the question of whether they *should* be cataloged remains somewhat at issue. Some public service staff strongly resist adding electronic resources that are not also added to the OPAC. This is not the book in which to explore this complex issue. We note it here because it is a concern for collection managers, library staff, and end users alike.

Great difficulty arises in attempting to answer Jul's last question about changing (or disappearing) locations or resources. Anyone with even limited experience using Internet resources has encountered the message "Error 404, File Not Found" at least once. According to 1997 data from the OCLC Inter-Cat project, an average of 3 percent of URLs could not be accessed during any given test,[20] and this percentage has risen with the growth of the Internet. The percentage of URLs that might "break" in a catalog will vary, depending on what types of resources the library chooses to catalog. A vendor-supplied URL will tend to be more persistent than the URL of a personal website, but vendors also end up changing their URLs eventually. The time and effort necessary to check and update records are considerable. There are products that can assist in checking URLs, but when there is a change in address for an item in the OPAC, someone has to make the required changes.

In addition to the other issues we have addressed, there are legal issues involved in the use of electronic resources that cannot be ignored. These issues encompass both copyright and licensing agreements. Copyright involves several topics: fair use, preservation, and production. Electronic (digital) material is easy to transmit, manipulate, and duplicate. These features make the medium popular but also raise serious copyright questions. According to Mark McGuire:

> One of many challenges in the digital realm is the problem of ensuring appropriate compensation in transactions involving intellectual property. Other considerations include: ascertaining and proving liability in information malpractice; safeguarding information integrity; ensuring respect for privacy; and maintaining equitable access to information.[21]

Achieving compliance with these copyright requirements and standards provides ongoing challenges for library and information center staffs. Some of the use issues are addressed by the licensing agreements accompanying the product or contract for online services. Rather like photocopying services, the library takes no responsibility for what users do with downloaded data after they leave the library. Whether posting signs regarding copyright in the electronic work area(s) will prove adequate to protect libraries and information centers remains to be seen. In any case, the staff must know what use rights exist for each product.

The entire question of preserving print material by converting it to a digital format is slowly being resolved. (See chapter 17 for a discussion of how this issue relates to copyright.) In all likelihood, if the digital material is not publicly accessible, except through the group preserving the material, that will be acceptable to everyone. The ease with which electronic data is manipulated and duplicated is one of the concerns regarding preservation of materials that are becoming too brittle or fragile to handle.

A complex area is that of author responsibility or ownership. Perhaps the idea put forward by McGuire,[22] or something similar—embedding codes in the data to link various information elements to their original producers, thus identifying authorship as well as assigning responsibility for content—will solve the problem. In addition, such coding could ensure that economic value is equitably attributed to the originators. Such a system would avoid the fair use concerns that Robert Kost identified as the key problem: "We have lost the control necessary for copyright law to be effective. Control over copies is hopeless."[23]

When the library or information center provides equipment or assists with multimedia production, under copyright law, it has some responsibility for assuring that the copied material is public domain or that permission is granted to reproduce the material. (See chapter 17 for a discussion of the Digital Millennium Copyright Act and library/institutional liability, especially regarding electronic resources.)

Copyright law requires libraries and information centers that supply public access equipment to post signs reminding users about the need to comply with copyright law. One further step to consider, if the equipment is in a secure area or locked cabinet that requires users to get a key from library staff, is for a staff person to have the user sign a statement assuming full responsibility for complying with copyright law. Obviously, if the library is producing products, it can make certain that compliance occurs. A question arises about accepting multimedia courseware from instructors without some type of protection for the library in the event the developer failed to get the required permission(s).

Licensing agreements are an important concern for libraries and collection development staff. Initially, library staff paid little attention to such agreements. Acquisition staff signed the agreements and returned them without fully understanding what they were signing. As Edward Warro stated,

> When is the last time you stood at the counter of a rental car agency and quibbled over various clauses on your rental agreement? . . . To make them even more unappealing to read, the agreements are normally printed in fine gray type on pink paper to maximize eyestrain. There is good reason for the fine print: the people who wrote these agreements would sooner have you die than read them. But if you do read them, you will probably die anyway when you realize what you have been signing.[24]

Anyone involved in the selection or acquisition of electronic materials should read Warro's article or the more recent piece by Kathryn Metzinger Miller.[25] These days, library staff study the license agreements in detail, sometimes with the legal department of the institution, and will make changes to the agreement before signing.

A final legal issue for libraries in relation to electronic resources is in providing access to patrons with a disability. Electronic resources that require the use of a mouse and do not have equivalent keyboard shortcuts, use small fonts, odd graphics or colors in text, or have flashing, audio, or video components may not be usable for a patron with a disability unless the library provides special equipment. In this case, a print equivalent of the resource may be needed.

Financial and technical considerations are what staff talk about most after they address other concerns. In times of tight budgets, which seem to be the norm, budgeting for high-priced electronic materials represents a challenge. Balancing quality, quantity, and cost is the fundamental task of collection development staff. The fact that electronic materials tend to be expensive for single-user agreements and even more expensive for multiple-user agreements makes it even more difficult to answer the question: How much benefit to how many users? Does enhanced searching capability justify the purchase? What must be given up in other areas?

Shifting resources from monographs, to serials, to electronic resources is a finite game for most libraries and information centers. Sometimes, additional funding is available for electronic materials, particularly when funding bodies view it as enhancing the image of the parent institution. As the glamour of electronic material delivered to individual workstations fades, so does the additional funding. Sometimes, the trade-off involves canceling low-use serials to gain enough money to cover the costs for acquiring both the occasionally needed article from the canceled titles and a few articles from titles never held. The question of formats is also a question of technology and money. Realistically, additional funding will come from direct and indirect charges paid by end users. These charges will, at best, cover only the cost of the information, not the support, training, staffing, equipment, and maintenance costs, thus creating an overall net cash drain and cost shift from other areas—often print collection funds.

Because electronic information access offers the potential of end users having full control of their searches and acquisition of data, cost containment will likely become an important consideration. For example, initial costs will vary depending on how the organization decides to handle its connections with electronic services, such as the Internet. In some cases such costs are covered by the parent organization; when they are a charge to the library, one needs to think the options through with care. Connection options include a regular dial-up connection through an ISP (Internet Service Provider), a DSL connection, or a T1 line, and new connection options are becoming available all the time. Most institutions should already have one of these in place for their employees' use of the Internet and e-mail. The choice of connection should also include a close look at the security of the connection, in order to protect the privacy of users in their searches, and should include virus checking and a strong firewall.

As one can see, the question of how to provide access is not just a library or information center decision; it involves substantial technical and financial resources. All options have implications for cost. One cost that is sometimes overlooked is user education, training, and support. That cost is ongoing and, depending on the turnover rate of users, can result in a large or small annual cost for training.

Collection Development and the Web

As most librarians are aware, Web materials are a mixed bag ranging from solid, scholarly material to junk. Developing an appropriate collection of websites brings to mind (at least for librarians who have been in the profession for a long time) the efforts to create and maintain the "vertical file pamphlet" collection. Print vertical files contained free or inexpensive items but were labor-intensive to maintain. Website collections are the same in those two regards. The difference is in usage: vertical files seldom did not, and certainly now do not, receive as much use as one would like. Because the Web is popular with the public, usage is higher, and if the library provides network access to its electronic material, the material is probably available 24 hours a day, which will further increase use.

The Web and print-world publishing are much the same in the range of material available. That is, some materials are pure vanity pieces, while others are very scholarly. Personal home pages are, in a sense, a form of vanity publishing. Experienced collection development officers know that not all self-publishing is poor quality or without value. What is different is that self-publishing does not go through the "vetting" process that takes place with other forms of publishing. The vetting/review process of print publishing serves the very useful purpose of imparting at least some degree of quality assurance. Websites that one knows are equally vetted are the equivalent of the scholarly print publications. The key is that one "knows" this to be the case. The Web also allows people to make any type of representations about themselves and what they are putting on the Web.

The following example illustrates many of the concerns that should be addressed when considering websites as information resources. A surprising number of people are what Native Americans call "wanabes," people who are not Native Americans but for some reason want to be identified as, or with, true Native Americans. Just because a website author claims to be Native American does not necessarily make it so. Sites filled with sophisticated graphics, sounds, and perhaps video clips and claiming to represent Native American views, ideas, or affiliation should raise questions. A great many Native Americans, especially those living on reservations, do not have access to such high-end technology and software. By itself, the sophistication of a site does not mean that the site is incorrect or exploitive—but it should suggest that further checking is in order. The URL can provide a useful clue; does it contain a nation name such as Navajo, Oneida, or Blackfeet? Even the address information does not necessarily mean that it is an official site or that the tribal government knows of its existence. The best approach is to locate a telephone number, mailing address, or e-mail address for the tribal government and contact them (guides such as Barry Klein's *Reference Encyclopedia of the American Indian* [Todd Publications] or *The Native North American Almanac*, edited by Duane Champagne [Gale], provide such information).

One should be particularly wary of supposed Native American websites that suggest they are providing information of a spiritual, religious, or mystical nature. Almost all true Native Americans would not think of publicly sharing such information. This does not mean that some native peoples are unwilling to share such information with a nonnative person who they believe has a serious interest in the subject. The print world has done a thriving business promoting pseudo-Native American spirituality, and that activity has spread to the Web.

One should be wary of sites that present a picture of *the* American Indian/Native American. There is no such group. There are more than 500 different Native American groups with different languages, values, and traditions. Even the "urban Indian" is not a single entity.

The essentials of website evaluation are the same as for print. The challenge arises from the fact that there are fewer quick clues to quality in the Web environment. Where Web and print publishing differ is in the amount of promotional/advertising material. That is not to say that print is not also filled with similar material, but it can be much more difficult to determine whether Internet data is actually promotional and advertising material. It is not too difficult to determine when something on television or a printed page is advertising, even the so-called television infomercials. With self-published material on the Web, it is often hard to tell where information ends and advertising begins. Thus, determining website quality is a bit more challenging than with printed material.

Determining quality is challenging for several reasons. First, there is the changing nature of Web material. What was good yesterday may be poor or bad today, and vice versa. This requires one to look for a last revised, modified, updated statement that one finds on quality websites, as well as some not-so-good sites. At least one gets some sense of the age of the material; naturally, a current date does not necessarily guarantee that the material was, in fact, modified.

Further complicating the search for quality websites are the popular search engines such as Google and Yahoo!. The websites that rise to the top of the search results might, in fact, be the best sites on that subject, but sometimes a site is at the top of the list through a pay-for-placement agreement or through other tricks done by website producers to ensure that the site is near the top of a result list (e.g., creating several pages that link to the site or mentioning the site several times in a weblog). Users need to be taught how to create a smart search, the different nuances of each search engine, and how to evaluate the search results that they receive.

Another factor making evaluation more challenging is lack of knowledge about the "publisher." With a book from a commercial or university press, selectors have a history of quality of prior publications to draw upon. (See pages 92–93 for a discussion of publisher reputation.) The best indicator one has for websites is information contained in the URL. If it implies it is from an academic institution, ".edu," one has a little stronger sense that the material is at least not promotional or advertising. Although most educational institutions do not closely monitor the content of pages posted, most do have rules against using the institutional resources in a manner that would harm the institutional image, as well as forbidding individuals from engaging in commercial activity.

An excellent site dealing with evaluation of Internet resources is Nicole Auer's "Bibliography on Evaluating Internet Resources" (<http://www.lib. vt.edu/help/instruct/evaluate/evalbiblio.html>). Two good sources to consult for vetted "reviews" of websites are "Librarian's Index to the Internet" (<http://www.lii.org>) and "KidsClick!" (<http://www.kidsclick.org/>). Both of these sites contain brief reviews of subject websites reviewed by librarians. A subscription-based resource worth consulting is Thomson/Gale's *Web Feet* (<http://www.webfeetguides.com/>).

Summary

Electronic materials will be an ever-growing part of collections and user expectations. As Mary Morley and Hazel Woodward aptly noted:

> In an era of restricted funding, decisions have to be made between the provision of printed and electronic information; between local holdings of material and remote access to external information; between "just in case" as opposed to a "just in time" strategy. Librarians dealing with electronic information are constantly confronted by questions about equipment requirements; pricing polices; bibliographic control; archival access; staffing implication; and user needs.[26]

Balancing these various elements demands constant adjustments in how libraries think about services and the most cost-effective approach. One must keep up-to-date on changing technology, changing players in the marketplace, and user needs and wants. Further, libraries must do what they can to maintain a balance between producers' economic interests and rights and users' rights to fair use. It will be an ongoing challenge to libraries and information centers for years to come. By engaging in careful planning (including the preparation of an electronic collection policy), employing sound selection criteria, and monitoring the use of the resources, libraries will meet the challenge.

Notes

1.   *Collection Development and the Internet: A Brief Handbook for Recommending Officers in the Humanities and Social Sciences Division at the Library of Congress.* Compiled by A. Yochelson et al. (Washington, DC: Library of Congress, 1997), <http://lcweb.loc.gov/acq/colldev/handbook.html>.

2.   Péter Jascó, "Tomorrow's Online in Today's CD-ROM: Interfaces and Images," *Online* 18 (March 1994): 41–47.

3.   William Fisher, "Now You See It; Now You Don't: The Elusive Nature of Electronic Information," *Library Collections, Acquisitions, & Technical Services* 27, no. 4 (2003): 463–72.

4.   Ibid., 464.

5.   "CPL Lending Ebooks via Phone to Smartphones and PDAs," *Library Hotline* 33, no. 17 (April 26, 2004): 5–6; "Libraries, Publishers, Vendors Address State of E-books," *Library Hotline* 33, no. 13 (March 29, 2004): 3–4.

6.   Kathleen Kluegel, "From the President of RUSA: Redesigning Our Future," *RQ* 36, no. 3 (Spring 1997): 330.

7.   University of Virginia Library, "Electronic Text Center Holdings," <http://etext.lib.virginia.edu/uvaonline.html>.

8.   Scott Carlson and Jeffrey R. Young, "Google Will Digitize and Search Millions of Books from 5 Top Research Libraries," *Chronicle of Higher Education* 51, no. 18 (January 7, 2005): A37–A40. See also Andrew Albanese, "Google to Digitize 15 Million Books," *Library Journal* 130, no. 1 (January 2005): 18–19, 22.

9.   Clifford Lynch, "Institutional Repositories: Essential Infrastructure for Scholarship in the Digital Age," *Portal: Libraries and the Academy* 3, no. 2 (2003): 328.

10.   Andrea Foster, "Papers Wanted," *Chronicle of Higher Education* 50, no. 42 (June 25, 2004): A37–38.

11.   Miriam A. Drake, "Institutional Repositories: Hidden Treasures," *Searcher* 12, no. 5 (May 2004): 41–45, <http://www.infotoday.com/searcher/may04/drake.shtml>.

12.   Thomas W. Cokling and Bonnie Anne Osif, "CD-ROM and Changing Research Patterns," *Online* 18 (May 1994): 71–74.

13.   Matthew Ciolek, "Today's WWW—Tomorrow's MMM," *Educom Review* 32, no. 3 (May/June 1997): 23–26.

14.   Shelley Arlen, Nanji Lindell, and Colleen Seale, "Web Tools for Collection Managers," *Collection Building* 17, no. 2 (1998): 65–70.

15.   Peter Young, "Changing Information Access Economics," *Information Technology and Libraries* 13, no. 2 (1994): 103–14.

16.   Douglas Badenoch et al., "The Value of Information," in *The Value and Impact of Information*, eds. M. Feeney and M. Grieves, 9–77 (London: Bowker, 1994).

17.   Karen Svenningsen, "An Evaluation Model for Electronic Resources Utilizing Cost Analysis," *Bottom Line* 11, no. 1 (1998): 18–23.

18.   Gary White and Gregory Crawford, "Cost-Benefit Analysis of Electronic Information," *College & Research Libraries* 59 (November 1998): 503–10.

19.   Erik Jul, "Cataloging Internet Resources: Survey and Prospectors," *Bulletin of the American Society for Information Science* 24 (October–November 1997): 6–9.

20.   Ibid., 8.

21. Mark McGuire, "Secure SGML: A Proposal to the Information Community," *Journal of Scholarly Publishing* 25 (April 1994): 146.

22. Ibid.

23. Robert Kost, "Technology Giveth . . . Electronic Information and the Future of Copyright," *Serials Review* 18, nos. 1/2 (1992): 69.

24. Edward A. Warro, "What Have We Been Signing? A Look at Database Licensing Agreements," *Library Administration and Management* 8 (Summer 1994): 173.

25. Kathryn Metzinger Miller, "Behind Every Great Virtual Library Stand Many Great Licenses," *Library Journal* Net Connect Issue 128, no. 1 (Winter 2003): 20–22.

26. Mary Morley and Hazel Woodward, eds., *Taming the Electronic Jungle* (Horsforth, UK: National Acquisitions Group and UK Serials Group, 1993), xiii.

Selected Websites*

(See also resources on the DLC5 website: <http://www.lu.com/dlc5>)

Digital Book Index
    <http://www.digitalbookindex.com/>
    An online listing of over 100,000 e-titles, a high percentage of which are available free of charge.

Directory of Electronic Text Centers
    <http://harvest.rutgers.edu/ceth/etext_directory/>
    Sponsored by Rutgers, this site provides a listing of electronic text resources hosted in the United States and worldwide.

Oxford Text Archive
    <http://ota.ahds.ac.uk/>
    An online archive of "digital resources of interest to those working in the literary and linguistic disciplines (including modern and ancient languages)."

U of M Digital Library Production Service
    <http://www.umdl.umich.edu/>
    Formed in 1996 as an outgrowth of the Digital Library Program at the University of Michigan to support digital library resources such as the Humanities Text Initiative.

*These sites were accessed May 5, 2005.

Further Reading

Ayers, E. L. "Doing Scholarship on the Web: 10 Years of Triumphs—and a Disappointment." *Chronicle of Higher Education* 50, no. 21 (January 30, 2004): B24–B25.

Balas, J. L. "The Way You Organize Your Electronic Resources Really Matters." *Computers in Libraries* 24, no. 1 (January 2004): 36–39.

Baudoin, P., and M. Branschofsky. "Implementing an Institutional Repository: The DSpace Experience at MIT." *Science & Technology Libraries* 24, nos. 1/2 (June 2004): 31–45.

Block, R. J. "Voices of the Future." *Serials Librarian* 45, no. 2 (2003): 27–38.

Casey, A. M. "Collection Development for Distance Learning." *Journal of Library Administration* 36, no. 3 (2002): 59–73.

Cassel, R. "Selection Criteria for Internet Resources." *College & Research Libraries News* 56 (February 1995): 92–93.

Castelli, D., P. Pagano, and C. Thanos. "OpenDLib: An Infrastructure for New Generation Digital Libraries." *International Journal on Digital Libraries* 4, no. 1 (2004): 45–48.

Chang, S. "Institutional Repositories: The Library's New Role." *OCLC Systems & Services* 19, no. 3 (2003): 77–79.

Chiorazzi, M., and G. Russell, eds. *Law Library Collection Development in the Digital Age*. Binghamton, NY: Haworth, 2004.

Davis, T. L. "The Evolution of Selection Activities for Electronic Resources." *Library Trends* 45 (Winter 1997): 391–404.

Dorner, D. G. "The Impact of Digital Information Resources on the Roles of Collection Managers in Research Libraries." *Library Collections, Acquisitions, & Technical Services* 28, no. 3 (2004): 249–74.

Garner, J. L. Horwood, and S. Sullivan. "The Place of ePrints in Scholarly Information Delivery." *Library Management* 25, no. 4 (2001): 250–56.

Grahame, V., and T. McAdam. *Managing Electronic Resources*. SPEC Kit 282. Washington, DC: Association of Research Libraries, 2004.

Hastings, S. K. "Selection and Evaluation of Networked Resources." *Acquisitions Librarian* 20 (1998): 109–22.

Johns, C. "Collection Management Strategies in a Digital Environment." *Collection Management* 28, nos. 1/2 (2003): 37–43.

Jordan, J. "New Directions in Electronic Collection Development." *Journal of Library Administration* 36, no. 3 (2002): 5–20.

Kovacs, D. K., and K. L. Robinson. *The Kovacs Guide to Electronic Collection Development*. New York: Neal-Schuman, 2004.

Krueger, J. M., and K. Matthews. "Copyright Law: Fact or Fiction?" *Serials Librarian* 46, nos. 3/4 (2004): 227–32.

Lee, S. D. *Electronic Collection Development: A Practical Guide*. New York: Neal-Schuman, 2002.

Lee, S. H. *Electronic Resources and Collection Development*. Binghamton, NY: Haworth, 2004.

LeFurgy, W. G. "Levels of Service for Digital Repositories." *D-Lib Magazine* 8, no. 5 (May 2002), <http://www.dlib.org/dlib/may02/lefurgy/05lefurgy.html>.

Lynch, C. A. "Institutional Repositories: Essential Infrastructure for Scholarship in the Digital Age." *ARL* 226 (February 2003): 1–7.

McCray, A. T., and M. E. Gallagher. "Principles for Digital Library Development." *Communications of the ACM* 44, no. 5 (2001): 49–55.

Medeiros, N. "E-prints, Institutional Archives and Metadata." *OCLC Systems & Services* 19, no. 3 (2003): 51–53.

Miller, R. H. "Electronic Resources and Academic Libraries." *Library Trends* 48, no. 4 (Spring 2000): 645–70.

Minchew, H. L. "Collection Development for an Electronic Library." *Mississippi Libraries* 66, no. 4 (2002): 110–12.

Misek, M. "eScholars of the World Unite!" *EContent* 27, no. 3 (2004): 36–40.

Pinfield, S., and H. James. "The Digital Preservation of e-Prints." *D-Lib Magazine* 9, no. 9 (September 2003), <http://www.dlib.org/dlib/september03/pinfield/09pinfield.html>.

Pratt, G. F., P. Flannery, and C.L.D. Perkins. "Guidelines for Internet Resource Selection." *College & Research Libraries News* 57 (March 1996): 134–35.

Schaffner, B. L. "Electronic Resources: A Wolf in Sheep's Clothing?" *College & Research Libraries* 62 (May 2001): 239–49.

Smith, M., M. Barton, M. Bass, M. Branschofsky, G. McClellan, D. Stuve, R. Tansley, and J. H. Walker. "DSpace: An Open Source Dynamic Digital Repository." *D-Lib Magazine* 9, no. 1 (January 2003), <http://www.dlib.org/dlib/january03/smith/01smith.html>.

Stefancu, M., and A.B.J. Lambrecht. "All About DOLLeR: Managing Electronic Resources at the University of Illinois at Chicago Library." *Serials Review* 30, no. 3 (2004): 194–205.

Tennant, R. "Beg, Buy, Borrow, License, or Steal." *Library Journal* 125, no. 11 (June 15, 2000): 30–32.

———. *Managing the Digital Library*. New York: Reed Press, 2004.

Thong, J.Y.L., W. Hong, and K. Y. Tam. "What Leads to Acceptance of Digital Libraries?" *Communications of the ACM* 47, no. 11 (November 2004): 78–83.

Tibbo, H. R. "Archival Perspectives on the Emerging Digital Library." *Communications of the ACM* 44 (May 2001): 69–71.

Witten, I. H., M. Loots, M. F. Trujillo, and D. Bainbridge. "The Promise of Digital Libraries in Developing Countries." *Communications of the ACM* 44, no. 5 (May 2001): 82–86.

Young, J. R. "Google Tests Search Engine for Colleges' Scholarly Materials." *Chronicle of Higher Education* 50, no. 33 (April 23, 2004): A36.

8
Government Information

Among the great many things that changed after 9/11 is the way governments, especially the federal government, handle access to information. The events of that day have significantly changed how much federal government information is available to private citizens, reporters, and organizations, including libraries. Significant changes have occurred in public access websites due to concerns of possible terrorist use of this information. The prevailing wisdom is that small, seemingly unimportant pieces of information (when viewed alone) from different government agencies become a potential threat when these pieces are combined.

Even prior to 9/11, there were major changes being planned in the federal government's approach to making information available. The planned shift was, and is, to increasing dependence upon electronic, rather than paper, distribution. Such a shift could mean that individuals, those without access to necessary technology, would find it increasingly difficult to find and use needed government information.

When it comes to understanding governmental actions and processes, having free access to information is essential if the people are to respond effectively. In chapter 5, we noted that commercial publishers need to make a profit on the majority of their publications. There is a host of information, data, and other materials that are useful, if not essential, to individuals and organizations but that are not commercially viable, due to the cost of collecting and compiling the material, as well as to its relatively limited sales appeal. Government publications can fill the gap between no profit and no information.

As James Madison wrote in 1832,

A popular government without popular information, or the means of acquiring it, is but a prologue to a farce or a tragedy;

or perhaps both. . . . And a people who mean to be their own governors, must arm themselves with the power that knowledge gives.[1]

As this quotation shows, interest in, and concern about, society's access to government information has a long history in the United States.

Without question, governments are the world's number one producers of information and publications. Despite major efforts aimed at trying to stem the flow of paper, starting with the Paperwork Reduction Act (PRA, 1980, 44 U.S. Code § 3501 et seq.) and its many revisions, the U.S. government still produces more publications than the combined total from U.S. commercial publishers. The relationship between the volume of government and commercial publications is probably the same in many countries. In many countries, all levels of government generate information and publications, not just the national level.

Government information comes in a variety of sizes, shapes, and media formats. There are books, technical reports, periodicals, pamphlets, microforms, posters, films, slides, photographs, CD-ROMs, online databases, and maps, to name but a few of the formats. They have no special subject focus, because they are the product of many diverse branches and agencies of government. Normally, they reflect the concerns of the agency that produced them. Predictably, an item produced by the U.S. Department of Agriculture (USDA) probably deals with a subject related to agriculture, such as livestock statistics, horticulture, or irrigation. However, the relationship may be less direct. For example, the USDA also publishes information about nutrition, forestry, and home economics. However, as remote as the connection may seem, most government publications do have some connection to the issuing agencies' purpose and function.

Although national government documents are frequently the only official publications easily identified or treated as government publications, all other levels of government—local, regional, state, foreign national, and international—also produce official publications that are government documents as well. Additionally, even though national government documents are the most numerous and important in the library's collection, other levels of government publications are also valuable and useful. A library may choose to include only one type or level of document in its government documents collection, or it may include several.

Defining what is government information is not always easy. Are reports prepared by nongovernmental agencies but required by a government agency truly government publications? What about the publications produced by short- and long-term multijurisdictional groups? Usually, discussions of government information include materials published by the United Nations, which is clearly not a governmental body in the usual meaning of the term. We take a broad view of this, and, for our purposes, any information that has government involvement, with or without direct government funds, is included in this chapter.

Government information, given its breadth of coverage, can be an excellent resource for building effective/useful collections. It is often free or costs very little compared to commercial items on the same topic. Often it contains more current information than its commercial counterparts. (Just because it is free or inexpensive does not mean there are no real costs involved. Staffing costs are high when one actively collects government information.)

As is true with any material in the collection, one must be certain that items selected meet a real need in a reasonably cost-effective manner. The manner in which the library handles government information has a direct impact on its cost-effectiveness.

Background

Starting in 1813, the U.S. government decided that some government information should be made available to the public through libraries. Since that time, the federal program expanded from modest beginnings into a gigantic publications program. Part of the growth came about as a natural process as government activities grew. Another factor was the expansion of the concept of what types of information the government ought to provide. That is, not only were the activities of the three major branches considered important to report to the people, but material for the "general good" of the country was also thought to be appropriate to produce and distribute.

The expansion was such that by the time of the Reagan administration, there were more than 1,300 U.S. government document full and partial depository libraries across the country containing hundreds of thousands of publications. During President Reagan's first term, the Office of Management and Budget (OMB) received authorization to develop a federal information policy as the result of the passage of the Paperwork Reduction Act of 1980 (PRA). OMB was given the responsibility to minimize the costs of government paperwork from collecting data to its dissemination.

One of OMB's initiatives supported the concept of disseminating federal information as raw data in an electronic format, often without software for using or searching for the desired data.[2] Certainly, OMB's role in shifting the emphasis from paper to an electronic means of dissemination was significant. Since 1980, Congress has amended the PRA, always with greater emphasis on moving away from paper. By 1998, changes in PRA had gone from "reduction" to "elimination" of paperwork. In 2002, Congress passed the E-Government Act (116 Stat. 2899), which added an emphasis on security systems for the information produced in electronic form.

One outcome of 9/11 was the federal government's reassessment of the classification of the information within its databases. The general sense of librarians is that there is much less information available as a result of the reassessment. Additionally, as reported by Harold Relyea, the Government Printing Office (GPO) ordered depository libraries to destroy at least one CD-ROM and other holdings as part of the reclassification activities.[3] Some withdrawals have not gone unchallenged, however, such as an attempt in mid-2004 by the GPO to withdraw Department of Justice documents, which was rescinded due to protests by libraries and the American Library Association.[4]

Relyea also noted that some of the government websites closed down post-9/11 and that when they returned, they were "bare bones" versions of the former site.[5] For example, in 2002 the federal government's portal, *FirstGov* (<http://www.firstgov.gov/>), was "overhauled" to better reflect the current state of affairs. *FirstGov*'s purpose is to serve as an intermediary between Web users and Web-based agency resources and services. It is a directory, a linking tool, and a search engine. Even with the tighter classification system in place, it searches millions of documents that government

agencies make available electronically. It is the best starting point for almost any search for federal government information. (A discussion of
sources to use for locating historical government documents is located on
the CD accompanying this text.)

One issue for agency information is that while there is a mandate to
go electronic, the manner in which it is done is up to each agency, based on
its assessment of what is appropriate given the agency's responsibilities.
The result is a host of variations, which in turn present service challenges
for libraries.

From a public service point of view, providing such assistance for all
the variations in U.S. government databases is a challenge that few libraries can fully meet. Even if the library confines itself to assisting with
CD-ROM products, the challenge is great, due to variations in approach and
the often minimal documentation accompanying these products. The products also have a history of changing without adequate advance warning
about the changes. This results in discovery of the changes only when one
tries to use the product in the same manner as one did in the past.

Another federal government Web tool is the Government Information
Locator Service (GILS, at <http://www.access.gpo.gov/su_docs/gils/>), which
is a federal-wide standard for describing information. However, even this
"standard" does, and will continue to, present complexities, for public service staff as well as for end users. GILS consists of two basic elements. One
is the centrally maintained "GILS Core," which is for "general" access to information. The second element relates to the fact that agencies maintain a
GILS designed to meet the special requirements of their primary constituencies. Specialized GILS are linked back to the Core, but a host of variations exist.

One of the major arguments from the federal government is that the
move to electronic formats is reducing costs. The reality is that it does *not*
reduce costs, just as it did not for commercial publishers, but rather shifts
the burden to end users and organizations such as libraries that support
the end user. Customers/end users face the loss of their favorite print publications as well as the challenge of learning new formats—often with less
than complete instructions from the producer on how to use the product.
Few commercial ventures would last long following the methods used by
some federal agencies in producing their electronic products.

Reference service in this "new age" of electronic government information presents some challenges for the staff. There is much to learn about
the idiosyncrasies of various agency databases, even in terms of such basics as how to search, display, and print or download. Also, some agencies
provide different or additional information in the electronic format than in
the print version. That means remembering which version supplies which
type of information.

Library staff must struggle to learn the new and seemingly endless
changing formats. In addition, the library must address equipment issues,
such as multiple-disk CD-ROM products that really require the availability of multiple disks on a tower to assure complete, or at least somewhat
efficient, searching. Extra equipment equals extra expense, as well as support and maintenance costs. Moving to Web-based products will reduce the
need for peripheral equipment such as CD towers. However, there will likely
be a need to provide upgraded computing and printing equipment as
graphics-intensive products require higher-end resolutions and download
times, and the presence of low-end machines will likely lead to dissatisfied

users (not to mention the staff and end-user time lost when access to the Internet is down).

Finally, there are hints that subscription fees for the databases are on the horizon. Depository libraries may be able to avoid some or all of these fees, but that is not certain. The question that remains unanswered is: Will these fees be as low as their former print versions were (and are)? A concern is that, as yet, there is no generally accepted model for pricing electronic materials. Commercial producers approach the pricing in a seemingly ad hoc manner; some use size of service population, some use size of collection budget, others link it to having the print version . . . the variations go on and on. The worry is that the federal interest in reducing and recovering costs will result in substantial fees and that agencies will use a myriad of ways of setting the fees.

Evaluating government electronic resources is actually no different from evaluating other electronic sites. Assessment of the content should include both ease-of-use issues and technical considerations. From the earlier discussion, one might expect the technical aspects to be highly important, given the variations in approach by different agencies. Also, unlike commercial information producers, government agencies may not be as responsive to user complaints about access problems.

Handling Government Information Resources

Government documents and information form a mysterious and frequently misunderstood part of a library's collection. Because of their unique nature, these materials can bewilder and confuse both staff and users. Yet they also constitute an important source of current, vital information. Although we use the term "documents" in a generic sense, people use various labels for this type of material, such as government publications, government information, official documents, federal documents, agency publications, legislative documents, or presidential documents. Libraries house the materials in several ways, ranging from a separate collection containing nothing but government material to complete integration into the general collection. How the library houses these materials affects their processing, from fully cataloged to partially cataloged to uncataloged, which in turn impacts usage.

To add to the confusion created by their diverse management, the documents themselves have only one common trait: they are all official publications of some government or international agency. Thus, they have corporate, rather than personal, authors, which can make it more difficult for users to locate material, unless there is representation in an OPAC. If government publications are included in the OPAC with subject or keyword searching capability, clients will identify and use more government information than they will if the material is cataloged in manual files or in a separate in-house database.

One of the ways depository libraries (further discussed on pages 193–97) are trying to maximize their investment in government information is to consolidate the service into other public services. In the past, depositories often created stand-alone departments. As the federal government has been moving away from paper-based publications, libraries have been rethinking their government documents services.

Types of Documents

U.S. Federal Documents

The executive, judicial, and legislative branches, as well as executive cabinet-level agencies and independent agencies, all issue documents. Most document librarians state that legislative/congressional information and statistical data are the most heavily used items. Other popular documents include presidential statements, reorganization plans, and executive orders. Sources used to identify such publications are the *Code of Federal Regulations—Title 2 (President)* and the *Weekly Compilation of Presidential Documents*. These can be consulted in print or are available online via *GPO Access* (<http://www.gpoaccess.gov/>). Presidential commission reports belong to this class of publications, as do the *Budget of the United States Government* and *Economic Report of the President Transmitted to the Congress* (both of which are available electronically through *GPO Access)*. Such documents are valuable for academic and general-interest purposes, and most large and medium-sized public and academic libraries collect some or all of them. School media centers may collect a few publications that relate to curriculum concerns.

The White House home page (<http://www.whitehouse.gov/>) has links to speeches, press briefings, executive orders, and much more. *POTUS: Presidents of the United States* (<http://www.ipl.org/div/potus>), sponsored by the Internet Public Library, provides bibliographical data on all the U.S. presidents, including election results, cabinet members, memorable events, inaugural addresses, and a host of other information.

Cabinet-level departments (e.g., Department of Agriculture or Department of the Interior) include administrative units, such as agencies and bureaus. Most of these units issue reports, regulations, statistics, and monographs; many issue educational and public relations materials as well. Some sample titles include *U.S. Statistical Abstract of the United States*, *Yearbook of Agriculture, Handbook of Labor Statistics*, and *The Smokey the Bear Coloring Book*. (There is a large body of material for elementary and secondary school-age children from various government agencies. A place to consult for such resources is "Web Pages for the Nation's Youth," Chapter 13 in P. Hernon, R. Dugan, and J. Schuler's *U.S. Government on the Web*, 3rd ed. [Westport, CT: Libraries Unlimited, 2003].) All types of libraries will find publications of interest from the various governmental units. Special libraries collect many of the technical publications. Most academic libraries collect heavily in this area, but media centers and public libraries are rather selective in their acquisition of such materials. In addition to cabinet-level agency publications, many independent agencies publish a similar range of items. The Tennessee Valley Authority, Federal Reserve Board, and Central Intelligence Agency are examples of independent agencies that publish documents.

Judicial documents (aside from case law reports) are not as numerous as those from the other two branches of government. A good starting point for judicial information available electronically is a site maintained by Administrative Office of the U.S. Courts (<http://www.uscourts.gov/>). This is essentially a clearinghouse for information from and about the judicial branch of the U.S. government. It also contains links to a variety of documents. The best-known and most important title is the *United States Reports*, which contains Supreme Court opinions and decisions. (Private commercial publishers issue the decisions of lower federal courts; these are not normally considered government documents.) Although large law libraries must have a set of the *United States Reports*, other libraries' patrons may find them useful for historical, political, or personal reasons. As a result, many larger public and academic libraries acquire a set for the general collection, even when there is a good law library nearby.

Users often seek information about members of Congress and their activities. A very sound starting point for electronic access to information are the House (<http://clerk.house.gov/members/index.html>) and Senate (<http://www.senate.gov/general/contact_information/senators_cfm.cfm>) websites. These sites include access to biographical data, committee assignments, staff member information, and home district contacts. Other online equivalents of standard print publications are the *Congressional Directory* (<http://www.gpoaccess.gov/cdirectory/index.html>) for current information and the *Biographical Directory of the United States Congress 1774–Present* (<http://bioguide.congress.gov/biosearch/biosearch.asp>).

Congressional publications are second in number and popularity only to executive publications. In addition to the text of proposed and passed legislation, these publications include materials documenting House and Senate deliberations. Floor debates appear in the *Congressional Record*; assessments of the need for legislation are available in congressional committee reports; testimony before congressional committees appears in documents that bear the words *Hearings of* or *Hearings on*. There are also several important reference books: *Official Congressional Directory*, *Senate Manual*, and *House Rules*.

The *Congressional Record* provides a semiverbatim transcript of the proceedings on the floor of each house of Congress—semiverbatim, because it is possible for a congressperson to add or delete material in the *Congressional Record*. Thus, it is not an accurate record of what actually transpired on the floor of Congress. Many libraries, including large public libraries, see a strong demand for the *Congressional Record*. Like many GPO publications, the *Congressional Record* is available online at: <http://www.gpoaccess.gov/crecord/index.html>.

House and Senate committee hearings offer a surprising wealth of material for libraries, because many hearings address controversial issues. The reports become a source examining the pros and cons about the subject, as well as information about what groups support or oppose proposed legislation. Often the hearings contain the first detailed reporting of topics under consideration in Congress. Though such hearings may have immediate general interest for library clients, they also are important for scholars of legislative history.

Reports that accompany bills out of committee form another important information resource for libraries. These reports document recommendations concerning the proposed legislation and background on the need for it. Often these reports are central in interpreting the law after the bill becomes law. Many of the current practices regarding copyright law are the result of interpretation of such reports (see chapter 18 for a discussion of this topic).

The Government Printing Office's *GPO Access* home page (<http://www.gpoaccess.gov/>) allows one to search the *Catalog of U.S. Government Publications* (CGP) for recent publications, as well as locate the nearest depositories that own the selected item. The New Electronic Titles (NET) feature of the CGP includes Web-accessible U.S. government publications and is available at <http://www.access.gpo.gov/su_docs/locators/net/index.html>.

The CGP also provides access to other government websites and provides links to other federal agency home pages.

Earlier we mentioned that end users face the prospect of losing their favorite print publications as federal agencies move into electronic dissemination of their information. Joe Morehead, who is certainly one of the most preeminent scholars, if not *the* leading scholar, of government publications and their distribution, wrote an article in 1997 about the migration of federal periodicals from print to electronic formats.[6] He labeled the electronic versions "govzines." His baseline was the *U.S. Government Periodical Index* (CIS/LexisNexis) and information taken from the University of Memphis Government Documents Department's website, in particular its database of "migrating government publications." In all, he discussed fourteen govzines. When describing *The Third Branch*, he noted that "with this govzine (and others, especially *FDA Consumer*, encountered in my cybersurfing expedition), the print version turned out to be considerably more current than the electronic version, a refutation of a guiding Internet principle, the rapid access to information."[7] (Some agencies, such as the Government Accountability Office [GAO, formerly the General Accounting Office], no longer automatically send out printed GAO reports. It is now up to the user to monitor the GAO's site, at <http://www.gao.gov>, and either download the materials in PDF format or request a print copy.)

An ongoing concern about electronic resources, whether government or commercial, is, How permanent is permanent? Who will archive and assure continued access to electronic information as operating systems, software, and hardware change time and time again? In classic Moreheadian prose, he concluded his sermon with:

> It seems that while the GPO gets a grand makeover, the using public suffers a bad hair day. To change the metaphor, the migration to the Internet and the concomitant extirpation of print-equivalent sources will falter if it proceeds with the frenetic exigency exhibited by the thundering herds of wildebeest across the Serengeti plains.[8]

It would appear that Morehead's words may not go unnoticed. In December 2004, the GPO issued a plan entitled "A Strategic Vision for the 21st Century," which outlined a series of strategic activities GPO intends to implement in order to reorganize itself into a "digital information factory." This plan, available online at <http://www.gpo.gov/congressional/pdfs/04stra tegicplan.pdf>, also includes such initiatives as the development of a Digital Content System for federal documents, which is slated for completion by late 2007.

Regardless of the method in which government publications are made available, when the public service staff is aware of the variety of information contained in federal information sources, especially those that are not reporting on government activities, they can direct the public to these useful sources. All types of libraries can find some useful material for patrons in the annual pool of federal publications. Even at higher prices, these materials not only enrich the collection but also help stretch the collection development funds. The extra material, in turn, will benefit the individual and the institution or community being served.

State and Local Governments

Several differences exist between state and federal information. One difference is that there is still a very strong print orientation at the state level. Certainly, there is a movement to having more and more state information available through the Web; however, it was not until 1996 that all states had a Web presence, and even then not all the sites were "official." Very few states produce audiovisual materials; thus, *state publication* or information refers to textual material, whether printed, mimeographed, or occasionally in microformat or some type of electronic format. A second and often overlooked difference is that states can, and frequently do, copyright their publications. Some shared characteristics of state and federal information are diversity of subject matter, relatively low purchase price, and increasing difficulty in identifying "official" publications.

Although many state publications are in the public domain, states do have the right to copyright some or all of their publications. Some states elect to use this option, whereas other states do not, so there is some confusion in this area. In Michigan, for example, the state *may* copyright materials, whereas in Pennsylvania state law *requires* copyrighting. Undoubtedly, one major reason for securing copyright is the hope that the material will generate revenue. From a library point of view, state documents are no different from any other copyrighted material. The staff and the public should assume that the concept of fair use, rather than the concept of public domain, applies to state publications. Staff need to understand the copyright differences in order to provide effective advice and service.

Like the federal publishing program, most state programs now produce materials mandated by law; that is, they record government activities and release a variety of statistical data and general information about the state. Many of the federal statistical publications are compilations of state data, which means that the most current information, by as much as two or three years, is in the state publications. The volume of general information and how-to publications from states is low compared to federal output.

The availability of documents of state and local government agencies is limited in most libraries and information centers. In the last twenty years, most states established or passed legislation to establish depository library programs that roughly parallel the federal depository program (see pages 193–94).

Access to state publications can be difficult. Some states do publish lists of their new titles (e.g., *California State Publications*); however, not all states do so. Two Web resources that help locate state and local information are "State and Local Government on the Net" (<http://www.state localgov.net/index.cfm>) and Yahoo!'s "Government: State Government (<http://dir.yahoo.com/Government/U_S_Government/State_Government/>).

Variations in access to electronic state information are as wide as for federal agencies. In terms of websites, some states have well-organized and well-coordinated home pages. Some examples are Minnesota's North Star page (<http://www.state.mn.us>) and North Carolina's (<http://www .ncgov.com>) and Utah's (<http://www.utah.gov>) websites. Others take a more *laissez-faire* approach. Many of these tend toward just promoting state tourism and why one should move one's business to their state. In other instances, the legislators appear more interested in marketing and selling state data than in providing public access to information.

The Council of State Governments (<http://www.csg.org>) has provided states with products that assist in governing. It also publishes items such as *The Book of the States* and *Trend Alerts* (based on fifty state surveys). Most of their products are available in print, disk, and online.

State and local governments tend to take greater advantage of the Web's interactive and graphic potential than does the federal government. For example, for a time the California home page (<http://www.state.ca.us >), in addition to providing information from more than thirty departments, featured an interactive "game" that allowed the public to see what would happen to the state budget when one employed different strategies and assumptions. Maryland's home page (<http://www.maryland.gov>) contains not only state information but also data about all counties and many cities, as well as links to a number of online services.

Depository practices and requirements differ from state to state. The statutes of any particular state set the frequency of deposit and the framework of the depository program. The state library can provide more detailed information about its state depository program, including a list of depositories, sales and acquisition information, and information about which materials are available from a central source and which are available only from individual agencies.

Historically, the most effective method for acquisition of state and local documents has been through direct agency contact. Like the federal government, most state agencies produce and sell publications at or near cost. Often, complimentary copies are available to libraries. One problem in acquisition of state documents has been their short press runs, which results in state documents being out of print practically before they are off the press. Although state and local agencies are usually willing to provide copies of their available publications, they rarely accept standing orders, deposit accounts, and other convenient methods of library acquisition. Usually, acquisition is possible only on a case-by-case basis, which is time-consuming and frustrating. Frequently, the only way a library learns about a timely document is through a newspaper article or a patron request.

Privately published indexes provide additional guidance. CIS/Lexis-Nexis' *Statistical Reference Index* (*SRI*) contains a large section of state-government-published statistics. *SRI* is available in print, with current and retrospective information (including links to selected documents) found online via *LexisNexis Statistical*. Another resource for statistical information is Fedstats (<http://www.fedstats.gov>), a resource point for statistics from over 100 U.S. federal agencies. The accompanying "Mapstats" tool (<http://www.fedstats.gov/qf/>) similarly provides a means of accessing summary statistics for states, counties, and major cities.

The *Index to Current Urban Documents* (*ICUD*), published by Greenwood Press, offers both bibliographic control of state and local documents and access to the documents themselves in PDF format. (*ICUD* documents are available in PDF from volume 29 forward; materials in volumes 1–28 are available in microfiche.) Given the poor bibliographic control of state and local documents, these sets, though expensive, sometimes offer the most cost-effective option for collection development.

Local Government Publications

Collecting local documents is something almost all public and academic libraries do, if not through intent, then by accident. Even if there is nothing about acquiring local documents in the library's collection development policy, local governments often view the library as a distribution mechanism. A better approach is to plan on collecting local documents, as they are often high-interest items for the community. Perhaps the major question to answer is how long to retain such documents.

In general, local government publications offer even fewer selection tools and less bibliographic control than state publications. However, some major publications of special interest, such as long-range county plans, demographic studies, or almost anything with local impact, get local publicity. Often, inexpensive or free copies are available to local libraries. The problems of acquisition roughly parallel those for state documents; that is, there are no agency mailing lists or standing orders and no effective acquisition options (such as deposit accounts). Furthermore, there is the need to negotiate individually with agencies to acquire reports and short-run publications. The strategic problems are almost identical to those for state documents, but without the advantage of the state documents depository programs. In many communities, the central public library becomes an unofficial local documents depository, and it may offer support to other libraries seeking local documents.

Collecting and retaining local city and perhaps county documents are reasonable for a central public library and perhaps a local academic library. Collecting from more than two or three local governments becomes expensive in terms of staff time. Very few libraries attempt to collect from more than twenty local governments, unless they are buying microforms through the Greenwood Press program, through which documents listed in *ICUD* are made available on microfiche (volumes 1–28), while the online subscription includes an annual paper index and CD-ROM for archiving.[9]

The *ICUD* covers over 500 cities in Canada and the United States and is updated every six to eight weeks. Very few cities or counties set up depository programs, and most do not have a central publications office. Tracking down reports of various departments and programs is obviously time-consuming. Adding to the problem are various short- and long-term associations formed by several local governments.

As one might expect, local and regional government use and organization of electronic information are highly varied. One early effort took place in Santa Monica, California, in 1989 with the development of PEN (Public Electronic Network, <http://pen.ci.santa-monica.ca.us/>). The name PEN suggests the fact that the initial purpose of the network was conferencing and e-mail service, designed to provide electronic interaction between the citizens and local government. Today, that concept is embedded in a much larger system linking all major city departments, including the public library's online catalog. The Riverside County, California, website (<http://www.co.riverside.ca.us/>) provides links to over 100 county, city, and school agencies. Another well-publicized site is the Blacksburg Electronic Village (BEV) in Virginia (<http://www.bev.net>), which provides access to government and commercial material.

Foreign and International Documents

National governments in almost every country issue at least a few publications each year, and a great many now have Internet sites. In many countries, the government publication program equals the U.S. program in volume and complexity. The good news is that these large-scale programs generally use an agency, like the U.S. GPO, as the primary distributor of the publications. Very few countries offer a depository program to foreign libraries. Only the large research libraries actively collect foreign documents, because few patrons need the material. If the public service staff know the location of the nearest foreign document collection, they can adequately serve the few patrons with an interest in, or need for, these publications. The University of Michigan maintains a website about national government information, called *Foreign Government Resources on the Web* (<http://www.lib.umich.edu/govdocs/forcomp.html>). Another source of information is the *World Fact Book* (<http://www.odci.gov/cia/publications/factbook/index.html>), which is prepared by the Central Intelligence Agency.

International documents, especially United Nations publications, however, have a wider appeal. The major source of international publications and information are IGOs (intergovernmental organizations). An IGO may be defined as a group of three or more member countries working together on one or more long-term common interests. Without doubt, the largest IGO is the United Nations. There are also nongovernmental organizations (NGOs), such as the World Health Organization, that issue publications and information of interest to a fairly large number of library users. Good starting points for such organizations are the *Geneva International Forum* (<http://geneva.intl.ch/index.htm>) and Northwestern University's *International Governmental Organizations* (<http://www.library.nwu.edu/govpub/resource/internat/igo.html>) sites. Another starting point is Yahoo!'s *Government: Countries* listing (<http://dir.yahoo.com/Government/Countries>), which provides links to Internet sites of 100-plus countries. Though some of these sites have little information, they may contain links to other helpful electronic resources.

The United Nations (UN) has an extensive publications program and, like other governmental bodies, is beginning to issue material in electronic formats. The UN website provides a variety of information about the organization, including the *UN Publications Catalogue* (<http://unp.un.org>), which contains ordering information. The site also has a listing of all UN depository libraries worldwide. For most libraries that have some UN documents, the material is part of the regular collection, circulating or reference, rather than held in a separate document area, simply because they do not acquire very many titles.

UNESCO also publishes some excellent reference titles dealing with statistics, education, science, etc. Some other titles published by agencies related to the UN are the International Labor Organization's *Yearbook of Labour Statistics*, the UNICEF *State of the World's Children Report*, and the Food and Agriculture Organization's (FAO) *State of Food and Agriculture*.

The international document collection development situation has benefited from the existence of Bernan Associates, a private distributor that collects international documents, creates catalogs, and offers the documents for sale from a central facility. This vendor offers a unique opportunity to build an international documents collection from a variety of agencies; Bernan provides all the conveniences found in the trade book field, such as standing orders, sales catalogs and subject pamphlets, deposit accounts, and a central sales office. An important fact to keep in mind is that Bernan handles many intergovernmental agency publications, such as the International Atomic Energy Agency, World Trade Organization (WTO), the United Nations University Press, the World Bank, and the International Monetary Fund (IMF).

Like state and federal documents, international documents profited from inclusion in computerized bibliographic databases. Privately published indexes, such as CIS/LexisNexis' *Index to International Statistics (IIS)*, are among the tools creating some degree of bibliographic control and collection development assistance. As with CIS/LexisNexis' state and federal documents program, *IIS* offers companion fiche collections, and materials are also available online via *LexisNexis Statistical*.

Each type of document has its own place in a collection development program, and each has special acquisition problems, collecting methods, and advantages. Depository programs offer free documents but may pose problems resulting from depository status requirements, such as being open to the public. A library may also not wish to assume depository responsibilities in order to acquire documents, especially given the wide variety of items available to nondepository libraries.

The GPO and Sale of Government Publications

Only agency publications chosen for the sales program are available from the GPO. These are documents that the GPO has screened and evaluated for sales potential and public interest. The GPO produces these documents in quantities sufficient for sale and adds them to the sales program. In 1999, GPO operated twenty-four regional bookstores as well as three sales offices in Washington, D.C. All bookstores, except for the main bookstore in Washington, D.C., and a retail outlet in Laurel, Maryland, were closed in September 2003.[10] On April 28, 2004, Bruce James, public printer of the United States, testified at a congressional hearing and reported on the results of GPO's closing of the "failing bookstores" in a cost-cutting move.[11] Publications in the sales program are available for purchase from the GPO website (<http://bookstore.gpo.gov>) or the Washington, D.C., bookstore. GPO deposit accounts are available to minimize purchasing problems, and the GPO also accepts major credit cards for purchases of GPO publications.

The GPO website offers a series of subject bibliographies and "best seller" lists that are frequently updated, adding new publications and deleting out-of-print items. In addition, GPO provides a "New Titles by Topic" e-mail alert service that provides updates of selected new publications available for sale from the superintendent of documents (<http://bookstore.gpo.gov/alertservice.html>). The subject bibliographies are particularly useful as acquisition tools for libraries that have particular subject interests or strengths. The bibliographies (available at <http://bookstore.gpo.gov/sb/about.html>) provide users with ordering information and an idea of the availability of documents that they might wish to acquire.

Libraries acquire government documents in a variety of ways. Some assume the responsibilities of depository collections, if they can. Others purchase documents to match a collection profile. Some have standing orders through official or commercial vendors; others purchase documents individually or acquire most of their documents free of charge.

Another common method of acquisition is purchase through the agency's official sales program. The agency may or may not offer a standing order program. Some commercial jobbers and bookstores do deal in documents, and some booksellers, especially those of used or rare books, may stock some documents. One large vendor of government documents is the aforementioned Bernan Associates (<http://www.bernan.com>), based in Maryland. Bernan Associates handles federal as well as UNESCO, UN, and other international organization publications.

Of course, many documents are available free of charge from issuing agencies and congressional representatives. They also are available as gifts or exchanges from libraries that have held them for the statutory period and wish to dispose of them or from libraries with extra nondepository or gift copies.

Public Access and the Federal Depository Library Program

Free, unrestricted access is the cornerstone of library public service programs, at least for the library's primary service population. In the case of information in depository libraries, there is a legal requirement that the documents collection be open to *all* persons, not just the primary service population. Thus, privately funded libraries that have depository status must allow anyone to come in and use the government material, even if the library limits access to its other collections. This requirement can create some problems for public service staff, especially if the library requires the patron to show a valid identification card to enter the library. Lacking that practice, the library may decide to escort such individuals to and from the government documents area. Most private institutions that have depository status do not attempt to monitor entrances and in-house use of the collection.

We have mentioned depository libraries at several points in this chapter, noting that national, some state, and international bodies have depository programs. Here we focus on the U.S. federal program, because it is so widespread. It is, however, very much in a stage of flux at the time we prepared this edition. It is very likely it will be a considerably different program by the time of the next edition. An article whose title could not have forecast the future more accurately appeared in the September 2001 issue of *American Libraries*, "Government Documents at the Crossroads."[12] The article appeared in response to GPO's October 2000 policy statement, which announced that in the future, the primary method of making publications available would be online dissemination. In the end, a core list of approximately forty titles would remain in paper, "so long as they are published in paper by the originating agency."[13] It appears this announcement makes the depository program redundant, since many users would be able to access documents online, anywhere. However, in the spring of 2003, the public printer of the United States and the superintendent of documents asked depository libraries to join in a three-year "visioning" process to shape the future of the program.[14] Updates and further details regarding this process are available on the Depository Library Council web page (<http://www .access.gpo.gov/su_docs/fdlp/council/index.html>).

Regardless of its future, the Federal Depository Library Program (FDLP) has had a long history; its formal start was in 1861. Since its inception, the FDLP has been successful in getting government information to the public through its approximately 1,279 depositories. A full depository agrees to accept all items available to FDLP participants, whereas selective (or partial) institutions take only a portion of the material. At one time the selective libraries were encouraged to take a minimum of 15 percent of the items available, although this is no longer a requirement. Regardless, the depository program does *not* include all publications issued by federal agencies and organizations.

The GPO is responsible for operating the program, and all the items in the *Catalog of U.S. Government Publications* are part of the program, so locating an entry in that product means that the item should be available at the closest full-member library and might be available at a selective member. (To locate the nearby members electronically, use <http://www .gpoaccess.gov/libraries.html>.) The GPO provides government information products at no cost (at least at present) to members of FDLP. Member institutions are, in turn, required to provide local, no-fee access in "an impartial environment" to the public and to provide professional assistance in using the material.

The composition of FDLP is heavily weighted toward academic libraries (50 percent), with public libraries a distant second (20 percent). The breakdown for the balance of members is: 11 percent academic law libraries, 5 percent community college libraries, 5 percent state and special libraries, 5 percent federal and state court libraries, and 4 percent federal agency libraries. As one can determine from the preceding data, the academic and law libraries dominate the program in terms of numbers. Many people view academic libraries as intimidating, so increasing the number of public libraries in the program might well increase usage by the general public.

As the federal government moves toward greater and greater dependence on electronic dissemination of information, some people raise questions such as:

- Is the FDLP still necessary?
- Is the FDLP a remnant of the 19th century?
- Is the FDLP really the best way to get information to people in the 21st century?
- Is there a way to change the system to make it more cost-effective?

A good article that explores the challenges facing FDLP is Patrick Wilkinson's "Beyond the Federal Depository Library Program." Wilkinson concluded, "The traditional FDLP is dead. . . . The new entity will be created to fill the country's need for free and open access to government information in the twenty-first century."[15] In contrast, Prudence Adler believes that FDLP "has stood the test of time because of the role that it has played in promoting access to government information, and in support of teaching and learning and in stimulating economic development. That role continues and, indeed, should be strengthened and reaffirmed."[16] The authors of "Government Documents at the Crossroads"[17] also believe the program is essential, and it will be interesting to see the results of the "visioning" process initiated in 2003.

Earlier we mentioned that, all too often, separate government documents collections are housed in low-use areas of the library. The primary issue is not the physical location but rather integration versus separation of government information and the general collections. In essence, intellectual access is the primary concern.

For the majority of libraries that do not actively collect government documents, the integrated approach is the only reasonable option and is the one most libraries employ. If the library is a partial depository, taking 25 percent or less of the items available, and there is no full-time public service documents staff, we believe the integrated approach is best. The reason is that, without experienced public service documents staff, the separate collection is too often forgotten and vastly underused for the shelf space occupied. Undoubtedly, the large separate collection with a full-time staff will be more effective if the general reference staff remembers to direct patrons to the document collection. There is no problem when a person asks about government documents. The public service staff, however, often forgets to suggest the government documents collection when responding to a general subject request. It is vital that *all* the public service staff remember to suggest this source of information when there is a separate collection.

As governments move toward ever-greater dependence on electronic formats for the dissemination of information, the issue of how to handle print materials is less critical to increasing usage. Nevertheless, at least in the near term, FDLP members will continue to receive some material in print formats. Even when, or if, all government information is available only in electronic format, there will be the question of what to do with more than 190 years' worth of print publications. Thus, there will still be a few challenges for depository libraries regarding traditional formats.

A reminder about public access to federal documents is appropriate here. Any depository library, partial or full, *must* allow anyone access to the federal documents, regardless of the library's policies about public use of its other collections. (The *U.S. Code* states, "Depository libraries shall make government publications available for free use of the general public."[18] In the *Instructions to Depository Libraries*,[19] "free use" is further defined, and the *Federal Depository Library Manual*[20] [*FDLM*] addresses issues of access to electronic materials.) If the library restricts public access to its general collections, and few people request access to the documents collection, staff members, especially new staff, may unknowingly deny legally required access. It is important that all public service staff understand this legal requirement.

Another requirement is that there be a library staff member primarily responsible for handling the depository material, but this does not necessarily mean a public service person. Very often, when there is just one person, that staff member is part of the technical services section, because of the high volume of record keeping and processing associated with maintaining a documents collection. In such cases, occasional miniworkshops for the public service staff on use of government publications and access tools (indexes, abstracts, and so forth) will help increase use of the material.

FDLP members have an obligation to promote their federal information collections and services. The *FDLM* states that when it comes to promotion, the "most important group to target for public awareness is the general public."[21] In essence, the library's primary service population may not be the target group that GPO is interested in reaching. A survey by David Heisser[22] and another by Charles McClure and Peter Hernon[23] demonstrated a lack of public awareness about FDLP and the service available through the program. Heisser surveyed nonprofit and small business organizations and found that 77 percent were unaware of the existence of depository libraries. McClure and Hernon looked at users of depository libraries. Their findings showed that only 12 percent of all academic depository users were from outside the institution.

Another aspect of the depository program is mandated retention. Adequate collection space is a chronic problem in most libraries. One method for gaining space is deselecting material from the collection. A traditional weeding/deselection technique is to remove the lowest-use items and either store them in less expensive space or discard the material. Government publications, more often than not, fall into the low-use category, yet the depository may not be as quick to remove these items as it might be with low-use purchased materials. All depository libraries must retain items for at least five years after receipt, although official electronic versions may be substituted for tangible items. Regional (full) depositories *must* retain their collections, and selective depositories must offer items identified as discards to the regional library and local partial depositories before discarding. On the plus side, periodic reviews of the documents collection may also encourage a review of the general collection's low-use items, which also occupy valuable shelf space.

Preservation problems are the same as found in the general collection. Print government publications are just as likely to be printed on acidic paper as their commercial cousins. There was, in 1990, a congressional resolution under consideration to encourage, if not require, all agenicies to use acid-free paper for important publications. Nonprint government materials also suffer from the same problems as their commercial counterparts, for example, poor processing—especially microformats—and poor bonding of the emulsion layer to the carrier film base in both photographs and motion picture film. All the materials need the same care in handling by staff and patrons, as well as the appropriate environmental controls (temperature and humidity), as discussed in other chapters (see especially chapter 16).

In early 2004, the GPO convened a meeting of experts in digitization to discuss the prospect of preserving "legacy" materials. This meeting was the first step in

> an initiative with the federal depository library community to digitize the entire legacy collection of U.S. government documents currently held in depositories, estimated to be about 2.2 million items (excluding microfiche). The intent is to ensure that the collection is digitally reformatted for preservation purposes and that access copies are derived from the digitized preservation copies. GPO is committed to the preservation of this information and to making it available, in the public domain, for permanent public access.[24]

Another project initiated by the GPO is the creation of a "Collection of Last Resort," or CLR, designed to serve as a "'dark archive' that will become, over time, a comprehensive collection of tangible and electronic titles that will backstop the regional library collections and future shared repositories."[25] Institutions participating in the pilot project include the University of Arizona (<http://www.library.arizona.edu/library/teams/sst/pol/guide/gpo-pilot/>) and the University of South Florida (<http://library.ucf.edu/GovDocs/ntis>). The success of these initiatives remains to be seen, although it may be the primary means of preserving a number of valuable materials.

In January 2005, the superintendent of documents proposed radical changes to the FDLP. Although the appropriations request to be submitted for fiscal year (FY) 2006 was to remain essentially the same, the request would include changes in the way materials were distributed, beginning in October 2005. One of the most significant changes would be that only those titles from the "Essential Documents" list (see page 193) would be published, excluding such items as maps, legal documents, and geological information. A second change would be the creation of a "Print on Demand"

Allowance Program, where selective and regional depository libraries would be allocated a small amount to purchase other titles.[26] The Government Documents Round Table (GODORT) of ALA passed a resolution opposing these proposed changes.[27] Although the ultimate fate of this issue was unclear as this text went to press, it is likely that if the FY 2006 appropriation is passed as suggested by the superintendent of documents, the face of the FDLP would be radically changed.

The preceding discussion provides an overview of access issues in a depository environment. A thoughtful reader may wonder about the costs associated with being a depository library. A 1993 study by Duggan and Dodsworth indicated that the Georgetown University library expended $217,970 in direct, support, and overhead costs on its depository program.[28] For smaller depository programs, the dollar costs would be much smaller, but we wonder if the proportions of depository costs to total operating expenses might not be very similar. There is no question but that substantial dollar and staff costs are associated with depository status. For at least some selective depositories in southern California, those costs and related issues are causing second thoughts about the value of being a selective depository.

Some existing depository libraries are thinking about dropping, or have dropped, out of the program. The LMU library was a selective depository that decided it would not be cost-effective to remain in the program. Several other southern California private academic libraries are also considering withdrawing. The GPO inspection reports were one of the factors that triggered the LMU decision to drop out of the program. Although no longer conducted, FDLP on-site inspections administered by GPO personnel allowed both the federal government and the library to assess how well the site was meeting program requirements. For the library, it was also an opportunity to think about the actual value of the program in meeting the library's primary mission and goals, as well as the service needs of the primary service population.

Summary

Government information is an important element in any collection development program. It is fundamentally important for society to have such information easily available, even if people do not use it heavily. All types of libraries can acquire useful information from government agencies at a reasonable cost. The idea that private, for-profit firms would provide the variety and depth of information and keep the costs reasonable seems naive. One has only to look at the cost of scholarly serials to see how privatization might affect the cost of government information. The effect of 9/11 on the availability of government information remains an issue of concern and will likely need to be monitored for some time. However, the popularity of some government publications, such as the 9/11 report,[29] unequivocally proves that the availability of such items meets a very real need for information on the part of library users.

Notes

1. James Madison, letter written in 1832.

2. U.S. Congress, Office of Technology Assessment, *Informing the Nation* (Washington, DC: Government Printing Office, 1988), 9.

3.   Harold Relyea, "E-Gov Comes to the Federal Government," in *U.S. Government on the Web* 3rd ed., ed. Peter Hernon, Robert Dugan, and John Schuler (Westport, CT: Libraries Unlimited, 2003), 395.

4.   "GPO Rescinds Docs. Withdrawal amid Growing Librarian Protest," *Library Hotline* 33, no. 32 (August 9, 2004): 1; "Senators Raise Questions over GPO Document Recall," *Library Hotline* 33, no. 37 (September 13, 2004): 7.

5.   Relyea, "E-Gov Comes to the Federal Government," 395.

6.   Joe Morehead, "Govzines on the Web: A Preachment," *Serials Librarian* 23, nos. 3/4 (1997): 17–30.

7.   Ibid., 25.

8.   Ibid., 29.

9.   "Index to Current Urban Documents," Greenwood Press <http://www.urbdocs.com/>.

10.   U.S. Government Printing Office, "U.S. Government Bookstores," <http://bookstore.gpo.gov/locations/>.

11.   Bruce R James. "Prepared Statement Before the Subcommittee on Legislative Appropriations, Committee on Appropriations, U.S. House of Representatives on the Appropriations Request of the U.S. Government Printing Office For Fiscal Year 2005," April 28, 2004 (Washington, DC: U.S. Government Printing Office), 1, <http://www.gpoaccess.gov/cr/testimony/4_28_04.pdf>.

12.   Karrie Peterson, Elizabeth Cowell, and Jim Jacobs, "Government Documents at the Crossroads," *American Libraries* 32 (September 2001): 52–55.

13.   U.S. Government Printing Office, "Essential Titles for Public Use in Paper Format," <http://www.access.gpo.gov/su_docs/fdlp/pubs/estitles.html>.

14.   U.S. Government Printing Office, "Envisioning the Future of Federal Government Information: Summary of the Spring 2003 Meeting of the Depository Library Council to the Public Printer," <http://www.access.gpo.gov/su_docs/fdlp/council/EnvisioningtheFuture.html>.

15.   Patrick Wilkinson, "Beyond the Federal Depository Library Program," *Journal of Government Information* 23, no. 3 (1996): 411–17.

16.   Prudence Adler, "Federal Information Dissemination Policies and Practice," *Journal of Government Information* 23, no. 4 (1996): 441.

17.   Peterson et al., "Government Documents at the Crossroads."

18.   44 U.S.C. § 1911 (1944).

19.   "Physical Facilities," in *Instructions to Depository Libraries* (Washington, DC: Government Printing Office, 2000), <http://www.access.gpo.gov/su_docs/fdlp/pubs/instructions/in_ch6.html>.

20.   *Federal Depository Library Manual* (Washington, DC: Government Printing Office, 1993).

21.   Ibid., 112.

22.   David Heisser, "Marketing U.S. Government Depositories," *Government Publications Review* 13 (January/February 1986): 58.

23.   Charles McClure and Peter Hernon, *Users of Academic and Public GPO Depository Libraries* (Washington, DC: Government Printing Office, 1989), 61.

24.   *Report on the Meeting of Experts on Digital Preservation* (Washington, DC: U.S. Government Printing Office, March 12, 2004), 1–2, <http://www.gpoaccess.gov/about/reports/preservation.pdf>.

25. *Collection of Last Resort*, Discussion Draft (Washington, DC: U.S. Government Printing Office, April 6, 2004), 4, <http://www.access.gpo.gov/su_docs/fdlp/pubs/clr.pdf>.

26. American Library Association, "Call for Oversight on GPO Initiatives," *Washington Office Newsline (ALAWON)* 14, no. 6 (January 27, 2005), <http://www.ala.org/ala/washoff/washnews/2005ab/006jan27.htm>.

27. American Library Association, Government Documents Round Table, "GODORT Resolution [Resolution Opposing GPO's Decision to Eliminate Print Distribution of Important Government Information]," endorsed by the American Library Association's Committee on Legislation, January 17, 2005 <http://sunsite.berkeley.edu/GODORT/resolutions/20050117301.html>.

28. Robert Duggan and Ellen Dodsworth, "Costing a Depository Library," *Government Information Quarterly* 11 (1994): 268.

29. *The 9/11 Commission Report: Final Report of the National Commission on Terrorist Attacks upon the United States* (Washington, DC: U.S. Government Printing Office, 2004).

Selected Websites and Discussion Lists*

(See also resources on the DLC5 website: <http://www.lu.com/dlc5>)

American Library Association—Government Documents Roundtable (GODORT)
> <http://sunsite.berkeley.edu/GODORT/>
> Website for GODORT, the ALA roundtable devoted to issues of concern for librarians working with government documents. Includes access to professional resources for government documents librarians, as well as information on the activities of the organization.

Data access tools—From FedStats
> <http://www.fedstats.gov/toolkit.html>
> A listing of statistical sources by agency.

Decision Framework for Federal Document Repositories
> <http://www.access.gpo.gov/su_docs/fdlp/pubs/decisionmatrix.pdf>
> Prepared by the Center for Research Libraries (CRL) for the GPO, this matrix is intended for use in creating specifications for a system of regional repositories for tangible federal government documents.

Documents Data Miner
> <http://govdoc.wichita.edu/ddm>
> Developed through a partnership between the University Libraries at Wichita State University and the National Institution for Aviation Research, this resource provides a means to locate items selected by FDLP members.

FDLP Electronic Collection
> <http://www.access.gpo.gov/su_docs/fdlp/ec/index.html>
> The Federal Depository Library Program Electronic Collection (FDLP/EC) is a comprehensive digital library of U.S. government information, including legislative and regulatory publications, products from related agencies, and electronic products distributed to depository libraries.

GOVDOC-L
> A discussion forum for issues related to government information and the Federal Depository Library program. To subscribe, send the following message to LISTSERV@LISTS.PSU.EDU: SUB GOVDOC-L Yourfirstname Yourlastname.

Government Information Table of Contents
   <http://www.arl.org/info/frn/nsletter/govtoc.html>
   The government information web page provided by the Association of Research Libraries (ARL), which includes links to resources related to access to government information post-9/11, as well as initiatives for data sharing and the FDLP.

Web-Based Government Information Project
   <http://www.cdlib.org/inside/projects/preservation/govinfo/>
   Website of the California Digital Library's initiative to study technologies and approaches for management of Web-based government information.

*These websites were last accessed May 5, 2005.

Further Reading

Bertot, J. C., and W. E. Moen. "Information Policy: FirstGov.gov/org/net/com." *Journal of Academic Librarianship* 26, no. 6 (November 2000): 422–26.

Block, M. "Dealing with Digital," *Library Journal* 128, no. 12 (July 15, 2003): 40–43.

Cain, C. C. "Permanent Public Access to State Electronic Government Information Project." *Louisiana Libraries* 66, no. 3 (Winter 2004): 13–16.

Halchin, L. E. "Electronic Government: Government Capability and Terrorist Resource." *Government Information Quarterly* 21, no. 4 (2004): 406–19.

Hartnett, C. "Discarding Documents, Filling in Gaps." *DttP* 30, no. 2 (Summer 2002): 19–21.

Hernon, P., H. C. Relyea, R. E. Dugan, and J. F. Cheverie. *United States Government Information: Policies and Sources*. Westport, CT: Libraries Unlimited, 2002.

Hernon, P., R. E. Dugan, and J. A. Shuler. *U.S. Government on the Web*. 3rd ed. Westport, CT: Libraries Unlimited, 2003.

Lopresti, R., and M. Gorin. "The Availability of US Government Publications on the World Wide Web." *Journal of Government Information* 29, no. 1 (January–February 2002): 17–29.

Marcum, B. "Preserving Government Documents, What Does the Future Hold?" *Kentucky Libraries* 67, no. 2 (Spring 2003): 16–20.

McCullough, M. "Web Clearinghouse Promotes Displays of Government Information." *College & Research Libraries News* 62, no. 5 (May 2001): 487.

Pierce, J. B. "What Ails Access to Government Health Information?" *American Libraries* 34 (December 2003): 58–63.

Relyea, H., and L. E. Halchin. "Homeland Security and Information Management." In *The Bowker Annual of Library and Book Trade Information*, 231–50. Medford, NJ: Information Today, 2003.

Roper, F. W. "U.S. Government Documents and Technical Reports." In *Introduction to Reference Sources in the Health Sciences* compiled and edited by J. A. Boorkman, J. Huber, and F. Roper, 99–107. New York: Neal-Schuman, 2004.

Shuler, J. A. "Libraries and Government Information: The Past Is Not Necessarily Prologue." *Government Information Quarterly* 19, no. 1 (2002): 1–7.

———. "Beyond the Depository Concept." *Journal of Academic Librarianship* 27, no. 4 (July 2001): 299–301.

———. "Government Information Locator Services and Systems." *Journal of Academic Librarianship* 27, no. 3 (May 2001): 224–28.

————. "New Economic Models for the Federal Depository System—Why Is It So Hard to Get the Question Answered?" *Journal of Academic Librarianship* 30, no. 3 (May 2004): 243–49.

Singer, C. A. "The Transition of U.S. Government Publications from Paper to the Internet: A Chronology." *Internet Reference Services Quarterly* 8, no. 3 (2003): 29–45.

Smith, L. L. "Government Documents." Theme issue. *Louisiana Libraries* 66, no. 3 (Winter 2004): 3–35.

Wilson, P. "Electronic Documents to the People." *Public Libraries* 42, no. 6 (November–December 2003): 362–63.

9
Audiovisual Materials

Although the most obvious components of library collections may be monographs and serials (either in print or electronic format), based upon circulation data, videos and sound recordings are among the most popular items in many types of libraries. While the major exceptions are corporate and research libraries, even in these libraries, nonprint media can, and do, have a role in serving the community.

Several years ago, Will Manley wrote an opinion piece in which he suggested that videos were the "Twinkies" of library collections: expensive, draining much-needed funding from the important materials, attracting only nonreaders, creating more potential censorship issues, and acting as unnecessary competition for video rental operations.[1] There are few librarians in school, public, and small libraries to fairly large academic libraries today who would agree with his views about videos in libraries. Manley's views may have had some merit when written, but attitudes have certainly changed during the intervening years. At present, there is recognition that the various formats have important specialized roles to play in disseminating information. A goal of libraries is to serve the entire service population, which means providing people with different ways of learning and using information.

Why Audiovisual Collections?

For many purposes, textual material is not the most effective or most reasonable method of conveying a particular message. For teaching, research, and recreation, more and more people consider collections of graphic and audio materials appropriate and useful, if not essential. A few people still consider these materials less intellectually sound than print—as "toys," or fit only for recreational purposes—and they resist adding such formats to a collection. However, as the number of people who have effectively used various formats increases, there is pressure to include all appropriate formats in a collection. Librarians need to remind the public, and sometimes themselves, that libraries are in the information business, not the book business.

With each passing year, as multimedia computer systems combine text, graphics, audio, and video clips, the distinction between books and audiovisuals becomes more and more blurred. Information that once was available only in printed formats is now available in several forms, including books, microfiche, CD-ROM, and online. Book publishers, especially publishers of scholarly journals, are thinking about and (in more and more cases) actually publishing their material electronically (see chapter 5). Many publishers expect to use, and are using, CD-ROM packages or the Web to distribute reference material.

Certainly, anyone reading *Publishers Weekly* (*PW*) knows that publishers and booksellers no longer limit themselves to just books and magazines. Regular columns in *PW* on audio as well as video releases indicate that both producers and vendors view themselves as being in the information business. Articles on compact disc technologies provide additional evidence of their thinking about any economical and marketable format for delivering information. The use of computerized typesetting and scanning equipment, which produces a record of the text in a digital format, opens up a number of options for delivering the information, including the Internet. If libraries confine themselves to just the traditional paper and print formats, they will quickly lose ground to organizations that define their business in the same manner as the producers.

As noted in chapter 4, primary, secondary school, and community college libraries took the lead in incorporating all formats into their service programs. In these library settings the instructional aspect to media existed, along with the recognition that many ideas are best expressed using a form other than the printed word. Further, the media were integrated into the library's collection. Undoubtedly, one reason for this, at least in the case of schools, was the relatively small size of the organization and the need to keep things simple from an administrative point of view. Why have two units, one for books and magazines and one for media, when one unit could handle the workload for both? Use of media in classrooms has been a long-standing tradition in these institutions, unlike four-year colleges and universities.

In academic institutions, the pattern was to establish separate units to handle media needs. Academic institutions tended to view media, essentially films, as solely classroom material; even then there were doubts about its real instructional value. Some professors believed—a few still do—that use of media in classroom is the lazy persons' way of not "doing" the teaching themselves. Certainly, art, film, music, and theater departments were exceptions, but they tended to create their own departmental collections for staff and majors' use only.

Public libraries were early collectors of sound recordings, and a number developed large film collections. Sound recordings circulated, and over time the collections expanded from just classical music to all forms of music and the spoken word. Motion picture films (primarily 16mm) attracted groups for in-house showings and were also available for loan to groups such as Scouts, churches, and occasionally schools. Today, few libraries collect films except in a video format, but the number of public libraries doing so is growing.

In short, media play an important role in meeting the educational and recreational needs of the service community. Some people are print-oriented, whereas others prefer audio or graphic presentations of information. For many types of information, a print format is inappropriate. Limiting a collection to one or two formats seldom provides the range of services appropriate to the service community's needs.

Sally Mason, although specifically addressing public libraries, summed up the situation for all types of libraries when she wrote: "Clearly, the visual media will only become more important to library service in the future. . . . It is not enough for librarians to 'capitulate' on the issue of visual media. We must become leaders and advocates . . . helping the public to learn what is available, to sort through multiple possibilities, and offering guidance in the use of media to obtain needed information."[2]

Goals of Media Service

Some type of equipment is necessary to use most of the media that we cover in this chapter. One goal of media services is to make the use of equipment so simple that it is "transparent." This means that the users can focus their attention on the information presented rather than on operating the equipment. In the past, using some equipment was so complicated that some people refused to learn how. Now most of the equipment is easy to use, as long as all one wants to do is play back the information. One important issue in keeping equipment simple to use is maintaining it in good working order.

A second goal of media service would be to integrate these materials within collections. The ideal OPAC would reflect the total holdings of the library, regardless of format, and we are getting close to that goal. Thus, a subject search for Native American basketry would produce a listing of books, journals, films and videotapes, oral histories, and, perhaps, in a museum setting, even some indication of holdings of actual baskets.

A third goal is to collect and provide access to all of the appropriate formats. Thus, collection development officers must know and appreciate the value of all the formats collected. Also, the staff must know how to operate the appropriate equipment and be able to assist the public. Recognizing that some individuals have strong preferences for a particular format is also important, as is not letting the staff personal preferences influence the service provided. Ranganathan, a leading figure in librarianship, proposed five laws of librarianship to which media services staff might add a sixth law—or perhaps modify his existing law "Each book its user" to read "Each format its user."

Media Formats

Media formats, like print formats, exist in a variety of sizes and shapes. Unlike the print forms, each media format requires special equipment or handling for an individual to gain access to its information. Thus, a decision to add sound recordings to a collection requires additional decisions about which type of recordings to acquire, CDs, tape, audio files on the Internet, or all of these. In this chapter, we discuss only six of the most commonly collected media formats (audio recordings, film, maps, microfilm, slides, and video) and some of their implications for public service. We devote most of the space in this edition to video and spoken-word recordings, as those formats have had the greatest growth in use and impact on media services. Today, video is part of almost all library collections; even special libraries are building this type of material into their collections.

General Evaluation Criteria

To a degree, the same factors that we discussed in chapter 4 that determine inclusion or exclusion of books apply to other formats. Obviously, one omits factually incorrect items unless there is a sound reason to buy them. Poorly organized and badly presented material seldom becomes part of the collection.

If the quality of a book is difficult to assess, assessing the quality of other media is even more difficult. All of us have seen a film we enjoyed only to hear a friend claim that it is "absolutely *the* worst film" ever made. Thus, subjectivity is a major concern. Although bias is also a problem with literature, we receive more training or exposure to good literature through formal schooling. Few of us receive formal training in evaluating nonprint materials. Basically, the issues of authority, accuracy, effectiveness of presentation or style, and value and usefulness to the community are as valid for all other formats as they are for books.

Before embarking on a program to develop a media collection, one should carefully evaluate each format in terms of its unique utility to the service community. Each format has its strong and weak points, and similar information may be available in a variety of formats. The following paragraphs offer general guidelines for assessing the strengths and weaknesses of various forms.

Formats that involve motion (such as 8mm, 16mm, and 35mm films, and video) are among the more expensive formats to purchase on a per title basis, after STM titles. Therefore, an important question to ask is whether motion really adds information. There are films in which there is no action, just "talking heads," or if there is motion, it may not be very relevant. In contrast, one can read hundreds of pages and look at dozens of still photographs of cell division and still not fully understand how it occurs. A short, clearly photographed film combined with a good audio track can sometimes produce a more accurate understanding than one can achieve through hours of reading.

With both motion and still graphic formats, color is an important consideration. Full-color reproduction is more costly than black-and-white reproduction; the question is whether the color is necessary or merely pleasing. In some instances, color is necessary. Certainly, anything that attempts to represent the work of a great artist must have excellent color quality, as is also the case with medical and biological materials.

Audio formats also can provide greater understanding and appreciation of printed material. One's own reading of a poem is never the same as hearing the poet's recitation of the work. Tone, emphasis, inflection, and so forth can change the meaning of a printed text dramatically. On a different level, there are literally millions of people in the world who cannot read music scores and yet get enormous enjoyment from listening to music. Audio recordings are a must in any collection serving the visually impaired. Spoken-word recordings can be an important service for such persons as well as for commuters who want to listen to a book as they travel.

Other general selection factors include cost, flexibility and manipulation, and user preference. Audiovisual formats frequently require expensive equipment in addition to rather costly software. When thinking about cost factors, one needs to know what types of equipment users own (e.g., slide projectors, videotape or DVD players, CD or tape players, or even—occasionally—record players). The selector should also consider what formats users prefer.

Once one's library decides to develop a media collection, how does one select appropriate items? There are four sets of factors to consider—programming, content, technical aspects, and format—with criteria related to each factor. The following paragraphs highlight major selection criteria.

Programming Factors

Programming (i.e., use of material) is important in deciding what to acquire. Many articles and books about this topic are available (see the bibliography at the end of this chapter). Programming questions include:

- Will the medium be used in formal instructional situations?
- Is it only for recreational use?
- Who is the primary audience: adults, children, or all ages?
- Will the item circulate, or will it be available only for in-house use? If used in-house, will it be available to individuals or only to groups? Will group use involve a library staff member or an expert in the field to guide group discussions before or after the item's use?
- Will the library be a member of a resource-sharing network? If so, will the item become part of the shared material pool?

Answers to these questions will affect the type of media purchased and the prices paid. For example, many videos for home use are less expensive than videos for instructional use, even when both packages are the same title (more about this later in the chapter).

Content Factors

Content is the next concern in the selection of any format. In the past, audiovisual selection was a group process rather than the responsibility of one selector. This was especially true in the case of expensive formats. Today, with the prices of videos dropping and increasing numbers of titles needed for the collection, the selection process is more like book selection, that is, an individual process. School media centers still emphasize the group process, in part because of limited funds but also because the possibility of someone objecting to an item's presence in the collection is higher than in other types of libraries.

Whether selection is a group or individual process, using an evaluation form is helpful. Keeping the forms for several years, for titles rejected as well as those purchased, can save selectors' time in the long run. Unlike print material, most media are sequential in nature; this means that it takes fifty minutes to review a fifty-minute program. An evaluation form indicating that the library reviewed and rejected an item three years ago should help selectors decide whether the item is worth reconsidering. No matter what questions are on the form—and not all items listed in this chapter will be on any one form—one ought to consider all of the following points:

1. What is the primary purpose of the item? If there is a user's guide, does it provide a specific answer to this question?

2. Given the purpose(s) of the item, is the length of the program appropriate? Items can be too short, but more often than not, they are too long.

3. Is the topic a fad, or is it likely to have long-term interest? Long-term interest and lasting value are not always the same.

4. Is the material well organized?

5. Is the story line easy to follow?

6. If the item is of relatively short duration and is an attempt to popularize a subject, does it do this with sufficient accuracy? (I.e., does the simplification cause misunderstandings or, worse, create a misrepresentation?)

7. When was the material copyrighted? Copyright information can be difficult to find for some formats. Films usually provide this information somewhere in the credits, often in roman numerals. Sales catalogs may or may not provide the date of production. Unfortunately, a large number of dated products are, or have been, sold as if they were current (rereleases).

8. Will the visuals or audios date quickly? In many educational films, the subject matter is appropriate, but the actors' dress makes the film appear old-fashioned. If one does not present the material as historical, many viewers may miss its true purpose. Audience attention is easily drawn away from the real subject, especially students. This ties into the need for accurate copyright information.

9. Are there multiple uses for the item, in addition to those identified by the producer? If there are a number of ways to use the format (with various types of programs or audiences), it is easier to justify spending money on the item.

Technical Factors

Technical issues vary in importance from format to format, but some general considerations apply to several formats. In most instances, judging technical matters is less subjective than judging many other selection criteria. Nevertheless, it will take time and guidance from experienced selectors to develop a critical sense of these factors. Most individuals entering the field of library and information work are more attuned to good literature, well-manufactured books, and the various methods of literary review and criticism than the average person. Although our exposure to television, film, and video recordings may be greater than to books, few of us have the background to assess the technical aspects of these formats. This fact is evident during film and television awards ceremonies—the public interest is in the best film or program and performance categories. It is the rare individual who can name the winners in the technical areas (direction, production, special effects, cinematography, and so forth). The following are some questions to consider regarding technical features:

1. Are the visuals, assuming that there are visuals, necessary?

2. Are the visuals in proper focus, the composition effective, and the shots appropriate? (These questions must be asked because out-of-focus shots, strange angles, and jarring composition may be used to create various moods and feelings.)

3. Is the material edited with skill?

4. Does the background audio material contribute to the overall impact?

5. Is there good synchronization of visuals and audio?

6. How may the format be used—can it be viewed by small or large groups or by both? Can it be viewed in a darkened, semilighted, or fully lighted room?

7. If there are subtitles, can they be read easily?

8. Are closed or open captions available, and (in the case of DVDs) are captions available in multiple languages?

Format Factors

Questions to consider about format are:

1. Is the format the best one for the stated purposes of the product?

2. Is the format the least expensive of those that are appropriate for the content?

3. Will the carrier medium (the base material that supports the image or sound layer) stand up to the amount and type of use that people would give it?

4. If damage occurs, can it be repaired (locally or by the producer), or must one buy a replacement copy? Does it require maintenance? If so, what kind?

5. What equipment is needed to use the medium? How portable is the equipment, and how easy is it to use?

Additional Considerations

It is possible to group all audiovisual materials into six broad categories: still images (filmstrips, slides, microformats, transparencies); moving images (film and video); audio recordings; graphic materials (maps, charts, posters, etc.); three-dimensional materials (models, realia, dioramas); and other formats (games, software, etc.). Each type has some equipment or storage implications that one needs to take into consideration. For example, microform storage cabinets are heavy when empty and become even heavier as they are filled. Until one knows that the floor was designed to carry such weight, which is greater than book stacks, one should be cautious about starting a major collecting program in that format.

Audio Recordings:
Discs and Tapes

In reviewing additional considerations for media formats, we begin with a widely held format, audio recordings, where we encounter great diversity and incompatibility. Sound recordings were among the first nonprint formats collected by libraries. In public libraries, the recordings are usually part of the circulating collection. For educational libraries, the purpose is usually instructional, with limited use outside the library. As we will show, this is the media category that most clearly reflects the long-term influence of a changing technology on a library media collection.

Although a few music libraries and archives have collections of early cylinder recordings, by the time most libraries began actively collecting recordings, the standard format was the flat disc. Many libraries built up extensive collections of 78 rpm (revolutions per minute) records by the end of the 1950s. For a period of time there were four common playing speeds for records: $16\frac{1}{2}$, $33\frac{1}{3}$, 45, and 78 rpm. Although the $16\frac{1}{2}$ rpm speed was not widely used, most record players had that setting as well as the other "standard" speeds. From a library point of view this was fine; record speed was not a consideration in building the collection. Then in the late 1950s and early 1960s, the recording industry shifted to $33\frac{1}{3}$ rpm "long play" records and the 45 rpm speed for popular, "single" recordings (i.e., one track per side).

The substantial investment in 78 rpm albums was not lost because the newer equipment still played the recordings, even if you could not buy new 78-speed albums and records. One problem with the older format was that the sound quality was not as good as that of the $33\frac{1}{3}$. Also, more material would fit on a single side of the new recording. The public began to expect the newer format to be in the library's collection, just as it was in their personal collections.

Eventually, equipment manufacturers stopped including 78 rpm as a standard speed. As older players wore out and could not be repaired, some libraries attempted to transfer the 78 rpm recordings to tape format; others sold or, in some cases, gave away the records. At almost the same time, the "new" $33\frac{1}{3}$ format had a challenger in the form of tape formats, mostly reel-to-reel, because of tape's better sound reproduction qualities. With increased portability of radios, tape decks, and CD players, the popular music industry dropped the 45 rpm recording in favor of cassette tapes and, later, CDs and CD minidiscs. CDs are one of today's most popular formats for sound recordings, with MP3s following closely behind.

The life span of each new and better recording method (except possibly the CD) is getting shorter and shorter, and most are not compatible with other forms. An old sound recording collection could consist of cylinders, discs ($16\frac{1}{2}$, $33\frac{1}{3}$, 45, 78 rpm, and compact), tapes (reel-to-reel, with both acetate and wire recordings recorded at a variety of speeds), and cassettes (both dual-track and 8-track, and recorded on tapes with different characteristics that may or may not cause equipment problems). Each format uses its own equipment or older, more flexible equipment, either of which requires special skills to maintain. It seems every time you turn around, another change is taking place, which will probably mean yet one more format to collect.

A circulating collection will need to keep closer pace with changing technology than will an instructional collection. Part of the problem, from a library point of view, is that the recording industry focuses on the individual and home markets rather than the institutional market. The new technologies tend not to be too expensive. They cannot be if mass sales are the goal. Most individuals do not invest as heavily in sound recordings as libraries and can switch to a new format and equipment more easily; libraries, however, may have collections of several thousand titles in a particular recording format. The librarian who finds that she or he suddenly has a "historical" collection or to whom the music department chairperson says, "Get rid of the 33⅓s; they are dinosaurs. Replace them with CDs" may wonder where to find the funds. Also, how soon will the CD become the next dinosaur? The library with an instructional collection may be able to move slowly into the new format, as long as the old equipment is serviceable. The shift for the circulating collection will have to be faster and certainly will be more costly.

For public libraries, spoken-word tapes (the preferred trade term is *audiobooks*) have become almost as important as the video collection. (It should be noted that *audiobooks* is truly the best term to use for these items, as many of the other shorthand labels used are, in fact, copyrighted names, including Books on Tape, Talking Book, Recorded Book, BookCassette, and Talking Tape.) Automobile and portable, handheld and CD players have created a market for audiobooks. Even reading a small paperback book on a crowded subway or bus can be difficult. "Popping a CD" into a small player that fits in one's jacket pocket and has a small headset allows one to close out the noise, to some degree, and enjoy a favorite piece of music or listen to a current best-seller book. The same is true for those commuting in cars or just out for their "power walks."

The audiobook format has substantial sales to individuals as well as libraries. In a 1996 article in *Publishers Weekly*, one of the titles on tape passed the 1 million copy mark (*The Seven Habits of Highly Effective People*, by Stephen R. Covey, from S&S Audio).[3] This same article listed twenty-nine titles that had surpassed the 175,000 sales mark. An interesting feature of the list was that seventeen of the titles were nonfiction. The fact that *PW* has a regular section on audiobooks is an indication of their importance to the trade.

Donna Holovack wrote an article outlining the popularity of audiobooks in *Public Libraries*, in which she suggested that audiobooks are "a good marketing aid, [and] a loss leader extraordinaire."[4] She noted that libraries have supplied recorded books (and, we note, current magazines as well) for the visually impaired for some time. (The Library of Congress' service for the visually and physically impaired is a most valuable program and one that perhaps led publishers to think there was a bigger market for audiobooks.) The question of the "suitability" of libraries making abridged versions of works of fiction available is one for the profession; some people prefer abridged versions. The idea that people are looking for only the latest work of fiction is belied by the data from Holovack's *PW* article.

One of the drawbacks of audiocassettes and CDs, whether spoken word or music, is that they have a relatively short life span, five to six years, even under optimal usage conditions. Both cassettes and CDs are vulnerable to damage during use. They are also small objects that have few places upon which a library can attach a security strip/device, so their loss rate (shrinkage in retail terms) can be rather high. Nor, for that matter, is there much room to apply barcodes or other property markings. Replacing lost items can be costly. The fact that a single, unabridged audiobook can have as many as six to eight cassettes means that keeping everything sorted in its proper order can be a problem, from both the public's and staff's point of view. Certainly, the staff must check each title that has multiple cassettes each time it is returned. If, in fact, a person is listening to the cassettes in the car and is using more than one title, there is a very good chance that a cassette will end up in the wrong container. No one wants to have the ending of a "whodunit" delayed because the last cassette is for Shakti Gawain's *Creative Visualization Meditations* (New World Library).

On the technical side, because of different tape types, there can be problems. Some companies attempt to reduce the amount of tape required for a title, thus reducing the number of cassettes, by recording using multichannel technology. The user needs good "balance control" capability for this to work properly; few portable players or car tape decks have such control, and lacking such control, one hears two tracks, neither of which is clear. Often when a person returning an item complains that something is wrong with the tape, it is a multichannel recording. The tape itself is fine, but the necessary balance control was lacking. However, the staff must still listen to the tapes to be certain that they are, in fact, all right. Another aspect of the multiple-cassette question is, Given a choice, what approach is better for the library? Some companies offer the same title on different lengths of tape, perhaps a choice between six and eight cassettes. There is a trade-off for the library. The fewer the cassettes, the less checking staff will need to do on returning materials. The fewer the cassettes, the thinner the tape used; the thinner the tape, the greater the chances are that a player will "eat" the tape. That is, the tape stretches and may become stuck in part of the player, or it simply breaks and really becomes entangled in the deck's mechanisms. Even CDs are not indestructible, as they can be scratched.

Before ending our coverage of audio recordings, we should say a word or two about musical recordings. Some of the same issues covered earlier about tape length, etc., apply to music recordings as well. We noted earlier that libraries have had music recording collections for a great many years. Some have also collected music scores; a question for the library is whether the scores and recordings should be together. Certainly, in the case of academic institutions, the music department, if it does have a separate library, would like the two together. The reality for most libraries is that if the two are combined, scores probably will get moved to the media department, first, because that is where the equipment to play back the recordings is located and where the staff has the training to assist the public in using the equipment. Second, few libraries have the resources to buy additional playback equipment and find space for it where the scores are located (usually in the main book collection stacks). Third, the storage needs of the formats are very different. In the 1997 edition of *A Basic Music Library*, the editors noted that:

> ... differences reflect inherent, practical distinctions between print and recordings: printed music is typically sought by players or students of a particular instrument (bassoon) or medium (choral), while recordings tend to be thought of in relation to a stylistic category (salsa) with less concern towards details of instrumentation.[5]

This view may or may not help libraries that are attempting to provide both recordings and scores for their service population, at least in terms of deciding whether to integrate the two formats.

Many audio recording collections that have been in place for any length of time contain a wide variety of formats, including vinyl discs, reel-to-reel tapes, cassette tapes, and compact discs. No other format more clearly demonstrates changing technology. In little more than forty years, the technology has evolved considerably from the days of 78-rpm disc recordings to today's compact disc. Each change required new equipment and new recording formats. In libraries that support music programs, it is not uncommon to find fairly large collections of two or three different formats that more or less duplicate content. That is, a library may have all of Bach's cantatas on 33⅓-rpm vinyl discs, on audiocassette, and on compact disc. The cost of duplicating the information can be substantial; however, users demand the newer format because of the improved quality of sound. (At LMU, a new music department chair demanded that the library replace all the 33⅓-rpm albums and the audiocassettes with compact discs. To have done so would have cost the library more than $40,000. The library has been replacing the recordings slowly over the last five years but still has about 25 percent of the collection on what the music department chair calls "the dinosaurs.") Unlike secondhand books, there is not a strong used recording trade, making it more difficult to resell or even give away materials in the old format. The commercial music and spoken-book trade is reasonably well controlled in a bibliographic sense; certainly, there is more control than in any other nonbook format. Where will it go from here? At this writing, the compact disc is the major format. However, the MP3 format is gaining popularity and may present a new collection issue for media librarians in the near future.

Reviews of popular music recordings are relatively easy to locate in both mass-market and professional publications. *Booklist* (American Library Association), *Library Journal* (Reed Business Information), *SLJ* (Reed Business Information), and *Notes* (Music Library Association) are a few of the professional sources that review sound recordings. *Sound and Vision* (formerly *High Fidelity*, published by Hachette Filipacchi Media), *Billboard* (VNU Business Publications), and *Down Beat* (Maher Publications) are mass-market publications one can consult for music reviews. For audiobooks, *PW* publishes a regular section of reviews; *Audio File* magazine is also an excellent source for reviews and announcements, and occasionally one can find such reviews in *Booklist* as well. Additional resources include Bowker's *Books Out Loud*, which provides detailed listings of over 115,000 titles as well as contact information for wholesalers and distributors, and *CD Hotlist* (<http://cdhotlist.btol.com>), which provides reviews written by librarians for new CD resources.

Regardless of the format, there are some general questions to keep in mind during the selection process:

1. How much use can the format withstand without distorting the quality of the sound?

2. How easily damaged is the format? Can people erase it by mistake?

3. Does the recording cover the full range of sound frequencies?

4. Is there any distortion of the sound?

5. Is the recording speed constant? (This is seldom a problem with major producers, but it can be significant with smaller producers.)

6. If the recording is multiple-channel, were the microphones properly placed to ensure a balanced recording?

7. Was the recording site suitable for the purposes? (E.g., if the goal is to produce an excellent recording of a musical composition, then a recording studio or a concert hall with excellent acoustics and no audience, rather than a concert, is the best location. Live performances do not produce the best sound quality.)

Film and Video

We include film and video in this section because video has taken over most of the role films used to play in libraries. Most educational/instructional films are now available as videos. Libraries have shifted almost completely to video formats and found them to be increasingly popular with users.

Some years ago, Pamela Hancock wrote a short article about 16mm film service in public libraries.[6] (Until the 1980s, most of the libraries with film collections were schools, community colleges, and public libraries. All of the films were educational/documentary in character, and public libraries tended to use them for programming purposes rather than circulation.) Hancock noted that, at that time, film usage was increasing by 20 percent per year, and the video collection had even higher numbers. She made the point that there are similarities and differences in the two formats and that they complement, rather than compete with, one another. Further, there are valid reasons to have some titles in both formats, in order to meet different needs.

Hancock listed several strengths of 16mm film, starting with portability in the sense that it serves *group* needs. Another strength is that it provides better quality images in a large room setting (however, current video projection systems are changing that), and the film image is (or was) vastly superior to a video image. (It will be interesting to see if high-definition television/video changes this.) Finally, the cost of the equipment is less than for a video projection system. She believed the weakness for the format was isolation from other library services. She might have included that film can be more easily damaged and more often than not more expensive to replace. It is still the best format for teaching cinema studies. Hancock noted two threats to the film format. First is a lack of understanding about the differences between film and video on the part of librarians as well as the public. The second threat was that even producers/distributors have the idea that libraries are not interested in buying films, which is true except for libraries that engage is programming for moderate to large groups.

Our purpose in covering the Hancock material is to emphasize the fact that the two formats are related but different. Both can play an important role in meeting the community information needs for some time to come.

Video Recordings

A number of video recording formats exist for home and commercial usage. The good news is that today libraries need consider purchasing only two formats—VHS and DVD. (Many video collections still contain several other formats—U-Matic, laser discs, and perhaps Beta.) Although VHS is still a viable format, especially for documentary and educational videos, DVDs are *the* format for motion pictures. (DVDs will be discussed in more detail later in this chapter.)

In terms of "legacy" video formats, anyone who has had a home VCR for any length of time is aware of the marketing battle that occurred between the VHS and Beta formats. VHS and Beta tapes were not compatible, and Beta died out in spite of an edge in picture quality. A few individuals still own Beta machines, and a very few libraries still have some

Beta cassettes. The $\frac{3}{4}$-inch format, sometimes called U-Matic, was, and is, yet another option for video collections in the library. Intended for institutional use, the design of both cassette and player was intended to withstand the heavy use, and sometimes abuse, that occurs in schools, colleges, and business settings.

Videos in libraries have a history of about thirty years. Schools, community colleges, and public libraries quickly adopted video as an appropriate part of their collections. Usage of videos increased even when book circulation declined. Academic and corporate libraries were slower to add the format to their collections.

Initially, some public libraries charged a fee for each video that circulated (hence Will Manley's point about unnecessary competition with video stores, at least in a sense). The fee, although low compared to those charged by commercial stores, was still a charge. The purpose in the early days was based on the idea that tapes damaged easily and required replacement. Another stated reason was to provide funds to expand the video collection—perhaps a reflection of the idea that the format was marginal and not worthy of operating funds? Today, few, if any, libraries charge for video loans.

There are two types of commercial videos—theatrical and "special interest." Drawing a parallel with books, theatrical videos are fiction, and "special interest" videos are nonfiction. One can more or less equate theatricals with the production of the motion picture industry. Special interest videos are everything else—how-to-do-it, *Barney*, and sets such as *The Civil War*. Just as is true with the print market, titles expected to have mass appeal have lower prices than those that probably will sell only to institutions.

One problem with video collections, of whatever format, is the cost of replacing damaged titles. People expect to see fairly recent (six to ten months old) theatrical films released on video (or DVD) and often priced well under $30. Video clubs, like book clubs, seldom offer a single video at more than $50 or $60. When confronted with a replacement bill of $150 or $200 for a damaged instructional title, people get angry. They often are not aware that the size of the potential market plays a major role in pricing. Theatrical movie releases and a small percentage of educational and instructional videos are distributed widely enough to be low-cost items. The majority of educational and instructional videos, however, are usually well over $100 each and often as high as $300 to $500 or more for business and science titles.

One of Will Manley's concerns, increased potential for complaints and censorship challenges, can also be an issue with video collections. Other than special libraries, there is probably no library with a video collection that has not had at least one person question the suitability of a title or two in the collection. School libraries have somewhat less exposure to challenges, due to the instructional nature of the collections; however, even here it is possible to have a parent complain about a video (such as one dealing with evolution).

Public libraries face the greatest challenge. Their public is, in fact, anyone, children to seniors. Very often the individuals who raise a question about the suitability of certain titles will do so in the context of "protecting the children."

In addition to the broad service community, public library video collections have, in general, a high percentage of theatrical titles. As most people know, for better or worse, the Motion Picture Association of America (MPAA) has a rating system for its releases—the familiar G, PG, PG-13, R, and NC-17 one sees in the movie section of the newspaper.[7] The Classification and Rating Administration (CARA) handles the rating of each title. Although these ratings have no legal force and, in fact, are based on the somewhat subjective opinions of the eight- to thirteen-member CARA board, the general public accepts them as appropriate. The key is the content of the film in terms of its suitability for children. A 1998 *LJ* survey of public library media collections indicated that some libraries do not purchase R-rated videos. Others do so on the ground that R-rated films are not that different from many of the novels in their collections. Still others avoid the entire issue by purchasing only educational and documentary videos.[8]

Although ALA has a statement opposing labeling,[9] the majority of public libraries that responded to a national video survey indicated that the MPAA/CARA ratings did influence acquisition decisions.[10] The unfortunate fact is that even a collection of G- and PG-rated titles would not ensure that there would be no complaints. One possible way to handle the situation, though not always easy to accomplish, is to create two sections for video, one in the children's/young adult area and another in the adult area. Again, this will not forestall all complaints, but it could help. From the staffing point of view, making certain that the videos are in the proper section will be something of a challenge, unless the video containers are clearly color-coded or marked in some way that makes sorting easy.

The Indianapolis-Marion County Library reaffirmed its video policy in 1996 after a customer's concerns about "potential effect on minors."[11] The library formed a "Community Video Task Force" to review the current policy and make recommendations, if any, for changes. The task force's report concluded that the policy should retain the parents' right to restrict a child's borrowing to the juvenile videos and that the staff should continue to receive training in the current policy. The basic policy is that anyone can borrow any video, unless the person is a child with a card stamped "JV," which indicates a parental restriction. The person who raised the issue wanted the policy to require parents to give written permission for a child to borrow anything but juvenile titles.

Perhaps the greatest problem with videos is copyright. What can and cannot a library do with video? For example, can one use a video sold for home use in a classroom? What is meant by *public performance?* Public performances are any performances the public may attend, even when there is no fee. Library programs, including story hours and senior discussion groups, as well as programs sponsored by any formal group (such as Scouts, churches, and service organizations), are public performances. To be safe, in library programs one should not use any video for which the library has not purchased performance rights.

The issue of performance rights is equally important in classroom settings, and this is a growing area of use. According to Lillian Gerhardt, classroom use of videos in educational institutions, elementary through graduate school, is the steadiest growing area of video use.[12]

Performance rights (the right to give a "public" performance of a program) have both legal and cost implications for libraries. From a legal point of view most uses of a video outside the home may be a copyright violation, unless the video carries with it performance rights. Face-to-face instructional use without performance rights *may* be legal under the concept of "fair use" (see pages 391–93 for a discussion of fair use concept). For any group use (noninstructional) in or out of the library, performance rights are a must.

Gray areas abound when performance rights are not acquired. We will mention only two of the more typical, both related to individual usage of a video. If the library has public access video players, does it constitute "public performance" for a person to watch a "home use" video? Many, if not most, copyright holders would say yes. Most librarians would disagree, suggesting the individual viewing of a video is no different from the person reading one of the magazines in the collection. Another situation is perhaps even grayer. A teacher uses a video in face-to-face instruction, and one or more students miss that class session. When the student(s) go to the library to independently view the material, is that a possible violation? Again, many copyright holders would say yes. Most school and academic libraries would allow such usage as an extension of the face-to-face instruction. None of the above has led to court cases and may never do so; however, acquiring performance rights as part of the acquisition process, when there is a reasonable expectation much of the probable usage will not be home use, is probably a wise move.

Performance rights are not free. Videos aimed at the institutional market normally include the rights, one of the reasons for their higher cost. Few, if any, of the theatrical or mass market special interest videos come with the rights. One source for securing those rights to theatrical videos is the Motion Picture Licensing Corporation (<http://www.mplc.com>), which offers an *Umbrella License*®, which

> allows [for] unlimited use of all MPLC authorized motion picture titles within licensed facilities. The license period is generally one year and there is a low, annual fee. The license does not cover showings where an admission is charged or where specific titles have been advertised or publicized.[13]

For most libraries, the fact that there are several television standards is a nonissue. However, for educational and some corporate libraries that collect internationally it is a selection concern. A video program (VHS or DVD format) released in the U.K. will not play on a machine manufactured for use in the United States. There are three broad standards, two of which have subvariations—NTSC, PAL, and SECAM. Just collecting from Canada, France, the U.K., and the United States requires dealing with all three standards. Having one or two "universal" video players is the least expensive way to handle this challenge.

Selection of videos is very much like book selection, at least for lower-priced titles. More often than not, one person makes the decision about titles costing less than $100. The decision may be based on information in a producer's catalog or a journal review, as well as a preview of the item. Identifying potentially useful videos is becoming easier and easier. *Bowker's Complete Video Directory* (available on CD as *Bowker's Audio and Video Database*) and Gale's *Video Source Book* (Thomson Gale) both provide long lists of available video titles. Unfortunately, no one source is comprehensive, so one must consult several sources when building a subject collection.

Access to theatrical films is reasonably easy because of the number of retail video stores and their need to have bibliographic control. Documentary film access also is fairly good, in the sense that a number of guides are available. However, independent filmmakers come and go with great speed; many "indie" films never appear in a guide, and others remain in the guides long after the producers are out of business. Keeping current with changes in the independent filmmakers' field could become a full-time occupation for a person, if serious collecting is a goal. One resource for this area of filmmaking is *Independent Film and Video Monthly* (Foundation for Independent Video and Film), whose accompanying website provides information on independent film distributors (<http://www.aivf.org/resources/faq/dist_faq.html>).

Reviews of mainstream videos are becoming common, appearing alongside book reviews in professional journals. *Video Librarian* (Video Librarian) is probably the single best source and is supplemented online (<http://www.videolibrarian.com>). Additionally, *Library Journal, School Library Journal*, and *Booklist* cover a number of formats. However, it should be noted that these publications tend to cover items that have broad appeal, and they do not cover many titles in the course of a year. A sampling of journals that cover a wide range of subjects and levels of treatment includes *American Film & Video Review* (Eastern College), *AV Video & Multimedia Producer* (Access Intelligence), *Educational Technology* (Educational Technology), *Children's Video Report* (Children's Video Report), and *Media & Methods* (American Society of Educators).

Some questions to bear in mind when selecting videos and films are:

- Does the motion add to the message?
- Are variable speed capabilities (fast, normal, slow, and stop) used effectively?
- Is the running time appropriate to the content? Too long? Too short?
- Do recreational films using performers or animation present an accurate picture of the events depicted?
- Is the sound properly synchronized with the visuals?
- Are the images dated, and would this interfere with the message being conveyed?
- Does color add to the material, or is it just nice?

DVDs

Videos are beginning to emulate sound recording in the rise and fall of formats. Beta is gone, and U-Matic is barely still around, while laser discs hardly existed. Can VHS be far from going away now that DVD is here? The long-term answer is probably not. Although some popular theatrical and television programs are available only in DVD format, in the near term VHS will likely be with us for a while.

Why the shift to DVD? Beyond the fact that we are in the digital age and can digitize almost anything, there are good reasons for the changeover. As with any format, there are pluses and minuses. Without question the picture quality for DVDs is superior to that of VHS (500 lines compared to 250 for VHS), and when high-definition televisions are less costly and more widely available, the quality difference will be even more apparent. In terms of size and durability, the matter is not as clear-cut. The small size means one can get at least twice as many DVDs into the same shelf space as VHS. On the other hand, the size does make theft easier, and the packaging makes it difficult to add security tags. (This may result in the need to devote a secure space to the DVD itself, such as behind a service counter.) On the positive side, since there is no physical contact between the play heads and surface of the disc, there is no wear unlike the case of VHS tapes, which are slightly worn with each playback. On the downside, discs are easily scratched or pitted, and occasionally they will even crack.

In addition to the superior picture quality, DVDs themselves have substantial storage capacity. A DVD-5 (the typical disc) can store almost 5 gigabytes of data. A standard video DVD is capable of holding up to 260 minutes of playback on its two sides. For the typical feature film, that means ample space for supplementary material, including director's commentaries and deleted scenes. The flexibility of DVDs is another advantage, as the format allows for access to individual scenes on demand, and a single image may be held for as long as desired without damage to the disc.

Like VHS, there are television standard (NTSC, PAL, and SECAM) issues for DVDs. Currently, there are six "country" codes for DVDS. For example, Region 1 is Canada and the United States, while Region 2 is Japan, Europe, South Africa, and the Middle East. Most DVDs carry the country code somewhere on the packaging. Like VHS, the disc and the playback unit must match, or playback cannot occur. As with VHS, there are multiregion players available.

Many of the same tools used to select VHS titles include reviews of DVDs. For instance, the *Video Librarian* website (<http://www.video librarian.com>) contains separate DVD reviews. By the time of the next edition of this book, it is likely DVDs will be the dominant format for video, unless, of course, there will be something newer and better by then. An excellent and fairly recent book on videos and libraries worth consulting is *Video Collection Development in Multi-type Libraries* 2nd ed., edited by Gary Handman (Westport, CT: Greenwood Press, 2002).

Microforms

Where do microformats belong—with books or with audiovisuals? The answer is, probably in both places. It is rare for a microformat title to contain original (new) material. The major exception to this is technical reports, which may be available only in microform.

One problem for people doing retrospective selection is finding paper copies of all of the items they might wish to add to the collection. Usually, if one waits long enough (perhaps years), the book or periodical will turn up in an out-of-print shop. Sometimes the need for the item is too great to wait. If reprint dealers do not have the item, then a microform copy may be the answer.

Microforms are also a means of access to primary research material or to items that are very rare and may be available, in their original form, in only one or two libraries in the world. Thus, though many librarians and most of the public view microforms with some degree, or a great deal, of displeasure, they do serve a useful function in providing access to materials that would not otherwise be available locally.

One major drawback to using microforms is user resistance. Many persons claim that they cannot read anything in a microformat and that it gives them headaches and causes eyestrain and other problems. Occasionally, someone will complain that it causes nausea. To date, none of these concerns are supported by research. Usually, when the only source for the information is microform, an individual is able to use the material without a problem. Admittedly, it takes time to get used to using microforms; it is more difficult in some formats, such as reels, to locate a specific portion of text than in the traditional book format. Without proper maintenance, the image quality will be poor, and that will cause eyestrain. Equipment breaks down and malfunctions at times, causing user and staff frustration. As noted in chapter 6, microforms can be converted to digital images, but this requires additional equipment, which can be difficult to justify given the low use of microformat materials in general.

Despite their relatively infrequent use, it is nonetheless important to be familiar with the guides to microformats. Two guides to in-print micro-formats are *Guide to Microforms in Print* (K. G. Saur Verlag) and *Online National Register of Microform Masters* (<http://www.arl.org/preserv/nrmm.html>). Both titles try to be international in scope, include both commercial and noncommercial sources of supply (e.g., libraries and historical associations), and cover more than sixteen types of microformats. The *National Register* includes only U.S. suppliers, but the material available is international in scope. A major source of reviews of microform series, both current and retrospective, is *Microform and Imaging Review* (K. G. Saur Verlag). In addition to these resources, major producers (such as UMI) offer extensive catalogs of what they have available. It is necessary to keep a file of their catalogs, because it is even less common for micropublishers than for book publishers to contribute information to the in-print guides.

The two most common microform formats found in libraries are reels and fiche. Reel formats are the older of the two and are still widely used for newspapers and serials. Reel microfilms are long strips of film on reels that come in several sizes: 16, 35, and 70mm. The film can be positive (clear with black text) or negative (dark with white text). Library staff and selection officers need to know about these different types because microfilm readers require adjustment for different film sizes and types. Failure to use the correct size of take-up reel can damage film. Failure to adjust the reader for positive or negative film will make it difficult to produce a readable paper copy on a reader-printer machine. (Most people prefer not to read at the machine but rather to make paper copies and leave the machine as quickly as possible.)

Most libraries try to confine the microfilm collection to one or two sizes (35mm and 70mm) and one type (positive). With any large-scale collection, however, more variety is inevitable—inevitable because the information needed by the library is available only in a particular size and type of microfilm. The choice is often either not to get the information or to accept yet another variation in format.

Microfiche are sheets of film with the images of the original document arranged in columns and rows. Fiche can be a great space-saving device while providing much greater access by breaking up the file into smaller units, somewhat like drawers in the card catalog. Eye-legible titling of each fiche assists users in locating the desired material as well as helping the staff keep the fiche in order. The most useful headers are those with numbers and different colors to distinguish content (e.g., white headers for author entries, blue for title entries, and yellow for subject entries).

Like other media, microfiche comes in a variety of sizes as well as reduction ratios. Common sizes are 3 by 5 inches, 3 by 6 inches, and 6 by 7 inches; reduction ratios range from 12 to more than 200. The greater the reduction ratio, the more information the producer can fit on a single fiche. An item marked *10×* means the image is $\frac{1}{10}$ the size of the original. Currently, producers use five categories of reduction: low (up to 15×), medium (16–30×), high (31–60×), very high (61–90×), and ultra high (greater than 91×). Reduction ratios are important because one must, in most cases, change lenses in the reader as one uses microforms at various reduction ratios. Most microform collections contain materials produced using various reduction ratios.

Another concern is whether the film treatment is silver halide, diazo, or vesicular. The latter two are less expensive but have relatively short shelf lives, even with good storage and handling conditions. Silver halide, although more expensive, is the option to choose when there is a choice and long-term retention is an issue. A related issue is the polarity of the film (positive or negative). A negative film produces a black image on a white background (the traditional image people expect) in hard copy. Some of the more expensive reader-printers automatically produce the traditional image, regardless of polarity, and most require the user to select the film's polarity before printing. This is yet one more step that many users resent having to undertake.

Microformats are best for low-use materials, for older materials that need only a black-and-white image, and as second copies of materials with high demand or high loss and mutilation rates. Backfiles of journals are excellent candidates for storage on microfilm. Color microforms are expensive, and few libraries have equipment capable of making hard color copies from color microforms.

Still Pictures
(Slides and Other Graphic Material)

Slides

For most people, the term *photographic slides* brings to mind the traditional family collection of 35mm slides from various vacation trips and family events. Indeed, the common 35mm slide is a part of many library collections, but it is not just a matter of collecting the garden-variety, paper-mounted 2-by-2-inch 35mm slide. Like all the other media formats, there are several variations on a common theme. Large slide collections are likely to consist of 2×2-inch, $2\frac{1}{4} \times 2\frac{1}{4}$-inch, and 3×4-inch slides, perhaps with even a few old glass lantern slides. In a sense, slides are simply strips of film cut into individual frames and mounted for projection onto a screen. The larger the size, the better the image will project for large audiences.

Slide mountings vary from paper to plastic to metal to glass. Each type of mounting material results in a different thickness for the final slide, which may create some projection and projector problems. Many projectors are capable of handling the various thicknesses but are better with one or two types of mounts (paper and plastic). Problems of jamming, with potential damage to the slide, and the need to adjust the focus for each type of mount are common.

Although the 35mm slide is satisfactory for most general purposes, high-definition slides require a larger film format. Such slides are commonly found in special libraries, especially those supporting scientific, medical, and art museum work. Historical picture collections may include stereo slides as well as a variety of still photographs and negatives. Stereo slides and photographs may also be part of a map collection. (Stereo slides or photographs are slightly overlapping images that, with special viewers, give the illusion of three dimensions.)

Only special and academic libraries collect extensively in the slide format. Special libraries (museums, medical, technical, art, and architecture) will have working slide collections. It is rare for a public library to have a slide collection, even in the standard 35mm format, despite the number of homes that have, or had, slide projectors. Some high school and most academic libraries will have instructional collections. Anyone teaching an art appreciation course will want slides or access to digital images for classroom use as well as for students to view independently. A constant problem for the staff members who are responsible for the slide collection is keeping track of thousands of small, thin, square, and rectangular pieces of film and mounting material. Another problem is loss of color when slides are exposed to light, including the projector's lamp. Efforts to "copy" slides into a digital database or CD-ROM—via scanning—can result in a well-preserved collection but may violate copyright.

Perhaps the greatest problem in collecting slides is the large number of sources, which may produce packages of highly variable quality. A major issue with slides is color quality and the quality of lighting and exposure. Slow exposure using a fine-grained film produces the best-quality slides, assuming that the photography (focus, composition, and so forth) and film processing were performed competently.

Reviews of slide sets appear, irregularly at best, in such standard sources as *Booklist*, *LJ*, and *SLJ*. Sandra C. Walker and Donald W. Beetham's *Image Buyers' Guide*, 7th ed. (Englewood, CO: Libraries Unlimited, 1999) is a source for detailed information on this topic, while *Image Providers Directory* (<http://www.rci.rutgers.edu/~beetham/vendor.htm>) supplements the Walker and Beetham title.

Maps

Maps are a form of pictorial material, and most libraries have at least a small collection, in addition to atlases in the reference collection. Small collections of local-area maps pose no particular problem other than having them disappear into an individual's books or briefcase. Large public libraries, academic libraries, and many business and industrial libraries have extensive map collections. Maps, as graphic representations of geological, physical, and natural features, take many forms and shapes, from folded road maps to raised relief globes. Any major map collection must determine its scope and define what to collect. Most would include aerial photographs, including satellite photographs—but should they also house the remote sensing data from satellites? Are raised relief maps worth including in a collection, or are they a commercial product of no real information value? Clearly, the users' needs will determine the answers to these and many other questions about the collection.

Depending on the collection's purpose, maps can be organized in a simple geographic location sequence or by some more complex system. An individual asking, "Do you have a map of X?" may (and usually does) mean he or she wants a map showing streets, roads, and other man-made features. It could also mean interest in seeing a topographic map that provides elevation information in addition to cultural features. Or the individual may really want a soils map to get information for agricultural or construction purposes.

Most map users who want a contour map, however, will ask for "the topo map of X." Normally, persons with specialized maps needs are knowledgeable about maps and will be precise in their requests. In a large collection it is common to keep types of maps together, for example, topographic, cultural, political, and geologic maps. In addition to map content, factors such as projection and scale may be important in their organization and storage. Staff working with large map collections will need special training to properly handle this format.

Globes and maps, although different in form and requiring different handling, usually are available from the same sources. Most libraries have always had a small collection of local maps and atlases, along with a globe or two. Increased leisure time and increased interest in outdoor recreational activities have generated a demand for maps of recreational areas for boaters, campers, and hikers. However, the control of map production is very uneven. There are not many commercial sources of maps, and these are easy to identify. Unfortunately, the largest producers of maps are government agencies. Though federal agency maps are reasonably well controlled, state and local agencies have little central control. Acquisition departments need to develop and maintain their own lists, if map collecting becomes a significant activity.

Some of the selection issues for maps and globes are:

1. Is the level of detail presented appropriate, or is it confusing given the scale of the map?

2. If a color map, are the colors aligned (registered) properly with the lines outlining an area?

3. Are the symbols clearly defined?

4. For world political maps, do the names on the map reflect the current or appropriate names of the countries represented?

5. Will the map or globe be able to withstand the type of use that the library anticipates it will receive?

A variety of professional journals publish reviews to assist selection officers. *Cartographic Journal* (U.K., Maney Publishing), *Cartographica* (University of Toronto Press), *Geographical Review* (United States, American Geographical Society), and *Geographical Journal* (U.K., Blackwell) are but a few of the professional journals that publish evaluative reviews.

An interesting development is the growing use of computer-based geographic and demographic data. Geographic Information Systems (GIS) opens a new and challenging area of image collecting for many libraries. (GIS is a computer-based tool for analyzing and mapping features. It combines database operations, such as statistical analysis, with unique visualization and geographic analysis capability to create maps.) However, it requires equipment that is capable of handling the images and color graphics these products contain. Another option for maps, at least for general information or recreational use, is Internet-based services such as *MapQuest* (<http://www.mapquest.com>) for destinations in the United States and Canada and *Mappy* (<http://www.mappy.com/>) for locales in Europe and Great Britain. Although such services will not replicate the physical map collection, they allow individuals to find information about places for which the library does not collect maps. Another option for Web-based maps is the Perry-Castañeda Library Map collection, available at <http://www.lib.utexas.edu/maps/index.html>.

Previewing

The actual process of selecting audiovisual materials can be a group, rather than an individual, activity. This is particularly true of films and expensive video sets. To some degree, the cost of the material under consideration, rather than the usual collection development factors, drives the issue. In essence, making a mistake about a twenty-minute sound, color, 16mm film or educational video has more serious economic consequences for the library budget than most single mistakes with a book, transparency, or sound recording. Educational videos can cost $200 to $500 per title; in a multiple-cassette package, the total cost can be substantial. Given that the selection process can be highly subjective, having multiple opinions about a prospective purchase can help avoid costly mistakes. In public libraries and school media centers, a selection committee is the typical mechanism employed for securing multiple points of view. In academic libraries, often a single faculty member makes the recommendation, assuming that the purchase will be made with departmental funds, or the head of the library's media program selects titles on the basis of reviews and a knowledge of instructional needs.

How does the audiovisual selection committee differ from the book selection committee? Audiovisual selection committees usually function as a true group decision-making body. Normally, the group previews audiovisual materials under consideration as a group. They view the material from beginning to end. (With book selection, the typical approach is for committee members to divide the items among group members and have individuals give oral reports about each item. Thus, only one member of the committee reviews the item completely.) A group discussion usually takes place after each screening, and each person expresses a reaction to, and evaluation of, the item. Everyone sees the same material, and group interaction ends in a decision to buy or not to buy. Sometimes the product is rerun several times when there are strong differences in opinion.

An important difference in the two formats affects the selection process. This is the sequential nature of video formats. It is not possible to effectively skim a video as one does a book. One must view videos at their normal speed to get the proper impression. A 20-minute running time means 20 minutes of previewing time. Simple arithmetic indicates that a group previewing 20-minute films could view only 24 films in an 8-hour workday. A book selection committee meeting would be a disaster if only 24 titles were discussed in 8 hours. Realistically, no group can preview 24 titles in 8 hours, as the figure does not provide for discussion time or breaks. Finally, it is not feasible to expect people to view materials for four hours straight; they need a break. All of this means, more realistically, that the group could preview 10 to 12 items per day.

Additional Selection Aids

Despite the desirability of previewing audiovisual materials, published evaluations (especially when combined with previewing) are important in this field. Each year, there is a little more progress toward bibliographic control of the field, including reviews of most formats. Perhaps when multiple published reviews of a majority of formats are available, there will be less and less need for hundreds of audiovisual librarians to spend hours and hours in preview screening rooms.

At this time, no comprehensive source for audiovisual materials similar to *Book Review Digest* or *Book Review Index* exists. *Media Digest* (National Film and Video Center) has developed into the best source for locating reviews in all formats, with *Media Review Digest* (Pierian Press) being another resource worth consulting.

Identifying potentially useful audiovisual materials also presents a problem. The National Information Center for Educational Media (NICEM) focuses on educational materials; however, because NICEM employs a rather broad definition of education, the publications are useful to all types of libraries. *NICEM Film and Video Finder Online* (<http://www.nicem. com>) allows one to search the entire database by subject, age level, and media type. The 2004 subscription was $500 for a single-user license for a year. The database contains almost 630,000 records in English and 130 other languages. Its primary strengths lie in the video, film, audio recording, filmstrip, and CD-ROM formats, although there are records for every format discussed in this chapter, as well as some that were not covered. This database is as close as one can come to an audiovisual equivalent of *Books in Print*. The website also provides useful links to professional media groups, guidelines, and other resources media librarians.

Although the preceding list of sources provides a general overview, there is a slight emphasis on films. One reason for this is historical. After microforms and phonograph records, motion picture films and videos are the most commonly held audiovisual forms in libraries. Also, 16mm films and educational videos cost significantly more than either of the other two formats, making previewing all the more important. Because of film's popularity, cost, and longer history of use, film review and evaluation have had more time to become established. Increased popularity of other formats will, in time, make it economically feasible to publish journals covering other audiovisual formats. Some of the most active nonprint discussion lists are: <videolib@library.berkeley.edu>, archived at: <http://www.lib. berkeley.edu/pipermail/videolib/>; Videonews <VIDEONEWS@library .berkeley.edu>, archived at: <http://www.lib.berkeley.edu/pipermail/video news/>; and Media-L <MEDIA-L@BINGVMB.CC.BINGHAMTON.EDU>, archived at: <http://listserv.binghamton.edu/archives/media-l.html>. These lists provide information on how to handle various media issues, as well as information about sources.

Ordering Media

For all practical purposes, the process of ordering materials in the formats discussed in this chapter is the same as for ordering books and serials, with a few exceptions. One difference is that libraries place most of the orders directly with the producer, because there are no general audiovisual jobbers as there are for books and serials. Some book jobbers, such as Baker & Taylor, Folletts, and Ingram handle some of the most widely collected formats (e.g., videos and audiotapes), but they do not handle the full range of audiovisual materials or, for that matter, a wide selection of "special interest" or independent videos. Of course, *Amazon.com* is another source that many video librarians use.

There is a major difference between review copies of books and preview copies of other media. With books, if the purchasing librarian likes what he or she sees, the library keeps it, pays the invoice, and perhaps orders multiple copies at the same time. With audiovisual materials, for a number of reasons (risk of loss, damage, and so forth), the library usually requests a preview copy from the supplier, views the copy, and then returns the item. (Some producers now send a new copy—especially for videos—and expect the library to keep the copy if it decides to buy the item. Other producers charge for previewing but deduct the charge from the purchase price. A few film vendors ship an approval copy with a 10 percent discount if the library buys the film.) One must request the preview copy well in advance of the preview date. Normally, a librarian writes to the producer or supplier asking for preview copies of certain titles and listing a number of alternative dates. This becomes an issue when previewing with a group, because of scheduling problems. One also must know when specific items will be available for previewing. A preview file thus becomes a very important aid in the selection process; it contains a listing of each title requested, the dates requested, scheduled preview dates, and the result of the preview.

One should keep in mind several other factors for previewing as well. A preview copy may have had some prior use; therefore, the quality may not be as high as that of a new copy. If one can determine from the supplier how often the item went out for previewing, it is possible to gain insight into the durability of the product. In assessing this information (assuming one can get it), the librarian must remember that the preview copy's use was by individuals who know how to properly handle the material (unlike many library users).

Upon receiving the purchased copy, a staff member should view the item to be certain it is (1) a new print, (2) the item the library ordered, and (3) technically sound (checking for breaks or scratches, sound quality, and quality of processing). Checking for technical soundness upon receipt should be standard procedure for all audiovisual items, not just for previewed items. Generally, other media are not mass-produced in the same manner as are books. Many are produced on demand, that is, in response to orders. The producer has several preview copies and a master copy; when an order arrives, the producer uses the master copy to produce a new print.

One issue to decide before ordering is that of performance rights. Does the library pay an additional fee for public performance rights, or are they part of the quoted price? (This is a typical issue for videos.) There may be some justification for paying a somewhat higher price for performance rights in an educational setting, but there is hardly any when the videos are for circulating home use. The classic example of the confusion between "the home market" and "the library market" was Public Broadcasting System's (PBS) release of its series *The Civil War* in 1990. Initially, it was available to libraries for $450; only a few months later, PBS released it to the "home market" for just under $200. Another example, from 1995, was *Malcolm X: Make It Plain:* $99.95 from PBS Video (with public performance rights) and $29.95 from MPI Home Video (with home video rights).[14] Failure to have public performance rights and using a film or video in a "public performance" setting could lead to a very costly lawsuit. Knowing how the item is most likely to be used, acquiring the appropriate rights, and maintaining a record of what was purchased can be important in building media collections.

With some formats, there may be still another decision: to buy or rent. Normally, the rental fee is 10 percent of the list price. If there are doubts about the level of demand, it may be best to rent a copy. (Ten uses in five years would be more than enough to justify buying the item.) Remember that, when calculating the cost, it will be necessary to include staff time for preparing rental forms, as well as time for mailing and handling activities. In many cases, with film, video, and software, the library is not buying an item in the same sense that it purchases books and serials. Often the library must sign an agreement that outlines what the library may or may not do with the item. These agreements cover duplication and resale and, in some cases, place restrictions on where performances are possible. Vendors do enforce these agreements, which are legal contracts, so the librarian must understand what he or she is signing. If something is not clear, or if a clause should be modified, the librarian should discuss it with the vendor and the library's legal counsel before signing.

Summary

Building a media collection for the library is a time-consuming and expensive undertaking, but it is important and worthwhile for both the library and its service population. Each new format is capable of doing certain things that no other format can do, but each also has its limitations; as a result, they supplement, rather than replace, each other. It is clear that patrons have various preferences in seeking, using, and enjoying information. If the library is to be responsive to the community, it must build a collection of materials that reflects that community's various interests and tastes. As noted by Walt Crawford:

> Video tells stories differently than books, which tell stories differently than songs; all have their roles. It's a lot more complicated to make a good video or film than to write a good book. Fortunately, in a world of many media, we—librarians and users—can appreciate, collect, and preserve many forms of storytelling.[15]

Notes

1. Will Manley, "Facing the Public," *Wilson Library Bulletin* 65 (June 1991): 89–90.

2. Sally Mason, "Libraries, Literacy and the Visual Media," in *Video Collection Development in Multitype Libraries*, ed. G. P. Handman (Westport, CT: Greenwood Press, 1994), 12.

3. "*Seven Habits* Reaches Million-Selling Milestone for S&S," *Publishers Weekly* 243 (September 2, 1996), 43.

4. Donna Holovack, "The Popularity of Audiobooks in Libraries," *Public Libraries* 35 (March/April 1996): 115.

5. The Music Library Association, comp., *Basic Music Library: Essential Scores and Sound Recordings*, 3rd ed. (Chicago: American Library Association, 1997), xii.

6. Pamela Hancock, "16 MM Film Services in Public Libraries: A S.O.W.A.T. Analysis," *Sightlines* 23 (Fall 1991): 29.

7. For information on the history of MPAA ratings, visit "MPA Movie Ratings: How It Began," December 2000, <http://www.mpaa.org/movieratings/about/index.

htm>. Film ratings explanations are available online at <http://www.filmratings.com>, <http://www.mpaa.org>, and <http://www.parentalguide.org>.

8. Norman Oder, "AV Rising: Demand, Budgets, and Circulation Are All Up," *Library Journal* 123 (November 15, 1998): 30–33.

9. American Library Association. "Statement on Labeling: An Interpretation of the Library Bill of Rights," June 1990, <http://www.ala.org/ala/oif/statementspols/statementsif/interpretations/statementonlabeling.pdf>.

10. Oder, "AV Rising," 32.

11. "Indianapolis PL Reviews Video Policy," *Library Journal* 121 (June 1, 1996): 20.

12. Lillian Gerhardt, "Sharpening the AV Focus," *School Library Journal* 37 (April 1991): 4.

13. Motion Picture Licensing Corporation home page (<http://www.mplc.com>).

14. Randy Pitman, "The Outer Limits of Video Pricing," *Library Journal* 120 (May 15, 1995): 34.

15. Walt Crawford, "Thinking about Complex Media," *American Libraries* 34, no. 10 (November 2003): 59.

Selected Websites*

(See also resources on the DLC5 website: <http://www.lu.com/dlc5>)

ALA's "Best" Lists
> <http://www.ala.org/ala/booklist/alasbestlists/Best.htm>
> Annual Lists of publications selected by *Booklist* magazine. The 2004 media entries include "Notable Children's Media," "Selected DVDs and Videos for Young Adults," and "Notable Videos for Adults."

ALA Video Round Table
> <http://www.ala.org/ala/vrt/vrt.htm>
> An ALA roundtable that "addresses issues related to video collections and services in all types of libraries."

Audiovisual Useful Links
> <http://www.ala.org/ala/pla/committeework/audiovisualuseful.htm>
> A listing of online resources, maintained by the Public Library Association Audiovisual Committee.

CD Hotlist Guide
> <http://www.btol.com/pdfs/Guide_CD_Hotlist.pdf>
> An online users guide for CD Hotlist (<http://cdhotlist.btol.com>).

Educational Media Reviews Online
> <http://libweb.lib.buffalo.edu/emro/search.html>
> An outgrowth of AV Review Database, this resource provides reviews of videos, DVDs, and CD-ROMs. "The reviews are written primarily by librarians and teaching faculty in institutions across the United States and Canada. The reviews are given one of three ratings: Recommended, Highly Recommended, or Not Recommended."

Guidelines for Media Resources in Academic Libraries
> <http://www.ala.org/ala/acrl/acrlstandards/guidelinesmedia.htm>
> Guidelines prepared by members of the Media Resources Committee (formerly the Audiovisual Committee) of the Association of College and Research Libraries and approved by the ACRL Board and the ALA Standards Committee in 1999.

National Library Service for the Blind and Physically Handicapped: Talking Book Topics
<http://www.loc.gov/nls/tbt/index.html>
Sponsored by the Library of Congress, this resource lists recorded books and magazines available through a network of libraries in the United States.

*These sites were accessed May 7, 2005.

Further Reading

Baird, S. *Audiobook Collections and Services: A Guide for Libraries*. Fort Atkinson, WI: Highsmith, 2000.

Brulliard, K. "For Libraries, an Influx of Outmoded CDs." *Washington Post*, September 5, 2004, Maryland edition, sec. C.

Byers, F. R. *Care and Handling of CDs and DVDs: A Guide for Librarians and Archivists*. Washington, DC: Council on Library and Information Resources, 2003, <http://www.clir.org/pubs/abstract/pub121abst.html>.

Caron, S. "Transitioning to DVD." *Library Journal* supplement 129 (May 15, 2004): 4–6.

De Stefano, P. "Moving Image Preservation in Libraries." *Library Trends* 52, no. 1 (Summer 2003): 118–33.

Handman, G. "A View Outside the Mainstream: Boldly Go beyond Popular Home Video to Build an Exciting and Diverse Video Collection." *American Libraries* 34, no. 10 (November 2003): 38–40.

Hsieh-Yee, I. *Organizing Audiovisual and Electronic Resources for Access: A Cataloging Guide*. Englewood, CO: Libraries Unlimited, 2000.

Laskowski, M. S. "Stop the Technology, I Want to Get Off: Tips and Tricks for Media Selection and Acquisition." *The Acquisitions Librarian* 16, nos. 31/32 (2004): 217–25.

Luttmann, S. "Selection of Music Materials." *The Acquisitions Librarian* 16, nos. 31/32 (2004): 11–25.

Minkel, W. "They Want Their MP3." *School Library Journal* 50, no. 7 (July 2004): 22–23.

Oder, N. "Feeling a Squeeze." *Library Journal* 129, no. 19 (November 15, 2004): 34–36.

Pennavaria, K. "Nonprint Media Preservation: A Guide to Resources on the Web." *C&RL News* 64, no. 8 (September 2003): 529–32.

Pitman, R. "Making Room for DVD: The Tipping Point." *American Libraries* 34, no. 10 (November 2003): 40–42.

Snider, M. "DVDs Success Steals the Show." *USA Today* (January 8, 2004): A1–A2.

Walters, W. H. "Video Media Acquisitions in a College Library." *Library Resources & Technical Services* 47 (October 2003): 160–70.

10
Acquisitions

Change was one of the themes for acquisition departments in the last decade. However, there seems to be no letup in the need to change and the pace of change in the field at the start of the 21st century. In the last edition we started this chapter with the following, and it seems as appropriate now as it did then.

"Morphing," if that is a valid word, is something moviegoers and television watchers frequently see. Computers and other technologies allow filmmakers to easily cause objects and people to change shape before our eyes. Those same technologies are changing, if somewhat more slowly than in a film, the way we structure and operate acquisition units in libraries and information centers. Change is a natural aspect for any dynamic organization, and we believe that most libraries and information centers are dynamic organisms. (S. R. Ranganathan's fifth law of librarianship was that "a library is a growing organism."[1] A growing organism is a changing one.) Though change has always been part of the field, today is a period of very rapid change in the nature and character of collections and how one goes about developing them.

One outcome of these changes is that some people in the acquisition area have begun questioning the role and character of their work. A surprising amount of time has gone into exploring the question, Is acquisitions a profession? Some people—for example, Alex Bloss[2]—believe strongly that it is; others, such as Ron Ray,[3] do not. Although a number of significant changes have taken place in collection development, everyone agrees that the basic function of the acquisitions unit remains as it has been for the past thirty years: that is, acquisitions work involves locating and acquiring the items identified as appropriate for the collection.

Changing Environment of Acquisitions Work

As one might expect, it is the electronic materials—more specifically the networked/Web materials—that are creating most of the changes in the environment for library acquisitions units. Carol Diedrichs reported that between 1995 and 1998, the Ohio State University libraries' serials librarian shifted her time commitment to almost 50 percent conducting licenses reviews and negotiations for electronic products.[4] One can imagine the percentage is now approaching 70 to 80 percent. Electronic products, as we have noted in several earlier chapters, call for a different acquisitions approach, such as having trial periods and leasing rather than owning materials. While one might think of a trial period as somewhat like an approval plan for books, previewing other media—in other words, looking before buying—is very different, especially when you consider who needs to be involved and the requisite communication for a successful trial process.

Joyce Ogburn noted that managing an acquisitions program calls for a special set of skills and activities—assessment, prediction, control, choice, validation, and quantification. In doing so, libraries

> [a]ssess the risk and feasibility of acquisition, the availability of the resources, and the chances of success, control the system and methods needed, the choice of the source, the supporting services, and the resources themselves; and quantify the resources, work, and costs involved to conduct the business of acquisitions and measures of success.[5]

We believe that these skills and activities are a constant, but today libraries may need to draw on the expertise of a number of staff members to acquire the desired resources. Further, we fully agree with Ron Ray's concluding comment:

> Library administrators cannot afford to leave acquisitions expertise out of their considerations as libraries navigate into new technology environments and unconventional patterns of information distribution. But neither should they feel constrained to continue organizing acquisitions expertise as it historically developed in libraries.[6]

A 2002 article by Linda Lomker[7] reported on the work of "technical service teams" at the University of Minnesota library. Although that situation is different from that of the majority of libraries due to size of the UM library, teams or work sharing across traditional technical services departmental lines is becoming commonplace, especially as libraries use services such as *PromptCat*.

To be fully effective, selection and acquisitions personnel must have a close, cooperative work relationship. Poor coordination will result in wasted effort, slow response time, and high unit costs. Achieving coordination requires that all parties understand the work processes, problems, and value of each other's work. Beyond the obvious purpose of supporting overall library objectives, the acquisitions department has both library-wide goals and departmental goals. One can group the library-wide goals into five broad areas of purpose:

- Assist in developing a knowledge of the book, media, and electronic resources trade.

- Assist in the selection and collection development process.

- Assist in processing requests for items to be added to the collection.

- Assist in monitoring the expenditure of collection development funds.

- Assist in maintaining all the required records and produce reports regarding the expenditure of funds.

By disseminating material from the various information producers and vendors, the acquisitions department aids in the selection process, even if there is duplication, as there is likely to be. While many publishers now use e-mail announcements in place of mailed flyers for new titles or editions, the question of getting the information to the correct person remains and probably increases duplication. However, not forwarding the announcement can lead to missed titles and opportunities (e.g., discounts). Most information producers are uncertain who in the library makes purchasing decisions. With electronic materials, the process is generally even more complex, with two or more persons involved in the decision making. Thus, it is not surprising that producers buy a number of mailing lists to use when promoting a new or revised product and that several copies of the promotional literature or online announcements will be sent.

Traditionally, acquisitions departments maintained collections of publishers' catalogs, prepublication announcements, and vendors' catalogs. Today more and more publishers depend on online catalogs rather than their costly mass mailing of a print version. Monitoring the websites of publishers that the library buys from on a regular basis is something that selectors and acquisitions staff should do. (A good article that looks at how one can incorporate publishers' and others' catalogs electronically into departmental work activities is by Sue Wiegand.[8]) Despite the changing environment, there is no particular reason to change the location of such activities unless there is a major reorganization, and even then the activities ought to be retained in some form somewhere.

Processing requests for materials involves several activities to ensure that the library acquires the needed items as quickly and inexpensively as possible. Libraries would waste time and money if they simply forwarded requests to the assumed/stated publisher or a vendor. Inaccurate information, duplicate requests, unavailable material, and similar problems would generate unacceptable costs for both the library and the supplier (and would probably cause considerable ill will). Each acquisitions department develops its own set of procedures to reduce such problems. Though there are hundreds of variations, the basic process is the same: preorder searching, ordering, receiving, fiscal managing, and record keeping.

Acquisitions departments also have internal goals. Four common goals are:

1. To acquire material as quickly as possible.

2. To maintain a high level of accuracy in all work procedures.

3. To keep work processes simple, to achieve the lowest possible unit cost.

4. To develop close, friendly working relationships with other library units and with vendors.

Internal goals are important to the achievement of the broader, library-wide goals, because all of the department's decisions regarding internal goals will have some impact on other operating units in the library.

Speed is a significant factor in meeting user demands and determining user satisfaction. An acquisitions system that requires three or four months to secure items available in local bookstores will create a serious public relations problem. A system that is very fast but has a high error rate will increase operating costs and will waste time and energy for both departmental staff and suppliers. Studies have shown that, in many medium-sized and large libraries, the costs of acquiring and processing an item are equal to, or greater than, the price of the item. By keeping procedures simple and by periodically reviewing work flow, the department can help the library provide better service. Speed, accuracy, and thrift should be the watchwords of acquisitions departments. Certainly, online ordering, electronic invoicing, and credit card payments greatly enhance the speed with which the department can handle much of the traditional paperwork. What has not changed very much is the speed with which items actually arrive. The label "snail mail" is still all too often appropriate for the shipping speed, unless one is willing to pay a premium price for faster service.

Staffing

The rapidly changing electronic environment also has an impact on staff. New technologies and applications put pressure on the staff to quickly learn new skills because the workload seldom decreases, and there is a need to maintain a steady flow of materials into the library. Keeping a flow of materials as even as possible allows other units, such as cataloging, to plan their work more effectively.

One popular label for the technology pressure on staff is *technostress*. Technology pressures exist for all the library staff, not just in acquisitions. Kalin and Clark suggested: "The rapid change of technology necessitates a different approach to training. . . . Staff also have to make a commitment to learn new skills. Training must become an integral part of their work life, not an adjunct."[9]

Given the need for training, as well as time to become reasonably comfortable in using the new skill(s) and have such activities become integral to daily work activities, there is a need to rethink duties. Certainly, many of the new technologies and applications make the process of acquisitions less paper-based and in some ways more efficient. Each new upgrade, much less a whole new system, of the acquisitions module means training and stress, and it seems as if the time between upgrades gets shorter and shorter. Funding sources are more willing to spend money on technology than they are to commit resources to additional positions. What this means is that one should not just move the traditional paper-based methods over to a computer system. One should rethink activities and duties that, more often than not, lead to still more change for the staff to handle.

Efficient staffing usually involves using three classes of employees: professionals, support staff, and part-time help. Persons in each category supply certain skills and knowledge required for optimum operation of the department.

Librarians provide in-depth knowledge of library operations and the information trade, in all its various guises. They set departmental objectives and goals, prepare operating plans, develop policies, and supervise departmental operations. They also carry out tasks requiring special skills or knowledge, such as negotiating license agreements, monitoring and forecasting possible price increases for budget requests, and working with vendors to secure discounts. If the acquisitions department does not have any selection responsibility (and few do), only the largest departments need to have many professionals. With properly planned procedures, support staff can handle a large percentage of the department's activities.

Several surveys indicate that this staffing pattern is typical of U.S. libraries. One of the more comprehensive studies was done by Karen Schmidt.[10] Her data showed that support staff performs at least 75 percent of each of the major acquisitions activities (preorder searching, ordering, claiming, and receiving). Another study, by James Coffey, reviewed personnel costs of library acquisitions. His message was that there is a need to carefully consider staffing patterns when one tries to control the cost of acquisitions work.[11] Similar studies done today would have much the same results, despite the changes brought about by technology.

An interesting aspect of the Schmidt article is her data showing the continuing division of acquisitions and serials work in the majority of the responding libraries.[12] (We did not identify any similar later study, but our sense is that more merged units exist today.) A somewhat dated, but still sound, review of technical service reorganization efforts, including merging acquisitions and serials departments, is by Gomez and Harrell.[13] There is a trend toward merging the departments, as LMU did when the library installed an integrated automation system (a result of rethinking how the process is completed).

As noted earlier, few acquisitions departments have any selection responsibility. Most libraries divide selection responsibility among all librarians and, in some instances, users. Many large public and research libraries employ full-time subject specialists for collection development work. Even in such libraries, the individuals involved in the process must cover broad subject areas or select materials published in many countries. Chapter 1 outlined the six major collection development functions; each function has many elements. Beyond those basic functions, excluding acquisitions, selectors perform ongoing liaison activities with their primary user groups:

- Review gift and exchange materials.
- Review acquisition programs, such as approval plans and standing orders.
- Take part in fund allocation discussions.
- Conduct various user and circulation studies.
- Be involved in deselection decisions.
- Plan and implement collection evaluation studies.
- Identify needed retrospective materials.

When one adds these duties to other full-time activities, as is typical in most libraries, it is not surprising to find that not all the selector duties are performed as often as everyone might wish. The result is that some activ-

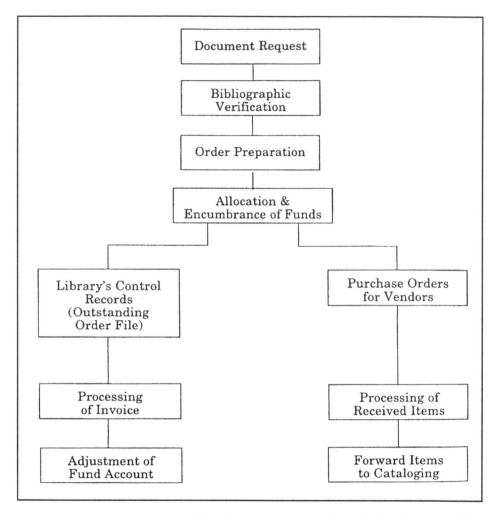

Fig. 10.1. Acquisitions process. From *Introduction to Technical Services*, 7th ed., by G. Edward Evans, Sheila Intner, and Jean Weihs. Greenwood Village, CO: Libraries Unlimited, 2002, p. 99.

ities receive little attention; deselection and user studies are two areas commonly given less time and effort than is desirable. This chapter covers only the basic functions of the acquisitions department staff (see figure 10.1).

Before leaving the discussion of staffing, we should provide a few comments about outsourcing, as it has also become a staff stress factor, especially in the area of technical services. If one read only the 1998–2004 literature about library outsourcing, one might think this was a radical departure for libraries as well as a major threat. To the degree it is being done to reduce staff ("downsizing" in current management jargon), it is relatively new. We are not aware of any libraries that used outsourcing as a means to reduce staff. However, libraries have outsourced a variety of activities for many years—using jobbers/vendors to consolidate order placement for books and/or serials, for example. When used for what Arnold Hirshon and Barbara Winters labeled "strategic reasons"[14]—that is, to supplement existing staff efforts or to handle ever-increasing workloads without benefit of additional staff—outsourcing can be a useful tool in the acquisitions department.

Acquisitions Processing

Acquisitions departments, merged with serials or not, acquire materials using several methods, each carrying with it somewhat different processing. Essentially, there are eight standard methods of acquisition: firm order, standing order, approval plans, blanket order, subscriptions (for serials departments), leases (increasing in use), gifts, and exchange programs. A *firm order* is the usual method for acquiring many titles that the library *knows* it wants—with order form(s) sent to either a vendor or the producer of the item sought. Ordering directly from the individual producers takes substantially more staff time than placing an order for a number of titles, from different producers, with a jobber/wholesaler. The major drawback of this method is the time it takes to prepare the individual orders.

Standing orders work best for items that are somewhat serial in nature. That is, they appear on a regular or irregular basis. Some are a numbered or unnumbered series from a publisher that deals with a single subject area. The library places the order for the series/items, rather like placing a journal subscription. The supplier (vendor or producer) automatically sends the items as they appear, along with an invoice. If the library knows it wants all the items, then a standing order will save staff time and effort due to the automatic shipments. However, especially in academic libraries, standing orders are often the result of one person's request, and if the library does not periodically review its standing orders, it may find that the requester (who may have been the lone user) left the institution years ago. The result is money spent on less useful items. The greatest drawback to standing orders is their unpredictable nature in terms of both number and cost. Certainly, there is no problem about quantity for the regular series, but their cost per item may vary. When it comes to publishers' series or irregular series, one may go several years without receiving a title and then receive several in one year. This is one of the areas where Joyce Ogburn's (see page 230) prediction skills come into play, as one must "guestimate" how much money to set aside at the start of the budget year to cover standing order expenses. Looking at past experience and using an average amount are a safe approach; however, one is seldom able to set aside exactly the right amount. Committing (encumbering) money for too long may result in lost opportunities to acquire other useful items. Committing too little can result in having invoices arrive and not having the funds available to pay them and having to cancel some items in order to pay the invoice(s). Standing orders are a valuable acquisition method but requires careful monitoring throughout the year.

Approval plans are, in a sense, a variation of the standing order concept. They involve automatic shipment of items to the library from a vendor, along with automatic invoicing after the library accepts the items. The differences are that the approval plan normally covers a number of subject areas, and the library has the right to return any items it does not want. Approval plans are usually available from book jobbers, for example, Yankee Book Peddler, Blackwell, and Coutts. Saving staff time and effort is one of the major advantages of such plans. Another advantage is the right to return unwanted items; the underlying assumption is that selectors can make better decisions about an item's appropriateness by looking at the item before committing to its purchase. However, research evidence indicates that the approval plan can result in a higher number of very low or no-use items being added to the collection.[15]

As noted in chapter 4, the key element in making the approval plan a cost-effective acquisition method is in developing a sound "profile" with the plan vendor. A profile outlines the perimeters of the plan and covers issues such as subjects wanted, publishers wanted or not wanted, levels of treatment (undergraduate, graduate, etc.), countries covered, no reprints, no collections of reprinted articles, and so forth. The more time spent in preparing the profile, as well as in monitoring the actual operation of the plan and making adjustments, the greater the value of an approval plan is to the library and the acquisitions unit. The monitoring of operations and carefully reviewing shipments are also obvious keys to success. Given today's staffing situation in most libraries, there is a real danger that the plan will shift from approval to blanket order, simply because the staff has to attend to more pressing duties. An excellent overview article about approval plans is Audrey Fenner's "The Approval Plan: Selection Aid, Selection Substitute."[16]

Blanket order is a combination of firm order and approval plan. It is a commitment on the library's part to purchase all of something, usually the output of a publisher, or a limited subject area, or from a particular country. In the case of a subject area or country, a profile is developed between the library and the blanket order vendor. The materials arrive automatically along with the invoice, thus saving staff time. Another advantage, for country blanket order plans, is that they ensure that the library acquires copies of limited-print-run titles. (It is not uncommon to have very limited print runs of scholarly items in most countries. Waiting for an announcement or a listing in a national bibliography may mean that there are no copies available to purchase.) Like the standing order, the major drawback of blanket order plans is predicting how much money one should reserve to cover the invoices. There is even less predictability with blanket order plans because there are more variables.

We covered subscriptions and leases in earlier chapters (chapters 6 and 7) and will cover gifts and exchange programs later in this chapter. Level and Myers wrote a fine article that outlines the development and implementation of Web-accessible acquisition and collection development tools [17] that is well worth reading.

Request Processing

The first step in the acquisitions process is to organize the incoming requests. The form of requests ranges from oral or e-mail requests, to a scrawled note on a napkin, to a completed formal request card, to an online form. Eventually, the staff organizes all requests so they can carry out an efficient checking process. Each library will have its own request format. Sometimes a card produced by a library supply firm such as Gaylord or Brodart will be used, while other times a locally developed form is preferred. More and more often, an online request form is available for use by requesters. At times, when selectors use a trade or professional review source (such as *Booklist*), they simply check desired items in the publication, and the searchers work with the entire publication rather than transferring everything to request cards. (Despite all the electronic aspects of today's acquisitions work, there is a rather large dependence on paper-based forms. It may be a long time before that dependence disappears.)

Commercially produced request cards cover all the categories of information called for in the *Guidelines for Handling Library Orders for In-Print Monographic Publications*,[18] that is, author, title, publisher, date of publication, edition, International Standard Book Number (ISBN) or International Standard Serial Number (ISSN), Standard Address Number (SAN), price, and number of copies. Many provide space for other information that is of interest only to libraries, such as requester's name, series, vendor, funding source, and approval signature. For any person not familiar with library or book trade practice, the most confusing item on the request card is the space labeled "date/year." Many nonlibrary requesters often assume that the library wants the date they filled out the form, rather than the items' copyright or publication date. Anyone with acquisitions department experience knows how often this confusion takes place. If the form specifically calls for the date of publication, there will be no problem.

Many users request items already in the collection because they do not know how to use the catalog. People (including full-time selectors) occasionally combine or confuse authors' names, titles, publishers, and so on. Therefore, bibliographic searching is an important step in acquisitions work.

Preorder Work

Bibliographic verification or searching consists of two elements. First is establishing the existence of a particular item, that is, *verification*. Second is establishing whether the library needs to order the item, that is, *searching*. In verification, the concern is with identifying the correct author, title, publisher, and other necessary ordering data. Searching determines whether the library already owns the item (perhaps received but not yet represented in the OPAC), whether there is a need for a second copy or multiple copies, and whether the item has been ordered but not received. Integrated automated library systems make searching quick and easy, except for determining the need for additional copies. Many systems show ordered and received status in the online public catalog, which tends to reduce the number of duplicate requests.

Where to begin the process? The answer depends on the collection development system employed by the library. Although it is true that all requests require searching, it also is true that not all request cards have sufficient correct information to search accurately. If the majority of information comes from bibliographies, dealers' catalogs, publishers' flyers, or forms filled out by selection personnel, then searching may be the most efficient way to start. However, a survey by Karen Schmidt of preorder searching indicated that between 30 percent and 40 percent of nonlibrarian requests are duplicates or for items already in the collection.[19] When a large percentage of the requests are from nonlibrarians, it is advisable to start with the verification process.

One of the major activities for preorder searchers is establishing the correct author (main entry). Some selectors, usually nonlibrarians, know little about cataloging rules of entry. Even bibliographers may not keep up-to-date on rule changes. Knowing something about main entry rules, as well as how the standard bibliographic sources list titles, will save search time.

As can be expected, corporate authors, conference papers, proceedings, or transactions are the most troublesome to search. If the department maintains its paper order files, assuming they still exist, by title rather than main entry order, it may be possible to reduce bibliographic training to a minimum while improving accuracy. Titles generally do not change after publication. However, catalogers' decisions about the proper main entry may change several times between the time of selection and the time the item is on the shelf. Main entry searching requires a greater knowledge of cataloging rules, which, in turn, requires more time for training searchers and more time spent searching.

Occasionally, it is impossible to verify an item using the submitted information. All the department can do is contact the requester to try to secure additional information. If the requester cannot provide additional information, a subject search *may* produce a verification. The success rate of subject searches is low. Because of its low success rate, subject verification is a last resort for urgently needed items.

There are several files to check when establishing the library's need for an item; this is true whether the file is paper or electronic. The most obvious starting point is the OPAC. A searcher should look first under the assumed main entry; if the results are negative, and there is some doubt as to the validity of the main entry, then a title search is appropriate. Many librarians suggest that checkers begin with the title, because there tends to be less variation and doubt. In some libraries, even if there is an online public catalog, there may be several other public catalogs to search (e.g., special collections or a nonprint catalog), and all should be part of the checking process, if appropriate. Audiovisual materials, government documents, serials, and collections in special locations often are not fully represented in the OPAC. Other public service files that searchers need to consider are those for lost, missing, or damaged items (replacement files). The searcher would not examine all of these files for all items, but merely for those popular items not marked "added copy" or "replacement."

There are files that are unavailable to the public that searchers may have to examine to determine whether the item is already somewhere in the acquisitions/cataloging process. If the library has a manual system, normally there are three files to consult: the in-process file, the verified requests file (items awaiting typing on order forms), and the standing order file. The in-process file represents books on order, books received but not yet sent to cataloging, and books in the cataloging department. The standing order file represents items that will arrive automatically from a supplier, and that fact may end the search.

Online systems are available in many libraries to speed preorder checking. *Books in Print* is available in both online and CD-ROM formats, as well as in the traditional print version. Other commercial bibliographic selection aids are also available in electronic formats. Bibliographic utilities such as OCLC (*WorldCat*) and RLIN provide large bibliographic databases that are useful in verification and searching. Integrated automation systems have eased the workload on acquisitions. For example, it is possible to download bibliographic data directly from a bibliographic utility. With some systems, the staff can use the downloaded data to prepare a computer-generated order form, provide an online status report, and create the basis for local cataloging work. In some libraries, a person responsible for preorder activities may be able to do substantially more of the work at one terminal merely by logging on and off the integrated system and the bibliographic utility.

Ordering

We noted earlier in this chapter that libraries employ several acquisitions methods (see page 235). Each method has a useful role to play in developing a collection in an efficient, cost-effective manner. Today a majority of libraries use computer-generated orders and store the data electronically, thus reducing the volume of paper associated with ordering activities. For a few libraries, there is no order form for current trade books, because the libraries handle the entire order process electronically, storing the transaction in both the library's and the supplier's computers. In the future, this may be the way all libraries place their orders; however, for thousands of libraries, the paperless order is far from reality.

Regardless of the method used to order material, the vendor must receive enough information to assure shipment of the correct materials: author, title, publisher, date of publication, price, edition (if there are various editions), number of copies, order number, and any special instructions regarding invoicing or methods of payment. Also, more suppliers are asking for the ISBN or ISSN. In time, International Standard Numbers (ISNs) may be all the library needs to send, because ISNs are unique numbers representing a specific journal or a specific edition of a specific title.

A useful publication for all aspiring collection development officers is *Guidelines for Handling Library Orders for In-Print Monographic Publications*. Prepared by the Book Dealer-Library Relations Committee of the Resources and Technical Services Division of ALA, it reflects the needs of both groups and contains recommendations for establishing and maintaining good working relationships. One suggestion is that libraries use the American National Standards Institute (ANSI) Committee Z39 single-title order form, which measures 3×5 inches. At present, there is no equivalent standard for electronic order transmission.

Another standard of ANSI Committee Z39 (Z39.43-1993) is the Standard Address Number (SAN). Like the ISBN, the SAN is a unique number (of seven digits) that identifies each address or organization doing business in the American book trade. For example, the SAN of the Charles Von der Ahe Library at LMU is 332-9135; Brodart is 159-9984; and Libraries Unlimited is 202-6767. Perhaps, in time, all that will be necessary to order a title electronically will be three sets of unique numbers: the ISBN or ISSN and the SANs for the supplier and the buyer. Again, such ease of ordering will take some time off the process, if it ever becomes reality. Nevertheless, these unique numbers are useful as a cross-check for accuracy. Keys to SANs appear in a variety of sources, such as the *American Library Directory* (Information Today), which includes library SANs in its entries. The *Directory* is available in print as well as online (OVID) and CD-ROM (SilverPlatter).

With a manual system or with approval plans, libraries commonly use a multiple-copy order form for placing orders. Some vendors offer a "forms selection" option with an approval plan, in which preprinted order forms are sent instead of books. This approach can be useful for areas of modest interest to the library (not high enough to warrant sending books but high enough to want to see what is available on an ongoing basis).

While almost any computer-based acquisition system can handle all of the following tasks with little or no paper, print order forms are available in a number of formats and contain from four to as many as twelve copies. The 3×5-inch size is standard in the United States, with each copy being a different color, for easy identification. There is no standard dictating a

particular color for a certain purpose. A minimum of four copies is typical:
(1) outstanding order copy, (2) dealer's copy, (3) claiming copy, and (4) accounting copy.

The in-process file may contain several copies of the order form. For
example, after sending the order, the staff might place all remaining copies
in the in-process file. These copies represent on-order status or possible
claims requests, while one copy is forwarded to cataloging with the item
when it arrives, and the final one remains in the file, indicating that the
item is being processed but is not yet ready for public use. Upon receipt, a
staff member pulls all slips except the in-process slip. When the item is
ready for circulation, the cataloging department returns a slip to acquisitions to prompt the removal of the in-process slip. Presumably, at this point
the title is in the OPAC or public catalog, indicating that the item is available for use.

Claiming and handling supplier reports are one of the more time-
consuming and frustrating aspects of the order function, whether manual
or online. Purchasers have every reason to expect U.S. commercial publishers, or vendors supplying titles from such publishers, to deliver the item
or report its status within 90 days. For noncommercial publishers (e.g., university presses or professional associations), an additional 30 days (120
days total) is common for delivery or a report. Western European titles delivered to the United States normally require 180 days, but for items from
countries with a developing book trade, a year or more is not uncommon.
When there is an active collecting program from developing countries, one
must expect a certain percentage of nonresponse. Learning how long to wait
for delivery or a status report takes experience.

When dealing with a U.S. publisher, allowing for the normal two-way
postal time, it is reasonable to send a claim in 60 days if there has been no
response. Many order forms have a printed note stating "cancel after x
days." Although such statements are legally binding, most libraries send a
separate cancellation notice. Certainly, cancellation should not take place
until after the normal response time passes, unless there are unusual circumstances, such as unexpected reductions in the budget. Unfortunately,
over the past twenty years, many such cuts have taken place, and most vendors have been cooperative about making the adjustments. By establishing
a regular cancellation timeline, libraries that must expend funds within a
fixed period can avoid or reduce the last-minute scramble of canceling outstanding orders and ordering materials that the vendor can deliver in time
to use the funds.

Vendors should respond with a meaningful report when they cannot
fill an order within a reasonable period. One less-than-helpful report that
vendors did, and occasionally still do, use is "temporarily out of stock"
(TOS). How long is "temporarily"? What has the vendor done to secure the
item? Poor or inaccurate reporting costs the library money, as Audrey Eaglen pointed out in "Trouble in Kiddyland: The Hidden Costs of O.P. and
O.S."[20] In periods of rapid inflation, each day that the funds remain committed but unexpended erodes buying power, because producers and suppliers raise prices without notice.

Recommended vendor reports are "not yet received from publisher"
(NYR); "out-of-stock, ordering" (OS, ordering); "claiming"; "canceled"; "not
yet published" (NYP); "out-of-stock, publisher" (OS, publisher); "out-of-print"
(OP); "publication canceled"; "out-of-stock indefinitely" (treat this one as a
cancellation); "not our publication" (NOP); "wrong title supplied"; "defective
copy"; and "wrong quantity supplied." After one learns how long a vendor
takes to supply items first reported in the recommended manner, it is pos-

sible to make an informed decision regarding when to cancel and when to wait for delivery.

Before placing an order, the staff must make three important decisions:

1. Which acquisition method to use.

2. What vendor to use.

3. Where to get the money.

The remainder of this chapter explores the methods of acquiring materials. Chapter 11 discusses vendors—when and how to use them and what to expect from them. Chapter 12 covers the fiscal side of acquisitions work.

For most current items, the firm order is the logical method to use. It is often the best method for the first volume in a series, even if the selectors are thinking about requesting a standing order. When the selectors know that the reputation of the publisher or editor of the series is sound, it is probably best to place a standing order. If there is some question about suitability or content of the series, a firm order or approval copy order for the first volume is the better choice.

Order Placement and Receiving

After selecting a vendor, a staff member assigns an order number and decides which fund to use for payment. Order numbers assist the staff in tracking the order. The assignment process is simply a matter of checking the last order number and using the next number in the sequence. As soon as the department head signs the orders, they are ready to be sent to the vendor either electronically or by mail.

Receiving orders, though not difficult, requires careful planning. If not handled properly, receiving can be more complex and time-consuming than ordering. As strange as it may seem, proper unpacking of shipments will save everyone in the department a great deal of time, energy, and frustration. Finding the packing slip or invoice is the key first step in the process. A *packing slip* lists all the items in a particular shipment. An *invoice* is an itemized bill, which business offices require before they will issue a voucher or check. For receivers' convenience, most vendors attach a clearly marked envelope containing the packing slip to the outside of one of the boxes. One technique is to enclose the slip inside one of the items, and another favorite hiding place is under a cardboard bottom liner on the bottom of the box. If no packing slip is found, it is essential to keep the items separated from other materials in the receiving area. Mixing shipments can create seemingly endless problems.

A second important step is to check each item against the packing slip as it comes out of the box. This serves as a check on what the shippers think they sent against what the library actually received. After all, boxes go astray in shipment, shipping room clerks overlook items, and sometimes, items disappear from the library before processing. Checking the physical condition of each item is another step in the receiving process. Defective materials may be returned for credit or replacement without prior approval from the vendor. Imperfections can be of many kinds. With books, typical problems are missing or blank pages or improperly collated texts. Staff members need to check audiotapes and videotapes for gaps, blank or fogged sections, and proper recording speed. Microforms must be examined to assure that the producer processed them properly; sometimes they have fogged, streaked, or spotted areas, and occasionally there is hypo (developing solution) residue, which can ruin the film. The following list highlights some common receipt problems:

- The wrong edition sent. (The checker must be aware of the difference between an edition and a printing. A new edition means that there are substantial changes—material added or deleted; a new printing merely indicates that the publisher sold out the previous printing and reprinted more copies with no changes in the text.)

- Items ordered but not received.

- Items not ordered but shipped.

- Too many or not enough copies sent.

- Imperfect copies received.

Vendors usually are good about accepting returns of unwanted items, even when it turns out to have been the fault of the library—as long as the library has not property-marked them.

After determining that the shipment is complete, property marking (such as stamping or embossing) takes place. As noted earlier, sometimes items disappear, so the sooner property marking takes place, the more difficult it will be for materials to vanish without a trace. Property marking takes many forms. Stamping the fore edge and the title page of books is a common practice. (Rare books are handled differently.) Another method is to *accession* items, that is, to give each item a unique number. A staff member records the number and title of the item in an accessions log (either print or online). Today, linking the barcode in an item to its item record in a database accomplishes the same type of inventory control with much less effort.

The last step in processing is approving the invoice for payment. Normally, this requires the signature of the head of the department or that person's representative. Usually, only a completely filled order may be approved for payment. The library bookkeeper passes the approved invoice on to the agency that actually issues the check. Rarely does a library itself write such checks; it is done by the governing agency.

Gifts and Deposits

In most cases, acquisitions departments are the ultimate recipients of unsolicited gifts of books, serials, and other materials (including a variety of molds and insects) that well-meaning people give to the library. Both solicited and unsolicited gifts can be a source of out-of-print materials for replacement, extra copies, and the filling of gaps in the collection. The collection development policy statement on gifts will help acquisitions personnel process the material quickly. (One example is the "Gifts to the Collection" statement developed by the University of Maryland Libraries: <http://www.lib.umd.edu/CLMD/Gifts/donate.html>). A good article outlining all aspects of handling gifts is Mary Bostic's "Gifts to Libraries: Coping Effectively."[21] Another excellent survey of both gift and exchange programs, by Steven Carrico,[22] covers all management aspects of the work.

Reviewing gifts is important, as a library should not discard valuable or needed items that arrive as gifts. However, one must keep in mind the fact that a library should not add unnecessary items just because they were "free." David Fowler and Janet Arcand's article[23] provides detailed information about the time and costs of book acquisition activities. The two factors are substantial, and the only real difference for gifts is their lack of a purchase price. Processing and storage costs are the same for a gift as for a purchased item. Older books require careful checking, as variations in printings and editions may determine whether an item is valuable or worthless. (Usually, a second or third printing is less valuable than the first printing of a work.) Persons with extensive training and experience in bibliographic checking must do searching.

There are some legal aspects about gifts that staff must be aware of. Essentially, these issues are related to tax deductions and Internal Revenue Service regulations, which we address in chapter 17 on legal issues. At a minimum, staff should make a count of the gift items, noting hardcover, soft cover, and, if magazines are included, the number of issues and if any are bound. Beyond the minimum, there are several steps to take, which we cover in chapter 17.

There are two basic types of exchange activity: the exchange of unwanted duplicate materials and the exchange of new materials between libraries. Usually, only large research libraries engage in exchanging new materials. In essence, cooperating institutions trade institutional publications. Tozzer Library (Harvard University's anthropology library) has exchange agreements with several hundred organizations. These organizations send their publications to Tozzer, which, in turn, sends them Peabody Museum publications. Often this method is the only way a library can acquire an organization's publications. Occasionally, libraries use this system to acquire materials from countries in which there are commercial trade restrictions. Where government trade restrictions make buying and selling of foreign publications difficult or impossible, the cooperating libraries acquire (buy) their local publications for exchange. Exchanges of this type are complex and difficult to manage, and this is a method of last resort. Libraries can exercise better quality control when they trade for known organizational series or titles than when the choice of publications from the organization is more or less left to chance. Exchanges of this type exist on the basis of formal agreements between the cooperating organizations. They play an important role in developing comprehensive subject collections.

Libraries normally add only a small percentage of gifts to the collection. This means that the library must dispose of a great many unwanted items. Disposition of unwanted gift materials is an activity that almost every library engages in at some time. One method is to post the list of unwanted items on a discussion list such as Back Issues & Exchange Services (<http://www.uvm.edu/%7ebmaclenn/backexch.html>). The first library to request an item gets it for the shipping cost (usually book-rate postage). This method is time-consuming, but it does offer other libraries an opportunity to secure some needed materials for minimal cost.

Another method is to arrange with an out-of-print dealer to take the items, usually as a lot rather than for a per-item price. It is unusual to receive cash; instead, the dealer gives the library a line of credit. The library uses the credit to acquire materials from the dealer. This system works well when the library has specialized materials the dealer wants and when the dealer stocks enough useful material that the library can use its credit within a reasonable time (less than eighteen to twenty-four months). Holding a book sale is yet another method of disposing of unwanted material, one that is gaining in popularity as dealers resist the credit memo system. However, this is not a "free" venture, as staff must select the items for sale, establish a fair price, find a suitable location, and monitor the sale. Depending on the volume of gifts, annual, semiannual, or monthly sales are appropriate. Sales can be an excellent Friends of the Library project that can save some staff time. A few libraries use an ongoing sale tactic, especially when they have limited staff and space and a high volume of unwanted gifts. The Boston Public Library has entered into an arrangement that allows it to sell unwanted duplicates through *Amazon.com*.[24] There is, as one might expect, a website devoted to listing book sales (<http://www.book-sales-in-america.com>).

Future Developments

Undoubtedly, hardware and software technology, especially in the area of small, relatively inexpensive business computer systems, will make it increasingly possible for even the smallest libraries to benefit from technology, as well as to tie into regional and national systems. The idea that all homes and offices will have access to a library's online catalog is no longer a daydream. With each new subsystem bringing the total integrated library system closer to reality, collection development can become more effective and efficient. But, despite the marvels of technology, there will always have to be intelligent, widely read, humanistic, and service-oriented information professionals making the decisions and planning the systems.

Summary

This chapter touched on only the basic activities and problems in acquisitions work. The following three chapters cover vendors and suppliers, fiscal management related to collection development, and an overview of how materials are removed from collections once they have outlived their usefulness.

A very sound and relatively recent book that provides detailed information about all aspects of acquisitions work is Francis Wikerson and Linda Lewis' *The Complete Guide to Acquisitions Management* (Westport, CT: Libraries Unlimited, 2003).

Notes

1.   S. R. Ranganathan, *The Five Laws of Library Science* (Bangalore, India: Sarada Ranganathan Endowment for Library Science, 1988), 326.

2.   Alex Bloss, "The Value-Added Acquisition Librarian: Defining Our Role in a Time of Change," *Library Acquisitions: Practice and Theory* 19 (Fall 1995): 321–30.

3.   Ron L. Ray, "Where Is the Future of Acquisitions Expertise Written in the Future of Libraries?" *Journal of Academic Librarianship* 24 (January 1998): 80–82.

4.   Carol Diedrichs, "Acquisitions: So What and Where?," *Journal of Academic Librarianship* 24 (January 1998): 74.

5.   Joyce L. Ogburn, "T2: Theory in Acquisition Revisited," *Library Acquisitions: Practice and Theory* 21 (Summer 1997): 168.

6.   Ray, "Where Is the Future of Acquisitions Expertise," 82.

7.   Linda Lomker, "Nimble as Cats, Dependable as Dogs: Subject-based Technical Services Teams and Acquisitions," *Library Collections, Acquisitions & Technical Services* 26 (2002): 343–44.

8.   Sue Wiegand, "Incorporating Electronic Products into Acquisitions Workflow in a Small College Library," *Library Collections, Acquisitions & Technical Services* 26, no. 4 (Winter 2002): 363–66.

9.   Sally Kalin and Katie Clark, "Technostressed Out?," *Library Journal* 121 (August 1996): 32.

10.   Karen Schmidt, "Acquisition Process in Research Libraries," *Library Acquisitions: Practice and Theory* 11, no. 1 (1987): 35–44.

11.   James Coffey, "Identifying Personnel Costs in Acquisitions," in *Operational Costs in Acquisitions*, ed. J. Coffey, 55–74 (New York: Haworth Press, 1990).

12.   Schmidt, "Acquisition Process in Research Libraries."

13.   Joni Gomez and Jeanne Harrell, "Technical Services Reorganization: Realities and Reactions," *Technical Services Quarterly* 10, no. 2 (1992): 1–15.

14.   Arnold Hirshon and Barbara Winters, *Outsourcing Library Services: A How-to-Do-It Manual* (New York: Neal-Schuman, 1996).

15.   G. Edward Evans, "Book Selection and Book Collection Usage in Academic Libraries," *Library Quarterly* 40 (July 1970): 297–308; G. Edward Evans, "Approval Plans and Collection Development in Academic Libraries," *Library Resources & Technical Services* 18 (Winter 1974): 35–50.

16. Audrey Fenner, "The Approval Plan: Selection Aid, Selection Substitute," *The Acquisitions Librarian* 16, nos. 31/32 (2004): 227–40.

17.   Allison Level and Sarah Myers, "Creating Internal Web Tools for Collection Development," *Collection Building* 22, no. 4 (2003): 162–66.

18.   *Guidelines for Handling Library Orders for In-Print Monographic Publications*, 2nd ed. (Chicago: American Library Association, 1984).

19.   Karen Schmidt, "Cost of Pre-Order Searching," in *Operational Costs in Acquisitions*, ed. J. Coffey (New York: Haworth Press, 1990), 5–20.

20.   Audrey Eaglen, "Trouble in Kiddyland: The Hidden Costs of O.P. and O.S.," *Collection Building* 6 (Summer 1984): 26–28.

21.   Mary Bostic, "Gifts to Libraries: Coping Effectively," *Collection Management* 14, nos. 3/4 (1991): 175–84.

22.   Steven Carrico, "Gifts and Exchanges," in *Understanding the Business of Library Acquisitions*, 2nd ed., ed. K. Schmidt, 205–23 (Chicago: American Library Association, 1999).

23.   David Fowler and Janet Arcand, "Monographs Acquisitions Time and Cost Studies: The Next Generation," *Library Resources & Technical Services* 47 (July 2003): 109–24.

24.   Jennifer B. Pierce, "Weeding the Amazon Way," *American Libraries* 35 (August 2004): 90.

Selected Websites
and Discussion Lists*

(See also resources on the DLC5 website: <http://www.lu.com/dlc5>)

"Acquisitions, Serials, and Collection Development."
        <http://www.itcompany.com/inforetriever/acqsercd.htm>
        "A portal designed for librarians to locate Internet resources related to their profession. A popular information resource site for librarians since 1994." From the *Internet Library for Librarians*.

ACQNET—Acquisitions Librarians Electronic Network
> To subscribe, send the following e-mail message to listproc@listproc.app
> state.edu: SUBSCRIBE ACQNET-L YOURFIRSTNAME YOURLASTNAME

ACQWEB
> <http://www.acqweb.org>
> A website of acquisitions and collection development information, which in-
> cludes links to reference resources, verification tools, and vendor directories.

Association for Library Collections and Technical Services: Acquisitions Section:
Statement on Principles and Standards of Acquisitions Practice
> <http://www.ala.org/ala/alctscontent/alctspubsbucket/alctsresources/acqui
> sitionsres/ethicsacq/principlesstandards.htm>
> A brief statement prepared by the ALCTS Acquisitions Section Ethics Task
> Force and adopted by the ALCTS Board of Directors in 1994.

Back Issues & Exchange Services
> <http://www.uvm.edu/%7ebmaclenn/backexch.html>
> A detailed listing of resources for acquisitions librarians, compiled by Birdie
> MacLennan.

BACKMED
> A forum for the listing of both available and desired serial issues and books
> in primarily medical subject areas. To subscribe, e-mail backmed@lists.swetsb
> lackwell.com or visit <http://lists.swetsblackwell.com/mailman/listinfo/back
> med>.

BACKSERV
> A forum for the listing of both available and desired serial issues and books
> in all nonmedical subject areas. To subscribe, e-mail backserv@lists.swetsb
> lackwell.com or visit <http://lists.swetsblackwell.com/mailman/listinfo/back
> serv>.

EUROBACK
> <http://www.lists.ulg.ac.be/mailman/listinfo/euroback>
> A discussion list devoted to exchange issues for European libraries and infor-
> mation centers.

GIFTEXCH
> To subscribe, send an e-mail message to: giftexch-request@umich.edu subscribe
> YourFirstName YourLastName

SERIALST
> <http://www.uvm.edu/~bmaclenn/serialst.html>
> A discussion list devoted to serials issues.

*These sites were accessed May 7, 2005.

Further Reading

American Library Association. *Acquisitions Guidelines Series*. Nos. 1–10. Chicago:
American Library Association, 1994.

———. Association for Library Collections and Technical Services. *Statement of
Standards and Principles of Acquisitions Practice*. Chicago: American Library
Association, 1994.

Bartolo, L. M., D. A. Wicks, and V. A. Ott. "Border Crossing in a Research University:
An Exploratory Analysis of a Library Approval Plan Profile of Geography."
Collection Management 27, nos. 3/4 (2002): 29–44.

Bobkoff, M. "A Bookworm's Eye-view of Collection Development: Making Use of Gift Books." *Public Libraries* 38 (November–December 1999): 364–70.

Brantz, M. "Role of the Bookstore in the Acquisitions Process." In *Charleston Conference Proceedings 2002*, edited by R. Bazirjian and V. Speck, 102–5. Westport, CT: Libraries Unlimited, 2003.

Cooksey, E. B. "Out to Sea But with a Rudder: Acquisitions Advice for the Solo Science Librarian." *The Acquisitions Librarian* 15, no. 29 (2003): 23–30.

Fenner, A. "The Approval Plan: Selection Aid, Selection Substitute." *The Acquisitions Librarian* 16, nos. 31/32 (2004): 227–40.

Janosko, J. "Acquisitions on the Web." In *Charleston Conference Proceedings 2002*, edited by R. Bazirjian and V. Speck, 115–18. Westport, CT: Libraries Unlimited, 2003.

Jasper, R. C. "Collaborative Roles in Managing Electronic Publications." *Library Collections, Acquisitions & Technical Services* 26, no. 4 (Winter 2002): 355–61.

Kistler, J. M. "Special Acquisitions: Collecting African Materials." *The Acquisitions Librarian* 15, no. 29 (2003): 31–50.

Kruse, T., and A. Holtzman. "Web Booksellers—Their Usefulness to Libraries." *Library Collections, Acquisitions & Technical Services* 27, no. 1 (Spring 2003): 121–29.

Langendorfer, J. M., and M. L. Hurst. "Comparison Shopping: Purchasing Continuations as Standing Orders or on Approval." *Library Collections, Acquisitions, & Technical Services* 27, no. 2 (Summer 2003): 169–73.

McHugo, A., C. Magenau, and J. M. Langendorfer. "Reinventing Acquisitions with a 'Forget-to-Do' List." *Serials Librarian* 46, nos. 3/4 (2004): 269–73.

Montgomery, J. G. "Management of Gifts to Libraries, Part III, Consignment/Trade-for-Credit Agreements." *Against the Grain* 13, no. 4 (September 2001): 80–81.

Norris, J. G. "A Subject Approach to Gifts Management and Donor Relations." *Collections Management* 27, no. 1 (2002): 41–57.

Plodinec, L., and J. Schmidt. "Which Worked Better for Mississippi State: Standing Order or Approval Plan?" *Library Collections, Acquisitions & Technical Services* 26, no. 4 (Winter 2002): 439–48.

Wachel, K. "Management of Gifts to Libraries, Part IV, Selling Gifts-in-Kind on Consignment: The University of Iowa Libraries Model." *Against the Grain* 14, no. 6 (December 2002/January 2003): 91–92.

Ward, J. "Web-based Acquisitions from Web-based Vendors: Pros and Cons." In *Charleston Conference Proceedings 2002*, edited by R. Bazirjian and V. Speck, 149–52. Westport, CT: Libraries Unlimited, 2003.

11
Distributors and Vendors

Librarians in acquisitions and collection development have a love-hate relationship with vendors. There are some issues for which vendors get the deserved blame and others for which they get underserved responsibility. (An example of undeserved blame is when producers change their minds about making an item available through an aggregator package.) The truth is that libraries could not manage the workload without the assistance and services that vendors provide. This is not to say there are no issues; there are, but we need them, and they need us, so developing an understanding of one another is essential.

Like all other organizations involved in the information business, library vendors and distributors are facing a changing environment, in large measure due to technology. Another factor in their changing environment is what has been happening to the majority of libraries; the past twenty years or so have not been the best of times for library funding and support in general. Library staffs are under pressure to do more with less, including personnel, and libraries have turned to vendors for assistance. Because they want to continue to do business with libraries, as well as take advantage of new business opportunities, many vendors and suppliers offer an increasing range of services to libraries. Taking advantage of such services is where libraries are expanding their outsourcing activities. We mention a few of these new "services" later in this chapter.

In chapter 5, we identified three major problems for materials producers: economics, copyright infringement, and distribution. Knowledge of the information product distribution system is essential for developing the most cost-effective collection of information materials. Wholesalers, retailers, and remainder houses are major sources of material for the library collection. Often, several different sources can supply the same item. Is there an important difference among these sources? What services does each provide? For example, if one is looking for a book published last year, it is possible to acquire a copy from many sources. Would it matter which source is used? How likely is it that all would have the book? For that matter, what function does each source perform?

Jobbers and Wholesalers

Librarians refer to *jobbers* or *vendors* rather than wholesalers. There is a technical difference between a wholesaler and a jobber, but for libraries, the difference is insignificant. Jobbers purchase quantities of books from various publishers, then sell the copies to bookstores and libraries. Because they buy in volume, they receive a substantial discount from publishers (50 to 60 percent is fairly common).

When the jobber sells a book, the purchaser receives a discount off the producer's list price, but it is much lower than the discount that the jobber received. For instance, if the jobber received a 40 percent discount from the producer, the discount given the library will not be more than 15 to 18 percent. If the library or bookstore orders the book directly from the publisher, the discount may be just as high.

Discounting is a complex issue in any commercial activity, and it is highly complex in the book trade. Every producer has a discount schedule that is slightly different, if not unique. Some items are *net* (no discount); usually, these are textbooks, science/technology/medical (STM) titles, or items of limited sales appeal. *Short discounts* are normally 20 percent; these are items the producers expect will have limited appeal, but with more potential than the net titles. *Trade discounts* range from 30 to 60 percent or more; items in this category are high-demand items or high-risk popular fiction. Publishers believe that by giving a high discount for fiction, bookstores will stock more copies and thus help promote the title. Jobbers normally receive 50 to 60 percent discounts, primarily because of their high-volume orders (hundreds of copies per title rather than the tens that most libraries and independent bookstore owners order).

Jobbers have encountered financial problems at much the same time as libraries in the form of rising costs and declining sales. A number of publishers are requiring prepayment or have placed jobbers on a *pro forma* status. Pro forma status requires prepayment, and suppliers extend credit on the basis of the current performance in payment of bills. Much of the credit and order fulfillment extended by publishers depends on an almost personal relationship with a jobber. This means that libraries must select a jobber with care. It is not inappropriate to check a prospective jobber's financial status (through a rating service, such as Dun & Bradstreet). Even longtime, "major" vendors fail (see "Publishers Hurt in Divine Fallout,"[1] which discusses the bankruptcy of RoweCom/Faxon).

One very pertinent question for the library is how many vendors to use. There are pros and cons to consolidating one's business with only one or two vendors, just as there are to using a number of vendors for the same type of product. Consolidation usually means that the vendor gains a better sense of the library's requirements, perhaps a better discount for the library and some "free" services from the vendor. Today's environment requires substantial investment in technology on a regular basis, which, combined with libraries' budget woes, means that smaller firms may not be able to survive—or at the least not be able to keep up with technological developments in the field. In contrast, having several vendors for one type of product may also yield a higher discount, because there is a degree of competition for the library's business. On the downside, the service may not be as good, and perhaps the vendors will not have the resources to invest in newer technology. The primary concern should be service, followed by financial strength. As stated earlier, privately held companies can be checked in a service such as Dun & Bradstreet, and publicly held firms file 10K reports that one can locate via a service like the Security Exchange Commission's *EDGAR* database (<http://www.sec.gov/edgar.shtml>).

What Can Jobbers Do?

Why buy from an indirect source that charges the same or a higher price than the direct source would? Service! Jobbers provide an important service in that they can save a library a significant amount of time and money. Although jobbers do not give high discounts, the time saved by placing a single order for ten different titles from ten different publishers (instead of ten different orders) more than pays for the slightly higher price. Other savings can result from the batch effect of unpacking only one box and authorizing only one payment. Most jobbers also promise to provide fast, accurate service. It is true that a few publishers, if they accept single-copy orders (and most do), handle these orders more slowly than they do large orders. But it is also true that jobbers do not always have a specific title when the library wants it, which means that the library must allow additional time to secure the desired item.

Many jobbers promise 24-hour shipment of items in stock. Do they make good on such claims? Generally, yes; however, the key phrase is *in stock*. Frequently, there can be delays of three to four months in receiving a complete order because some titles are not in stock. When talking with jobbers, do not be impressed by numbers quoted in their advertising, for example, "more than 2 million books in stock." What is important is how many *titles* and which publishers they stock. For various reasons, from economic to personal, some publishers refuse to deal with a particular jobber. Some important questions to ask any jobber before a library contracts for that firm's services are:

1. Will you give me a list of all the publishers that you do not handle?

2. How does your firm handle a request for a title not in stock?

3. Will you give me a list of series that your firm does not handle?

4. Do you have any service charges on any category of material? (If so, ask if the charge is indicated on the invoice as a separate cost.)

5. What other libraries use your firm?

6. From what location would our orders ship?

7. Would we have a permanent account representative/contact person for concerns?

8. What is the average shipment turnaround time for items in stock?

9. Can you accommodate a single billing address with multiple ship-to addresses?

10. If we change to your firm, what type of assistance can you provide in handling the transfer?

Often the answer to the first question is difficult to obtain. Sales representatives want to say they can supply any title from any publisher, with only minor exceptions, as well as meet the library's needs in terms of the account. However, libraries in the same system may simultaneously receive different lists from representatives of the same firm about publishers not supplied or warehouse/service location. The issues are important, and the acquisitions department must resolve the question if it is to operate effectively.

Speed of service is significant. Some jobbers order a single title from a publisher when it is not in stock. Others say they will do this, but they may actually wait until they have received multiple requests before placing the order. By placing a multiple-copy order, the jobber receives a better discount. For the library, the delay may be one to several months, because it will take that long for the jobber to accumulate enough individual requests for the title to make up an order of sufficient size. Usually, jobbers that place single-copy orders for a customer offer a lower discount on those items. Again, the acquisitions staff must weigh service and speed against discount. Occasionally, a jobber will have a title in stock after the publisher has listed the item as out-of-print (OP). On occasion, a jobber can supply out-of-print material, and a few jobbers will even try to find out-of-print items for their best customers. This is a special service that is never advertised and is offered only to favored customers.

Beyond fast, accurate service, jobbers should provide personal service. A smooth working relationship is based on mutual understanding and respect. When those are present, it is much easier to solve problems, even the difficult ones. The jobber, because of the smaller base of customers, normally can provide answers more quickly than a publisher's customer service department. Even the small-account customer receives a jobber's careful attention (in order to hold the account), something that seldom happens with publishers.

No single jobber can stock all of the in-print items that a library will need. However, most large firms do carry the high-demand current and backlist items. Book trade folklore says that 20 percent of the current and backlist titles represent 80 percent of total sales. All of the good jobbers try to stock the right 20 percent of titles. Some are more successful than others. Bookstores find this useful for maintaining their stock of bestsellers. Libraries, however, must acquire a broader range of titles. Thus, the opinion of bookstore owners about the best jobbers is useful only if librarians and bookstores agree about whether 20 percent of all titles will fill 80 percent of all needs.

One problem with a jobber that has limited stock is in invoicing and billing procedures. A small jobber may ship and bill for those items in stock, then back order the remainder of the titles. In this case, the jobber expects to receive payment for the partial fulfillment of the order. However, some funding authorities allow payment only for complete orders. That is, the library must receive or cancel every item on an order before the business office will issue a check. This procedure can cause problems for small jobbers and libraries alike. Few small vendors are able or willing to wait for payment until a particular order is complete. For small libraries with small materials budgets, the challenge is to find a jobber that will accept complicated procedures and delays despite low volume. It is becoming harder to find such firms, and libraries are attempting to persuade their funding authorities to simplify ordering and payment procedures.

One useful service that many large jobbers offer is a periodic report on the status of all of a library's orders. Many provide a monthly report on all items not yet shipped. They provide a list of back ordered items along with the reason that each item is unavailable. A timely and complete status report will save both library and jobber unnecessary letter-writing campaigns and telephone calls. Most large jobbers offer a flexible order and invoicing system; that is, they try to adapt to the library's needs, rather than force the library to use their methods.

Status reports are an area of concern for both the acquisitions and collection development staff. Almost everyone in the field has been frustrated by these reports. Does a report stating that a book is out of print mean that the book is *really* out of print? It should, but occasionally, by contacting the publisher, the library may have the item in hand in less than thirty days. This happens often enough to keep alive doubts about the quality of jobber reports. Perhaps two of the most frustrating reports are out-of-stock (OS) and temporarily out-of-stock (TOS) reports. Exactly what these two reports mean varies from jobber to jobber. The basic meaning is clear: the book is not available at present. Beyond that, however, doubt exists. How long will the title be out of stock? Some cynics suggest that these reports really mean "We are waiting until we get enough orders from buyers to secure a good discount from the producer." The cynics propose that the difference between the two reports is that TOS means "We expect to have enough soon," and OS means "Don't hold your breath." Those interpretations are much too harsh, but they do indicate some problems with the quality and content of the reporting system. (Not all blame for faulty reporting lies with jobbers; sometimes producers change their plans after reporting a status to a jobber.) An article in a 1989 issue of *School Library Journal* reported that 10 percent of all school library orders and 7 percent of public library orders are unavailable for some reason.[2] This figure has not changed much over the years; if anything, the percentages have increased slightly.

Does it really matter how accurate the reports are? Yes, it does matter, and the result can have an impact on collection development. An item on order encumbers (sets aside) the necessary funds for payment. The acquisitions staff cannot determine the precise cost of the item until the invoice arrives; the price may change, the exact discount is unknown, and shipping and handling charges vary. One hopes to set aside slightly more than the total cost. Most libraries and information centers have annual budgets and operate in systems where any monies not expended at the end of the fiscal year revert to the general fund (i.e., the funds do not carry forward into the next fiscal year). In essence, the library loses the unspent money. Having large sums of money tied up (encumbered) in outstanding orders that are undeliverable before the end of the fiscal year can result in a real loss for the collection. In a sense, the library loses twice: wanted items go unreceived, and the library loses funds. Accurate reports assist in avoiding this unpleasant situation.

Another problem commonly encountered is the paperwork involved in cancellations and reordering. Many people have estimated the cost of normal library paperwork; these estimates range from four dollars for a simple, two-paragraph business letter, to more than twenty-one dollars for placing an order, to even more, depending on the complexity of the task, the organization, and the cost elements included in the calculation. Regardless of how one calculates the costs, one must consider the staff time, forms, letters, and postage involved in each transaction. Though these costs do not come out of the acquisitions budget, they represent a loss in the sense that the order did not result in the library receiving the desired material.

Finally, the library does lose some buying power, as funds remain encumbered, especially during periods of high inflation. Unlike money in a savings account, which earns a small amount of interest each day, encumbered funds lose a small amount of purchasing power each day. If inflation is rapid, or if one is buying foreign books, and the currency's value is fluctuating widely, losses can be large. Producers raise prices without notice, and in times of inflation one can count on regular price increases. The less time funds remain encumbered, the more purchasing power the library has. Thus, the accuracy of vendor reports is important. If the vendor cannot supply an item (OP, OS, or TOS) in time and so informs the library, the library can cancel the order and use the funds for something that is available for delivery. Monitoring of vendor performance in report accuracy and speed of delivery can help control the problem.

Where does one learn about vendors and services? One method that allows one to talk directly with a variety of vendors in a short time period is to attend an American Library Association summer or winter meeting. At ALA, one will find just about every major vendor doing business with U.S. libraries; and yes, firms from many other countries are also present. In addition to the "majors," there are always a surprising number of smaller firms present that are trying to break into the library market. Larger vendors also attend state library conventions, as well as specialized library conferences.

Beyond library association conference contacts and word-of-mouth suggestions from one's peers, several guides to vendors are available. General publications such as *Literary Market Place* and *International Literary Market Place* (Information Today) or specialized lists by format, region of the world, and subject matter will provide a long list of possibilities. One can also post questions about who uses whom on acquisitions discussion lists or refer to websites such as AcqWeb's "Library Vendors" (<http://www.acqweb.org/pubr.html>).

A number of jobbers offer their services to U.S. libraries. Some of the larger firms that are active in marketing their programs are Brodart, Baker and Taylor, Ingram, Yankee Book Peddler (YBP), Coutts, Emery-Pratt Company, and Blackwell North America. There are also specialized jobbers, such as Majors, a leading firm for medical, science, and technical books. Serials jobbers include EBSCO and Basch Subscriptions, Inc. Websites for each of these jobbers may be found at the end of this chapter.

When selecting a vendor, one should keep several factors in mind. We have mentioned them earlier, but a summary list is useful.

- Service—a representative, toll-free numbers, website features, etc.
- Quality of service—ask for and check references, ease of handling "problems."
- Speed of fulfillment—including accuracy.
- Discounts and pricing.
- Vendor's financial viability.
- Vendor ability to work with the library's automation system.
- Special services available—free and at a cost.

These are the same factors one should use to evaluate the vendor(s) after selection.

Vendor-Added Services

Today, most vendors offer services beyond the basics of supplying books, serials, media, and electronic resources at "wholesale" prices. Some of the more common services are:

- Acquisition assistance—such as searches and verification.
- Automated selection assistance programs (some including book reviews).
- Book rental plans.
- Cataloging and shelf-ready processing.
- Customized management data.
- Electronic financial transactions beyond the basics of ordering and invoice payment.
- Ability to provide materials in a variety of formats—print, AV, electronic, etc.
- Provision of electronic tables of contents or machine-readable data.
- Library furniture.
- Library supplies.

As this list suggests, vendors are entering the outsourcing market, and some are attempting to offer most of the supplies and services necessary for library operation.

Many small libraries and today more and more large libraries find it beneficial to buy books shelf-ready. Normally, the technical services offered by vendors allow the library a number of choices. Processing kits that include catalog cards, pockets, labels, jackets, and so forth are available for purchase; the library staff uses the kit to complete the processing routines. Some firms offer completely processed, ready-for-shelf products and in cooperation with OCLC provide records for the library's OPAC (*PromptCat*). Flexibility is essential in these services; yet, to make them cost-effective or profitable for the vendor, there are limits on the variations allowed or, at least, a high sales volume for each variation. Thus, one can expect to receive a degree of personalized customer service but not custom processing.

One jobber, Brodart, offers a rather unusual service, the McNaughton Plan (<http://www.books.brodart.com/onlinetools/mcnaughtonbooks.htm>), to help solve the problem of providing an adequate number of high-demand titles for both books and audiobooks. Most libraries have suffered the problem of high demand for a popular book, with the demand lasting only a few months. Should the library buy many copies and discard all but one or two after the demand subsides or buy only a few copies and take reservations? The McNaughton Plan offers another alternative: rent multiple copies for the duration of the title's popularity. Brodart describes the plan as a leasing program. The plan offers high-demand items that Brodart's staff selects. One cannot order just any book; it must be on Brodart's list of high-demand titles. Savings occur in several areas. There are no processing costs, because the books come ready for the shelf, and the leasing fee is considerably lower than the item's purchase price. Users will be happier about shorter waiting times for the high-interest books. All in all, anyone involved in meeting recreational reading interests will find the program worth investigating. College and university libraries may use it to stock a variety of materials for recreational reading without taking too much money out of the book fund.

Other services many vendors offer are electronic ordering and, especially useful for serials, electronic invoicing. Access to an electronic version of *Books in Print* is often part of the service as well. With electronic ordering, acquisitions staff has dial-in or Web access to the vendor's inventory database. This allows one to learn the availability of a title, place an order, receive confirmation of receipt of the order, and receive the invoice electronically, with the entire process taking only a few seconds. One problem with electronic ordering is that most acquisitions departments use many different vendors, and each vendor offering this type of service seems to have a number of variations in the system. This is an area where standards could be beneficial to everyone. Learning and remembering or consulting manuals for several different electronic ordering systems cuts into the time that could be saved by using such systems.

Some vendors offer useful management reports based on their electronic systems. An example from a book vendor is illustrated in figure 11.1, page 256; figure 11.2, page 257, is a report from a serials vendor. Such reports assist the library in making budget requests and estimating encumbrances for standing orders and blanket orders.

We discussed Brodart's TIPS program (<http://www.books.brodart.com/services/tips.htm>) in the chapter on selection and mention it again here as an example of vendor-assisted selection.

What Should Jobbers and Librarians Expect from Each Other?

Librarians are responsible for helping to maintain good working relationships with vendors. Simply stated, a vendor's profits are the difference between the price it pays producers and the resale price. Is this any different than for any other type of business? Not in the fundamentals, but there are some special aspects to the book trade and library market. One such variation is that any buyer can buy directly from the materials producer. This is seldom true in other fields. Another difference is that, to a large degree, libraries can find out the maximum price of any item by checking in-print lists, such as *Books in Print*, or by consulting the producer. When every buyer knows the maximum price, as well as any producer discount, vendors must at least match the maximum price and provide superior service to hold customers.

Volume buying and selling are the only ways a jobber can make a profit. Efficient plant operations and low overhead can help, but no matter how efficient the operation, it will fail without high volume. One order for fifteen or twenty titles in quantities will yield a high discount for the jobber, perhaps as high as 60 percent. Even after giving a 20 to 25 percent discount to the library, the jobber has a comfortable margin with which to work. In the library market, such orders are usually the exception rather than the rule. More often, the jobber's discount is 50 percent. A smaller margin is still acceptable if all the items sell—but not all of them do! Many

LC CLASSIFICATION#	DESCRIPTION	NUMBER OF TITLES	TOTAL PRICE	AVERAGE PRICE	
AM		Museums.Collectors(Genl)	1	9.95	9.95 **
AM	10-101	Museography. Individual	2	78.95	39.48 **
AM	200-501	Collectors & collecting	1	65.00	65.00 **
AS		Academies & learned soc.	8	416.95	52.12 **
AY	30-1730	Almanacs	1	19.95	19.95 **
AZ		History of scholarship	1	78.50	78.50 **
		A'S SUBTOTALS	14	669.30	47.81 ****
B		Philosophy (General)	8	397.45	49.68 **
B	69-5739	History & systems	16	849.90	53.12 **
B	108-708	Ancient	29	1,561.75	53.85 **
B	720-765	Medieval	8	439.90	54.99 **
B	770-785	Renaissance	2	103.95	51.98 **
B	790-5739	Modern	34	1,889.20	55.56 **
B	850-5739	By region or country	132	7,228.85	54.76 **
BC		Logic	15	831.90	55.46 **
BD	10-41	Gen'l philosophical wks.	5	253.85	50.77 **
BD	95-131	Metaphysics	4	279.50	69.88 **
BD	143-236	Epistemology	14	804.30	57.45 **
BD	300-450	Ontology	20	919.25	45.96 **
BD	493-701	Cosmology	13	644.50	49.58 **
BF		Psychology	20	819.50	40.98 **
BF	173-175	Psychoanalysis	11	655.35	59.58 **
BF	180-210	Experimental psychology	5	282.95	56.59 **
BF	231-299	Sensation. Aesthesiology	5	365.00	73.00 **
BF	309-499	Cognition. Perception	21	1,153.85	54.95 **
BF	511-593	Emotion	7	289.85	41.41 **
BF	608-635	Will. Choice	2	140.00	70.00 **
BF	636-637	Applied psychology	6	264.80	44.13 **
BF	660-685	Comparative psychology	1	50.00	50.00 **
BF	698-698.9	Personality	3	84.85	28.28 **
BF	699-711	Genetic psychology	2	64.95	32.48 **
BF	712-724.85	Developmental psychology	2	113.00	56.50 **
BF	721-723	Child psychology	7	439.90	62.84 **
BF	1001-1389	Parapsychology	2	99.00	49.50 **
BF	1404-1999	Occult sciences	14	822.65	58.76 **
BH		Aesthetics	24	1,313.00	54.71 **
BJ		Ethics. Social usages	12	602.85	50.24 **
BJ	71-1185	History and systems	13	683.25	52.56 **
BJ	1188-1295	Religious ethics	6	336.90	56.15 **
BJ	1518-1697	Individual ethics.Charac	7	289.45	41.35 **
BJ	1801-2195	Social usages. Etiquette	1	16.95	16.95 **
BL		Religions. Mythology	25	1,140.85	45.63 **
BL	74-98	Religions of the world	2	87.95	43.98 **
BL	175-290	Natural theology	7	276.95	39.56 **

Fig. 11.1. Sample book vendor management report. Reprinted with permission of the Midwest Library Services.

Historical Price Analysis by Title Code

Section 1 - SHOWS TITLES FOR WHICH A FULL FIVE-YEAR PRICE COMPARISON IS AVAILABLE

9/13/2004

TITLE	FREQ	SUB	PRICE 2000 JAN	% INCR	PRICE 2001 JAN	% INCR	PRICE 2002 JAN	% INCR	PRICE 2003 JAN	% INCR	PRICE 2004 JAN	% INCR	TOTAL INCREASE %
TITLE CODE 973894058													
YOUNG EXCEPTIONAL CHILDREN HEGIS - 000EDP TSC # INDICES: NO INDICES GIVEN	QR	AA	35.00	00.0	35.00 COMM 1	00.0	35.00	00.0	35.00 COMM 2	00.0	35.00	00.0 COMM 3	0.00 / 00.0
975249004													
YOUTH & SOCIETY /J210/ /AALL EXCEPT EUR MID AFR IND PAK BGD BTN MDV LKA AUA NPL/ /FOR INSTITUTIONS/ HEGIS - 000EDP TSC # INDICES: NO INDICES GIVEN	QR	AA	284.00	14.4	325.00 COMM 1	12.3	365.00	07.9	394.00 COMM 2	17.5	463.00	COMM 3 - VLS CHANGE IN	179.00 / 63.0
982296105													
ZYGON - INCLS ONLINE - STANDARD ACCESS / FOR AMERICAS / HEGIS - 000THP TSC #/ INDICES: NO INDICES GIVEN	QR	AA	108.00	05.6	114.00 COMM1	12.3	128.00	10.9	142.00 COMM 2	09.2	155.00	47.00 COMM 3	43.5
CUSTOMER TOTAL			385,759.72		411,944.38		443,748.43		481,914.47		525,631.73		139,872.01 / 36.3
** 1538 TITLES AVERAGE PRICE			250.81		267.84		288.52		313.33		374.76		
AVERAGE % INCREASE			06.8		07.7		08.6		09.1		09.0 %		

BASED ON THE CUMULATIVE TOTAL INCREASE OF FOUR YEARS OF COMPARABLE DATA, THE AVERAGE YEARLY INCREASE IS EQUAL TO 09.0 %

Fig. 11.2. Historical price analysis. Based on data from EBSCO for the Charles Van der Ahe Library, LMU.

257

publishers have a return policy (in which a publisher buys back unsold books). However, many producers are changing or dropping the return policy, thus increasing the risk for the vendor. Returns normally result in credits against the current account or future purchases. They seldom result in a cash refund for book jobbers.

Jobbers, being dependent on volume sales, must know their markets very well to project sales and maintain proper stock in their warehouses. When a vendor representative stops by, the purpose is not merely public relations or, necessarily, an attempt to sell more books. Rather, it is an attempt to determine the library's plans for collection development. It is not curiosity or an attempt to make conversation that generates questions like, "How does next year's materials budget look?" The collection development librarian should take time to explain new programs and areas to be worked on or describe how budget prospects look for the next year. This type of information helps vendors plan their buying policies for the coming months.

Selection officers should ask jobbers' representatives about what is available in any field the library is developing, even if the selection officers think they know. The answers may be surprising. One should ask what the vendor could do to supply the items. Is it a field the vendor carries as part of the normal inventory, or is the field one for which the jobber has listed publishers? (Listed publishers indicate that the vendor has an established relationship with the publisher but does not stock its titles. If the library uses a vendor for listed publishers, there will be a delay in receiving the material, because the jobber must forward the order to the publisher.) Such discussions take time but result in better service.

To get the maximum discount, some librarians dump their "problem" orders on vendors and order easy items directly from the publishers. Nothing could be more shortsighted. Without the income from easy, high-volume items, no jobber can stay in business. Someone has to handle the problem orders, and most vendors will try to track down the difficult items, especially for good customers. However, libraries should give jobbers easy orders as well. Almost all of the problems facing jobbers involve cash flow. Lack of cash has been the downfall of many businesses, and it becomes critical for jobbers when they handle only problem orders; staff expenses go up, but income does not. Failure of jobbers would lead to higher labor costs for most acquisitions departments as a result of having to place all orders directly with publishers.

Whenever possible, the library should use the order format preferred by the vendor and not plead legal or system requirements for a particular method of ordering, unless it is impossible to change the requirement. Most vendors and publishers go out of their way to accommodate the legal requirements of library ordering procedures. If libraries could come closer to a standardized order procedure, jobbers could provide better service, because they would not have to keep track of hundreds of variations. If libraries keep all paperwork to a minimum, everyone will benefit.

Although most jobbers accept a few returns from libraries, even if the library is at fault, returns create a lot of paperwork. If an item serves no purpose in a library's collection, perhaps it would save time and money to accept the mistake and discard the item rather than return it, assuming mistakes are infrequent. Frequent mistakes signal a problem in the acquisitions department or selection procedures. (This discussion refers to errors; the library should return any defective copy received for replacement.)

Finally, libraries should process invoices promptly; the acquisitions department should not hold them longer than necessary. Most library systems require at least two approvals before issuing a payment voucher: the library's approval and the business office's approval. Some systems have three or more offices involved in the approval process. The collection development officer should know the system, from approval to final payment. If payment takes longer than six weeks, the library should inform any new jobber of that fact so the firm can decide whether it can do business with the library. There is also a need to inform jobbers of any changes in the system that may affect the speed of payment. Most jobbers would like to receive payment within thirty days, because they are on a thirty-day payment cycle with publishers.

Jobbers provide a valuable service to libraries. Given a good working relationship, both parties benefit. Following is a summary of the basic factors at work in establishing such a relationship.

What Do Libraries Expect from Jobbers?

A collection development officer has reason to believe that a chosen jobber will provide

- a large inventory of titles;
- prompt and accurate order fulfillment;
- prompt and accurate reporting on items not in stock; and
- personal service at a reasonable price.

What Do Jobbers Expect from Libraries?

By the same token, jobbers should be able to expect

- time to get to know what the library needs;
- cooperation in placing orders;
- paperwork kept to a minimum; and
- prompt payment for services.

Vendor Evaluation

A trend in the 1990s was toward creating a formal contract between vendor and library. The contract is the result of either a formal bidding process or a response to a Request for Proposal (RFP). If one has a choice— and often public libraries have to employ a bidding process—the RFP is the better option. Often the bid process is out of the library's hands and is conducted by business officers who do not fully understand that information materials are *not* the same as pencils, paper, or even computers. With the RFP there should be at least some library input to the requirements, if the library is not solely responsible for the document. An RFP will, or should, contain all the elements and aspects the library will use to evaluate the vendor's performance and often specifies performance parameters. An excellent source on the RFP process is Francis Wilkinson and Connie Thorson's *The RFP Process: Effective Management of the Acquisitions of Library Materials*.[3]

Even without a formal contract, acquisitions departments and collection development officers must monitor vendor performance. In the past, monitoring vendors was time-consuming and difficult, and it still is if one is working with a manual acquisitions system. However, today's automated acquisitions systems can produce a variety of useful management/vendor reports very quickly and in various formats. Knowing what to do with the quantity of data the systems can produce is another matter. (There are two types of evaluation that acquisitions staff undertakes. One is more a monitoring of vendor performance, with an eye to identifying small concerns that, left unnoticed, could become a major issue. The other is a formal assessment of the vendor, with an eye toward changing vendors or renewing a contract.)

One obvious issue that arises in evaluation is which vendor performs best on a certain type of order (examples are conference proceedings, music scores, or video recordings). The first thing to do is to decide what *best* means. Highest discount? Fastest delivery? Most accurate reports? Highest percentage of the order filled with the first shipment? All of the above? The answer varies from library to library depending on local needs and conditions. Once the library defines *best*, it knows what data to retrieve from the system. This is an example where the RFP process is of assistance, because the answers to these questions should be in that document. Other questions to consider are:

- Who handles rush orders most efficiently?

- Who handles international orders most effectively—a dealer in the country of origin or a general international dealer?

- Are specialty dealers more effective in handling their specialties than are general dealers?

Figure 11.3, on pages 261–62, is a systems report covering three years' performance of some of LMU's book vendors on some typical areas of concern. It shows quantities of titles ordered; total expended; average delivery time; percentage of the order received; average cost of each order; shipping/handling charges, if any; and the discount for each of the vendors. In addition to system reports based on normal operating procedures, one can conduct some experiments by placing a random sample of a type of order with several vendors to assess their performance.

When conducting a test or experiment, one must be certain that each vendor receives approximately the same mix of titles so that no vendor receives more or fewer easy or hard items to handle. Often, the normal procedure data reflect the use of a particular vendor for only one type of order. This makes comparing vendor performance rather meaningless because one is not comparing like groups. One can use the test method to select a vendor for a particular type of order and use the operating data approach to monitor ongoing performance.

Checking on the performance of serials vendors is more difficult. Most libraries use only domestic serials vendors, because of the complexity of changing ongoing subscriptions. A library that is just establishing a current subscription list or is starting a large number of new subscriptions might consider splitting the list between two or more vendors for several years to determine which would be the best sole source for the long term.

A limited amount of checking is possible through comparisons with other libraries. Often, this type of checking is done in a casual manner, that is, by merely asking a colleague in another library, "Do you use vendor *X*? How do you like them?" or "How much is your service charge?" To make

	Ave Deliv Time	# orders received in					
		02 wks	04 wks	08 wks	12 wks	16 wks	17+ wks
a&e	12.0	4	2	6	3	0	8
abc	13.0	321	177	1822	1573	513	904
abca	0.0	5111	2	0	1	1	0
abcc	1.4	177	0	5	13	1	5
acrl	13.0	0	0	0	0	1	0
ais	0.0	1	0	0	0	0	0
ala	0.3	60	2	0	1	0	0
alibr	5.1	318	345	76	3	4	38
ama	?	0	0	0	0	0	0
amazc	4.6	178	79	105	55	27	1
amb	9.9	5	169	1328	467	104	249
ambr	6.0	0	0	1	0	0	0
ams	?	0	0	0	0	0	0
ann	3.3	10	0	1	0	1	0
ared	0.0	31	0	0	0	0	0
asppi	0.0	2	0	0	0	0	0
astm	?	0	0	0	0	0	0
auxam	11.7	1	0	0	0	9	0
bagc	0.0	1	0	0	0	0	0
bagch	2.5	1	1	0	0	0	0
barni	1.0	2	0	0	0	0	0
bbs	10.3	15	161	211	53	55	134
bbsa	0.0	415	0	0	0	0	0
berna	0.0	10	0	0	0	0	0
bfrog	5.8	2	15	3	4	0	1
bh	6.4	97	1256	1017	177	83	153
blk	?	0	0	0	0	0	0
blkc	1.0	26	1	0	0	0	1
blkna	11.0	0	0	0	2	0	0
bowk	?	0	0	0	0	0	0
bracp	23.3	1	0	0	0	0	2
brepo	0.0	4	0	0	0	0	0
brou	0.0	3	0	0	0	0	0
cabpc	17.0	0	0	0	0	0	3
cam	38.0	0	0	0	0	0	1
cara	2.0	1	0	0	0	0	0
cch	0.5	4	0	0	0	0	0
ccsce	0.0	4	0	0	0	0	0
ceel	0.0	1	0	0	0	0	0
cios	?	0	0	0	0	0	0
cistp	0.0	2	0	0	0	0	0
colbo	0.0	1	0	0	0	0	0
conf	0.0	2	0	0	0	0	0
conqi	2.0	1	0	0	0	0	0
corup	0.0	1	0	0	0	0	0
cqpre	0.0	2	0	0	0	0	0
davbr	0.0	1	0	0	0	0	0
dia	0.0	1	0	0	0	0	0
dir	5.4	673	273	139	70	34	63
dirc	6.0	1	0	1	1	0	0
dover	6.0	0	0	2	0	0	0
easbc	8.6	33	1027	2156	471	143	351
ebscb	1.0	1	0	0	0	0	0

(continued)

Fig. 11.3. Vendor performance statistics.

Vendor Performance Statistics—Percentages
Processed Record #: 1000007 to 282498x
Count orders Placed in period 06-01-2001 to 04-20-2004

Claims	# Orders	Ave Est Price/ Order	Ave Est Price Recd Order	Ave Amt Paid/ Order	% Orders Recd	% Orders Cancld	% Total Orders Claimed
1 a&e	23	$30.16	$30.16	$34.53	100.00	0.00	0.00
2 abc	5399	$54.92	$55.76	$94.93	98.35	1.57	0.00
3 abca	5135	$12.67	$12.72	$43.35	99.61	0.05	0.00
4 abcc	210	$92.68	$94.27	$87.34	95.71	0.00	0.00
5 acrl	1	$55.00	$55.00	$119.08	100.00	0.00	0.00
6 ais	1	$42.00	$42.00	$44.95	100.00	0.00	0.00
7 ala	63	$64.72	$64.72	$67.21	100.00	0.00	0.00
8 alibr	835	$42.68	$38.39	$49.66	93.89	4.07	0.00
9 ama	1	$0.00	?	?	0.00	100.00	0.00
10 amazc	463	$37.52	$38.33	$40.33	96.11	2.37	0.00
11 amb	2458	$58.37	$59.63	$60.03	94.46	1.46	0.00
12 ambr	1	$295.00	$295.00	$325.60	100.00	0.00	0.00
13 ams	1	$5,156.00	?	?	0.00	0.00	0.00
14 ann	12	$128.77	$128.77	$149.37	100.00	0.00	0.00
15 ared	31	$97.32	$97.32	$52.28	100.00	0.00	0.00
16 asppi	3	$480.83	$577.93	$981.57	66.66	0.00	0.00
17 astm	2	$75.00	?	?	0.00	0.00	0.00
18 auxam	10	$66.56	$66.56	$69.15	100.00	0.00	0.00
19 bagc	1	$65.00	$65.00	$69.13	100.00	0.00	0.00
20 bagch	3	$84.90	$100.35	$100.78	66.66	0.00	0.00
21 barni	2	$37.86	$37.86	$37.86	100.00	0.00	0.00
22 bbs	708	$59.01	$58.08	$58.48	88.84	0.98	0.00
23 bbsa	419	$165.24	$166.61	$283.29	99.04	0.23	0.00
24 berna	10	$549.29	$549.29	$599.06	100.00	0.00	0.00
25 bfrog	25	$208.08	$208.08	$220.09	100.00	0.00	0.00
26 bh	2956	$49.67	$51.28	$52.73	94.14	3.01	0.00
27 blk	2	$0.00	?	?	0.00	0.00	0.00
28 blkc	29	$55.10	$53.67	$84.53	96.55	0.00	0.00
29 blkna	2	$90.20	$90.20	$82.45	100.00	0.00	0.00
30 bowk	1	$3,875.00	?	?	0.00	0.00	0.00

Vendor Performance Statistics—TOTAL
Processed Record #: 1000007 to 282498x
Count orders Placed in period 06-01-2001 to 04-20-2004

Average Estimated Price per Order: $3,327,190.85 / 44084 = $75.47

Average Paid Amount of Receipts: $3,816,454.43 / 42711 = $89.35

Average Estimated Price for Received Orders: $2,505,553.17 / 42711 = $58.66

Average Delivery Time: 253204 / 42711 = 5

% Orders Received in 2 weeks: 15813 / 42711 = 37.02%

% Orders Received in 4 weeks: 6424 / 42711 =15.04%

% Orders Received in 8 weeks: 11973 / 42711 = 28.03%

% Orders Received in 12 weeks: 4516 / 42711 = 10.57%

% Orders Received in 16 weeks: 1459 / 42711 = 3.41%

% Orders Received in 17+ weeks: 2526 / 42711 = 5.91%

% Cancelled: 501 / 44084 = 1.13 %

% Claimed: 0 / 44084 = 0.00 %

Average Claims per Claimed Order: 0 / 0 =?

Average Claims per Order: 0 / 44084 = 0.00

Fig. 11.3—*Continued*.

valid and useful comparisons, one needs to know the other library's title mix. Recent developments of union catalogs based on OPAC data suggest that collections, even in apparently similar libraries, have surprisingly different holdings. At one time a comparison was made of the monograph holdings of LMU, Santa Clara, University of San Francisco, and the University of San Diego libraries for a ten-year period, using the AMIGOS CD-ROM collection analysis software. The university librarians thought the collections would have a large percentage of overlap because the institutions are similar in size and programs. All were surprised to learn that more than 80,000 titles of the 159,000 titles in the database were unique; that is, only one of the four schools held the title. Although the results were not as striking for serials holdings, the number of titles held by just one library was a surprise. These discoveries reinforced the idea that casual, impressionistic assessments are suspect.

One way to compare serials vendors is to take a sample of commonly held titles. Items to investigate include the service charges on those titles, the effectiveness of claims processing, and other issues such as vendor follow-up and handling of credit memos.

In any vendor evaluation, keep in mind some of the problems vendors have with producers. These bear repeating:

- Changes in title, or not publishing the title.
- Not being informed when publishing schedules change or when publishers suspend or cease publication.
- Incorrect ISBNs or ISSNs.
- Producers refusing to take returns.
- Producers refusing to sell through vendors.
- Producers reducing discounts or charging for freight and handling when those were free in the past.
- Poor fulfillment on the producer's part.
- Constantly changing policies on the producer's part.
- Producer price increases without prior notice.

We provide references to several "models" for conducting vendor evaluation studies in the Further Reading section.

Libraries depend on vendors; they offer services that save libraries time, effort, and staffing. Libraries need vendors and need to understand the vendors' problems. That said, one must monitor their performance, question charges, and challenge charges that seem inappropriate. Maintaining good relations is everyone's business. If librarians, vendors, and producers take time to learn about one another's businesses, working relationships will be better. The senior author met a new regional manager of our serials vendor who had no prior experience in the library-marketing sector. He asked if he could spend a week in our library learning how we handle journals and how our customers use the journals. We said yes, and he spent three days in technical services with the serials acquisition staff and two days in public services. Even if our operations are not completely typical, his experience made him more aware of the problems libraries face in handling serials. Another outcome has been that several of our staff have spent two or more days observing the vendor's operations. Increased understanding of one another's problems solidified an already good working relationship. It is not necessary to go to such lengths, but reading about developments in each other's fields and asking informed questions help build mutual understanding and respect. Having realistic expectations for one another is the key, just as it is in personal relationships. Be professional and ethical in working with vendors and publishers; expect and demand the same from them.

Retail Outlets

Several articles appeared in the late 1990s about the potential competition between bookstores and libraries, in particular, public libraries.[4] Essentially, the articles suggested that bookstores have a great advantage over libraries. In some ways, this message is surprising, as one often hears that public libraries, in particular, hurt the sales of bookstores because they offer large quantities of popular titles for free. Authors and bookstores have both made such claims in the past. Why buy a copy of the latest bestseller that everyone is talking about, especially if it is not a topic one has a long-term interest in, when one can get a copy for free in the library? For some countries this claim, at least from authors, has given rise to legislation that compensates authors for "lost income" due to the presence of their books in libraries—public lending right laws (we cover this topic in chapter 17).

Public libraries and bookstores have existed side by side in communities for close to 200 years. Both have been in the book and magazine business, and now both see themselves as being in the information business. Both generally stock a variety of formats, not just print-based materials. Despite the long association and similarity in activities, neither side seems to have taken much time to learn about the other. We believe that libraries can learn some useful lessons from bookstores and, further, that there are potentially useful library/bookstore partnership opportunities. Certainly, bookstores can be, and often are, a source for acquisitions units, especially when the item is popular and has to be in-house today.

How Do New Bookstores Operate?

Bookstores are interesting places to visit, whether or not one is responsible for collection development. Many librarians started haunting bookstores long before they became librarians. (If there is a bibliographic equivalent of alcoholism, many librarians have it.) *Bibliomania* is defined as "excessive fondness for acquiring and possessing books."[5] Most bibliomaniacs (librarians included) cannot stay out of bookstores and consider it a great feat of willpower and self-control if they manage to leave one without buying a book or two.

Although most librarians have undoubtedly visited many bookstores innumerable times, one should make a special visit to at least two local stores that have existed for many years to answer some specific questions. What are the environmental and operating conditions necessary for a successful bookstore? How does the store display and market its materials? What is for sale? How wide a range of materials is available? Could this shop be of any value in developing the collection?

One consideration for any bookstore owner is location. Many owners live and work in the community for a long time before they open their stores. Just as the person responsible for library collection development needs to know the community, so does the bookstore owner. Bookstores, like libraries, must face the "Law of Least Effort," which means having a location that is easy to find and convenient to use.

A few librarians harbor the dream of finding a quaint little town where they will retire and then open up a small bookstore. Most use it as a nice daydream on the occasional "bad library day." Of those who go further and try to implement the idea, few succeed. Those who *do* succeed do so by locating the store in a community they know that knows them as a result of frequent visits and extended stays. A successful bookstore is a busy, people-oriented organization. It is not a quiet retreat for persons who do not like working with people, anymore than a library is. Furthermore, owning a bookstore requires physical work on the part of the owner and a fairly large population base to support the required volume of sales, assuming that one hopes to live off the income.

The educational level of the population is another factor in store location. As the average level of education in a community rises, so do the chances of a bookstore's succeeding with a smaller population base. College graduates represent the largest segment of book buyers. Where one finds a high concentration of college-educated people living near a large shopping center, one is also likely to find a bookstore.

There are striking similarities between a successful bookstore and a successful library. Both require solid knowledge of the community. If librarians could select sites as do bookstore proprietors, library circulation would skyrocket. A public library branch in the center of Stockholm provides an example of an almost ideal bookstore location: on a shopping mall in the center of the main business district, with a high volume of foot traffic, near a concourse to a major subway station. This branch is the most active of all the service points in a system where high use is the norm.

Store owners attempt to stimulate buyers through a variety of sales methods. Owners employ store window and entryway displays to provide clues about the basic stock before customers enter. Only very large stores can afford to purchase newspaper advertisements on a weekly basis, and radio and television advertising costs are prohibitively high for most owners. An occasional newspaper advertisement and a good storefront display are the best they can do to promote business.

One can make a fair assessment of a bookstore merely by looking through its windows, without even walking in the door (of course, this is an assessment of the type of material sold, not the level of service). Observing is not the same as casually looking. If a store's windows do not provide enough clues to its stock, looking in the door can provide another quick visual check. Tables of books with banners such as "Top 20!," "55% to 75% Off!" or "Giant Discounts!" are almost certain signs of a store that will be of limited value to a library, especially if most of the window displays have favored the latest and best sellers. A store with a good, wide range of stock cannot afford to devote much floor area to such sales methods. All stores have sales from time to time—books that have not sold and may be past their return date, some remainders—and of course, there is always the pre-inventory sale. However, the store that is always having a sale is never really having a sale and is seldom of value to libraries.

Another quick visual check is for sideline items. A new bookstore selling only new books needs a minimum community population of 25,000, but almost all bookstores now sell some sidelines: greeting cards, stationery and office supplies, posters, art supplies, audio and video recordings, magazines and newspapers, calendars, games, and so forth. Why the sideline? It is difficult to make a good living just selling books, because there are few buyers, and the margin of profit on books is much smaller than the margin on sideline items.

The possible profit on books is a complex subject given the various discount arrangements available to booksellers. Publishers offer the same general discounts (trade, long, short, new, mass-market) to bookstores that they offer to jobbers. Bookstores receive long discounts (40 percent or more) on most trade hardback books. In the case of large orders (multiple copies), discounts of 50 percent or more are possible. Normally, the discount is 40 percent, and even then the store may have to buy a required minimum number of copies (five or more) to receive this amount. A few publishers offer 33 to 40 percent off an order of ten different single titles under the Single Copy Order Plan (SCOP). Librarians ordering a sizable number of single copies from one publisher may find bookstores eager to place such orders. However, it is important to remember that such an agreement requires the bookseller to prepay and to do all the paperwork. Thus, if the library is slow in issuing payments, only large bookstores can afford to carry its accounts.

Some stores will order short-discount (20 to 25 percent) items but add a service charge. If the order contains enough short-discount items from a single publisher, most stores will handle the order without a service charge. On a twenty-dollar book with a 25 percent discount, the bookstore has only a five-dollar margin with which to work. After covering the clerical time and record-keeping costs, the owner is lucky if the transaction has not cost the store more money than it received from the customer, so a service charge is not unreasonable.

There are two classes of paperbacks: quality and mass-market. Quality paperbacks (the term does not necessarily apply to the content of the book) generally sell for more than fifteen dollars and are found only in bookstores. Mass-market books are those in drugstores, grocery stores, airports, and so forth, that usually sell for six to eight dollars. Most publishers give a long discount on quality paperbacks when ordered in groups of five to ten or more. A store must order twenty-five to fifty assorted titles of the mass-market type to begin to approach a 40 percent discount. Orders for less than that amount will get discounts of 25 to 35 percent.

The book distribution system in the United States is cumbersome and frequently adds to the cost of books. A simplified system would benefit everyone. Perhaps the best illustration of the complexity of the system is in the area of discounts, returns, billings, and so forth. Each year the American Booksellers Association (ABA) publishes an extensive guide titled *ABA Book Buyer's Handbook* (New York: American Booksellers Association, 1947–   ). Pity the poor bookseller, confronted with all the other problems of a bookstore, who also must work through a mass of legal forms and sales conditions for purchasing from various publishers. It does create extra work for both bookseller and publisher, and they undoubtedly pass their costs on to the buyer.

Thus, when a sideline item offers a 70 to 80 percent discount, it is not surprising to find a mixed store; as much as 30 to 40 percent of the total store income comes from nonbook sales. A store that devotes more than one-third of the available floor space to nonbook items probably will not be of much use to a library for developing collections, so the librarian should be sure to observe the percentage of floor space devoted to sidelines. In addition to quick visual checks, some acquaintance with the store's personnel will provide additional information about a store. Although more and more stores must use a self-service arrangement as labor costs rise, getting to know what staff there is can pay dividends in getting service. Most self-service operations emphasize paperbacks, sidelines, and popular trade books. Obviously, such stores offer little that will be of value to the library.

When a general bookstore exists nearby, the library ought to talk to the owner to determine what, if any, business relationship might be possible. It may take time for the relationship to fully develop, but it can prove mutually beneficial. (Most of the preceding discussion does not apply to the large national chains, such as Borders, Barnes & Noble, and Waldenbooks. Their operations are very different.)

We cannot leave this section without commenting on Internet bookstores. When *Amazon.com* went online in 1995, it was the only e-store that was "independent." A late 2004 search on Google of "new book sellers" resulted in more than 4.3 million hits. Even reducing that number by 90 percent for false hits, the online book sales market is very large. Certainly, these stores are popular, but note that there are challenges for the acquisitions department trying to use them. There is always the question of reliability of the vendor if not well known. Perhaps the biggest challenge is that most want to carry out the transaction by credit card, which is something of a problem for many libraries. Not too many departments have institutional credit cards, and using a personal card can create problems with the funding authorities.

The LMU library has been using *Amazon.com* for several years for the purchase of some popular items. (We should note that it did take some effort to develop a workable means of payment.) Monica Fusich wrote a brief article on the use of *Amazon.com* and other e-stores that appeared in *College & Research Libraries News*.[6] She outlined several services that she had found useful, in her role as a collection development officer who has other duties as well. (Being a reference librarian or some other "full-time" assignment as well as having selection responsibilities is very common in today's library environment.) The features she mentioned were:

- Cumulated book reviews (one must remember that some of the reviews are from the general public).
- Search and browsing capability.
- Size of the database(s).
- Coverage of both in- and out-of-print titles, as well as recorded music.
- Notification services (such as "Available to Order" notices for newly released titles or items that were listed as "out-of-stock").

Certainly, e-stores are *not* the answer to the challenges facing busy librarians with a number of duties besides collection development; however, they are of assistance. In particular, they are a boon for retrospective collection development.

Out-of-Print, Antiquarian, and Rare Book Dealers

Retrospective collection building is one of the most interesting and challenging areas of collection development work. It was also one of the last to experience the impact of technology and the Internet. However, since 2000 it has more than made up for its slow start. Today there are hundreds of out-of-print dealers with a Web presence, one of the reasons for the large number of Google hits mentioned above.

Libraries buy retrospectively for two reasons—to fill in gaps in the collection and to replace worn-out or lost copies of out-of-print titles. There has been a steady decline in retrospective buying over the past twenty years, due to limited book budgets, as well as the need to increase purchases of nonprint and electronic formats. Another factor in the decline has been the existence of ever-growing bibliographic databases, such as OCLC, that make locating a copy of an out-of-print title to borrow through ILL much easier. As a result, acquisitions staff and selectors have less and less experience to draw upon when they need to work in this field. (Dealers in this field are a special breed, unlike other vendors with which the library has more experience.)

One outcome of the decline is that this field, which was always very dependent on collectors, is now even more driven by collector interests, as well as by the online access to information about titles thought to be in short supply. It is now very easy to compare prices and select the best price for an item based on its condition and expected usage. To some degree the Web has kept prices down or slowed their increase. Checking prices through a site such as Abebooks (<http://www.abebooks.com>) is very easy. For example, searching Charles Dickens' *Pickwick Papers* in September 2004 turned up 2,058 hits ranging in price from $1.00 (U.S.) to $13,818 (U.S.) for a copy of the first edition in book form (1837). Sellers were from many countries (a total of twenty-one—for example, Australia, Canada, Denmark, India, Norway, Scotland, and the U.K.) and in cities across the United States. As was, and is, true of dealer's catalog descriptions, one must be careful to read the description with a critical mind, at least for the rare book purchases. Despite the need for caution, the Web has indeed changed the nature of retrospective collection development.

Allowing for overlap, there are two broad categories of out-of-print (OP) dealers. (It should be noted that most of these dealers dislike the label "secondhand dealer.") One category focuses primarily on general OP books, that is, with buying and selling relatively recent OP books. Often, these books sell at prices that are the same as, or only slightly higher than, their publication price. The other category of dealer focuses on rare, antiquarian, and special (e.g., fore-edge-painted, miniature, or private press) books. Prices for this type of book range from around $100 to several thousands of dollars per title.

There is a changing face to the field. Margaret Landesman[7] provided an excellent, detailed outline of the six major types of dealers, and although the Web has had an impact on their business methods, the categories she identified continue to be sound:

- Book scouts, working part-time or full-time, searching out desirable books and selling them to dealers and collectors primarily through websites. Such individuals are one of the primary reasons one gets so many hits when searching the Web for OP titles. They carry little or no stock.

- Operators of neighborhood stores that have limited service hours, often only one or two days a week. Stores are in low-cost areas. Today, many operators use the facility only as a storage unit and depend on selling through the Web, rather than walk-in trade and a few very loyal customers. Their stock is generally recent materials and covers a variety of subject areas.

- Specialized dealers that often issue catalogs in addition to their Web postings and do searching in their specialty. Their stock is limited in scope, but successful dealers do have depth of coverage in their specialties.

- General out-of-print dealers with a substantial store who have a rather large stock in varied areas—what most people think of when thinking about OP dealers. Today with the Web, searching for titles is a common service, and a few do issue catalogs.

- Mixed in-print and out-of-print stores—often a store that was an independent new bookshop that is trying to survive the competition from the "superstores" by diversifying. A good example of the mixed store is Powell's City of Books of Portland Oregon (<http://www.powells.com/>).

- Academic library book vendors that also offer out-of-print search services.

- Rare book dealers specializing in rare and expensive titles. Most established rare book dealers do not handle the more ordinary, scholarly, out-of-print titles, but many general, out-of-print dealers also handle some rare books.

The vast majority of dealers have small shops in low-rent areas or operate out of their homes. Because of this diversity, it is difficult to make many generalizations about this group. Sol Malkin painted a cheery picture of at least part of the out-of-print trade:

> Imagine a separate book world within the world of books where dealers set up their businesses where they please (store or office, home or barn); where the minimum markup is 100 percent; where they can call upon 5,000 fellow dealers throughout the world and a stock of over 200 million volumes, practically from the beginning of the printed word; where books are safely packed and mailed with no extra charge for postage; where there is no competition from the publishers and discount houses; where colleagues help one another in time of need to provide fellow dealers with a unique service that makes customers happy all the time—an ideal imaginary book world that never was nor ever will be? Perhaps . . . but the above is 99 percent true in the antiquarian book trade.[8]

Most libraries will have occasion to use the services of these dealers. Collection development officers working with large research collections spend much of their time, or did in the past, engaged in retrospective collection development. Changes in organizational goals and programs may result in developing whole new areas of collecting, of both current and retrospective materials. Public libraries also buy from OP dealers, especially for replacement copies and occasionally for retrospective collection building. School libraries make limited use of this distribution system, and when they do, it is for replacement copies; scientific and technical libraries rarely need to worry about acquiring retrospective materials.

Several directories to antiquarian or rare book dealers provide information about specialties (e.g., Information Today's *American Book Trade Directory* and Omnigraphics' *Antiquarian, Specialty and Used Book Sellers Directory*), and anyone concerned with selection and acquisition needs to get to know these directories. Some major metropolitan areas have local directories or guides to special bookstores. In any case, a person will find it worthwhile to develop a listing of the local shops. This can provide quick information about search services, hours, and true specialties. One can go to a shop that advertises itself as a Western Americana store only to find the specialty stock very limited or overpriced. Nevertheless, one should examine the shop's stock to identify its true specialties and assess its general pricing polices. Maintaining this private directory can prove well worth the time required to keep it up-to-date. This is not to say that the published sources are worthless. However, if an owner changes emphasis, and his or her stock turns over and is subject to local economic conditions, such factors result in changes faster than published sources can monitor.

Historically, selectors used *AB Bookman's Weekly* (*AB*) to access advertisements from dealers offering or searching for particular titles. *AB* ceased publication in 1999, but resources of this type have been an essential ingredient in the OP book trade, because they served as a finding and selling tool. Without services like this, the cost of acquiring an OP item would have been much higher (assuming the library could locate a copy without the service). Luckily for selectors, the Web version (<http://www.abbookman.com/>) remains active and has links to condition guidelines, book sales, book values, glossaries, literary awards, and other useful resources for buyer and seller alike.

Selectors also use the *AB* website in their work. Other useful publications for both dealers and libraries are *Bookman's Price Index* (Gale), *American Book Prices Current* (Bancroft Parkman), and *Library Bookseller* (Antiquarian Bookman). We list some of the more useful websites at the end of this chapter; however, one very good site is Bibliofind (<http://www.bibliofind.com>).

One requisite for an OP dealer that a library should use is a reputation for honesty, service, and fair prices. To gain such a reputation requires a considerable period of time in this field. In today's Web-based environment, this issue is a challenge for libraries. If one is purchasing only a twenty- to thirty-dollar replacement copy, the risks of dealing with an unknown dealer are not all that high. For higher-priced materials, there are real risks. The risks were there in the pre-electronic environment as well, but ease of posting an item for sale on the Web has magnified the opportunities for less than honest sellers to make a sale.

When you search for a title on such a site as *Abebooks.com*, your result appears as a listing of sellers, prices, and a brief description of the book's condition. While it is possible to order directly from the result pages, it is advisable to follow the available link to the seller's page and, if there is one, the home page for the seller. One of the best assurances of a reputable dealer is membership in one of the bookseller associations such as ABAA (Antiquarian Booksellers Association of America). That is not to say that not being a member is necessarily a negative sign, but its presence is a positive one. Also, going to the seller's pages provides important information about terms and conditions, as well as contact information where you can attempt to clarify issues and perhaps try to negotiate the price. (Yes, it is possible to try to get a better price—you will not get one if you don't ask. It is probably not worth the time to try this with inexpensive items.)

One element in the OP trade is very mysterious to the outsider and even to librarians who have had years of experience with these dealers: How do dealers determine the asking price? (The rule of thumb of paying one-third or less of the expected sales income is probably ignored more than it is practiced. The "or less" is the key.) As Malkin indicated, the markup is at least 100 percent, but how much more? One may find a book in an OP store with no price on it, take it to the salesperson (often the owner), ask the price, and receive, after a quick look, the answer, "Oh, yes. That is *X* dollars." Sometimes the amount is lower than one expects and other times much higher, but most of the time it is close to the price the library is willing to pay. Some salespersons seem to be mind readers, to know exactly how much a customer is willing to pay. Malkin summed up the outsider's feeling about pricing in the OP trade: "Many new book dealers think of the antiquarian bookseller as a second-hand junkman or as a weird character who obtains books by sorcery, prices them by cannibalistic necromancy, and sells them by black magic."[9]

As amusing as Malkin's theory may be, prices are in actuality based on a number of interrelated factors:

1. How much it costs to acquire the item.

2. The amount of current interest in collecting a particular subject or author.

3. The number of copies printed and the number of copies still in existence.

4. The physical condition of the copy.

5. Any special features of the particular copy (e.g., autographed by the author or signed or owned by a famous person).

6. What other dealers are asking for copies of the same edition in the same condition.

In the past it might have appeared that magic is the essential ingredient in successful OP operations—getting the price right. To a large degree, dealers set prices after they know the answers to the questions of supply and potential sales. The OP dealer has several sources of supply, but only two consistently produce new stock. One major source is personal or business collections. Placing an ad in the telephone directory and now online (saying, "I buy old books") will generate a number of inquiries. Two of the most frequent reasons a private collection comes onto the market are household moves and the settling of estates. Only when outstanding private collections of a well-known collector come on the market will dealers enter into a bidding contest. They may come to look at a collection, but only after determining by telephone or e-mail that it is large and has potential value. After a quick review of the collection, they make a flat offer with a take-it-or-leave-it attitude. A person who has no experience with the OP trade is usually unhappy with what that person believes is too low an offer. After one or two such offers, a prospective seller might conclude that there is a conspiracy of OP dealers to cheat owners out of rare items. Going online to check prices would probably convince most prospective sellers that the offered price was reasonable, if one takes into account the labor the dealer will have to put into the process. The other fact that will likely jump out from online searches of the title offered is how many copies are for sale and the range in price—remember the earlier example of the *Pickwick Papers*.

Such a search, with careful review of the results, will indicate the book's condition as well as its printing history and has a significant impact on prices. Yes, a first edition *may* be more valuable than a later edition, and it may not. A signed first printing of a book will make it more valuable than an unsigned second printing volume. The *Pickwick Papers* example illustrates the difference that condition and publication history make in the price of OP items.

For collectors and libraries, the quality of the item descriptions and the care taken in preparing that information, be it a catalog or online description, are critical. Some descriptions are nothing more than the very basic bibliographic information—author, title, and price. A few catalogs contain so much bibliographic information as well as useful condition information that research libraries add them to their permanent bibliography collection. Catalogs of high quality are less and less common today, and the trend is likely to continue because of rising printing costs and use of the Web as the dominant sales method. To recover the cost, it is necessary to sell the catalog to buyers who are not regular customers, which also usually means that the prices for all the items in the catalogs will be rather high ($300 and up). Only the longtime major dealers can afford to issue such catalogs today—and even these dealers have shifted over to Web commerce for the bulk of their business.

One may assume that most OP dealers sell their stock as described or "as is." If there is no statement about the item's condition, one may assume it to be in good or better condition. A common statement in catalogs or on websites is "terms—all books in original binding and in good or better condition unless otherwise stated." How the book is described is highly variable, and there are many OP terms that need defining for the newcomer. Some of the meanings become clear only after one gets to know the particular dealer, but some guidance can be found in books like Carter and Baker's *ABC for Book Collectors*[10] and Allen and Patricia Ahearn's *Book Collecting 2000*.[11] Carter and Baker provide illuminating and entertaining notes about dealer adjectives describing the condition of a book, while the Ahearns' work surveys the basics of book collecting and includes a listing of estimated market values for over 6,000 texts.

Because dealer catalogs are so important, and the manner in which they describe an item's condition is central to a buying decision, a former student of the senior author conducted a small "experiment" in describing some out-of-print books. The student worked for an antiquarian book dealer and helped prepare sales catalogs. The student selected three items that were to appear in a forthcoming catalog. The dealer's description of each book was one element in the study. Two other antiquarian dealers who worked in the same subject areas were then given the three items to describe as if they were going to list the books in one of their catalogs. In addition, the books were given to two librarians (both were in charge of large rare book collections in major research libraries), asking them to describe the condition of each item. Five major conditions (water stains, mildew, tears, and so forth) were previously identified in each book before the librarians and other dealers described the items. Both librarians noted all of the conditions for each book and gave precise information. All three dealers' descriptions had to be combined to have a complete list of all the conditions for each item. No one dealer described all the conditions for all the items. It was also interesting, but not surprising, to find that the dealer descriptions tended to downplay the faults. One would expect this, because their goal is to sell the items. Professional associations (such as ALA) and antiquarian dealer associations attempt to develop guidelines to help reduce the tensions that often arise between libraries and dealers as a result of catalog descriptions.

This section, like the one on new bookstores, can only briefly outline some of the more significant points about the OP book trade. It provides some basic information upon which one can continue to build while buying and collecting books for oneself or a library.

Summary

The distribution system for books and other library materials is varied and complex. One must know something about the system before beginning to develop a library collection. This chapter merely highlighted what one needs to know; it portrays just the beginning of a long, challenging, but enjoyable learning process. Jobbers, book dealers, and media vendors are more than willing to explain how they modify their operations to accommodate library requirements, when they know that a librarian has taken time to learn something about their operations.

Notes

1. Andrew Albanese, "Publishers Hurt in Divine Fallout," *Library Journal* 128, no. 16 (October 1, 2003): 17.

2. Lotz Wendall, "Here Today, Here Tomorrow: Coping with the OP 'Crisis,'" *School Library Journal* 35 (July 1989): 25–28.

3. Francis Wilkinson and Connie Thorson, *The RFP Process: Effective Management of the Acquisitions of Library Materials* (Englewood, CO: Libraries Unlimited, 1998).

4. Renee Feinberg, "B&N: The New College Library?" *Library Journal* 123 (February 1, 1998): 49–51; Steve Coffman, "What If You Ran Your Library Like a Bookstore?," *American Libraries* 29, no. 3 (March 1998): 40–46; J. Raymond, "Libraries Have Little to Fear from Bookstores," *Library Journal* 123 (September 1998): 41–42.

5. *Random House Dictionary of the English Language* (New York: Random House, 1996), 153.

6. Monica Fusich, "Collectiondevelopment.com: Using Amazon.com and Other Online Bookstores for Collection Development," *College & Research Libraries News* 59 (October 1998): 659–61.

7. Margaret Landesman, "Out-of-Print and Secondhand Market," in *The Business of Library Acquisitions*, ed. K. A. Schmidt, 186–88 (Chicago: American Library Association, 1990).

8. Sol Malkin, "Rare and Out-of-Print Books," in *A Manual on Bookselling*, 208 (New York: American Booksellers Association, 1974).

9. Ibid.

10. John Carter and Nicholas Baker, *ABC for Book Collectors* (New Castle, DE: Oak Knoll Press, 2000).

11. Allan Ahearn and Patricia Ahearn, *Book Collecting 2000: A Comprehensive Guide* (New York: G. P. Putnam, 2000).

Selected Websites*

(See also resources on the DLC5 website: <http://www.lu.com/dlc5>)

Advanced Book Exchange (Abebooks)
<http://www.abebooks.com>

ALIBRIS
<http://www.alibris.com>

Antiquarian Booksellers Association of America (ABAA)
<http://www.abaa.org>

Baker and Taylor
<http://www.btol.com>

Barnes and Noble.Com
<http://www.bn.com>

Basch Subscriptions
<http://www.basch.com/>

Biblio Magazine
<http://www.bibliomag.com>

Blackwell's Online
<http://bookshop.blackwell.com/bobus/scripts/welcome.jsp>

BookFinder.Com
<http://www.bookfinder.com>
Also provides a service called "BookFinder.Com Report" (<http://report.book
finder.com>, which provides updates on the most frequently requested OP titles.

Coutts
<http://www.coutts-ls.com/>

EBSCO
<http://www.ebsco.com>

Emery-Pratt
<http://www.emery-pratt.com/>

Ingram Book Group
<http://www.ingrambook.com/home.asp>

International League of Antiquarian Booksellers
<http://www.ilab-lila.com/>

Majors
<https://www.majors.com/>

ProQuest/UMI Books On Demand
<http://wwwlib.umi.com/bod>

Yankee Book Peddler (YBP)
<http://www.ybp.com/>

*These sites were accessed May 7, 2005.

Further Reading

American Library Association, Collection Development and Management Committee. *Guide to Performance Evaluation of Library Materials Vendors.* Acquisitions Guidelines no. 5. Chicago: American Library Association, 1993.

Blessinger, K., and M. Olle. "Comparison of Three Primary Aggregator Databases." *Serials Librarian* 45, no. 1 (2003): 53–58.

Brown, L. A. "Approval Vendor Selection—What's the Best Practice?" *Library Acquisitions* 22, no. 3 (Fall 1998): 341–51.

Flood, S. *Evaluation and Status of Approval Plans.* SPEC Kit 221. Washington, DC: Association of Research Libraries, 1997.

Flowers, J. L. "Specific Tips for Negotiations with Library Materials Vendors Depending upon Acquisitions Method." *Library Collections, Acquisitions, and Technical Services* 28, no. 4 (Winter 2004): 433–48.

———. "Negotiations with Library Material Vendors: Preparation and Tips." *The Bottom Line: Managing Library Finances* 16, no. 3 (2003): 100–105.

Flowers, J. L., and S. Perry. "Vendor—Assisted E-Selection and Online Ordering." *Library Collections, Acquisitions, & Technical Services* 26, no. 4 (Winter 2002): 395–407.

Harwood, P. "Courting Controversy: Views of a Not-So-Secret Agent." *Serial Librarian* 45, no. 1 (2003): 71–74.

Hirshon, A., and B. Winters. *Outsourcing Library Technical Services: A How-to-Do-It Manual.* New York: Neal-Schuman, 1996.

Hoyle, M. S. "Managing Electronic Journals from a Vendor's Perspective." *Serials Librarian* 45, no. 2 (2003): 135–44.

Kent, P. "How to Evaluate Serial Suppliers." *Library Acquisitions: Practice and Theory* 18, (Spring 1994): 83–87.

Kruse, T., and A. Holtzman. "Web Booksellers—Their Usefulness to Libraries." *Library Collections, Acquisitions, & Technical Services* 27, no. 1 (Spring 2003): 121–28.

Langendorfer, J. M., and M. L. Hurst. "Comparison Shopping: Purchasing Continuations as Standing Orders or on Approval." *Library Collections, Acquisitions, & Technical Services* 27, no. 2 (Summer 2003): 169–73.

Langston, D. "Collection Development: Use a Wholesaler!" *School Libraries in Canada* 21, no. 4 (2002): 30–31.

Levine-Clark, M. "Distributors and Vendors: An Analysis of Used-Book Availability on the Internet." *Library Collections, Acquisitions, and Technical Services* 28, no. 3 (Autumn 2004): 283–97.

Lorbeer, E. R. "Selecting the Appropriate Book Distributor for Your Library." In *Charleston Conference Proceedings 2002*, edited by R. Bazirjian and V. Speck, 128–30. Westport, CT: Libraries Unlimited, 2003.

Overmier, J. A. *Out-of-Print and Special Collection Materials: Acquisitions and Purchasing Options.* Binghamton, NY: Haworth, 2002.

"Preparing a Quotation (Request for Proposal) for Jobbers." *School Libraries in Canada* 21, no. 4 (2002): 38.

Presley, R. L. "Firing an Old Friend, Painful Decisions: Ethics between Librarians and Vendors." *Library Acquisitions: Practice and Theory* 17, no. 1 (1993): 53–59.

Richards, D. T. "Library/Dealer Relationships: Reflections on the Ideal." *Journal of Library Administration* 16, no. 3 (1992): 45–55.

Rogers, M. "Barnes and Noble Launches Library Bookstore Service." *Library Journal* 128, no. 7 (April 15, 2003): 25–27.

Rumph, V. A. "Vendor Selection Using the RFP Process—Is It for You? One Library's Experience." *Indiana Libraries* 20, no. 1 (2001): 26–28.

Shedenhelm, L., and B. A. Burk. "Book Vendor Records in the OCLC Database—Boon or Bane?" *Library Resources and Technical Services* 45 (January 2001): 10–19.

Van Orsdel, L., and K. Born. "Big Chill on the Big Deal?" *Library Journal* 128 (April 15, 2003): 51–56.

Walther, J. "Assessing Library Vendor Relations: A Focus on Evaluation and Communication." *Bottom Line* 11, no. 4 (1998): 149–57.

Ward, J. "Web-based Acquisitions from Web-based Vendors: Pros and Cons." In *Charleston Conference Proceedings 2002*, edited by R. Bazirjian and V. Speck, 149–52. Westport, CT: Libraries Unlimited, 2003.

Zeugner, L. "Negotiating Rare Book Purchases." *Library Collections, Acquisitions, & Technical Services* 26, no. 4 (Winter 2002): 367–68.

12
Fiscal
Management

Without funding, most library collections would be relatively small, consisting of items individuals no longer wanted and probably of little value to other people. With funding, the potential is almost unlimited, if one monitors the funds, uses them wisely, and can secure adequate amounts. This chapter addresses these issues—securing adequate funding, allocating funds provided, and controlling expenditures.

Monies spent on materials for the collection constitute the second largest expense category for the majority of libraries and information centers. Traditionally, in U.S. libraries, salaries represent the largest percentage of the total budget, followed by the materials (book) budget and, finally, all other operating expenses. That order remains today, but the percentage spent on materials has decreased as salaries have risen. Although percentages vary, the order also remains the same in any type of information environment or for any size collection. As is often the case, most of the literature on the topic of collection budgeting reflects a large research library orientation. However, the same issues exist in other libraries. Similarly, most of the ideas and suggestions contained in such articles apply equally well to other information settings.

In the recent past, there has been constant pressure on the materials budget of most libraries. This pressure resulted in a decline in the percentage of the total budget spent on acquiring items for the collection. The almost yearly double-digit inflation of serials prices further skewed the traditional balance in collection fund allocations. In many libraries in the United States, serials expenditures exceed monographic purchases, even in institutions that have traditionally emphasized book collections.

If one compares the total amount of money expended on materials thirty years ago with the current funding levels, today's total is considerably higher. Unfortunately, the total expenditures do not tell the entire story. When one looks at the number of items acquired for the money, one sees that the increase in acquisitions is not proportional to the funding increases. We are spending more and acquiring less. Since the 1970s, many libraries, along with many other organizations, have dealt with budgets that some persons call "steady state," others call "zero growth," and still others call "static." Yes, there have been the occasional "good" years, when increases have actually exceeded inflation, but for most libraries these have been the rare and badly needed exceptions. At best, budgeting of this type uses the previous year's inflation rate as the base for the next fiscal year's increase. An average inflation rate, like all averages, contains elements that increase at both above and below the average rate. For libraries this is a problem, because the inflation rate for information materials has been running well ahead of the overall inflation rate.

A 2004 *Library Journal* article[1] reporting results of a survey on public library funding noted that while budgets were slightly up overall, only 31 percent had increases in the adult book budget, while 33 percent reported decreases. Overall, there has been a steady drop in funding for adult books over the past six years, and it seems likely the trend will continue. Even when there is an increase, it seldom matches inflation, so the number of titles acquired declines. Libraries of all types face similar challenges.

Problems in Fiscal Management

Over the years, collection development staffs in the United States have faced several problems. We mentioned the inflation issues above and its impact on acquisition rates. Serials prices increased even more rapidly than did monographic prices. To maintain serials subscriptions, libraries took monies from book funds, thus further reducing the number of monographs acquired. Eventually, libraries started canceling subscriptions. Today, one also has to factor in the increased costs of e-resources, which seem to be patterning their cost increases along the lines of print journals. Thus, differential inflation rates and the use of national average rates as the basis for calculating budgets have contributed to declining acquisition rates for many libraries.

A second problem was, and still is, that the materials budget is vulnerable in periods of tight budgets. For most libraries the two biggest categories of expenditure are salaries and collection development. Unfortunately, expenditures on materials are somewhat discretionary in that (in theory) one could wait to buy an item until the next fiscal year.

Institutions set staff salaries on an annual basis, and staff reductions are rare during the middle of a fiscal year, unless the organization faces a major financial crisis. In essence, salaries are the last item organizations cut when attempting to save money. Without heat, light, and water (utility bills), the organization cannot remain open, so those generally are not cut during a fiscal year. Some operating expenses are discretionary: pens, pencils, paper, print cartridges, and other office supplies. Professional development and travel reimbursements may likewise be frozen, in an attempt to save funds. Institutions may achieve small savings, in terms of percentage of the total budget, by cutting back in such areas, but not very much—usually less than 2 percent.

Institutions with relatively large library collections view the materials budget as one of the largest available pools of funds to cut in an emergency. (Even a medium-sized library such as the Von der Ahe Library at LMU has a materials budget of well over $2.5 million. This amount is large enough to make the financial officers look at it as a source of significant funds if needed.) Further, the reality is that the monograph materials budget is the only place where significant cuts are easy to make, because of the non-ongoing nature of the material. All too often, the long-term impact of such decisions does not receive enough consideration, and the other choices appear, at least in the short run, to be even less acceptable. These issues are institutional and apply to corporate and special libraries as much as to publicly funded libraries.

What happened in collection development in the 1970s and 1980s was a shift in emphasis from monographs to trying to maintain periodical collections. Today, that shift is slowly reversing, and through careful library budget preparation and presentation, funding authorities appear to be more willing to accept differential budget increases that more closely reflect the actual expense experience. If nothing else, the problems of the past thirty years caused collection development officers to become better planners and to develop more accurate methods for calculating budgetary needs. As a result, they have more credibility with funding authorities.

Library Fund Accounting

The vast majority of libraries and information centers are part of not-for-profit (NFP) organizations. Being not-for-profit affects how the library maintains its financial records, particularly when contrasted with for-profit organizations. Libraries that are part of a governmental jurisdiction receive most revenues through an annual budget. Collection development officers must have accurate information about the monies available, and they need accurate data to assist in the preparation of budget requests. The funding authorities review the budget requests and authorize certain levels of funding for various activities. The three most common forms of income for libraries are appropriations (monies distributed by the governing body to its agencies to carry out specific purposes), revenue generated by the library as a result of service fees and fines, and endowment/donations.

Because of the nature of the financial activities, certain accounting terms and concepts are different for NFP organizations than for for-profit organizations. However, some general accounting rules and practices do apply. One special term for NFP accounting is *fund accounting*. (Fund accounting has been defined as a set of self-balancing account groups.) Another difference is that the profit-oriented bookkeeping system equation uses *assets*, *liabilities*, and *equity*; in NFP accounting, the elements used are assets, liabilities, and *fund balance*. One of the equations for NFP bookkeeping is that assets must equal liabilities plus the fund balance; another is that the fund balance is the difference between assets and liabilities. Substituting equity for fund balance would make the equation apply to for-profit organizations. A difference between these equations is that an increase in fund balance carries with it no special meaning, whereas an increase in equity is a positive signal in a for-profit organization. Other terms, such as *debit*, *credit*, *journalizing*, *posting*, and *trial balance*, have the same meaning, regardless of the organization's profit orientation.

In most libraries, the major fund is the operating fund. Other funds may be endowment and physical plant funds. The operating funds are the group of accounts used to handle the day-to-day activities of the library for a given time, usually one year, covering such items as salaries, materials purchases, and utility bills. Within the operating fund there may be two categories of accounts: restricted and unrestricted.

Restricted accounts require that one use the monies only for specific purposes. Collection development and acquisition staff often works with such accounts (frequently referred to as funds in the monetary rather than the accounting meaning of the term). More often than not, these accounts are the result of donations by individuals who have definite ideas about how the library should spend the money. Some libraries have endowments that are a combination of individual and corporate or foundation gifts; an example is endowments developed under the National Endowment for the Humanities Challenge Grant program. (Sometimes gifts are for current use, and sometimes they are for an endowment. Endowments should generate income for the library indefinitely. The normal procedure for endowments is to make available some percentage of the interest earned. The balance of the interest is returned to the endowment to increase its capital base. Private libraries and an increasing number of publicly funded libraries have one or more endowments.) Often the donor's restrictions are narrow. When the restrictions are too narrow, it is difficult to make effective use of the available monies. Most collection development officers prefer *unrestricted* book accounts (used for any appropriate item for the collection) or broad-based restricted accounts.

The purpose of the accounting system is to assure the proper use of monies provided and to make it possible to track expenditures. That is, one must record (charge) every financial transaction to some account and keep a record of what the transaction involved. With a properly functioning fund accounting system, it is possible to tie every item acquired to a specific account and to verify when the transaction took place. With a good accounting system, one can easily provide accurate reports about all financial aspects of collection development activities. Furthermore, it is a great planning aid. It takes time to understand accounting systems, but one must understand them if one wishes to be an effective and efficient collection development officer. A good book to consult for accounting is G. Stevenson Smith's *Managerial Accounting for Libraries and Other Not-for-Profit Organizations.*[2] For budgeting, another very sound title is *Basic Budgeting Practices for Librarians*, by Richard S. Rounds.[3]

Estimating Costs

Several factors influence the funding needs for collection development. Changes in the composition of the service community may have an important impact in either a positive or a negative sense (see chapter 2). Another factor is changes in collecting activities, such as the scope or depth desired in a subject area (see chapter 3). The two cost factors that come up year in and year out are the price of materials and inflation. They become the key factors in estimating collection development funding needs.

From time to time, libraries have had some problems establishing the credibility of collection development funding requirements. Although a good accounting system will assist in justifying budget requests, additional data about book expenditures are often necessary. One example of the problems caused by inflation, stable budgets, and rapidly rising prices for materials (and perhaps limited credibility) is what happened to the expenditures and acquisition rates for academic libraries. Between 1993 and 1998, monograph prices rose just over 25 percent. For serials, the data were almost shocking; between 1986 and 2000 prices rose 226 percent.[4] Libraries of every type and size experienced similar problems during this time. *Library Journal* periodically publishes surveys of spending and other activities of various types of libraries. Although the surveys do not appear predictably, when they become available, they provide useful national data to compare where your library falls.

For more than forty years, collection development/acquisitions librarians have been publishing cost indexes for books and serials. The indexes have proven useful in providing hard data for funding requests, even if they have not always led to budget increases. Today there is concern that the indexes and surveys have outlived their usefulness. It is true that electronic resources are taking up an ever-greater share of collection development funding, and the fact that there are no cost tracking indexes for them does complicate the cost estimation process. Nevertheless, print books and serials are still being acquired in substantial numbers, and the existing indexes do still have value. It probably will not be long before one or more e-resources cost indexes become available.

James Neal provided a good summary of why one would/should use indexes and some of their limitations.[5] Although he uses academic library examples, one can easily see how his points apply to any type of library. His list of uses included the following:

- to influence campus administrative support;
- to strengthen campus budget presentations;
- to analyze library purchasing power;
- to plot trends and plan budgets;
- to provide support for new academic programs;
- to educate faculty and secure their support;
- to assist with journal cancellation projects;
- to influence state budget agencies;
- to value collections for insurance purposes;
- to support asset accounting for collection discards;
- to determine charges for lost books; and
- to assist in training new selectors.[6]

One finds the most recent data in journals; historical data appear in *The Bowker Annual* (Information Today). Using *The Bowker Annual* may be adequate for some purposes, but one needs to be aware that the information appearing in the "current" volume is almost two years old. Preliminary data for books published during a calendar year appear in *Publishers Weekly* (often in late February or early March). Final data appear some months later (September or October). The major problem with the published indexes is that up-to-date data may not be readily available when one must prepare a budget request.

Vendors can sometimes provide more current data. Some vendors will provide custom pricing information, and others may provide a general set of data based on their experience, such as the Yankee Book Peddler material illustrated in figure 12.1, page 283. These information sheets contain price data about books handled in the firm. Figure 12.2, page 284, illustrates pricing information from another major book vendor, Midwest Library Service.

It is also possible to secure information about serials subscriptions from a vendor. Figure 12.3, page 285, reproduced from EBSCO's *Serials Price Projections and Cost History,* illustrates the differences among types of libraries as well as the change in price over a series of years. This document also provides information about the impact of exchange rate variations (<http://www.ebsco.com/home/printsubs/priceproj.asp>).

Just as libraries prepare budget requests at different times of the year, pricing data appear at various times during the year in a variety of sources. The challenge is to find the most current data, which may determine whether the library receives requested funding.

For libraries that purchase a significant number of foreign publications, there is a need to estimate the impact of exchange rates. Volatile exchange rates affect buying power almost as much as inflation. For example, in January 1985, the pound sterling was at $1.2963 (U.S.); in January 1988 it was up to $1.7813 (U.S.); in 1992 it was $1.7653 (U.S.); by January 1994 it was down to $1.4872 (U.S.), in March 1999 it had moved up to $1.6064 (U.S.), and September 2004 found the pound at $1.7818. During the same period, the Canadian dollar went from $0.6345 to $0.7693 (U.S.), then to $0.7913 (U.S.), back to $0.736 (U.S.), and then to $0.5199 (U.S.); in September 2004 it was $0.7771. Although it is impossible to accurately forecast the direction and amount of fluctuation in the exchange rates for the next twelve months, some effort should go into studying the past twelve months and attempting to predict future trends. Naturally, one must have good data about the amounts spent in various countries during the past year. The country of publication may be less important than the vendor's location. For example, if the library uses the vendor Harrassowitz (<http://www.harrassowitz.de/>), prices will be in deutsche marks, regardless of the country of origin of the items purchased. After collecting the data, one can use them as factors in estimating the cost of continuing the current acquisition levels from the countries from which the library normally buys. An online source for checking/converting currency rates is the "Universal Currency Converter" at <http://www.xe.com/ucc/>.

Allocation of Monies

As stated earlier, collection development funds may be restricted or unrestricted. For most libraries, the unrestricted allocation represents the majority of monies available for collection development. Libraries employ internal allocation systems in an attempt to match monies available with needs and to assure that all collecting areas have some funding for the year. These systems provide guidelines for selection personnel; the allocation sets limits on, and expectations for, purchases in subject areas or for certain types of material. Sometimes there are different accounts for different types of material—books, journals, e-resources, etc.—that establish macrocategories. Within such a large grouping, there are often finer divisions, such as adult books, children's books, and reference books. Even the macro allocation decisions can be challenging, as the serials, book, and e-resources have substantial needs that go well beyond the available funding.

YBP Library Services
New Title Output by LC Subjects: University Press

| LC Subclass | Subject and Description | Fiscal Year 2002 - 2003 | | |
		Number of Titles	Total List Value ($)	Average List ($)
AC	Collections	1	19.95	19.95
AG	Dictionaries	1	300.00	300.00
AM	Museums	3	96.90	32.30
AP	Periodicals	2	24.00	12.00
AS	Learned Societies	1	45.00	45.00
AZ	History of Scholarship	2	143.50	71.75
	A Total	10	629.35	62.94
B	Philosophy	284	14,745.88	51.92
BC	Logic	17	1,018.79	59.93
BD	Speculative Philosophy	62	2,708.95	43.69
BF	Psychology	105	5,641.80	53.73
BH	Aesthetics	22	1,094.05	49.73
BJ	Ethics	59	2,629.05	44.56
BL	Religion	123	5,517.64	44.86
BM	Judaism	31	1,536.79	49.57
BP	Islam	49	2,124.60	43.36
BQ	Buddhism	33	1,604.65	48.63
BR	Christianity	92	4,051.64	44.04
BS	The Bible	40	1,760.12	44.00
BT	Doctrinal Theology	54	3,418.24	63.30
BV	Practical Theology	46	1,976.55	42.97
BX	Denominations	157	6,550.12	41.72
	B Total	1,174	56,378.87	48.02
CB	History of Civilization	18	856.05	47.56
CC	Archaeology	12	593.30	49.44
CD	Diplomatics. Seals	2	75.00	37.50
CE	Technical Chronology	1	120.00	120.00
CJ	Numismatics	1	50.00	50.00
CN	Inscriptions	2	225.00	112.50
CR	Heraldry	3	105.90	35.30
CS	Genealogy	5	372.90	74.58
CT	General Biography	24	841.20	35.05
	C Total	68	3,239.35	47.64
D	History, Eastern Hemisphere	178	6,849.73	38.48
DA	Great Britain	123	5,997.65	48.76
DB	Austria	13	544.25	41.87
DC	France	49	1,809.35	36.93
DD	Germany	28	1,568.00	56.00
DE	Greco-Roman World	4	271.95	67.99
DF	Greece	24	1,319.80	54.99
DG	Italy	36	2,028.15	56.34
DJK	Eastern Europe	6	369.95	61.66
DK	Russia. Poland	57	2,117.80	37.15
DL	Northern Europe	3	117.95	39.32
DP	Spain. Portugal	21	1,039.20	49.49

Fig. 12.1. YBP new title output by LC subjects. Reprinted with permission from YBP Library Services.

Midwest Library Service
All Press Publications Analysis by Subject
For the Period 1/1/2003 to 12/31/2003

LC CLASSIFICATION#		DESCRIPTION	NUMBER OF TITLES	TOTAL PRICE	AVERAGE PRICE
VK	1250-1299	Shipwrecks and fires	1	32.95	32.95 **
VK	1300-1491	Saving of life&property	2	79.90	39.95 **
VM		Naval architect.Shipbldg	5	215.75	43.15 **
		V'S SUBTOTALS	31	1,199.60	38.70 ****
Z	4-8	History books&bookmaking	2	230.00	115.00 **
Z	105-115.5	Paleography	3	290.00	96.67 **
Z	116-265	Printing	7	365.00	52.14 **
Z	278-549	Bookselling & publishing	6	210.85	35.14 **
Z	687-718.8	The collections. Books	1	45.00	45.00 **
Z	719-871	Libraries	3	364.95	121.65 **
Z	1001-8999	Bibliography	1	70.00	70.00 **
Z	1201-4980	National bibliography	4	480.00	120.00 **
Z	5051-7999	Subject bibliography	6	911.95	151.99 **
Z	8001-8999	Personal bibliography	1	34.95	34.95 **
ZA		Information resources	1	40.00	40.00 **
		Z'S SUBTOTALS	35	3,042.70	86.93 ****
		TOTAL NUMBER OF TITLES	9,456	488,227.97	51.63 ******

Fig. 12.2. Pricing. Reprinted with permission of the Midwest Library Serivces.

Five Year Journal Price Increase History (2000–2004)

Library Type	% of Total Titles	% of Total Expenditure	2000 Avg. Title Price	2001 Avg. Title Price	2001 % Increase	2002 Avg. Title Price	2002 % Increase	2003 Avg. Title Price	2003 % Increase	2004 Avg. Title Price	2004 % Increase	% Increase 00 - 04
ARL												
US Titles	67.1%	45.7%	$253.62	$275.11	8.47%	$297.23	8.04%	$320.55	7.85%	$347.17	8.31%	36.89%
Non-US Titles	32.9%	54.3%	$609.49	$647.93	6.31%	$697.65	7.67%	$759.64	8.89%	$840.12	10.59%	37.84%
Total Titles	100.0%	100.0%	$370.79	$397.86	7.30%	$429.07	7.84%	$465.12	8.40%	$509.47	9.54%	37.40%
College & University												
US Titles	75.4%	54.0%	$250.29	$270.63	8.13%	$293.45	8.43%	$316.73	7.93%	$342.89	8.26%	37.00%
Non-US Titles	24.6%	46.0%	$639.29	$687.83	7.59%	$741.24	7.77%	$807.63	8.96%	$895.85	10.92%	40.13%
Total Titles	100.0%	100.0%	$345.91	$373.18	7.88%	$403.52	8.13%	$437.39	8.39%	$478.80	9.47%	38.42%
Academic Medical												
US Titles	67.5%	49.0%	$418.90	$455.69	8.78%	$495.98	8.84%	$539.34	8.74%	$585.88	8.63%	39.86%
Non-US Titles	32.5%	51.0%	$919.65	$989.07	7.55%	$1,050.16	6.18%	$1,144.26	8.96%	$1,262.96	10.37%	37.33%
Total Titles	100.0%	100.0%	$581.78	$629.18	8.15%	$676.24	7.48%	$736.10	8.85%	$806.11	9.51%	38.56%
Corporate												
US Titles	85.7%	59.9%	$186.12	$196.83	5.75%	$209.09	6.23%	$222.25	6.30%	$235.32	5.88%	26.43%
Non-US Titles	14.3%	40.1%	$684.04	$730.43	6.78%	$785.69	7.57%	$859.82	9.44%	$946.25	10.05%	38.33%
Total Titles	100.0%	100.0%	$257.25	$273.06	6.14%	$291.46	6.74%	$313.34	7.50%	$336.88	7.51%	30.95%
Public Library												
US Titles	95.8%	87.6%	$55.51	$57.17	2.99%	$59.49	4.05%	$62.38	4.86%	$64.53	3.44%	16.25%
Non-US Titles	4.2%	12.4%	$156.05	$162.72	4.27%	$171.84	5.60%	$187.21	8.94%	$207.60	10.89%	33.03%
Total Titles	100.0%	100.0%	$59.74	$61.61	3.14%	$64.21	4.22%	$67.63	5.32%	$70.54	4.31%	18.09%

Fig. 12.3. EBSCO five-year journal price history. Reprinted with permission of EBSCO.

Ordinarily, the allocations reflect the collection development policy statement priorities. If the library employs a collecting intensity-ranking system in the collection development policy, it is reasonable to expect to find those levels reflected in the amount allocated to the subject or format. Almost all allocation methods are complex, and how one goes about matching the needs and monies available requires consideration of several factors. Also, one can be certain there will be a political aspect to the process. Generally, it will not be as significant an issue when the process is completely internal as when there are users involved—educational settings with teaching departments trying to stake out "their rightful share."

Among the factors one must consider are past practices, differential publication rates, unit cost and inflation rates, level of demand, and usage of the material. Implementing a formal system takes time and effort. Some professionals question whether it is worthwhile allocating the monies. Opponents to allocation claim it is difficult to develop a fair allocation model, and it is time-consuming to calculate the amounts needed. They also claim that, because the models are difficult to develop, libraries tend to leave the allocations in place too long and simply add in the next year's percentage increase rather than recalculate the figures annually. They suggest that selectors may not spend accounts effectively because there is too much or too little money available. Finally, they argue that it is difficult to effect transfers from one account to another during the year.

Proponents claim that allocations provide better control of collection development and are a more effective way to monitor expenditures. Some allocation does take place, regardless of the presence or absence of a formal allocation process. When there is no formal system, selectors engage in informal balancing of needs and funds available for various subjects or classes of material. (In the worst case, the more influential/active selectors have greater access to the funds, regardless of actual collection or user needs.) It seems reasonable, if the process is going to take place one way or another, to have the formal process provide the best opportunity for achieving a fair balance.

A good allocation process provides at least four outcomes. Obviously, its overall purpose is to match available funds with needs. Second, it provides selectors with guidelines regarding how they should allocate their time. That is, if one is responsible for three selection areas with funding allocations of $15,000, $5,000, and $500, it is clear which area requires the most attention. (In some cases, it is harder to spend the smaller amount, because one must be careful to spend it wisely.)

Third, the allocation process provides a means of assessing the selector's work at the end of the fiscal year. Finally, it provides clients with a sense of collecting priorities, assuming the allocation information is made available to them. The library can communicate the information in terms of percentages rather than specific monetary amounts if there is a concern about divulging budgetary data.

The allocation process should be collaborative, with input from all interested parties. Two things are certain: whether the library uses a formal or informal approach to gaining the input, the process has political overtones, and the outcome will invariably disappoint some individual or group. This is particularly true when introducing a revised allocation in a static budget environment. Those who receive more money will be happy, but those who lose funds will object to the method used to reallocate the funds. Unfortunately, sometimes the objectors are influential enough to get the allocations changed, which defeats the purpose of the process—matching funds to needs.

What allocation method the library selects is influenced, in part, by internal library practices, institutional needs, and extrainstitutional requirements (such as those of accreditation agencies). Internal factors include operational practices that determine what type of information is readily available to those making the allocation decisions (vendor's country of origin, number of approval titles versus firm orders, format and subject data, and use are some examples). How the library organizes its services—centralized or decentralized—also plays a role in the allocation decision. Other internal factors affecting the allocation process include past practices for allocation and the purpose of allocation (i.e., its use as a control mechanism or guideline). Institutional factors, in addition to the obvious importance of the institution's mission and goals, include the type of budget control it employs, its organization, and its overall financial condition. Extrainstitutional factors are the political atmosphere (e.g., the degree of accountability), economic conditions, social expectations and values regarding information services (such as equal access and literacy levels), and outside agencies (such as accreditation bodies or governmental bodies) that monitor or control the institution.

One can think of allocation methods as being a continuum with impulse at one end and formula at the opposite end. Between the two extremes are several more or less structured methods. Impulse allocation can take the form of allowing active selectors to have greatest access to available funds or, with a slightly more structured approach, to allocate on the basis of perceptions of need. History of past use and some annual percentage increase for each allocation area are a little more formal; this is probably one of the most widely employed methods. Allocating on the basis of organizational structure (main and branch units) is still more formal (often, the allocation is a fixed percentage of the fund pool). If one adds to that method some incremental funding based on workload (such as circulation data), one moves even closer to the formula end of the continuum. Also, somewhere in the middle of the continuum is the format allocation method (including books, serials, audiovisual, electronic, and reference).

Libraries employ several category allocation methods in addition to format, such as subject, unit, users, language, and formula. Most libraries that use a format allocation system use several approaches. Many small libraries, including most school media centers, employ the format system using monographs, serials, and audiovisuals as the broad groupings. The library divides these funds by subject (language arts), grade level (fifth grade), or user group (professional reading). Occasionally, libraries divide monograph funds into current, retrospective, and replacement categories. In libraries using approval, blanket-order, or standing-order plans, it is normal practice to set aside monies for each program before making any other allocations. A typical approach would be to set aside an amount equal to the prior year's expenditure for the category with an additional amount to cover expected inflation. The reason for setting aside these funds first is that they are ongoing commitments.

Formula allocations have become more and more popular, especially in large libraries. Librarians have proposed many formulas over the years, but no one formula has become standard. Each library must decide which, if any, formula is most appropriate for its special circumstances. A 1992 article by Ian R. Young described a project that compared seven formulas.[7] His results showed that, though each formula employed one or more unique variables, there were no statistically significant differences among the formula results in terms of a single institution. He concluded that there was a high degree of similarity among the seven formulas, at least when applied to his institutional setting. Based on our experience with formulas and the selection of a formula in several institutional settings, we would say the library selects the formula that contains all the variables necessary to satisfy all interested parties. (Thus, political rather than practical considerations dictate which formula is used.) Only quantifiable factors (e.g., average price, number of titles published, and use data) can be used as variables in formulas. This does not mean that subjective judgments do not play a role, but the allocation process as a whole depends on weightings, circulation data, production figures, inflation and exchange rates, number of users, and so forth. Figure 12.4 shows the allocation formula used at LMU.

ALA's *Guide to Budget Allocation for Information Resources* indicates that there are six broad allocation methods: historical, zero-based (no consideration of past practice), formulas, ranking (a variation of formulas), percentages, and other modeling techniques.[8] The book also outlines some of the variations in formulas by type of library. For example, academic libraries might consider enrollment by major or degrees granted in a field (the factors used in figure 12.4 are widely used in academic libraries as well). Public libraries might factor in differences in the service communities being served, the ratio of copies per title of bestsellers to general titles, or the demand (in terms of use or requests) in popular subject fields. Special libraries employ factors like delivery time expectations of the clients, service chargebacks, and the number of clients or departments served. Many school media centers use factors like changes in curriculum, number

Department	Use	Average Cost	Cost-Use	Percent Cost-Use	Formula Allocation	Present Allocation
Psychology (BF& RC 435–577)	4,674	$38.55	180,183	0.07	$12,693	$15,033
Sociology (HM-HX)	5,311	$37.85	201,021	0.09	$14,542	$6,587
Theater Arts (PN 1600– 1989, 2000– 3310)	144	$38.14	5,492	0.003	$361	$3,908
Theology (BL-BX)	6,503	$36.49	237,294	0.1	$16,258	$7,409
Totals			2,491,436		$181,342	$180,652

Use = Circulated use of the class numbers associated with the department

Average Cost = Price listed as average for that discipline in *Choice*

Cost-Use = Average cost times use for the field

Percent Cost-Use = Percentage of library's total cost-use for the field

Formula Allocation = Amount of new allocation under new formula

Present Allocation = Amount of current allocation

Fig. 12.4. Loyola Marymount University library book allocation formula. Courtesy of Loyola Marymount University.

and ability of students by grade level, and loss and aging rates of various subject areas in the collection. The guide provides a starting point for anyone thinking about changing the allocation process a library uses.

Allocating funds is an involved process, and changing an existing method is almost more difficult than establishing a new method. Often, past practices and political issues keep the process from moving forward or evolving. How much to allocate to current materials and how much to allocate to retrospective purchases are related, in part, to the serials inflation rate. If the decision is to maintain serials at the expense of monographs, in time, there will be a significant need for retrospective buying funds to fill in gaps in the monograph collection. Subject variations also complicate the picture: science materials are very expensive; social science materials are substantially less costly but are more numerous. Electronic access, rather than local ownership, also clouds the picture, especially because electronic access often involves cost at the individual level, something with which allocation models have not dealt. Although allocation work frequently involves political issues and occasionally involves upset individuals, in the long run careful attention to this process will produce a better collection for the organization that the library or information center serves.

Encumbering

One aspect of accounting and financial management in collection development that differs from typical accounting practice is the process of *encumbering*, which allows one to set aside monies to pay for ordered items. When the library waits 60, 90, or 120 or more days for orders, there is some chance that the monies available will be over- or underspent if there is no system that allows for setting aside monies.

The following chart shows how the process works. Day 1, the first day of the fiscal year, shows the library with an annual allocation of $1,000 for a particular subject area. On day 2, the library orders an item with a list price of $24.95. Although there may be shipping and handling charges, there probably will be a discount. Because none of the costs and credits are known at the time, the list price is the amount a staff member records as encumbered. The unexpended column reflects the $24.95 deduction, though there is still nothing in the expended category. Sixty-two days later, the item and invoice arrive; the invoice reflects a 15 percent discount ($3.74) and no shipping or handling charges. The bookkeeper records the actual cost ($21.21) under expended and adds the $3.74 to the unexpended amount. The amount encumbered now is zero.

	Unexpended	Encumbered	Expended
Day 1	$1,000.00	0	0
Day 2	$ 975.05	$24.95	0
Day 62	$ 978.79	0	$21.21

This system is much more complex than the example suggests, because libraries place and receive multiple orders every day. With each transaction the amounts in each column change. *One seldom knows the precise balance, except on the first and last day of the fiscal year.* If the funding body takes back all unexpended funds at the end of the fiscal year (a cash accounting system), the collection development staff will want to know their fund(s)' balances as they enter the final quarter of the year.

Several factors make it difficult to learn the exact status of the funds, even with the use of encumbrance. One factor is delivery of orders. Vendors may assure customers that they will deliver before the end of the fiscal year but then fail to do so. Such a failure can result in the encumbered money being lost. With a cash system, the collection development staff must make some choices at the end of the fiscal year if there are funds in the encumbered category. The main issue is determining if the items still on order are important enough to leave on order. An affirmative answer has substantial implications for collection development. Using the foregoing example and assuming that day 62 comes after the start of a new fiscal year and that the new allocation is $1,000, on day 1 of the new fiscal year, the amount unexpended would be $975.05 ($1,000 minus $24.95), encumbered $24.95, and expended zero. In essence, there is a reduction in the amount available for new orders, and the library lost $24.95 from the prior year's allocation. (The senior author once took over as head of a library on June 25, and on July 1 the system financial officer reported that the entire acquisitions allocation was encumbered for the coming fiscal year. To have some funds for collection development over the next twelve months, it was necessary to cancel 347 orders.)

With an accrual system, the unexpended funds carry forward into the next fiscal year. Under such a system, using the example, the day 1 figures would be unexpended $1,000, encumbered $24.95, and expended zero. (There is often a limit as to how much one can carry forward. For example, the LMU library may carry over only $100,000; thus, there can be the same year-end issues as with a cash system if the encumbered amount exceeds the limit during the last eight weeks of the fiscal year.)

The staff also needs to consider how reliable the vendor or producer is, because occasionally an item never arrives. How long should one wait? The answer varies from producer to producer and country to country. If the library buys substantial amounts from developing countries, waiting several years is not unreasonable. Because print runs tend to be very close to the number of copies on order, the chance of never being able to acquire the item makes it dangerous to cancel the order.

There is a problem in leaving funds encumbered for long periods under either system, especially when there is rapid inflation or when exchange rates are unfavorable. These are two reasons why a firm, but reasonable, date for automatic cancellation of unfilled orders is important.

Other factors making it difficult to know the precise fund balance during the year are pricing and discounts. Prices are subject to change without notice on most library materials, particularly online resources, which means that the price may be higher on delivery than when ordered. In addition, discounts are unpredictable. Because of the uncertainty, most libraries encumber the list price without freight charges and just hope that the amount will be adequate. Exchange rates enter the picture for international acquisitions, and the question of when the rate is set can be a critical issue. Certainly, the rate is not firm when one places the order, but is it firm at the time of shipment? The date of the invoice? The date the library receives the invoice and items? The date the financial office makes out the check? Possibly even the date the supplier deposits the check? With international orders, one can expect four months or more to elapse between order placement and delivery. In periods of rapid rate changes, even a four-month difference can significantly affect the amount of money available for purchases.

Moving monies back and forth, especially in a manual system, can lead to errors, so the acquisitions department needs a good bookkeeper. Automated accounting systems speed the recording activities and provide greater accuracy, as long as the data entry is correct. Despite the uncertainty that exists with the encumbering system, it is still better than having unexpended and expended categories, because without it one would not know how much of the unexpended balance was actually needed for items on order.

Audits

We have a favorite Robert Frost poem[9] about accounting that goes:

Never ask of money spent
Where the spender thinks it went.
To remember or invent
What he did with every cent.

Robert Frost,
"The Hardship of Accounting"

One outcome of having the authority to manage and expend substantial amounts of money is fiscal accountability. Actually, the amount of money need not be "substantial," if it is public or private funds. The process of establishing how well one has handled the monies one is responsible for expending is the audit.

A rather legalistic definition of an *audit* is the process of "accumulation and evaluation of evidence about quantifiable information of [an] economic entity to determine and report on the degree of correspondence between the information and established criteria."[10] More simply put, it is the process of assuring that the financial records are accurate and that the information is presented accurately, using accepted accounting practices; and of making recommendations for improvements in how the process is carried out. The basic questions and required records relate to: Was the purchase made with proper authorization? Was it received? Was it paid for in an appropriate manner? Is the item still available? (If the item is not still available, there should be appropriate records regarding its disposal.) Today, with automated acquisitions systems, undergoing an audit is less time-consuming than in the past, where the "paper trail" was, in fact, a number of different paper records that had to be gathered up and compared. At least now the system can pull up the necessary material fairly quickly.

Are audits really necessary in libraries? Must we remember how, where, on what, and when we spent every cent? Unfortunately, the answer is yes. Not many years ago Herbert Synder and Julia Hersberger published an article outlining embezzlement in public libraries.[11]

There is another accounting/collections issue that comes up from time to time. Should the collection be depreciated like other durable major expenditures? Opinions vary as to whether or not to perform this practice as well as what the time frame should be if one does. Where it is done, the time frame ranges from five to fifteen years—straight-line depreciation. The question of "should one do it" is usually answered by the parent jurisdiction/body. Very few individual items cost enough by themselves to warrant depreciating them; however, the aggregate expenditure on the collection is substantial. Some jurisdictions depreciate the acquisitions costs, but insurance purposes appreciate the value.

Summary

One must be constantly aware of changes in prices and in invoicing practices to gain the maximum number of additions to the collection. It is important to watch for changes and demand explanations of freight and handling charges, inappropriate dual-pricing systems, or other costs that may place additional strain on the budget. By understanding basic accounting principles and using the reports and records generated by the library's accounting system, one will be better able to monitor the use of available monies and to use them effectively to meet the needs of the public.

Notes

1.   Barbara Hoffert, "Facing Down the Crunch," *Library Journal* 129 (February 15, 2004): 38–40.

2.   G. Stevenson Smith, *Managerial Accounting for Libraries and Other Not-for-Profit Organizations,* 2nd ed. (Chicago: American Library Association, 1999).

3.   Richard S. Rounds, *Basic Budgeting Practices for Librarians*, 2nd ed. (Chicago: American Library Association, 1994).

4.   Claudia Weston, "Breaking with the Past: Formula Allocation at Portland State University," *Serials Librarian* 45, no. 4 (2004): 43–53.

5.   James Neal, "Predicting Publication Prices: An Academic Library Perspective," *Library Resources & Technical Services* 47, no. 4 (2003): 189–90.

6.   Ibid., 190.

7.   Ian R. Young, "A Quantitative Comparison of Acquisitions Budget Allocation Formulas Using a Single Institutional Setting," *Library Acquisitions: Practice and Theory* 16, no. 3 (1992): 229–42.

8.   Edward Shreeves, ed., *Guide to Budget Allocation for Information Resources,* Collection Management and Development Guides no. 4 (Chicago: American Library Association, 1991).

9.   Robert Frost, "The Hardship of Accounting," in *Collected Poems, Prose and Plays* 282 (New York: Library of America, 1995).

10.   Alvin Arens and James Loebbecke, *Auditing: An Integrated Approach* (Englewood Cliffs, NJ: Prentice-Hall, 1994), 1.

11.   Herbert Synder and Julia Hersberger, "Public Libraries and Embezzlement: An Examination of Internal Control and Financial Misconduct," *Library Quarterly* 67 (January 1997): 1–23.

Selected Websites*

(See also resources on the DLC5 website: <http://www.lu.com/dlc5>)

Library Materials Budget Survey
        <http://www.arl.org/scomm/lmbs/index.html>
        An annual survey prepared by the Association for Research Libraries.

Library Research Service Tools
        <http://www.lrs.org/tools.asp>

A selection of budget calculators and comparison resources for academic and public library settings.

Price and Title Output Reports for Collection Management
    <http://www.library.yale.edu/colldev/index.html>
    A comprehensive list of "regularly issued national and international price reports and price indexes, in print and on the Internet" maintained by the Yale University Library.

*These sites were accessed May 7, 2005.

Further Reading

Albanese, A. "In Tough Budget Times, Grants Aid Collections." *Criticas* 3 (September–October 2003): 12–14.

"Ann Arbor Audit Reveals Big Deficit." *Library Journal* 125 (March 15, 2000): 13, 16.

"Auditors Urge Feds and City to Investigate Detroit PL Finances." *American Libraries* 33 (December 2002): 20–21.

Barker, J. W. "What's Your Money Worth?" *Journal of Library Administration* 16, no. 3 (1992): 25–43.

Berger, S. "The First Audit." *Bottom Line* 5 (Summer 1991): 28–30.

Bluh, P., J. G. Neal, and J. R. Call. "Predicating Publication Prices: Are the Old Models Still Relevant?" *Library Resources & Technical Services* 36, no. 4 (2003): 188–91.

Budd, J. "Allocation Formulas in the Literature." *Library Acquisitions: Practice and Theory* 15, no. 1 (1991): 95–101.

Burdick, A. J. "Citation Patterns in the Health Sciences: Implications for Serial/Monograph Fund Allocation." *Bulletin of the Medical Library Association* 81 (January 1993): 44–47.

Carrigan, D. P. "Improving Return on Investment: A Proposal for Allocating the Book Budget." *Journal of Academic Librarianship* 18 (November 1992): 292–97.

Christianson, E. "When Your Parent Dictates Your Accounting Life." *Bottom Line* 7 (Summer 1993): 17–21.

Christianson, E., and S. Hayes. "Depreciation of Library Collection: Terminology of the Debate." *Bottom Line* 5, no. 3 (1991): 35–37.

Crotts, J. "Subject Usage and Funding of Library Monographs." *College & Research Libraries* 60 (May 1999): 261–73.

Cubberly, C. "Allocating the Materials Funds Using Cost of Materials." *Journal of Academic Librarianship* 19 (March 1993): 16–21.

Ferguson, A. "Georgia Librarians Defend School Collection Against Audit." *School Library Journal* 45 (February 1999): 14.

Fowler, D. C., and J. Arcand. "Monographs Acquisitions Times and Cost Studies." *Library Resources & Technical Services* 47 (July 2003): 109–24.

Gleeson, M. E., and J. R. Ottensmann. "A Decision Support System for Acquisitions Budgeting in Public Libraries." *Interfaces* 24 (September–October 1994): 107–17.

Granskog, K. "Basic Acquisitions Accounting and Business Practice." In *Business of*

Acquisitions, 2nd ed., edited by K. Schmidt, 285–320. Chicago: American Library Association, 1999.

Hawks, C. P. "The Audit Trail and Automated Acquisitions." *Library Acquisitions: Practice and Theory* 18 (Fall 1994): 333–39.

Johnson, P. "Preparing Materials Budget Requests." *Technicalities* 15 (April 1995): 6–10.

Lawrence, S. R., L. S. Connaway, and K. H. Brigham. "Life Cycle Costs of Library Collections." *College & Research Libraries* 62 (November 2001): 541–53.

Lynden, F. C. "Impact of Foreign Exchange on Library Materials Budgets." *Bottom Line* 9, no. 3 (1996): 14–19.

McCabe, G. B., and R. N. Bish. "Planning for Fund Management in Multiple System Environments." *Library Administration and Management* 7 (Winter 1993): 51–55.

Murray, M. S., and M. T. Wolf. *Budgeting for Information Access: Managing the Resource Budget for Absolute Success.* Chicago: American Library Association, 1998.

Park, L. M. "Endowed Book Funds." In *Library Fund Raising.* Annual. Chicago: American Library Association, 1995.

Petrick, J. "Electronic Resources and Acquisitions Budgets." *Collection Building* 21, no. 3 (2002): 123–33.

Rein, L. O., F. P. Hurley, and J. C. Walsh. "Formula-Based Subject Allocation: A Practical Approach." *Collection Management* 17, no. 4 (1993): 25–48.

Roberts, S. A. "Financial Management of Libraries: Past Trends and Future Prospects." *Library Trends* 51 (Winter 2003): 462–93.

Schmitz-Veitin, G. "Literature Use as a Measure for Funds Allocation." *Library Acquisitions: Practice and Theory* 8, no. 4 (1984): 267–74.

Smith, M. I. "Using Statistics to Increase Public Library Budgets." *Bottom Line* 9, no. 3 (1996): 4–13.

Stanley, N. M. "Accrual Accounting and Library Materials Acquisitions." *Bottom Line* 7, no. 2 (1993): 15–17.

Waznis, B. "Materials Budget Allocation Methods at San Diego County Library." *Acquisitions Librarian* 20 (1998): 25–32.

Weston, C. V. "Breaking with the Past: Formula Allocation at Portland State University." *Serials Librarian* 45, no. 4 (2004): 43–53.

13
Deselection

Although most libraries have not had significant increases in purchasing power in recent years, even steady state acquisitions rates will, in time, fill up the available collection space. Given the lack of funding for collection building, it is not surprising that funds to expand an existing building (much less build a new facility) were, and are, the rare exceptions rather than the rule. A collection space "crunch" does not happen overnight; it is relatively easy to predict when the shelves will be at full capacity. Multiplying the number of linear feet of empty shelving by the average number of items per linear foot (ten to twelve for books) gives a fairly accurate estimate of when a major crisis will take place if something is not done. The "something" usually takes the form of deselection/weeding.

"Selection in reverse" is one way to think about weeding or collection control. Deselection, or weeding, is something many librarians thought about but seldom did in the past. However, this process is as important as the other steps in collection development and one that most libraries now engage in. Without an ongoing weeding program, a collection can quickly age and become difficult to use, which are important issues for public and school libraries. Although the major function of libraries is to acquire, store, and make available knowledge resources, it is obvious that no library can acquire and store the world's total production of knowledge resources for any current year.

Some of the world's largest libraries (the Library of Congress, the British Library, Bibliothèque Nationale, and others) do acquire the most important items. Nevertheless, even these giants of the library world cannot do it all. Eventually, when they reach the limit of their growth, they confront, as the smallest library does, three alternatives: (1) acquire new physical facilities, (2) divide the collection (which also requires space), or (3) weed the collection (which may or may not require new space). Only with new, adequate storage area can a librarian avoid selecting items for relocation.

The need to find space for collections is a problem as old as libraries themselves. One of the earliest references to the problem in the United States was a letter from Thomas Hollis to Harvard College's Board of Governors in 1725. He wrote, "If you want more room for modern books, it is easy to remove the less useful into a more remote place, but do not sell them as they are devoted."[1] More than 100 years passed before Harvard followed Hollis' advice; today, like most major research libraries as well as many medium-sized academic libraries, remote storage is part of everyday collection development activities at Harvard.

What is Deselection/Weeding?

H. F. McGraw defined *weeding* (called *stock relegation* in the United Kingdom) as "the practice of discarding or transferring to storage excess copies, rarely used books, and materials no longer of use."[2] He defined *purging* as "officially withdrawing a volume (all entries made for a particular book have been removed from library records) from a library collection because it is unfit for further use or is no longer needed."[3] The word *purging* applies more to the library's files than to items in the collection. Libraries seldom destroy purged items. Slote's definition of *weeding*, from the fourth edition of his book, is "removing the noncore collection from the primary collection area [open stack area]."[4] (The topic of records retention is addressed on the CD accompanying this text.)

Disposal takes several forms: exchange programs, Friends of the Library book sales, or sale to an out-of-print dealer for credit against future purchases. Occasionally, the material goes into a recycling program. The result is that a user who may later request a purged item will have to use interlibrary loan to secure a copy.

Storing, in contrast, retains the item at a second level of access. Second-level access normally is not open to the client and is frequently some distance from the library. Most second-level access storage systems house the materials as compactly as possible to maximize storage capacity. Compact shelving for low-use material is coming into widespread use as libraries attempt to gain maximum storage from existing square footage. Generally, a staff member retrieves the desired item from the storage facility for the user. Depending on the storage unit's location and the library's policy, the time lapse between request and receipt ranges from a few minutes to several days. Nevertheless, this arrangement is normally faster than interlibrary loan.

Before implementing a deselection program, the collection development staff should review deselection policies and goals. This review should include an analysis of the present staffing situation, consideration of alternative approaches, the feasibility of a weeding program in terms of other library operations, user interest and cooperation in such a project, types of materials collected, and cost. Some of the data for the program should come from collection evaluation projects that the selection officers and others undertake on a regular basis. An active (i.e., ongoing) deselection program should be part of the library's collection development policy, which will help the library avoid crisis deselection projects.

Collection policies, if properly prepared, help reduce space problems by controlling growth. Nevertheless, the time eventually comes when collection space no longer accommodates additional material. As mentioned earlier, when this happens, some hard, costly decisions confront the library:

build a new building, split the collection and use remote storage, or reduce the collection size. All three alternatives involve time-consuming and expensive processes. A policy of continuous deselection is more effective in the long run. Lazy librarians, like lazy gardeners, will find that the weeding problem only gets larger the longer they wait to do the job.

One of collection development's proverbs is that one person's trash is someone else's treasure. This is the fundamental problem confronting collection development staffs every day. When the library bases its collection building on current user needs, deselection can be a major activity, because those needs change.

Some years ago, in *Current Contents*, Eugene Garfield noted that weeding a library is like examining an investment portfolio. Investment advisers know that people do not like to liquidate bad investments. Just like frustrated tycoons, many librarians cannot face the fact that some of their guesses have gone wrong. They continue to throw good money after bad, hoping, like so many optimistic stockbrokers, that their bad decisions will somehow be undone. After paying for a journal for ten years, they rationalize that maybe someone will finally use it in the eleventh or twelfth year.[5]

Deselection by Type of Library

Because different types of libraries have significantly different clientele and goals, they approach deselection from different points of view. Although the basic problems, issues, and methods of deselection apply to all libraries, variations occur in how they select the weeds and what they do with the weeds after pulling them.

Public Libraries

Most public libraries are primarily supplying materials that meet the current needs and interests of a diverse community of users and in most cases have limited collections that are of long-term preservation concern. In the public library, user demand is the important factor influencing selection and deselection. Therefore, materials no longer of interest or use to the public are candidates for storage or disposal, which is the more typical outcome. Usually, only large municipal public libraries consider storage, because their collections include research materials. As for discarding, a public library rule of thumb is that collections should completely turn over once every ten years. Actual practice probably falls far short of that goal. Storage, when undertaken, usually involves separating little-used books from the high-use working collection and discarding duplicates, worn-out volumes, and obsolete material. Some people claim that a collection containing many items of little interest is less useful, because high-demand items are not readily visible or accessible. Costs involved in maintaining a large collection are also a consideration.

Certainly, there are differences due to size. Small and branch public libraries generally focus on high-demand materials, with little or no expectation that they will have preservation responsibilities. (An exception would be in the area of local history, where the library may be the only place one might expect to find such material.) Large public libraries have different responsibilities that often include housing and maintaining research collections. Thus, they have to consider a wider range of issues, more like those confronting academic libraries, when undertaking a deselection program.

Sometimes a deselection project can have unexpected results; an example was the Free Library of Philadelphia. In chapter 12, we noted that auditors expect to find items purchased still available. When the Philadelphia city controller's office conducted its review of the library, it concluded that the library was in violation of the city charter by "destroying hundreds of thousands of books." Although the report acknowledged that weeding was a generally accepted practice in libraries, it also stated that "this practice had gone awry."[6] At issue was the library's failure to try to find takers for the worn books it had withdrawn (admittedly, the numbers involved were substantial—360,000 volumes).

An interesting 2002 survey of North American public libraries' weeding practices[7] indicated that they are committed to the process and engage in it frequently. Over 60 percent weed on some type of schedule, while 33 percent do so on an irregular basis (294 libraries in Canada and the United States responded to the survey). Many respondents noted that if they did not weed on a regular basis, their space problems would become insurmountable. The five top reasons for weeding, in rank order, were (1) accuracy/currency of information, (2) physical condition, (3) space needs, (4) usage history, and (5) duplicate copy. Maintaining useful collection(s) and space considerations were the underlying factors for the weeding activities.

Two books are especially useful in planning public library weeding projects: Stanley J. Slote's *Weeding Library Collections* (actually this book can be considered the book for planning and implementing a deselection project in any type of library) and Belinda Boon and Joseph P. Segal's *The CREW Method: Expanded Guidelines for Collection Evaluation and Weeding for Small and Medium-Sized Public Libraries*.[8] Both works emphasize the use of circulation data, with Slote's system relying on circulation data (shelf-life) to identify candidates for weeding. Boon and Segal's system uses age of the publication, circulation data, and several subjective elements labeled as MUSTIE (M = misleading, U = ugly [worn out], S = superseded, T = trivial, I = irrelevant to your needs, and E = available elsewhere). The word CREW in the title represents Continuous Review Evaluation and Weeding. Ideas and methods described in both books are useful in all types of small libraries, especially school media centers.

Special Libraries

The category "special libraries" encompasses such a range of libraries as to make the category almost meaningless. Nevertheless, special libraries have to exercise the most stringent deselection programs, because of strict limits on collection size, usually the result of fixed amounts of storage space. Paula Strain examined the problem of periodical storage and cost of industrial floor space and found, not surprisingly, that the cost is so high that libraries must make efficient use of each square foot.[9] The special library must operate with the businessperson's eye toward economy and efficiency. Also, the collections of such libraries usually consist of technical material, much of it serial in character and often with a rapid and regular rate of obsolescence, at least for the local users.

Not surprisingly, the major concern of special libraries is meeting the current needs of clients. In such a situation, deselection is easier because of comparatively straightforward and predictable use patterns, the small size and homogeneous nature of the clientele, and the relatively narrow service goals for the library. Deselection takes place with little hesitation because costs and space are prime considerations. Many of the bibliometric measures described earlier can be valuable in establishing deselection programs in special libraries. A book addressing the special requirements of weeding in some types of special libraries and worth reviewing, is Ellis Mount's *Weeding of Collections in Sci-Tech Libraries*.[10] In addition, an equally noteworthy article describing an actual special library weeding project is Richard Hulser's "Weeding in a Corporate Library as Part of a Collection Management Program."[11]

Academic Libraries

Traditionally, the purposes of the academic research library have been to select, acquire, organize, preserve (this has had special emphasis), and make available the full record of human knowledge. Collection development officers in these institutions seldom view demand as a valid measure of an item's worth. Potential or long-term research value takes highest priority. This being said, why are deselection programs part of academic library collection development?

The role of the college and university library is evolving. Whenever librarians discuss the changing role, they cite the information explosion as one cause. It is clear to most collection development staffs that it is futile to expect any one institution to locate and acquire all of the printed matter that comes into existence. Nor can they organize it, house it, or make it readily accessible to their public. No one person can manage to absorb all the relevant material that would be available, even if libraries could collect and preserve everything.

Although academic libraries have a slightly better track record of securing funding for additions to their buildings or even occasionally a new building, they, too, face finite collection space and a mission goal of preserving information resources. Thus, deselection has become a part of the academic library life cycle. The difference between public and academic library weeding projects is that the bulk of the academic "weeds" go into some type of lower-cost storage unit either on or off campus.

There are several options for such storage (most of these are not open to the public). Usually, the first storage efforts involve maintaining the material in call number order in stacks that have narrower aisles than required for open/public access. Such an approach does not gain much storage capacity and is quickly followed by some type of "high-density shelving"— shelving mounted on rails which allows one to "open" an aisle where needed. (E.g., instead of devoting floor space to an area of stack ranges with six aisles with public access spacing, with compact shelving one could add five ranges with just one aisle.) Such systems require floors that can carry the extra weight, which in older facilities probably means basements or areas that are "on grade." Also, they are not inexpensive, especially if one goes with the electronic system with safety floors. Using such systems can increase storage capacity by 40 percent or more depending on the number of aisles one can eliminate. Often the space needs are such that maintaining call number order is too costly, and fixed location and size become the shelving method. Maximum "high density" storage units (automated warehousing systems) are now being designed into many new academic library buildings. In these systems, materials are stored in bins that are retrieved by mechanical means and are not stored in a particular order. The item barcode is linked to a bin barcode, and the bin is retrieved by the system when a request for a specific item is placed. Two examples of such systems include the Automated Storage and Retrieval System at California State University, Northridge (<http://library.csun.edu/asrs.html>), and Sonoma State University's (<http://libweb.sonoma.edu/about/ars.html>) Automated Retrieval System.

Naturally, such high-density systems are expensive, especially the automated retrieval and the electronic compact shelving systems. However, their cost is always less than that of constructing traditional open-access shelving space.

When compact shelving is closed to the public, one has the option of changing how one houses the stored material. (Usually, the library attempts to use on-campus options before going with off-campus storage.[12]) It is possible to gain an extra 40 to 50 percent storage capacity by shelving the material by size in a "fixed location" arrangement—that is, not in call number order. That type of plan would require additional shelves but would delay having to move materials off campus.

Off-campus options range from constructing facilities designed for housing collections, to leasing existing commercial space, to storing the material in a commercial documents storage company. All the options are currently in use by one or more academic libraries. (LMU uses on-campus compact storage as well as having 30 percent of the collection at a commercial documents storage company.)

Deselection for storage is somewhat easier than for purging, but in either case one can expect to have some unhappy users. Even waiting only 48 to 72 hours for an item is "too long" for some people, especially students who waited until the last minute to do their assignment(s).

School Media Centers

School libraries and media centers employ highly structured collection development practices. In most schools and school districts, the media center expends its funds with the advice of a committee consisting of teachers, administrators, librarians, and, occasionally, parents. The need to coordinate collection development with curriculum needs is imperative. Typically, media centers lack substantial floor space for collections. Thus, when there is a major shift in the curriculum (new areas added and old ones dropped), the library must remove most of the old material. To some degree, the media center's deselection problems are fewer because there are usually other community libraries or a school district central media center that can serve as backup resources.

In addition to the Slote and Segal books, two excellent articles about weeding school media collections are Anita Gordon's "Weeding: Keeping up with the Information Explosion" and the Calgary Board of Education, Educational Media Team's "Weeding the School Library Media Collection."[13] Gordon's article, though short, provides a good illustration of how one may use some standard bibliographies (e.g., *Senior High Catalog*) in a deselection program. The Calgary article provides a detailed, step-by-step method for weeding the school collection.

A very interesting website for school libraries is "Weed of the Month Club"—<http://www.sunlink.ucf.edu/weed>. It is designed to assist K–12 library media specialists weed their collection a little at a time. Each month a subject section is selected for weeding, such as "Presidential Elections" or "Short Stories." It would appear this site could also be useful for public libraries.

Reasons for Deselecting

Four reasons for implementing a deselection program appear regularly in the literature:

- to save space;
- to improve access;
- to save money; and
- to make room for new materials.

Additionally, libraries may engage in deselection activities as a result of acquiring online resources, simultaneously addressing several of the items listed above.

Do theory and practice concerning space-saving coincide? Definitely! Compact storage systems save space. The conventional rule of thumb allows 15 volumes per square foot (500,000 volumes would require more than 33,000 square feet). A compact shelving system using a sliding shelf arrangement can store 500,000 volumes in slightly more than 14,000 square feet (an average of about 35 volumes per square foot)—a savings of more than 50 percent. Using a rail system of moving ranges, such as one provided by Spacesaver (<http://www.spacesaver.com/>), some libraries achieve savings of more than 80 percent. The following are some approximate cost/space factors:

	Volumes per Square Foot	Cost per Volume
Standard shelving	10–15 vols.	$11.00
Compact shelving	20–30 vols.	$ 4.00
Automated retrieval	175–250 vols.	$ 2.50

Thus, one can lower the unit cost for stored items by using some form of high-density storage. (The cost cited covers only the building and shelving, not ongoing operational expenses.)

One basic theme of this book is that libraries exist to provide service. Archival libraries provide service, so our discussion naturally includes them, as they, too, eventually run out of space. However, service and size frequently do not go together. Anyone who has used a major research library knows that it takes time and effort to locate desired items. Often, such a library is the only location for certain materials, which is clearly an important service. However, few people claim that such libraries are easy to use. Most people still like everything to be convenient and easy to use. Thus, it is possible for a smaller, well-weeded collection to provide better service than a larger collection—as long as the smaller collection contains popular items. One interesting fact is that shelf location does seem to affect usage patterns—books on the middle shelves have higher circulation than those on the top or bottom shelf.

Does deselection improve access? Here theory and practice start diverging. Some staff members and users give enthusiastically positive answers. Others give equally definite negative responses. For those who require quick, easy access to high-use, current materials, the thoughtfully maintained collection becomes the ideal. However, for older, seldom-used materials housed in a remote storage facility, it may take some time to determine whether the library even owns the item, in addition to the time needed to retrieve it. Thus, the answer to the question of whether weeding improves access is sometimes yes, sometimes no.

Finally, does weeding maintain currency? Here the answer is probably yes with a big "if." It does so only so long as the deselection is ongoing, at least once a year. Theory and reality can be far apart in terms of cost saving. It may delay building a new library, but the delay comes at a cost. As indicated, the cost per volume stored is usually lower using a compact storage system. However, one should consider several other important costs. The process of weeding probably adds to the library's operational costs.

For example, it is possible to quickly reduce the size of a collection by some arbitrary figure (5,000 volumes) or percentage (20 percent). Just withdrawing the items from the shelves does not, however, complete the process. Staff must also change all the public and internal records to reflect the new status of the items. Although online catalogs and databases allow rapid record updating, there are still labor costs to consider.

In addition to the cost of record modification, one must consider:

- the cost of deciding which items to remove;
- the cost of collecting and transporting them to their new location; and
- the cost of retrieving items when needed.

Even if the storage system is less expensive per volume than conventional stacks, these costs can quickly mount.

Another cost, often overlooked, is the cost to users. Delayed access to desired materials carries a user cost, if nothing more than negative public relations. Almost every user wants items now, not in a few hours, much less days. In a research and development environment, retrieval delays may cost researchers valuable time and, perhaps, cost the organization money. Although it is difficult to determine or measure accurately, user cost should be taken into account when evaluating the costs of deselection.

An article by Jennifer Teper and Stephanie Atkins details the time and cost factors for deselection projects in an academic library setting.[14] Anyone planning a large-scale deselection and storage project should read the article.

Barriers to Deselection

A story that is of questionable veracity but that highlights the major deselection barrier concerns a collection development teacher. The teacher insisted that there was only one possible test to determine a person's suitability for becoming a collection development officer. Candidates would visit a doctor's office, where office staff would immediately take the candidate's blood pressure. The doctor would then hand the candidate a new book and tell the person to rip out one page and throw the book in a wastebasket. If the candidate's blood pressure rose above the initial reading, he or she would fail the test. True or not, the story does emphasize one of the most significant barriers to deselection—the psychological one.

Parents and teachers teach most of us to treat books and magazines with respect. In fact, we learn a great respect for anything printed. The idea of tearing pages or otherwise damaging a book goes against all we have learned. The problem for those engaged in deselection is that we are confusing the information contained in a package with the packaging. Some material becomes dated and should go, or people will act on incorrect information (prime examples are a loose-leaf service with superseding pages or dated medical or legal information). Travel directories and telephone books are other examples of materials that should be removed from the collection. Long-term value of other materials is less clear, and it is easy to find reasons to save them. In essence, our childhood training adds to the difficulties in removing items from a collection. If the library's goal is to purge rather than store the item, the problem is even greater.

Some of the more common excuses for not thinning a collection are

- lack of time;
- procrastination;
- fear of making a mistake;
- fear of adverse or embarrassing publicity; and
- fear of being called a "book burner."

These reasons are, to a greater or lesser extent, psychological. No matter how long the candidate for storage or removal has remained unused, a collection development officer's reaction is, "Someone will need it tomorrow." Also, an unused book or audiovisual title raises two questions: Why wasn't it used? and Why did the library buy it? Like anyone else, collection officers are reluctant to admit to making mistakes. The possibility of erroneously discarding some important items always exists. But to use fear of making a mistake as the reason for not engaging in deselection is inexcusable.

Another barrier, which is political as well as psychological, is created by users and governing boards. An academic library staff may feel that it needs to institute a weeding and storage program but fails to do so because of possible faculty opposition. If experience is any indication, one can count on people's being in favor of removing the deadwood—but not in their areas of interest.

Sometimes, librarians are reluctant to suggest deselection because they assume that there will be opposition from faculty, staff, general users, board members, or others. Often there will be opposition. However, if no one raises the issue, there is no chance of gaining user support. The possibility also exists that the assumed opposition will never materialize and that users from whom one least expects help turn out to be strong supporters. This is especially true when the space problems reach crisis status and there will be no room for new materials. Fear of possible political consequences has kept libraries from proposing a deselection program until the crisis stage, when projects become complex and very costly.

Loyola Marymount University's library has had to undertake several extensive deselection projects over the past eight years as major problems arose in getting funding for a new building. The most recent project added all bound journals to a remote storage facility that already contained 82,000 books. The librarians responsible for collection development had solid working relationships with the academic departments and so had little trouble gaining support for the project as everyone awaited the new building. Gaining active participation in the book deselection process was another matter. To gain faculty involvement, the librarians told them that a book that circulated at least four times would be returned to the on-campus collection. As an additional incentive, the librarians warned the faculty that, after a certain date, the librarians would decide what to store and what to discard. Every department claimed that nothing in its subject area should be discarded.

Related to the political barrier is the problem of size and prestige. Many librarians, library boards, and users rate libraries by size: the bigger the better. This brings us back to the epigraph of this book: "No library of one million volumes can be all BAD!" Quantity does not ensure quality. Collecting everything and throwing away nothing are much easier than selecting and deselecting with care. Librarians risk no political opposition, their prestige remains high, and only the taxpayers and users pay the price of maintaining everything the library ever acquired.

Practical barriers to deselection also exist. Time can be a practical as well as a psychological barrier. The processes of identifying suitable deselection criteria, developing a useful program, and selling that program require significant amounts of time. Beyond those steps, time is required for staff training, as is time to identify and pull the candidate items, to change the records, and, finally, to dispose of the weeds. (LMU estimates indicated that the library committed a minimum of 2.5 FTE (full-time equivalent) staff [from an FTE of 39.5] for ten months to its deselection project. That estimate covers all staff time; no staff member was full-time on the project.)

With a small library staff, it is difficult to mount a major deselection project because there are too many things to do with too few people. Starting a program is, inevitably, a major project for any size library. After completing the first project, the library should establish an ongoing deselection procedure and incorporate it into the normal work flow. The ideal approach to a major project is to seek special funds and temporary staff to support the work.

Occasionally, libraries encounter legal barriers. Although not a common problem, when it does arise, it is time-consuming. The problem arises in publicly supported libraries where regulations may govern the disposal of any material purchased with public funds, as noted earlier in the chapter. In some cases, the library must sell the material, even if only to a pulp dealer. Any disposal that gives even a hint of government book burning will cause public relations problems; this stems from general attitudes toward printed materials. The library should do all it legally can to avoid any such appearance.

Deselection Criteria

Deselection is not an overnight process, and it is not a function that one performs in isolation from other collection development activities. Some of the most important issues are library goals, the availability of acquisition funds for new titles, the relationship of a particular book to others on that subject, the degree to which the library functions as an archive, and potential future usefulness of an item. Only when one considers all the factors can one develop a successful deselection program.

After the staff recognizes the need for a deselection project, lists of criteria can help in the deselection process. H. F. McGraw developed the following, fairly comprehensive list:

- duplicates;
- unsolicited and unwanted gifts;
- obsolete books, especially science;
- superseded editions;
- books that are infested, dirty, shabby, worn out, juvenile (which wear out quickly), and so forth;
- books with small print, brittle paper, and missing pages;
- unused, unneeded volumes of sets; and
- periodicals with no indexes.[15]

The mere fact that a book is a duplicate or worn out does not necessarily mean that one should discard it. Past use of the item should be the deciding factor. Also, consider whether it will be possible to find a replacement copy. The books and articles cited earlier provide additional criteria.

Three broad categories of deselection criteria exist, at least in the literature: physical condition, qualitative worth, and quantitative worth. Physical condition, for most researchers, is not an effective criterion. In most cases, poor physical condition results from overuse rather than nonuse. Thus, one replaces or repairs books in poor physical condition. (There is little indication in the literature on deselection that poor condition includes material with brittle paper. As discussed in chapter 16, brittle paper is a major problem.) Consequently, if the library employs physical condition as a criterion, it will identify only a few items, unless brittle paper is part of the assessment process.

Qualitative worth as a criterion for deselection is highly subjective. Because of variations in individual value judgments, researchers do not believe that this is an effective deselection method. Getting people to take the time to review the material is difficult. As noted earlier, LMU's library staff were only moderately successful in enlisting faculty input. Also, the faculty did not always agree about what to reclass and what to store, and few faculty recommended that the library discard anything. When all is said and done, the same factors that govern the buying decision should govern deselection judgments.

Any group assessment will be slow. Researchers have shown that a library can achieve almost the same outcome it would from specialists' reviewing the material by using an objective measure, such as past circulation or use data, if one wishes to predict future use. Also, the deselection process is faster and cheaper when past-use data are available.

C. A. Seymour summed up the issues regarding deselection as follows:

When the usefulness and/or popularity of a book has been questioned, the librarian, if the policy of the library permits discarding, must decide

a. If the financial and physical resources are present or available to provide continuing as well as immediate housing and maintenance of the book;

b. If the book can be procured, within an acceptably short time, from another library at a cost similar to, or lower than, the cost of housing and maintenance within the library;

c. If allowing the book to remain in the collection would produce a negative value.[16]

The problems that plague monograph weeding also apply to serials. A major difference, however, is that journals are not homogeneous in content. Another difference is that the amount of space required to house serial publications is greater than that required to house monographs. Thus, cost is often the determining factor in weeding (i.e., although there may be some requests for a particular serial, the amount of space that a publication occupies may not be economical or may not warrant retaining the full set in the collection). We have more to say about journals later in this chapter.

Criteria for
Deselection for Storage

Large libraries, particularly research libraries, deselect for storage rather than for discarding. These are two different processes. Often, criteria useful in making discard decisions do not apply to storage decisions. The primary objective of storage deselection is to maximize, by employing economical storage facilities, the amount of research material available to the user. The two main considerations for a storage program are: (1) What selection criteria are most cost-effective? and (2) How will the library store the items?

Although the project occurred more than forty years ago, the Yale University Library Selective Book Retirement Program still has value for today's deselection project planners. The project funding came from the Council on Library Resources, with the expectation that the results would be useful to other libraries, as they have proven to be. Project staff were to determine how best to cope with the problem of limited shelf space while continuing to build quality research collections and provide good service. The council outlined the following objectives for Yale in Yale's Selective Book Retirement Program:

a. to expedite the Yale University Library's Selective Book Retirement Program (from 20,000 to 60,000 volumes per year) and to extend it to other libraries on the campus;

b. to study (in collaboration with the faculty) the bases of selection for retirement for various subjects and forms of material;

c. to study the effects of the Program on library use and research by faculty and graduate and undergraduate students;

d. to ascertain what arrangements may compensate for the loss of immediate access caused by the program;

e. to explore the possible effectiveness of the program toward stabilizing the size of the immediate-access collection; and

f. to publish for the use of other libraries the policies, procedures, and results thus discovered.[17]

According to the report, the project staff fulfilled all the objectives but "d."

The Yale staff based their decisions about which books to move to storage on several factors:

1. A study of books on the shelves.

2. Value of a title as subject matter.

3. A volume's importance historically in the field.

4. Availability of other editions.

5. Availability of other materials on the subject.

6. Use of a volume.

7. Physical condition.[18]

Clearly, the selection process depended upon the subjective judgment of individual librarians, some of whom were subject bibliography specialists. The librarians determined that general policies regarding weeding were easier to formulate than those that applied to specific fields; that it was easier to recommend weeding of specific titles than groups or kinds of books in specific fields; and that unanticipated mechanical problems greatly affected weeding procedures. These last problems included:

1. Lack of regularity in weeding (i.e., finding an adequate number of faculty and staff members and the time to keep the process going satisfactorily).

2. Diminishing returns over the long period (i.e., the longer the program existed, the more difficult the weeding process became).

3. The "Ever-Normal-Granary" theory (one of the purposes of the selective retirement program was to discover whether a library can control the growth of its collection by annually removing from the stacks the same number of volumes it adds). It was discovered that for the theory to be practical, either fragmentation into department libraries must occur, or the library administration must be willing to manage its collection and facilities solely on the principle of stabilization—neither of which Yale was willing to do.

4. Disagreement among weeders (i.e., the narrower viewpoint of faculty because of subject specialty versus the broader viewpoint of the librarian).[19]

Another unforeseen problem was a general feeling of discontent among faculty members and students. Neither group really understood the storage problem, and both objected to any change. Students particularly disliked the fact that they could not browse in the storage area. This problem will exist for most libraries embarking upon a storage project. After two or more such projects users come to understand the issues and are more supportive.

The Yale approach is labor-intensive and becomes more so over time. In response, academic libraries looked for methods that could help speed up the deselection process. In *Patterns in the Use of Books in Large Research Libraries*, Fussler and Simon reported some interesting ideas and statistical findings concerning the use factor in selective weeding of books for storage.[20] Although they recognized that frequency of circulation or use of books is not always an accurate measure of the importance of books in large research libraries, Fussler and Simon hoped to determine whether some statistical method could identify low-use books in research library collections. One of their goals was to sort the collection into high- and low-use materials. High-use items would remain in the local collection, and low-use items would go to a remote storage facility. They found that use and circulation data were effective for the first cut, that is, to identify potential materials. The final judgment of what to send to storage or discard remained with the collection development staff and other interested persons. Blindly following use data can create more problems than it solves.

Based on their data, Fussler and Simon concluded that past use of an item was the best predictor of future use. Given the nature of a large research library, they thought a fifteen- to twenty-year study period provided the best results, but a five-year period provided adequate data.

Fussler and Simon suggested that their methods would produce similar percentages of use in other libraries regardless of type, clientele, and collection size. They concluded that scholars at various institutions have similar reading interests. Finally, they identified three practical alternatives for selecting books for storage:

1. Judgment of one or a few expert selectors in a field.

2. An examination of past use of a book and/or its objective characteristics.

3. A combination of these two approaches.[21]

Of these alternatives, they concluded that an objective system (i.e., a statistical measure) ranks books more accurately in terms of probable value (future use) than does the subjective judgment of a single scholar in the field. They did recommend, however, that subject specialists and faculty review the candidate books identified using objective means before moving the books to remote storage. This is the most typical method for selecting materials for storage.

Many other deselection studies exist, and they all generally agree that deselection based on past-use data provides the most cost-effective results. Although most of the studies were from academic libraries, Stanley Slote found that the method also worked in public libraries. (A U.K. study by J. A. Urquhart and N. C. Urquhart has taken exception to these findings, especially for serials.[22]) Past use is a reasonable criterion if one is selecting for storage. However, the questions raised by the Urquharts indicate that librarians should go slowly in applying the past-use criterion when selecting items for purging.

Researchers have investigated almost every conceivable combination of objective criteria at one time or another in hope of finding the best. For example, they have examined language; date of publication; subject matter; frequency of citation; and listing in bibliographies, indexes, and abstracting services. Citation analysis and presence or absence of indexing or abstracting were, and are; most effective for print serials; however, e-journals are forcing libraries to rethink the use of indexing and abstracting as a useful tool for making deselection decisions.

An interesting method for deselecting periodicals is to calculate a density-of-use value. The method requires establishing a unit of space occupied (perhaps one linear foot of shelf space) for each periodical title. Next, one determines the number of uses the title receives during a fixed time (perhaps one month). A ranking of the titles by use will produce one list, whereas a ranking by space occupied will probably result in a different list. Because one common objective of deselection programs is cost-effective use of existing collection space, calculating a ratio of space occupied to use (density of use) will help determine which periodicals to move to storage. An interesting article about weeding journals in a special library environment is by Richard Hunt.[23]

McBride and Behm reported on a yearlong study of journal usage at Southern Illinois University, Edwardsville.[24] Their study had three purposes, to identify possible candidates for cancellation, storage, and high-use "core" journals. An article examining the role of e-journals and journal usage is by Betty Galbraith.[25] It highlights some of the challenges in getting useful data about e-resource usage patterns.

The preponderance of evidence points to the past-use criterion as the one most reliable for storage purposes. If the library has a circulation system that leaves a physical record of use in each book or in a database, one can easily collect the needed data. Today's automated circulation systems can provide detailed information about items, including frequency of circulation, class of borrower, use by class number, age of the item, language, and producer, as well as almost any other physical or intellectual content characteristic.

Although circulation data are as sound a predictor of future use as one can find, they rest upon several assumptions that staff must understand and accept. One assumption is that circulated use is proportional to in-house use. What that proportion is depends on local circumstances. Assumption two is that current use patterns are similar to past and future patterns. A third assumption is that statistically random samples provide an adequate base for determining use patterns. One known limitation of circulation data is that a few users can have a major impact on circulation (otherwise known as the 80/20 rule). Failure to take in-house use into account in a deselection program dependent on use data as the main selection criterion will have skewed results.

One factor to keep in mind is that the automated circulation systems now in use in many libraries will make it possible to collect valuable data for a project. With many systems, it is possible to collect data about in-house use by using a handheld reader and then downloading the data to the system. In the past, in-house use data were particularly time-consuming to collect. The fourth edition of Slote's book has an excellent chapter on using computer data in a deselection project.

Although the widespread use of e-resources is still in its "adolescent" stage, as costs escalate, decisions to drop some of these resources (purging) will have to take place. The literature on this topic is slim at the start of the 21st century but is likely to grow fairly quickly. Perhaps because e-books do not take up valuable shelf space, it is easy to ignore them. However, the same issues of currency and accuracy exist for virtual books as they do for physical books. Including e-books in an ongoing deselection program is one way to assure they receive the same level of attention as print books. One question about the value of usage data for e-books is how well the library promotes its e-book program. An article worth consulting that explores the weeding of e-books is by A. Paula Wilson.[26]

Summary

Deselection is an important part of a collection management program. All types of libraries have to engage in the activity at some time. Regardless of the setting, shelf space is finite unless one can secure funds to expand a facility as needed. Today when that expansion occurs, if it happens, more often than not it is away from the main library, which means there must be decisions made about what stays and goes from the primary facility. Thus, even with new space, deselection must still take place.

In 2002, ALA published the 2nd edition of *Guide to the Review of Library Collections, Preservation, Storage and Withdrawal*, a resource for deselection projects.[27] This work contains a very complete bibliography of relevant deselection articles and books and concludes with the following statement:

> An ongoing and systematic review of collections based on the library's collection policy and utilizing appropriate criteria and methodologies can optimize prime shelf space, save staff time by speeding retrieval and simplifying shelf maintenance, and enhance the usefulness of a library's collection.[28]

Notes

1.   Kenneth E. Carpenter, *The First 350 Years of the Harvard University Library* (Cambridge, MA: Harvard University Library, 1986), 122.

2.   H. F. McGraw, "Policies and Practices in Discarding," *Library Trends* 4 (January 1956): 270.

3.   Ibid.

4.   Stanley J. Slote, *Weeding Library Collections*, 4th ed. (Englewood, CO: Libraries Unlimited, 1997), 228.

5.   Eugene Garfield, "Weeding," *Current Contents* 15 (June 30, 1975): 26.

6.   Evan St. Lifer, "City Rebukes Philadelphia Library on Weeding Practices," *Library Journal* 121 (May 15, 1979): 12.

7.   Juris Dilevko and Lisa Gottlieb, "Weed to Achieve: A Fundamental Part of the Public Library Mission?" *Library Collections, Acquisitions & Technical Services* 27, no. 1 (Spring 2003): 73–96.

8.   Slote, *Weeding Library Collections*; Belinda Boon and Joseph P. Segal, *The CREW Method: Expanded Guidelines for Collection Evaluation and Weeding for Small and Medium-Sized Public Libraries* (Austin: Texas State Library, 1995).

9.   Paula M. Strain, "A Study of the Usage and Retention of Technical Periodicals," *Library Resources & Technical Services* 10 (Summer 1966): 295.

10.   Ellis Mount, ed., *Weeding of Collections in Sci-Tech Libraries* (New York: Haworth Press, 1986).

11.   Richard P. Hulser, "Weeding in a Corporate Library as Part of a Collection Management Program," *Science and Technology Libraries* 6 (Spring 1986): 1–9.

12.   Elka T. Shlomo, "Nicholson Baker Wasn't All Wrong: A Collection Development Policy for Remote Storage Facilities," *Acquisitions Librarian* 15, no. 30 (2003): 117–30.

13.   Anita Gordon, "Weeding: Keeping up with the Information Explosion," *School Library Journal* 30 (September 1983): 45–46; Calgary Board of Education, Educational Media Team, "Weeding the School Library Media Collection," *School Library Media Quarterly* 12 (Fall 1984): 419–24.

14.   Jennifer Hain Teper and Stephanie Atkins, "Time and Cost Analysis of Preparing and Processing Material for Off-Site Shelving at the University of Illinois at Urbana-Champaign Library," *Collection Management* 28, no. 4 (2003): 43–65.

15.   McGraw, "Policies and Practices in Discarding," 269–82.

16.   C. A. Seymour, "Weeding the Collection," *Libri* 22 (1972): 189.

17.   L. Ash, *Yale's Selective Book Retirement Program* (Hamden, CT: Archon, 1963), ix.

18.   Ibid., 66.

19.   Ibid.

20.   H. H. Fussler and J. L. Simon, *Patterns in the Use of Books in Large Research Libraries*, rev. ed. (Chicago: University of Chicago Press, 1969), 4.

21.   Ibid., 208.

22.   J. A. Urquhart and N. C. Urquhart, *Relegation and Stock Control in Libraries* (London: Oriel Press, 1976).

23.   Richard Hunt, "Journal Deselection in a Biomedical Research Library," *Bulletin of the Medical Library Association* 78 (January 1990): 45–48.

24.   Regina McBride and Kathlyn Behm, "A Journal Usage Study in an Academic Library: Evaluation of Selected Criteria," *Serials Librarian* 45, no. 3 (2003): 23–37.

25.   Betty Galbraith, "Journal Retention Decisions Incorporating Use-Statistics as a Measure of Value," *Collection Management* 27, no. 1 (2002): 79–90.

26.   A. Paula Wilson, "Weeding the E-Book Collection," *Public Libraries* 43, no. 3 (May–June 2004): 158–159.

27.   *Guide to the Review of Library Collections, Preservation, Storage and Withdrawal*, 2nd ed., ed. D. K. Lambert, W. Atkins, D. A. Litts, and L. H. Olley ([Chicago]: Association for Library Collections & Technical Services; Lanham, MD: Published in cooperation with Scarecrow Press, 2002).

28.   Ibid., 32.

Further Reading

Austin, B., and S. Seaman. "Temporary Remote Book Storage at the University of Colorado, Boulder Libraries." *Collection Management* 27, no. 1 (2002): 59–77.

———. "Establishing Materials Selection Goals for Remote Storage: A Methodology." *Collection Management* 27, nos. 3/4 (2002): 57–68.

Banks, J. "Weeding Book Collections in the Age of the Internet." *Collection Building* 21, no. 3 (2002): 113–19.

Bazirjiian, R. "Ethics of Library Discard Practices." In *Legal and Ethical Issues in Acquisitions*. Edited by K. Strauch and B. Strauch, 213–34. New York: Haworth Press, 1990.

Block, D. "Remote Storage in Research Libraries: A Microhistory." *Library Resources & Technical Services* 44, no. 4 (2000): 184–89.

Boss, R. W. "Automated Storage/Retrieval and Return/Sorting Systems." *PLA Tech-Notes*, June 2002, <http://www.ala.org/ala/pla/plapubs/technotes/asrsystems.htm>.

Bromann, J. "Letting Go: How One Librarian Weeded a Children's Magazine Collection." *School Library Journal* 48, no. 7 (July 2002): 44–46.

Cerny, R. "When Less Is More: Issues in Collection Development." *School Library Journal* 37, no. 3 (March 1991): 130–31.

Davis, V. R. "Weeding the Library Media Center Collection." *School Library Media Activities Monthly* 17, no. 7 (March 2001): 26–28.

Diodato, V. P., and F. Smith. "Obsolescence of Music Literature." *Journal of the American Society of Information Science* 44 (March 1993): 101–12.

Donovan, C. A. "Deselection and the Classics." *American Libraries* 26 (December 1995): 110–11.

Doylen, M. "Experiments in Deaccessioning." *American Archivist* 64 (Fall–Winter 2001): 350–62.

Drake, C. S. "Weeding of a Historical Society Library." *Special Libraries* 83 (Spring 1992): 86–91.

Enssle, H. R., and M. L. Wilde. "So You Have to Cancel Journals? Statistics That Help." *Library Collections, Acquisitions, & Technical Services* 26, no. 3 (2002): 259–81.

Fang, X. "A Study of the Problems of Aging Books in University Libraries." *Journal of the American Society of Information Science* 43 (August 1992): 501–5.

Farber, Evan I. "Books Not for College Libraries." *Library Journal* 122, no. 13 (August 1997): 44–45.

Harbour, D. "Collection Mapping." *Book Report* 20, no. 5 (March/April 2002): 6–11.

Hazen, D. "Selecting for Storage." *Library Resources & Technical Services* 44, no. 4 (2000): 176–83.

Hill, D. S. "Selling Withdrawn and Gift Books on eBay: Does It Make Sense?" *Journal of Interlibrary Loan, Document Delivery & Information Supply* 14, no. 2 (2003): 37–40.

Jacob, M. "Weeding the Fiction Collection: Or Should I Dump Peyton Place?" *Reference & User Services Quarterly* 40, no. 3 (Spring 2001): 234–39.

Jaguszewski, J. M., and L. K. Probst. "The Impact of Electronic Resources on Serial Cancellations and Remote Storage Decisions in Academic Research Libraries." *Library Trends* 48, no. 4 (Spring 2000): 799–820.

Kennedy, J. R., and G. Stockman. *The Great Divide: Challenges in Remote Storage*. Chicago: American Library Association, 1991.

Kerby, R. "Weeding Your Collection." *School Library Media Activities Monthly* 18, no. 2 (February 2002): 22.

Mount, E., ed. *Weeding of Collections in Sci-Tech Libraries*. New York: Haworth Press, 1986.

Oberhofer, C.M.A. "Information Use Value." *Information Processing and Management* 29 (September–October 1993): 587–600.

Pao, M. L., and A. J. Warner. "Depreciation of Knowledge." *Library Trends* 41, no. 4 (Spring 1993): 545–709.

Pongracz, S., G. D. Ellern, and N. Newsome. "Collection Development and Long-Term Periodicals Use Study." *Serials Review* 28, no. 1 (2002): 38–44.

Scigliano, M. "Serial Use in a Small Academic Library." *Serials Review* 26, no. 1 (2000): 43–53.

Shirato, L., Cogan, S., and S. G. Yee. "The Impact of an Automated Storage and Retrieval System on Public Services." *Reference Services Review* 29, no. 3 (2001): 253–61.

St. Lifer, E., and M. Rogers, "Jury Rules Corporate Library Willfully Destroyed Documents." *Library Journal* 118, no. 2 (February 1, 1993): 14.

Tobia, R. C. "Comprehensive Weeding of an Academic Health Sciences Collection: The Briscoe Library Experience." *Journal of the Medical Library Association* 90, no. 1 (January 2002): 94–98.

Triolo, V. A., and D. Bao. "A Decision Model for Technical Journal Deselection with an Experiment in Biomedical Communications." *Journal of the American Society for Information Science* 44 (April 1993): 148–60.

Tyler, D. C., and D. L. Pytlik Zillig. "Caveat Relocator: A Practical Relocation Proposal to Save Space and Promote Electronic Resources." *Technical Services Quarterly* 21, no. 1 (2003): 17–29.

Vogel, B. D. "The Adventures of Molly Keeper, a Cautionary Tale." *School Library Journal* 38 (September 1992): 136–42.

"Weeding Media " *School Library Workshop* 14 (November 1993): 8–9.

Wezeman, F. "Psychological Barriers to Weeding." *ALA Bulletin* 52 (September 1958): 637–39.

14
Evaluation

In the last edition of this text, we opened this particular chapter with a reference to a statement by Sheila Intner and Elizabeth Futas that the 1990s was the decade of evaluation.[1] Whether it was *the* decade of evaluation/assessment may be debatable; however, an annotated bibliography on the topic by Thomas Nisonger[2] suggests it was a decade of very, very high interest in the subject. Nisonger started updating his prior bibliography on academic library collection evaluation but found that the volume of literature on the topic for all types of libraries published in the 1990s was so large it warranted a separate work. His update covers the years 1992 to 2002 and includes over 600 entries!

If the 1990s was not the decade of evaluation, what is not debatable is that *evaluation*, *assessment*, *outcomes*, and *accountability* were words and activities that many librarians were, and are, addressing. Certainly, accreditation bodies were, and are, demanding evidence that institutional expenditures were more than just expenditures; that is, they wanted to know the result of spending the funds. Long statistical lists of books added, journal subscriptions started, and items circulated were no longer acceptable. Accreditation visiting teams started asking questions like, "So you added x thousands of books, have x hundreds of subscriptions, and your users check out an average of x items per month. Have you any evidence that this has made any difference and helped meet the institutional mission and goals?" They also asked, "What evidence of quality do you have, and how do you and your institution define that concept?"

Answering such questions is difficult unless you have systematically collected a body of data with such questions in mind. What this means is that some of the measures of evaluation we have employed in the past, such as collection size, will not be acceptable in some circumstances when outcome and accountability are at issue. Certainly, the questions asked go beyond just our collections, both physical and virtual, but carefully evaluating our collections will help us address the broader issues (such as, Is the library worth the money expended on it?).

What are the strengths of the collection? How effectively have we spent our collection development monies? How useful are the collections to the service community? How do our collections compare to those of our peers? These are but a few of the questions one may answer by conducting a collection evaluation assessment project. Evaluation completes the collection development cycle and brings one back to needs assessment activities. Although the term *evaluation* has several definitions, there is a common element in all of them related to placing a value or worth on an object or activity. Collection evaluation involves both objects and activities, as well as quantitative and qualitative values.

Hundreds of people have written about collection evaluation—Stone, Clapp-Jordan, Evans, Bonn, Lancaster, Mosher, McGrath, Broadus, and Hall, to name a few. Though the basics remain unchanged, the application of the basics has become more and more sophisticated over the years. Computers make it possible to handle more data, as well as a wider variety of data. Bibliographic and numeric databases can provide valuable data that in the past would have been exceedingly difficult, if not impossible, to obtain (e.g., see Metz's older, but still interesting, *Landscape of Literatures*[3]). Bibliographic utilities, such as OCLC, and products for assessing and comparing collections are more widespread today than in the past. Despite the assistance of technology and increasingly sophisticated systems of evaluation, as Betty Rosenburg, a longtime teacher of collection development, repeatedly stated, the best tool for collection evaluation is an intelligent, cultured, experienced selection officer with a sense of humor and a thick skin. Because there are so many subjective and qualitative elements involved in collection development, Rosenburg's statement is easy to understand and appreciate. Although this chapter will not help one develop the personal characteristics she identified as important, it does outline the basic methods available for conducting an evaluation project and provides a few examples.

Background

Before undertaking any evaluation, the library must carefully define the project's purposes and goals. One definition of *evaluation* is a judgment as to the value of X, based on a comparison, implicit or explicit, with some known value, Y. If the unknown and the (presumably) known values involve abstract concepts that do not lend themselves to quantitative measurement, there are bound to be differences of opinion regarding the value. There are many criteria for determining the value of a book or of an entire collection: economic, moral, religious, aesthetic, intellectual, educational, political, and social, for example. The value of an item or a collection fluctuates depending on which yardstick one employs. Combining several measures is effective as long as there is agreement as to their relative weight. So many subjective factors come into play in the evaluation process that one must work through the issues before starting. One important benefit of having the goals defined and the criteria for the values established ahead of time is that interpretation of the results is much easier. It may also help to minimize differences of opinion about the results.

Libraries and information centers, like other organizations, want to know how they compare with similar organizations. Comparative data can be useful, but they can also be misleading. Like all other aspects of evaluation, comparative data present significant problems of definition and interpretation. What, for example, does library A gain by comparing itself with library B, except, perhaps, an inferiority complex—or a delusion as to its own status? Without question, some libraries are better than others, and comparisons may well be important in discovering why this is so. Two key issues in interpreting comparisons are that (1) one assumes a close approximation of needs among the comparative groups and (2) one assumes the existence of standards or norms that approximate optimum conditions. Neither assumption has a solid basis in reality. If the library or its parent organization is considering starting a new service or program, comparative data from libraries already supporting similar services can provide valuable planning information. Though comparisons are interesting and even helpful in some respects, one should be cautious in interpreting the significance of the findings.

Robert Downs, an important historical figure in the field of evaluation, noted:

> From the internal point of view, the survey, if properly done, gives one an opportunity to stand off and get an objective look at the library, to see its strengths, its weaknesses, the directions in which it has been developing, how it compares with other similar libraries, how well the collection is adapted to its clientele, and provides a basis for future planning.[4]

Downs believed that, in addition to their internal value, surveys are an essential step in preparing for library cooperative acquisitions projects and resource sharing.

Organizations conduct evaluations for several reasons, including

- to develop an intelligent, realistic acquisitions program based on a thorough knowledge of the existing collection;
- to justify increased funding demands or for particular subject allocations; and
- to increase the staff's familiarity with the collection.

It is possible to divide collection evaluation purposes into two broad categories: internal reasons and external reasons. The following lists provide a variety of questions or purposes for each category.

Internal Reasons

Collection development needs

- What is the true scope of the collections (i.e., what is the subject coverage)?
- What is the depth of the collections (i.e., what amount and type of material constitute the collection)?
- How does the service community use the collection (i.e., what are the circulation and use within the library)?
- What is the collection's monetary value? (This must be known for insurance and capital assessment reasons.)

- What are the strong areas of the collection (in quantitative and qualitative terms)?
- What are the weak areas of the collection (in quantitative and qualitative terms)?
- What problems exist in the collection policy and program?
- What changes should be made in the existing program?
- How well are collection development officers carrying out their duties?
- Provide data for possible cooperative collection development programs.
- Provide data for deselection (weeding) projects.
- Provide data for formal cancellation projects.
- Provide data to determine the need for a full inventory.

Budgetary needs

- Assist in determining allocations needed to strengthen weak areas.
- Assist in determining allocations needed to maintain areas of strength.
- Assist in determining allocations needed for retrospective collection development.
- Assist in determining overall allocations.

External Reasons

Local institutional needs

- Is the library's performance marginal, adequate, or above average?
- Is the budget request for materials reasonable?
- Does the budget provide the appropriate level of support?
- Is the library comparable to others serving similar communities?
- Are there alternatives to space expansion (e.g., weeding)?
- Is the collection outdated?
- Is there sufficient coordination in the collection program (i.e., does the library really need all those separate collections)?
- Is the level of duplication appropriate?
- Is the cost/benefit ratio reasonable?

Extraorganizational needs

- Provide data for accreditation groups.
- Provide data for funding agencies.
- Provide data for various networks, consortia, and other cooperative programs.
- Provide data to donors about collection needs.

Having undertaken numerous evaluation projects, as staff members and consultants, the authors have found that these reasons inevitably surface in one form or another. Not all the reasons apply to every type of information environment, but most have wide applicability.

After the library or evaluators establish the purposes for carrying out the evaluation, the next step is determining the most effective methods of evaluation. A number of techniques are available, and the choice depends, in part, upon the purpose and depth of the evaluation process. George Bonn's article "Evaluation of the Collection" lists five general approaches to evaluation:

1. Compiling statistics on holdings.

2. Checking standard lists—catalogs and bibliographies.

3. Obtaining opinions from regular users.

4. Examining the collection directly.

5. Applying standards [which involves the use of various methods mentioned earlier], listing the library's document delivery capability, and noting the relative use of a particular group.[5]

Most of the methods developed in the recent past draw on statistical techniques. Some of the standards and guidelines of professional associations and accrediting agencies employ statistical approaches and formulas that give evaluators some quantitative indicators of what is adequate. Standards, checklists, catalogs, and bibliographies are other tools of the evaluator.

ALA's *Guide to the Evaluation of Library Collections*[6] divides assessment methods into collection-centered measures and use-centered measures. Within each category are a number of specific evaluative methods. The *Guide* summarizes the major techniques currently used to evaluate information collections. These methods focused on print resources, but there are elements that one can also employ in the evaluation of electronic resources.

Collection-Centered

- Checking list, bibliographies, and catalogs;
- expert opinion;
- comparative use statistics; and
- collection standards.

Use-Centered

- Circulation studies;
- user opinion/studies;
- analysis of ILL statistics;
- citation studies;
- in-house use studies;
- shelf availability;

- simulated use studies; and
- document delivery tests.

Each method has its advantages and disadvantages. Often it is best to employ several methods that will counterbalance one another's weaknesses. We will touch on each of these; however, the use-centered methods all share the same broad characteristics as circulation studies. Each is valuable in its own way to evaluate some aspect of use, but due to space limitations, we will not address all of the variations. One should also consult items listed in the Notes and Further Readings sections before planning an evaluation project.

Collection-Centered Methods

List Checking

The checklist method is an old standby for evaluators. It can serve a variety of purposes. Used alone or in combination with other techniques— usually with the goal of coming up with some numerically based statement, such as "We (or they) have X percentage of the books on this list"—it provides objective data. Consultants frequently check holdings against standard bibliographies (or suggest that the library do it) and report the results. Checklists allow the evaluator to compare the library's holdings against one or more standard lists of materials for a subject area (*Business Journals of the United States*), for a type of library (*Books for College Libraries*), or for a class of user (*Best Books for Junior High Readers*).

When asked to assess a collection, we use checklists as part of the process, if appropriate lists are available. Whenever possible, we ask a random sample of subject experts at the institution to identify one or two bibliographies or basic materials lists in their specialty that they believe would be reasonable to use in evaluating the collection. The responses, or lack of responses, provide information about each respondent's knowledge of publications in her or his field and indicate the degree of interest in the library collection. When appropriate, we also use accreditation checklists, if there is doubt about the collection's adequacy.

As collections increase in size, there is less concern with checking standard bibliographies. However, it is worthwhile for selectors to occasionally take time to review some of the best-of-the-year lists published by various associations. Such reviews will help selectors spot titles missed during the year and can serve as a check against personal biases playing too great a role in the selection process. Selectors quickly identify items not selected and can take whatever steps are necessary to remedy the situation. Often such lists appear in selection aids; it takes little extra time to review the list to conduct a minievaluation.

Self-surveys by the library staff frequently make use of checklist methods. M. Llewellyn Raney conducted the first checklist self-survey, at least the first reported in the literature, in 1933 for the University of Chicago libraries. This survey used 300 bibliographies to check the entire collection for the purpose of determining future needs. There is little question that this pioneering effort demonstrated the value of using checklists to thoroughly examine the total collection.

Obviously, one can use a variety of checklists in any situation. The major factor determining how many lists to employ is the amount of time available for the project. Today's OPACs make list-checking a faster process, but it still requires a substantial amount of time. Many evaluators have their favorite standard lists, but there is a growing use of highly specialized lists in an effort to check collection depth as well as breadth. Most evaluators advocate using serials and media checklists in addition to book checklists. Large research libraries (academic, public, or special) seldom use the basic lists; instead, they rely on subject bibliographies and specially compiled lists. One of the quality control checks supported by the RLG/ARL in the past is a conspectus project using a specially prepared checklist technique (see chapter 3 for discussion of the conspectus). Specially prepared bibliographies are probably the best checklist method. However, preparing such lists takes additional time, and many libraries are unwilling to commit that much staff effort to the evaluation process.

Using any checklist requires certain assumptions; one is that the selected list reflects goals and purposes that are similar to those of the checking institution. Normally, unless an examination of a collection is thorough, the checklist method merely samples the list. Thus, the data are only as good as the sampling method employed.

The shortcomings of the checklist technique for evaluation are many, and eight criticisms appear repeatedly:

- Title selection was for specific, not general, use.
- Almost all lists are selective and omit many worthwhile titles.
- Many titles have little relevance for a specific library's community.
- Lists may be out-of-date.
- A library may own many titles that are not on the checklist but that are as good as the titles on the checklist.
- Interlibrary loan service carries no weight in the evaluation.
- Checklists approve titles; there is no penalty for having poor titles.
- Checklists fail to take into account special materials that may be important to a particular library.

To answer these criticisms, the checklist would have to be all things to all libraries. All too often, there is little understanding that not all works are of equal value or equally useful to a specific library. Though some older books continue to be respected for many years, an out-of-date checklist is of little use in evaluating a current collection.

Obviously, the time involved in effectively checking lists is a concern. Spotty or limited checking does little good, but most libraries are unable or unwilling to check an entire list. Checklist results show the percentage of books from the list that is in the collection. This may sound fine, but there is no standard proportion of a list a library should have. How should one interpret the fact that the library holds 53 percent of some list? Is it reasonable or necessary to have every item? Comparing one library's holdings with another's on the basis of percentage of titles listed is of little value, unless the two libraries have almost identical service populations. In a sense, the use of a checklist assumes some correlation between the percentage of listed books held by a library and the percentage of desirable books in the library's collection. This assumption may or may not be warranted. Equally questionable is the assumption that listed books not held necessarily constitute desiderata and that the proportion of items held to items needed (as represented on the list) constitutes an effective measure of a library's adequacy.

This lengthy discussion of the shortcomings of the checklist method should serve more as a warning than a prohibition. There *are* benefits from using this method in evaluation. Many librarians believe that checking lists helps to reveal gaps and weaknesses in a collection; that the lists provide handy selection guides if the library wishes to use them for this purpose; and that the revelation of gaps and weaknesses may lead to reconsideration of selection methods and policies. Often, nonlibrary administrators respond more quickly and favorably to information about gaps in a collection when the evaluators identify the gaps by using standard lists than when they use other means of identifying the weaknesses.

Expert Opinion

As its name implies, this method depends on personal expertise for making the assessment. What are the impressionistic techniques used by experts? Some evaluators suggest examining a collection in terms of the library's policies and purposes and preparing a report based on impressions of how well the collection meets those goals. The process may involve reviewing the entire collection using the shelf list; it may cover only a single subject area; or, as is frequently the case, it may involve conducting shelf examinations of various subject areas. Normally, the concern is with estimating qualities like the depth of the collection, its usefulness in relation to the curriculum or research, and deficiencies and strengths in the collections.

Very rarely is this technique used alone. It occurs most frequently during accreditation visits, when an accreditation team member walks into the stacks, looks around, and comes out with a sense of the value of the collection. No consultant who regularly uses this technique limits it to shelf reading. Rather, consultants prefer to collect impressions from the service community. Though each person's view is valid only for the individual's areas of interest, in combination, individuals' views should provide an overall sense of the service community's views. (This approach falls into the category of user satisfaction.) Users make judgments about the collection each time they look for something. They will have an opinion even after one brief visit. Thus, the approach is important, if for no other reason than that it provides the evaluator with a sense of what the users think about the collection. Further, it encourages user involvement in the evaluation process.

The evaluation draws on information compiled from various sources—personal examination of the shelves, qualitative measures, and the impressions of the service community. Subject specialists give their impressions of the strengths and weaknesses of a collection. Sometimes, the evaluator employs questionnaires and interviews to collect the data from many people. Less frequently, specialists' impressions may constitute the entire evaluation. Library staff member opinions about the collection add another perspective to the assessment; often, these views differ sharply from those of the users and those of an outsider.

Because many large public libraries employ subject specialists, most special libraries have in-depth subject specialists available, and school libraries can draw on teachers for subject expertise, this method is viable in any library environment.

The major weakness of the impressionistic technique is that it is overwhelmingly subjective. Obviously, the opinions of those who use the collection regularly and the views of subject specialists are important. Impressions may be most useful as part of an evaluation when used in connection with other methods of examining a collection, but their value depends on the objectives of the individual evaluation project, and their significance depends on their interpretation.

Comparative Use Statistics

Comparisons among institutions can offer useful, if sometimes limited, data for evaluation. The limitations arise due to institutional differences in objectives, programs, and service populations. For instance, a junior college with only a liberal arts program requires one type of library, whereas a community college with both a liberal arts curriculum and strong vocational programs requires a much larger collection. Comparing the first library to the second would be like comparing apples and oranges. There simply is no basis for comparison and no point in it unless one can effectively isolate the liberal arts components.

Comparing libraries is difficult because of the way some libraries generate statistics about their collections and service usage. On paper, two libraries may appear similar, yet their book collections may differ widely. Some years ago, Eli Oboler documented this problem:

> One library, without any footnote explanation, suddenly increased from less than twenty-five thousand volumes added during 1961–62 to more than three times that number while the amount shown for books and other library materials only increased approximately 50 percent. Upon inquiry the librarian of this institution stated that, "from storage in one attic we removed forty thousand items, some of which have been catalogued, but in the main we are as yet unsure of the number which will be added. The addition of a large number of volumes also included about one-fourth public documents, state and federal, and almost fifty thousand volumes in microtext."[7]

No one suggests that it is possible to determine the adequacy of a library's collection solely in quantitative terms. Number of volumes is a poor measure of the growth of the library's collection in relation to the programs and services it provides. However, when standards fail to provide quantitative guidelines, budgeting and fiscal officers, who cannot avoid quantitative bases for their decisions, adopt measures that seem to have the virtue of simplicity but are essentially irrelevant to the library's function. Therefore, it is necessary to develop quantitative approaches for evaluating collections that are useful in official decision making and that retain the virtue of simplicity while being relevant to the library's programs and services.

Some useful comparative evaluation tools have been developed as a result of technology and growth of bibliographic utilities. Two widely used products were produced by AMIGOS and WLN. The AMIGOS product employed data from OCLC, and the WLN product uses its own bibliographic database. Due to the merger of OCLC and WLN, only the product that WLN developed is currently available. Such products allow one to compare one collection against one or more other collections in terms of number of titles in a classification range. One could, with either product, identify "gap" titles, items not in the collection but in the collection(s) of the other libraries.

The product that still exists is OCLC/WLN's "Automated Collection Analysis Service" or ACAS (<http://acas.oclc.org>). There are four possible analyses available. One analysis is a useful benchmarking and planning tool that analyzes the collection by subject, age, language, and format and for public libraries breaks the data down between adult and juvenile materials. This analysis is appropriate for a single library or a consortium. The second and third services are comparisons of two or more libraries—overlap analysis and gap analysis. The last analysis is a comparison of an academic library's holdings against the third edition of *Books for College Libraries*. At the time this edition was being prepared, OCLC was developing a new tool for collection analysis, which was released in March 2005 as a part of the *WorldCat* and *FirstSearch* service (<http://www.oclc.org/coll ectionanalysis/>). At first glance, it appears this service holds great potential for any library that has access to *WorldCat*.

LMU used the AMIGOS product for several years to evaluate various subject areas and work with the appropriate academic department to strengthen the collection in that area. We used two CD-ROMs, one disc containing data from a "peer group" consisting of forty libraries that are comparable to the LMU library or to which we wished to compare ourselves. The other disc contained data for the four California Catholic universities. The discs were used for several projects. One project was to explore the possibilities for resource sharing and cooperative collection development among the California Catholic universities. Another use was to assist in assessing the collection to support proposed new academic programs. The library also used the material, in combination with other data, to respond to various accreditation and self-study reports that were done every year. Using these products took time, because the manual was large, and learning how the product worked and how to interpret the results had a steep learning curve. It also took time to teach the recipients of the data how to use the material effectively.

Table 14.1 presents a sample of the type of data one can secure from such a product. An article by Marcia Findley (LMU's collection development officer) described in detail a project assessing the art history collection.[8]

The term *peer* in table 14.1 refers to the group LMU is comparing itself to; the term *evaluator* refers to LMU. The Subcollection Counts notes that in the areas denoted BL1–BL9999, the peer group of forty libraries holds 2,821 titles with a total of 18,774 copies. There are 922 unique titles (i.e., only one library has a copy); of those, 672 are at LMU. In addition, LMU has 647 titles that other libraries in the peer group hold. For the Subcollections Proportions for B1–B68, LMU has 80 titles; the average peer library holds 54. LMU's collection is 48.15 percent larger than the average size for these class numbers. The Subcollection Gap Table shows that LMU does not own 131 books that 80 to 89 percent of the peer libraries (in this case, three libraries) hold. If LMU were to buy the 131 titles, its comparative rank would increase to 73 percent of that of the peer group. The Bibliographic Lists portion of the CD-ROM program allowed LMU to generate a list of the 131 books it did not own.

Collection Standards

There are published standards for almost every type of library. The standards cover all aspects of a library, so there is at least one section that addresses collections. Additionally, some standards have one section about print collections and another section dealing with other formats. The stan-

Subcollection Counts
Peer Group: PEER GROUP 1 (40)
LC Division: BL-BX Religion

| | Peer Group | | Evaluator | | Overlap | |
NATC	Titles	Holdings	Unique	Titles	Titles	Holdings
BL1-BL9999	2,821	18,774	922	672	647	8,520
BM1-BM9999	1,157	6,680	324	204	189	2,242
BP1-BP9999	746	4,539	274	94	88	1,359
BQ1-BQ9999	710	3,293	284	93	89	976
BR1-BR9999	2,626	16,205	862	643	626	8,529
BS1-BS9999	4,166	23,597	1,274	946	914	10,564
BT1-BT9999	3,194	17,957	1,239	760	737	8,785
BV1-BV9999	3,341	12,412	1,447	458	444	4,314
BX1-BX0799	344	1,323	153	36	36	382
BX0800-BX4795	4,144	20,951	1,635	924	903	10,368
BX4800-BX9999	1,774	7,904	752	287	277	3,012
Totals	25,023	133,635	9,166	5,117	4,950	59,051

Subcollection Proportions
Peer Group: PEER GROUP 1 (40)
LC Division: B-BJ Philosophy/Psychology

| | Titles | | Comparative | | % of Subcollection |
NATC	Evaluator	Avg Mbr	Size	Peer Group	Evaluator
B1-B68	80	54	148.15	2.23	2.09
B69-B789	386	241	160.17	9.96	10.08
B790-B5739	937	606	154.62	25.00	24.47
BC1-BC9999	60	49	122.45	2.01	1.57
BD1-BD9999	336	196	171.43	8.08	8.78
BF1-BF1000	1,500	939	159.74	38.71	39.17
BF1001-BF1400	48	37	129.73	1.54	1.25
BF1401-BF1999	38	37	102.70	1.51	0.99
BH1-BH9999	68	44	154.55	1.81	1.78
BJ1-BJ1800	372	217	171.43	8.95	9.72
BJ1801-BJ2195	4	5	80.00	0.19	0.10
Totals	3,829	2,425	157.88	100.00	100.00

Subcollection Proportions
Peer Group: CALIFORNIA CATHOLIC (3)
LC Division: D-DZ History: General & Old World

| | Titles | | Comparative | | % of Subcollection |
NATC	Evaluator	Avg Mbr	Size	Peer Group	Evaluator
D1-D0899	470	823	57.11	15.62	16.50
D0900-D2009	16	37	43.24	0.70	0.56
DA-DA9999	469	654	71.71	12.41	16.47
DAW1001-DAW	1051	0	0	0.00	0.00
DB-DB9999	31	53	58.49	1.01	1.09
DC-DC9999	133	262	50.76	4.96	4.67
DD-DD9999	152	191	79.58	3.62	5.34
DE-DE9999	20	19	105.26	0.36	0.70

(continued)

Table 14.1. Subcollection counts, proportions, and gaps. Based on data from OCLC/AMIGOS for the Charles Von der Ahe Library, LMU.

Subcollection Proportions
Peer Group: CALIFORNIA CATHOLIC (3)
LC Division: D-DZ History: General & Old World

NATC	Titles Evaluator	Avg Mbr	Comparative Size	Peer Group	% of Subcollection Evaluator
DF-DF9999	140	103	135.92	1.95	4.92
DG-DG9999	137	183	74.86	3.47	4.81
DH-DH9999	4	8	50.00	0.15	0.14
DJ-DJ9999	5	0	100.00	0.09	0.18
DJK-DJK9999	7	50	14.00	0.94	0.25
DK-DK9999	130	373	34.85	7.07	4.56
DL-DL9999	9	22	40.91	0.42	0.32
DP1-DP0500	39	94	41.49	1.78	1.37
DP0501-DP0900	3	8	37.50	0.15	0.11
DQ-DQ9999	2	1	200.00	0.03	0.07
DR-DR9999	14	60	23.33	1.13	0.49
DS1-DS0040	31	69	44.93	1.30	1.09
DS0041-DS0329	278	659	42.19	12.50	9.76
DS0330-DS0500	67	211	31.75	4.00	2.35
DS0501-DS0937	368	857	42.94	16.25	12.92
DT-DT9999	294	433	67.90	8.21	10.32
DU-DU9999	28	96	29.17	1.81	0.98
DX-DX9999	1	3	33.33	0.05	0.04
Totals	2,848	5,271	54.03	100.00	100.00

Subcollection Gap
Peer Group: CALIFORNIA CATHOLIC (3)

Division	Holdings Range	Gap Titles In Range	Cumulative	Comparative Size
D1-D0899	90–100%	0	0	57.09%
History: General	80–89%	131	131	73.00%
	70–79%	0	131	57.09%
Current:	60–69%	0	131	57.09%
LMU Titles 470	50–59%	300	431	93.52%
Comparative Size	40–49%	0	431	57.09%
	30 39%	0	431	57.09%
	20–29%	0	431	57.09%
	10–19%	0	431	57.09%
	1–9%	0	431	57.09%
Unique		718	1,149	144.29%
Total	0–100%	1,149	1,149	196.64%

Table 14.1—*Continued.*

dards vary over time and sometimes shift from a quantitative to a qualitative approach and back again. These shifts make long-term comparisons problematic.

Quantitative standards have proven useful, in some instances, for libraries that do not achieve the standard or that have a low "score" or "grade." For example, an earlier edition of the *Standards for College Libraries* had a grading method for collection size based on the percentage held of the ideal size. The ideal size was the result of a calculation using so many books per category such as undergraduate majors and minors, with another number for each master's degree program. Meeting or exceeding the ideal was an "A" grade; anything less was a lower grade. For some funding authorities, such standards are important; for others, such standards are of little or no interest unless failure to achieve the standard has clear consequences for the institution.

Use-Centered Methods

Circulation Studies

Studying collection use patterns as a means of evaluating collections is increasingly popular. Two basic assumptions underlie user/use studies: (1) the adequacy of the book collection is directly related to its usage, and (2) circulation records provide a reasonably representative picture of collection use. Such pragmatic evaluations of collections or services are distasteful to some professionals. As L. Carnovsky stated:

> In general surveys of college and university libraries, where surveyors have devoted attention to use, they have focused on rules and regulations, physical convenience of facilities, and stimulation of reading through publicity, browsing rooms, open stacks and similar matters. They have not been concerned with circulation statistics, and in fact, the statistics for college and university libraries issued by the Library Services Branch do not include them at all. This is tacit recognition of the fact that circulation is largely a function of curriculum and teaching methods, and perhaps also of the realization that the sheer number of books a library circulates is no measure at all of its true contribution to the educational process. In spite of the fact that Wilson and Tauber advocated the maintenance of circulation records, Wilson and Swank, in their survey of Stanford University reported: "Because statistics of use are kept for only a few of the University libraries and those that are kept are not consolidated and consistently reported, it is impossible for the surveyors to present any meaningful discussion or evaluation of this significant aspect of the library program."[9]

Usage data, normally viewed in terms of circulation figures, are objective, and the legitimate differences in the objectives of the institution that the library serves do not affect the data. They also serve as a useful check on one or more of the other evaluation methods. They are helpful in deselection projects. An important factor is to have adequate amounts of data on which to base a judgment. With today's computer-based circulation systems, use data become relatively easy and inexpensive to gather. An example of an early study that made extensive use of circulation data is the aforementioned *Landscape of Literatures: Use of Subject Collections in a University Library*, by Paul Metz.[10]

Certainly, there are problems in interpreting circulation data in terms of the value of a collection. Circulation data cannot reflect use generated within the library, such as reference collections and noncirculating journals. Even for circulating items, there is no way of knowing how the material was used; perhaps the volume was used to prop open a window or press flowers. Also, the value derived by a user from a circulated item is unknown, making it difficult to accurately assess the collection's worth. Use factors are only a small part of the overall mission of research and archival libraries.

In the public library setting, circulation and use data can be useful in determining the need for multiple copies as well as subject areas of high use in which the library has limited holdings. Automated circulation systems allow one to gather such data quickly with little staff effort. The staff time goes to assessing the data and deciding what to do about the results.

User Perceptions

Surveys of users' opinions about collection adequacy, in terms of quantity, quality, or both, have been staples in evaluation programs for many years. On the positive side, users know, or think they know, if the material in the collection has met their needs. On the negative side, past experiences will affect their assessment. A person who has used material from only one collection may be more positive about the collection than it warrants because of lack of experience with any other collection. Likewise, a person who has experience with a large research collection may be overly critical of anything less. Knowing something about the individuals' past library experiences can help evaluators assess the responses more accurately. One must also be careful in interpreting self-selected samples; those volunteering information are a small, but vocal, segment of the user population and may unduly influence the evaluation.

If there is a high percentage of users with a negative attitude toward the collection, there may or may not be a problem with the collection. Certainly, if the results are from a proper random sample, there is a good chance it is a collection problem. However, other factors may be more significant; for example, poor marketing or ineffectual bibliographic instruction may be the more pressing issue. When developing a survey, one should ask one or two questions that will help "sort out" such variables. Sampling only actual users may leave out a large number of people in the service population and fail to discover basics: Why are nonusers nonusers? Is it because of collection inadequacies?

LibQUAL+™ (<http://www.libqual.org/>) is a Web-based user satisfaction instrument that is administered through the Association of Research Libraries (ARL). This assessment tool is currently used internationally and employs three "dimensions"—affect of service, information control, and library as place—to ascertain what users think about the library and its collections. One can use it over time for one's own library as well as using results over time to make comparisons to other libraries. Although developed for academic libraries, it has been used by at least one larger public library, as well as being used in hospital and large special libraries. A good article describing its use is one by Jan Kemp,[11] and an extensive bibliography on LibQUAL+™ is available online from ARL (<http://www.libqual.org/Publications/index.cfm>).

Use of Other Libraries (ILL Statistics)

One factor that is sometimes overlooked in the assessment process is the service population's use of other libraries. Heavy use of other libraries may or may not signal a collection issue for the users. There are at least three aspects to use of "other resources"—physical access to other facilities, traditional ILL, and document delivery services. People often use several libraries to meet their various information requirements: educational libraries for academic needs, special libraries for work-related information, and public libraries for recreational materials. They may also use such libraries for a single purpose, because no one type to which they have access can, or does, supply all the desired data. It is this latter group that has implications for collection development officers. Just knowing that some segment of the service population is using two or more libraries is not enough. The issue is why they are doing so. Again, the reasons may be something other than collection adequacy—closer proximity to where they live or work, different or more convenient service hours, more or better parking, and so forth. However, it is also possible that the problem *is* the collection, and learning from the users their reasons for securing information from other libraries will be of assistance in thinking about possible adjustments in collecting activities.

Collection development officers should periodically review ILL data for journal articles, if for no other reason than copyright compliance. There should be a careful consideration of whether it is better to add a paper subscription or depend upon a commercial service that pays a royalty fee for each item delivered. An overall review of ILL data may reveal areas of the collection that are too weak to meet all the demands or that may need greater depth of coverage.

Likewise, document delivery data may also provide useful clues for collection development officers, assuming one employs a broad definition that includes electronic full-text materials mounted on remote databases. Gaining useful evaluative data about online databases can be a challenge. The library needs to review/assess the use of the databases. Who is using what and for what purpose? The key issue is long-term versus short-term needs and how the archiving of the electronic information is or is not handled by the vendor(s).

As we noted earlier in chapter 6, aggregators add and drop titles with little or no notice. (It is important to note that the titles dropped are usually at the request of the producer of the title, not the aggregator.) Who is responsible for the loss is not an issue for end users; only the fact that it is no longer available matters. Unfortunately, most libraries are currently facing or have recently had to face one or more cuts in the acquisitions budget, and there is little reason to believe that such cuts are a thing of the past. Electronic resources will eventually be considered suitable for possible reductions, if they are not yet in that category. Vendors try to assure librarians that there will be adequate archiving. At present it is too early to say whether such assurances are warranted, but past experience suggests having some doubt is valid. (One electronic resource vendor, in a nationwide video conference, basically stated that a library would have access to backfiles for which that library had had a current subscription *at a rea-*

sonable per-item rate. Although there are storage costs and upgrade/migration costs to consider as systems change, as well as a record-keeping system for tracking what library subscribed to what title for what years, it seems likely the "reasonable rate" may be substantial. When we drop a paper-based subscription, we have the volumes we paid for and do not pay for later use of those volumes. Thus, it may be more cost-effective, for high-use titles, either to acquire a microform backfile or to keep or even start a paper-based subscription. It is not likely that libraries and vendors will agree on what is "a reasonable per-item price.")

Citation Studies

We touched on citation studies in chapter 4 (selection practice) in particular for journal selection purposes. One can also use this method to assess the collections of educational and STM libraries by using a sample of research publications appropriate to the library's overall purpose(s). Compiling a sample of appropriate studies often takes time as well as the cooperation of some scholars to assist in the identification process. One then checks the works cited against the library's catalog to determine how many of the items are in the collection. Essentially, this is a variation on the checklist method, but for research-level materials. The authors employ this method or suggest it to an academic department considering a new graduate degree program. (It can be useful in school settings as well.) Although a dissertation or thesis is normally original in character, it is expected to draw on some body of important literature in the broader field of interest. If the collection lacks a substantial percentage of a sample of "typical research" in the area of interest, the collection will be inadequate in its support of a program.

Citation studies are relatively easy to conduct and over time provide good measures of changes in the strength of the collections. We outlined the downside of this method in chapter 4. A relatively recent article by Margaret Sylvia[12] provides a good example of how one may use citation analysis for collection development purposes, while Erin Smith's report of a citation analysis evaluation project starts with a sound literature review, followed by the project description.[13]

One other evaluation technique is worth mentioning, although it is not primarily a collection development tool. Some years ago, T. Saracevic and others reported on a study of the causes of user frustration in academic libraries.[14] Since that time, many researchers have used variations of the original methodology in a variety of institutional settings. Whatever form the project takes, it requires substantial staff effort as well as user cooperation. This method requires a staff member or researcher to look over the user's shoulder as she or he searches for material. The focus is on material availability and reasons for its not being available.

With this method, one studies two types of searches: a search for a specific item (called a *known search*) and a search for material on a topic (a *subject search*). Within each search there are six decision points, or errors:

- Bibliographic error. (User has incorrect citation; the correct citation is verifiable in some source, and the item is correctly listed in the catalog.)

- Acquisition error. (User has correct citation, and library does not own the title.)

- Catalog use error. (User has correct citation but fails to locate the call number that is in the catalog or fails to record the number properly.)

- Circulation error. (The desired item is identified, but it is in circulation or being held for someone else.)

- Library malfunction error. (Library operations or policies block access to the desired item; such errors include items that are lost or missing, and no replacements are on order, or the items are misshelved, at the bindery, or waiting to be reshelved.)

- Retrieval error. (User has correct call number or location but cannot find the properly shelved item.)

For the subject search, instead of acquisition and bibliographic errors, there are

- Matched query error. (This occurs at the start of the search when the user fails to find a match between search topic and library subject headings or matches the topic to Library of Congress subject headings, but the library has no listings under that heading.)

- Appropriate title error. (This occurs at the end of the search when the user does not select any of the items listed under the matched subject heading or does not borrow any items after examining them.)

Clearly, this technique goes well beyond collection assessment, but it has obvious collection development implications in terms of specific titles needed, subject area weakness, and the issue of how many copies to have of a title.

What Your ILS May Provide

In our search for methods of assessing our collections, we often overlook the information our ILS (integrated library system) can provide with little effort. Most systems have the capability of selecting random samples

Table 14.2. Collection usage of education class numbers 2003–2004.

Class Number	Topic	Percentage of total circulation	Number of circulations
L-L9999	Education (General)	0.0%	2
LA-LA9999	History of Education	0.1%	91
LB-LB9999	Theory and Practice of Education	1.5%	989
LC-LC9999	Special Aspects of Education	1.3%	863
LD-LD9999	Individual Educational Institutions—US	0.2%	110
LE-LE9999	Individual Educational Institutions—Americas (not US)	0.0%	2
LJ-LJ9999	Student Fraternities and Societies	0.0%	10

Table 14.3. Patron usage patterns 2003–2004.

Patron Type	Percentage of Total Circulation	Number of Circulations
Undergrad: Freshman	14.4%	11,961
Undergrad: Sophomore	12.1%	10,012
Undergrad: Junior	14.2%	11,799
Undergrad: Senior	15.1%	12,560
Graduate: Non-degree	0.1%	102
Graduate: Credential	0.3%	224
Graduate: Masters	9.8%	8,140

from the database. Tables 14.2 through 14.4 illustrate some of the information one might extract from the ILS. Age of the collection is easy to determine, and often the result is surprising. Other questions the system can answer are who (classes of users, not individual names) is using what, what class numbers are heavily used, and solid data about the number of titles in class numbers that can be unearthed. Some systems also make it possible to calculate average price for titles or class numbers, which can be helpful for budget planning.

Electronic Resources

Although we are in the early stages of developing electronic information collections, it is not too soon to begin to think about evaluating those collections. It seems likely that over time we will develop as many, if not more, methods for evaluating e-collections as we have for print-based collections. In fact, many of the "print-based" methods apply just as much to electronic collections—usage data, end users' assessments, and citation studies, for example.

At present, the work of Charles McClure and his colleagues provides one of the most comprehensive approaches for evaluating e-resources.[15] They suggest a matrix approach that incorporates many of the elements one uses in the electronic selection process: technical infrastructure, information content, support issues, and management issues. To that they add that one should assess those elements in terms of their extensiveness, efficiency, effectiveness, service quality, impact, usefulness, and adoption. (One should read their publications, as we can only very briefly outline their major ideas here.) Efficiency and effectiveness elements are what they sound like. *Extensiveness* is defined as how much of the electronic service users access; this can be a major factor with aggregator packages. *Service quality* is how well the activity is accomplished; McClure et al. suggest that one measure would be the percentage of users who find what they need. *Impact* is a measure of what, if any, difference the service makes to other activities. *Usefulness* is a measure of how appropriate the service is for a class of users or an individual. *Adoption* is a measure of how much, if at all, users incorporate the service into individual or organizational activities.

As we noted in chapter 7, many electronic products provide, as part of the package or as an optional addition, report software that allows one to easily monitor who is using what and when. One can, and should, load management report software onto the servers that provide access to electronic

Table 14.4. Book checkouts over time—"T" (Technology).

Library of Congress range, definition	Total books in range	Zero checkouts		One checkout		Two checkouts	
		Total	%	Total	%	Total	%
T-T999—Technology (General)	700	274	39.14%	163	23.29%	101	14.43%
TA-TA9999—Engineering (General), Civil Engineering	1290	477	36.98%	316	24.50%	174	13.49%
TC-TC9999—Hydraulic Engineering, Ocean Engineering	250	75	30.00%	76	30.40%	40	16.00%
TD-TD9999—Environmental Technology	884	309	34.95%	145	16.40%	104	11.76%
TE-TE9999—Highway Engineering	40	20	50.00%	7	17.50%	5	12.50%
TF-TF9999—Railroad Engineering	33	9	27.27%	8	24.24%	4	12.12%
TG-TG9999—Bridge Engineering	60	17	28.33%	11	18.33%	16	26.67%
TH-TH9999—Building Construction	108	47	43.52%	24	22.22%	13	12.04%
TJ-TJ9999—Mechanical Engineering	625	192	30.72%	142	22.72%	104	16.64%
TK-TK9999—Electrical Engineering	1542	511	33.14%	375	24.32%	185	12.00%
T-TX9999: All Technology	8468	2863	33.81%	1832	21.63%	1129	13.33%

resources. Management reports will provide some of the data needed to evaluate electronic resources and the "value" of different products and services to local as well as remote users.

Summary

There is much research to do before collection evaluation becomes an objective science. Everyone agrees that collection evaluation is a difficult

Three checkouts		Four checkout		Five checkouts		Six+ checkouts	
Total	*%*	*Total*	*%*	*Total*	*%*	*Total*	*%*
63	9.00%	41	5.86%	14	2.00%	44	6.29%
119	9.22%	60	4.65%	50	3.88%	94	7.29%
16	6.40%	15	6.00%	12	4.80%	16	6.40%
67	7.58%	49	5.54%	44	4.98%	166	18.78%
3	7.50%	1	2.50%	1	2.50%	3	7.50%
5	15.15%	1	3.03%	4	12.12%	2	6.06%
6	10.00%	3	5.00%	3	5.00%	4	6.67%
11	10.19%	8	7.41%	2	1.85%	3	2.78%
65	10.40%	49	7.84%	20	3.20%	53	8.48%
153	9.92%	92	5.97%	53	3.44%	173	11.22%
793	9.36%	522	6.16%	324	3.83%	1005	11.87%

task, and the results are highly subjective. Thus, the evaluator must be willing to live with what are, at best, tentative results.

Because no one evaluation method is adequate by itself, a combined approach is most effective. Most evaluation projects employ several methods to take advantage of the strengths of each technique. Nancy Everhart[16] prepared an excellent book on evaluating the school library media center. It covers all aspects of library media center operations, including a chapter on collection assessment. One of the pluses of the book is the many useful forms that she provides. Another fine publication for assessment projects is

Carol Doll and Pamela Barron's *Managing and Analyzing Your Collection*,[17] which also provides useful forms. "Time to Tell the Whole Story" is an interesting article discussing outcome data ("Counting on Results"), developed in Colorado public libraries.[18]

When we serve as consultants on collection evaluation projects, we employ the following steps after determining the library's goals and objectives:

1. Develop an individual set of criteria for quality and value.

2. Draw a random sample from the collection and examine the use of the items (shelflist sample).

3. Collect data about titles wanted but not available (ILL requests).

4. Keep a record of titles picked up from tables and in stack areas (in-house use).

5. Keep a detailed record of interlibrary loan activities.

6. Find out how much obsolete material is in the collection (e.g., science works more than fifteen years old and not considered classics).

7. If checklists have some relevance to the library, check them; but also do some research concerning the usefulness of these checklists.

8. Relate findings to the library's goals and objectives.

Collection evaluation is time-consuming, but only after completing the task does the staff know the collection's strengths and weaknesses. With this knowledge, the collection development staff can formulate a plan to build on the strengths and correct the weaknesses. This assumes that the assessment of strengths and weaknesses took place in the context of the library's goals, objectives, and community needs. After the first effort, if the process is ongoing, the work will be less time-consuming, and with each assessment the judgments will come closer to accurately assessing the collection's true value.

Notes

1. Sheila Intner and Elizabeth Futas, "Evaluating Public Library Collections," *American Libraries* 25, no. 5 (May 1994): 410–13.

2. Thomas Nisonger, *Evaluation of Library Collections, Access, and Electronic Resources* (Westport, CT: Libraries Unlimited, 2003).

3. Paul Metz, *Landscape of Literatures: Use of Subject Collections in a University Library* (Chicago: American Library Association, 1983).

4. Robert B. Downs, "Techniques of the Library Resources Survey," *Special Libraries* 23 (April 1941): 113–15.

5. George Bonn, "Evaluation of the Collection," *Library Trends* 22 (January 1974): 265–304.

6. B. Lockett, ed., *Guide to the Evaluation of Library Collections* (Chicago: American Library Association, 1989).

7. Eli Oboler, "Accuracy of Federal Academic Library Statistics," *College & Research Libraries* 25 (September 1964): 494.

8. Marcia Findley, "Using the OCLC/AMIGOS Collection Analysis Compact Disk to Evaluate Art and Art History Collections," *Technical Services Quarterly* 10, no. 3 (1993): 1–15.

9. L. Carnovsky, "Survey of the Use of Library Resources and Facilities," in *Library Surveys*, eds. M. F. Tauber and I. R. Stephens, 68, (New York: Columbia University Press, 1967).

10. Metz, *Landscape of Literatures*.

11. Jan H. Kemp, "Using the LibQUAL+ Survey to Assess Users Perceptions of Collections and Service Quality," *Collection Management* 26, no. 4 (2001): 4–14.

12. Margaret J. Sylvia, "Citation Analysis as an Unobtrusive Method for Journal Collection Evaluation Using Psychology Student Research Bibliographies," *Collection Building* 17, no. 1 (1998): 20–28.

13. Erin T. Smith, "Assessing Collection Usefulness; An Investigation of Library Ownership of the Resources Graduate Students Use," *College & Research Libraries* 64 (September 2003): 344–55.

14. T. Saracevic et al., "Causes and Dynamics of User Frustration in an Academic Library," *College & Research Libraries* 38 (January 1977): 7–18.

15. John Carlo Bertot and Charles McClure, "Measuring Electronic Services in Public Libraries," *Public Libraries* 37 (May/June 1998): 176–80; Charles McClure, John Carlo Bertot, and Douglas Zweizig, *Public Libraries and the Internet: Study Results, Policy Issues, and Recommendations* (Washington, DC: National Commission on Libraries and Information Science, 1994); John Carlo Bertot, Charles McClure, and Douglas Zweizig, *The 1996 National Survey of Public Libraries and the Internet* (Washington, DC: National Commission on Libraries and Information Science, 1996); John Carlo Bertot, Charles McClure, and Patricia D. Fletcher, *The 1997 National Survey of Public Libraries and the Internet* (Washington, DC: National Commission on Libraries and Information Science, 1997).

16. Nancy Everhart, *Evaluating the School Library Media Center* (Westport, CT: Libraries Unlimited, 1998).

17. Carol A. Doll and Pamela Patrick Barron, *Managing and Analyzing Your Collection: A Practical Guide for Small Libraries and School Media Centers* (Chicago: American Library Association, 2002).

18. Nicole Stoffer, Keith Lance, and Rochelle Logan, "Time to Tell the Whole Story: Outcome-Based Evaluation and Counting on Results Project," *Public Libraries* 41 (July–August 2002): 222–28.

Selected Websites*

(See also resources on the DLC5 website: <http://www.lu.com/DLC5>)

CDT: Collection Assessment
    <http://www.dlapr.lib.az.us/cdt/collass.htm>
    Part of the Collection Development Training (CDT) program, sponsored by the Arizona State Library, Archives and Public Records.

Collection Assessment
    <http://www-lib.uwyo.edu/cdo/collass.htm>
    An extensive listing of collection assessment techniques, prepared by the Uni-

versity of Wyoming Libraries. Includes a description of collection assessment procedures.

Evaluating Library Collections: An Interpretation of the *Library Bill of Rights.*
<http://www.ala.org/ala/oif/statementspols/statementsif/interpretations/eval uatinglibrary.htm>
From the American Library Association.

*These sites were accessed May 7, 2005.

Further Reading

Bell, G. "System-Wide Collection Assessment Survey (Birmingham Public School System)." In *School Library Media Annual 10*, 135–47. Englewood, CO: Libraries Unlimited, 1992.

Bremer, T. A. "Assessing Collection Use by Surveying Users at Randomly Selected Times." *Collection Management* 13, no. 3 (1990): 57–67.

Bruggeman, L. "'Zap! Whoosh! Kerplow!' Build High-Quality Graphic Novel Collections with Impact." *School Library Journal* 43, no. 1 (January 1997): 22–27.

Budd, J. M., and C. Wyatt. "'Do You Have Any Books On . . .' An Examination of Public Library Holdings." *Public Libraries* 41, no. 2 (March–April 2002): 107–12.

Carlson, B. A. "Collection Development Assessment for Biomedical Serials Collections." *Serials Librarian* 23, nos. 3/4 (1993): 289–92.

Carpenter, K. H. "Evaluating Library Resources for Accreditation." *Bulletin of the Medical Library Association* 80 (April 1992): 131–39.

Clark, P. M. "Patterns of Consistent, Persistent Borrowing Behavior by High-Intensity Users of a Public Library." *Public Libraries* 37, no. 5 (September–October 1998): 298–306.

Davis, B. "How the WLN Conspectus Works for Small Libraries." *Acquisitions Librarian*, 20 (1998): 53–72.

D'Elia, G., and E. Rodger. "Customer Satisfaction with Public Libraries: Surveys in Five Urban Library Systems with 142 Libraries." *Public Libraries* 35 (September–October 1996): 292–97.

Doll, C. A. "Quality and Elementary School Library Media Collections." *School Library Media Quarterly* 25 (Winter 1997): 95–102.

Doll, C. A., and P. P. Barron. *Managing and Analyzing Your Collection: A Practical Guide for Small Libraries and School Media Centers.* Chicago: American Library Association, 2002.

Emanuel, M. "A Collection in 150 Hours." *Collection Management* 27, nos. 3/4 (2002): 79–93.

Garland, K. "Circulation Sampling as a Technique for Library Media Program Management." *School Library Media Quarterly* 20 (Winter 1992): 73–78.

Gaylor, R. H. "Collection Analysis at a Junior College Library." *OCLC Systems and Services* 10, no. 1 (1994): 9–12.

Gottlieb, J., ed. *Collection Assessment in Music Libraries*. New York: Music Library Association, 1994.

Guise, J., and D. Feinmark. "ARL's Collection Analysis Project: Continuing Feasibility for a Medium-Sized Academic Library." *Library Management* 24, nos. 6/7 (2003): 332–36.

Hacken, R. D. "Statistical Assumption-Making in Library Collection Assessment: Peccadilloes and Pitfalls." *Collection Management* 7 (Summer 1985): 17–32.

"Health Libraries: Checklist Will Boost Quality." *Library Association Record* 100 (December 1998): 620.

Hiller, S. "Another Tool in the Assessment Toolbox: Integrating LibQUAL+ ™ into the University of Washington Libraries Assessment Program." *Journal of Library Administration* 40, nos. 3/4 (2004): 121–38.

Holleman, C. "Study of the Strengths, Overlap, and National Collection Patterns: The Uses of the OCLC/AMIGOS Collection Analysis CD and Alternatives to It." *Collection Management* 22, nos. 1/2 (1997): 57–69.

Kachel, D. E. *Collection Assessment and Management for School Libraries: Preparing for Cooperative Collection Development*. Westport, CT: Greenwood Press, 1997.

Lee, S. H. *Collection Assessment and Acquisitions Budgets*. New York: Haworth Press, 1992.

Lockett, B., ed. *Guide to the Evaluation of Library Collections*. Chicago: American Library Association, 1989.

McClure, C. R., and B. Reifsnyder. "Performance Measures for Corporate Information Centers." *Special Libraries* 75 (July 1984): 193–204.

Nisonger, T. E. *Collection Evaluation in Academic Libraries: A Literature Guide and Annotated Bibliography*. Englewood, CO: Libraries Unlimited, 1992.

Ochola, J. N. "Use of Circulation Statistics and Interlibrary Loan Data in Collection Management." *Collection Management* 27, no. 1 (2002): 1–13.

O'Connor, D. O., and E. R. Dyer. "Evaluation of Corporate Reference Collections." *Reference Librarian* 29 (Summer 1990): 21–31.

Pancheshnikov, Y. "Course-centered Approach to Evaluating University Library Collections for Instructional Program Reviews." *Collection Building* 22, no. 4 (2003): 177–85.

Richards, D. T. *Collection Development and Assessment in Health Sciences Libraries*. Lanham, MD: Medical Library Association, 1997.

Sandler, M. S. "Quantitative Approaches to Qualitative Collection Assessment." *Collection Building* 8, no. 4 (1987): 12–17.

Seeds, R. S. "Impact of a Digital Archive (JSTOR) on Print Collection Use." *Collection Building* 21, no. 3 (2002): 120–22.

Senkevitch, J. J., and J. H. Sweetland. "Evaluating Public Library Adult Fiction: Can We Define a Core Collection?" *RQ* 36 (Fall 1996): 103–17.

Smith, M., and G. Rowland. "To Boldly Go; Searching for Output Measures for Electronic Services." *Public Libraries* 36 (May–June 1997): 168–72.

Stebelman, S. "Using Choice as a Collection Assessment Tool." *Collection Building* 15, no. 2 (1996): 4–11.

Tenopir, C. "Online Databases: Database and Online System Usage." *Library Journal* 12, no. 6 (October 2001): 41–45.

Urquhart, C. "Comparing and Using Assessment of the Value of Information to Clinical Decision-Making." *Bulletin of the Medical Library Association* 84 (October 1996): 482–89.

Weber, J., and D. Ridley. "Assessment and Decision Making: Two User-Oriented Studies: Borrowing/Browsing Patterns in Academic Libraries." *Library Review* 46, nos. 3/4 (1997): 202–9.

Weber, M. "Effects of Fiction Assessment on a Rural Public Library." *Collection Building* 13, nos. 2/3 (1994): 83–86.

Wood, R. J. "Building a Better Library Collection." *Library Software Review* 15 (Spring 1996): 22–24.

15
Resource Sharing

There have been a number of significant changes over the past eight to ten years in how people think about cooperative collection development. Perhaps a better label for what is now taking place is "shared" collection development. The growth of consortia and availability of technology combine to change the ease of gaining access to collections in other libraries. Paula Kaufman may well have predicted the future when she wrote that "there will be fewer consortia, but they will be larger in size and scope and more powerful than they are today. There will also be many new types of partnerships and collaborative activities that will extend and enhance access for our users."[1]

Library literature is full of discussions about cooperative collection development. Based on the volume of material, a newcomer to the field might think that libraries have been successfully engaged in such activities for a long time. However, just the opposite is the case. Libraries have tried mounting everything from local to national programs, with modest success[2] at best; most of the success has come at the local and regional levels. What has changed in the last few years is a rapid growth of consortia that purchase electronic resources. There is growing evidence that consortia members are using their technological capabilities to modify how they go about collection development. We see little on the horizon leading us to believe that "traditional" cooperative collection development will change for the better. Rather, there will be a different form of resource sharing, which we discuss later in this chapter.

Shortly after the beginning of World War II, U.S. research libraries learned that their collections were not as strong as they had believed. The weakness lay in their holdings of publications from other countries and in all formats, not just books. After the war there was an effort, the Farmington Plan, to get research libraries across the United States to divide up the collecting responsibility for all of the knowledge from most countries. The plan was ambitious, to say the least, and in the end it failed for a variety of reasons, not just because of its scale. However, that elusive goal of comprehensiveness remains, to many, a desirable mission for research libraries. Smaller-scale efforts to reduce duplication and expand breadth of coverage grew out of early efforts such as Farmington. Regional and local groups with various types of resource-sharing arrangements exist, but there has been little progress in establishing a coordinated national program that will assure that one copy of almost any research item will be available somewhere in the United States. Technology helps us know who has what, and other tools, such as the now-defunct RLG conspectus, have helped librarians determine who thinks they have strong collections in various subject fields. However, many barriers exist when it comes to developing a workable plan. As Edward Shreeves stated, "There is, however, widespread belief that cooperation in building collections can significantly improve the quality of library service by broadening and deepening the range of materials collectively available."[3]

Webster's Third New International Dictionary defines *cooperative* in part as "given to or marked by working together or by joint effort toward a common end"; it defines *coordinate* as "to bring into a common action, movement, or condition; regulate and combine in harmonious action."[4] Some years ago, John Berry wrote an editorial in *Library Journal* about how the then-current tight funding situation was causing cooperative ventures to cease. Unfortunately, the situation has changed little since Berry wrote:

> The pressure is reported by public, academic, and school librarians from across the United States. One state's fine multitype systems are near collapse. Cooperative county systems in another have been reduced to bickering disarray from years of no-growth funding. Consortia members are scrapping over slices of a shrinking pie. New, harsh limitations on interlibrary loan crop up. Stiff nonresident fees and interlibrary charges proliferate. Old battles between small and large libraries in shared jurisdictions flare anew. State agency and cooperative system operating budgets are openly attacked by constituent librarians. . . . Librarians, torn between professional commitment to library cooperation and local pressure to provide service with deeply diminished resources, have to make the choice to cut service to outsiders.[5]

Today, what seems to be the most likely outcome of e-resources and consortia efforts is best described as "resource sharing." ALA's *Glossary* defines *resource sharing* as "activities engaged in jointly by a group of libraries for the purposes of improving services and/or cutting costs. Resource sharing may be established by informal or formal agreement or by contract and may operate locally, nationally, or internationally. The resources shared may be collections, bibliographic data, personnel, planning activities, etc."[6] That definition is wide-ranging enough to encompass almost any activity.

Essentially, we are looking at four concepts in this chapter:

1. *Cooperative collection development*, a mechanism whereby two or more libraries agree that each one will have certain areas of "primary collecting responsibility" and that they will exchange such materials with one another free of charge (the Farmington/Scandia models).

2. *Coordinated acquisitions*, whereby two or more libraries agree to buy certain materials and/or share the associated cost(s), and one or more of the members house the material (LACAP/CRL model).

3. *Joint acquisitions*, whereby the members place a joint order for a product or service, and each member receives the product/service, such as systemwide agreements to purchase electronic database subscriptions (including such projects as VIVA—the VIrtual Library of Virginia <http://www.viva.lib.va.us>).

4. *Shared collection information*, a system in which members use information in a shared database about collection holdings to influence their selection/acquisitions decisions.

All four can, and generally do, lead to resource sharing among the members.

While each of these concepts will be examined in turn, the fourth element is relatively new and involves consortia that link OPACs and has some form of document delivery system in place to speed up the traditional ILL borrowing process (such as OhioLINK and LINK+). As we see later in this chapter, even if there is no formal agreement among the member libraries regarding collection development activities, collection development officers frequently check the holdings of the member libraries when considering the possible purchase of an item they think will be of low use in their library. If another member has the item, they often do not purchase the item, thus depending on the document delivery system to supply the item when the need arises. This has been a growing activity over the past five years.

The Something-for-Nothing Syndrome

True library cooperative collection development systems operate on a series of assumptions that one should examine with considerable care. Perhaps the most important assumption, although the one least often stated, is that all of the participants in the system are, or will be, equally efficient in their collection development operations. No one assumes that every member will achieve the same benefits or contribute materials at an equal volume. Rather, the assumption is that each library is somewhat unusual, if not unique (i.e., each library has different clientele, collections, and service programs).

Data from consortial projects such as OhioLINK and LINK+ suggest this is true, at least in terms of holdings. Why, then, assume that each is *equally* efficient? It is clear that one cannot legitimately make such an assumption. However, if libraries do not make that assumption, it is difficult to believe that every library will gain something or at least receive a value equal to its contribution. Each library hopes that it will be the one to receive more than it puts into the system. If a library enters into a cooperative program with the something-for-nothing goal in mind, there is little hope of success. During periods of low funding from outside sources, libraries have a tendency not to cooperate. According to Boyd Rayward, "Networks (consortia) are a phenomenon of relative affluence. They cannot be created unless each member at the local level has sufficient resources of time, staff, materials, and basic equipment and supplies to participate."[7]

Cooperative planners sometimes factor in the extra work of a staff member filling out one or more forms or answering extra questions for the library but almost never do so for the customer. Too often, the planners think of these as small, insignificant increases for an individual to absorb. However, although a single increase may be small, in time or in aggregate such increases become significant. Today's shared approaches do, in fact, benefit users and save them time, assuming there is a good delivery system in place.

Today, librarians discuss developing agreements to allow free ILL services to one another. One interesting outcome of more and more libraries having OPACs and being part of regional or statewide networks is that large libraries are actually borrowing more material from smaller institutions than they are lending. This suggests that in the past it was lack of information rather than weak collections that led to the imbalance of ILL activity. Additionally, the availability of courier services delivering materials between member libraries has greatly improved user services.

What Can Be Gained Through Cooperation?

Why is it necessary to discuss the benefits of cooperation in collection development? The benefits of increased access should be obvious. The reason is that most cooperation projects are highly political and that costs, financial and political, are high. "Selling" the concept can be more complex than one might expect.

One can identify six general benefits that could arise from any library cooperative effort. First is the potential for improving access—improving in the sense of making available a greater range of materials or better depth in a subject area. In the past, in the days of card catalogs and limited computer networking, it was difficult to know what library owned what. Adding the slow ILL service into the mix made true sharing problematic. That became less and less of a problem as libraries automated their catalogs and joined various networks. Some networks are statewide, such as for OHIO-Link (<http://www.ohiolink.edu/>) and LINK+ (<http://csul.iii.com/screens/whatslink.html>) in California, and include both public and private institutions. LMU joined LINK+ in 1999, with the result that its service population went from having access to a collection of just under 400,000 volumes to having online access to a collection of more than 4 million titles and 6 million copies. Although the LMU collection was the smallest added to the database up to that time, more than 37 percent of the items were unique additions to the system. (The experience has been that each new member contributes between 30 and 40 percent unique titles, according to the firm that handles both OHIOLink and LINK+. This suggests that, to some degree, the claim that each library is "special" is true, at least in terms of its collections.)

A second benefit is that it may be possible to stretch limited resources. One danger in suggesting that cooperation may benefit the public or the professional staff is that the idea of getting something for nothing becomes ingrained. Too often, people view cooperation as a money-saving device. In truth, cooperation does not save money for a library. If two or more libraries combine their efforts, they will not spend less money; an effective cooperative program simply divides the work and shares the results.

Sharing results leads to some benefits, such as greater staff special-ization. A person can concentrate on one or two activities rather than on five or six. The resulting specialization should produce better overall per-formance. Naturally, better performance should lead to better service and thus greater customer satisfaction. Reducing unnecessary duplication is a second result of sharing work. The reduction may be in work performed or materials purchased, but planners should study just how much duplication they can eliminate before drawing up a formal agreement. Vague discus-sions about reducing duplication, without an in-depth study of the situa-tion, usually lead to high expectations and, all too often, dashed hopes. Nevertheless, reduced duplication of low-use items is a real potential bene-fit.

By actively advertising its presence and services, a cooperative pro-gram may reduce the number of places a customer will need to go for ser-vice. However, in most systems, this benefit is more theoretical than real. In the past, a lack of union lists generally negated this potential benefit. Today, networked OPACs provide a real benefit in terms of better directing clients to the correct source of information.

A final benefit, one not frequently discussed, is the improvement in the working relationships among cooperating libraries. This is particularly true in a multitype system. Persons can gain a better perspective about others' problems as a result of working together on mutual problems. Also, learn-ing about the special problems that another type of library encounters helps one to know what its staff can or cannot do. Some systems have found this to be so important that they have set up exchange internships for staff members, both professional and nonprofessional.

As for many other areas of collection development, ALA's Resources and Technical Services Division (now the Association for Library Collections and Technical Services) created a set of guidelines for cooperative collection development, "A Guide to Cooperative Collection Development."[8] The guide-lines provide specific details about benefits, problems, and recommenda-tions that fit easily into this chapter's more general concepts.

In terms of collection development, cooperative programs force li-braries to have better knowledge of their collections. In a cooperative pro-gram, a library must know both what it has and what the other member libraries have. In the 1980s until the late 1990s, the RLG conspectus and ARL's National Collection Inventory Project (NCIP) served such a purpose. The ARL project also used the conspectus model and attempted to identify who has what and in what strength. Although developed for academic li-brary use, the conspectus concept has been used in all types of libraries.

If there is to be a division of collection responsibility by subject area, each library must have an in-depth knowledge of its own collection before entering into a meaningful cooperative agreement, and that is but the first step in the process of developing a workable program. Even if there is no final agreement, the process of examining the collection will be of great value. Also, the opportunity to share problems and solutions should improve each participant's capabilities.

Resource Sharing Issues

We will briefly discuss several issues that can impact a resource-sharing project/program. Some of them are most important during the start-up phase, while others become critical during the ongoing operational period. The material that follows is a highly condensed and reworked version of what appeared in the fourth edition of this book (the full text of the material is on the accompanying CD).

Institutional issues are a key factor in both start-up and ongoing operations. Matching/modifying the missions and goals as well as the policies of participating libraries is seldom as easy in practice as it seems it would be when thinking about it in the abstract. Compromise is the key to getting successful sharing projects off the ground. That and sharing authority/power are two significant stumbling blocks to achieving an effective working group. Talking about creating a "partnership" is easy; making it an effective partnership takes hard work.

"People" issues are linked to the institutional issues, both library staff and users. Users want their local library to meet all their needs, even when they know that is highly unlikely, if not impossible. Longtime library users have deeply ingrained views about how much time it takes (or took) to get materials from another library (traditional ILL). Those views tend to lead to opposition to any resource-sharing program that might, in their view, result in any reduction in local acquisitions. Staff members may also be reluctant to give up on the idea of local self-sufficiency. In addition, they often fear a loss of autonomy when it comes to selection decisions. Both users and staff may engage in passive resistance during start-up stages. Another tactic both groups may employ is to question reliability or quality of the proposed partners.

Accrediting agencies can have an impact on resource-sharing projects. For example, the Western Association of Schools and Colleges (WASC) includes the following statements in its standards:

> 6.B.1 Basic collections *held* by the institution are sufficient in quality to meet *substantially all* of the needs of educational programs on and off campus.

> 6.B.2. Interlibrary loan or contractual use arrangements may be used to *supplement* basic holdings *but are not* to be used as the main source of learning resources.[9]

Although such statements do not preclude cooperative collection building, they certainly add another layer of complexity to an already complex issue.

The role of the WASC as an institutional accrediting body has had a mixed influence on cooperative collection building. WASC's accreditation standards, particularly 6.B.1, were designed, in part, to control institutions that were establishing widely scattered off-campus programs. One concern was that students were not receiving proper support—in particular, library support—at the off-campus sites. This standard has proven to be a two-edged sword for cooperative collection building. In a few instances, it motivated the library and its parent institution to enter into formal agreements with the libraries near the off-campus instructional sites. Usually, such agreements state that the institution needing access to material will pay an annual fee, which the receiving library agrees to use towards subscribing to certain journals or to buy books about certain subjects. Given that most libraries do not have large amounts of excess collection growth space, it appears clear that the receiving library believes its primary customers will also benefit from the acquired material. This form of cooperative collection building is often overlooked.

The standard also resulted in libraries acquiring technologies that would allow the remote sites to have access to the main campus library. Undoubtedly, for many of the libraries, the accreditation pressure regarding off-campus students having access to library support resulted in funding for online catalogs, fax machines, and remote access to Web-based resources. In many cases, most of the technology would have been much slower in arriving in the library had it not been for the accreditation concerns.

Legal and *administrative* factors create theoretical and practical challenges for resource sharing. To be effective, cooperative programs need to be more than a local matter. However, expanding beyond the local area usually means cutting across jurisdictional lines—city to county, county to counties, counties to state, etc. The more lines crossed, the more rapidly the complexities multiply, and all of them raise issues of funding and control. Perhaps the most significant issue is transferring funds and who may be authorized to expend them. Another area where issues always seem to arise is when the group is a mix of public and private libraries. Multitype projects can also present challenges. Often, it requires "joint power agreements," which means politicians become involved.

Physical access occasionally can be a small problem for "in-person" resource sharing. Reciprocal borrowing rights are often put forward for local area sharing programs. These work well when there is adequate user space in all the participating libraries. As long as the "law of least effort" does not become too big a factor, it can be an effective approach. However, there are instances where libraries in high traffic areas or with the strongest collection become overwhelmed with users. Some private libraries have restrictions on who may physically use their facilities.

Technology has had an impact on cooperative collection development and resource sharing. There were many reasons why true cooperative collection development never succeeded over the long term and on a large scale. One of the reasons was not having up-to-date information about what was available where and its availability. Another reason was the slow nature (snail mail ILL) of the delivery service. The two reasons were interrelated in that often an ILL request had to go to two or three libraries before it could be filled. That was because even when one knew a library owned an item, one had no way of knowing if it was available for lending. Knowledge about ownership quickly improved as bibliographic utility databases such as OCLC grew in size and more libraries contributed holdings information. What was lacking was information about availability. OPACs now provide information on the status of items in the collection. Add to this the fact that computer memory has increased dramatically while its cost has declined, which in turn makes large databases economically viable. The result is that statewide databases, with availability data, are becoming more and more common.

What technology has done is to shift the focus away from formal cooperative programs to resource-sharing programs. The ILS allows for knowledge of item availability to be quickly shared. This, in turn, allows for faster access for the end user since this information is almost instantly known. Today there are several statewide programs that allow relatively quick resource-sharing services (three-day delivery is fairly common).

As noted previously, LMU belongs to a consortium known as LINK+, which consists of thirty-seven sites throughout California and the University of Nevada, Reno. Within LINK+, there are public and private academic libraries (the original members), public libraries, and community colleges. Our combined unique holdings are over 5 million titles and 14 million copies. End users search their local OPAC, and if they do not find what they are looking for, they can click on "Search LINK+" and the search is automatically rerun on the union database. If the person finds what she or he wants, the individual directly requests the item from the system, and it will arrive at the person's library within three days by courier delivery. When there is more than one copy of the item available, the LINK+ software has a "load balancing" program that provides as even a distribution of the lending work as possible across the membership.

Directors of the LINK+ libraries have talked about actually using the system to develop a formal joint collection development program. However, at present there is just informal use of the system by a few libraries when making selection decisions. A few libraries occasionally are deciding not to acquire a title when they see there are two or more copies already in the system. They then use the funds for something that is unique or has only a single copy in the system. Other libraries are using the database to make decisions about gift items; if there is a copy available, they don't add the gift item to their collection. Because the courier service charges more for items going back and forth between northern and southern California, at least one library also factors in the location of the item(s) when deciding if it should purchase a title. The idea is to have at least one copy of a title in both regions. Although the activities are informal, they are expanding resources for all the members. None of this would be feasible if it were not for the technology now available.

Libraries that belong to OhioLINK, using the same technology, have developed a more formalized procedure to increase the range of titles available to members. In this case, it involved developing a partnership with a book dealer (YBP Library Services) and producing what is called the "Not-Bought-in-Ohio Report."[10] The article about this program is worth reading, especially as it addresses some of the issues that can make it difficult to get cooperative projects up and running.

What to Avoid When Establishing a Resource-Sharing Program

The following seven points about what to avoid in order to establish a successful cooperative program come from the literature on the topic. Avoid these pitfalls, and your system has an excellent chance of succeeding:

- Avoid thinking of the cooperative as "supplementary" and an "add-on"; instead, consider it as something it is impossible to do without.

- Have planners spend time working out operational details.

- Realize that the system *should* cause major operational changes in the member libraries.

- Avoid thinking of the system as providing the library with something for nothing.

- Have the cooperative's funding and operation handled by an independent agency.

- Realize that it takes time; careful, complete communication; and one or two persons who take on the leadership role with patient understanding for such a project to succeed.

- Remember that, above all else, forming a cooperative is a political process.

Although these are complex points within themselves, they exemplify common reasons resource-sharing programs are not as successful as intended.

A number of resource-sharing models have been experimented with over the years, with varying degrees of success. This is largely due to the above-named factors. The aforementioned ALA guidelines identified seven models for cooperative collection development: the Farmington Plan, the National Program for Acquisitions and Cataloging (NPAC) system, the Library of Congress system, the Center for Research Libraries model, the mosaic overlay of collection development policies, the status quo, and the combined self-interest models. Each of these holds valuable lessons for anyone considering a resource-sharing program.

The Farmington Plan, mentioned earlier, was a valiant, but unsuccessful, effort. It was an attempt by major American research libraries to have one copy of any currently published research work available somewhere within the United States. After years of effort, it was abandoned in the 1970s. The plan originally assigned acquisition responsibility on the basis of institutional interests. In twenty years, those interests changed, but the goal of one copy remained. Another problem was that some areas were not of major interest to any institution. Sufficient national interest existed to warrant coverage, but deciding which institution should have the responsibility for buying such materials was a constant problem. A careful study of why the Farmington Plan failed provides invaluable data for future cooperative ventures. In the final analysis, it failed as a result of not avoiding the pitfalls discussed earlier.

A European example was the Scandia Plan, implemented in the Scandinavian countries, which experienced similar problems. This plan never achieved the same level of activity as the Farmington Plan, primarily because of problems of changing needs and the assignment of responsibilities.

The NPAC system was another attempt at acquiring quantities of research materials from outside the United States and assuring that cataloging data would be available for the material. (Cataloging was one of the stumbling blocks for the Farmington Plan.) The Library of Congress (LC) was the focal point in NPAC, but there was consultation with other research libraries in the United States about what subjects to include in the program. Public Law 480[11] was an element of the NPAC program in which LC "was authorized by Congress to acquire books abroad by using U.S.-owned nonconvertible foreign currency under the terms of the Act."[12] Again, the Library of Congress was responsible for operating the program, including cataloging and distributing the materials to participating academic libraries. Public Law 480 was not a cooperative collection development project in the usual sense of the term; it was a centralized acquisition and cataloging program.

A related, joint acquisition program that also failed was the Latin American Cooperative Acquisition Plan (LACAP). LACAP was a commercial undertaking designed to share costs and problems of acquiring quantities of research material, on a regular basis, from Latin American countries. Although some research libraries in the United States still collect extensively from Latin America, they could not sustain the program. Three factors played an important role in the demise of LACAP. First, most of what the libraries acquired was low-use material. Tight funding requires hard choices, and low-use items are always a prime area for cuts. Second, the plan started in a period when many institutions were developing area study programs, and there was an expectation that this would be a growing field. Economic conditions changed; institutions stopped planning for new programs and often cut some of the most recently established programs. As a result, not as many institutions were interested in participating in LACAP. Finally, the book trade in many Latin American countries matured, and it was no longer as difficult to locate reliable local dealers. If one can buy directly and reliably at a lower cost, it is reasonable to buy the most material possible with the funds available.

The ALA guidelines describe the LC system as "a variation of the Farmington Plan." In general terms, it is a centralized (coordinated) system in which the national library and the research libraries in a country work together to ensure that at least one copy of all relevant research material is available.

Two of the most successful cooperative programs are the Center for Research Libraries (CRL) in the United States and the British Library Document Supply Service (formerly the British National Lending Division or BLD). One reason for their success is that they operate as independent agencies. Their purpose is to serve a diverse group of member libraries; in essence, they have no local constituency to serve. Another major difference for CRL is that there is no attempt to acquire high-use items; in fact, just the opposite is true. With no local service population, the fiscal resources can go to acquiring low-use items of research interest to the member libraries.

The CRL does face some major decisions regarding its collection policies. One issue is whether it should build a broad-based selective collection, with many subjects and areas, or whether it should attempt to be comprehensive in a few areas. A second issue relates to the need for a single source of low-use periodicals (the "National Periodicals Center" concept) and what role CRL should play. What of the future? One would hope that the center will continue to develop as the holder of unique materials. With better delivery systems, perhaps libraries can supply low-use items quickly enough from CRL and let patrons know about the system, which would allow less duplication of low-use items. We explore a new CLR project in the next chapter.

A "mosaic overlay of collection development policies" is what the RLG conspectus and ARL National Collection Inventory Project (NCIP) tried to accomplish. Their purpose was to assure national coverage; to identify collection gaps nationally; to serve as a basis for libraries taking on collecting responsibilities (primary collecting responsibility, or PCR); to assist in directing scholars to strong collections; to create a consistent basis for collection development policies; to function as a communication device signaling changes in collection activities; to serve as a link among collecting policies and processing and preservation policies; to serve as a possible fund-raising tool; and finally, to stimulate interest in, and support for, cooperative programs. Whether NCIP and RLG efforts will succeed in achieving that long list of purposes, only time will tell, but as of 2004 it seems highly unlikely. The final product will be an assessment of collection strength in almost 7,000 subject categories by the participating libraries, giving each appropriate subject category a value of 0 to 5. When that is done, we shall know which libraries think they have strong or weak collections in each area, but we will not know exactly what is in each collection. The assessment will identify gaps and will be useful for referral purposes, and perhaps for ILL if the library is online and the library seeking the information can tap that database. The possibility of each of some 200 or so research libraries (a generous estimate of potential participants) accepting its share of the potential 5,000 PCRs, about 25 PCRs each, is grand. Will it happen? It would be wonderful if it did; however, it has not happened yet.

Shared Purchases

An example of resource sharing on a more limited scale is the University of California Library System's "Shared Collections and Access Program." The program has a twenty-year history of shared buying. When initiated as the "Shared Purchase Program," its purpose was:

> to acquire materials which, because of their high cost (or anticipated frequency of use), should be shared among the campuses without unnecessary duplication. The program has also been instituted to reduce competition for, and to promote sharing of, manuscript and subject area collections among the various campuses of the University of California. Stanford University is a full member of the program. However, state funds will not be used to acquire materials housed at Stanford (except for necessary indexes). Materials acquired with shared funds are to be shared among the campuses either statewide or on a regional (North and South) basis.[13]

Any campus library can recommend items for the committee to acquire, and membership on the committee rotates so that every campus has representation from time to time.

Creating a pool of funds for group purchases is usually a complex issue when it cuts across jurisdictional lines. One of the most successful shared purchase programs is that of the Center for Research Libraries (CLR). Libraries pay a membership fee to belong to CLR, and a portion of that fee goes into a fund to acquire materials that are housed in the CLR facility. This avoids one of the issues in shared purchases—who will house what is likely to be *very* useful material.

To some degree one could consider various consortia projects to lease e-resources as a form of shared purchasing. It is less valid when one looks at databases, but there have been consortial purchases of e-books in which member libraries agree to a package of titles. In one case, the Statewide California Electronic Library Consortium's (SCELC) purchase of e-books went well for the initial package, but follow-on collections have proven to be as problematic as print book cooperative purchases.

Local and International Projects

A current project illustrates most of the points discussed in this chapter. Los Angeles County has a number of libraries with theology collections that support one or more degree programs. None of the libraries are well-off financially, and combining acquisition budgets would be of assistance to all customers. Certainly, there is interest in cooperative work at the directors' level. Thus, there is enough institutional and library support to at least explore cooperative ventures. It is still much too early to know how many, if any, of the specific institutional barriers will arise.

Because all of the schools are private institutions, they should not encounter any legal barriers. Because the project remains in the "what-if" stage, it is unknown whether any administrative barriers may appear. However, it seems likely that administrative barriers could be quickly resolved.

Technology has been on our side, at least so far. In 1999, those of us from the twenty-three theology libraries that use EBSCO as our serials agent agreed to have the firm produce a union list of our serials subscriptions (quarterly or more frequent titles). The listing is comprehensive, not just theology and philosophy titles, so we have a fairly sound knowledge of our joint serials holdings. Naturally, there are a few direct-order titles that do not appear on the list. We could use this listing as the starting point for cooperative serials collection management. We have agreed to an annual update of the listing. This could not have been done fifteen years ago without the expenditure of large sums of money. The next step will be to agree that any theology or philosophy title held by only one of us would not be canceled without first consulting the other libraries.

Most of us have a fax machine, and for those that do not, an investment of a few hundred dollars would provide a Los Angeles-area theological library fax network. Assuming that the libraries could agree to giving member libraries priority ILL fax service for theology or philosophy articles, they would achieve a journal document delivery service that should satisfy most customers.

All but a few of the libraries have OPACs. For a relatively modest cost, each could provide dial-in access, at least by member library staff. This would allow the libraries to share information about what each library has in its monograph collections. Certainly, it would be ideal to have a union OPAC, but that is unrealistic at this time. Without question, having to dial into ten or more individual OPACs to determine whether a library owns a desired title would be time-consuming. Nevertheless, it would appear that such an approach would provide better service than the libraries now provide. Even without entering into formal subject buying agreements, this approach would allow the libraries to make some selection decisions on the basis of knowing who has what in the local area. Some of the libraries have automation systems that reflect information about items on order in the OPAC. This would provide additional data for selectors, if all the libraries could agree to activate such a capability in their systems.

The lack of a union catalog will make it more difficult for the Los Angeles-area theology libraries to determine strengths, weaknesses, and, perhaps of greatest importance, degree of overlap. One option that exists to solve this problem, for the libraries using OCLC, is to use the Collection Analysis service that we discussed in the last chapter. The major drawback to the product as it now stands is that one cannot determine which library in the peer group holds which titles. Nevertheless, it could be a useful tool if the project goes forward. (This was still a project under discussion as we completed this edition. The lengthy time frame for considering such a project is not unreasonable, if the project becomes a success.)

Thus, we have most of the necessary pieces available to set up a cooperative collection-building program:

- managerial interest;
- institutional interest (unknown as to strength);
- union list of serials;
- OPACs;
- collection assessment tool;

- document delivery capability;
- fax capability;
- courier service; and
- limited geographic service area.

Why is it taking so long, if all these positives exist? Lack of knowledge and people are to blame. We have not progressed far enough in our thinking to know exactly what we do and do not know. It is doubtful that many of us have much data about our collection use patterns. We probably would be hard-pressed to produce much data about our core collections, much less our high- and low-use research material. There is no sense of the costs involved. Thus, lack of knowledge and the time and money to collect the information are serious barriers.

However, the people concerns will pose the major problems. Customer resistance will be particularly hard to overcome. Some years ago, the senior author approached a member of the LMU faculty library committee, who is in the theology department, about this project. He was given a brief outline of the major points, which was presented to his department colleagues at their last meeting of the academic year. His report on the outcome of the discussion was depressing. The faculty said that they would prefer a mediocre collection in all areas at LMU, rather than having certain areas of great strength while depending on other libraries in the area for in-depth, noncurriculum, or course subjects. If other institutional faculty respond in a similar way, it will be difficult to get the project off the ground, even if the library staffs are fully supportive. Will it succeed? It will depend on how much we want it to work and how well we market the idea to our customers and our funding authorities.

Every information professional knows there is a long way to go in achieving that goal, even in countries with strong library systems and economies, let alone in developing countries. One only needs to look toward one extremely complex initiative to implement—the UNESCO Universal Availability of Publications (UAP) program. As Maurice Line stated,

> One of the main reasons why the situation with regard to UAP is so unsatisfactory is that availability has been approached piecemeal; particular aspects such as acquisitions and interlending have been tackled by individual libraries or groups of libraries, but uncoordinated piecemeal approaches can actually make things worse. . . . UAP must ultimately depend on action with individual countries.[14]

UAP is a very ambitious program designed to make published knowledge, in whatever form it is produced, available to anyone whenever he or she wants it. Since its formulation, UAP has undergone some significant changes, especially in terms of e-resources. During the early 1980s, few people had a clear idea what the volume of information would be in the digital world. The Web did not exist, home computers were not all that common, and few schools of libraries had more than terminals connected to a mainframe. National libraries around the world have made it clear they cannot acquire and maintain all the information resources produced in their country, much less do much about materials from other countries. We explore the issue of maintaining cultural heritage in the next chapter.

Summary

There are four main points to keep in mind about the subject of this chapter. First, the concept of cooperation is subject to many varying interpretations, even among the library staff—public service staff see it as more access, selection officers have both positive and negative views, and, often, top administrators see it as a way to save money. Second, status and budgets are still major issues, if there is a chance that cooperating might have a negative impact on size. Third, multitype or multisize library efforts are unlikely to succeed because of the libraries' different goals and what each library can contribute to a true cooperative venture. Finally, technology is making it increasingly easy to share collections, even with multitype consortia.

Cooperative collection development is not an easy task. Local needs often seem to be at odds with broader needs of the area or nation. However, problems of funding and local practices can be overcome. As new delivery systems become available, we may be able to break down the need for local self-sufficiency and expand resource-sharing programs beyond levels currently seen. It will be a long, slow process, but it is necessary to keep striving for this goal.

Ross Atkinson summed up this chapter, although he did not know it, when he wrote:

Many collection development officers of a certain age no doubt feel, as I do, that they have been reading about cooperation for most of their adult lives. Oceans of ink have been spilled in arguments over the rationale and practicability of cooperation—how future cooperative agreements might work, and why past ones have not. What is in fact so fascinating about cooperative collection development is why it is so plausible in theory—and yet so problematic to implement in practice.[15]

Notes

1.   Paula Kaufman, "Whose Good Old Days?" *Journal of Library Administration* 35, no. 3 (2001): 13.

2.   J. J. Branin, "Cooperative Collection Development," in *Collection Management: A Treatise*, 87 (Greenwich, CT: JAI Press, 1991).

3.   Edward Shreeves, "Is There a Future for Cooperative Collection Development in the Digital Age?" *Library Trends* 45 (Winter 1997): 373–91.

4.   *Webster's Third New International Dictionary* (Springfield, MA: G. & C. Merriam, 1976), 501.

5.   John Berry, "Killing Library Cooperation: Don't Let Professional Principles Become the Economy's Next Victim," *Library Journal* 117 (August 1992): 100.

6.   *ALA Glossary of Library and Information Science* (Chicago: American Library Association, 1983), 194.

7.   Boyd Rayward, "Local Node," in *Multiple Library Cooperation*, ed. B. Hamilton and W. B. Ernst (New York: R. R. Bowker, 1977), 66.

8.   Bart Harloe, ed., *Guide to Cooperative Collection Development*, Collection Management and Development Guides, no. 6 (Chicago: American Library Association, 1994).

9.   Western Association of Schools and Colleges, *Handbook of Accreditation* (Oakland, CA: Western Association of Schools and Colleges, 1988), 62.

10.   Julia Gammon and Michael Zeoli, "Practical Cooperative Collecting for Consortia: Books-Not-Bought in Ohio," *Collection Management* 28, nos. 1/2 (2003): 77–105.

11.   Pub. L. No. 480, The Agricultural Trade Development and Assistance Act, *codified at* 7 U.S.C. § 41.

12.   *A Historical Guide to the U.S. Government*, ed. George T. Kurian and Joseph P. Harahan (New York: Oxford, 1998), 366.

13.   University of California, Library Council, Collection Development Committee, *Guidelines for University of California Library Acquisitions with Shared Purchase Funds* (Berkeley: University of California Press, 1984), 1.

14.   Maurice Line, "Universal Availability of Publications: An Introduction," *Scandinavian Public Library Quarterly* 15 (1982): 48.

15.   Ross Atkinson, "Uses and Abuses of Cooperation in a Digital Age," *Collection Management* 28, nos. 1/2 (2003): 3–4.

Selected Websites*

(See also resources on the DLC5 website: <http://www.lu.com/dlc5>)

Center for Research Libraries
       <http://wwwcrl.uchicago.edu/>
       Provides information on CRL activities, including collaborative programs.

BOCES School Library Services—Cooperative Collection Development
       <http://www.oneida-boces.org/sls/cooperative_collection_developme.htm>
       Website for the Board of Cooperative Educational Services (BOCES) for Oneida/Herkimer School Library System, New York. Provides an example of a cooperative collection development program in the school library setting. Includes a policy statement and FAQ.

Statewide California Electronic Library Consortium
       <http://scelc.org/>
       Website of SCELC, providing background information on the consortium and links to member websites.

University of California Libraries: Shared Collections
       <http://libraries.universityofcalifornia.edu/planning/shared_collections.html>
       A listing of shared collection activities in the UC system.

*These sites were accessed May 7, 2005.

Further Reading

Anderson, K. J., R. Freeman, and J.V.M. Hérubel. "Buy, Don't Borrow: Bibliographers' Analysis of Academic Library Collection Development Through Interlibrary Loan Requests." *Collection Management* 27, nos. 3/4 (2002): 1–10.

Atkinson, R. "Uses and Abuses of Cooperation in a Digital Age." *Collection Management* 28, nos. 1/2 (2003): 3–20.

Ballard, T. H. *Failure of Resource Sharing in Public Libraries and Alternative Strategies for Service*. Chicago: American Library Association, 1986.

Bosch, S., L. Lyons, M. H. Munroe, Anna H. Perrault, and C. Sugnet. "Measuring Success of Cooperative Collection Development." *Collection Management* 28, no. 3 (2003): 223–39.

———. "Public Libraries and Resource Sharing." *Encyclopedia of Library and Information Science* 44, supplement 9 (1989): 257–74.

Bright, S. K. "New York City School Library System: Resource Sharing Network." *Bookmark* 50 (Fall 1991): 54–55.

Brown, L. A. "Strategic Duplication: The OhioLINK Perspective." In *Charleston Conference Proceedings 2002*, edited by R. Bazirjian and V. Speck, 153–55. Westport, CT: Libraries Unlimited, 2003.

Burgett, J., J. Haar, and L. L. Phillips. *Collaborative Collection Development: A Practical Guide for Your Library*. Chicago: American Library Association, 2004.

Childs, M., and W. Weston. "Consortia and Electronic Journals: An Overview." In *E-Serials Collection Management: Transitions, Trends, and Technicalities*, edited by D. C. Fowler, 91–110. New York: Haworth, 2004.

Curl, M. W. "Yours? Mine? Ours? Duplication in Consortia." In *Charleston Conference Proceedings 2002*, edited by R. Bazirjian and V. Speck, 156–60. Westport, CT: Libraries Unlimited, 2003.

Diamant-Cohen, B., and D. Sherman. "Hand in Hand: Museums and Libraries Working Together." *Public Libraries* 42 (March–April 2003): 102–5.

Dickinson, G. K. "Effect of Technology on Resource Sharing in a School Media Program." In *Advances in Library Resource Sharing*, edited by J. S. Cargill and D. J. Graves, 97–105. Greenwich, CT: Meckler, 1992.

Doyle, C., C. Millson-Martula, and S. Stratton. "Stone Age Consortia, New Age Consortia: The Place for Coordinated Cooperative Collection Management." In *Charleston Conference Proceedings 2001*, edited by K. Strauch, 157–67. Westport, CT: Libraries Unlimited, 2003.

Edelman, F. "Death of the Farmington Plan." *Library Journal* 98 (April 15, 1973): 1251–53.

Edwards, P. M. "Collection Development and Maintenance across Libraries, Archives, and Museums." *Library Resources & Technical Services* 48, no. 1 (2004): 26–33.

Fosbender, L. "University of California Collection Management Initiative." *California Libraries* 12, no. 2 (2002): 11.

Gammon, J. A., and M. Zeoli. "Practical Cooperative Collecting for Consortia: Books-Not-Bought in Ohio." *Collection Development* 28, nos. 1/2 (2003): 77–106.

Haar, J. "Assessing the State Cooperative Collection Development." *Collection Management* 28, no. 3 (2003): 183–90.

Hannesdottir, S. K. *Scandia Plan*. Metuchen, NJ: Scarecrow Press, 1992.

Hayes, R. M. "Cooperative Game Theoretic Models for Decision-Making in Contexts of Library Cooperation." *Library Trends* 51, no. 3 (2003): 441–61.

Hughes, C. A. "Resource Sharing." In *Librarianship and Information Work Worldwide*. General ed. Maurice Line; edited by Graham Mackenzie and Paul Sturges, 209–42. London: Bowker Saur, 1999.

Johns, C. "Collection Management Strategies in a Digital Environment." *Collection Development* 28, nos. 1/2 (2003): 37–44.

Karris, R. "Consortium Level Collection Development." *Library Collections, Acquisitions, & Technical Services* 27, no. 3 (2003): 317–26.

Kohl, D. F. "Doing Well by Doing Good." *Journal of Academic Librarianship* 29, no. 4 (July 2003): 205–6.

Kulleseid, E. "Cooperative Collection Development in the School Library Revolution." *Bookmark* 50 (Fall 1991): 21–23.

Langston, M. "The California State University E-book Pilot Project." *Library Collections, Acquisitions, & Technical Services* 27, no. 1 (2003): 19–32.

Lord, J., and B. Ragon. "Working Together to Develop Electronic Collections." *Computers in Libraries* 21 (May 2001): 40–44.

Luquire, W., ed. *Coordinating Cooperative Collection Development: A National Perspective.* New York: Haworth Press, 1986.

Lynden, F. C. "Will Electronic Information Finally Result in Real Resource Sharing?" *Journal of Library Administration* 24, nos. 1/2 (1996): 47–72.

Miller, K. L. "Library Consortia Change the Rules." *Computers in Libraries* 16 (November–December 1996): 20–21.

Mirsky, P. S. "The University of California's Collection Development Collaboration." *Collection Development* 28, nos. 1/2 (2003): 55–62.

Morgan, E. L. "Resource Sharing and Consortia, or, Becoming a 600-Pound Gorilla." *Computers in Libraries* 18, no. 4 (1998): 40–41.

Munroe, M. H., and J. E. Ver Steeg. "The Decision-Making Process in Conspectus Evaluation of Collections: The Quest for Certainty." *Library Quarterly* 74, no. 2 (2004): 181–205.

Oberlander, C., and D. Streeter. "LibStatCAT: A Library Statistical Collection Assessment Tool for Individual Libraries & Cooperative Collection Development." *Library Collections, Acquisitions, and Technical Services* 27, no. 4 (Winter 2003): 493–506.

Perrault, A. H. "The Role of WorldCat in Resources Sharing." *Collection Development* 28, nos. 1/2 (2003): 63–76.

Peters, T. "Is Collaboration an Unnatural Act?" In *Charleston Conference Proceedings 2001,* edited by K. Strauch, 173–80. Westport, CT: Libraries Unlimited, 2003.

Potter, G. "Recent Trends in Statewide Academic Library Consortia." *Library Trends* 45, no. 3 (1997): 416–33.

Reilly, B. F., Jr. "The Case for Belts and Suspenders: Risk Management Aspects of Cooperative Collection Development." *Collection Development* 28, nos. 1/2 (2003): 121–34.

Rosen, F. "Infinite Collections, Almost." *Library Journal* 130 (Spring 2005): 4–11.

Scigliano, M. "Consortium Purchases: Case Study for a Cost-Benefit Analysis." *The Journal of Academic Librarianship* 28, no. 6 (2002): 393–99.

Scott, S. "Cooperative Collection Development: A Resource Sharing Activity for Small Libraries." *Colorado Libraries* 18 (June 1992): 27–28.

Seaman, S. "Collaborative Collection Management in a High-Density Storage Facility." *College & Research Libraries* 66, no. 1 (January 2005): 20–27.

Severt, L. C. "The Once and Future Union List." *The Serials Librarian* 45, no. 1 (2003): 59–69.

Shales, N. C. "Cooperative Collection Management Succeeds in Illinois." *Resource Sharing and Information Networks* 12, no. 1 (1996): 49–53.

Shelton, C. "Best Practices in Cooperative Collection Development." *Collection Management* 28, no. 3 (2003): 191–222.

Shreeves, E. "Is There a Future for Cooperative Collection Development in the Digital Age?" *Library Trends* 45, no. 3 (1997): 373–91.

Sloan, B. "Evolution Takes a Leap." *Library Journal* 130 (Spring 2005): 2–3.

Waldhart, T. J. "Resource Sharing by Public Libraries." *Public Libraries* 34, no. 4 (1995): 220–24.

16
Protecting
the Collection

Nicholson Baker's *"Double Fold: Libraries and the Assault on Paper"*[1] gained a surprising amount of press coverage when it appeared in 2001. Perhaps one reason for this attention was the fact that much of his book focused on how libraries are handling newspaper backfiles. In the book, he took exception to many aspects of what he saw as inappropriate library preservation activities. He complained about microfilming newspapers followed by their disposal, as well as claiming that the "brittle book" issue is overstated by librarians.

In some way, librarians may owe Mr. Baker a thank-you for raising the issue of preserving the artifact as well as the content. At about the time Baker's book appeared, there was an increase in the volume of literature dealing with the need to do more with our cultural heritage.[2] This is not to say that protecting our investment in the collection has faded, as it has not; however, there is once again concern about the artifact.

A major premise of this book is that collection development is the central function of collection management. However, collection management involves several other functions as well, including preservation and conservation of the collection. As there should be a concern for preservation and conservation throughout the collection development process, it is appropriate to place responsibility for preservation with the collection managers. More and more libraries are placing preservation and binding under the direction of the chief collection development officer.

There are several aspects to protecting the collection, including proper handling of materials, environmental control, security (to protect against theft and mutilation) and disaster preparedness planning, binding, preservation, and insurance. Most of these issues are broad concerns, and detailed discussion of them is beyond the scope of this book; however, this chapter briefly touches on each topic. In a sense, all these factors work together to prolong the useful life of the materials in the collection. Even insurance fulfills this function, because claims payments help the library replace lost or damaged items.

Problems of acidic paper have long been the major concern of those involved in conservation activities in the library, in spite of what Mr. Baker believes and wrote. However, there is now a new challenge that may be more difficult to resolve than neutralizing the acid in paper. (In fact, many books are now printed on acid-free paper.) This challenge involves electronic resources and their long-term preservation. We explore this issue later in the chapter.

Two terms, conservation and preservation, are in common use but have different meanings for different people. We use the definitions that appeared in the *ALCTS Newsletter* in 1990.[3] *Conservation* can be defined as "[t]he treatment of library or archive materials, works of art, or museum objects to stabilize them chemically or strengthen them physically, sustaining their survival as long as possible in their original form."[4] Meanwhile, *preservation* refers to "[a]ctivities associated with maintaining library, archival or museum materials for use, either in their original physical form or in some other format. Preservation is considered a broader term than Conservation."[5] Another term, *restoration*, is not often used in reference to library and archival work because it involves changing the original item. It is defined as "[t]reatment procedures intended to return cultural property to a known or assumed state, often through the addition of nonoriginal material."[6]

Essentially, we see most "good housekeeping" practices as part of the preservation program. Our discussion starts with print materials and follows the preservation-to-conservation concept. (It is beyond the scope of this book to explore restoration in any detail.)

Preservation

Proper Handling

Storage and handling are the first two steps in protecting a collection. Neither step requires extra expenditures on the part of the library. Libraries purchase storage units from time to time; the purchaser needs to give some thought to what is the most appropriate type of storage unit for the format. (This does not necessarily translate into the most expensive unit.)

For example, using too narrow and/or too shallow a shelf will result in items being knocked off and damaged. Filling shelves and drawers too tightly is a poor practice. Equally harmful is allowing the material to fall over on the shelf (because proper supports are lacking) or slide around in a drawer, because either practice will lead to damage in time. Buying adjustable storage units provides the library a measure of flexibility.

Anyone with extensive experience in shelving books (except a conservation specialist) probably has found a way to squeeze "just one more book" onto a shelf when good practice calls for shifting the material to provide proper space. This often happens when shelvers are under pressure to finish shelving a full book truck within a certain time period (or when space is at a premium). Having sound performance standards is proper management; however, libraries must be certain that the shelving standard includes time for shifting materials. Not factoring that in will result in cracked and damaged book spines, as well as torn headbands resulting from users' attempts to pull books out from a fully packed shelf. Books should be vertical or horizontal on the shelf, not leaning this way and that. Fore-edge shelving should be avoided because it places undue strain on the binding (which is designed for horizontal or vertical storage). Proper supports and bookends help to keep materials in good order. Poorly constructed or finished supports can be more damaging to materials than having none at all.

Teaching people how to handle material properly is important. Training public service staff is an ongoing task; teaching proper handling techniques, if not already taught, will cost some time but will pay off in longer-lasting materials. One should make an effort to educate users in proper handling of materials as well. Some librarians regard housekeeping issues as bad for the library's image. If the library effectively communicates the fact that monies spent on repair and replacement of materials damaged through improper handling ultimately means less money to buy new material, people will understand the importance of housekeeping. It does not take more than two or three items sent for rebinding to equal the cost of a new book. Additionally, like everything else related to collection development, bindery fees are constantly increasing.

Environmental Control

Climate control in the library is essential to any successful preservation program. Few libraries are able to follow the example of the Newberry Library in Chicago, where a stack area ten stories high is double-shelled, windowless, and monitored by a computerized environmental system. Something less complex, however, will still help extend the useful life of most materials. The major concerns for environmental control are humidity, temperature, and light. Architects and librarians should take these issues into account when planning a library building. This is often easier said than done, because the ideal environmental conditions for human comfort and for preserving materials do not match. For example, the design specifications of the book stacks for the Newberry Library storage facility call for a constant temperature of 60°F +/–5°F and a relative humidity (RH) of 35 percent.[7]

Few people would be happy to engage in sedentary work all day in a room with a 60-degree temperature. As a result, most library designs place human comfort ahead of material preservation. The only time designers can effectively meet both sets of requirements is in situations like the Newberry, where the stacks are closed to the public and even employees are in the stacks for only short periods. Still, this arrangement does not answer all concerns about the environment for preserving materials. There are also differences in the ideal conditions for preserving various types of materials. Thus, building design characteristics may present some problems for implementing a good preservation program.

Institutional emphasis on energy conservation can lead to cooler winter temperatures and warmer summer temperatures. Cooler winter temperatures are better for materials, but normally the temperature is still well above 65 degrees. The greatest damage occurs in summer, when reducing air-conditioning costs becomes an institutional priority. (A related problem is that changes in air temperature affect relative humidity.) One way to reduce air-conditioning costs is to turn off the system when the library is closed, but overnight shutdowns are damaging to materials. When the system is off for some time, such as the weekend, the temperature can rise dramatically. When the air-conditioning is turned back on, the temperature falls fairly quickly. This "roller coaster" temperature swing is more damaging to materials than storing them at a steady, somewhat higher temperature. Temperature cycling is damaging (it ages paper prematurely), but so are high temperatures. For every rise of 10°C, book paper deteriorates twice as fast. With rapid fluctuations in temperature, the primary problem is the humidity level, which causes damage to the materials.

The Library of Congress Preservation Leaflet no. 2 (*Environmental Protection of Books and Related Materials* [Washington, D.C., 1975]) recommends a temperature of 55°F in book storage areas and a maximum of 75°F (below 70°F, if possible) in reading areas, all with a 50 percent relative humidity. Paul Banks, a well-known preservation specialist who set the standards for the Newberry storage area, also recommended 50 percent relative humidity. For most libraries constructed after World War II, there is little chance of having temperature differentials in storage and reading areas, because the design concept called for integrating readers and materials. Also, in most libraries, the temperature and humidity range is much greater than +/–5°F.

Why the concern with humidity? Because changes in humidity can physically weaken materials, which, in turn, can create added costs for repair or replacement. Books (including bound periodicals) consist of a number of different materials—paper, cloth, cardboard, thread, man-made fabrics, adhesives, and sometimes metal (e.g., staples). Often, a single book is made up of several different types of material from each category; for example, heavy endpapers, a moderate-weight paper for the text, and coated paper for illustrations. Each component absorbs and loses water vapor (humidity) at a different rate. Materials expand as they absorb moisture and shrink as the humidity falls. As the amount of water vapor in the air goes up or down, there is constant shrinking and swelling of the materials. With each expansion and contraction, the material weakens slightly. Overall, paper deterioration is the main problem with cycling. Humidity and heat combine to accelerate deterioration from paper acidity.

The differences in the rates of expansion and shrinkage for the different components in the book weaken the bonds between the components, making the book more likely to fall apart. (Humidity is also an issue with photographic materials.) Constant humidity stabilizes the materials. How much water vapor is normally present is important; paper fibers are subject to deterioration when humidity is somewhere below 40 percent. At 65 percent or higher, the chances of mildew and mold formation increase. The musty smell of the antiquarian bookshop may contain more than a hint of mildew or mold, something one does not want in the library.

Other materials (microfilms, videotapes, photographs, and so forth) have somewhat different ideal temperature and humidity storage requirements. The ideal range for microforms is 70°F +/–5°F with humidity at 40 percent +/–5 percent. The same ranges apply to still photographs and safety motion picture film. In contrast, nitrate-based motion picture film must be stored below 55°F but can tolerate humidity up to 45 percent. Videotapes do best at 65°F +/–5°F and no more than 45 percent humidity. Audiodiscs (LPs, 45s, and so forth) can handle temperatures up to 75°F and 50 percent humidity. However, the upper limits for audiotapes are 70°F and 45 percent humidity. Electronic media (CDs and DVDs) are best stored at temperatures between 14°F and 73°F, with a relative humidity between 20 and 50 percent.[8]

The National Archives has set even higher standards for its facility in College Park, Maryland. Text and map storage areas call for 70°F and 45 percent relative humidity. Black-and-white film, audiotapes, and sound recordings have a 65°F and 30 percent relative humidity limit. Glass negative, black-and-white photographs, slides, negatives, posters, and electronic materials are in areas with 65°F temperature and 35 percent relative humidity. Storage areas for color photography film, slides, and photographs are still cooler—38°F and 35 percent relative humidity. Coldest of all are storage areas for color motion picture film and color serial film, at 25°F and 30 percent relative humidity.

Recalling basic chemistry, we know that increasing the temperature also increases chemical activity. Roughly, chemical reactions double with each 10°C increase in temperature. Freezing books would be the best way to preserve them; however, it is not likely that readers would be willing to sit about in earmuffs, overcoats, and mittens. One is fortunate to achieve a controlled temperature below 70°F in areas where people work for extended periods. One reason for wanting the lower temperatures is to slow down the chemical decomposition of wood pulp paper, which the majority of books and journals contain. However, lower temperatures only slow the process; they do not stop it. All formats are sensitive to temperature variations, and the ideal storage condition is an environment with minimal changes.

Lighting, both natural and artificial, influences preservation in two ways. First, it contributes to the heat buildup in a building. Naturally, designers take this into account when specifying the building's heating, ventilating, and air-conditioning system. Fluorescent lighting is not a major heat contributor, but in older libraries where incandescent fixtures exist, the heat generated by the fixtures can be a problem. If the light fixtures are close to materials (i.e., in exhibit cases), there can be significant temperature differentials from the bottom to the top shelf in a storage unit. Windows and sunlight generate heat as well, and they create miniclimates. The Newberry Library's windowless storage unit eliminates the sunlight problem. Many libraries have designs featuring numerous windows to provide natural lighting (thus reducing electric costs) and to satisfy users' desire to see outside. The cost of these designs has been high in terms of money spent after a few years to reduce the sunlight problem and to repair damaged materials.

The second concern is ultraviolet radiation, a result of sunlight, fluorescent, and tungsten lights. Ultraviolet light is the most damaging form of light because it quickly causes materials to fade, turn yellow, and become brittle. Windows and fluorescent light fixtures should have ultraviolet screens or filters built in or installed. Tungsten lighting has the lowest levels of ultraviolet radiation, but even these lights should have filters. The longer one exposes materials to unfiltered light, the more quickly damage occurs. Nonprint materials are even more sensitive, and they require greater protective measures than do print materials.

Air filters that reduce the gases in the air inside the library are useful, if expensive. Urban activities pump a variety of harmful gases into the air every day. Some enter the building as people come and go. Few buildings have airlocks and ventilating systems that remove all harmful gases. Whenever it is economical, the ventilation system should remove the most harmful substances. Sulfur dioxide is a major air pollutant and a concern for library preservation programs, because it combines with water vapor to form sulfuric acid. Hydrogen sulfide, another common pollutant, also forms an acid that is harmful to both organic and inorganic materials. In addition to gases, air filters can reduce the number of solid particles contained in the building air. Dust and dirt include mold spores, which can cause problems if the air-conditioning fails in warm, humid weather. Solid particles act as abrasives, contributing to the wearing out and wearing down of materials. Dusty, gritty shelves wear away the edges of bindings—and, all too often, dusting book shelves is not in anyone's job description.

Mold can be a serious problem for paper-based collections and people as well. For example, *Aspergillas furnigatus* can be toxic, in sufficient quantities, and many molds can cause serious (even debilitating) allergy problems for some people. A good source of information about how to deal with a mold outbreak is the Northeast Document Conservation Center's "Technical Leaflet: Emergency Salvage of Moldy Books and Paper" (<http://www.nedcc.org/plam3/tleaf39.htm>).

Finally, insects contribute to the destruction of books and other items in the collection. Silverfish enjoy nothing more than a feast of wood pulp paper, flour paste, and glue. Cockroaches seem to eat anything but have a particular taste for book glue. Termites prefer wood, but wood pulp paper is a good second choice. Larder beetle larvae (book worms), though lacking intellectual curiosity, can devour *War and Peace* in a short time. Finally, book lice enjoy the starch and gelatin sizing on paper. Other, less destructive insects can infest collections in the temperate zones; in a tropical setting, the numbers and varieties increase dramatically. Control of insects presents a few challenges, because pesticides create pollution problems. Naturally, the best control is to keep the insects out. One way to control insects, especially cockroaches, is to keep food and drink out of the library. A second step is to keep the temperature and humidity as low as possible, because insects multiply faster and are more active at higher temperature and humidity levels. If the library faces a significant insect infestation, it is better to call on a commercial service rather than attempt to handle the problem with library staff.

What are the signs of insect infestation? Most of the insects that cause damage prefer the dark and to stay out of sight. When one sees them, it is a signal that the population may be so large that there is nowhere to hide. Obviously, if one finds "remains" of insects on shelves, windowsills, or the floor, it is a sign of potential trouble. Unusual dust, "sawdust," or colored powder on bookshelves is likely to be "frass" (insect droppings), and is a clear indication of a problem. A good source of information about pest management in libraries and archives is Chicora Foundation, Inc.'s *Managing Pests in Your Collection* (<http://palimpsest.stanford.edu/byorg/chicora/chicpest.html>). Another resource is Conservation OnLine's "Pest Management" bibliography at <http://palimpsest.stanford.edu/bytopic/pest/index.html>.

Gifts to the library require careful examination before being stored in any area where insects could get into the general collection. Shipments that arrive by sea mail also need careful study. As the concern for the environment increases, many in-library fumigation units have ceased to operate or been extensively (and expensively) modified. This may mean using commercial systems, with additional costs and delays in getting and keeping material on the shelf.

Security

We include physical security of the collection in our discussion because some of the issues are preservation issues—for example, mutilation and water/smoke damage.

A full library security program involves several elements. Broadly, the program's goals are to assure the well-being of people and to protect the collections and equipment from theft and misuse. This discussion emphasizes the collections, with only passing mention of the people and equipment issues; topics covered include theft, mutilation, and disaster preparedness. (For a fuller discussion of security programs, see chapter 14 in *Introduction to Library Public Services*, 5th edition.[9])

We tell people, only half in jest, that if a library wishes to identify its true core collection, all it has to do is prepare a list of all the lost and missing books and mutilated journal titles. Normally, these are the items that, for one reason or another, are (or were) under pressure from users, including high-use or, in the case of missing books, potentially high-use materials.

Every library loses materials each year to individuals who, if caught by the security system, say they forgot to check the material out. Journals and other noncirculating materials are subject to some degree of mutilation. Each incident of theft and mutilation means some small financial loss for the library, if nothing more than the cost of the material and the labor expended to make the item available. Other costs are the cost of staff time to search for the item, to decide how or whether to replace it, plus actual replacement and processing costs. Although a single incident seldom represents a significant cost, the total annual cost may be surprising, even if one calculates only the amount paid for replacement materials. The LMU library spends about $10,000 per year on replacement materials, and few of those replacements are for items that have become too worn to remain in circulation. This rate of loss occurs despite a high-quality electronic security exit system and targeting every book and every issue of every journal that goes into the collection. Time and money expended to prevent theft or replace materials are time and money not spent on expanding the resources available to users.

There are several givens to any security program. First, there will be some level of loss no matter what the library does. Second, the systems help basically honest people stay honest. A professional thief will circumvent almost any library security system, as Stephen Blumberg and David Siegelman demonstrated some years ago.[10] Therefore, the library must decide how important the problem is and how much loss it can tolerate. The goal is to balance the cost of the security program against the losses. The less loss the library will accept, the higher the security costs, so finding the proper balance is important.

Most libraries employ some mix of people-based elements and electronic systems for security. Door guards or monitors who check every item taken from the library are the most effective and most costly option. This method works well only when the person doing the checking is not a peer of the people being checked. That is, using students to check fellow students, much less their teachers, does not work well. Retired individuals are very effective. They interact well with users but also do the job without favoring anyone. The major drawback to exit monitors, after the cost, is, when there are peaks and valleys in the exit flow, there can be long queues during the peaks.

Electronic systems are common and may give a false sense of security. Every system has a weakness that the person who regularly "forgets to check out books" eventually discovers and that the professional thief knows. Also, some materials (e.g., magnetic tape and videotape) cannot have the "target" deactivated without damaging the content, and some materials simply do not have a place for a target. Such systems are susceptible to electronic interference, such as frequencies generated by computers or even fluorescent light ballasts. Finally, the inventive thief can jam the operating frequency, and no one on the staff will know the difference.

Mutilation is another ongoing problem, which, during a year, can generate a surprisingly large loss for the library. There are few cost-effective options for handling this problem. Having copy services available and at competitive prices will help. Monitors walking through the building will solve or reduce many other security problems but will do little to stop mutilation. Studies suggest that even users who see someone mutilating library materials will not report the activity to library staff.[11] One option that users do not like but that does stop the mutilation of journals is to supply only microform backfiles of journals that are subject to high mutilation. This option does not safeguard the current issues, and it requires providing microform reader-printers, which are more expensive than microform readers. There is also the occasional title that does not make its backfiles available in a microformat. Full-text CD-ROMs or Web-based services are a partial answer to some of the problems, because there is little user resistance to electronic material. However, if the person is seeking a color photograph or any color image, there may still be a problem, especially if the library does not provide color printing or copier service. Another option is to acquire multiple copies of high-use titles. Here again, one trades some collection breadth for a possible reduction in mutilation. Theft and mutilation are a part of doing business. How much they cost the library depends on the local situation. Those costs come at the expense of adding greater variety to the collections, and, in the long run, they hurt the user.

Disaster preparedness planning is vital for the protection of people, collections, and equipment. Planners must think in terms of both natural and man-made disasters. Earthquakes, hurricanes, tornadoes, heavy rains, and floods are the most common natural disasters for which one should plan. The most common man-made disaster is water damage, which can be caused by a broken water pipe or sprinkler head, a faulty air-conditioning system, or broken windows. In the case of a fire, water may cause more damage than the flames.

The following are the basic steps to take in preparing a disaster plan:

1. Study the library for potential problems. Often, the institution's risk management officer (insurance) is more than willing to help in that assessment.

2. Meet with local fire and safety officers for the same purpose.

3. Establish a planning team to develop a plan. This team may become the disaster-handling team.

4. Establish procedures for handling each type of disaster and, if appropriate, form different teams to handle each situation.

5. Establish a telephone calling tree, or other fast notification system, for each disaster. A *telephone tree* is a plan for who calls whom in what order.

6. Develop a salvage priority list for the collections. If necessary, mark a set of floor plans and include them in the disaster planning and response manual. Most plans do not have more than three levels of priority: first priority is irreplaceable or costly materials, second priority is materials that are expensive or difficult to replace, and third priority is the rest of the collection. (The LMU

plan includes a category for hand-carrying one or two items from the immediate work area, if the disaster strikes during normal working hours.) Establishing priorities can be a challenge for planners, because everyone has some vested interest in the subject areas with which he or she works.

7. Develop a list of recovery supplies the library will maintain on-site (e.g., plastic sheeting and butcher paper).

8. Include a list of resources—people and companies—that may assist in the recovery work.

After the planners finish the disaster plan, the library must put copies in the hands of each department and in the homes of the disaster team. It is also important to practice some of the procedures before disaster strikes. The LMU plan has been in place since 1991 and has been used three times, twice for water problems and once for an earthquake. With the water problems, the library was able to save all but eight books out of more than 15,000 that got wet. Had the staff not practiced its disaster response plan ahead of time, the loss rate would have been much higher. The library did not fare as well in the earthquake, because it is impossible to practice having book stacks collapse. Although LMU certainly fared better than libraries closer to the epicenter, it lost 1,237 books. Unfortunately, these losses could have been avoided if the shelving had been properly braced. The library staff knew where the problem stacks were and was waiting for funds to have the stacks retrofitted; however, the earthquake was quicker than the funding authorities.

Locating water, gas, and electrical system shutoffs is a good starting point for training the disaster team. Next, the team should check fire extinguisher locations to determine whether the units are operational and are inspected regularly. The team also should implement a program to train staff in use of the extinguishers. Usually, the local fire department will do this at no charge. There are three types of fire extinguishers: "A" for wood and paper fires, "B" for oil and electrical fires, and "C" for either type of fire. It is important to match the type of extinguisher to the location and anticipated problems. It is equally important to prepare floor plans, clearly identifying locations of shutoffs and extinguishers, ahead of time, before such information would be needed in a crisis.

Salvage operations require careful planning and adequate personnel and materials. It is a good idea to develop a list of potential volunteers if the situation is too large for the staff to handle within a reasonable time. Keep in mind that the library can count on only about 72 hours of assistance from volunteers—that is, 72 hours from the time the first request for assistance goes out. Thus, there should be planning for what to do after 72 hours, if the disaster is major.

Water damage is a potentially destructive problem, as is the development of mold and mildew. Mold can develop in as little as 48 hours, depending on the temperature. What basic steps should one follow in a water emergency? The best way to handle large quantities of water-soaked paper is to freeze it and process the material as time and money allow. Planners should identify companies with large freezer facilities and discuss with them the possibility of using or renting their freezers in case of emergency. Often, such companies are willing to do this at no cost, because of the good publicity they gain from such generosity. Large grocery store chains and meatpacking plants are possible participants. Refrigerated trucks can be most useful, if costly to rent. Getting wet materials to the freezing units is a problem: milk crates, open plastic boxes, or clothes baskets work well, because they allow water to drain. Cardboard boxes absorb water. Plastic interlocking milk crates are ideal, because they are about the right size for a person to handle when three-fourths full of wet material. Sometimes, local dairies are willing to assist by supplying free crates for the duration of the emergency. Freezer or butcher paper is best for separating the materials; never use newsprint, because it tends to stick, and the ink comes off. Finally, find some drying facilities. There are three primary methods of drying wet books: (1) freezing/freeze-drying, (2) vacuum drying, and (3) vacuum freeze-drying. Vacuum freeze-drying is the best way to handle wet items. Often, vacuum drying facilities are difficult to locate and can handle only a small volume of material at a time, so materials may be in the freezer for a long time while a small quantity is done whenever the source and funding permit. A variety of disaster-related online information, including Peter Waters' *Procedures for Salvage of Water-Damaged Library Materials*, is available from Conservation OnLine (CoOL, <http://palimpsest.stanford .edu>).

Two other steps are important when designing a disaster preparedness plan. One is to identify the nearest conservation specialist(s). Most are willing to serve as a telephone resource, and often they will come to the scene. A second important step is to arrange for special purchasing power. Although some groups, organizations, and companies may be willing to assist free of charge, many will not, and the library may need to commit quickly to a specific expense. Having to wait even a few hours for approval may cause irreversible damage.

While most disasters are relatively minor—a few hundred water-damaged items—a large disaster is always possible. One example was the April 1986 fire that struck the Los Angeles Public Library. For more than ten years, there had been concern about the fire danger, but the hope that a new building would be constructed forestalled major modifications in the existing building. According to *Library Hotline*, it took 1,700 volunteers working around the clock to shrink-wrap and freeze the 400,000 water-soaked books (about 20 percent of the Central Library's collection).[12] In addition, the city paid a salvage contractor $500,000 for his firm's services. As we were preparing this volume, the Hamilton Library at the University of Hawaii at Manoa was recovering from a flash flood that caused considerable damage to collections, computing equipment, and facilities alike.[13]

Although incidents such as those named above were devastating at the time, one can only speculate what the costs and problems might have been at both of these institutions had disaster preparedness plans not existed. In preparing a plan for your institution, it is helpful to review plans developed by similar institutions. A number of plans are available online, including that of the University of Maryland Libraries (<http://www.lib .umd.edu/TSD/PRES/disasterplan.html>).

Conservation

By having the collection properly stored and handled in a controlled climate and with sound security practices as well as a disaster preparedness plan in place, the library will lengthen the useful life of its materials and reduce conservation problems. However, if the library fails to employ good preservation methods, much of what it gains from those practices will be lost as items fade, decompose, or become unusable. Preservation should start with the purchase decision (which ought to include consideration of how well the material will stand up to the expected use) and should end with the question of what to do about worn, damaged materials and items identified in the deselection process.

One element in a library's conservation program is the basic binding and repair program. In-house repairs are fine as long as they employ good conservation methods and use materials that will not cause more harm. Repairers should do nothing that cannot be undone later, if necessary. For example, one should avoid using any adhesive tape other than a reversible adhesive, nonacidic tape to repair a torn page.

Most commercial binderies follow sound practices and employ materials that will not add to an already serious problem of decomposing books. An excellent overview of library binding practices, in a commercial setting, is Paul Parisi's "An Overview of Library Binding."[14] Selecting a commercial binder should involve the chief collection officer, if the bindery operation is not under the supervision of that person. Most libraries spend thousands of dollars on bindery and repair work each year, and having a reliable and efficient binder who uses the proper materials benefits the library and its users. Knowing something about bindery operations and the process the materials undergo can help the library staff responsible for selecting materials for binding to make better judgments about the type of binding to order, given the probable use of the material. Most commercial binders are pleased to explain their operations and give customers and new library employees tours of their plant.

A current challenge facing conservation programs is acidic wood pulp paper. William J. Barrow is the person most often associated with identifying acid as the cause of the deterioration of wood pulp paper.[15] The problem is not new, but people are now seeing the full implications of the findings of Barrow and other researchers. Estimates vary as to just how big the problem is. One project estimated that there were more than 600,000 brittle or moderately brittle books in a collection of 2 million books in the UCLA library system in 1979. (A *brittle book* is one in which a corner of a page breaks off when folded back and forth once or twice.) The estimate was based on a random sample of books in the collection. An estimated 1 million volumes in Widener Library (Harvard University) were reported to be in similar condition.[16] In the early 1980s, the Library of Congress estimated that it had 6 million brittle volumes.[17] According to Richard Dougherty, the Commission on Preservation and Access estimated that "more than 25 percent of the world's greatest monographic collections are already embrittled beyond redemption."[18] The problem grows with each passing day, and nothing is done to stop the process. Unfortunately, few libraries have sufficient funding to do more than address a small percentage of the items needing attention.

Deanna Marcum published a short article in the *New York Times* in 1998 about the ever-growing problem of conservation. She outlined the stark facts and made a strong case that technology may be a greater problem than acidic paper. In the article, she noted that the U.S. national archivist had advised government agencies that they "could delete certain computer files *if they kept paper copies*" (emphasis added).[19] She also noted that the acidic paper issue was still a problem.

In the case of brittle books, short fibers and chemical residues from the paper-manufacturing process are the culprits. The longer the fibers in the paper, the stronger it is. When ground wood pulp became the standard source for paper manufacturing, the long-term strength of paper dropped sharply. A weak paper combined with the acidic residue from sizing and bleaching, as well as lignin (a component of the wood used for paper), creates self-destructing material. At one end of the scale is newsprint, which is very acidic; at the other end is the nonacidic paper that more and more publishers are using in books. The Council on Library Resources' efforts to establish some guidelines for publishers, manufacturers, and librarians regarding the use of alkaline paper in book production are paying off. The CLR report stated that "alkaline paper *need not be more expensive* than acidic paper of the quality normally used in hardbound books."[20]

What can be done about materials that are self-destructing in the stacks? Maintaining environmental factors (temperature, humidity, and light) at the recommended levels slows the chemical processes; thus, this is a first step to take. For the already-brittle materials in the collection, the two concerns are permanence (shelf life) and durability (use). Permanence is the first issue, and there are several ways to stop the acidic activity. After the acidic action is under control, several options exist to enhance durability.

Several mass deacidification systems on the market are designed to process large numbers of books at one time. The only one with a reasonably long history of use is the Wei T'o process, developed by Richard Smith. Probably the second best known system is the DEZ system. Developed with the support of the Library of Congress, the process received widespread press coverage after it encountered several problems, the most notable being an explosion at the test site.[21] A good review of the history of deacidification systems is found in Michèle V. Cloonan's "Mass Deacidification in the 1990s."[22]

Options for Handling Brittle Materials

Given the magnitude of the acid paper problem, almost every library will be faced with a variety of decisions on what to do. Here, if nowhere else, collection development staff must enter the preservation picture. When an item in the collection deteriorates to the point that it cannot be rebound, what should one do? Ten options exist:

- Ignore the problem and return the item to storage.
- Withdraw the item from the collection and do not replace it.
- Seek a reprint edition on alkaline paper.
- Convert the material to microfilm and decide what to do with the original.
- Convert the material to an electronic format.
- Photocopy the material on alkaline paper and decide what to do with the original.
- Seek a replacement copy through the out-of-print trade.
- Place it in an alkaline protective enclosure made for the item and return it to the collection.
- Withdraw the item from the main collection and place it in a controlled access storage facility.
- Deacidify and strengthen the item and return it to use.

Ignoring the problem is the most reasonable alternative for materials about which one is confident that long-term retention is unnecessary or undesirable and only a limited amount of use is probable. If there is little or no probability of use in the near future, withdrawing the item is probably the most effective option.

Seeking a reprint edition printed on alkaline paper is the least expensive option for materials that are worth long-term storage and probably will experience moderate to heavy use. Reprints are not available for all the items that are self-destructing; only the high-demand titles are reprinted. Several companies exist to serve the reprint market, for example, Primary Source Microfilm, Dover Publications, and Replica Books (Baker & Taylor), while *Guide to Reprints* (K. G. Saur), *Books on Demand* (University Microfilms, <http://wwwlib.umi.com/bod>), and *Guide to Microforms in Print* (K. G. Saur) are three sources of information about a broad range of titles. (Just because an item is a reprint does not mean that it is printed on alkaline paper. Be certain to specify alkaline paper when ordering.)

Microformat and electronic storage of the brittle material are other options. Until the mid-1980s, microfilming was the most common way of storing the content of brittle materials in a secondary format. The cost of making the master negative is high, but once made, duplicate copies are relatively inexpensive to produce. Thus, if the primary collection development concern is with preserving the intellectual content of the brittle material and not with the item as an artifact, a microformat is a good solution. It may be possible to locate a master copy of an item, thereby reducing costs. One place to check is the *Guide to Microforms in Print*, which lists titles from commercial publishers around the world.

Digitization of an item for preservation or access purposes is another option, although, as we will note later, there are some doubts as to the long-term stability and accessibility of digital objects. Digitization can occur either by scanning the original object, taking a digital photograph, or transcribing the text into word-processing software. Additional advantages of this method include the ability to digitally restore damaged materials.[23] An article exploring the various facets of digital preservation is by Lavoie and Dempsey.[24]

One method of preservation that can be considered as being related to digitization is taking a photocopy of the original. This may be the best option when the library anticipates moderate use and cannot locate a reprint. There are commercial firms that will produce a bound photocopy on alkaline paper from an individual volume on demand. This is an especially good alternative when it is not necessary to preserve the original item. Photocopying and microfilming cause physical wear on bound materials, and a bound item may have to be taken apart to be duplicated properly. Generally, in the photocopy process, there is some loss in image quality; obviously, this may not be acceptable for items with high-quality photographs and illustrations. Several paper manufacturers offer buffered (alkaline) paper for use in photocopy machines. When binding the photocopies, it is necessary to specify that the binder use buffered materials. If alkaline paper or deacidified paper comes into contact with acidic material, the acid will migrate into the alkaline paper and start the process all over again.

The staff should think carefully before going to the out-of-print market for replacement copies. Although a replacement copy may be available at the lowest price of any of the options, will the replacement be in any better condition than the one it is to replace? Unless the replacement copy had better storage conditions than the library's copy, both will be in about the same state of deterioration. It is probable that the replacement copy will be less worn (as long as it is not an ex-library copy), but there will be little difference in the acidic state. Normally, the replacement copy's storage history is worse than the library's copy, and thus the replacement copy will be in greater need of conservation.

Protective enclosures or containers provide a stopgap treatment. Enclosing the brittle item in an alkaline container (made of paper, plastic, or cardboard) protects it from unnecessary handling and light. This is a common method of storage for the original (hopefully deacidified) item when a surrogate copy is available for general use. The most common approach is to make custom-sized phase boxes for the item using alkaline cardboard. Bindery/archival supply firms and commercial binderies offer a wide range of prefabricated, standard-sized phase boxes, as well as materials for constructing custom-sized boxes. Unfortunately, the materials, including alkaline mending tapes and adhesives, are expensive. To save a small amount of money, some libraries decide not to use the proper materials. Certainly, there is no need to use expensive mending materials on items that the library is likely to discard in time, but, all too often, librarians do not know which items will be kept and which will be discarded.

The following are some basic guidelines for preparing materials for storage:

1. Remove extraneous materials, such as paper clips, rubber bands, wrapping material, old folders, and any other material that is not pertinent. If foreign matter, such as pressed flowers, must be saved as documentary evidence, place it in a separate enclosure.

2. Unfold and flatten papers wherever possible without causing damage to the folds. If the paper is brittle or inflexible, it may have to be humidified before unfolding. Remove surface soil with a soft brush.

3. Isolate newsprint because it is highly acidic and will stain adjacent paper. Newspaper clippings can be replaced with photocopies on alkaline paper or placed in a separate envelope. Fax copies are similarly unstable and should be reproduced or isolated, unless they are plain-paper faxes.

4. Note any badly damaged items; place them within individual folders and set them aside for professional conservation treatment. Do not undertake any first aid unless you have received training and are qualified to do so.

5. If it is necessary to place identifying information on the object itself, use a soft (no. 2) pencil and write on the verso or in the lower right margin. Repeat the identification on the storage folders and envelopes in pencil or typing. Never use ballpoint or felt-tip pens, which might stain or bleed.

6. Identify boxes with labels that contain adequate information about the contents. This curtails unnecessary browsing and rifling through documents.[25]

If materials should be humidified (see step 2), consult Mary Lynn Ritzenthaler's *Preserving Archives and Manuscripts*.[26]

Restoration is expensive, and libraries will never be able to restore all or even most of the brittle items they own. As noted earlier, the deacidification process is also expensive, and added to that are costs of restoring strength to the individual pages and binding. For a good description of the advantages and disadvantages of the various methods of preservation, see Robert Mareck's "Practicum on Preservation Selection."[27]

To end this section on an upbeat note, in 1996 the Library of Congress (LC) began a major program to deacidify books in its collection. Prior to 1996, LC had had a series of evaluation programs, one of which led to the destruction of its test facility in 1986. Between 1996 and 1998, more than 100,000 books had gone through the process, and the Library of Congress awarded an updated contract in 2002, with the goal of treating over 250,000 books per year by the end of the contract.[28] More information on this program is available at <http://www.loc.gov/preserv/deacid/massdeac.html>.

Nonpaper Preservation Issues

Although this chapter emphasizes books and paper, other library materials also require preservation and conservation. In many cases, librarians, as well as technicians, do not fully understand how long a format may last without loss of information or what problems may arise. However, various groups, such as the Council on Library Resources (CLR), the Mellon Foundation, and the National Endowment for the Humanities, are actively exploring the issue.

Like paper products, all photographic products (microfilm, photographs, motion picture films) are self-destructing on the shelves and in the cabinets of libraries and archives. There was some hope that electronic technologies would prove a more stable storage medium for older materials, and longevity testing is still under way. We already know that there are serious concerns about the long-term value of digitization of print materials. Issues of changing technology cloud the hopes of a digital solution.[29] No one can predict what it will cost to periodically check the data and restore them as necessary. One major question is who will be responsible and have the necessary funding to carry out the work.

A 1998 article in *U.S. News & World Report* had a title that sums up current concerns about electronic data: "Whoops, There Goes Another CD-ROM."[30] The author of the article described the frustration of NASA's Jet Propulsion Laboratory scientists when, in 1996, they tried to read magnetic data from the 1976 Viking Mars mission. What they found was that 10 to 20 percent of the data was missing—this in spite of the fact that the laboratory had tried to maintain the tapes according to "standard guidelines."

Anyone who has been a computer user for more than a few years knows something of the problem. Just try opening a word-processing document that was created two or more versions before the current version, one that had not been opened in the later versions. Even when one does open all the old documents in the newer version, one usually sees a warning message about the danger of possible loss of formatting and other information. Although the loss due to the migration from one version to the next may be small, the cumulative loss over ten or more versions could be significant. Given the speed with which software and hardware companies "improve" their products, it does not require too many years to reach potentially troubling losses.

Gerd Meissner wrote an article for the *New York Times* about problems in preserving data in the German Federal Archives.[31] In that piece he touched on many of the problems. "While shellac records or damaged microfilms can still be put to use today, one faulty data bit on a 10-year-old magnetic tape or a scratched optical disk often renders the rest of the stored information useless." Tracking down documentation, even from the company that produced the software or hardware, for old versions is difficult and sometimes impossible.

The NASA Jet Propulsion Laboratory and the German Federal Archives cases are just a sample of the problems that can arise with electronic data and serve as cautionary examples of the dangers in committing to digitization as *the* preservation solution. We have doubts about the effectiveness of digitization—"long-term" in the preceding cases was less than twenty-five years. We agree with Roy Tennant's assessment: "Digital libraries are sitting on a time bomb. Yes, libraries are already familiar with deteriorating materials, but digital libraries face an even graver threat."[32]

Librarians do have some recommended guidelines for checking some of these special formats. Staff should inspect and rewind motion picture film once every three years, inspect and rewind videotapes and audiotapes every two years, and inspect still photographs every three years. Peter Graham's paper dealing with electronic preservation is an excellent source of information about the issues related to preserving intellectual content in an electronic environment.[33] The Commission on Preservation and Access (which later evolved into the National Digital Library Federation) published a mission and goals statement for digital consortia that should help resolve some of the unanswered questions about digitized data and long-term retention. Although established some time ago, the goals are still useful guidelines. They are:

1. Verify and monitor the usefulness of digital imagery for preservation and access.
   a. Establish the convertibility of preservation media.
   b. Foster projects to capture special types of documents.
   c. Ensure the longevity of digitized images.
   d. Cultivate research on the application of intelligent character recognition.
2. Define and promote shared methods and standards.
   a. Sponsor forums to define production quality standards.
   b. Promote the development and use of the document structure file.
   c. Create appropriate bibliographic control standards.
   d. Address copyright issues.
   e. Organize a document interchange project.
3. Enlarge the base of materials.
   a. Encourage the involvement of service bureaus.
   b. Focus on the conversion of thematically related materials.
   c. Mount a large interinstitutional collaborative project.

4. Develop and maintain reliable and affordable mechanisms to gain access to digital image documents.

    a. Involve a broad base of constituents in technology development.

    b. Forge effective support structures for end users.

    c. Determine the efficacy of access to digital materials in the context of traditional library collections.[34]

Cooperation

Because of the magnitude of the problems confronting libraries and scholars, it seems clear that cooperative preservation is essential. In the mid-1980s, under the leadership of CRL, the profession created the Commission on Preservation and Access. This later evolved into the aforementioned Digital Library Federation (<http://www.diglib.org/>). Two groups, ARL and RLG, have been collecting statistics on research library preservation activities and developing guidelines. (ARL's statistics are available online at <http://www.arl.org/stats/pres/>, while RLG has focused on digital preservation and publishes a bimonthly electronic newsletter, *DigiNews* <http://www.rlg.org/>.) The National Endowment for the Humanities has provided funding for microfilming and digitization projects. A program for educating preservation librarians was started at the Columbia University Library School; after that school closed, the preservation program was transferred to the University of Texas Library School of Information (<http://www.ischool.utexas.edu/programs/pcs/>). Many large libraries are hiring full-time preservation specialists. One newsletter that allows one to keep up-to-date on conservation matters is *The Abbey Newsletter,* <http://palimpsest.stanford.edu/byorg/abbey/>. The American Institute for Conservation of Historic and Artistic Works (AIC, <http://aic.stanford.edu>) provides a forum for concerned individuals to discuss preservation and conservation issues, as well as sponsoring workshops and other continuing education programs. OCLC also has an interest in preservation activities (<http://digitalcooperative.oclc.org/preserve/default.htm>). Naturally, ALA and many of its divisions have an active interest in this area, as do most other library associations around the world. A comprehensive source of information is the aforementioned Conservation OnLine (CoOL). We list some additional websites and resources at the end of this chapter.

As we noted at the beginning of this chapter, there is a growing concern about how much of our cultural heritage we are preserving in its original artifact and, in some cases, even collecting/saving it at all. Michèle Cloonan noted:

> Current approaches to preservation are being influenced by new technologies that are eliciting a disproportionate amount of emphasis on technical problems. At the same time, new modes of collaboration among cultural heritage institutions provide a perfect opportunity to add core meaning of preservation from a broad cultural perspective.[35]

National libraries as well as the other libraries in their countries can collect and preserve everything. One approach has been to take "samples" during the year of websites, films, videos, and other widely held materials.

In 2003, the Council on Library and Information Resources issued a report that emphasized the need for more shared preservation and access.[36] The Institute of Museum and Library Services, an example of institutional collaboration that Cloonan mentioned, funded a conference that led to creation of a national print preservation project by the Center for Research Libraries (CRL). Entitled "Preserving America's Print Resources" (PAPR), the project goal is "to establish a viable national strategy for ensuring the long-term survival of important paper-based library materials."[37]

As of late 2004, the initiative is focused on five categories of material—books, government publications, U.S. legal publications, journals, and newspapers. The hope is to create a structure to assist libraries in making difficult decisions about what to save or not and to coordinate their preservation activities. In the last chapter, we discussed the space challenges facing all types of libraries but particularly those in academic institutions. To recapitulate, costs for e-resources and print journal subscriptions strain library operating budgets, especially preservation funds. Space is in short supply, and the cost of additional space is such that it is less and less likely a library will secure needed funding for facilities. This makes it difficult to save materials that are in both digital and print formats. Staffing also suffers, if in nothing more than having vacant positions held open for long periods. Essentially, the concern is that the "last copy" of something of importance will be lost because local issues well outweigh national concerns.

There are two broad objectives for PAPR:

1. synchronize and expand archiving and "collection of record" efforts and

2. enable informed local preservation and retention decision making by libraries and consortia.[38]

A "collection record" is a library/organization that is committed to retaining a "last copy." Organizations such as the Library of Congress, Center for Research Libraries, American Antiquarian Society, JSTOR, and some of the major research libraries (e.g., New York Public Library, Harvard, Stanford, and University of California system) are likely sites for collections of record.

Some examples of programs under way that one hopes will expand to a true collection of record are as follows:

• American Antiquarian Society's pre-1877 U.S. newspaper imprints;

• Library of Congress' Heritage Copy Preservation Repository program; and

• JSTOR's "dark archive" (page-by-page authentication, optimal storage, and no public access).

While they are important initiatives, more needs to be done to save U.S. cultural heritage. For this to happen, most of the problems discussed in the last chapter must be effectively addressed. Although technology has been a great boon to cooperative activities, there is still a lack of item-level (vol. XX, no. XX, date) information about holdings for newspapers and journals. Who will pay for what? Who will coordinate the process? Can items be transferred across jurisdictional lines? These are but some of the issues that libraries must resolve if the initiative is to succeed. Perhaps the biggest challenge is to find a way for libraries to take on the financial obligations of being a library of record. Just because most of them are large does not mean they do not face financial pressures.

It is clear that someone/some organization will need to become the "leader" of the preservation effort. It is hoped that CRL will be that body. As noted in the PAPR conference report:

> The Center for Research Libraries is in many ways positioned to play such a role. . . . To actively promote coordinated action and inter-reliance among libraries and consortia, however, CRL will have to build upon this base of archiving and preservation activities and actively catalyze the formation of partnerships among libraries and repositories to accomplish broader archiving and collection of record functions.[39]

By the time the next edition of this text is prepared, we should have a clearer picture of how much has been accomplished.

Insurance

Careful planning, proper handling, and the other elements discussed in this chapter will help prolong the useful life of collections. A good disaster preparedness plan will help reduce the scope of loss when disaster strikes. Because the odds are rather high that a disaster will strike eventually, where will the library get the funds to replace the materials damaged beyond salvaging? In fact, where will the library get the funds to salvage what it can? The obvious answer is some type of insurance. The section on developing a disaster preparedness plan suggests that one early contact for the planning team should be the institution's risk manager. This is the person who monitors safety conditions in the workplace and oversees the insurance programs that cover various loss situations, from fires, to slippery floors, to actions of the institutional officers. The risk manager for LMU visits the library once a year to discuss any new or outstanding problems, as well as to review the values assigned to the collections, equipment, and building.

The LMU risk manager and library staff have discussed and clarified the fact that there will be insurance coverage for salvage operations, after the institution's deductible limit is surpassed. Discussions regarding the collection valuation have been interesting, especially when it comes to what to do about coverage for special collections and archives materials. If a Shakespeare folio is stolen or destroyed by fire, it is highly unlikely that the library could ever replace it, even if the library insured each folio for several million dollars. The risk manager sees no point in paying an extra premium for something that cannot be replaced. That moved the discussion to facsimile works and the appropriateness of replacing an original with a top-of-the-line facsimile. To date, this is a topic of ongoing debate. Anyone who has dealt with homeowners' or renters' insurance representatives and policies can understand the complexities involved. Does the collection valuation increase or decrease over time? What does *replacement* mean? Will there be funds to process the material or merely to acquire it? What damage is covered?

An example of the complexities involved in insuring collections occurred in 1989, when twelve ranges of shelving containing 20,000 volumes collapsed at the Columbia University library annex. Many, if not most, of the volumes were brittle, so the fall was very damaging. However, the embrittlement was a preexisting condition. After some long negotiations, the insurer agreed to pay for volumes with damage to the cover or text block attachments, but not for volumes with broken pages. There were questions about serial runs as well; this was finally resolved with the insurer paying for the entire run of backfiles, if more than one-third of the run was damaged.[40]

Earlier, we mentioned the recent flooding at the University of Hawaii. It is too soon to determine the cost or long-term effects of the disaster, although given the nature of the collections affected, it would not be surprising if the totals were staggering. However, a similar major disaster took place in late July 1997 at Colorado State University. After an unusually heavy rainstorm, major flooding occurred on the campus, with much of the water damming up against the wall of the lower level of the library. The wall collapsed as the result of the water pressure, and a huge wave of water poured into the building. All of the materials on the lower level became water-soaked: more than 500,000 items, with an estimated value of more than $100 million.[41] Although the library responded to the immediate need via InterLibrary Loan and by providing electronic resources to researchers, collection recovery efforts lasted several years after the facility was repaired. Even though insurance helped cover some of the costs, the final recovery efforts were assisted by donations of materials from libraries and publishers.[42]

Working out reasonable arrangements in advance, such as who pays for salvage work, will reduce the pressure on everyone during a disaster. One cannot anticipate everything, but some issues are bound to arise, and, to the extent one can deal with those concerns ahead of time, there will be fewer distractions during recovery operations. Another element that bears predisaster discussion is how to value the collection. One common way is to use averages, such as one finds in *The Bowker Annual* (Information Today), and multiply that figure by the number of units held. The problem with that approach, as was noted in an unsigned comment on the collection development discussion list, is that local circumstances also determine the value of an item; "a single volume of *JAMA* from 1952 is probably worth $2.00, but as part of a set that is missing from 1952, it's worth $500!"[43]

For a good discussion about replacement, actual cash value, average replacement cost, valuable papers, and records coverage, as well as other basic insurance topics and libraries, see Judith Fortson's "Disaster Planning: Managing the Financial Risk."[44] Having insurance is a sound practice, because almost every library at some time will have a disaster of some type and size. Having insurance is one more step in protecting the library's and institution's investment.

Summary

This chapter highlights the many aspects of protecting the collections on which libraries and information centers expend large sums of money. Many of the issues raised are ones that virtually any library staff member can implement without major changes in duties or in training. Preparing for trouble always makes it easier to handle the trouble when, or if, it happens. Knowing what type of financial help one can expect to assist in recovering from a disaster can provide some peace of mind, if nothing else. Long-term preservation, though the primary responsibility of the large libraries, is also a concern, or should be, of all libraries and information centers. Working together, we will solve preservation problems, even if it takes a long time and great effort.

Notes

1. Nicholson Baker, *Double Fold: Libraries and the Assault on Paper* (New York: Random House, 2001).

2. Michèle V. Cloonan, "W(h)ither Preservation," *Library Quarterly* 71, no. 2 (2001): 239.

3. "Glossary of Selected Preservation Terms," *ALCTS Newsletter* 1, no. 2 (1990): 14–15.

4. Ibid., 14.

5. Ibid., 15.

6. "AIC Definitions of Conservation Terminology," *Abby Newsletter* 20, nos. 4–5 (September 1996): 48, <http://palimpsest.stanford.edu/byorg/abbey/an/an20/an20-4/an20-405.html>.

7. Newberry Library, "Conservation at the Newberry," <http://www.newberry.org/collections/conservationhome.html>.

8. Fred R. Byers, *Care and Handling of CDs and DVDs* (Washington, DC: Council on Library and Information Resources and National Institute of Standards and Technology, 2003), 16.

9. G. Edward Evans, Anthony Amodeo, and Thomas Carter, *Introduction to Library Public Services*, 5th ed. (Englewood, CO: Libraries Unlimited, 1992).

10. Susan Allen, "The Blumberg Case: A Costly Lesson for Librarians," *AB Bookman's Weekly* 88 (September 2, 1991): 769–73; "Rare Document Thief Sentenced," *Library Journal* 123 (June 1, 1998): 20.

11. Terri L. Pederson, "Theft and Mutilation of Library Materials," *College & Research Libraries* 51 (March 1990): 120–28.

12. *Library Hotline* (May 12, 1986): 2.

13. "Major Flood Damages U of Hawaii Library," *Library Hotline* 33, no. 45 (November 8, 2004): 5–6; "Community Pulls Together Around UH Manoa Library," *Library Hotline* 33, no. 47 (November 22, 2004): 6–7.

14. Paul A. Parisi, "An Overview of Library Binding: Where We Are, How We Got Here, What We Do," *New Library Scene* 12 (February 1993): 5–9.

15. W. J. Barrow, *Manuscripts and Documents: Their Deterioration and Restoration* (Charlottesville: University Press of Virginia, 1972); W. J. Barrow, *The Manufacture and Testing of Durable Book Papers* (Richmond: Virginia State Library, 1960).

16. *Harvard Crimson* (October 23, 1986): 1.

17. *Book Longevity* (Washington, DC: Council on Library Resources, 1982).

18. Richard Dougherty, "Redefining Preservation and Reconceptualizing Information Service," *Library Issues* 13 (November 1992): 1.

19. Deanna Marcum, "We Can't Save Everything," *New York Times*, Op-Ed section, July 6, 1998, 11.

20. *Book Longevity*, 9.

21. "LC's Mass Deacidification Facility Destroyed," *Wilson Library Bulletin* 60 (May 1986): 8–9.

22.   Michèle V. Cloonan, "Mass Deacidification in the 1990s," *Rare Books and Manuscripts Librarianship* 5, no. 2 (1990): 95–103.

23.   W. Brent Seales, James Griffioen, and Kevin Kiernan, "The Digital Atheneum—Restoring Damaged Manuscripts," *RLG DigiNews* 3, no. 6 (December 15, 1999), <http://www.rlg.org/preserv/diginews/diginews3-6.html#technical1>.

24.   Brian Lavoie and Lorcan Dempsey, "Thirteen Ways of Looking at . . . Digital Preservation," *D-Lib Magazine* 10, nos. 7/8, July–August 2004, <http://80-www.dlib.org.researchport.umd.edu:2050/dlib/july04/lavoie/07lavoie.html>.

25.   *Gaylord Preservation Pathfinder No. 2, Archival Storage of Paper* (Syracuse, NY: Gaylord Brothers, 1993), 5.

26.   Mary Lynn Ritzenthaler, *Preserving Archives and Manuscripts* (Chicago: Society of American Archivists, 1993).

27.   Robert Mareck, "Practicum on Preservation Selection," in *Collection Management for the 1990s*, ed. J. J. Brain, 114–26 (Chicago: American Library Association, 1993).

28.   Kenneth Harris, "Library of Congress Mass Deacidification Program," *New Library Scene* 17 (September 1998): 8–9; "Saving the Written Word: Library Awards Deacidification Contract," *Library of Congress Information Bulletin* 61, no. 1 (2002): 15, <http://www.loc.gov/loc/lcib/0201/preserve.html>.

29.   Scott Carlson, "The Uncertain Fate of Scholarly Artifacts in a Digital Age," *Chronicle of Higher Education* 50, no. 21 (January 30, 2004), A25–27.

30.   Laura Tangley, "Whoops, There Goes Another CD-ROM," *U.S. News & World Report* (February 16, 1998): 67–68.

31.   Gerd Meissner, "Unlocking the Secrets of the Digital Archive Left by East Germany," *New York Times*, March 15, 1999, D5.

32.   Roy Tennant, "Time Is Not on Our Side: The Challenge of Preserving Digital Materials," *Library Journal* 124 (March 15, 1999): 30–31.

33.   Peter Graham, *Intellectual Preservation: Electronic Preservation of the Third Kind* (Washington, DC: Commission on Preservation and Access, 1994).

34.   *Digital Preservation Consortium: Mission and Goals* (Washington, DC: Commission on Preservation and Access, 1994), <http:/www.clir.org/pubs/reports/dpcmiss/dpcmiss.html>.

35.   Cloonan, "W(h)ither Preservation," 231.

36.   B. Reilly and B. DesRogiers, *Developing Print Repositories: Models for Shared Preservation and Access* (Washington, DC: Council on Library and Information Resources, 2003).

37.   "Preserving America's Print Resources: Toward a National Strategic Effort," Conference Report, Chicago: Center for Research Libraries, 2003, <http://www.crl.edu/content/PAPRreportdraft.pdf>.

38.   Ibid.

39.   Ibid.

40.   Janet Gertz, "Columbia Libraries Annex Disaster," *Archival Products News* 1 (Summer 1992): 2.

41.   Leonard Kniffel, "Flood Toll at Colorado State Could Reach $100 Million," *American Libraries* 28 (September 1997): 16; "The Silver Lining: Recovering from the Shambles of a Disaster," *Journal of Library Administration* 38, nos. 1/2 (2003): 101–7.

42.   Thomas Delaney, "The Day It Rained in Fort Collins, Colorado," *Journal of Interlibrary Loan, Document Delivery & Information Supply* 8, no. 4 (1998): 59–70.

43. "Number 570—Collection Valuation (Summary of Responses)," e-mail to COLLD-LUSCVM discussion list, August 8, 1994.

44. Judith Fortson, "Disaster Planning: Managing the Financial Risk," *Bottom Line* 6 (Spring 1992): 26–33.

Selected Websites
and Discussion Lists*

(See also resources on the DLC5 website: <http://www.lu.com/dlc5>)

Conservation DistList
> An online forum sponsored by Conservation OnLine (<http://palimpsest. stanford.edu>). To subscribe, send the following message to consdist-request@lindy.stanford.edu: subscribe consdist YourFirstName YourLastName.

Conserve O Grams
> <http://www.cr.nps.gov/museum/publications>
> A series of publications created by the Museum Management Program of the National Park Service.

Library Preservation at Harvard: Resources
> <http://preserve.harvard.edu/resources/index.html>
> Guidelines, readings, and related resources prepared by the Weissman Preservation Center at Harvard.

National Digital Information Infrastructure and Preservation Program (NDIIPP)
> <http://www.digitalpreservation.gov/>
> A federally funded (Public Law 106-554) collaborative project to preserve digital information led by the Library of Congress.

National Preservation Office (NPO)
> <http://www.bl.uk/services/npo/npo.html>
> A service of the British Library, the NPO oversees preservation activities in the United Kingdom and Ireland.

Northeast Document Conservation Center (NEDCC)
> <http://www.nedcc.org/>
> A nonprofit, regional conservation center. The NEDCC website contains a number of resources of use to conservationists, including *Preservation of Library & Archival Materials: A Manual*, edited by Sherelyn Ogden.

OCLC Best Practices: Digitization
> <http://www.oclc.org/community/topics/digitization/bestpractices/>
> A collection of resources, readings, and useful links for digitization of materials.

Preserving Access to Digital Information (PADI)
> <http://www.nla.gov.au/padi/>
> An initiative of the National Library of Australia. The PADI website provides links to a series of international resources on preservation of electronic materials.

Regional Alliance for Preservation (RAP)
> <http://www.rap-arcc.org/>
> RAP began as a pilot project of the Commission on Preservation and Access to foster cooperation among Preservation Field Service programs funded by the National Endowment for the Humanities and was later continued by program participants. The RAP website provides links to disaster assistance, surveys, and training resources.

Society of American Archivists (SAA)
    <http://www.archivists.org/>
        A professional organization for archivists. The SAA website includes links to continuing education programs and other resources of interest.

*These sites were accessed May 7, 2005.

Further Reading

Abifarin, A. "Library Stock Security." *Library and Archival Security* 14, no. 1 (1997): 11–19.

Adelstein, P. Z. *IPI Media Storage Quick Reference*. Rochester, NY: Image Permanence Institute, 2004.

Alire, C., ed. *Library Disaster Planning and Recovery Handbook*. New York: Neal-Schuman, 2000.

Applebaum, B. *Guide to Environmental Protection of Collections*. Madison, CT: Sound View Press, 1991.

Baird, B. J. "Brittle: Replacing Embrittled Titles Cooperatively." *College & Research Libraries News* 58 (February 1997): 83–84+.

———. "Motivating Student Employees: Examples from Collection Conservation." *Library Resources & Technical Services* 39 (October 1995): 410–16.

Balloffett, N., and J. Hille. *Preservation and Conservation for Libraries and Archives*. Chicago: American Library Association, 2004.

Banks, P. N., and R. Pilette. *Preservation: Issues and Planning*. Chicago: American Library Association, 2000.

Bansa, H. "New Media: Means for Better Preservation or Special Preservation Problem?" *Restaurator* 12, no. 4 (1991): 219–32.

Beagrie, N. *National Digital Preservation Initiatives*. Washington, DC: Council on Library and Information Resources and National Institute of Standards and Technology, 2003, <http://www.clir.org/pubs/abstract/pub116abst.html>.

Berges, C. "Risk Management: The Unrecognized Necessity." *Rural Libraries* 13, no. 1 (1993): 53–66.

Brawner, L. B. "Insurance and Risk Management for Libraries." *Public Library Quarterly* 13, no. 1 (1993): 5–15.

Child, M. *Directory of Information Sources on Scientific Research Related to the Preservation of Sound Recordings, Still and Moving Images and Magnetic Tape*. Washington, DC: Commission on Preservation and Access, 1993.

Clark, L., ed. *Guide to Review Library Collections: Preservation, Storage and Withdrawal*. Chicago: American Library Association, 1991.

Cloonan, M. V. "Monumental Preservation: A Call to Action." *American Libraries* 35 (September 2004): 34–38.

———. "Preservation of Knowledge." *Library Trends* 41 (Spring 1993): 594–605.

Council on Library and Information Resources. *Building a National Strategy for Preservation: Issues in Digital Media Archiving*. Washington, DC: Council on Library and Information Resources and the Library of Congress, 2002, <http://www.clir.org/pubs/abstract/pub106abst.html>.

Croft, J. "The Preservation Evolution." *Library Resources & Technical Services* 47, no. 2 (2003): 59–70.

Cunha, G. M. "Disaster Planning and a Guide to Recovery Resources." *Library Technology Reports* 28 (September–October 1992): 533–623.

Dane, W. J. "A Major Challenge to Security." *Art Documentation* 10 (Winter 1997): 179–80.

Delong, L. R. "Valuating Library Collections." In *Conference on Acquisitions, Budget, and Collections*, 89–95. St. Louis, MO: Genaway & Associates, 1990.

De Stefano, P. "Moving Image Preservation in Libraries." *Library Trends* 52, no. 1 (Summer 2003): 118–32.

Drewes, J., and K. Smets. "Deacidification of Journals." *Serials Librarian* 38, nos. 3/4 (2000): 269–76.

Drewes, J. M., and J. A. Page, eds. *Promoting Preservation Awareness in Libraries: A Sourcebook for Academic, Public School and Special Libraries*. Westport, CT: Greenwood Press, 1997.

Eden, P., and G. Graham. "Disaster Management in Libraries." *Library Management* 17, no. 3 (1996): 5–12.

Edwards, P. M. "Collection Development and Maintenance across Libraries, Archives, and Museums." *Library Resources & Technical Services* 48 (January 2004): 26–33.

Foot, M. "Housing Our Collections: Environment and Storage for Libraries and Archives." *IFLA Journal* 22 (1996): 110–14.

Fortson, J. *Disaster Planning and Recovery*. New York: Neal-Schuman, 1992.

Gilliland-Swetland, A. J. *Enduring Paradigm, New Opportunities*. Washington, DC: Council on Library and Information Services, 2000.

Graham, P. S. "Long-Term Intellectual Preservation." *Collection Management* 22, nos. 3/4 (1998): 81–98.

Hain, J. E. "A Brief Look at Recent Developments in the Preservation and Conservation of Special Collections." *Library Trends* 52, no. 1 (2003): 112–17.

Harris, C. L. "Preservation Considerations in Electronic Security Systems." *Library and Archival Security* 11, no. 1 (1991): 35–42.

Henderson, K. L., and W. T. Henderson. *Conserving and Preserving Materials in Nonbook Formats*. Urbana: University of Illinois, Graduate School of Library and Information Science, 1991.

Higginbotham, B. B., and J. W. Wild. *The Preservation Program Blueprint*. Frontiers of Access to Library Materials Series 6. Chicago: American Library Association, 2001.

Holland, J., and S. Benz. "Unanticipated Outcomes: A Large-Scale Digitization Project Offers Surprising Benefits." *Library Journal* 129, no. 13 (August 2004): 30–31.

Kahn, M. B. *Protecting Your Library's Digital Sources*. Chicago: American Library Association, 2004.

Kellerman, L. S. "Out-of-Print Digital Scanning." *Library Resources & Technical Services* 46, no. 1 (January 2002): 3–10.

Kenny, A. R., and P. Conway. "From Analog to Digital: Extending the Preservation Tool Kit." *Collection Management* 22, nos. 3/4 (1998): 65–79.

Lambert, D. K., W. Atkins, D. A. Litts, and L. H. Olley. *Guide to the Review of Library Collections: Preservation, Storage and Withdrawal*. 2nd ed. Collection Management and Development Guide 12. Lanham, MD: Scarecrow, 2002.

Lynn, M. S. "Digital Preservation and Access." *Collection Management* 22, nos. 3/4 (1998): 55–63.

Maroso, A. L. "Digitization as a Preservation Practice." *The Serials Librarian* 45, no. 2 (2003): 27–37.

Matthews, G., and J. Feather, eds. *Disaster Management for Libraries and Archives*. Aldershot, U.K.: Ashgate, 2003.

Matthews, G., and P. Eden. "Disaster Management Training in Libraries." *Library Review* 45, no. 1 (1996): 30–38.

Morris, J. *Library Disaster Preparedness Handbook*. Chicago: American Library Association, 1986.

Muir, A., and S. Shenton. "If the Worst Happens: The Use and Effectiveness of Disaster Plans in Libraries and Archives." *Library Management* 23, no. 3 (2002): 115–23.

National Film Preservation Foundation. *The Film Preservation Guide*. San Francisco: National Film Preservation Foundation, 2004.

Nelson-Strauss, B. "Preservation Policies and Priorities for Record Sound Collections." *Notes* 48 (December 1991): 425–36.

Newman, J., and C. Wolf. "The Security Audit." *Colorado Libraries* 23 (Spring 1997): 19–21.

Reilly, B., and J. Porro, eds. *Photograph Preservation and the Research Library*. Stanford, CA: Research Library Group, 1991.

Schneider, J. A. "Mold: Recovery from a Potential Collection Disaster and Environmental Hazard." *Journal of Interlibrary Loan, Document Delivery & Information Supply* 14, no. 4 (2004): 49–66.

Sitts, M. *Handbook for Digital Projects: A Management Tool for Preservation and Access*. Andover, MA: Northeast Document Conservation Center, 2000.

———. *A Practical Guide to Preservation in School and Public Libraries*. Syracuse, NY: Information Resources Publications, 1990.

Slide, A. *Nitrate Won't Wait*. New York: McFarland, 1992.

Smith, A. "Common Cause: Taking Care of Print Collections." *Library Collections, Acquisitions, & Technical Services* 28, no. 1 (Spring 2004): 8–12.

———. "The Digital Preservation Conundrum, Part 1." *The Serials Librarian* 46, nos. 1/2 (2004): 107–13.

Stoker, D. "The Case of the Disappearing Books." *Journal of Librarianship and Information Science* 23 (September 1991): 121–24.

Stranger, C., and L. Brandis. "Insect Pests and Their Eradication." *Australian Library Journal* 41 (August 1992): 180–83.

Swartzburg, S., H. Bussey, and F. Garretson. *Libraries and Archives: Design and Renovation with a Preservation Perspective*. Metuchen, NJ: Scarecrow Press, 1991.

Teper, T. H. "PAPR: Preserving America's Printed Resources." *Library Collections, Acquisitions, & Technical Services* 28, no. 1 (Spring 2004): 5–7.

Vargas, M. A. "Using a Third-Party Vendor for Off-Site Storage of Library Materials." *Library Administration & Management* 19, no. 1 (Winter 2005): 26–30.

Weaver-Meyers, P.L., W.A. Stolt, and B. Kowaleski. "Controlling Mold on Library Materials with Chlorine Dioxide." *Journal of Academic Librarianship* 24 (November 1998): 455–58.

Wellheiser, J., and J. Scott. *An Ounce of Prevention: Integrated Disaster Planning for Archives, Libraries and Record Centres*. 2nd ed. London: Scarecrow Press, 2003.

Wilhelm, H.G., and C. Brower. *The Permanence and Care of Color Photographs.* Grinnell, IA: Preservation Publishing, 1993.

17
Legal Issues

A relatively recent book, *The Library's Legal Answer Book*,[1] suggests librarians encounter legal issues almost every day. At least some of those issues relate to collection management activities, particularly as related to e-resource contracts, copyright/ILL, donation/IRS concerns, and Internet access questions. Thus, having some knowledge of legal concerns in terms of collection development is important for selection officers. Additionally, with the passage of the Digital Millennium Copyright Act (DMCA) in October 1998 (P.L. 105-304, 112 Stat. 2860), much has changed for libraries and collection development officers. One issue that remains unknown is just what the concept of "fair use" will mean in the future. Another legal issue that is becoming ever more important for libraries and collection managers is license agreements.

National laws and regulations influence collection development activities. Two of the topics discussed in this chapter are of concern only to U.S. libraries. However, most of the chapter addresses copyright, lending rights, licensing agreements, and other concepts of interest to libraries around the world. One legal issue specifically relating to U.S. libraries concerns Internal Revenue Service (IRS) regulations.

IRS Regulations

We noted in earlier chapters that libraries of all types receive gifts from time to time. Some gifts are useful and occasionally even very valuable; however, much of the time they are of little interest to the library. Nevertheless, the individuals giving the material generally believe that it is very valuable. People often expect, want, and/or request a document from the library indicating the value of their gift.

Valuing Gifts

There are regulations relevant to gifts and donations to a library or not-for-profit information center. Any library or its parent institution that receives a gift-in-kind (books, journals, manuscripts, and so forth) with an appraised value of $5,000 or more must report the gift to the IRS. A second regulation forbids the receiving party (in this case the library) to provide an estimated value for a gift-in-kind. A third disinterested party or organization must make the valuation. The latter requirement grew out of concern that recipients were placing unrealistically high values on gifts. The donor received a larger tax deduction than was warranted, and it did not cost the receiving organization anything to place a high value on the gift. Normally, an appraiser charges a fee for valuing gifts, and the donor is supposed to pay the fee. Most often, the appraisers are antiquarian dealers who charge a flat fee for the service unless the collection is large or complex. If the appraisal is complex, the appraiser charges either a percentage of the appraised value or an hourly fee.

Typically, with gifts thought to be less than $4,999 in value, the library may write a letter of acknowledgment indicating the number and type of items received. For gifts of less than $250, the IRS does not require a letter. The donor can set a value on the gift for tax purposes. (The best practice is to provide a letter for any accepted gift.) If asked, the library can provide dealer catalogs so that donors can review retail prices for items similar to their donation. However, the donor and her or his tax accountant establish the final value of the gift. The collection development staff should be involved in the acceptance of gifts and must have a sound knowledge of material prices. Just because the gift is small in terms of number of items does not mean that the fair market value is below $5,000. Not too long ago, LMU received a gift of 483 books about Japanese art, architecture, and landscape design; its appraised value was $39,743. The donor might well have accepted a letter simply stating the number of books given and thus have lost a substantial tax deduction. (For additional discussion about gifts, see chapter 10.)

To meet IRS requirements, an acknowledgment letter must contain the library's name, the date of the contribution, and the location or place of the gift. At a minimum, that description should state the number and kind of gift (e.g., 100 mass-market paperbacks, 40 hardcover books, 6 complete and 20 unbound volumes *of National Geographic*).

Copyright

Is copyright an issue in collection development? Yes. Cooperative collection development efforts depend on sharing resources through interlibrary loan or other reciprocal borrowing agreements. There are also questions about how many photocopies one can use for course reserve purposes in educational institutions. What about making a copy of an out-of-print work for preservation purposes: how does the copyright law affect these programs? Clearly, libraries have modified copying policies as well as interlibrary loan practices. For example, under the present law, a library in a not-for-profit setting may borrow no more than five articles per year from any given journal. If the library borrows more than five articles, the assumption is that the borrowing is in lieu of placing a subscription and thus is a violation of the law. If libraries cannot freely exchange books, periodicals, or photocopies of copyrighted items, it is difficult to develop and maintain effective cooperative systems.

Copyright grants the creators of works certain rights that protect their interest in the work. Originally, copyright's purpose was to provide protection against unauthorized printing, publishing, importing, or selling of multiple copies of a work. In essence, it was protection from the unauthorized mass production and sale of a work. It was a straightforward and seemingly reasonable method of encouraging individuals or businesses to take a financial risk to produce and distribute information. Libraries, in contrast, exist to disseminate information on a mass, usually free, basis. Until photocopiers appeared on the scene, the relationship between copyright holders and libraries was cordial, if not always friendly.

With the development of fast, inexpensive photocopying, problems arose. Although the library might make only a single copy of an article for a user, the aggregate number of copies could be very high. By the mid-1960s, the volume of copying was so great that copyright holders became convinced that libraries, schools, and individuals were violating their rights at unacceptable levels—and in some cases they were correct.

In the past, copying printed matter for personal use was not a problem. Word-for-word hand-copying of extensive sections of books or complete magazine articles was uncommon—people took notes. Today, quick and inexpensive copy services, as well as the ability to download digitized copyrighted material, exist everywhere. All of us have made photocopies of complete journal articles or printed many pages of Internet material rather than take notes; some of those items were from current issues of periodicals that we could have purchased for not much more than its photocopy cost. All of us have done it, and, if we thought about it at all, we thought that just one copy is not going to hurt anyone. Unfortunately, as the number of such copies and printing increases, so does the problem.

With audiovisual materials (e.g., videotapes and audiotapes), the problem is acute. Institutions and individuals who own the hardware to play these materials also have copying capabilities. Control of copying is even more difficult to achieve for audiovisual materials than for books or journals. Preview copies help control the institutional buying situation, because they tend to show wear to such an extent that many persons would not want to reproduce a copy. If the preview copy shows too much wear, however, the library's buyer may decide not to buy the item because it lacks technical quality. There is also an issue of "performance rights" (see chapter 9) that is both a legal and cost issue.

The public still does have some rights to gain access to, and to use, copyrighted material. Where to draw the line between creators' and users' rights is a complicated problem and has become more so with digitization of material and scanning devices. An old, but still valid, editorial by John Berry in *Library Journal* summed up the complex issues involved in fair use. Today, the issues are even more complicated than they were when he wrote the editorial.

> Here at *LJ* we are often asked why the magazine has not come out strongly on one side or the other of the copyright issue. We are after all a library magazine. . . . In the case of copyright, however, our library-mindedness is somewhat blunted by the facts of our existence as a publication which is in copyright and is published by an independent, commercial publisher. Not only is copyright protection fundamental to our continued fiscal health, [but]

we believe that authors and publishers deserve compensation for their creative work and for the risks taken to package and deliver that creative effort to users of it.

Like any magazine publisher we have winced when it was obvious our rights in our published material have been violated. . . . Yet there is the other side, the flattery in the notion that people want to read what we print, and the gratification that so many share our view of its importance.

So the issue of copyright, particularly of library copying, is deeply complicated for us. . . . We don't believe that "fair use" should be eliminated, but we can't subscribe to the view that wholesale copying should be allowed for "educational purposes."

The answer has to be compromise.[2]

Several points about copyright require emphasis. First, the problem of how to handle the rights of creators and users is worldwide, in the sense that each country has to deal with both its own copyright problems and international copyright issues. Second, in the past, much of the controversy centered on educational and library copying. Today, with computer technology so readily available, the problem has increased far beyond libraries and educational institutions. Third, copyright disputes divide authors, publishers, and producers from libraries, schools, and users, almost destroying what were once friendly working relationships. The relationship has not yet deteriorated to the point of hostility, but unless true compromises emerge, hostility may be the result. The recent efforts of the Recording Industry Association of America to enforce copyright have, in fact, generated hostility.

Most librarians agree that creators' rights need and deserve protection and that those rights have occasionally been violated in and by libraries. However, direct daily contact with users and their needs tempers that recognition just as it did John Berry's views.

There is no question that some people copy materials for commercial purposes, especially music and video products. However, much of the "improper" usage is a function of not understanding the nature of copyright and what fair usage may be in various circumstances. There are many misconceptions about copyright, and we can touch on only a few of them. *Note: None of the following discussion of copyright or licensing should be thought of as legal advice. When in doubt, contact a legal specialist in the field of copyright, intellectual property, or contract law.*

One of the most common misunderstandings of copyright concerns notice of copyright. ("It did not indicate that it was copyrighted, so it must be public domain.") Part of the reason for confusion about the need to have a notice of copyright is that, in the United States, it *was* necessary until April 1, 1989. After that date, the United States joined most of the rest of the world as a signatory to the Berne copyright convention (an international agreement), which grants copyright with or without notice. Thus, the only safe assumption now is that everything is copyrighted, unless one has definite knowledge to the contrary.

A related technical misconception is that if an item is on the Internet, it is in the public domain. This is clearly untrue. For anything to be in the public domain, the creator or owner must include a statement putting the material into the public domain.

There is also a common belief that if one does not charge for, or gain financially from, the usage, there is no violation of copyright. We noted earlier that libraries should also purchase performance rights for the films and videos they purchase, if they are to be used in library programming. Even a free "public performance" during a children's program requires permission, if one did not pay for performance rights. Use in face-to-face instruction has been thought to be "fair use," but even that idea is questioned by many copyright holders. As a reminder, it is better to acquire performance rights if at all possible.

Fair use is an area full of "yes, you can/no, you can't." Now that the United States has passed the Digital Millennium Copyright Act, the issue of what will, and will not, be deemed fair use is unclear, as of late 2004. (We explore this concept further later in this chapter.) Older guidelines seem to be under scrutiny, and the goal appears to be a further lessening of fair use rights.

Another aspect of the situation seems to be people's attitudes. There appears to be a sense that infringing copyright is not really a crime. The attitude is rather like drivers who know that the speed limit is 65 miles per hour but think that it *really is okay to drive* 70 miles per hour. Related to that belief, which is inaccurate, are the notions that copyright holders are greedy and that the cost for permission to use copyrighted material is much too high. Therefore, using the material without permission is reasonable. Legally, it is not okay either to exceed the speed limit or to infringe copyright, even if no one is looking.

Libraries are caught in the middle of these issues. Librarians may agree that prices are high, but they also know that if there were no income and profit for the producers and creators, there would be no information. They believe in free access to information, especially for educational purposes, once the library acquires the material or information. Finding the balance, or John Berry's compromise, is the challenge. In many ways, the only organized voice for users is library and educational associations.

For further background information, a section about the historical aspects of copyright that appeared in earlier editions may be found on the CD accompanying this text.

International Copyright Conventions

At the international level, there have been two important copyright conventions: the Berne Convention (1886) and the Universal Copyright Convention (1952). Until the signing of the Berne Convention, international copyright was in chaos, with reciprocity only on the basis of bilateral treaties. Some countries, like the United States, made no such agreements. As a result, during the nineteenth century, a new form of piracy appeared: literary piracy. Some countries signed the Berne Convention, notable exceptions being Russia and the United States (although the United States later did sign this agreement). Basically, the signatories agreed to give one another the same copyright protection they provided their own citizens. A 1908 revision required this coverage to be automatic—copyright owners did not have to file any forms to secure coverage. The Internet brought chaos back to copyright, as different countries have very different concepts of fair use (United States) or fair dealing (U.K.).

The United States did sign the Universal Copyright Convention (UCC) in 1954. How is it that the United States was able to sign one international convention but not the other? There were two important differences between the conventions. First, the UCC did not provide automatic copyright without formalities. The formalities, however, were that a work carry the copyright symbol (©), the name of the owner, and the date of first publication. That satisfied the U.S. notice requirement and, presumably, made life easier for American librarians. The second difference was that the term of copyright could be whatever term the country granted its citizens at the time of signing; the only minimum was twenty-five years for all works other than photographs and applied arts. (Photographs and applied arts must have at least ten years' protection.)

In 1971, modifications to both the Berne Convention and the UCC ensured that developing countries would receive certain licensing rights. The revisions provided a mechanism for forcing a copyright owner to grant use rights to developing countries under certain conditions—in effect, it was compulsory licensing. Most of the signatories to the two conventions approved the revisions by 1990. Certainly, the revisions helped control what was becoming the second era of international piracy of literary and creative works. Nevertheless, some countries are not party to any copyright agreement, nor do the publishers in those countries bother to seek a license; hence, piracy is still alive in the 21st century.

To understand current U.S. copyright law, it is also necessary to look at, and understand, the international aspects of intellectual property protection. This is because the 1998 DMCA was in part motivated by the need to conform to new international requirements.

The Berne Convention members set up an administrative group to handle its activities. That group evolved into today's World Intellectual Property Organization (WIPO), which is also one of the United Nations' specialized agencies. WIPO has 181 member countries and administers twenty-three treaties. Two of its goals are to "harmonize national intellectual property legislation and procedures" and to "marshal information technology as a tool for storing, accessing, and using valuable intellectual property information."[3] (*Intellectual property* in the case of WIPO also means industrial property, such as inventions, trademarks, and industrial design, as well as copyright covering such material as literary, musical, artistic, photographic, software [as a literary work] databases, and audiovisual works.)

A WIPO meeting in Geneva in December 1996 led to the approval of two treaties: the WIPO Copyright Treaty and the WIPO Performances and Phonograms Treaty. A third proposed treaty, dealing with databases, was held over for later discussion. In part because of the lack of WIPO discussion, the matter of databases was not part of the DMCA either.

Digital Millennium Copyright Act and Earlier Copyright Laws

The purpose of the DMCA was to update existing U.S. copyright law in terms of the digital world, as well as to conform to the 1996 WIPO treaties. Congress also passed a Copyright Term Extension Act in 1998 (also known as the Sonny Bono Copyright Term Extension Act, PL 105-298, 112 Stat 2827), which added twenty years to the protection term for both individuals and corporate bodies. The old protection terms were life plus fifty years for individuals and seventy-five years for corporate entities. (There was an exception for libraries, archives, and nonprofit educational institutions during the last twenty years of protection. Essentially, these groups would have greater levels of fair use during the last twenty years if the work was not commercially available. One must wonder just how often that will be necessary. How many requests do libraries receive for special fair usage of material that is seventy years old?)

The 1978 copyright law is still in force but changed dramatically as a result of amendments and the DMCA. The fair use doctrine is given statutory recognition for the first time in the 1978 law. Traditionally, fair use has been a judicially created limitation on the exclusive rights of copyright owners, developed by the courts because the 1909 copyright law made no provision for any copying. In the law (as codified in Title 17 of the *U.S. Code*), fair use allows copying of a limited amount of material without permission from, or payment to, the copyright owner, when the use is reasonable and not harmful to the rights of the copyright owner (17 *U.S. Code* § 107).

The law extends copyright protection to unpublished works. Instead of the old dual system of protecting works under common law before publication and under federal law after publication, the law establishes a single system of statutory protection for all works, whether published or unpublished (§ 301).

Every librarian should have some knowledge of all of the following sections of the law. The sections of the law and the content of handbooks on the law can be helpful in developing a collection; however, when questions arise, the best source of information is an attorney who handles copyright cases. What follows *is not* legal advice—merely an outline of the sections and their content:

§§ 102–105 define works protected by copyright.

§ 106 defines the exclusive rights of the copyright owner.

§ 107 establishes the basis of the right of fair use.

§ 108 authorizes certain types of library copying.

§ 108(g) identifies library copying not authorized by the current law.

§ 602(a)(3) relates to the importation of copies by libraries.

Works Protected by Copyright

Copyright protection extends to literary (including computer software) works; dramatic works; pantomimes and choreographic works; pictorial, graphic, and sculptural works; motion pictures and other audiovisual works; and sound recordings (§ 102).

Unpublished works by U.S. and foreign authors receive protection under the copyright statute, as do published works by U.S. authors. The published works of foreign authors are subject to copyright under certain conditions, including coverage under national treaties such as the Universal Copyright Convention (§ 104) and now the WIPO Copyright Treaty.

U.S. government works are not copyrightable. The law did not change the basic premise that works produced for the U.S. government by its officers and employees are not subject to copyright (§ 105). However, contractors working for the federal government generally own the copyright to works created under contract, unless otherwise specified in the contract itself.

Exclusive Rights of Copyright Owners

Section 106 states the exclusive rights of copyright owners. Subject to §§ 107 through 118, the owner of copyright under this title has the exclusive rights to do and to authorize any of the following:

1. To reproduce the copyrighted work in copies or phonorecords.

2. To prepare derivative works based upon the copyrighted work.

3. To distribute copies or phonorecords of the copyrighted work to the public by sale or other transfer of ownership or by rental, lease, or lending.

4. In the case of literary, musical, dramatic, and choreographic works, pantomimes, and motion pictures and other audiovisual works, to perform the copyrighted work publicly.

5. In the case of literary, musical, dramatic, and choreographic works, pantomimes, and pictorial, graphic, or sculptural works, including the individual images of a motion picture or other audiovisual work, to display the copyrighted work publicly.

It is important to understand the significant limitations on the exclusive rights stated in § 106, which are stated in §§ 107 through 118.

Fair Use

In previous editions of this text we noted, "Even the most adamant copyright holder advocate acknowledges that at least some kinds of copying are fair and permissible. The problem lies in defining what constitutes fair use." This statement is still true today. Although the existing law did recognize fair use, copyright holders have become less and less happy with the concept. Reading statements from representatives of copyright holders over the past decade or so makes one wonder how long "fair use" will exist. For example, in 1992, the Association of American Publishers (AAP) asserted:

> The copyright law provided the copyright holder with the exclusive right to control the making of copies of a copyrighted work. Exceptions to the exclusive right are intended to permit limited, occasional copying for individuals in particular circumstances which will not impair the rights of the copyright holder, nor generate regular business-like activities based upon usurpation of copyright owners' rights, markets, or materials.[4]

Richard Schockmel commented about the AAP statement in a 1996 article on fair use and use fees:

> [T]his 1992 AAP statement . . . in effect nullifies fair use: Copyright holders have exclusive rights to control all copying and no exceptions are allowed which would impair these rights. It is difficult to imagine any copying made without permission and/or fee which would not impair the exclusive right to control making copies.[5]

Perhaps a more worrisome statement was that made by Marybeth Peters, U.S. register of copyrights, in a 1998 interview with *Library Journal* staff. She was asked about ALA's concern that proposed changes in the law would mean that fair use would not exist in the 21st century. Her response was, "I disagree. What the library community is arguing is that if a copyright owner employs technological protection measures to safeguard his work, they may never be able to get around that protection to exercise their fair use rights. My point is you can't argue fair use to get access to a work."[6] Later in the interview she said, "Fair use is a defense to copyright infringement to the unauthorized exercise of any of the exclusive rights of a copyright owner."[7] We are not clear how exercising the permission given in § 107 for fair use is a defense against infringement, but then we are not lawyers. She went on to say, in relation to what was to become DMCA, "That is why the act of circumventing a technological protection measure that prevents unauthorized exercise of any of the copyright owners' rights *is not* prohibited. For example, if a librarian obtained legal access to a work."[8]

If all of that seems confusing, it is because the matter is confusing. It is also the reason there are ongoing discussions about the concept. Attempts have been made to help define what really constitutes fair use. After passage of the 1976 law, the Conference on Technological Use (CONTU), drawing on the House Judiciary Committee report, developed some guidelines. Though helpful, neither users nor owners have been pleased with its results as technology evolved. Another effort, in 1994, by the Conference on Fair Use (CONFU) attempted to resolve some of the technological concerns. (Several groups—e.g., the American Association of University Professors and the Association of American Law Schools—had opposed the existing guidelines as not representing the needs of higher education well.) CONFU negotiators spent two years developing the report they issued in 1996.[9] The proposed guidelines generated expressions of concern from a substantial number of educational organizations, unlike the earlier guidelines. Perhaps the most important point to keep in mind is that the fair use guidelines do *not* have the force of law. They are only interpretations of the law, and they are not the only possible interpretation. A good article on this issue is Kenneth Crews' "Fair Use and Higher Education: Are Guidelines the Answer?"[10] Another resource is the "Reproduction of Copyrighted Works by Educators and Librarians," Circular 21 from the U.S. Copyright Office (<http://www.copyright.gov/circs/circ21.pdf>).

Carrie Russell, ALA's copyright specialist in Washington, D.C., wrote in 2003 that "by choosing guidelines over fair use, librarians are establishing a new norm that suggests 'we do not need fair use, the guidelines are sufficient.' Eventually, fair use would lose its meaning and worth, and guidelines would be considered law . . ."[11]

Fair use doctrine was codified in general terms in § 107. That section refers to such purposes as criticism, commentary, news reporting, teaching, scholarship, or research, and it specifies four criteria to use in determining whether a particular instance of copying or other reproduction is fair. The statutory criteria in § 107 are

1. the purpose and character of the use, including whether such use is of a commercial nature or is for nonprofit educational purposes;

2. the nature of the copyrighted work;

3. the amount and substantiality of the portion used in relation to the copyrighted work as a whole; and

4. the effect of the use upon the potential market for, or value of, the copyrighted work.

Depending on the circumstances, fair use might cover making a single copy or multiple copies. For example, multiple copying for classroom use may be considered fair use under certain circumstances. In deciding whether any particular instance of copying is fair use, one must always consider the statutory fair use criteria.

Guidelines for Copying

The 1976 Guidelines developed by educators, publishers, and authors provided some indication of what various parties believe is reasonable fair use. The guidelines are not part of the statute, but they are part of the House Judiciary Committee's report on the copyright bill.[12] They are *Guidelines for Classroom Copying in Not-for-Profit Educational Institutions* and *Guidelines for Educational Uses of Music*. As noted earlier, there is much debate about fair use and use of the guidelines as "safe harbors." However, until there is a clear court decision or Congress clarifies the meaning of fair use, the guidelines are all that users have to go by.

Library Copying Authorized by Section 108

In addition to copying that would fall within the fair use section of the statute, certain types of library copying that may not be considered fair use are authorized by § 108. Section 108 in no way limits the library's fair use right (§ 108[f][4]).

Section 108(a) contains general conditions and limitations that apply to the authorized copying outlined in the rest of the section. These general conditions apply:

1. The copy is made without any purpose of direct or indirect commercial advantage.

2. The collections of the library are open to the public or available not only to researchers affiliated with the library but also to other persons doing research in a specialized field.

3. The copy includes a notice of copyright.

The House Judiciary Committee's report clarified the status of special libraries in for-profit institutions with respect to the criterion "without direct or indirect commercial advantage" (§ 108[a][1]). It is the library or archives within the institution that must meet the criteria, not the institution itself.

In addition to the general conditions of § 108(a), it is possible for contractual obligations between a publisher or distributor and a library to limit copying that would otherwise be permissible under § 108. Furthermore, the limited types of copying authorized by § 108 can be augmented by written agreement at the time of purchase (§ 108[f][4]).

Possible Contractual Limitations on Section 108

Section 108(f)(4) states that the rights of reproduction granted to libraries do not override any contractual obligations assumed by the library when it obtained a work for its collection. In view of this provision, librarians must be especially sensitive to the conditions under which they purchase materials. Before executing an agreement that would limit their rights under the copyright law, they should consult legal counsel. *This is the key section with regard to licensing agreements.*

Single Copy of Single Article or Small Excerpt

Section 108(d) authorizes the making of a single copy of a single article or a copy of a small part of a copyrighted work in the library's collections provided that (1) the copy becomes the property of the user; (2) the library has no notice that the use of the copy would be for any purpose other than private study, scholarship, or research; and (3) the library both includes on its order form and displays prominently at the place where users submit copying requests a warning about copyright in accordance with requirements prescribed by the register of copyrights.

On November 16, 1977, the *Federal Register* published the new regulation and provided the form for the warning signs that the library must post near all library copy machines (see figure 17.1).

The *Federal Register* (February 26, 1991) later printed the text for a second warning sign for computer software. The warning is similar to the first warning, but the wording differs slightly (see figure 17.2).

NOTICE: WARNING CONCERNING COPYRIGHT
RESTRICTIONS

The copyright law of the United States (Title 17, United States Code) governs the making of photocopies or other reproductions of copyrighted material.

Under certain conditions specified in the law, libraries and archives are authorized to furnish a photocopy or other reproduction. One of these specified conditions is that the photocopy or reproduction is not to be "used for any purpose other than private study, scholarship, or research." If a user makes a request for, or later uses, a photocopy or reproduction for purposes in excess of "fair use," that user may be liable for copyright infringement.

This institution reserves the right to refuse to accept a copying order if, in its judgment, fulfillment of the order would involve violation of copyright law.

Fig. 17.1. Official text of the required copyright warning sign. From *Federal Register* (November 16, 1977).

NOTICE: WARNING CONCERNING COPYRIGHT
RESTRICTIONS

The copyright law of the United States (Title 17, United States Code)
governs the reproduction, distribution, adaptation, public performance,
and public display of copyrighted material.

Under certain conditions specified in law, nonprofit libraries are authorized to lend, lease or rent copies of computer programs to patrons on a
nonprofit basis and for nonprofit purposes. Any person who makes an
unauthorized copy or adaptation of the computer program, or redistrib-
utes the loan copy, or publicly performs or displays the computer program, except as permitted by Title 17 of the United States Code, may be
liable for copyright infringement. This institution reserves the right to
refuse to fulfill a loan request if, in its judgment, fulfillment of the request would lead to violation of the copyright law.

Fig. 17.2. Official wording of the required copyright notice for computer software.
From *Federal Register* (February 26, 1991).

Copying for Interlibrary Loan

Section 108(d) authorizes the making of a single copy of a single article or a copy of a small part of a copyrighted work for purposes of interlibrary loan provided that it meets all the conditions previously listed
regarding a single copy of a single article from the library's own collections
and further provided (§ 108[g][2]) that requests for interlibrary loan photocopies are not in such aggregate quantities as to substitute for purchases
or subscriptions. The wording of the statute places responsibility for compliance on the library requesting the photocopy, not on the library fulfilling
the request. The National Commission on New Technological Uses of Copyrighted Works (CONTU), in consultation with authors, publishers, and librarians, developed guidelines to assist libraries in complying with this
provision. A library or archive may receive no more than five photocopies
per year of articles published in the restricted issues of a periodical. (They
may be five copies of one article or single copies of five different articles.)
The restriction applies only to issues published within the last five years.
Duplication of older issues is limited only by the broad provisions of §
108(g)(2), which prohibit copying that by its nature would substitute for a
subscription. We should note that not all journal publishers agree with
those guidelines. Also, in the late 1990s there was a ruling that has clouded
the picture, at least for document delivery services.

UnCover (now ingenta) faced a serious legal ruling in a copyright lawsuit in 1998 (*Ryan v. Carl Corporation*, 23 F.Supp. 2d 1146). UnCover/in-
genta provides copies of journal articles as part of a document delivery
service. One reason for using such a service for ILL requests is that part of
the fee goes to cover royalty charges, based on a negotiated rate between
the supplier and the various journal publishers. A San Francisco U.S. District Court judge issued a summary judgment in favor of the five freelance
authors who filed the suit. Daniel Reidy, attorney for the plaintiffs, said, "In
essence, the lawsuit is a copyright infringement action because UnCover

typically only seeks permission from publishers, without seeking permission from freelance authors. Our position is that unless the authors have either assigned their copyrights or given the publisher express permission to sell individual copies of their articles, UnCover would need to get permission from authors."[13] He also indicated that the law firm was working on developing the case into a class action suit. One wonders why the suit was not filed against the publishers in order to receive a share of the revenue the publishers received from UnCover.

A related case is the *New York Times v. Tasini* (206 F.3d 161), in which the plaintiffs (freelance authors, Tasini et al.) argued that articles they had written in back issues of publications were sold to online databases without their consent (and without additional compensation). Tasini won on appeal. As a result, some articles written by freelance authors are no longer available in online databases. (The Tasini ruling does not apply to employees of publishers or to those authors who have assigned copyright to the publisher.)

Coin-Operated Copying Machines

Section 108(f)(1) and (2) make it clear that *neither libraries nor library employees* are liable for the unsupervised use of reproducing equipment (this does include microform reader/printers) located on library premises, if the machine displays the required notice (see fig. 17.1). The person making the copy is, of course, subject to liability for copyright infringement, if his or her copying exceeds the provisions of § 107.

Library Copying Not Authorized by Section 108

With the exception of audiovisual news programs, § 108 does not authorize a library to make multiple copies. Two general types of library copying that are not clearly defined in the statute are specifically not authorized by § 108. Stated only in the most general terms, the definitions of these types of library copying are susceptible to many interpretations.

The first type is "related or concerted reproduction or distribution of multiple copies." This related or concerted copying by libraries is illegal, whether the library makes the copies all on one occasion or over a period of time and whether the copies are intended for aggregate use by one individual or for separate use by individual members of a group (§ 108[g][1]).

The second type of library copying not authorized by § 108 is "systematic reproduction or distribution of single or multiple copies." Because many librarians feared that this term might preclude a wide range of interlibrary lending systems, Congress amended this section of the bill to clarify that, whatever may be meant by the term *systematic*, copying for purposes of interlibrary loan as specifically authorized by § 108(d) is not illegal under § 108(g)(2) as long as it does not substitute for purchases or subscriptions. The wording of the statute places responsibility for copyright compliance on the library requesting the photocopy, not on the library filling the request (§ 108[g][2]).

It is important to remember that the copyright law does not establish licensing or royalty payment schemes for library copying. It focuses primarily on the kinds of copying that libraries can do without such schemes. Section 108(g) merely states the two types of library copying that are *not* authorized by § 108.

Importation of Copies by Libraries

In general, the law prohibits the importation of copies of works without the permission of the copyright holder. There are, however, certain exceptions to this general prohibition, one of which directly relates to libraries. Section 602(a)(3) states that a nonprofit scholarly, educational, or religious organization may import no more than one copy of an audiovisual work for archival purposes only and no more than five copies of any other work "for its library lending or archival purposes, unless the importation of such copies or phonorecords is part of an activity consisting of systematic reproduction or distribution, engaged in by such organization in violation of the provisions of Section 108(g)(2)."

Infringement

A person who violates the rights of the copyright owner is a *copyright infringer*. Remedies available to the copyright holder for infringement include damages (actual or statutory, the latter set by statute at from $100 to $100,000 per infringement), injunction, and recovery of court costs and attorney's fees. There is also criminal infringement (done willfully for commercial advantage or private financial gain), which is subject to a maximum penalty of $150,000 and/or one year imprisonment per infringement.

There is a waiver of statutory damages for a library or nonprofit educational institution when the institution or one of its employees acting within the scope of his or her employment "believed or had reasonable grounds for believing that his or her use of the copyrighted work was a fair use under Sec. 107" (§ 504[c][2]).

Librarians and media specialists have a professional responsibility to learn about provisions of the copyright law that relate to libraries and to frequently review their practices in light of such provisions. If current practices seem likely to constitute infringement, librarians should plan now for needed changes and make sure that library users understand the reason for such changes. Above all, it is important to take the time and trouble to master the basic provisions of the statute, so the library will fully exercise the rights it has under the copyright law. Anything short of this would be a disservice to library users. Online resources for copyright information appear at the end of this chapter.

DMCA and Technology Issues

Earlier we noted that the DMCA amended U.S. law to comply with WIPO treaties. It did more than that; it also addressed a great many of the technology aspects of copyright. One of the education/library community's concerns about the decline of fair use rights related to § 1201. This section prohibits gaining unauthorized access to material by circumventing any technological protection measures a copyright holder may have put in place. The implementation of this section began two years after the legislation became law—about the end of 2000. During the two-year period, the Library of Congress conducted a rule-making procedure to determine what, if any, exceptions would be appropriate. LC will conduct similar proceedings every three years.

Section 1201 is not intended to limit fair use, but fair use is *not* a defense to circumventing technological protection measures. Other elements in the section have limited implication for collection development, at least at the time we wrote this chapter.

Section 1202 prohibits tampering with "Copyright Management Information" (CMI). The DMCA identified the following as constituting copyright management information:

- Information that identifies the copyrighted work, including title of the work, the author, and the copyright owner.

- Information that identifies a performer whose performance is fixed in a work, with certain exceptions.

- In the case of an audiovisual work, information that identifies the writer, performers, or director, with certain exceptions.

- Terms and conditions for use of the work.

- Identifying numbers or symbols that accompany the above information or links to such information, for example, embedded pointers and hypertext links.

- Such other information as the register of copyrights may prescribe by regulation, with an exception to protect the privacy of users.[14]

One aspect of the DMCA that will probably be very important to libraries is "Title II: Online Service Provider Liability." The reason for this is that the DMCA defines "online service provider" (OSP) very broadly, and libraries that offer electronic resources or Internet access could be considered OSPs. The law creates some "safe harbors" for certain specified OSP activities. When an activity is within the safe harbor, the OSP qualifies for an exemption from liability. One should read the most current material available about this title, as it is complex, and legal interpretation of it is likely to evolve.

Title IV provides some clarification about library and archival digitization activity for preservation purposes. It allows the creation of up to three digital preservation copies of an eligible copyrighted work and the electronic loan of those copies to qualifying institutions. An additional feature is that it permits preservation, including in a digital form, of an item in a format that has become obsolete.

Distance education activities are also addressed in Title IV. The register of copyright provided Congress with a report on "how to promote distance education through digital technologies." The outcome of this report was the Technology, Education, and Copyright Harmonization Act (TEACH).

The TEACH Act and Digital Rights Management

President Bush signed the TEACH Act in November 2002 (Public Law 107-273). Essentially, this law outlines what is expected from educational institutions when/if they plan to employ copyrighted material with their electronic course work and claim fair use. As was true with DMCA, this law focuses on institutions (educational and libraries) as the enforcement mechanism. The emphasis here is on limited/short-term usage and only by those enrolled in the course. Additionally, fair use and public domain are more tightly controlled in the digital than in the print world.

Although the law is a clear recognition of the importance of "distance education," it does not address one of its important features—flexibility of time and place. Rather, it is "built around a vision that distance education should occur in discrete installments, each within a confined span of time, and with all elements integrated into a cohesive lecture-like package."[15] Although much will need to be resolved over the coming years, it appears as if the expectation is that students will use/view the material during a narrow time frame and probably will not be able to save or go back to the material after the allotted time has passed.

The ALA website cited above lists four benefits/improvements that arise from the TEACH Act—a greater range of allowed works and an expansion of receiving sites that qualify, specifically allowing for storage (at least for a limited time) and permitting digitization of analog works. There are, of course, requirements to gain such benefits. The TEACH act applies only to accredited nonprofit organizations that institute copyright policies that include providing material about copyright to students, faculty, and staff. The act further requires that students must "receive notice" that the material is copyrighted. Finally, the material may be available only to enrolled students.

During the time the TEACH Act was under consideration, producers were busy with what is called digital rights management (DRM). DRM technology allows the producer to control who has access to what content. The technology translates the producer's rules (who and how access is gained) in an encrypted code that then encrypts the content. A bill addressing these issues was introduced in the Senate during the 108th Congress (Consumer, Schools, and Libraries Digital Rights Management Awareness Act of 2003, S.1621) but remained in committee at the time this chapter was prepared. Carrie Russell raised the question of to what degree DRM, by defining the who and how of access, could/will replace the concept of fair use.[16] As one might expect, circumventing the encryption is specifically prohibited by Section 1201 of DMCA. More information about DRM, including a summary of legislation related to the topic, is available from the ALA website.[17]

Enforcement

Copyright holders are quick to enforce their rights. One of the early suits was instituted just four years after the 1976 legislation became law. A group of book publishers filed a complaint against the Gnomon Corporation for alleged copyright infringements. Gnomon operated a number of photocopy stores in the eastern United States, many located near academic institutions. The publishers claimed that the company encouraged copyright violations by promoting its Micro-Publishing service with university and college teachers. By May 1980, publishers had their first favorable ruling and announced that their next target would be large, for-profit corporations with libraries that did not use the Copyright Clearance Center (see page 400 for more about the Copyright Clearance Center). Although the publishers won their case against Gnomon, many photocopy service firms continued to promote similar services. By the early 1990s, publishers and commercial copy services had worked out a system for providing academic institutions with custom readers. The system uses an electronic copyright approval procedure that permits a copying service or other company to quickly secure the requisite permissions and legally produce the reader in the needed quantities. Many academic campus bookstores offer similar services, and most of them use the services of the Copyright Clearance Center. However, issues regarding "course packages" and copyright remain. A late 1990s case involved the University of Michigan.[18]

In 1982, various publications carried announcements that the AAP had moved forward with infringement suits against several corporate libraries. The AAP had an out-of-court settlement with E. R. Squibb and Sons Corporation, a large pharmaceutical company, after filing suit. Squibb agreed to pay royalty fees when copying articles from technical journals, including ones to which the corporation library subscribed. Before the Squibb suit, the publishers had also been successful in a suit against American Cyanamid Company. More recently, Texaco lost a copyright suit.[19]

After their success against for-profit organizations, the AAP focused on the not-for-profit sector. On January 5, 1983, the *Chronicle of Higher Education* published an article about an AAP suit in the New York district court against New York University, nine faculty members, and a photocopy shop near the university. New York University settled out of court, agreeing to follow the 1976 guidelines and agreeing that faculty members who did not do so would not receive legal assistance from the institution if they were named as parties in a future copyright infringement suit. At about the same time, a Los Angeles secondary school teacher lost an infringement suit on the same grounds, namely, failure to follow the 1976 guidelines. In 1984, the National Music Publishers Association persuaded the University of Texas at Austin to stop allegedly illegal photocopying of music by its music department. Of course, almost everyone is aware of lawsuits filed against individuals for file sharing of music (such as the *A&M Records v. Napster* case, 114 F. Supp 2d 898). Between legal actions and implementing DRM technology, copyright holders are enforcing their rights.

Though it is true that copyright holders do have rights, the law clearly states that libraries and other users do, too. As Scott Bennett wrote:

> We should respect the copyright law. This means understanding the law so that we can obey it and benefit from it. It means a refusal to wink at violations of the law, however widespread, just as it means advancing no untenable claims either to copyright protection or to fair use. Most important, it means acknowledging there are many genuinely debatable issues before us that will need to be resolved through negotiation, legislation, and litigation. Respecting the copyright law means making judicious use of these methods of resolving differences.
>
> We should keep the Constitutional purposes of copyright in view; honor those purposes; and work to give them vitality.[20]

Contractual Compliance

Following the various guidelines is one obvious way to achieve a limited form of compliance. (To date, there have been no suits in which the defendants claimed that they followed the guidelines; however, that does not mean there will not be such a suit.) For some libraries, the guidelines are too narrow, and the cost of acquiring, processing, and housing the needed copyrighted material is high. Are these libraries and information centers cut off from needed information? Not if they have enough money.

The Copyright Clearance Center (CCC) is a not-for-profit service designed to serve libraries and other users of copyrighted material by providing a central source to which to submit copying fees. It is, in a sense, a licensing system; CCC does not copy documents but functions as a clearinghouse. Several thousand organizations are members; many, if not most, of these are libraries and information services. The CCC handles both U.S. and foreign publications (it can grant permission to use more than 1.75 million publications).

The address/contact information for CCC is 222 Rosewood Drive, Danvers, MA 01923; telephone (978) 750-8400, and <http://www.copyright.com>. There is also a Canadian equivalent, the Canadian Copyright Licensing Agency (Access Copyright). Contact information for Access is 1 Yonge Street, Suite 1900, Toronto, ON M5E1E5, Canada; telephone (416) 868-1620, and <http://www.accesscopyright.ca/>. Another service is the Television Licensing Center (5547 N. Ravenswood Ave., Chicago, IL 60640), which assists in legal off-the-air videotaping, an area of concern for school media centers as well as other educational institutions.

The fees can be substantial when one realizes that the charge is for just one article; however, the cost of a lawsuit would be higher, and if the organization lost, it could be forced to pay as much as $50,000 plus other costs and fees.

When in doubt, ask for permission. The process can be complicated when one must go directly to the copyright owner, but that is often the only option. Libraries can help make it easier in various ways. Tom Steele reported on a project at Wake Forest University that has helped make the process easier, if not painless.[21] Two library staff members designed a website with a list of publishers, a list of journals, a set of form letters for permission requests, and links to sites that provide information about copyright (<http://www.wfu.edu/Library/copyright/>). Although the site has evolved from its original format, it still provides a concise listing of resources useful in this area.

Licensing Agreements

Licensing is another method to achieve compliance. The CCC offers an annual license for publications it handles. Robert Oakley suggested a potentially useful approach to some of the copyright and preservation concerns in terms of journals.[22] His suggestion was based on the idea that many, if not most, publishers do not have significant backfiles in a digital format. (Perhaps one could go further and suggest that they do not want to commit too many resources to maintaining very low revenue material in either print or digital formats.) According to Oakley, this situation presents an opportunity for joint ventures between libraries and publishers. Libraries engage in what they have always done, preserve information, and publishers produce it. In return, libraries would receive access to the backfile materials. Such arrangements would probably be through a contract or license.

What is the relationship between copyright and licenses? Perhaps the best short description of the similarities and differences was written by Ann Oakerson:

- Copyright represents a set of general regulations negotiated through statutory enactment. The same laws and guidelines apply to everyone in the country.

- Licenses are contracts . . . [that] represent [a] market-driven approach to such regulation. Each license is arranged between a willing surveyor and willing licensee, resource by resource. The owner of a piece of property is free to ask whatever price and set whatever conditions the market will bear.[23]

More and more producers and libraries are turning to contracts or licenses to handle access and use, as well as employing DRM to assure compliance.

Typical licensing agreements outline the lessee's responsibility for such things as security, customer service, payment and delivery, limitations and warranties, termination, indemnification, and assignment. All of these factors can affect the expected use. Although having to add attorney fees to the cost of building a collection is unappealing, the fact is that most of the producers will negotiate changes, and librarians should demand changes that benefit, or at least do not create unreasonable demands on, libraries and users.

The library should maintain a master file of copies of all the licensing agreements and contracts. There should be a contact person who is responsible for knowing the terms of these documents as well as for being able to answer or secure answers to questions about the agreements. Compliance is a key issue, and the library or information center must do what it can to ensure compliance. However, some licensing agreements contain language that places responsibility on the library (subscriber) to monitor what users do with material after they leave the premises. Such clauses are beyond any library's or information center's ability to handle, and librarians should insist that they be deleted from the agreement.

The key is knowing what is in the agreement before purchasing. As with computer software, the licensing agreement often comes with the product, that is, after the purchase. It is sealed in a package with a warning message to the effect that opening the package constitutes accepting the terms of the agreement inside the package. (Courts have ruled that both "click" and "shrink-wrapped" licenses are legally binding.) When considering a product from a new vendor, ask for a copy of the licensing agreement before making a final decision to purchase. This gives the staff an opportunity to review the document. It also provides an opportunity to request changes that the vendor may or may not be willing to make. In any event, it will give the library a chance to consider whether it can live with the conditions of the licensing agreement before committing to the purchase.

Licensing is becoming a major and ever-growing issue for libraries. Two resources to consult when developing licensing agreements are "Liblicense," sponsored by Yale University Library (<http://www.library.yale.edu/~llicense/index.shtml>), and "Licensing Electronic Resources," available from ARL (<http://www.arl.org/scomm/licensing/licbooklet.html>). Additionally, a series of "Principles" for licensing electronic resources proposed by a number of library associations in North America is available from the ARL website and is worth reviewing (<http://www.arl.org/scomm/licensing/principles.html>).

Public Lending Right

Public lending right (PLR) is a system that allows an author to be compensated for the circulated use of his or her copyrighted work from libraries. Many people, including librarians, are not fully aware of this right. It is better known outside of the United States, and in most countries where it exists, it operates successfully. In view of copyright owners' increasing attempts to charge a fee for types of usage that were free in the past, it may not be too long before the public lending right will come to the United States.

In this system, authors are compensated in some manner for the circulated use or presence of their works in a library. Where does the money come from? There are only three logical sources: the user, the library, or the funding authority. In most countries, the money comes from a separate fund established for that purpose by the national government. Does the presence of a lending right program have any negative impact on library budgets? No one really knows, but it seems likely that there is some spillover that ultimately reduces library funding. However, a 1986 report from England indicated no adverse effects on library budgets as a result of PLR. Collections built using the demand principle will increase the pressure on the PLR fund, and a self-feeding cycle may begin that makes less money available to buy low-use titles.

The PLR system started in the Scandinavian countries after World War II. Initially, it was considered a way to encourage writers to write in languages that had a small number of native speakers (e.g., Danish, Finnish, Icelandic, Norwegian, and Swedish). For more than twenty years, the concept did not spread beyond Scandinavia. Starting in the early 1970s, the idea spread to the Netherlands (1972), the Federal Republic of Germany (1972), New Zealand (1973), Australia (1974), the United Kingdom (1983), and Canada (1986). Although some legislation contains the provision that all libraries are to be included, in most countries only public libraries are involved in data collection. Details of the systems utilized vary, but some form of sampling is used to collect the data, unless there is a single source from which the public libraries buy their books. (Online acquisition systems are frequently capable of providing such data.) A good, but somewhat dated, source of detailed information about PLR is a 1981 issue *of Library Trends*.[24] Several websites of PLR resources worldwide are included at the end of this chapter and on the website accompanying this text (<http://www.lu.com/dlc5/>).

In Canada, the system is called Payment for Public Use (PPU). A $2.5 million fund was established by the national government to compensate authors for the circulation of their books by Canadian public libraries. In 1985, the Council of Writers Organizations was able to get U.S. senator Charles Matthias of Maryland to submit PLR-enabling legislation. Nothing has happened in the intervening years. Does such legislation have much chance of becoming law? Assuming that the plan would copy other countries' practice of federal funding, and as long as the federal deficit and budget cutting remain congressional priorities, establishment of a PLR system is unlikely. However, this assumption may not be valid, for several reasons. First, two other sources of funding are possible: the user and the library. Second, the worrisome § 106 of the copyright law lists as an exclusive right of the copyright owner "to distribute copies or phonorecords of copyrighted works to the public by sale or other transfer of ownership, or by rental, lease or *lending*" (emphasis added). Third is the attitude exemplified by a 1983 statement in *Publishers Weekly:* "The fate of a book after it is sold is an important one for the book industry, reflecting as it does the possibility of lost sales; pass-along readership of a book, unlike that of a magazine, does not translate into potential revenue."[25] If publishers, authors, and others, such as music producers (audio collections) and motion picture producers (video collections), join forces, we might well see another cost imposed on libraries and their users.

Summary

Copyright provides persons or organizations several rights, including the right to seek tangible rewards from the production of creative or informative works. Without users of copyrighted materials, the producers would realize little or nothing from their efforts. Producers and users need to work together, or everyone will lose. It would be desirable if once again we became partners in the dissemination of information and knowledge, rather than antagonists. Whatever does occur, it will not change the fact that it will not be possible to develop a library collection without considering the impact of copyright laws. Librarians should work to maintain a fair balance, but they must work primarily for the users because users have few spokespersons.

We agree with the ideas that Ann Prentice expressed in an article about WIPO, copyright owners, and users:

> Digital library projects are moving ahead in many libraries and much has been said about the benefits of being able to access information once it is in digital form. Because of copyright restriction, there are limitations on what can be digitized. . . . What will happen when [we] look to digitize material[s] of greater mainstream interest that are under copyright? What kinds of charges will be suggested by copyright holders? Can libraries afford them?[26]

All the legal issues discussed in this chapter do have implications for collection development. For example, issues of who, how, and where access/use will take place can impact the number of copies acquired, the need to maintain print subscription, and what access one might need to purchase. Keeping up with the legal issues is a part of being an effective collection development officer.

Notes

1. Mary Minow and Thomas Lipinski, *The Library's Legal Answer Book*. Chicago: American Library Association, 2003.

2. J. Berry, "Copyright: From Debate to Solution," *Library Journal* 100 (September 1, 1975): 1459.

3. World Intellectual Property Organization, "General Information: WIPO Today," <http://www.wipo.int/about-wipo/en/gib.htm#P52_8261>.

4. Association of American Publishers, *Statement of the AAP on Commercial and Fee-Based Document Delivery* (New York: Author, 1992).

5. Richard Schockmel, "The Premise of Copyright, Assaults on Fair Use, and Royalty Use Fees," *Journal of Academic Librarianship* 22 (January 1996): 17.

6. Evan St. Lifer, "Inching Toward Copyright Détente," *Library Journal* 123 (August 1998): 43.

7. Ibid.

8. Ibid.

9. *Conference on Fair Use: An Interim Report to the Commissioner* (Washington, DC: U.S. Patent and Trademark Office, 1996).

10.   Kenneth Crews, "Fair Use and Higher Education: Are Guidelines the Answer?," *Academi* 83 (November–December 1997): 38–40.

11.   Carrie Russell, "Understanding and Protecting Fair Use," *Public Libraries* 42 (September–October 2003): 289.

12.   U.S. Congress, House of Representatives, *Conference Report on General Revision of the Copyright Law 94-553* (September 29, 1976), 55.

13.   Michael Rogers, "Judge Rules Against UnCover in Copyright Suit," *Library Journal* 123 (November 15, 1998): 19.

14.   Title 17, U.S.C. § 1202(c) (1998).

15.   American Library Association, "Distance Education and the TEACH Act," <http://www.ala.org/ala/washoff/WOissues/copyrightb/distanceed/distanceeducation.htm>.

16.   Carrie Russell, "Fair Use Under Fire," *Library Journal* 128 (August 2003): 32–34.

17.   American Library Association, "Digital Rights Management," <http://www.ala.org/ala/washoff/WOissues/copyrightb/digitalrights/digitalrightsmanagement.htm>.

18.   Sarah K. Wiant, "Coursepack Copying," *Virginia Libraries* 43 (July–August–September 1997): 13–14.

19.   Sarah K. Wiant, "Texaco Settles Suit," *Virginia Libraries* 42 (April–May–June 1996): 18–19.

20.   Scott Bennett, "Copyright and Innovation in Electronic Publishing," *Library Issues* 14 (September 1993): 4.

21.   Tom Steele, "The Copyright Permission Pages: Making a Frustrating Experience More Convenient," *Campus-wide Information Systems* 15, no. 2 (1998): 61–62.

22.   Robert Oakley, "The Copyright Context," *Collection Management* 22, nos. 3/4 (1998): 177–84.

23.   Ann Oakerson, "Copyright or Contract?," *Library Journal* 122 (September 1, 1997): 136–39.

24.   "Public Lending Right," *Library Trends* 29 (Spring 1981): 565–719.

25.   "The Pass-Along Market for Books: Something to Ponder for Publishers," *Publishers Weekly* 224 (July 15, 1983): 20.

26.   Ann Prentice, "Copyright, WIPO and User Interests: Achieving Balance among the Shareholders," *Journal of Academic Librarianship* 23 (July 1997): 309–12; see also University of California Libraries, Collection Development Committee, "Principles for Acquiring and Licensing Information in Digital Formats" (Archived at Indiana University) <http://www.indiana.edu/~libsalc/policies/ucal.html>.

Selected Websites*

(See also resources on the DLC5 website: <http://www.lu.com/dlc5>)

Copyright/Intellectual Property

Berne Convention for the Protection of Literary and Artistic Works
      <http://www.wipo.int/clea/docs/en/wo/wo001en.htm>
   Text of the Berne Convention treaty, provided by the World Intellectual Property Organization (WIPO).

Canadian Intellectual Property Office (CIPO)
> <http://cipo.gc.ca/>
> Administers the Intellectual Property system in Canada, including copyright, trademarks, and patents.

Copyright Advisory Network
> <http://www.librarycopyright.net/>
> An electronic bulletin board sponsored by the American Library Association Office for Information Technology Policy, designed to answer copyright questions by librarians.

Copyright Law of the United States
> <http://www.copyright.gov/title17/>
> The complete text of the law, from the U.S. Copyright Office.

Digital Millennium Copyright Act (10/98)
> <http://www.copyright.gov/legislation/hr2281.pdf>
> The full text of the DMCA, in PDF format.

Information Policy: Copyright and Intellectual Property
> <http://www.ifla.org/II/cpyright.htm>
> Website produced by the International Federation of Library Associations (IFLA), with an international point of view.

Legal Information Institute: Law about . . . Copyright
> <http://www.law.cornell.edu/topics/copyright.html>
> Cornell University's Legal Information Institute copyright home page.

Promoting Innovation and Economic Growth: The Special Problem of Digital Intellectual Property
> <http://www.ced.org/docs/report/report_dcc.pdf>
> Policy statement developed by the Committee for Economic Development addressing digital intellectual property laws and their consequences.

Public Law 107-273 (TEACH ACT)
> <http://www.copyright.gov/legislation/pl107-273.html>
> Full text of the Technology, Education, and Copyright Harmonization Act (TEACH), approved in 2002.

Stanford Copyright & Fair Use Center
> <http://fairuse.stanford.edu>
> An extensive site maintained by the Stanford University Libraries.

United States Copyright Office—Registration
> <http://www.copyright.gov/register/>

University of St. Francis—A Visit to Copyright Bay
> <http://www.stfrancis.edu/cid/copyrightbay/>
> An entertaining and informative site developed for use in nonprofit educational settings.

U.T. System Crash Course in Copyright
> <http://www.utsystem.edu/ogc/intellectualproperty/cprtindx.htm#top>
> A detailed tutorial on all aspects of copyright policy, from the University of Texas. Includes a checklist for implementation of the TEACH act (<http://www.utsystem.edu/ogc/intellectualproperty/teachact.htm#checklist>).

Software & Information Industry Association (SIIA)
> <http://www.siia.net>
> The website of the SIIA, the trade association for this industry.

When U.S. Works Pass Into The Public Domain
> <http://www.unc.edu/~unclng/public-d.htm>
> Concise chart created by Lolly Gasaway, University of North Carolina.

World Intellectual Property Organization
      <http://www.wipo.int>
      The website of WIPO, an organization responsible for the promotion and protection of intellectual property throughout the world.

Public Lending Right (PLR)

Public Lending Right Commission
      <http://www.plr-dpp.ca/>
      Website of the Canadian PLR organization.

PLR International Network Website
      <http://www.plrinternational.com/>
      Includes background and contact information for PLR resources worldwide.

Public Lending Right UK Website
      <http://www.plr.uk.com/>
      Home page for PLR in the United Kingdom. Includes extensive background of the PLR, as well as procedures for authors to use in registering their works.

*These sites were accessed May 7, 2005.

Further Reading

Association of American Publishers et al. *Questions and Answers on Copyright for the Campus Community*. 6th ed. New York: Association of American Publishers, 2003.

Biskup, P. "Libraries, Australian Literature and Public Lending Right." *Australian Library Review* 11 (May 1994): 170–77.

Burke, M., and S. J. Heron. "Copyright Issues and 'For Profit' Libraries: Problems and Solutions." *Journal of Interlibrary Loan, Document Delivery & Information Supply* 14, no. 4 (2004): 5–21.

Burnham, S. J. "Copyright in Library-Held Materials: A Decision Tree for Librarians." *Law Library Journal* 96, no. 3 (2004): 425–48.

Cheverie, J. F. "Managing Technology." *The Journal of Academic Librarianship* 28, no. 5 (2002). 325–31.

Davis, T. L. "Licensing in Lieu of Acquiring." In *Understanding the Business of Library Acquisitions*. 2nd ed. Edited by K. A. Schmidt, 360–78. Chicago: American Library Association, 1999.

"Digital Copyright Protection: Good or Bad for Libraries?" *Information Outlook* 3 (January 1999): 32–33.

"Electronic Reserves and Fair Use." *ARL* 232 (February 2004): 7–8.

Fernández-Molina, J. C. "Licensing Agreements for Information Resources and Copyright Limitations and Exceptions." *Journal of Information Science* 30, no. 4 (2004): 337–47.

Fisher, C. "Internet Issues in Elementary School Library Media Centers." *PNLA Quarterly* 68, no. 4 (2004): 22, 40–43.

Gadd, E., and R. Gaston. "Copyright Questions Asked by Libraries." *Library Management* 22, nos. 8/9 (2001): 387–94.

Gadd, E., C. Oppenheim, and S. Probets. "The Intellectual Property Rights Issues Facing Self-archiving," *D-Lib Magazine* 9, no. 9 (September 2003) <http://www.dlib.org/dlib/september03/gadd/09gadd.html>.

Gasaway, L. *Growing Pains: Adapting Copyright for Libraries, Education and Society*. Littleton, CO: Fred B. Rothman, 1997.

Harris, L. E. *Licensing Digital Content: A Practical Guide for Librarians*. Chicago: American Library Association, 2002.

Hoon, P. E. "Who Woke the Sleeping Giant? Libraries, Copyrights, and the Digital Age." *Change* 35, no. 6 (2003): 28–33.

Hyatt, D. "Public Lending Right in the U.S.: An Active Issue." *Public Libraries* 27 (Spring 1988): 42–43.

Karlsen, G. "Copyright Reminder: PPR—Public Performance Rights for Video-tapes for Classroom Use." *School Libraries in Canada* 18, no. 2 (1998): 23–24.

Lariviere, J. "Le Droit de Pret Public au Canada." *Documentation et Bibliotheques* 37 (April–June 1991): 53–58.

"License Agreements in Lieu of Copyright: Are We Signing Away Our Rights?" *Library Acquisitions: Practice and Theory* 21, no. 1 (1997): 19–27.

Linke, E. "On Beyond Copyright." *Serials Libraries* 33, nos. 1/3 (1998): 71–81.

Lipinksi, T. A. "The Climate of Distance Education in the 21st Century." *The Journal of Academic Librarianship* 29, no. 6 (2003): 362–74.

Marcon, T. "Electronic Reserves." *Library Acquisitions* 22 (Summer 1998): 208–9.

Marley, J. L. "Guidelines Favoring Fair Use: An Analysis of Legal Interpretations Affecting Higher Education." *The Journal of Academic Librarianship* 25, no. 5 (1999): 367–71.

Ogden, R. S. "Copyright Issues for Libraries and Librarians." *Library Collections, Acquisitions, & Technical Services* 27, no. 4 (Winter 2003): 473–81.

Okerson, A. "Copyright or Contract?" *Library Journal* 122 (September 1, 1997): 136–39.

———. "The Current National Copyright Debate: Its Relationship to Work of Collection Managers." *Journal of Library Administration* 22, no. 4 (1996): 71–84.

Peloso, J. *Intellectual Property*. New York: H. W. Wilson, Co., 2003.

Poulain, M. "Le Droit de Preter." *Bulletin des Bibliotheques de France* 37, no. 3 (1992): 84.

"Public Lending Right." *Library Association Record* 99 (February 1997): 61.

Rogríguez Pardo, J. *Copyright and Multimedia*. New York: Kluwer Law International, 2003.

Russell, C. *Complete Copyright: An Everyday Guide for Librarians*. Chicago: American Library Association, 2004.

———. "A Tough Act to Follow." *School Library Journal* 49, no. 11 (2003): 52–54.

Sanville, T. "A License to Deal." *Library Journal* 124 (February 15, 1999): 122.

Schuler, J. A. "Distance Education, Copyrights Rights, and the New TEACH Act." *The Journal of Academic Librarianship* 29, no. 1 (2003): 49–51.

Shyu, J. "Preliminary Study on the Issue of Public Lending Right." *Journal of Library and Information Science* 17 (October 1991): 64–92.

Sturges, P., V. Teng, and U. Iliffe. "User Privacy in the Digital Library Environment: A Matter of Concern for Information Professionals." *Library Management* 22, nos. 8/9 (2001): 364–70.

Swaffield, L. "Public Lending Right: Online Links for PLR." *Library Association Records* 100 (April 1998): 182.

Totka, V. A., Jr. "Preventing Patron Theft in the Archives: Legal Perspectives and Problems." *American Archivist* 56 (Fall 1993): 664–73.

Wherry, T. L. *The Librarian's Guide to Intellectual Property in the Digital Age: Copyrights, Patents, and Trademarks*. Chicago: American Library Association, 2002.

Wiant, S. K. "Copyright and Government Libraries." *Information Outlook* 3 (February 1999): 38–39.

Wolverton, R. E., Jr. "E-Journal Licensing and Legal Issues: A Panel Report." *The Serials Librarian* 45, no. 2 (2003): 153–59.

18
Censorship, Intellectual Freedom, and Collection Development

As part of our preparation for this new edition, we contacted individuals who used the fourth edition in order to gain input about what to add and what to drop. When it came to this chapter, several individuals suggested dropping it as a stand-alone chapter. After due consideration, we concluded that the issues were too complex not to have a separate chapter (although we have moved a discussion of bibliotherapy to the CD accompanying this text). The complexity arises from the fact that the issues of censorship and intellectual freedom are both organizational and individual in character. Providing Internet access to end users adds yet another layer to the complexities.

All of the collection development topics discussed thus far have been complex, and some touch on a wide variety of social issues and concerns. However, none are more complex than intellectual freedom and censorship. *Free speech*, *freedom to read*, and *open access to information* are alternative terms used for *intellectual freedom*, which ALA defines as

> the right of every individual to both seek and receive information from all points of view without restriction. It provides for free access to all expressions of ideas through which any and all sides of a question, cause or movement may be explored.[1]

Likewise, *censorship* is defined by ALA as

> a change in the access status of material, based on the content of the work and made by a governing authority or its representatives. Such changes include exclusion, restriction, removal, or age/grade level changes.[2]

410

Obviously, First Amendment rights are the cornerstones on which librarians and information managers build collections. Thus, the concepts of intellectual freedom and censorship must be addressed in the collection development process.

There is not enough space in this chapter to fully explore all the aspects of intellectual freedom, censorship, and free speech. Although they are interesting and important concepts for anyone involved in collection development, they are so complex that each has been the subject of numerous books and articles. (The bibliography at the end of this chapter provides a starting point for exploring these topics in more depth.) All librarians must have an understanding of these areas, but it is essential that all selection personnel fully comprehend the issues relating to censorship.

Many library associations have membership-approved statements and public positions on the questions of free speech and intellectual freedom. The ALA's *Freedom to Read* statement (available online at <http://www.ala.org/ala/oif/statementspols/ftrstatement/freedomreadstatement.htm>) is a classic example. Most of the statements contain fine-sounding phrases. The statements *look* useful when one is discussing the theory or philosophy of intellectual freedom in the classroom or in a meeting. However, on a daily basis, these statements provide little assistance in collection development and provide only limited assistance in fighting off a censor.

Background

On the organizational side, censorship arises from laws and regulations, government policies and actions, library policies and actions, and pressures for organized groups. From the individual point of view, censorship comes from individual users and, perhaps most significantly, from the individuals making the decisions about what to include and exclude from the collection.

The concept of a "balanced collection," one representing all the views of a pluralistic society, is relatively recent for U.S. libraries. For the better part of 100 years (1870s to 1970s) legal regulations enforced, or attempted to enforce morality, at least in terms of literary materials. Anthony Comstock was a person of strong beliefs and personality whose efforts to control the reading materials of Americans were so vigorous and successful that his name is now part of the lexicon of intellectual freedom and censorship discussions—Comstockery.

Indeed, Comstock was so vocal in his efforts that, in 1873, Congress passed a law that attempted to create a structure for national morality. For almost seventy-five years, this law went unchallenged, with the U.S. Postal Service designated as the government agency primarily responsible for enforcement at the national level. At the local level, several elements were at work. State and local governments passed similar regulations, and, thus, local police departments became involved in the control of vice. Law enforcement agencies had ample help from two citizen groups: the Society for the Suppression of Vice and the Watch and Ward Society. The Society for the Suppression of Vice was the vehicle Comstock used to gain popular support and show the depth of national support for his views. A primary activity of the society was checking on printed material available to local citizens, whatever the source (bookstores, newsstands, and libraries both public and private). Occasionally, when the society felt that local law enforcement officials were not moving quickly enough, it took matters into its own hands. Book burnings did take place, and the society applied pressure to anyone involved in buying or selling printed material to stock only items it deemed moral. The phrase "banned in Boston" originated as a result of the society's activity.

From 1873 until well into the 20th century, the United States experienced a mix of all three types of censorship: official censorship because of the 1873 law; group pressure from organized societies concerned with the moral standards of their communities; and self-censorship on the part of publishers, booksellers, and librarians. A public or even a private stance by librarians against such censorship was almost unheard of; in fact, professional groups sponsored workshops and seminars to help librarians identify improper books. Most of the notable librarians of the past are on record (in ALA proceedings, speeches, or writings) in favor of this type of collection development. As Evelyn Geller noted, Arthur Bostwick felt it was reasonable to purchase books like *Man and Superman* for the New York Library's reference collection (noncirculating), but not for branch libraries.[3] Bostwick's inaugural speech as president of the ALA (1908) was about the librarian as censor; as censor the librarian performed a positive act, if not an act of "greatness," Bostwick said.[4]

An interesting situation arose with foreign-language titles. Many authors were available in their own languages, but not in English. Apparently, if one could read French, German, Spanish, Russian, or any other language, one was reading a "moral" book—but that same work in an English translation was immoral. The censorial atmosphere caused a few American authors to live abroad, and some had a larger foreign readership than English-speaking readership. (Henry Miller is a prime example.) At the time, librarians were no more vocal in protesting this situation than anyone else in the country.

The period between 1873 and the mid-1950s exhibited all of the censorship problems one can encounter. From the 1930s to the mid-1950s, various federal court decisions, including several by the U.S. Supreme Court, slowly modified the 1873 law. (It was during the 1930s that ALA took a stance for more open access.) The 1873 Comstock Act remains a part of the U.S. Code, but it is so modified as to be a completely different law. During this time period, most court cases dealing with censorship were between the government and publishers or booksellers. Librarians and their associations occasionally entered the suits as *amici curiae* (friends of the court), but seldom as defendants or plaintiffs.

Major changes in the interpretation of the law began with the U.S. Supreme Court's 1957 *Roth* decision.[5] This decision established a three-part test for obscenity. First, the dominant theme of the work as a whole had to appeal to a prurient interest in sex. Second, the work had to be patently offensive because it affronted contemporary community standards in its representation of sex. Third, the work had to be utterly without redeeming social value. With that interpretation, more sexually explicit material became available in the open market. Not unexpectedly, some people objected to the new openness, and in 1973, the Supreme Court, in deciding the *Miller* case,[6] modified the three-part test. The Court suggested a new three-part test. First, would an average person applying contemporary community standards find that the work as a whole appealed to prurient interest in sex? Second, does the work depict or describe in a patently offensive way sexual conduct specifically prohibited in a state's law? Third, does the work, as a whole, lack serious literary, artistic, political, or scientific value? The effect of the decision was to reduce the impact of national mores by employing tests that emphasize local standards. This test is in place today.

Does the shift in emphasis matter? Yes, especially in terms of production and distribution of materials. One example of what the changed interpretation could do to distribution occurred in 1982. *Show Me: A Picture Book of Sex for Children and Parents* (New York: St. Martin's Press, 1975), a children's book by Will McBride, was taken out of distribution by its American publisher/distributor, St. Martin's Press. It stopped distribution because the U.S. Supreme Court upheld a New York state child pornography law.[7] The book contained photographs of nude children. The New York law contained a strict provision barring the use of children in all sexually explicit films and photographs, obscene or not. St. Martin's had already successfully defended *Show Me* in Massachusetts, New Hampshire, and Oklahoma. However, the publisher decided that determining which of the fifty states it could legally ship the book to, as well as keeping track of individual orders, was much too difficult, so it stopped all distribution. Perhaps the most interesting aspect of this incident is that the book was written by a Swiss child psychologist (Helga Fleischhauer-Hardt), and the photographs were taken by an American photographer (Will McBride). They prepared the book for a Lutheran church-sponsored children's book company in West Germany in 1974. The English-language edition appeared in 1975, and St. Martin's stated that it had sold almost 150,000 copies in hardback and paperback before it ceased distribution.[8]

Some distributors and book clubs started using labeling systems in an attempt to protect themselves from lawsuits. For example, one book club used labels that state: "Warning: explicit violence" or "Warning: explicit sex and violence." A few people speculated that the purpose was to increase sales rather than avoid a lawsuit. Perhaps it served a dual purpose. For a time, one of the library distributors that serves many school media centers included warnings with "problem" books it shipped. For example, in children's books acquired for courses in children's literature, librarians at LMU have found slips bearing the warning, "This book is not up to our usual standards." (The standards referred to do not relate to the quality of the physical volume itself, and it was unclear what the "standards" were.) Such labeling violates the ALA *Statement on Labeling* (see <http://www.ala.org/ala/oif/statementspols/statementsif/interpretations/statementlabeling.htm>); however, it also reflects the growing concern on the part of vendors with social values and with pressures to influence those values.

Today, just as during the period 1873–1950, most of the problems libraries encounter are with individual and group attempts to censor material. Although no active Society for the Suppression of Vice exists today nationally, librarians increasingly face organized pressure groups. What may at first seem to be a person's objection to one book can become a major confrontation between a library and an organized pressure group. Much depends on the energy and time that the would-be censor is willing to devote to the issue. Influential persons may be able to organize a group to generate even greater pressure than the average person could. A librarian may encounter organized pressure groups based on local interests and views (often, views that are religious or politically oriented), but seldom does a librarian face a challenge from a local group with broad national support. If such a group were to exist, it would be extremely difficult to avoid at least an occasional debate (if not an all-out battle) over some materials in the collection. Policy statements about controversial materials, ALA's *Freedom to Read* statement, and other support materials will help to slow the process, but they will not stop it. Local groups are particularly hard to resist, because they can have a fairly broad base of community support, and their existence indicates some active interest in certain problems.

A few examples illustrate the problems that confronted many librarians in the United States during recent years. For example, a 1993 report about censorship in U.S. schools, released by People for the American Way, indicated that in 41 percent of the 395 reported attempts at censorship, censors succeeded in having the objectionable material removed or restricted in some manner.[9] The report indicated that the majority of the reported attempts were by groups identified as religious right or "pro-family." It went on to report school personnel as acknowledging that they were being careful in what they added to the collections, a form of self-censorship. Between 1990 and 2001, ALA's Office for Intellectual Freedom recorded 6,364 challenges and noted there was an increase in almost all types of challenges between 1999 and 2000.[10] In February 2005, Alabama state representative Gerald Allen introduced a bill to his state legislature to prohibit educational institutions—libraries, schools, and universities—in Alabama from purchasing "textbooks or library materials that recognize or promote homosexuality as an acceptable lifestyle."[11] Although this bill failed in committee in April 2005, had it succeeded, it likely would have been met with a great deal of opposition from ALA and other groups. It is also proof that such challenges still do occur—and these challenges are not limited to K–12 educational institutions. Much of the censorship pressure arises from a concern about children, and the concern is not limited to sex. Some parents do not believe they are capable of judging the materials that their children are exposed to in school or the library. As a result, several organizations review materials for worried parents. These groups include Educational Research Analysts, Inc., founded by Mel and Norma Gabler (<http://members.aol.com/TxtbkRevws>); America's Future in St. Louis, MO (<http://www.americasfuture.org>); Fairfax, Virginia-based Parents Against Bad Books In Schools (<http://www.pabbis.com/>); and the John Birch Society (<http://www.jbs.org>). These groups, especially Educational Research Analysts, are particularly active in the area of elementary school textbooks and required reading material, but they also assess what is in the general collections that support the curriculum.

Supporters of biblical creationism suggest that libraries are censoring Christian materials and especially creationism literature (or creation science). Anyone thinking about going into school media center work needs to be fully aware of what is taking place and to beware the dangers and pitfalls. The *Island Trees Union Free School District* decision of the U.S. Supreme Court,[12] which limited the power of school boards to limit access to materials, did not solve all the problems.

Not all censors are concerned about children's welfare. Challenges to materials based on their racist or sexist content arise fairly often. One of the more unusual cases was "The Incredible Case of the Stack o' Wheat Murders" photograph incident in 1980.[13] The case illustrates that censorship battles are not limited to public and school libraries. The Stack o' Wheat incident occurred in the special collections room at the University of California, Santa Cruz library. Ten 4×5-inch photographs, called "The Incredible Case of the Stack o' Wheat Murders," were taken by photographer Les Krims. The collection was a parody of theme murders intended for use in a marketing project. Each photograph showed a "gruesomely" murdered nude woman dripping blood alongside a stack of wheat pancakes. The dripping blood was chocolate syrup; the chocolate represented the "epitome of the series humor," according to the text that accompanied the photographs. A young woman who viewed the photographs demanded their removal from the library's collection on the ground that they represented the sexploitation of women. When the library took no action, she went to the special collections room, ripped up the photographs and accompanying material, and poured chocolate syrup over the debris. The case quickly escalated into a significant problem for the campus, encompassing many complex issues, such as freedom of expression, censorship, status of women, vandalism, and social justice.

Another, more recent case involving photographs, one that gained national attention, was the Robert Mapplethorpe controversy. This case went to trial and led to the resignation of a museum director, as well as an individual who had once won ALA's intellectual freedom award.[14]

A variation on the censorship/intellectual freedom issue occurred in 1999, when the National Endowment for the Arts (NEA) withdrew funding for a book-publishing project.[15] The publisher was a small press in El Paso, Texas, that had applied for, and won, a grant from the NEA to help cover the color publishing cost of $15,000 for 5,000 copies. *The Story of Color* is a children's book based on a Mexican folktale about the gods that remade a gray world into one of many colors. The "problem" was the author, Subcomandante Marcos. Marcos is one of the major leaders of the Zapatista guerrilla movement in Mexico. According to the newspaper article, William Ivey, chairmen of the NEA, canceled the funding after learning about the book from a reporter. His decision overturned many levels of approval for the funding. The reason given for the reversal was concern that some of the funds might eventually reach the Zapatistas. "There was uncertainty about the ultimate destination of some part of the funds," according to Mr. Ivey.[16]

The above examples illustrate how censorship can be organizational as well as individually based. ALA's *Freedom to Read* statement suggests today's collection managers should present all major points of view. That is the goal collection managers should strive for. What are the challenges? Some of the challenges are of a practical nature, and others are ethical and philosophical in character.

At several places in this text we have made the point that no library can acquire everything. Thus, at the logical extreme, it is clear that no library presents all points of view on all subjects. One can ignore such an extreme situation, and on the realistic level, two very practical issues exist—money and physical space. Almost all libraries face these practical limitations. Beyond those two are two other important limitations—the library's purpose/mission and the level of treatment. It is unlikely that anyone would seriously suggest that a school teaching geometry should collect materials on why one does not need to study geometry. The collection policy should clearly identify the range of topics collected and depth of collecting. Thus, not acquiring materials that fall outside those limits is not censorship. Likewise, no one should expect a K–12 library to collect graduate-level treatments, even of topics covered in the school's curriculum. These are all issues we addressed in earlier chapters.

Where the issues begin to blur is when the topic, treatment level, and price all are within the acceptable range, but the author's approach may reflect minority perspective. We believe the real difference between selection and censorship resides in the decision makers' frame of reference in making the judgment. A selector is *positive*, looking for reasons to *acquire* while the censor is *negative*, looking for reasons to *reject*. The reasons are driven by *internal factors* (collection policy) for the selector. In the case of the censor, the factors are very often external to the library. Selectors use *professional judgment*, whereas the censor employs value judgments. The goal of the selector is to increase access; for the censor the goal is to limit or provide no access. Items not selected are often in that category because of limited funds; the censor rejects items because of content.

Again, the above are easy to talk and think about. In practice, when one has deeply held beliefs and values, it is often difficult not to let them become a key factor in one's decision. Also, when one is dependent upon the job, can/does one risk that job over a decision to buy or not to buy an item? (Yes, librarians have lost their jobs as a result of censorship challenges.) When confronted with an item one is fairly certain will raise questions and could cause trouble, it is all too easy not to purchase the item on the grounds "we need to save our money for more important titles," "we already have enough material on this topic," etc. Such reasons are not the result of censorship but are based in reality; one just needs to check occasionally to be sure it is reality and not some other reasons. One check is to see how many of the challenged titles/authors one has in one's collection. (The Office of Intellectual Freedom reported that some of the most challenged authors between 2000 and 2003 were John Steinbeck, Toni Morrison, Maya Angelou, and J. K. Rowling.) Studies have shown that self-censorship is an issue in library collection building.[17]

Examples of Censorship

Almost every type of library encounters a challenge or two. However, school media libraries are the ones that have the most challenges. These challenges usually relate to sexuality, drug use, rights of "minority" groups, religious values, and sometimes political views. The Office of Intellectual Freedom reported that 71 percent of the challenges between 1990 and 2000 were in school settings and that parents filed 60 percent of those challenges.[18] An interesting fact is the success rate (restricting access or removal) is over 40 percent, in spite of the *Island Trees/Pico* decision.[19]

As might be expected, public libraries receive the second largest number of challenges. Academic and special libraries are far behind in the number of challenges, but often these are some of the more complex challenges to resolve. The following highlights are but a few of the hundreds of attempts at censorship in libraries and information centers in the United States and represent examples from each type of library. ALA's *Newsletter on Intellectual Freedom* (<http://members.ala.org/nif/>) provides an ongoing source of news about this field.

Journals

In the late 1960s, two periodicals, *Ramparts* (Noah's Ark) and *Evergreen Review* (*ER*, <http://www.evergreenreview.com/>), caused libraries and librarians to confront the censorship issue head-on. These confrontations illustrate the variety of ways libraries deal with controversy. In Los Angeles, the public library had to fight a city councilman's efforts to have *ER* removed from the library.[20] The councilman was unsuccessful, but the library removed the current *ER* issues from public areas while the controversy raged. Eventually, the journal was returned to the open shelves after the parties reached a final decision. This was a short-term victory for censorship but, in the end, a victory for free access.

Not all librarians were so lucky. Richard Rosichan lost his position as director of the Kingston Area (New York) Public Library because he fought to keep *ER*, despite both library board and John Birch Society pressure to drop it.[21] At the same time, the American Legion demanded that he remove *Ramparts* because of what the Legion considered its un-American stance. Groton (Connecticut) Public Library managed to retain its staff but lost its subscription to *ER;* after a four-month fight, the library's board of trustees ordered the removal of all issues from the library and the subscription canceled. This was done under the threat of fines and jail sentences for both the library board and staff. Head librarian John Carey issued a statement to the effect that this decision would affect the general acquisition policy.[22] One can only hope that he was wrong.

Between keeping an item on the shelves and removing it is the compromise position to which librarians sometimes resort—restricted availability. The Philadelphia Free Library used this approach for *ER* when pressure began to be applied. The library renewed the subscription for the main building and one regional branch, but it kept the issues in closed-stack areas, and no one under the age of eighteen could examine the title.[23] Emerson Greenaway, who was at that time the director of libraries for the Philadelphia Free Library, said this was done because *ER* was "important sociologically." Who was the winner here, the censor or the librarian?

The foregoing are a small sample of the problems that arose with *Evergreen Review* and *Ramparts*, and they are only two of hundreds of periodicals that have been attacked over the years. In fact, groups frequently question *Newsweek* and *Time*. Some other journals that have been questioned by an individual or group in recent years include *The Advocate*, *People*, *Penthouse*, *Playgirl*, *Reader's Digest*, *Rolling Stone* (removed from the Livingston Park High School Library in October 2002 after an unsuccessful attempt to simply restrict use to students with parental permission), and *Young Miss*.

Books

The list of books that have caused trouble over the years is immense. The Office of Intellectual Freedom's website (<http://www.ala.org/ala/oif/bannedbooksweek/bbwlinks/100mostfrequently.htm>) lists the 100 books most frequently challenged between 1990 and 2000. Steinbeck's *Of Mice and Men* is in sixth place, while Maya Angelou's *I Know Why the Caged Bird Sings* ranked in third place. *The Catcher in the Rye*, a long-standing challenged title, was thirteenth while *To Kill a Mockingbird* was forty-first. It is clear that although schools face most of the challenges, some highly regarded literary works also can cause problems.

I Know Why the Caged Bird Sings faced challenges because of passages dealing with child molestation and rape. In most instances, the objectors were successful in forcing its removal or restricting its use by requiring parental approval in writing.

The Adventures of Huckleberry Finn (fifth on the ALA list) has a long history of complaints. The complaints are a perennial problem. The usual charge is that the book contains racist material. Complaints are also frequently filed over J. D. Salinger's *Catcher in the Rye* and its profanity; occasionally, someone objects to sexual references.

Other books may not rank on the current "Top 100" list but nonetheless draw complaints because of the point of view they present, for example, Dee

Brown's *Bury My Heart at Wounded Knee*. Still others encounter problems for reasons that are hard to understand. Try to find the offending nudity in *Where's Waldo?* or determine why some school media centers have *Snow White* on the list of books that may be read only with signed parental approval.

Some "problem" titles challenged in the past are equally hard for many people to understand:

- *Twelfth Night* (due to a school district's ban on alternative lifestyle instruction).
- *Origin of the Species* (once again the Tennessee legislature attempted to limit the teaching of evolution).
- *Little Red Riding Hood* (because the basket of goodies included wine).
- *My Brother Sam Is Dead* (too much violence in a story about a family split apart by the American Revolution).
- *The Chocolate War* (due to language and sexual content—this book is beginning to catch up to *Catcher in the Rye* in terms of challenges).
- *My Friend Flicka* (due to cruelty to animals).

One recent case involved a Wisconsin school district's banning of four books dealing with gay themes—*When Someone You Know Is Gay*, *The Drowning of Stephen Jones*, *Baby Be-Bop*, and *Two Teenagers in Twenty*.[24] What is interesting about this case is that the complaint that led to banning was filed by a parent of a former student in the school.

Music and Recordings

Although in the past there had been fewer problems with music than with other formats, that is no longer the case. Rap music, hard rock, and music lyrics in general now generate controversy quite regularly. In the late 1990s, 2 Live Crew recordings and performances drew national attention, and the concern continues to grow. Early in 1990, the recording industry instituted a labeling program similar to the motion picture rating system. This occurred after years of debate, even in Congress, and opposition from a variety of groups, such as the ALA. Anna Thompson's article "Lyric Censorship" provides some good insights into this area.[25] A good article that gives one a sense of how long people have been trying to censor music in the United States is Edward Volz's "You Can't Play That."[26]

In August 2004, the American Civil Liberties Union (ACLU) was seeking additional information about the Kansas attorney general banning over thirty music CDs from Kansas libraries. The attorney general's office reportedly said, ". . . we feel we removed most of the albums that did not mesh with the values of the majority of Kansans."[27] This goes back to the *Roth* decision and the emphasis placed on local values.

Games

Nothing in the collection is immune from challenge, as several libraries have learned the hard way. Aurora Public Library (Colorado) had to deal with controversy over *Dungeons and Dragons* (D&D) players' books. A woman presented an official complaint and a petition with 150 signatures supporting the complaint. She claimed the game promotes "violence, Satanism and blasphemy of Christian terms." The complaint was withdrawn a short time later because the woman said she feared reprisals against her and her widowed mother. However, the publicity sparked a rash of complaints about other items in the library, and a local evangelist began checking area public library collections for D&D players' books. He tried to pursue the Aurora complaint, but, because he did not live in the community, he could not file a complaint. At about the same time, in Hanover, Virginia, the parents of a sixteen-year-old who committed suicide sued a public school system. The parents alleged that the suicide was a direct result of his playing D&D in a school building. Wrongful death lawsuits related to games, movies, and television programs have been increasing. None have involved libraries, but there is no reason to suppose that libraries will be immune from such a suit, particularly when many collections have materials about suicide. The November 1983 issue of *American Libraries* published some responses to the ALA Ethics Committee question, "Should you give a student a copy of *Suicide Mode D'Emploi?*" The book is said to be linked to at least ten suicides. If one believes in freedom to read, what should one do?

Film and Video

As library collections of theatrical videos grow, so do the odds that someone will demand the removal of one or more titles. Educational videos, especially those dealing with reproduction, abortion, and alternative lifestyles, also present problems. Even foreign-language videos, such as a Portuguese-language film, can draw protests.[28] During the Gulf War, some libraries rejected an antiwar video, raising the question of whether the librarians were acting as censors and not providing both sides of an issue.[29] A short, but informative, article about issues of accessibility to video collections is by John Hurley.[30]

LMU's large video collection has drawn several complaints. None of the challenges have been serious enough to warrant attention outside the library, as no one from the university has raised the issue. To date, the complaints have been from community users who think the collection should contain only "Christian if not solely Roman Catholic" materials. Films such as *Jesus Christ, Superstar* and *The Last Temptation of Christ* have drawn highly negative comments from several community members. What might happen if a student's parents or major donor were to complain is difficult to say. We rather expect the issue would go beyond the walls of the library.

Some years ago, librarians put on an amazing performance of self-censorship. The situation surrounding the film *The Speaker* includes almost every element one is likely to encounter in any censorship case. To fully understand all of the paradoxes that this event represents, one must review the background of the situation and view the film.

The problem with *The Speaker* began when ALA's Committee for Intellectual Freedom received funds to produce a film about the issues of censorship and intellectual freedom. Shown for the first time to membership at the June 1977 annual convention, the film generated one of the longer debates in ALA history. Seldom has there been as long or as bitter a debate within the ALA about an issue that is, presumably, an article of faith in the profession. Many of the African American members labeled the film racist. Many other members agreed that the film was a problem for that or other reasons. An attempt to have the ALA's name disassociated from the film failed, but not by much. Is that a move to censor? Does that really differ from a publisher's deciding not to release a title because the work is found not to be in the best interest of the owner of the company?

As with every other problem of this type, we have no objective data on which to base a judgment. Not all African Americans or other persons of color who viewed the film saw it as racist. Just because one (albeit large) group claims that an item is this or that, does the claim make it so?

Is this really different from the Citizen's Committee for Clean Books saying that *The Last Temptation of Christ* is sacrilegious, or the John Birch Society claiming that *Ramparts* and the *Evergreen Review* are anti-American? One hopes that most librarians will agree with Dorothy Broderick regarding *The Speaker:*

> Let librarians across the country decide for themselves: If they find the film boring, let them not buy it. If they feel that using it will stir up trouble in their community—as if they had invited *"The Speaker"*—let them ignore its existence. If the film is as bad as its opponents claim, it will die the natural death of an inadequate work in the marketplace.[31]

Many persons believed that if the ALA removed its name from the film, the association would have taken the first step toward suppressing the film, thus practicing censorship, the very thing it tries to avoid.

Happily, the ALA has produced, or taken part in the production of, an excellent video, *Censorship v. Selection: Choosing Books for Public Schools.*[32] Although the focus is on public schools, the issues covered are broad enough to make the film valuable for use with any group to generate a discussion of intellectual freedom and censorship.

One rather different situation came up in 1996 in a rather unexpected place—medical libraries. *Pernkopf Anatomy: Atlas of Topographic and Applied Anatomy* was a critically acclaimed anatomical atlas containing more than 800 detailed paintings of dissections that doctors, especially surgeons, used for many years. The first volume was published in Vienna in 1937, part two was printed in 1943, and the final volume appeared in 1952.[33] Urban & Schwarzenberg of Baltimore issued a two-volume set in 1989; later, Wavery Inc. acquired the rights to the title. Both the original and reissue volumes were (and still are) widely held by medical libraries. Reviewers in 1990 used phrases such as "in a class of its own" and "classic among atlases."[34] Anyone thinking about the date and place of the initial publication probably can guess why the controversy arose. Dr. Eduard Pernkopf was a Nazi Party member from 1933 forward and was named dean of the medical school at the University of Vienna after the anschluss of 1938. He also spent three postwar years in Allied prisoner of war camps but was never charged with any war crimes. Some doctors in the 1990s wanted medical libraries to withdraw, or at least not allow access to, the work until there was an investigation into whether concentration camp victims had been used for the dissections upon which the paintings were based. In 1998, the University of Vienna presented the results of their investigation of the matter, in which they were unable to make a conclusive determination in the case. The debate over the use of the text continued among practitioners nonetheless.[35]

What to Do Before and After the Censor Arrives

Knowing the dangers of censorship and having a commitment to avoid it are not enough in today's world. Information professionals must prepare for the censor long, long before there is a perceived threat or before the threat becomes real. The first step in preparing for the censor is to expect to have to face a censor. Prepare a policy statement about how the library will handle complaints and have the policy approved by all the appropriate authorities. Facing an angry person who is complaining about library materials and having no idea how to handle the situation are highly uncomfortable. Even with policies and procedures, the situation may escalate into physical violence; without procedures, the odds of physical confrontation increase. A typical procedure is to have the individual(s) file a formal complaint or fill out a form that specifies what is at issue. (Figure 18.1, page 422, is one such form.) Several organizations, such as the ALA and the National Council of Teachers of English, have recommended forms that are equally effective.

After the library develops the policies and procedures, and they are approved, everyone working in public services needs to understand the system and receive training in implementing the system. (Sometimes role-playing is helpful in reinforcing the training.) ALA's Office for Intellectual Freedom has an excellent manual that provides details about what to do before censors arrive as well as providing material on their website. Another good source is Frances Jones' *Defusing Censorship: The Librarian's Guide to Handling Censorship Conflicts*.[36]

The ALA's organizational structure for dealing with intellectual freedom concerns is somewhat confusing. The Intellectual Freedom Committee (IFC) is responsible for making recommendations to the association regarding matters of intellectual freedom. The Office for Intellectual Freedom (OIF), which has a full-time staff, has the charge of educating librarians and others about intellectual freedom and censorship matters. It also is the support service for the IFC, and it implements the association's policies related to intellectual freedom. As part of its educational function, the OIF produces several publications: *Newsletter on Intellectual Freedom* (news and current developments relating to intellectual freedom) and the *Intellectual Freedom Manual* (<http://www.ala.org/ala/oif/iftoolkits/ifmanual/intellectual.htm>).

Although the OIF does not provide legal assistance when a library faces a complaint, it does provide telephone consultation (occasionally with the addition of written statements or names of persons who might be able to testify in support of intellectual freedom). Very rarely, the OIF comes to the library to provide moral and professional support. Often, librarians are surprised to learn that the OIF does not provide legal aid. Legal assistance might be available from the Freedom to Read Foundation (FRF, <http://www.ala.org/ala/ourassociation/othergroups/ftrf/freedomreadfoundation.htm>). The FRF is not part of the ALA (it is a separate legal entity), but the two are so closely affiliated that many people have difficulty drawing the line between the two. The executive director of the FRF is also the director of the OIF; with such an arrangement, it is not surprising that

Since people differ, citizens may register their complaints by filling out the following form:

Author:

Title:

Publisher (if known):

Request initiated by _____
                     Name   Telephone No.

                     _____
                     Address

Complainant represents: Himself/Herself _____ Organization _____
If organization, give name:_____

1. Specify what you object to in the book (cite pages)_____
     _____

2. For what age group would you recommend this book?_____

3. What do you think might be the effects of reading this book?_____
     _____

4. What do you think is good about this book?_____
     _____

5. Did you read the whole book or just parts of it?_____

6. Do you know the literary critics' view of this book?_____

7. What is the theme of the book?_____

8. What action would you like the library to take about this book?
         Withdraw it from the shelves?_____
         Do not permit it in the children's room?_____
         Do not permit my child to sign it out?_____

9. What book would you recommend in its place?_____
     _____

                         _____
                         Signature of Complainant

                         _____
                         Date

Fig. 18.1. Patron's request for reconsideration of a book.

people think the FRF is part of the ALA. Be aware that there is no assurance of receiving financial or legal aid from the FRF; there are too many cases and insufficient funds to assist everyone.

Anyone interested in becoming involved in intellectual freedom activities should consider joining the Intellectual Freedom Round Table, which is the general membership unit of the ALA related to intellectual freedom. Although the ALA offers a variety of support services for handling censors' complaints, the best support is preparing before the need arises.

Filtering

We decided to place the discussion of filtering here because it is, in many ways, a very different concern from that of challenges to items that are part of one's collection(s). Filtering access to the Internet is a "hot topic" for the general public, government officials, and libraries. As we begin the 21st century, libraries appear to be "caught between a rock and a hard place" on this issue, as long as they offer Internet access to the public. Some of the general public, governing boards, and elected government officials want libraries to use filter software that will deny access to certain types of sites. Others, believing in free speech (First Amendment), do not want filtering. The primary reason for filtering is to keep children from having access to "unacceptable" sites. An excellent article describing how filtering works and the error rates of filter software is Paul Resnick, Derek Hanson, and Caroline Richardson's article in *Communications of the ACM*.[37]

Filtering Internet access revolves around protecting children and denying access to primarily sexual material. The major problem is that filtering softwares over and under block. Efforts to legislate a solution have had mixed results. The Communications Decency Act (CDA) (which made it a crime to send or post "indecent" material on the Internet) was ruled unconstitutional by the Supreme Court in 1997. Congress then passed the Child Online Protection Act (COPA, 47 U.S.C. § 231), which met much the same fate as the CDA, when the Supreme Court ruled in July 2004 to uphold an injunction placed on the act by a lower court.[38] In June 2003, CIPA (Child Internet Protection Act, P.L. 106-554) received a mixed judgment from the Supreme Court. It was mixed because although six of the judges found in favor of the law, only four agreed on a single opinion (it takes five to make a "controlling" decision). The positive opinions do, however, mean libraries (public and school) need to have filters,[39] as they presented the only realistic solution to the problem.

At the time we prepared this chapter (late 2004) it is not clear how public libraries would handle filtering. The challenge is meeting the legal requirements to protect children and still provide adult access to legitimate materials. There are three areas where filters are to block visual depictions—obscene material, child pornography, and those harmful to minors. (CIPA does not require filtering text.) While the act's title indicates the focus is children, if the library is covered by the CIPA mandate, all computers with Internet capability must have filtering software (including staff computers).

The law applies to public libraries and schools that have e-rate discounts for Internet access, receive funds under Title III of the Elementary and Secondary Education Act (ESEA) to purchase computers that will be connected to the Internet, or receive funds under state-operated LSTA (Library Services and Technology Act) for the purchase of Internet computers.

It does not apply to academic or special libraries. ALA has created an extensive website to track the effects of CIPA (<http://www.ala.org/cipa>), and a number of resources on CIPA and filtering are included in the Further Reading section at the end of this chapter.

Summary

The problem of censorship is complex, and it is necessary to do extensive reading and thinking about this topic. A theoretical example may help to illustrate just how complex the issue can be. Assume that a librarian is responsible for selecting materials for a small public library. Naturally, the librarian needs this job to cover living expenses. A small group of persons in the community wants the librarian to buy certain items for the library collection; but the librarian also knows of a large group of vocal and influential persons who would be upset and might even demand that the librarian be fired if the items were purchased. Should the librarian buy the item and risk his or her family's welfare and own career over this? If the librarian does not buy the item, what can be said to the people who asked for its purchase? Does telling them they can get it somewhere else or get it through interlibrary loan really address that librarian's problem?

Finally, an article in *American Libraries* raised the question: "Is it censorship to remove all copies of *The Joy of Gay Sex* because it advocates sex practices that are now felt to be dangerous in light of the AIDS epidemic?"[40] Several librarians responded to the question, and there was some difference of opinion. One wonders how the respondents would have answered had the question been: Is it censorship not to buy copies of Madonna's *Sex?* As with all real problems, there is no simple, completely satisfactory answer.

Notes

1. American Library Association, "Intellectual Freedom and Censorship Q&A," Chicago: American Library Association, <http://www.ala.org/ala/oif/basics/intellectual.htm>.

2. American Library Association, "Intellectual Freedom/Censorship," Chicago: American Library Association, <http://www.ala.org/Template.cfm?Section=if>.

3. E. Geller, "The Librarian as Censor," *Library Journal* 101 (June 1, 1976): 125.

4. A. Bostwick, "The Librarian as Censor," ALA *Bulletin* 2 (September 1908): 108.

5. *Roth v. United States*, 354 U.S. 476, 77 S. Ct. 1304 (1957).

6. *Miller v. California*, 413 U.S. 15, 93 S. Ct. 2607 (1973).

7. *New York v. Ferber*, 102 S. Ct. 3348 (1982).

8. "Children's Sex Book Removed from Sale," *Rocky Mountain News*, September 21, 1982, at 49.

9. "Censors Succeed in 41% of School Cases," *Library Hotline* 22 (September 27, 1993): 2.

10. Office of Intellectual Freedom, "Challenged and Banned Books," Chicago: American Library Association, <http://www.ala.org/ala/oif/bannedbooksweek/challengedbanned/challengedbanned.htm>.

11.   For more information, see "AL Legislator Would Ban Gay Books from Libraries," *Library Hotline* 33, no. 50 (December 13, 2004): 3; Gerald Allen, "HB 30," Alabama State Legislature, December 8, 2004, <http://alisdb.legislature.state. al.us/acas/ACASlogin.asp>; Kim Chandler, "Gay Book Ban Goal of State Lawmaker," *Birmingham News*, December 1, 2004, <http://www.al.com/news/birmingham news/index.ssf?/base/news/1101896768316400.xml>; "So Much for Plato," *Times-Picayune,* December 3, 2004, Editorial, <http://www.nola.com/news/t-p/editorials/ index.ssf?/base/news-1/1102057136171880.xml>); and "Legislature Briefs," *Birmingham News* 118, no. 40 (April 28, 2005): 4C.

12.   *Board of Education v. Pico*, 457 U.S. 853 (1981).

13.   "Stack o' Wheat Photos Uproar," *Los Angeles Times*, May 25, 1980, 1, 8, 22–24.

14.   "Director of Corcoran Resigns," *Newsletter on Intellectual Freedom* 39 (March 1990): 73; "Mapplethorpe Defender Wins Downs Award," *Newsletter on Intellectual Freedom* 41 (March 1992): 68.

15.   Julia Preston, "N.E.A. Couldn't Tell a Book by Its Cover," *New York Times*, March 10, 1999, A1, A8.

16.   Ibid., A1.

17.   Examples are L. B. Woods and Claudia Perry-Holmes, "Libraries Practice Prior Censorship to Avoid the Flak," *Library Journal* 107 (September 15, 1982): 1711–15; Frances McDonald, *Censorship and Intellectual Freedom* (Metuchen, NJ: Scarecrow Press, 1993); and Andrea Niosi, "An Investigation of Censorship and Selection in Southern California Libraries," *Public Libraries* 37 (September/October 1998): 310–15.

18.   Office of Intellectual Freedom, "Challenged and Banned Books."

19.   "Censors Succeed in 41% of School Cases," *Library Hotline* 22 (September 27, 1993): 2.

20.   *Wilson Library Bulletin* 48 (September 1969): 18.

21.   Ibid.

22.   *Wilson Library Bulletin* 50 (April 1971): 717.

23.   *Newsletter on Intellectual Freedom* 18 (January 1969): 5.

24.   "ACLU Press Release: 10-06-98—ACLU of Wisconsin Fights School Censorship of Gay-Themed Books," American Civil Liberties Union, <http://www. aclu.org/news/1999/n021699a.html>.

25.   Anna Thompson, "Lyric Censorship: The Risks of Dirty Disks," *Unabashed Librarian* 62 (1987): 5–7.

26.   Edward J. Volz, "You Can't Play That: A Selective Chronology of Banned Music, 1850–1991," *Colorado Libraries* 19 (Summer 1993): 22–25.

27.   American Civil Liberties Union, "Free Speech: Censorship," <http://www. aclu.org/FreeSpeech/FreeSpeechlist.cfm?c=83>.

28.   L. Kniffel, "N.C. County Commissioner Defends Effort to Ban Video," *American Libraries* 24 (January 1993): 14.

29.   B. Goldberg, "Librarians Called Censors for Declining Gulf War Video," *American Libraries* 22 (July–August 1991): 615–16.

30.   John Hurley, "Free Access Issues and Video Collections," *New Jersey Libraries* 22 (Fall 1989): 8–10.

31.   D. Broderick, "Son of Speaker," *American Libraries* 8 (October 1977): 503.

32.   *Censorship v. Selection: Choosing Books for Public Schools* (New York: Media and Society Seminars, 1982).

33.   Howard Israel, "Nazi Origins of an Anatomy Text," *Journal of the American Medical Association* 276 (November 27, 1996): 1633.

34.   Nicholas Wade, "Doctors Question Use of Nazi's Medical Atlas," *New York Times*, November 26, 1996, C1.

35.   Michel C. Atlas, "Ethics and Access to Teaching Materials in the Medical Library: The Case of the Pernkopf Atlas," *Bulletin of the Medical Library Association* 89, no. 1 (January 2001): 51–58.

36.   Frances Jones, *Defusing Censorship: The Librarian's Guide to Handling Censorship Conflicts* (Phoenix, AZ: Oryx Press, 1983).

37.   Paul Resnick, Derek L. Hansen, and Caroline Richardson, "Calculating Error Rates for Filtering Software," *Communications of the ACM* 47, no. 9 (September 2004): 67–71.

38.   Norman Oder, "Court: COPA Injunction Stands," *Library Journal* 129, no. 13 (August 15, 2004): 20.

39.   George Eberhart, "Libraries Choose to Filter or Not to Filter As CIPA Deadline Arrives," *American Libraries* 35, no. 7 (August 2004): 17.

40.   "Censorship in the Name of Public Health," *American Libraries* 17 (May 1986): 306.

Selected Websites*

(See also resources on the DLC5 website: <http://www.lu.com/dlc5>)

Banned Books Online
        <http://www.digital.library.upenn.edu/books/banned-books.html>
        A listing of books that have been targets of censorship, sponsored by the University of Pennsylvania.

Children's Internet Protection Act: The Recent Court Decision in Context
        <http://www.llrx.com/features/cipa.htm>
        A review of the practical implications of CIPA from the Law Library Resource Xchange (LLRX).

Colorado Filtering Clearinghouse
        <http://www.aclin.org/filtering/>
        Website sponsored by the Colorado State Library and the Colorado Department of Education. Provides access to resources about filtering and a guide to the Children's Internet Protection Act.

* These websites were accessed May 7, 2005.

Further Reading

Becker, B. C., and S. M. Stan, for the Office of Intellectual Freedom. *Hit List for Children 2: Frequently Challenged Books*. Chicago: American Library Association, 2002.

Berman, S. "Hot Stuff: Getting Sex in the Library." *Collection Building* 13, no. 1 (1993): 45–47.

Bocher, B. "A CIPA Toolkit." *Library Journal* 128 (August 2003): 35–37.

Bowen, C. F. "Preparing for the Censor's Visit." *Public Libraries* 36 (September–October 1997): 279–80.

Branin, J. J. "Collection Management and Intellectual Freedom." In *Collection Management for the 1990s*. Edited by J. J. Branin, 148–55. Chicago: American Library Association, 1993.

Brawner, L. B. "Protecting First Amendment Rights in Public Libraries." *Public Library Quarterly* 16, no. 4 (1997): 3–7.

Bright, L. "Censorship in a Small Town." *Colorado Libraries* 19 (Summer 1993): 15–17.

Burress, L. *Battle of the Books: Literary Censorship in the Public Schools (1950–1985)*. Metuchen, NJ: Scarecrow Press, 1989.

Busha, C. H. "Intellectual Freedom and Censorship." *Library Quarterly* 42 (July 1972): 283–84.

Bushman, J. "Librarians, Self-Censorship, and Information Technologies." *College & Research Libraries* 55 (May 1994): 221–28.

Cornette, L. "Intellectual Freedom Is a Concern for All Media Specialists." *Ohio Media Spectrum* 50 (Fall 1998): 13–14.

———. "A Censor: Do You Know One When You See One?" *Ohio Media Spectrum* 50 (Winter 1998): 13–14.

———. "Who Do You Call?" *Ohio Media Spectrum* 49 (Fall 1997): 10–11.

Deane, G. "Public Libraries, Pornography, and the Damage Done." *Library Administration & Management* 18, no. 1 (Winter 2004): 8–13.

Doyle, T. "Selection versus Censorship in Libraries." *Collection Management* 27, no. 1 (2002): 15–25.

———. "A Millian Critique of Library Censorship." *Journal of Academic Librarianship* 24 (May 1998): 241–43.

Elsner, E. J. "Legal Aspects of Internet Filtering in Public Libraries." *Public Libraries* 40 (July–August 2001): 218–22.

Foerstel, H. N. *Banned in the U.S.A.: A Reference Guide to Book Censorship in School and Public Libraries*. Westport, CT: Greenwood Press, 1994.

Harmeyer, D. "Potential Collection Development Bias: Some Evidence on a Controversial Topic in California." *College & Research Libraries News* 56 (March 1995): 101–11.

Heckart, R. J. "The Library as a Marketplace of Ideas." *College & Research Libraries* 52 (November 1991): 491–505.

Herring, M. "Libraries in the Cyberage: Filtering, Censorship and the First Amendment." *Against the Grain* 14, no. 4 (September 2002): 42–44, 46–47, 50–59.

Himma, K. E. "What If Libraries Really Had the 'Ideal Filter'?" *Alki* 19, no. 1 (March 2003): 29–30, <http://www.wla.org/alki/mar03.pdf>.

Hippenhammer, C. T. "Patron Objections to Library Materials: A Survey of Christian College Libraries." *Christian Librarian* 37 (November 1993): 12–17.

Hopkins, D. M. "A Conceptual Model of Factors Influencing the Outcome of Challenges to Library Materials in Secondary School Settings." *Library Quarterly* 63 (January 1993): 40–72.

Huston, K. "Silent Censorship." *UMKC Law Review* 72, no. 1 (Fall 2003): 241–55.

Jaeger, P. T., and C. R. McClure. "Potential Legal Challenges to the Application of the Children's Internet Protection Act (CIPA) in Public Libraries." *First Mon-*

day 9, no. 2 (February 2004), <http://www.firstmonday.org/issues/issue 9_2/jaeger/index.html>.

Kranich, N. "Why Filters Won't Protect Children or Adults." *Library Administration & Management* 18 (Winter 2004): 14–18.

Kravitz, N. *Censorship and the School Library Media Center*. Westport, CT: Libraries Unlimited, 2002.

LaRue, J. "Buddha at the Gate, Running: Why People Challenge Library Materials." *American Libraries* 35, no. 11 (December 2004): 42–44.

Lesesne, T. S., and R. Chance, for the Young Adult Library Services Association. *Hit List for Young Adults 2: Frequently Challenged Books*. Chicago: American Library Association, 2002.

Manley, W. "Instructions Not Included." *American Libraries* 34, no. 8 (September 2003): 112.

———. "The Manley Arts: Intellectual Freedom Begins at Home." *Booklist* 100, no. 3 (October 1, 2003): 278.

Mastroine, T. "Ten Good Things about a Censorship Challenge." *Ohio Media Spectrum* 50 (Spring 1998): 26–29.

McDonald, F. B. *Censorship and Intellectual Freedom: A Survey of School Librarians' Attitudes and Moral Reasoning*. Metuchen, NJ: Scarecrow Press, 1993.

Noble, W. *Book Banning in America: Who Bans Books and Why*. Middlebury, VT: Eriksson, 1992.

Oder, N. "Bumps on the CIPA Road." *Library Journal* 129 (October 1, 2004): 18–21.

Office for Intellectual Freedom. *Workbook for Selection Policy Writing*. Chicago: American Library Association, 1999, <http://www.ala.org/ala/oif/challenge support/dealing/workbook.pdf>.

Peace, A. G. "Academia, Censorship, and the Internet." *Journal of Information Ethics* 6 (Fall 1997): 35–47.

Peck, R. S. *Libraries, the First Amendment, and Cyberspace: What You Need to Know*. Chicago: American Library Association, 2000.

Pedersen, M. "They Censor, I Select." *Publishers Weekly* 241 (January 1994): 34–36.

Ratzan, J. S. "CIPA and the Roles of Public Librarians." *Public Libraries* 43 (September–October 2004): 285–90.

Reichman, H. *Censorship and Selection: Issues and Answers for Schools*. 3rd ed. Chicago: American Library Association, 2001.

Robbins, L. S. "Fighting McCarthyism through Film: A Library Censorship Case Becomes a Storm Center." *Journal of Education for Library and Information Science* 39 (Fall 1998): 291–311.

Sager, D. J. "Electronic Bowdlerites: Censorship in the Information Age." *Public Libraries* 36 (September–October 1997): 279–84.

Saunders, K. C. "Factors Affecting the Outcome of Challenges to Library Materials." *Texas Library Journal* 68 (Fall 1992): 84–86.

Schmitt, S. "The Battle of the Dumpster and Other Stories: Processing the Censorship." *The Serials Librarian* 44, nos. 3/4 (2003): 325–29.

Schrader, A. M. "Why You Cannot 'Censorproof' Your Public Library." *Public Library Quarterly* 16, no. 1 (1997): 3–30. Also in *Australasian Public Libraries and Information Services* 10 (September 1997): 143–59.

Selth, J. P. *Ambition, Discrimination, and Censorship in Libraries*. Jefferson, NC: McFarland, 1993.

Sherwill-Navarro, P. "Internet in the Workplace: Censorship, Liability and Freedom of Speech." *Medical Reference Services Quarterly* 17 (Winter 1998): 77–84.

Shields, G. R. "Censorship, Social Violence, and Librarian Ethics." *Library Quarterly* 62 (April 1992): 217–22.

Short, A. M. "Internet Policies & Standards in Indiana Public Libraries." *Indiana Libraries* 16, no. 2 (1997): 48–56.

Smolla, R. A. "Freedom of Speech for Libraries and Librarians." *Law Library Journal* 85 (Winter 1993): 71–79.

Woodward, D., ed. "Intellectual Freedom." *Library Trends* 39, nos. 1/2 (Summer–Fall 1990): 1–185.

Index

About the Authors

G. EDWARD EVANS is the Associate Academic Vice President for Information Resources, Von der Ahe Library, Loyola Marymount University, Los Angeles, CA.

MARGARET ZARNOSKY SAPONARO is Manager of Staff Learning and Development, University of Maryland Libraries, College Park, MD.